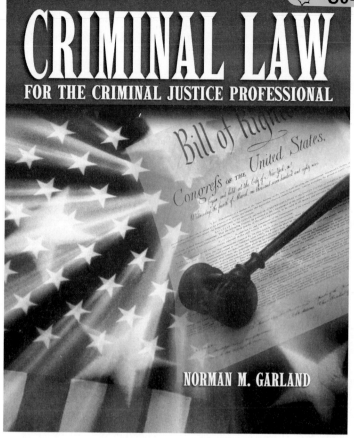

CRIMINAL LAW
FOR THE CRIMINAL JUSTICE PROFESSIONAL

NORMAN M. GARLAND

Norman M. Garland

Professor of Law
Southwestern University School of Law
Los Angeles, California

 **Glencoe McGraw-Hill**

New York, New York   Columbus, Ohio   Woodland Hills, California   Peoria, Illinois

Glencoe/McGraw-Hill

A Division of The **McGraw·Hill** *Companies*

Criminal Law for the Criminal Justice Professional

Printed in the United States of America.

Send all inquiries to:
Glencoe/McGraw-Hill
21600 Oxnard Street, Suite 500
Woodland Hills, California 91367

ISBN 0-02-800908-8

1 2 3 4 5 6 7 8 9 026 05 04 03 02 01

Brief Contents

www.cl.glencoe.com

Expanded Contents

Part 2   The Elements of Crime 81

Chapter 4

Classification of Crimes and Elements of Criminal Responsibility 82

Part 3   Types of Crime   253

Chapter 8

Criminal Homicide   254

Chapter 13

Crimes Against Public Order, Safety, and Morality   436

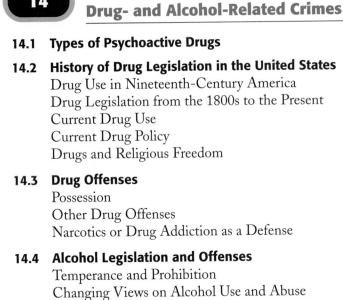

Chapter 16 — Organized Crime, Gangs, and Terrorism   542

Criminal Law for the Criminal Justice Professional

Learning System

This book is designed to help students learn. It contains 16 chapters, divided into five parts. You will learn more if you use the learning system. *Criminal Law for the Criminal Justice Professional* uses the following *integrated learning system:*

1. **Concept Preview**—The chapter opener introduces the key concepts to be learned.
2. **Concept Development**—The chapter text explains concepts in structured, visual format.
3. **Concept Reinforcement**—In-text examples, graphics, and special features enhance and strengthen your learning.
4. **Concept Review and Application**—End-of-chapter exercises and activities encourage you to apply what you learned.

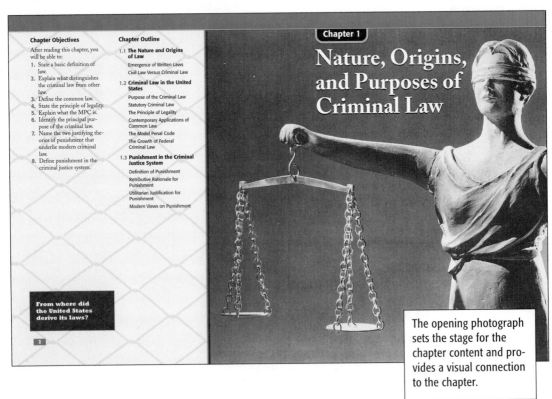

Chapter Objectives

After reading this chapter, you will be able to:
1. State a basic definition of law.
2. Explain what distinguishes the criminal law from other law.
3. Define the common law.
4. State the principle of legality.
5. Explain what the MPC is.
6. Identify the principal purpose of the criminal law.
7. Name the two justifying theories of punishment that underlie modern criminal law.
8. Define punishment in the criminal justice system.

Chapter Outline

1.1 **The Nature and Origins of Law**
Emergence of Written Laws
Civil Law Versus Criminal Law

1.2 **Criminal Law in the United States**
Purpose of the Criminal Law
Statutory Criminal Law
The Principle of Legality
Contemporary Applications of Common Law
The Model Penal Code
The Growth of Federal Criminal Law

1.3 **Punishment in the Criminal Justice System**
Definition of Punishment
Retributive Rationale for Punishment
Utilitarian Justification for Punishment
Modern Views on Punishment

Chapter 1

Nature, Origins, and Purposes of Criminal Law

From where did the United States derive its laws?

2

The opening photograph sets the stage for the chapter content and provides a visual connection to the chapter.

Concept Development

The heading structure shows the relationship among the topics in a section and breaks the material into easily digestible segments of information. Scan the headings to locate the information that will help you answer the questions you formed from the chapter objectives.

Key terms are defined when introduced and are printed in boldface to make them easy to find. Key Terms are also defined in the margin to make it easy for you to learn them.

Important concepts and data are depicted in visual format to make them easier to understand.

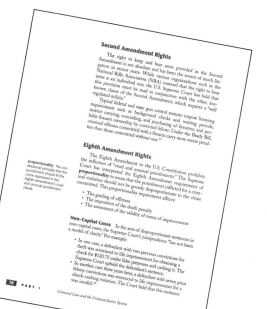

Second Amendment Rights

The right to keep and bear arms provided in the Second Amendment is not absolute and has been the source of much litigation in recent years. While various organizations such as the National Rifle Association (NRA) contend that the right to bear arms is an individual one, the U.S. Supreme Court has held that this provision must be read in conjunction with the other, lesser-known clause of the Second Amendment, which requires a "well regulated militia."

Typical federal and state gun control statutes impose licensing requirements such as background checks and waiting periods; restrict carrying, concealing, and purchasing of firearms; and prohibit firearm ownership by convicted felons. Under the Brady Bill, criminal offenses committed with a firearm carry more severe penalties than those committed without one.[15]

Eighth Amendment Rights

The Eighth Amendment to the U.S. Constitution prohibits the infliction of "cruel and unusual punishments." The Supreme Court has interpreted the Eighth Amendment **proportionality** to mean that the punishment inflicted for a criminal violation should not be grossly disproportionate to the crime committed. This proportionality requirement affects:

- The grading of offenses
- The imposition of the death penalty
- The assessment of the validity of terms of imprisonment

proportionality The constitutional principle that the punishment should fit the crime expressed in the Eighth Amendment's cruel and unusual punishment clause.

Non-Capital Cases

In the area of disproportionate sentences in non-capital cases, the Supreme Court's jurisprudence "has not been a model of clarity." For example:

- In one case, a defendant with two previous convictions for theft was sentenced to life imprisonment for obtaining a check for $120.75 under false pretenses and cashing it. The Supreme Court upheld the defendant's sentence.
- In another case three years later, a defendant with seven prior felony convictions was sentenced to life imprisonment for a check-cashing violation. The Court held that this sentence was invalid.[16]

70 PART 1

Criminal Law and the Criminal Justice System

Concept Reinforcement

Application Cases appear throughout the volume to help student focus on court applications of the theories introduced in the chapter. A brief account and analysis are followed by a critical thinking question.

On the Job features profile a profession in the field of criminal law and focus focus on duties, salary, and other pertinent facts.

People v. Kraft

In *People v. Kraft*, the defendant forced the victim's car off of the road when the victim attempted to pass him. The victim later noticed the defendant's vehicle and pulled up next to it to say something to the defendant. Before the victim had a chance to speak, the defendant pulled out a gun and fired several shots, some going above the car and one hitting the back of it. The victim then notified police of the incident, and, as a police officer approached the defendant's car, the defendant pointed a gun at the officer and later shot at him.

At trial, the defendant testified that when the victim approached his car he was scared and was only trying to scare the victim away. He stated that when he shot at the officer, he was in shock and only wanted to kill himself. The trial court instructed the jury that the defendant could be found guilty of attempted murder if he did "any act which constitutes a substantial step toward the commission of the offense of murder" with the *mens rea* to commit murder. The trial court further instructed the jury that the *mens rea* for murder included doing acts that create "a strong probability of death." The appellate court held that the jury instructions given were wrong for the charge of attempt and that "[t]he offense of attempted murder requires the mental state of specific intent to commit murder, to kill someone . . . ." On this basis, the appellate court overturned the defendant's conviction.

Critical Thinking Do you think the defendant had the necessary *mens rea* to be convicted of attempted murder?

SOURCE: *People v. Kraft*, 478 N.E.2d 1154 (Ill. App. Ct. 1985).

APPLICATION CASE

Attempted Murder

CRIMINAL LAW Online

Use of Force by Law Enforcement

You can learn how often law enforcement personnel use force in the line of duty by visiting the National Criminal Justice Reference Service Web site by clicking the link at cl.glencoe.com. As part of the Violent Crime Control and Law Enforcement Act of 1994, the National Institute of Justice and the Bureau of Statistics have combined efforts to collect data and research police-citizen contact. Is the use of force in police-citizen contacts rare or prevalent? Is it usually attributable to provocative behavior on the part of suspects?

Special features reinforce and enhance your understanding of concepts presented.

Ethics in Criminal Law

You are a prosecutor who is talking to the defense attorney of a man who has been arrested on rape charges. The defendant took a woman on a date, during which time they each drank five beers and became very drunk. He then told her that he would kill her if she did not agree to have sex with him. She tried to fight back, but passed out, during which time he had sex with her.

Critical Thinking

1. What elements of this act indicate that rape has taken place?

2. Does it matter that she agreed to get drunk? Why or why not?

Undercover Police Investigator

Private undercover investigator salaries range more widely, but an average estimate is $30,000 to $40,000.

Description and Duties: Investigate and regulate all vice, liquor, tobacco, gambling, and other vice-related criminal activities. Obtain physical evidence that others are committing crimes and obtain arrest warrants. Make large numbers of arrests by maximizing contacts in a crime ring, or by convincing a number of contacts to become informants. Undercover work can also include surveillance, eavesdropping, and espionage.

Other Information: Undercover officers are experienced police officers who have generally served in their departments before going undercover. Ethical issues in undercover work include entrapment, corruption, and the ethical management of informants.

Critical Thinking What kind of special training should undercover officers receive?

Average Salary: For undercover work in police departments, salaries can range from approximately $35,000 to $60,000, depending on the jurisdiction. Since undercover police are experienced, their salaries are somewhat higher than that of a rookie officer.

SOURCE: "Police Undercover Work," http://faculty.ncwc.edu/toconnor/205/205lect08a.htm. City of Everett (WA) Police Department, http://www.ci.everett.wa.us/EVERETT/police/investigations/smart.htm

Parties to a Crime CHAPTER 5 145

Concept Review and Application

Summary by Chapter Objectives sums up the chapter's major themes. The summary is organized by chapter objectives and provides you with general answers to the questions you posed when you began the chapter.

Key Terms consolidates the criminal law vocabulary presented in the chapter. If you cannot remember what a term means, the page reference alerts you to the location of its definition in the chapter.

Questions for Review re-examine key points presented in the chapter. These questions test your knowledge of the chapter concepts and can help you review for exams.

Problem-Solving Exercises and Workplace Applications encourage you to apply the concepts you have learned. Each scenario provides you the opportunity to analyze a situation, using the knowledge you have gained from the chapter, and to then propose a solution, evaluate a proposal, or make a decision.

Internet Applications offer opportunities for you to broaden your understanding of the material presented, prepare yourself to participate in classroom discussions, and enhance your performance on exams while learning to navigate this potent source of information.

Ethics Issues encourages students to focus on the ethical application of the law by requiring thought and analysis of real-life scenarios where the line between ethical conduct and wrong interpretation and procedure might be blurred.

Additional Study and Tutorial Resources

To assist you in learning and applying criminal justice concepts, Glencoe provides several resources in addition to the textbook.

Tutorial With Simulation Applications CD-ROM

This Tutorial With Simulation Applications CD-ROM is a comprehensive interactive study tool designed to assist you in learning and applying concepts. It contains:

Interactive Content Tutorial

This visually oriented tutorial covers all concepts in the textbook. Chapter content is divided into sections followed immediately by reinforcement and review questions.

Application Simulations

Chapter concepts and issues are applied through application simulations, which pose real-world problems. You receive immediate feedback regarding the appropriateness of your choices.

cl.glencoe.com

This site provides information on current trends, careers, research, and publications, links to relevant professional organizations as well as multiple reinforcement and assessment tools.

Student Success in Criminal Law

With the purchase of this volume, you have taken a major step toward achieving your career goals in your study of criminal law. To ensure your success, you must take full advantage of the many informational features, learning aids, and pedagogical structures that are provided. You will gain a broad and comprehensive understanding of criminal law and its applications in the criminal justice system. That knowledge will serve you well as a strong foundation for other more specialized courses in law, criminal justice, and the social sciences.

This book is divided into 16 chapters that are organized in five parts to provide a logical approach to understanding the history, theory, and applications of criminal law in the United States.

The first three chapters outline the history of criminal law and focus on how criminal law works within the American criminal justice system and within the frame of the U.S. Constitution. Established here is the use of Case Applications to illustrate the theoretical aspects introduced in each chapter. On-the-Job features also appear and zero in on one specific profession at a time.

Part 2 (Chapters 4, 5, 6, 7) discusses the elements of criminal responsibility, parties to a crime, attempted crimes, and defenses to crimes. You will learn about the liability and the extent of accomplice liability and instrumentality, as well as the meaning and interpretations of two basic criminal law concepts: *actus reus* and *mens rea*.

Chapter 7 explains the various approaches to defense and define proof, mitigation, justification, and the role each can play in the construction of a defense.

Part 3 (Chapters 8 and 9) lists and offers definitions for various types of crime (criminal homicide and other crimes against persons).

Part 4 (Chapters 10 and 11) focuses on crimes against habitation and property, while Part 5 (Chapters 12, 13, 14, 15, and 16) delves into crimes against the community and institutions which include white-collar crimes—from tax evasion to mail and securities fraud. Chapter 12 also presents key federal acts that bear on antitrust crimes and monopoly.

Chapter 14 gives a complete background on drug- and alcohol-related crimes including the types and classification of psychoactive drug and the history of drug legislation in the United States from the nineteenth century onward. Next, the chapter moves on to current legislation and applications of the law concerning alcohol and narcotics.

Chapter 15 examines crimes against the administration of justice, defines obstruction of justice, bribery, and contempt of court and outlines what these concepts mean in their current applications in the criminal justice system.

Finally, Chapter 16, elucidates the complexities of gangs and terrorism and the difficulties in defining them accurately. After giving a historical background on gangs and organized crime, this chapter tackles modern definitions of gangs and the variations in laws that target gangs and terrorism.

How to Study Criminal Law

As stated, here is a detailed and, we believe, foolproof strategy for succeeding in your criminal law course. (The strategy can also be applied successfully in other courses.) Before beginning, however, it is important to emphasize three qualities that are important in the learning process and that we cannot teach you: *desire, commitment, and perseverance.* If you are unwilling to apply those three qualities to your study of crimnal law, we cannot guarantee success.

Criminal law, like any other course, builds in stages. Information presented in later chapters often assumes knowledge of information introduced in earlier chapters. You cannot afford to fall behind and then expect to catch up in one massive cramming session.

To get off to a good start, prepare yourself before the course begins by setting learning goals, organizing your time, studying your syllabus, and examining your own learning style.

Set Learning Goals for Yourself

The purpose of setting goals is to understand exactly what you plan to accomplish. Ask yourself what you want out of this course. Is it a specific grade? Perhaps you need an A or a B to keep up your grade average. Perhaps you need a certain body of knowledge from this course to get into a higher level course. Perhaps you need a specific set of skills. You may be taking this course to meet a requirement for your job, to attain a personal career goal, or simply to satisfy your curiosity about the subject. Be forewarned, however—if you set your goals too low, you are likely to achieve only those low goals. For example, if you are not interested in the course but are taking it only because it is required of all majors, you should not be disappointed if you earn less than an A or a B.

Organize Your Time

Now that you have set your goals, you need to organize your time to accomplish them. Time management allows you to meet your goals and still have time for activities. It helps you work smarter, not just harder. As a rule of thumb, for every class hour, allow two study hours. If an exam is coming up, allow more study time. Plan to study when you are most alert. You will retain information longer if you study on a regular basis, rather than during one or two cramming sessions. Either before or after a study session, have some fun! Timely breaks from studying enhance the learning process.

Study Your Syllabus

Usually the course syllabus is available on the first day of class, but sometimes it is available sooner. If you can get a copy early, you will be that much ahead. The syllabus is your map for navigating the course. It should define the goals or objectives of the course, specify the textbook and supporting materials to be used, and explain course requirements, including the method or formula for determining final grades. The syllabus will also include a course schedule indicating when particular topics will be covered, what material needs to be read for each class, and when tests will be given. Other useful information on a course syllabus may include the instructor's name, office location, phone number, and office hours, and perhaps, the types of extra credit or special projects you may complete. Keep the syllabus in your notebook or organizer at all times. Review it at the beginning of each class and study session so you will know what course material will be covered and what you will be expected to know. Write down important due dates and test dates on your calendar.

Eight-Step Study Plan to Maximize Your Learning

This plan is based on research that shows people learn—and remember—best when they have repeated exposure to the same material. This technique not only helps you learn better but can also reduce anxiety by allowing you to become familiar with material step by step. You will go over material at least six times before you take an exam.

Step 1: Use a Reading Strategy

In most cases, you will be asked to read material before each class. The SQ3R (Survey, Question, Read, Recite, and Review) method can help you get the most out of the material in every chapter of your book. Reading the material before class will acquaint you with the subject matter, arouse your interest in the subject, and help you know what questions to ask in class.

Survey By surveying an assignment, you are preparing yourself for a more thorough reading of the material.

Read the Chapter Title, the Chapter Objectives, and the Chapter Outline What topics does the chapter cover? What are the learning objectives? Do you already know something about the subject?

Read the Summary by Chapter Objectives This will give you an overview of what is covered in the chapter.

Look for Key Terms Key terms are the names for or words associated with the important concepts covered in the chapter. Key terms are printed in boldface type in the text. Definitions of the key terms appear in the margins near the text in which they are introduced.

Question Turn the chapter objectives into questions. For example, if the objective is, "State a basic definition of law," turn it into a question by asking yourself, "What is a basic definition of law?" Look for the answers to your questions as you read the chapter. By beginning the study of a chapter with questions, you will be more motivated to read the chapter to find the answers. To make sure your answers are correct, consult the summary at the end of the chapter.

You can also write a question mark in pencil in the margin next to any material you don't understand as you read the chapter. Your goal is to answer all your questions and erase the question marks before you take an exam.

Read Before you begin a thorough reading of the material, make sure that you are rested and alert and that your reading area is well-lighted and ventilated. This will not only make your reading time more efficient, but help you understand what you read.

Skim the Material Generally, you will need to read material more than once before you really understand it. Start by skimming or reading straight through the material. Do not expect to understand everything at once. You are getting the big picture and becoming familiar with the material.

Read, Highlight, Outline The second time, read more slowly. Take time to study explanations and examples. Highlight key terms, important concepts, numbered lists, or other items that will help you understand the material. Most students use colored highlighting markets for this step. Put question marks in pencil in the margin beside any points or concepts you don't understand.

Outline the Chapter in your Notebook By writing the concepts and definitions into your notebook, you are using your tactile sense to reinforce your learning and to remember better what you read. Be sure you state concepts and definitions accurately. You can use brief phrases to take more extensive notes for your outline, depending on the material.

Apply What You Read In criminal law, as in other course, you must be able to apply what you read. The experiential activities and critical thinking exercises at the end of each chapter allow you to do this. Complete those activities and exercises when you have finished studying the chapter.

Recite In this step, you do a self-check of what you have learned in reading the chapter. Go back to the questions you formed from the chapter objectives and see if you can answer them. Also, see if you can answer the Questions for Review at the end of each chapter. Try explaining the material to a friend so that he or she understands it. These exercises will reveal your strengths and weaknesses.

Review Now go back and review the entire chapter. Erase any question marks that you have answered. If you still don't understand something, put a Post-it® by it or mark it in your text. These items are the questions you can ask in class.

Study Plan
1) Use a Reading Strategy
2) Combine Learning Styles in Class
3) Review Class Notes
4) Reread the Text
5) Get Help if Necessary
6) Study Creatively for Test
7) Develop Test-Taking Strategies
8) Review Your Results

Step 2: Combine Learning Styles in Class

Think of the time you spend in class as your opportunity to learn by listening and participating. You are combining visual, aural, and tactile learning styles in one experience.

Attendance: More Than Just Showing Up

Your attitude is a critical element. Attend class *ready to learn*. That means being prepared by having read and reread the assignment, having your questions ready, and having your note-taking materials organized.

Because criminal law, like other courses, builds in stages, it is important for you to attend every class. You cannot ask questions if you are not there. And you may miss handouts, explanations, or key points that often are included on a test.

One final note. If you cannot attend a class, call the instructor or a classmate to find out what you have missed. You do not want to show up the next day and find out the instructor is giving a test!

Attention: Active Listening and Learning During most classes, you spend more time listening than you do reading, writing, or speaking. Learning by listening, however, calls for you to become an *active listener* and to participate in the class. This means you come to class prepared, you focus on the subject, you concentrate on what the instructor or other students are saying, and you ask questions. Block out distractions such as street noises or people walking by the classroom.

Participation In reading the material before class, you will have made a list of questions. If those questions are not answered in class, then ask your instructor to answer them. If the instructor makes a point you do not understand, jot it down and ask him or her to explain it as soon as you can.

Note Taking Why take notes? We forget nearly 60 percent of what we hear within one hour after we hear it. Memory is highly unreliable. This is why taking notes during class is so important.

Note taking involves both listening and writing at the same time. You must learn not to concentrate too much on one and forget the other. Follow these tips for taking good notes:

Listen for and Record Main Ideas You do not need to write down everything your instructor or other students say. By reading your assignment before class, you will know what the main topics are. Listen for those topics when your instructor goes over the material in class, then take notes on what he or she says about them. If the instructor emphasizes the importance of a topic for a test, be sure to make a note of this information as well (for example, "This section really important for exam"). If you think you have missed a point, either ask your instructor to repeat or rephrase it right away, or mark the point with a question mark and ask your instructor about it later.

Use Outline Style and Abbreviations Set up your notes in outline style, and use phrases instead of complete sentences. Use abbreviations of symbols whenever possible (& for and, w for with, and so on). This technique will help you write faster to keep up with the instructor.

Step 3: Review Class Notes

Listening and taking notes are critical steps in Learning, but reviewing your notes is equally important. Remember—Repetition reinforces learning. The more times you go over material, the better you learn it.

Fill in the Blanks As soon as possible after a class, review your notes to fill in any missing information. Make sure you do it the same day. Sometimes you may be able to recall the missing information. If you can't, check your textbook or ask to see another student's notes to obtain what you need. Spell out important abbreviations that you may not recognize later.

Highlight Important Information Marking different types of information helps organize your notes. You want to find what you need when you need it. Try these suggestions for highlighting your notes:

1. Use different colored highlighting pens to mark key terms, important Supreme Court decisions, and other kinds of information. Then, you will know that green, for example, always indicates key terms; blue indicates Supreme Court decisions; and so on. This method will help you find specific information quickly and easily.
2. Write a heading such as "The Elements of a Crime" at the beginning of each key topic. These headings can either correspond to those in the chapter, or you may make up your own headings to help you remember key information.

Step 4: Reread the Text

After reviewing your notes, you are ready to reread the chapter to fix the concepts in your mind.

Read for Details
- Go over the key points and main ideas carefully. Make sure you understand them thoroughly and can explain them to someone in your own works.

- Review the Chapter Objectives (that you have turned into questions) and the Questions for Review. Make sure you can answer all the questions and that you understand your answers.

Mark Your Text
- Highlight any important terms or concepts you may have missed in your previous reading
- Highlight any Myth/Fact boxes, FYIs, case applications or figures you feel are important to remember.
- Erase any question marks in the margin that represent questions you have answered.
- Use Post-It® notes to mark anything of which you are still unsure. Ask questions about those points in the next class, talk them over with other students, or make an appointment to meet with your instructor to discuss your questions.

Step 5: Get Help if Necessary

What if you have read the material, taken notes, and asked questions, and you still do not understand the material? You can get further help. As soon as it becomes apparent that you need some help, ask for it. If you wait until the semester is nearly over, it may be too late. Here are several sources of help.

Your Instructors Most instructors are willing to spend extra time with students who need help. Find out what your instructor's office hours are and schedule an appointment to go over the material in more detail. You may need several sessions. Remember to take notes during those sessions.

Study Groups Join a study group in your class, or start your own. What one person does not learn, another does. Study groups take advantage of each member's expertise. You can often learn best by listening and talking to others in such groups. Chances are that, together, you will be able to master the material better than any one of you could alone. This is an example of power in numbers.

Learning Labs Many schools have learning labs that offer individual instruction or tutoring for students who are having trouble with course material. Ask your instructor or classmates for information about the learning labs in your college or university.

Private Tutors You might consider getting help from a private tutor if you can afford the fee. Although this route will cost you more, it may take only a few sessions to help you understand the material and keep up with the class. Check with your instructor about the availability of private tutors.

Step 6: Study Creatively for Tests

If you have read your assignments, attended class, taken notes and reviewed them, answered the Questions for Review, and completed the Experiential Activities and Critical Thinking Exercises, then you have been studying for tests all along. This kind of preparation means less stress when test time comes around.

Review: Bring It All Together You should enter all exam dates on your calendar so that you know well in advance when to prepare for a test. If you plan extra time for study during the week, you will not have to cram the night before the test.

During that week, bring together all your textbook notes, all your handouts, and other study materials. Reread them, paying particular attention to anything you marked that the instructor emphasized or that you had trouble understanding.

In addition to studying the Summary by Chapter Objectives, Key Terms, and Questions for Review at the end of each chapter, it is a good idea to make a summary sheet of your own that lists all the major points and other information that will be covered on the test. If you have quizzes or tests you have already taken, review them as well. Focus on the material you either missed or did not do well on before.

Do not hesitate to ask the instructor for information about the test, in particular:

- The types of test items he or she will use (multiple-choice, true-false, matching, fill-in-the-blanks, short answer, essay)
- What material, if any, will be emphasized, and what material, if any, will not be included
- How much time you will have to take the test

Step 7: Test-taking Strategies

No matter how well you prepare for a test, you will feel some anxiety just before and even during the exam. This is natural—*everybody* feels this way. The guidelines in this section will help you manage your anxiety so that you can do your best.

Before the Test: Get Ready Use this checklist to help you prepare the night before or a few hours before an exam.

- Gather supplies: unless instructed otherwise, at least two sharpened pencils with good erasers, a watch for timing yourself, and other items if you need them (such as a blue book for essay exams).
- If the test is in your first class, get up at least an hour before the exam to make sure you will be fully awake.
- Eat well before the test, but avoid having a heavy meal, which can make you sleepy.
- Arrive early to review your notes and study materials.

Remember: Luck favors the prepared!

During the Test: Go for It! Memorize these strategies to help you during the exam.

- Follow the directions. Listen carefully to the instructor's directions and read the printed directions carefully. Ask questions if the directions are unclear.
- Preview the test. Take a few minutes to look over the entire test. This will give you an idea of how much time to allot to each of the components.
- Do the easier sections first. If you get stumped on a question, skip it for now. You can come back to it later. Finish with the harder sections.
- Go back over the test. If you finish ahead of time, double-check your work and look for careless errors. Make sure your writing is legible if you are taking an essay exam or an exam that requires short answers. Make sure that your name and other information the instructor requires are on the test papers.

Step 8: Reviewing Your Results

Never throw away any of your quizzes or tests. Tests give you direct feedback on your progress in the courses. Whether the test is a weekly quiz or a mid-term, do not just look at the grade and put the paper in your file or notebook. Use the results of each quiz or test to help you achieve your goals.

Learn From Your Successes First review the test for those questions you answered correctly. Ask yourself the following questions:

- What are my strongest areas? You will know which topics to spend less time studying for the next exam.
- What types of items did I find easiest to answer (multiple-choice, true-false, etc.)? You might want to start with these types of items on the next exam, giving you more time to work on the harder items.

Learn From Your Mistakes Look over your errors, and ask yourself these questions:

- What types of items did I miss? Is there a pattern (for instance, true-false items, Supreme Court decisions)?
- Did I misunderstand any items? Was it clear to me what each item was asking for?
- Were my mistakes the result of carelessness? Did I read the items incorrectly or miss details? Did I lose track of time? Was I so engrossed in a test section that I forgot to allow myself enough time to get through the entire test at least once?

Look back through the textbook, your notes, class handouts, and other study materials to help you understand how and why you made the mistakes you did. Ask your instructor or classmates to go over your test with you until you know exactly why you missed the items. Evaluating your errors can show you where you need help and what to watch out for in the next test.

Refine Your Action Plan: The Learning Spiral You can think of the eight-step action plan as an upward spiral. Each time you travel a full cycle of the plan, you accumulate more knowledge and experience. You go one turn higher on the spiral.

Use your test feedback and classroom work to help you refine your plan. Perhaps you need to spend more time reading the textbook or reviewing key terms. Perhaps you did not allow enough time for study during the week. Or you might need extra help from your instructor, your classmates, or tutors. Make adjustments in your plan as you tackle the next part of the course.

About the Author

Norman M. Garland is Professor of Law at Southwestern University School of Law in Los Angeles, where he teaches evidence, constitutional criminal procedure, and trial advocacy. He received his J.D. from Northwestern University School of Law, and his L.L.M. from Georgetown Law Center where he was an E. Barrett Prettyman Fellow in trial advocacy. Professor Garland is a member of the Illinois, District of Columbia, and California Bars. He has had ten years of trial experience as a criminal defense attorney, mainly in federal felony cases. In 1968 he joined the faculty of Northwestern University School of Law where he helped establish the Northwestern University Legal Clinic. He joined the faculty of Southwestern University School of Law in 1975 to help establish the Southwestern Conceptual Approach to Legal Education (SCALE). In the mid-1980s, he spent two summers as a deputy district attorney in Ventura County, California, where he gained experience as a prosecutor. He is co-author of *Advanced Criminal Procedure In A Nutshell, Criminal Evidence for the Law Enforcement Officer* (Glencoe/McGraw-Hill 2000), and *Exculpatory Evidence,* 2d ed. He has also authored a number of computer interactive lessons for law students available through the Center for Computer-Assisted Legal Instruction (CALI).

Acknowledgments

A number of people were of substantial help to me in the production of this book. First are the research assistants from Southwestern University School of Law. They include Assaf Hami, Nancy Michael, Edie Rogoway, Joanie Roschlein, and El Mahdi Young. Very special thanks are due to one final research assistant, Melinda White, who contributed more than anyone. I would like to thank the dean, faculty, and board of trustees of Southwestern University School of Law. Part of this book was written with the aid of summer research grants from the law school and my research assistants were paid through the school's work-study program. I thank members of the support staff at Southwestern, Jeannie Nicholson and Martha Fink, for their assistance through the years that I have worked on this book. Finally, I wish to thank Dr. John Evans formerly of the International Centre for Criminal Law Reform of the University of British Columbia for his suggestion that I write this book.

Dedication

To my wife, Melissa Grossan, for her love, support, and understanding.

PART 1

Criminal Law and the Criminal Justice System

CHAPTER 1

Nature, Origins, and Purposes of Criminal Law

CHAPTER 2

The Structure and Operation of the Criminal Justice System

CHAPTER 3

Constitutional Limitations on the Criminal Law

Chapter Objectives

After reading this chapter, you will be able to:

1. State a basic definition of law.
2. Explain what distinguishes the criminal law from other law.
3. Define the common law.
4. State the principle of legality.
5. Explain what the MPC is.
6. Identify the principal purpose of the criminal law.
7. Name the two justifying theories of punishment that underlie modern criminal law.
8. Define punishment in the criminal justice system.

Chapter Outline

From where did the United States derive its laws?

2

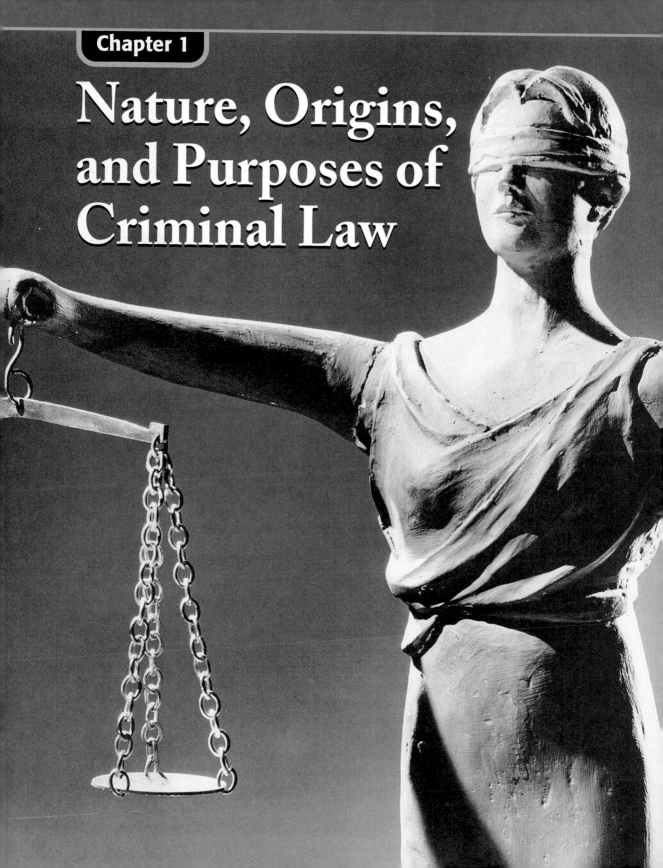

Chapter 1

Nature, Origins, and Purposes of Criminal Law

1.1 The Nature and Origins of Law

The definition of the word "law" is multifaceted and ranges from simple to complex. For example:

law The federal, state, or local enactments of legislative bodies; the known decisions of the courts of the federal and state governments; rules and regulations proclaimed by government bodies; and proclamations by executives of the federal, state, or local government.

- One dictionary definition of **law** is "A rule of conduct or procedure established by custom, agreement, or authority."[1]
- According to *Black's Law Dictionary*, law is "That which is laid down, ordained, or established." In this very general sense, law could consist of a culture's moral code, the commandments of a religion, or the regulations enacted by a political body to govern its members.

In the United States today, most citizens understand the concept of law to consist of:

- the federal, state, or local enactments of legislative bodies.
- the known decisions of the courts of the federal and state governments.
- rules and regulations proclaimed by administrative bodies.
- proclamations by executives of the federal, state, or local government.

Lawmakers distinguish between two types of rules: 1) religious and moral values, and 2) rules created by government to protect individuals and promote social welfare. People recognize that some actions may be immoral even though they are not illegal. In addition, people generally believe that they should be able to live according to their religious principles, as long as their actions do not violate the law.

Citizens of the United States may share a common view of the legitimate sources of law; but may also disagree about what behavior should be regulated by the government. For example, some people believe that abortion should be considered murder and thus should be prohibited by law; others hold that decisions about abortion should be made on personal religious or moral grounds, without governmental interference.

There is also disagreement on the role government should play in other matters of life and death, such as physician-assisted euthanasia, the use of reproductive technologies, and genetic screening. Other practices such as gambling and prostitution are considered immoral by some people, but morally acceptable by others. States differ in

Jury Nullification

Jury nullification occurs when a jury, having the power to acquit a criminal defendant, does so in complete disregard of the rules of law and facts before it. Even though the jury's decision may be incorrect, its decision is final. Jury nullification is legal, even though courts have held that the jury cannot be told of the power, nor can the defendant argue for it.

their approach to such practices: Gambling of all kinds is prohibited in some states, but in others, it is used through lotteries as a way of raising revenues for public schools.

Many cultures do not make the distinction between secular (non-religious) and religious law that is so central to American culture. For example, Islamic law, or Sha'ria, is derived from the sacred writings of the Koran. It provides the rules by which Muslim society is organized and governed, and the means for resolving conflicts between individuals and between individuals and the state. In the American colonies, witchcraft was an offense punishable by death under British law because of centuries-old church persecutions of people who were believed to practice beliefs other than Christianity. In Salem, Massachusetts, 20 persons (19 women and one man) were hanged as witches in 1692. The English statutes on witchcraft were not repealed until 1736, after thousands of women had been executed for the crime of practicing witchcraft.

Emergence of Written Laws

From time immemorial, humankind has sought to minimize turmoil and chaos by the imposition of some set of rules by which to live. From the edicts of kings and conquerors to the U.S. Constitution, rules of conduct for society have been proclaimed and enforced.

Ancient Law   Although human societies have always had rules of conduct, the first known written laws are believed to be those found on clay tablets in Ur, one of the city-states of Sumeria. They were created about 5,000 years ago. A much more extensive set of laws was established by King Hammurabi, who ruled Babylonia from 1792 to 1750 B.C. The Code of Hammurabi consisted of 282 laws that dealt with marriage, divorce, debt, wages, and the practice of slavery. It also defined criminal acts and penalties for committing them. The laws were carved on a black stone monument that was eight feet high.

English and American Common Law   Every ancient nation eventually developed formal legal codes, and the American legal code derives primarily from that of England. Before the Norman Conquest, the law in England was administered primarily according to Anglo-Saxon customs, with the church playing a major role. After William of Normandy conquered England in 1066, he established the *eyre*, that is, a court with judges who traveled throughout

➤ **The Origins of the Common Law**   Because the United States was originally an English colony, both countries share a common law heritage. *What is the common law, both historically and as it applies to modern law?*

common law   Law created by judicial opinion. Historically, law from America's colonial and English past, which has set precedents that are still sometimes followed today.

the kingdom once every seven years to hear cases as representatives of the king. The decisions of these judges and of other members of the central judiciary formed by the Normans to administer the law formed a large part of England's **common law**.

In England after the Norman Conquest, crimes and civil wrongs were less clearly defined at first. There was no penal code or even a set of criminal taboos discernable from a body of judicial decisions. Common law offenses simply consisted of the use of force against those who violated the King's peace, which could result in both punishment and the imposition of monetary sanctions. At common law, the use of violence was condemned, rather than the consequences of a violent act. In other words, the focus was on the violation of the King's peace, rather than on the harm done to the victim.

The common law developed from this foundation through judicial interpretation and elaboration of the concept of violence until crimes were recognized in such specific categories as homicide, robbery, arson, and assault. Eventually, especially from the sixteenth century on, enactments of Parliament added specific crimes to the array of common law offenses.[2]

Emergence of Modern Criminal Law   When the 13 colonies were established in America, they adopted England's common law. As the colonies developed and the United States was formed, the law of the United States developed separately from the English common law tradition. Eventually, **statutory law** replaced common law, also known as judge-created law. American statutory law was, and is, created through the state and federal legislatures. Today, the term common law refers to the body of law that is derived from judicial decisions rather than from legislative enactment. It can also refer to all of the laws that came from England and colonial America.

Today, virtually all criminal law is statutory law. This means that crimes are defined by the legislatures of the states and the federal government. You will learn about the two main types of law in the United States in the next section.

Civil Law Versus Criminal Law

Today, the United States judicial system provides for criminal law violations, also called crimes, and civil law violations, also called torts:

Criminal Law   **Criminal law** is different from other types of law, and from civil law in particular, because it involves a violation of public rights and duties, which create a *social harm*. Just as the common law considered a crime to be a violation of the King's peace, rather than a harm done to a victim, modern crimes are considered to be social harms that affect the entire community—and must be punished by the community in turn. In other words, what distinguishes the criminal law from all other law is that the criminal law

statutory law Law that is created through the American state and federal legislatures.

criminal law Law that involves the violations of public rights and duties, which create a social harm.

CRIMINAL LAW Online

For Law Students

Visit **cl.glencoe.com** for a link to **law.com**. Check out the section for law students under "News and More," and browse the three sections under "Cases and Filings." How do these sites provide useful information to law students and professionals?

Myth	Fact
The founders of the United States devised the legal system in order to protect citizens from those who did not obey the law.	Rather than protecting society from the offender, the original rationale for imprisonment was to insulate the lawbreaker from the temptations inherent in society.

seeks to regulate acts that are contrary to the community interest of the social or government unit—federal, state, or local.[3]

civil law Law that deals with matters that are considered to be private concerns between individuals.

tort A civil violation; the civil law's equivalent of a crime.

Civil Law   **Civil law** deals with matters that are considered to be private concerns between individuals. It includes laws dealing with personal injury, contracts, and property, as well as administrative law. A violation of civil law is called a **tort**. When a tort is committed, civil law provides a remedy in the form of an action for damages. The same is true for violations of contractual obligations.

For legal purposes, the same act may be both an offense against the state, which is a crime, and an offense against an individual, which is a tort. If someone steals another person's property, the offender may be punished under criminal law by imprisonment and/or a monetary fine, and may be required to pay restitution to the victim. In addition, the victim can sue in civil court for monetary damages. The trials of O.J. Simpson in the 1990s illustrate the overlapping of civil and criminal law. In October 1995, Simpson was acquitted of the murders of Nicole Brown Simpson and Ronald Goldman. However, in February 1997, in a civil trial brought by the family of Ronald Goldman against Simpson, the jury awarded $8.5 million in damages.

CRIMINAL
LAW
Online

Check your answers at
cl.glencoe.com.

Self Check   Why does the complexity of the definitions of law vary so much?

1.2 Criminal Law in the United States

The American and French revolutions stimulated a legislative movement in the area of criminal law. Of special concern was the severity of the criminal law: By 1800, more than 100 different kinds of offenses were punishable by death under English law.[4]

Much of the criminal law reform in England and the United States was influenced by the utilitarian legal philosopher, Jeremy Bentham. Bentham reorganized the law of crimes according to the amount of social harm they caused. As a result, the law of crimes in most American states has been recast into more or less coherent penal codes. At least since the late nineteenth century, the criminal law has been expressed in a penal code in all but a few American jurisdictions.

Purpose of the Criminal Law

The underlying purpose of the criminal law is to prevent and control crime. The criminal justice system seeks to carry out this goal by sanctioning behavior by an individual who violates the criminal law. To say this, however, is only to begin the subject of inquiry. Other questions can come up, such as:

- How do we know what conduct to sanction?
- Who, among those who may have engaged in the conduct, should be sanctioned?
- What sanction should be imposed?

The question of what conduct to sanction, which is also called the question of criminalization or decriminalization, is largely answered with respect to what most people think of as crime. This usually includes offenses such as murder, rape, assault, robbery, burglary, and traditional forms of theft. The modern focus of debate is on the question of criminalization in other areas, such as offenses designed to protect public morality, the economy, the environment, or generally to promote public welfare.

The question of who among those who have engaged in the conduct should be sanctioned involves consideration of the principles of basic elements of criminal culpability and criminal defenses. Generally, the criminal law seeks to sanction only those persons who intentionally violated the criminal law, under circumstances that did not involve excuse or justification. The question of what sanction to impose will be covered in a later section of this chapter, which will discuss punishment.

The Elements of a Crime A more complete definition of a crime includes the specification of five elements. A crime has been committed when the following elements are present:

1. A willed unlawful act, the ***actus reus***
2. A guilty mind, the ***mens rea***. The guilty mind element does not require intent to violate the law, but rather the intent to commit the act that the law prohibits.
3. A concurrence of act and mental state
4. The occurrence of harm to a person, property, or society
5. A causal relationship between the criminal act and the harm

Historical Perspectives on Crime

From 1820 to 1830, there was an increase in the construction of prisons, asylums, and reformatories. During the colonial period crime was accepted as a part of society, and criminal acts were considered the result of sinfulness. But in the Jackson era, reforming offenders and eliminating crime became social goals. "Another alternative then became not only feasible but essential: to construct a special setting for the deviant. Remove him from the family and community and place him in an artificially created and therefore corruption-free environment. Here he could learn all the vital lessons that others had ignored, while protected from the temptations of vice."

SOURCE: D. J. Rothman, *The Discovery of the Asylum: Social Order and Disorder in the New Republic.* Boston: Little, Brown 1971. 2nd edition 1990. Quote from 1971 edition, p. 71.

actus reus A willed unlawful act.

mens rea A guilty mind, or intent.

Statutory Criminal Law

The development of the common law of crimes that began in eleventh-century England continues to a smaller degree today, because some non-statutory crimes are still recognized in some jurisdictions. Otherwise, the criminal law develops and is redefined by legislative enactment, often in response to societal pressures. For example, in response to a public outcry against rising crime, the U.S. Congress adopted the Violent Crime Control and Law Enforcement Act of 1994, which related to a range of problems from sexual offenses to drive-by shootings. (See Figure 1–1 on page 12 for an excerpt of this act.) Congress, through such enactments, refines and redefines the criminal law. Similarly, state legislatures regularly redefine the criminal law in each state.

All of the 50 states and the federal government have their own separate set of criminal statutes. No state is bound by the criminal laws of another state, or by the laws of the federal government. For the most part, criminal law is a matter of state jurisdiction, although the reach of federal criminal laws has expanded in recent times. Nonetheless, federal criminal law can apply only to those matters where federal jurisdiction extends, such as national aspects of drug control or other crimes that involve interstate activities.

The Principle of Legality

legality The principle that no one can be punished for an act that was not defined as criminal before the person did the act.

Another reason for the decline of judicially created criminal law definitions is the principle of **legality**, which is a core concept of the American system of criminal justice. Under this principle, no one can be punished for an act that was not defined as criminal before the person did the act.

The principle of legality is *nullum crimen sine lege, nulla poena sine crimen,* which means "no crime without law, no punishment without crime." Basically, this means "that conduct may not be treated as criminal unless it has been so defined by an authority having the institutional competence to do so before it [the conduct] has taken place."[5] This principle is deeply imbedded in the American system of justice. If a court declares conduct criminal that has not previously been defined as criminal, then the principle of legality is violated.

There are three corollaries to the principle of legality:

1. Criminal statutes should be understandable to reasonable law-abiding people.

2. Criminal statutes should be crafted so as not to delegate basic policy matters to policemen, judges, and juries for resolution on an *ad hoc* and subjective basis.

3. Judicial interpretation of ambiguous statutes should "be biased in favor of the accused."[6]

Contemporary Applications of Common Law

Many states have abolished common law crimes, relying exclusively on statutory or code definitions. For example, Section 6 of the California Penal Code provides, "No act or omission . . . is criminal or punishable, except as prescribed or authorized by this Code."[7] But although modern criminal law is essentially statutory, the role of the courts continues. This is so because the criminal statutes often contain vague or general language that requires courts to interpret the statute's meaning when applied to a particular case.

A classic example is the statutory definition of burglary, which makes a "nighttime" burglary a more serious offense. The term

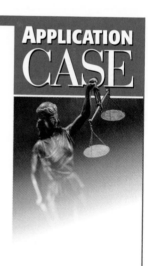

APPLICATION CASE

Defining Murder

Keeler v. Superior Court

At one time the definition of murder in California, which had abolished the common law, was the unlawful killing of a human being with malice aforethought. In the case of *Keeler v. Superior Court* (1970), the defendant was charged with murder of a fetus that was stillborn as a result of the defendant's attack on the mother, his ex-wife. The defendant approached his ex-wife, said he heard she was pregnant, and, stated "I'm going to stomp it [the baby] out of you," shoved his knee into her abdomen and struck her.

The Supreme Court of California looked to the common law in concluding that a fetus born dead was not a "human being." As a result, the defendant's murder conviction was set aside. Soon after the *Keeler* decision, the California legislature redefined "human being" in the Code section defining murder to include a fetus.

Critical Thinking Could the defendant have been charged with another crime in this case? If so, what?

SOURCE: *Keeler v. Superior Court* 470 P.2d 617 (Cal. 1970).

FIGURE 1–1

An Introductory Excerpt from the Violent Crime Control and Law Enforcement Act of 1994

U.S. Department of Justice Fact Sheet

The Violent Crime Control and Law Enforcement Act of 1994 represents the bipartisan product of six years of hard work. It is the largest crime bill in the history of the country and will provide for 100,000 new police officers, $9.7 billion in funding for prisons and $6.1 billion in funding for prevention programs which were designed with significant input from experienced police officers. The Act also significantly expands the government's ability to deal with problems caused by criminal aliens. The Crime Bill provides $2.6 billion in additional funding for the FBI, DEA, INS, United States Attorneys, and other Justice Department components, as well as the Federal courts and the Treasury Department.

SOURCE: www.ncjrs.org/txtfiles/billfs.txt

"nighttime" was not defined in some statutes, requiring the courts to decide when a burglary would be considered to have occurred at night. You will read more about how modern laws have adapted to this issue in Chapter 9.

Even though the common law is but an antecedent to today's modern statutory criminal law in most jurisdictions, the common law definitions of crimes continue to play a role in understanding the criminal law. Some states have not abolished common law crimes and still expressly recognize common law offenses, although prosecution of such offenses in those jurisdictions is rare.[8]

Moreover, many states' criminal laws are but codifications of the common law crimes. Therefore, if there is a question of statutory meaning, the courts will look to the common law definitions to help in understanding the term in question. One example of this is where the California Supreme Court looked to the common law definition of human being to determine that a fetus could not be a murder victim (see Application Case, page 11).[9]

The Model Penal Code

In 1923, the American Law Institute (ALI), an organization of lawyers, judges, and legal scholars, was founded for the purpose of clarifying and improving the law. One of the major factors leading to the establishment of the ALI was general dissatisfaction with the criminal law. (See Figure 1–2.) In 1931, a proposal for a model penal code was presented, but the Depression prevented funding the project. In 1950, a grant from the Rockefeller Foundation rekindled the model penal code project, which got under way in 1952. However, it was not until 1962, after 13 tentative drafts, that the American Law Institute published the Proposed Official Draft of the Model Penal Code.

The **Model Penal Code (MPC)** is a comprehensive recodification of the principles of criminal responsibility. The drafters of the MPC relied upon existing sources of the criminal law including codes, judicial opinions, and scholarly commentary. The ALI did not expect or intend that the MPC would be adopted in its entirety anywhere, or that it would result in a uniform national criminal law. The hope was that the MPC would generate a

Model Penal Code (MPC)
A comprehensive recodification of the principles of American criminal responsibility.

FIGURE 1–2

The American Law Institute

The American Law Institute was organized in 1923 following a study conducted by a group of prominent American judges, lawyers, and teachers known as "The Committee on the Establishment of a Permanent Organization for the Improvement of the Law." The Committee had reported that the two chief defects in American law, its uncertainty and its complexity, had produced a "general dissatisfaction with the administration of justice."

According to the Committee, part of the uncertainty of the law, as it then existed, was due to the lack of agreement among members of the profession on the fundamental principles of the common law. Other causes of uncertainty were reported as "lack of precision in the use of legal terms," "conflicting and badly drawn statutory provisions," "the great volume of recorded decisions," and "the number and nature of novel legal questions." The law's complexity, on the other hand, was attributed in significant part to its "lack of systematic development" and to its numerous variations within the different jurisdictions of the United States.

The Committee's recommendation that a lawyers' organization be formed to improve the law and its administration led to the creation of The American Law Institute. The Institute's charter stated its purpose to be "to promote the clarification and simplification of the law and its better adaptation to social needs to secure the better administration of justice, and to encourage and carry on scholarly and scientific legal work." Its incorporators included Chief Justice and former President William Howard Taft, future Chief Justice Charles Evans Hughes, and former Secretary of State Elihu Root; Judges Benjamin N. Cardozo and Learned Hand were among its early leaders.

SOURCE: www.ali.org/ali/thisali.htm

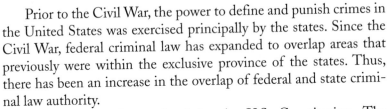

Myth	**Fact**
The American Law Institute wrote the Model Penal Code with the hope that it would be adopted in full throughout the United States.	The ALI did not expect or intend that the MPC would be adopted in full anywhere, or that it would result in a uniform national criminal law.

systematic reevaluation of the criminal law in the nation, and that hope has been fulfilled. An overwhelming majority of the states have adopted revised criminal codes as a result of the MPC. The MPC stands as a model in the reform of principles of American criminal responsibility.[10]

The Growth of Federal Criminal Law

Prior to the Civil War, the power to define and punish crimes in the United States was exercised principally by the states. Since the Civil War, federal criminal law has expanded to overlap areas that previously were within the exclusive province of the states. Thus, there has been an increase in the overlap of federal and state criminal law authority.

Federal power is restricted by the U.S. Constitution. The Constitution explicitly enumerates the federal crimes of treason, counterfeiting, crimes against the law of nations, and crimes committed on the high seas.[11] All other federal criminal jurisdiction emanates from the "necessary and proper" clause of article I, § 8 of the Constitution, which grants the power to Congress to pass legislation necessary to implement any enumerated federal power.

Since earliest times, the U.S. Supreme Court has upheld the exercise of this power. Especially since the Civil War, Congress has enacted criminal laws relating to a wide range of subjects, from civil rights, use of the mails, commerce, narcotics, extortion and robbery affecting interstate commerce, interstate travel to facilitate illegal activities associated with organized crime, organized crime itself, and racketeering.[12] Thus, the definition of federal crimes is an important aspect of the study of American criminal law.

State and Federal Liability

A person can be tried for both state and federal crimes if the offenses come under both jurisdictions. One example is kidnapping: If a person robs and kidnaps someone in one state, then takes the victim across the country, the kidnapper has violated state and federal laws.

Self Check

1. Explain the historical significance of the common law.
2. Why is statutory law taking the place of common law in many situations?

CRIMINAL LAW *Online*

Check your answers at **cl.glencoe.com.**

1.3 Punishment in the Criminal Justice System

The question of what sanction to impose upon those who should be sanctioned raises questions relating to punishment. The feature of the criminal law that distinguishes it from other law is the imposition of punishment for its violation. The stigma attached to the conviction for a crime is often, alone, sufficient to constitute a "punishment" in the eyes of society. Nonetheless, the criminal law "consists of prohibitions of antisocial behavior backed by serious sanctions."[13] Although not every person who suffers a criminal conviction is punished, a meaningful set of mandatory rules of conduct must provide for punishment of those who violate the rules. Thus, the meaning, theories, and possible justifications of criminal punishment are closely related to the meaning, theories, and possible justifications of the criminal law itself.[14]

Prisons Versus Schools

In 1980, California spent 2.3 percent of its budget on corrections and 9.2 percent for higher education. By 1996, however, it spent 9.4 percent on corrections, and 8.7 percent on higher education.

SOURCE: Elizabeth Alexander, "The Care and Feeding of the Correctional-Industrial Complex," in John P. May (Ed.) *Building Violence: How America's Rush to Incarcerate Creates More Violence*. Thousand Oaks, CA: Sage, 2000, p. 53.

punishment When an agent of the government, using authority granted by virtue of a lawful criminal conviction, intentionally inflicts pain, loss of liberty, or some other unpleasant consequence on the person who has been convicted.

Definition of Punishment

Punishment is not exclusively meted out through the criminal justice system, or the law, for that matter. Parents, teachers, religious leaders, and club presidents, to name a few, regularly punish their children, students, parishioners, and fellows. **Punishment** in the criminal justice system exists when an agent of the government, pursuant to authority granted to the agent by virtue of an accused's criminal conviction, intentionally inflicts pain on the accused or otherwise causes the accused to suffer some consequence that is ordinarily considered to be unpleasant.[15]

Punishment is relative and, thus, any definition of it may be criticized as being arbitrary. After all, if the punishment consists of payment of a fine that the convict can afford, then the punishment may seem inadequate. The same could be said for minimal sentences of imprisonment, probation, or community service. Similarly, noncriminal penalties, such as payment of a large civil judgment or loss of a license to practice a profession, may be very painful, but do not constitute punishment. They merely represent civil penalties.

The criminal law depends upon the threat of punishment to define it. Moreover, actual punishment must be delivered, at least enough of the time to make the threat meaningful. Thus, even though there are many reasons why threatened punishment may not be carried out—prosecutors may not pursue the case or the jury may acquit the accused—punishment is actually required in most cases.

Fundamentally, there are two justifying theories of punishment underlying modern criminal law:

Myth

The criminal justice system is operated by the government.

Fact

As early as the 1840s in New York, legislation was passed that curbed privately operated prison industries. By 1984, 80 percent of the states had contracted the services of private correctional companies. In 1990, more than 9,000 beds in adult correctional facilities were in private institutions.

SOURCE: *Punishment in America: Social Control and the Ironies of Imprisonment*, by Michael Welch. Thousand Oaks, CA:, Sage, 1999, p. 278.

- The **retributive theory** is that a wrongdoer deserves punishment, and the retributive view is easily expressed in the phrase "just deserts."
- The **utilitarian theory** is predicated on the notion that a social practice is desirable if it promotes human happiness more effectively than any other alternatives. Although it is a simplification, the hallmarks of the utilitarian view are general deterrence, individual deterrence, reform, and vengeance.

The moving force in American criminal law theory from approximately 1900 to 1970 was the utilitarian justification. Since the 1970s, however, the retributive justification has reemerged as a significant factor.

Retributive Rationale for Punishment

The simplest retributive analysis is that one who has violated the rights of others should be penalized. Punishment restores the moral order that has been breached by the original wrongful act. The eighteenth-century German philosopher, Immanuel Kant, made the point in stating that an island society about to disband should still execute its last murderer. Society's duty is to punish, or else the guilt remains upon society. Punishment of the deserving honors free will. Moreover, the imposition of a punishment in proportion to the degree of wrongdoing sets matters right. These retributive theories are all predicated on principles of moral wrong.

A different retributive explanation is that criminals deserve punishment because they violate social norms. By avoiding questions of morality, this theory fits better with modern approaches to criminal punishment. It avoids the criticism that the criminal law should not be in the business of correcting moral wrongs. Furthermore, this theory does not impose upon public officials the impossible task of deciding subtle degrees of moral guilt.

Utilitarian Justification for Punishment

The utilitarian justification is based upon Jeremy Bentham's test for moral desirability of an act or social practice: whether the act or practice promotes human happiness better than possible alternatives. The greatest good for the greatest number was the goal of this test. In modern usage, utilitarianism usually is employed to refer

retributive theory A justification for punishment based on the theory that a wrongdoer deserves punishment for punishment's sake.

utilitarian theory A justification for punishment based on the notion that a social practice is desirable if it promotes the greatest good for the largest number of people.

Capital Punishment: For the Greatest Good? Capital punishment is an example of individual deterrence, and some argue that it is a good example of utilitarian retribution.

Do you agree that capital punishment of certain offenders does the greatest good for the largest number of people?

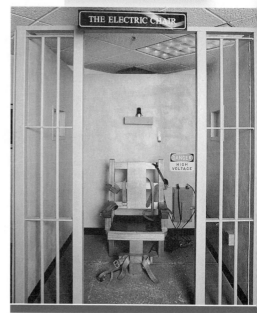

THE ELECTRIC CHAIR

Jail for the Mentally Ill?

The largest provider of mental health services in most states is the state prison system. The problem, of course, is that jails and prisons are not, either by intent or design, therapeutic environments.

SOURCE: Andrea Weisman, "Mental Illness Behind Bars," in John P. May (Ed.) *Building Violence: How America's Rush to Incarcerate Creates More Violence.* Thousand Oaks, CA: Sage, 2000, p. 106.

three-strike laws Laws that impose sentences of 25 years to life for those who have been convicted of certain serious offenses three times.

zero tolerance Laws that impose maximum penalties for certain crimes, such as particular sex offenses; also known as *one-strike laws*.

to theories that likely consequences determine the morality of action. Thus, the varieties of beneficial consequences that can be realized by punishment according to utilitarian theory include the following:

General Deterrence   General deterrence is the effect that punishment of the offender will have in causing other people in the community to refrain from committing the same crime. The offender cannot be reached, but the future offender can. A rational person will see that the benefits to be gained from criminal activity will be outweighed by the harms of punishment, even when those harms are discounted by the possibility of avoiding detection. On this theory, the greater the temptation to commit the crime and the less the chance of detection, the more severe the penalty should be.

Individual Deterrence   Individual deterrence is the effect that the imposition of punishment upon the wrongdoer will have in causing him or her to refrain from repeating the act. To achieve this result, the punishment must be severe enough to outweigh the benefits of the crime. More severe punishment for repeat offenders is justified because the first penalty was ineffective.

Incapacitation   Incapacitation is the removal or restriction of freedom of those who have violated criminal laws. The primary means used to achieve incapacitation is imprisonment. An intolerance for recidivist offenders and a desire to incapacitate such offenders have developed in the form of **three-strike laws**, which impose sentences of 25 years to life for those who have been convicted of certain serious offenses three times. **Zero tolerance**, or one-strike laws, have also been developed, which impose maximum penalties for certain crimes, such as particular sex offenses.

Myth

One-strike laws can be applied to any felony charges.

Fact

Although three-strike laws can be applied to most felony charges, one-strike laws target certain crimes. For instance, since child molesters are known to have high recidivism rates, California law has imposed one-strike laws for criminals that commit certain sexual offenses against children.

Reform Reform of the criminal so that he or she will no longer desire to commit crimes and will be a useful citizen may be sought as a by-product of punishment. Usually, conviction and imprisonment alone has been thought not to be enough to achieve reform. Therefore, rehabilitative therapy and education have been thought essential to the achievement of reform. In recent years, reform has fallen out of favor as an achievable beneficial consequence of punishment.

Vengeance Vengeance is the imposition of the punishment in the context of an "eye for an eye" or a "tooth for a tooth" and it is usually associated with retribution. The utilitarian, however, may see the benefit in vengeance whereas the retributivist believes that the wrongful act deserves punishment for punishment's sake. Vengeance is a beneficial consequence in that it satisfies victims, their families and friends, and members of the public. More specifically, the frustration generated in such people by the failure of punishment makes the imposition of punishment for their sake a worthwhile cause.

Modern Views on Punishment

During the 1970s, the American criminal justice system, reflecting broad public view, reacted against rehabilitation. The prison system was seen to have produced more hardened criminals than reformed persons. There developed a challenge to broad discretion in sentencing and unequal treatment of similar offenders as failing to produce desired results, while at the same time generating resentment. Thus, the trend developed and has continued to treat equal offenders equally, and to set the penalty to the seriousness of the offense. The result has been sentencing structures that are determined without broad discretion, such as mandatory sentencing and sentencing pursuant to set guidelines.

Rehabilitation is not a dead letter. However, the current trend in punishment theory is to set prison terms at the time of sentencing. Therapy, education, and training in prison should continue, but should not be factors considered in determining when a prisoner is released.

FYI

Vengeance Today

Vengeance can be seen today in several countries. One common example is the use of the death penalty for murder charges, which is still used in several countries. Another example is the actual or chemical castration of repeat sex offenders. A third, more extreme example is the practice in some Islamic countries of cutting off the hands of thieves.

CRIMINAL LAW *Online*

Consumer Advice

Billed as "the best law site for consumers," **FreeAdvice.com**, accessible through the link at **cl.glencoe.com**, offers information on almost all legal topics. Check out one section under Criminal Law, then write about what you have learned.

Self Check

1. Which do you prefer, retributive theory or utilitarian theory? Why?
2. Do you think that retributive theory is better for some crimes than utilitarian theory? For which crimes, and why?

CRIMINAL LAW *Online*

Check your answers at cl.glencoe.com.

Nature, Origins, and Purposes of Criminal Law

SUMMARY BY CHAPTER OBJECTIVES

1. State a basic definition of law.

Law is a rule of conduct or procedure established by custom, agreement, or authority. Law, in its generic sense, is a body of rules of action or conduct prescribed by controlling authority and having binding legal force.

2. Explain what distinguishes the criminal law from other law.

Criminal law seeks to regulate acts that are contrary to the community interest of the social or government unit—federal, state, or local. Therefore, a criminal act, though aimed at a personal victim usually, is perceived as involving a social harm and is prosecuted on behalf of the public.

3. Define the common law.

The common law means law created by judicial opinion. The law of the United States and England share a common heritage in the common law of England. When the 13 colonies were established in America, and when the United States gained independence, they adopted the common law of England.

4. State the principle of legality.

A core concept of the American criminal justice system, legality holds that no one can be punished for an act that was not defined as criminal before the person did the act. If a court declares conduct criminal that has not previously been defined as criminal, then the principle of legality is violated.

5. Explain what the MPC is.

The MPC (Model Penal Code) is a comprehensive recodification of the principles of criminal responsibility, drafted in reliance upon existing sources of the criminal law including codes, judicial opinions, and scholarly commentary. Though not adopted in any state, it has affected a reform of the criminal law in a majority of states and it stands as a model in the reform of principles of American criminal responsibility.

6. Identify the principal purpose of the criminal law.

The principal purpose of the criminal law is to sanction, usually by punishment, behavior by an individual that violates the rules of acceptable conduct within a community. The question of criminalization or decriminalization is largely answered with what most people think of as crime—offenses such as murder, rape, assault, robbery, burglary, and traditional forms of theft. The modern focus of debate on the question of criminalization is in other areas, such as offenses designed to protect public morality, the economy, the environment, or generally to promote public welfare.

7. Name the two justifying theories of punishment that underlie modern criminal law.

The two justifying theories of punishment underlying modern criminal law are the retributive justification and the utilitarian justification. The retributive justification is that a wrongdoer deserves punishment. The utilitarian justification is predicated on the notion that a social practice is desirable if it promotes human happiness better than other possible alternatives. The basic hallmarks of the utilitarian view are general deterrence, individual deterrence, reform, and vengeance.

8. Define punishment in the criminal justice system.

Punishment in the criminal justice system occurs when an agent of the government, using authority granted by virtue of a legal criminal conviction, intentionally inflicts pain, loss or liberty, or some other unpleasant consequence on the person who has been convicted.

KEY TERMS

law, page 4
common law, page 6
statutory law, page 7
criminal law, page 7
civil law, page 8
tort, page 8

actus reus, page 9
mens rea, page 9
legality, page 10
Model Penal Code (MPC) , page 13
punishment, page 16

retributive theory, page 17
utilitarian theory, page 17
three-strikes laws, page 18
zero tolerance, page 18

From where did the United States derive its laws?
Find it on page 5.

QUESTIONS FOR REVIEW

1. Name the various sources from which laws derive.
2. What is the difference between common law and statutory law?
3. What is the difference between criminal law and civil law?
4. What is the history of the common law?
5. How did Jeremy Bentham influence criminal law in England and the United States?
6. What is the Model Penal Code, and why was it created?
7. What document restricts federal law, and how?
8. Define *actus reus* and *mens rea*, and explain why they are needed for criminal charges.
9. How are retributive justification and utilitarian justification different? Similar?
10. How is punishment relative, and why?

PROBLEM-SOLVING EXERCISES

1. **Pre-Trial Detention** Immediately after being arrested and booked on drug charges or similar offenses, most white, middle-class people are released from custody as soon as a family member arrives to post bail. But unemployed people from a low socioeconomic class facing similar charges may be unable to post bail and may therefore remain in jail until their court appearance, which may be weeks or even months away. According to 1997 Bureau of Justice Statistics, 378 state correctional facilities (27 percent of the total) were under court order to reduce population or to improve conditions of confinement. Conditions in jails may include sleeping on the floor, long waits to call a family member or lawyer, and limited access to showers. In overcrowded jails, plumbing may fail, resulting in clogged toilets and flooding. Answer the following questions:
   a) Does being detained in such a setting prior to trial constitute punishment before before trial?
   b) What issues are raised by the fact that the poor are more likely to experience pre-trial confinement than upper- and middle-class suspects?

2. **Protection Against Cybercrime** You have heard that a new cybercrime has affected several other parts of the country, but that prosecutors are unable to press charges because the crime has not been added to their statutes and there is no legal precedent (i.e., common law). You do not want your jurisdiction to have the same problem, since it is clear that this crime could easily happen here. Answer the following questions:

a) How do you persuade legislators in you area to pass a law against this crime before it occurs?

b) How do you persuade law enforcement to educate people about this crime, since it is not yet a crime that they are legally required to enforce? What else can you do to help protect your jurisdiction?

3. **Sentencing Guidelines** You are a county judge who has been in your job for nearly a year. In that time, you have sentenced many drug offenders to the lengthy sentences that are within your options, and your community has strongly supported you. On the other hand, you are finding out from state prison authorities that their prisons are highly overcrowded, there are not enough funds to staff them properly, and nonviolent drug offenders are suffering from negative consequences, such as physical and sexual abuse from more hardened criminals. They strongly urge you to stop sentencing nonviolent drug offenders to any type of incarceration, and to instead use treatment-based alternatives.

a) Which option will you pick? Why?

b) Will you suggest or implement any changes to sentencing guidelines or options, so that more judges will pick treatment-based alternatives for drug offenders? Why or why not?

WORKPLACE APPLICATIONS

1. **Prison Budget** In 1995, for the first time in U.S. history, the total cost of state-issued bonds to finance prison construction surpassed the total for bonds to construct colleges. Compare the budgets for education and corrections in your county and state. Answer the following questions:

a) If you were a member of the state legislature, what recommendations would you make concerning funding for these areas?

b) How would you set funding priorities for these budget items compared to others?

2. **Find Out About Law School** Contact a professor at your local law school (it might be at your college or university) and ask him or her to explain how a law student could focus on his or her studies in criminal law.

a) What courses need to be taken, and what kind of internship or part-time work would help provide useful job experience?

b) If people specialize in criminal law, what are some of their job options after passing the bar? After gaining a few years' full-time case experience?

3. **Revise a City Ordinance** You are a judge who is hearing a case regarding a city ordinance that forbids more than five women from living in the same house together. The ordinance is obviously outdated, and it was created during the time that your state was a territory and large numbers of women were imported for purposes of prostitution. The ordinance,

therefore, was meant to attack brothels, not law-abiding citizens who are living together. The defendants in this case are six women who have been heavily involved in citywide police reform, and they have made some political enemies. The prosecutor is zealously trying to get them convicted, and has told you that he

would like to see all of them in jail. You, however, feel that the ordinance needs to be struck from the books.

a) How will you decide in this case? Why?

b) Should you ever let political factors influence your decision? Why or why not?

INTERNET APPLICATIONS

1. **Obtain Legal Information** Visit helpful sources of free legal information for those with little or no understanding of criminal law, by clicking the links at **cl.glencoe.com**. Click on the section for Criminal Law and browse some of the categories. What is covered here? Does anything appear to be missing, and if so, why? What crimes are here that you did not expect to see?

2. **Information for the Law Student** Visit The Law Student's Paradise through the link at **cl.glencoe.com**, then explore the search engines that are provided for federal and state court cases. What resources does this source provide, and how could it help a law student understand the use of common law in today's legal system?

ETHICS ISSUES

1. **Fireworks Ban** You are a county police officer patrolling the unincorporated areas of your county. While driving down a quiet road, you observe a fireworks stand that is selling fireworks to a long line of eager customers, who are loading their trunks with huge boxes of firecrackers, sparklers, roman candles, and even small (although legal) tubes of dynamite. It is June 29th, and your county has passed an ordinance prohibiting the sale of fireworks as of July 1 of this year. Answer the following questions:

a) Can you arrest the suspect? Why or why not? What can or should you do in response to this situation?

b) If you return two days later and witness any sales of fireworks, what can you do?

2. **Forensic Evidence** You are a prosecutor who is handling the case of a notorious child killer. It has taken investigators four years to build enough evidence to arrest him, and you are glad to see him off the streets. You have charged him with seven counts of murder and are asking for the death penalty. The public, which has been impatient to see this killer caught and punished, wants a quick resolution to this problem. Shortly after the trial begins, a forensic scientist who works for your county tells you that she has discov-

ered a problem: It appears that the evidence from three of the cases indicates that a completely different offender was involved in these crimes—not the defendant, even as an accomplice. This could slow down the court process and possibly create the idea among the general public that the defendant is innocent of the other crimes, as well.

a) Do you charge the defendant with these crimes anyway? Why or why not?
b) If the defendant is charged with these killings and the case is closed, what are the implications regarding arresting and charging the actual killer?

ENDNOTES

1 *The American Heritage Dictionary of the English Language* (3d ed. 1992, Houghton Mifflin Company).

2 G. Hazard, "Criminal Justice System: Overview," 2 *Encyclopedia of Crime and Justice* 450 (1983).

3 See Joshua Dressler, *Understanding Criminal Law* § 9.10[B], pp. 109–110 (3d ed. 2001).

4 *Keeler v. Superior Court*, 470 P.2d 617 (Cal. 1970).

5 *Keeler v. Superior Court*, as quoted in Dressler, note 3 at § 5.01[C][2], at p. 31.

6 Joshua Dressler, *Understanding Criminal Law* § 5.01[A], at pp. 39-40 (3d ed. 2001).

7 California Penal Code § 6 (West. 1997).

8 See Joshua Dressler, *Understanding Criminal Law* § 3.02[A], p. 28 (3d ed. 2001).

9 470 P.2d 617 (Cal. 1970).

10 See C. McClain, "Criminal Law Reform: Historical Development in the United States," 2 *Encyclopedia of Crime and Justice* 510–12 (1983) (McClain states that 30 states had adopted revised criminal codes affected by the MPC by 1980 and another nine had code revisions underway or completed and awaiting enactment. See also Joshua Dressler, *Understanding Criminal Law* § 3.03, p.

31, n.22 (3d ed. 2001), citing Peter W. Low, "The Model Penal Code, the Common Law, and Mistakes of Fact: Recklessness, Negligence, or Strict Liability?," 19 *Rutgers L.J.* 539 (1988) (stating that the MPC stimulated adoption of revised penal codes in at least 37 states).

11 See Sara Sun Beale, "Federal Criminal Jurisdiction," *Encyclopedia of Crime and Justice* 775–79 (1983).

12 Id.

13 Kent Greenwalt, "Punishment," 4 *Encyclopedia of Crime and Justice* 1336, 1337 (1983).

14 See Richard S. Frase, "Criminalization and Decriminalization," 2 *Encyclopedia of Crime and Justice* 437 (1983).

15 See Joshua Dressler, *Understanding Criminal Law* § 2.02, p. 12 (3d ed. 2001).

16 *Punishment in America: Social Control and the Ironies of Imprisonment*, by Michael Welch. Thousand Oaks, CA:, Sage, 1999, p. 90.

17 National Association of State Budget Officers, 1996, 1995 State Expenditures Report, pp. 77, 88. Washington, DC.

Chapter Objectives

After reading this chapter, you will be able to:

1. Describe the fundamental structure of the American criminal justice system.
2. Name the two basic police functions.
3. State what is required for a law enforcement officer to arrest a suspect.
4. State the purpose of a preliminary hearing.
5. Describe the two alternative methods for charging serious crimes.
6. List the three possible bases for a defendant's pre-trial motion to dismiss.
7. State the four possible grounds for appeal of a criminal conviction.
8. State when a defendant is entitled to an attorney at trial.

Chapter Outline

What are three ways a defendant can have his or her case dismissed?

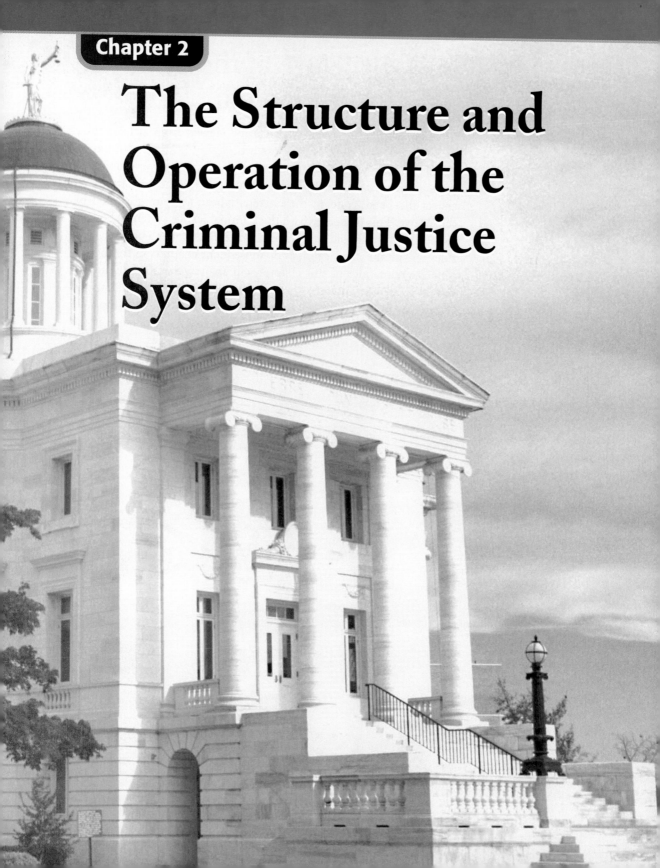

Chapter 2

The Structure and Operation of the Criminal Justice System

2.1 Structure of the Criminal Justice System

The criminal justice system can be viewed from at least three perspectives: as a social system, as a body of legal rules, and as an administrative system.[1] Viewed as a social system, the criminal justice system encompasses all levels of society, from the legislature that enacts the penal code to the citizens whose acts are governed by those laws. This perspective on the criminal justice system is beyond the scope of this book. The criminal justice system as a body of legal rules will be the primary focus of subsequent chapters in this book.

The remainder of this chapter will analyze the criminal justice system as an administrative system. In this role, the criminal justice system is the official apparatus for enforcing the criminal law. It consists of law enforcement agencies, prosecution and defense attorneys, courts, and correctional institutions and agencies.

FIGURE 2–1

Overview of the Criminal Justice System

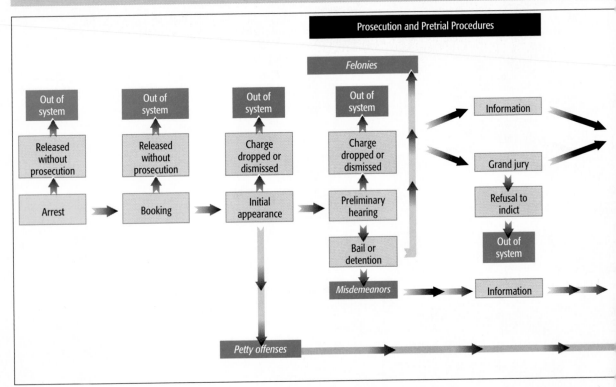

Law Enforcement

The main law enforcement agency in the United States is the police force. Police departments in cities, sheriff's departments in counties, state police, and state bureaus of investigation comprise the largest number of law enforcement officers in the country. In 1996, the national police-population ratio was 2.3 police officers per thousand citizens.[2] This statistic does not include the enormous number of private police (also known as private security) who are employed on private property such as office buildings, apartment buildings, shopping malls, and private residential communities. The number of private police who engage in patrol is larger than the number of law enforcement officers engaged in the same activity.[3]

The two basic police functions are prevention and detection:

Prevention Prevention is carried out by low-ranking officers assigned to cruise an area and watch for criminal activity. In the course of carrying out his or her duties, the police officer exercises

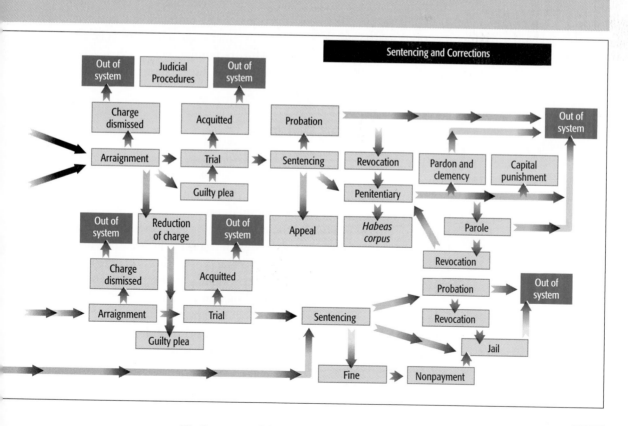

substantial discretion in deciding whether to arrest a person suspected of criminal wrongdoing. It is impossible for police officers to arrest all the offenders whom they encounter.

Detection Detection is usually performed by specialized squads consisting of older, more experienced, and higher-ranking officers. In addition to directly addressing crime, police departments spend a substantial amount of their time carrying out public services such as traffic control, crowd control, and emergency services.

Nationally, the Federal Bureau of Investigation (FBI) is charged with the responsibility of investigating federal law violations. There are a number of other federal law enforcement agencies, notably the Drug Enforcement Administration, the Bureau of Alcohol, Tobacco, and Firearms, the Customs Service, the Immigration and Naturalization Service, the United States Marshals Service, the Bureau of Postal Inspection, and the Secret Service.

All law enforcement agencies provide assistance to the prosecuting attorneys in presenting evidence in the courts to prosecute those arrested for criminal activities. Therefore, gathering evidence, maintaining evidence collected, and preparing evidence for presentation in a court of law are major functions of law enforcement agencies. For these purposes, most law enforcement agencies hire specially trained and educated personnel who are familiar with such specialized fields as ballistics, fingerprint analysis, blood stain analysis, and other areas of scientific methodology.

Prosecution and Defense

The American criminal justice system is an adversarial one. This means that the process by which guilt is determined is competitive, and the prosecution and defense are seen as adversaries, or rivals. In the American criminal justice system, the accused is presumed innocent until proven guilty, and the right to counsel attaches even before he or she is brought to court (at least with respect to an accused's decision whether or not to remain silent). The prosecuting and defending attorneys contend against each other, seeking a result favorable to their interests. The judge and jury function as independent judicial offices. Decisions from the point before arrest to the end of the process are shaped by this adversarial nature of the judicial system.

The chief prosecuting attorney in most state jurisdictions is a full-time, public, county official. He or she is usually elected to office and has a staff of assistant prosecuting attorneys. In some states and

Lawful Arrests

A police officer can make arrests for any felony for which he or she has probable cause to believe has been committed, but can only arrest for misdemeanors committed in the officer's presence. In many jurisdictions, a citizen who witnessed the misdemeanor may make a citizen's arrest, and later assert that he or she witnessed the crime being committed.

Public Defender

Duties and Description: Work with defendants, victims, witnesses, persons having interest in criminal cases, and varying levels of other governmental organizations. Interact with persons of diverse backgrounds and educational levels. Effectively manage the public in emotional and occasionally hostile situations. Work flexibly with changing deadlines and priorities. Higher job levels require experience as an attorney in the practice of criminal law. Occasionally, post-bar experience in a civil or general practice law office can apply.

Salary: Salaries vary from approximately $35,000 to $95,000, depending on location and experience.

Other Information: This job is usually a valuable stepping stone for young attorneys seeking to gain experience, but some attorneys make it their career. State applicants are required to have active membership in their states' bar association and must provide a bar number when applying. Federal applicants should be in good standing with a state bar and become admitted to whichever federal court for which they are applying. Spanish language proficiency is highly desirable in many locales.

Critical Thinking What qualities do you think an effective public defender should have?

SOURCE: Orange County (CA) Public Defender, http://www.oc.ca.gov/pd/emp.htm; Office of the State Public Defender, CO, http://www.state.co.us/gov_dir/pdef_dir/pd.htm.

in the federal system, the prosecutor is an appointed official. In some rural areas, the office of the prosecutor may be occupied by only one person, who may work only part-time at the job. In many urban areas, the prosecutor's office is very large. It is said that the Office of the District Attorney of Los Angeles County, with over 1,000 lawyers, is the largest law office in the country.

The chief prosecutor in the federal system is the Attorney General of the United States. In each of the 90-plus federal districts, the chief prosecuting officer is the U.S. Attorney for that geographic district. The Attorney General and the U.S. Attorneys are all appointed by the President of the United States. The assistant U.S. Attorneys are all federal employees.

It is the job of the prosecutor to take a case from the police and pursue it until the case terminates by trial, guilty plea, or dismissal.

The prosecutor must decide whether to pursue a formal charge and, if so, what crime to charge. The prosecutor is also responsible for conducting any plea negotiations, deciding whether to dismiss charges, and trying cases.

Since the 1960s, the U.S. Constitution has required that a defendant who is sentenced to more than six months in jail or prison is entitled to an attorney whether he or she can afford one. Moreover, any suspect who is interrogated by the police is entitled to warnings about the right to remain silent and to have an attorney present during interrogation, whether he or she can afford one. Therefore, many states and the federal government find it necessary to provide defense counsel to many criminal suspects and defendants. This is accomplished either through the private bar (the local attorneys association) or a public defender system.

Defense counsel must zealously represent the criminal defendant from the point of interrogation through the trial process, demanding that the prosecution respect the defendant's rights, treat the defendant fairly, and meet the burden of proof beyond a reasonable doubt in the event the case goes to trial.

Courts

There is a dual judicial system in the United States consisting of the federal and state courts. The federal courts exist throughout the nation while each state also has its own judicial system. All federal offenses are prosecuted in federal court and all state offenses are prosecuted in state courts. The **jurisdiction** of a court is the scope of its power or authority to act with respect to any case before it. The judicial power of U.S. courts, specified in Article II of the U.S. Constitution, "shall be vested in one Supreme Court, and in such inferior courts as the Congress may from time to time ordain and establish."

jurisdiction The power or authority of the court to act with respect to any case before it.

The staff of the courts, in addition to the judge, includes courtroom clerks, judge's clerks, and bailiffs. Bailiffs are law enforcement personnel assigned to keep order in the courtroom, attend to juries, oversee prisoners who are in custody during their court appearances, and otherwise provide security in the courtroom. In many jurisdictions, the bailiff is a deputy sheriff; in the federal courts, the bailiffs are deputy U.S. Marshals.

Federal Courts   There are currently federal trial courts in each state and 13 federal courts of appeal, arranged by circuits. Twelve of these are numbered circuits and one is a federal circuit (see

Figure 2–2 for an illustration). The federal courts have jurisdiction to consider cases charging defendants with violation of federal criminal laws.

State Courts   Each state also has its own court system. The structure of most state court systems is similar to that of the federal courts: a trial court, an intermediate appellate court, and a supreme court. In most states, the trial courts are organized by county. Furthermore, in most states, the trial courts are divided into two levels, an inferior and a superior court. The inferior court, often called the municipal court or justice of the peace court, conducts preliminary hearings in felony cases and trials in cases involving misdemeanors or petty offenses. The superior court, sometimes called the circuit or district court, is a court of general jurisdiction and has jurisdiction over felony trials.

FIGURE 2–2

The Federal Court Structure

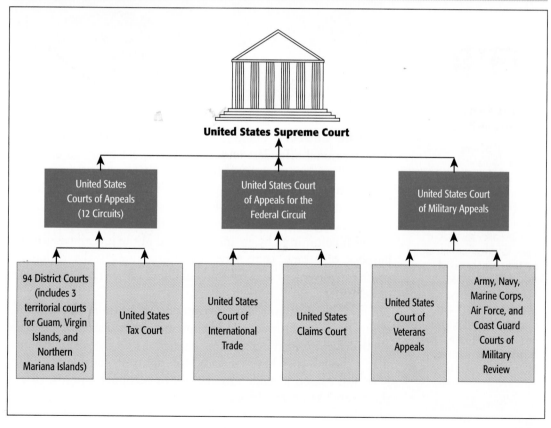

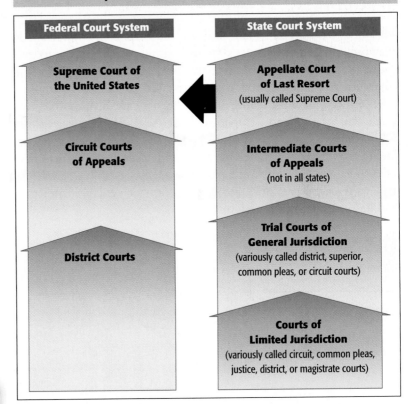

FIGURE 2-3

Dual Court System of the United States

Federal Court System

- Supreme Court of the United States
- Circuit Courts of Appeals
- District Courts

State Court System

- Appellate Court of Last Resort (usually called Supreme Court)
- Intermediate Courts of Appeals (not in all states)
- Trial Courts of General Jurisdiction (variously called district, superior, common pleas, or circuit courts)
- Courts of Limited Jurisdiction (variously called circuit, common pleas, justice, district, or magistrate courts)

Death Penalty for Juveniles

As juveniles have received greater due process rights over the years, juvenile court proceedings have also become more formal and juveniles have faced more severe punishment for their actions. As of this writing, the U.S. Supreme Court has allowed the death sentence for juveniles aged 16 and 17, although it has rejected it for juveniles any younger than 16.

Juvenile Courts There is also a juvenile court system in each state. Criminal offenders under a certain age, usually 18 or 16, are dealt with in juvenile courts by way of civil, rather than criminal proceedings. If the offense is particularly serious, the juvenile may be treated like an adult, and the case will be heard in the criminal court. Many youthful offenders who commit offenses that would be crimes if committed by an adult are tried in the juvenile courts, the purpose of which is to have specialized judges determine the youth's involvement and try to rehabilitate rather than punish him or her.

Juvenile court procedure was intended to be more informal than criminal courts. However, U.S. Supreme Court decisions since the 1960s have imposed due process restrictions on the juvenile courts that, although they have increased the rights of juvenile offenders, have also caused juvenile proceedings to become more formal and thus more like criminal courts.

◄ **Testimony and Evidence** Law enforcement officers frequently provide testimony for the prosecution. Anyone who gives testimony can be cross-examined by the opposing party. *Why is cross-examination an important part of the legal process?*

Courts and the Fourteenth Amendment Since about 1930, the U.S. Supreme Court has been interpreting the due process clause of the Fourteenth Amendment to incorporate constitutional criminal procedural requirements that apply to the states. These rights include:

- The right to trial by jury in cases involving serious offenses
- The right to assistance of counsel in any case in which a sentence of more than six months in jail or prison is imposed
- The privilege against self-incrimination, including a ban against comment by the prosecution on the defendant's failure to testify
- The presumption of innocence and requirement of proof beyond a reasonable doubt
- The freedom from unreasonable searches and seizures
- The right to silence and counsel during police interrogation
- The right to compel witnesses' attendance at trial, to confront them, and to cross-examine

- The right to a speedy and public trial
- Freedom from double jeopardy
- Freedom from cruel and unusual punishment
- Freedom from racial and sexual discrimination in substantive and procedural criminal law[4]

Violation of these constitutional requirements can be the subject of both state appeals and federal *habeas corpus* claims by prisoners.

Corrections

The American correctional system is made up of correctional institutions, such as jails and prisons, and correctional agencies, such as probation and parole offices. In addition, the broad term *community corrections* includes drug rehabilitation centers, halfway houses, community corrections centers, community service programs, and many other services that are available to less serious criminals or those who have shown significant rehabilitation.

Jails are used to maintain custody of persons arrested pending prosecution and of those sentenced to short periods of confinement, usually up to but not more than one year. Most jails are operated by cities, counties, or both. Jails provide few services, since most inmates are there temporarily. Usually, there are separate jail facilities for women and for juveniles.

All states maintain state penal institutions (prisons), consisting of state penitentiaries and juvenile training facilities. Often the institutions are graded according to level of security, ranging from maximum to minimum security. There are more than 500 state prison facilities in the United States,[5] with a total population in all the country's jails and prisons of 1.1 million.[6] Prison facilities are administered by a separate correctional agency of the state or federal government.

Two important features of the correctional system, which actually operate outside the walls of correctional institutions, are probation and parole.

Probation Most court systems have a probation department attached to them. The probation department investigates defendants prior to sentencing and provides a pre-sentence probation report to the court. In addition, the probation department provides supervision over those persons placed on probation after conviction. Probation is the most frequent disposition for first-time offenders.

Probationers are released back into the community and are required to stay out of trouble, avoid association with those involved in crime, attempt to find a job, avoid the use of alcohol and drugs, and report to a probation officer periodically. The probation service is designed to provide counseling, but because of the overwhelming caseload, probation officers usually are able to engage only in nominal supervision.

Parole Parole supervision is similar to probation supervision, except that the parole service is an agency of the state correctional system, rather than the court system. Violations of probation and parole lead to hearings that, in turn, lead to warning, incarceration, or re-incarceration.

1. Explain the differences between state and federal courts.
2. What roles do jails and prisons play in the criminal justice process? How do jails and prisons differ?

Check your answers at cl.glencoe.com.

2.2 Operation of the Criminal Justice System

The organization of the United States government is based on the principle of **federalism**, which states that power resides in the states unless expressly granted to the federal government. For this reason, the criminal justice system operates in 51 arenas. The basic system, however, is similar in each jurisdiction. The fundamental structure of the criminal justice system consists of law enforcement agencies, prosecution and defense attorneys, courts, and correctional institutions and agencies.

Law enforcement agents learn about most criminal acts through reports of victims or witnesses. Police also learn about crimes while working on patrol, surveillance, undercover, or other investigations to learn about crimes. The overwhelming majority of reported crimes are not solved. Investigations of crimes against persons, particularly homicides, take priority and, therefore, homicides are solved more often than other crimes.

federalism The system of government of the United States whereby all power resides in the state governments unless specifically granted to the federal government.

Arrest

probable cause Evidence that there is a fair probability that the suspect committed a crime—it is required for an arrest of a suspect by a law enforcement officer.

The criminal process most often begins with an arrest. An officer can arrest only if probable cause exists. **Probable cause** is evidence that there is a fair probability that the suspect committed a crime. An officer possessing probable cause may arrest the suspect without a warrant in a public place, unless the suspect is in his or her home. Alternatively, the officer can obtain a warrant from a court authorizing arrest of the suspect if there is a sufficient showing of probable cause. Arrests made by police on patrol are usually made without a warrant because of the need for a speedy response. Arrest with a warrant is likely to occur only when the arrest has resulted from investigation and there are no exigencies such as a crime in progress or "hot pursuit."

Not all arrests result in prosecution. The question of whether to prosecute is made not by the police officer but by the prosecuting attorney and the courts. Often, a perpetrator will have committed a major crime, usually a felony, and several lesser misdemeanors. For example, a suspect may have committed rape, which is the charge that the officer and prosecutor most want to be sure results in a conviction. But the suspect may have also committed the crimes of criminal trespass, breaking and entering into a dwelling, burglary, assault and battery, or theft. The arresting officer should be sure to include in the police report all elements of all the possible crimes that the officer finds the suspect committed. The decision whether to charge the suspect with those crimes is up to the prosecutor, and the lesser crimes may be used as bargaining chips by the prosecutor in plea negotiations.

Pre-Trial Procedures and Issues

After arrest and booking, and before the stage of the justice process at which the defendant may face a trial, the defendant must make several other court appearances. He or she will also most likely confer with his or her lawyer about plea bargaining, since approximately 90 percent of all felony cases are resolved in this manner. Plea bargaining, which you will learn more about shortly, is a process that helps expedite the justice system by enabling the courts to avoid a lengthy trial.

The key pre-trial procedures and issues are bail, charging the crime, the preliminary hearing, the handling of misdemeanor charges, the use of an indictment or information for felony charges,

FYI

Trials by Jury

In trials by jury in most jurisdictions, a 12-person jury must reach a unanimous verdict in felony cases. In some jurisdictions, however, the jury can be less than 12 and does not need to be unanimous to reach a verdict.

Myth	**Fact**
Every American jurisdiction is based upon English common law.	The state of Louisiana is the only American jurisdiction whose law is based on a source other than the English common law. It is based upon the Napoleonic Code.

arraignment and plea, plea bargaining, and (where applicable) dismissing the charges.

Bail   Most suspects are entitled to release after arrest and booking, either on the accused's own recognizance or on bail. **Recognizance** is a promise to appear in court. **Bail** is a deposit of cash, other property, or a bond, guaranteeing that the accused will appear in court. A **bond** is a written promise to pay the bail sum, posted by a financially responsible person, usually a professional bondsman. Bail is usually not very high, except in cases where it is shown that there is a risk that the accused will fail to appear for trial.

Charging the Crime   After arrest, the prosecutor will file a charge against the defendant if the prosecutor is satisfied that the evidence is sufficient to support the charge and that the case is worthy of prosecution.

Preliminary Hearing   After the prosecutor files the charge, a judge holds a **preliminary hearing** to determine whether probable cause exists. In some jurisdictions, the preliminary hearing is minimal, providing only a summary review of the sufficiency of the evidence. In other jurisdictions, the preliminary hearing is very extensive, amounting to a mini-trial.

At the preliminary hearing, an arresting officer has the first opportunity to present evidence to the court against the defendant. Many times, the officer will not get to testify at a trial because the defendant decides to enter into a plea bargain after hearing all of the evidence presented against him or her at the preliminary hearing. Therefore, the law enforcement officer should view the preliminary hearing as an important step in achieving the best result in a criminal case.

recognizance A promise to appear in court.

bail A deposit of cash, other property, or a bond, guaranteeing the accused will appear in court.

bond A written promise to pay the bail sum, posted by a financially responsible person, usually a professional bondsman.

preliminary hearing A post arrest, pre-trial judicial proceeding, at which the judge decides whether there is probable cause to prosecute the accused. In some jurisdictions, the preliminary hearing is minimal, in others it is a mini-trial.

Misdemeanor Charges   If the prosecution establishes probable cause, the defendant is required to answer to the charge in the trial court. If the crime charged is a misdemeanor or petty offense, the defendant will respond to the complaint filed by the prosecutor and enter a plea of guilty or not guilty. If the plea is not guilty, the case will be assigned to a court for trial.

Felony Charges: Informations and Indictments   Where the crime charged is a felony, the procedure is more complex. The common law rule required that a felony be charged only by a grand jury indictment. A **grand jury** is a panel of persons chosen through strict court procedures to review criminal investigations and, in some instances, to conduct criminal investigations. Grand juries decide whether to charge crimes in the cases presented to them or investigated by them. When a grand jury charges a person with a crime, it does so by issuing an **indictment**.

grand jury A panel of persons chosen through court procedures to review a criminal investigation and, in some instances, to conduct criminal investigations. Grand juries decide whether to charge crimes in the cases presented to them or investigated by them.

indictment The paper issued by a grand jury that charges an accused with a felony.

FIGURE 2–4

States That Use a Grand Jury, Information, or a Combination of Both in Their Preliminary Proceedings

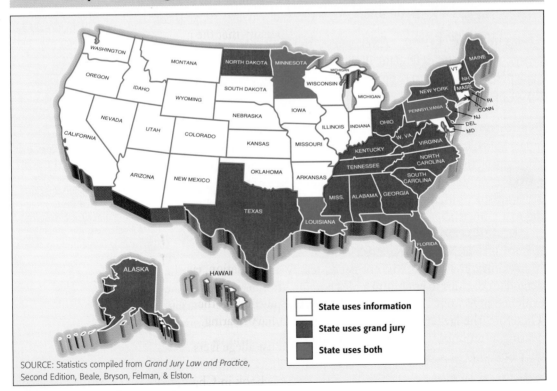

☐ State uses information

■ State uses grand jury

■ State uses both

SOURCE: Statistics compiled from *Grand Jury Law and Practice*, Second Edition, Beale, Bryson, Felman, & Elston.

In the federal system and in many states, felonies can still be prosecuted only by indictment of a grand jury. In those jurisdictions, after the police investigate a crime, the case is presented by the prosecutor to the grand jury. The grand jury hears testimony and decides whether to indict the accused. Where the defendant has been arrested on the street, in the process of committing a crime, the case can be immediately presented to the grand jury after arrest. In those jurisdictions that do not follow the grand jury procedure, prosecutors file a formal felony charge called an **information**. The information is merely a written statement of the formal charge, signed by the prosecutor.

information The paper issued by a prosecutor that charges an accused of a felony.

Arraignment and Plea After the formal charges have been filed against a defendant, either by indictment or information, the defendant appears in court at a proceeding called an arraignment or **arraignment and plea**. This is the defendant's appearance to respond formally to the charges. The defendant will enter a plea of guilty or not guilty. If the defendant pleads guilty, then the case will be set for sentencing. If the defendant pleads not guilty, the case will be set for trial.

arraignment and plea The defendant's appearance to respond formally to the charges.

Plea Bargaining Plea negotiations resolve a majority of all prosecutions filed.[7] Plea negotiations may result in a reduction of the original charge, which reduces the level of penalty that the judge may impose upon the accused. Another result of plea negotiations is that the prosecution recommends a specific sentence to the court, usually involving a lesser punishment than otherwise would be the case. In return, the defense enters a plea of guilty, and the prosecution does not have to go to the time and expense of taking the case to trial.

important

Dismissing Charges The defendant has a right to challenge the validity of the indictment or information by moving to dismiss the charges. There are only three bases for dismissal:

1. The crime charged is not a violation of the jurisdiction's law.
2. The facts asserted in the indictment or information, even if true, do not constitute the crime charged.
3. No reasonable jury could find the facts alleged on the basis of the evidence presented at the preliminary hearing.

In order to charge a crime, the prosecutor must allege facts as to each element of the crime as defined by law. (The definitions and elements of all major crimes are the focus of this book in Chapters

8 through 16.) The validity of a criminal charge is also determined by two other factors: the criminal statutes in effect in the jurisdiction, and federal and state constitutional law. In most jurisdictions, a valid criminal charge must allege that the defendant's acts violated some criminal statute. The federal constitutional provisions that relate to substantive criminal law issues include the due process clauses of the Fifth and Fourteenth Amendments and the cruel and unusual punishment clause of the Eighth Amendment. These issues are discussed in Chapter 3.

Trial of the Case

In the United States, an accused in a criminal case has a constitutional right to trial by jury for any crime for which the possible sentence is more than six months in jail or prison. The accused, however, can waive that right and have a trial before the judge alone. Before the trial commences, the judge will hear pre-trial matters, including motions to exclude evidence.

Where there is a jury, the actual trial process begins with jury selection. The trial proceeds with the prosecution making its opening statement, telling the story of the case and describing the evidence that will be presented. The defense can make its opening next, or it can reserve its opening statement until after the prosecution has presented its case. The prosecution then presents its case, consisting of witnesses, physical evidence, and documents. The defense has the right to cross-examine each prosecution witness. At the conclusion of the prosecution's case, the defense will ask the judge to decide whether the prosecution's evidence is enough to go to the jury, by making a motion for judgment of acquittal. If the motion is granted, the case is over, and the defendant cannot be charged again with that crime.

If the defense's motion for judgment of acquittal is denied, the defendant may rest without presenting any evidence, because the prosecution has the burden of proving the defendant guilty beyond a reasonable doubt. However, in most cases, the defense will present some evidence. The defendant may or may not choose to testify, and neither the court nor the prosecution can make any comment on the defendant's failure to do so. The defense's witnesses are subject to cross-examination by the prosecution. After the defense has presented all of its witnesses, physical evidence, and documents, the prosecution can offer evidence to rebut the defense's case. After that, the defendant has a chance to introduce rebuttal evidence as well.

Myth	**Fact**
A defendant has a constitutional right to a trial by jury for any criminal charges.	A defendant has a right to a trial by jury for any crime for which the possible sentence is more than six months in jail.

After the evidence for both the prosecution and defense has been completed—when each side has rested—both sides present closing arguments to the jury or, in a bench trial (a trial without a jury), to the judge. The judge then reads instructions on the law to the jury, after which the jury deliberates until it reaches a verdict.

In the event that the jury cannot reach a verdict on a charge, the judge will declare a mistrial and the prosecution may choose to retry the defendant. If the jury acquits the defendant, double jeopardy prohibits retrial or appeal by the prosecution. On the other hand, if the jury convicts, the accused can seek a new trial from the trial court or seek an appeal to an appellate court.

important

Post-Conviction Procedures and Issues

If a defendant is acquitted of the charges, he or she will be released from custody. Because of double jeopardy protections under the Fifth Amendment, the justice system cannot try the defendant twice for the same crime. Special exceptions to this exist when a defendant has violated different federal and state laws for the same crime, such as when a drug dealer violates state drug laws and federal organized crime laws simultaneously for the same crime. You will read about this more in Chapter 16.

If, however, a defendant is convicted, he or she must be sentenced. He or she has the right to appeal the sentence, although approximately 80 percent of appeals do not succeed. In addition, there are other types of post-conviction relief, such as filing a writ of *habeas corpus*.

Sentencing   If the defendant is convicted, the judge will ordinarily order a pre-sentence (or probation) report that will supply the judge with sufficient information upon which to base a decision on sentencing. Unless the charge carries a mandatory sentence, the

➤ **From Courtroom to Prison** After a defendant receives a prison sentence, correctional authorities process her arrival and she becomes an inmate. *What types of post-conviction relief are available for inmates?*

judge will hold a sentencing hearing, entertaining arguments from the prosecution and defense. The judge will then sentence the defendant in accordance with the statutory range. When the prosecution seeks the death penalty, the sentencing hearing will be a second trial before a judge or jury, who will hear evidence of aggravating and mitigating factors. In some states, the jury can also sentence the defendant for serious offenses other than the death penalty.

Appeal and Discretionary Review The bases for appeal of a criminal conviction on substantive grounds are limited to four possibilities:

1. The charge on which the accused was convicted is not a crime, either because the legislature did not proscribe the conduct or because the proscription is unconstitutional.
2. The evidence was insufficient to support a finding of fact on all the elements of the crime beyond a reasonable doubt.
3. Not all of the necessary elements of the crime were alleged.
4. The jury was improperly instructed.

CRIMINAL LAW Online

Justice Denied

Visit the Justice Denied Web site by clicking the link at **cl.glencoe.com**. Read at least two of the cases in the current monthly issue, then write a half-page report on whether you agree that these people have been denied justice. Explain your views objectively.

Other grounds for appeal, which do not relate to substantive criminal law issues, involve procedural and evidentiary errors alleged to have been committed by the trial court. In some jurisdictions, many claims to an appellate court are pursued by petition for *certiorari*, which allows the appellate court to decide, within its discretion, whether to hear the case.

Cases moving from the state courts to the U.S. Supreme Court are now only pursuable by a writ of *certiorari*, which is a written order from the U.S. Supreme Court to a lower court whose decision is being appealed, to send the records of the case forward for review. The Supreme Court receives thousands of petitions each year, but it reviews only a handful of criminal cases, mainly those that will settle a question that has been answered differently by different appellate courts or that present a substantial policy question that the Court wishes to address.

Post-Conviction Relief *Habeas corpus*, a common law remedy for an illegal confinement, exists in modern American criminal procedure to test the validity of a person's incarceration. ***Habeas corpus***, which literally means, "that you have the body," is a legal action separate from the criminal case. It can be brought only by a prisoner who has exhausted all of the usual appellate remedies. A federal prisoner can seek *habeas corpus* relief in the proper federal district court; state prisoners may seek such relief in the proper state court.

Under federal law, a state prisoner may seek *habeas corpus* relief in federal court if he or she alleges that the conviction violated the federal constitutional rights of the accused. As long as a defendant raises new grounds, he or she can file successive *habeas corpus* petitions. Just as with the original criminal conviction, these post-conviction petitions can be pursued from the trial court level all the way to the highest courts in the states and even the U.S. Supreme Court. Only rarely, however, can a prisoner seek post-conviction relief based on an issue relating to a substantive criminal law claim (such as the definition, or elements, of a particular crime).

habeas corpus Literally, that you have the body; it is a legal action separate from the criminal case, and can only be brought by a prisoner who has exhausted all the usual appellate remedies.

Self Check

1. What are the only three bases for dismissing a trial?
2. Explain the various grounds on which convicted criminals appeal their charges.

CRIMINAL LAW Online

Check your answers at cl.glencoe.com.

The Structure and Operation of the Criminal Justice System

SUMMARY BY CHAPTER OBJECTIVES

1. Describe the fundamental structure of the American criminal justice system.

The fundamental structure of the American criminal justice system consists of law enforcement agencies, prosecution and defense attorneys, courts, and correctional institutions and agencies. Moreover, the organization of American government is based on the principle of federalism, which holds that power resides in the states unless expressly granted to the federal government. For this reason, the criminal justice system operates in 51 arenas: the 50 state governments and the federal government (which includes the District of Columbia).

2. Name the two basic police functions.

The two basic police functions are prevention and detection. The prevention function is carried out by low-ranking officers assigned to cruise an area and watch for criminal activity. The detection function is usually performed by specialized squads who consist of older, more experienced, and higher-ranking officers.

3. State what is required for a law enforcement officer to arrest a suspect.

In the case of felonies, a law enforcement officer must have probable cause to believe that a person has committed a crime before he or she may arrest the suspect. In the case

of misdemeanors, an officer can only arrest for misdemeanors committed in the officer's presence.

4. State the purpose of a preliminary hearing.

The purpose of a preliminary hearing is for a judge to determine whether there is probable cause for the accused to answer to the crime charged. In addition, since many cases do not go to trial because of plea-bargaining, this is often the only chance that officers have to offer testimony and present evidence against the accused.

5. Describe the two alternative methods for charging serious crimes.

Felonies are charged either by an indictment or an information. An indictment is issued by a grand jury, which is a panel of citizens that decides whether to charge crimes in the cases presented to them (or investigated by them). An information, which is a piece of paper on which the charge appears, is filed and signed by the prosecutor.

6. List the three possible bases for a defendant's pre-trial motion to dismiss.

The three possible bases for a defendant's pre-trial motion to dismiss are:

- The crime charged is not a violation of the jurisdiction's law.
- The facts asserted in the indictment or information, even if true, do not constitute the crime charged.
- No reasonable jury could find the facts alleged on the basis of the evidence given at the preliminary hearing.

7. State the four possible grounds for appeal of a criminal conviction.

The four possible grounds for appeal of a criminal conviction are:

- The charge on which the accused was convicted is not a crime, either because the legislature did not proscribe the conduct or because the proscription is unconstitutional.

- The evidence was insufficient to support a finding of fact on all the elements of the crime beyond a reasonable doubt.
- Not all of the necessary elements of the crime were alleged.
- The jury was improperly instructed.

8. State when a defendant is entitled to an attorney at trial.

A defendant who is sentenced to more than six months in jail or prison is entitled to an attorney whether he or she can afford one. (Those who cannot afford an attorney are appointed one by the court.)

KEY TERMS

jurisdiction, page 32
federalism, page 37
probable cause, page 38
recognizance, page 39
bail, page 39

bond, page 39
preliminary hearing, page 39
grand jury, page 40
indictment, page 40

information, page 41
arraignment and plea, page 41
habeas corpus, page 45

What are three ways a defendant can have his or her case dismissed?
Find it on page 41.

QUESTIONS FOR REVIEW

1. Name some of the ways in which law enforcement agents learn about criminal acts.
2. Explain the difference between release upon recognizance and bail. What is a bond?
3. What is a grand jury, how does it work, and which jurisdictions use it?
4. What happens at an arraignment? What happens in response to the pleas of guilty or not guilty?
5. What is the burden of proof in a criminal trial?
6. What are the basic elements of the criminal trial? Include the different motions and actions of the prosecution and defense.
7. Name and define the three main perspectives from which the criminal justice system can be viewed.
8. Name the different types of departments in which police work, and give some examples of federal agencies.
9. What are the duties of the prosecutor? Of defense counsel?
10. What is jurisdiction? What is the jurisdiction of federal courts?
11. Name three or four of the constitutional due process rights that apply to state prisoners.
12. What are the general duties of a probation department?

PROBLEM-SOLVING EXERCISES

1. **Witness Treatment** A witness is called to court to testify against an individual charged with aggravated assault. The accused hit another man over the head with a cue stick in a barroom brawl, causing moderate injuries. The witness came to court on his day off, waited all morning and part of the afternoon to testify, then at 4:00 P.M. was informed that he could leave because the prosecution and defense agreed that the defendant would plead guilty to a lesser included offense. Answer the following questions:
   a) What has occurred here?
   b) Did the attorneys have a legal obligation to inform the witness of what was going on? What about an ethical right?
   c) Should the witness be angry? Why or why not?

2. **Disclosure** You are a federal officer who has arrested a key participant in an undercover drug transaction. You let him transfer the drugs to you and gave him money in exchange; in other words, you caught the perpetrator red-handed. In preparing for the preliminary hearing, the prosecutor tells you not to mention the fact that you were tipped by an informant to go the scene of the transaction. The prosecutor says that she wants to "spring" this information on the defense at trial.

a) Does the prosecutor have a legal right to do this? Why or why not?

b) What are the possible ramifications of such a move by the prosecutor?

c) Is such a move needed in this case? Why or why not?

d) What should you do? Why?

3. **Drug Possession** You are an appellate judge who is hearing the appeal of a convicted offender, who was given a 25-year sentence for possession with intent to distribute cocaine and transporting a controlled substance. Since the cocaine was found in the car that she was dri-ving, which was in her name but was shared with her two roommates, she insists that the drug was not hers and she had no idea that she was transport-ing it. On the other hand, police surveil-lance showed her visiting known drug dealers intermittently, and she had sev-eral bags in her car that would have been too large not to notice.

a) Does this defendant have a case? Why or why not?

b) Which factors influenced your deci-sion, and what other factors would help you make this decision?

WORKPLACE APPLICATIONS

1. **The Lesser of Two Evils** You are a police officer, working late at night. You are alone in a squad car, patrolling a resi-dential area that has been experiencing a rise in street crime. You observe a suspi-cious-looking group of three young men walking slowly down the street, carefully eyeing each house that they pass and talking with each other as they eye the houses. You pull over before any of the youths notice you. At this time, a car speeds by, exceeding the limit substan-tially. Answer the following questions:

a) Should you pursue the car or con-tinue observing the youths? Why?

b) Comparing the two possible dangers, which seems like it could have greater risk? Why?

c) What can you do to ensure that the crime you choose not to prevent is handled in an appropriate manner?

2. **Trial by Jury** You are a witness in a case that is on trial before a jury. The prosecution has called you, and you have testified and sat through cross-examination. The case for the prosecu-tion continues and you are permitted to sit in the courtroom and observe. Soon, the prosecution announces that the state "rests its case." The defendant makes a motion for a directed verdict, which is denied. The defense then states that it "rests its case." Answer the following questions:

a) What could happen next in this trial?

b) Is this unusual, and do you feel that the defense has provided an adequate defense? Why or why not?

c) Could the defendant ever make claims that his or her trial was mis-handled, due to the defense counsel's actions? Why or why not?

3. **Release and Bail** You are a judge who is hearing the first appearance of a 17-year-old defendant who has been arrested for stealing a car and causing a serious accident that killed two people. Because of the juvenile laws in your state, he will be tried as an adult. He has a history of drug abuse and violent crime, and his mother is mentally ill. Although he is upset about being arrested, he shows no apparent remorse for his crimes. His defense attorney, who is very persistent and well paid, is requesting that you allow his release upon recognizance. Your other options are to impose bail at whatever level you feel is appropriate, or to deny bail altogether.
   a) Which option will you choose, and why?
   b) Which of the above factors are considerations in your decision? Which are not?

INTERNET APPLICATIONS

1. **NAAG** Visit the National Association of Attorneys General through the link at **cl.glencoe.com**. Read two of their features, then answer the following questions:
   a) What were the cases you chose? What were their outcomes?
   b) How did the attorneys general involved in these cases choose to pursue them? Do you agree with them? Why or why not?
   c) What, if anything, would you have done differently? Why or why not?

2. **NAPSA** Check out the National Association of Pretrial Services Agencies by clicking on the link at **cl.glencoe.com**. Read some of the information posted on their front page, as well as the section entitled "Mission." Answer the following questions:
   a) What is the goal of NAPSA?
   b) What services do they provide, and how do these impact the criminal justice system?
   c) How could an organization such as NAPSA help a defendant facing trial? A defense attorney? A prosecutor?
   d) What is your opinion of the services offered by NAPSA? Why?

ETHICS ISSUES

1. **Defense Attorney** You are a criminal defense attorney who typically defends low-income adults facing drug charges and other nonviolent charges; your success rate is well known in your community. You receive a visit from the girlfriend of a man who is facing trial for a particularly brutal and heinous robbery-homicide. The victim was a seven-year-old child who was sexually assaulted and tortured before being murdered. The evidence against the accused is overwhelming, including a voluntary confession given to the arresting officer. In addition, it is clear that the confession was given without any prompting and all procedures were followed. Nonetheless, the defendant has had a change of heart and is going to trial to zealously fight a conviction. The girlfriend offers you an enormous sum of money as a retainer, and makes it clear that you can name your price for defending this person. Answer the following questions:
   a) Would you defend this person? Why or why not?
   b) What if you were offered a sum that was the equivalent of five times your regular annual salary? Why or why not?
   c) What ethical issues could you face as the defense counsel for such a person?
   d) Is the case winnable? Why or why not? If it is not winnable, do you have anything to lose?

2. **Prosecution** You are a prosecutor who is closing a case against a man charged with murdering his wife. The defendant has introduced evidence that he is a recovering alcoholic. You have the option of bringing in character witnesses who can testify to his violent behavior while he drank. You feel that this evidence will guarantee a conviction. You know that the defense will protest this as irrelevant, but you also know that your personal friendship with the judge will cause him to allow the evidence.
   a) How does such evidence affect the jury's understanding that the defendant committed the crime "beyond a reasonable doubt"? Why?
   b) Is it ethical to bring in such character evidence? Why or why not?

ENDNOTES

1 See Geoffrey C. Hazard, Jr., "Criminal Justice System: Overview," 2 *Encyclopedia of Criminal Justice* 450 (1983).

2 Sanford H. Kadish & Stephen J. Schulhofer, *Criminal Law and Its Processes* 3 (7th ed., 2001).

3 See Geoffrey C. Hazard, Jr., "Criminal Justice System: Overview," 2 *Encyclopedia of Criminal Justice* 450, 456 (1983).

4 *Id.* at 465.

5 *Id.* at 467.

6 Leslie Helm, "Factories With Fences," *Los Angeles Times*, Jan. 5, 1997, at D1.

7 See Geoffrey C. Hazard, Jr., "Criminal Justice System: Overview," 2 *Encyclopedia of Criminal Justice* 450, 461 (1983).

Chapter Objectives

After reading this chapter, you will be able to:

1. Identify who determines whether a legislative enactment violates a constitutional prohibition.
2. List those areas of the Constitution that limit criminal law enactments.
3. Identify the one crime defined in the U.S. Constitution.
4. List the provisions of the Bill of Rights that limit the government's ability to prohibit and punish crimes.
5. State three categories of unprotected speech.
6. Name three areas of personal privacy protected by the U.S. Constitution as it affects crimes.

Chapter Outline

Why can falsely yelling "Fire!" in a crowded movie theatre result in criminal prosecution?

Chapter 3

Constitutional Limitations on the Criminal Law

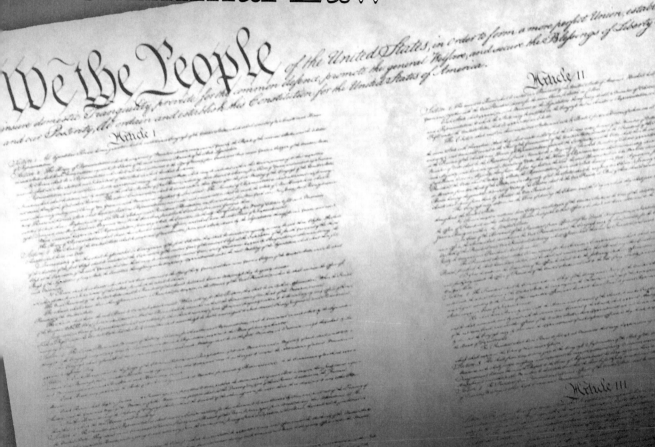

3.1 Criminal Law and the U.S. Constitution

American criminal law is mostly statutory, with courts interpreting the meaning of the penal codes when necessary. However, both the codes and the court decisions are limited by the U.S. Constitution. In this chapter, we examine the limitations imposed upon the criminal law by the Constitution.

Drafting, enacting, and enforcing criminal law involves action by government officials such as legislators, judges, police, and prosecutors. The content and the implementation of all criminal laws must be consistent with the federal Constitution and the constitution of the state in which the law is enacted and applied. Theoretically, neither the U.S. Congress nor state legislatures can enact laws that violate the Constitution; however, in reality, many laws are enacted but are later found to raise constitutional problems.

The Question of Constitutionality

Laws may be declared unconstitutional if they violate any of the following:

- Any dictate of the main body of the federal Constitution
- Any federal constitutional amendments
- Any provision of the constitution of the individual states

Criminal statutes may be unconstitutional in either of two ways:

1. Because of their *content*, which is known as a violation "on its face"
2. By the way in which they are *enforced* by government officials, which is known as a violation "by application"

Any state or federal law that violates the Constitution is legally unenforceable and will be declared invalid. Any criminal conviction based on such a law will be reversed. A state may provide protection for individuals within its borders that is greater than the protection provided by the U.S. Constitution. Situations involving greater state protection often arise with respect to criminal procedure law. For example:

- In the case of *United States v. Place* (1983), the U.S. Supreme Court ruled that dog sniffs are not searches and therefore need not be preceded by probable cause.[1]

- In contrast, in the later case of *Commonwealth v. Johnston*, a Pennsylvania court declared that for the purpose of state prosecutions, dog sniffs are searches and can be conducted only if state or local police have probable cause to believe the person, place, or thing to be sniffed is connected to criminal action. Thus, in this case, the concept of a lawful search was more narrowly defined than under federal law.[2]

Article III of the U.S. Constitution gives the power to determine the constitutionality and validity of a law. State courts determine the constitutionality of state laws and can also enforce federal constitutional principles in state cases. Federal courts decide the validity of state and federal laws that appear to violate the U.S. Constitution. In other words, the judiciary has the power to interpret, apply, or invalidate a law as it pertains to rights expressly created under the state or national constitution.

The U.S. Supreme Court has the final authority to interpret the federal Constitution. Cases reach the U.S. Supreme Court when at least four of the nine justices have elected to consider a certain case. In such instances, the Court grants a writ of *certiorari*, which is an order to the lower court to send the case forward for review.

The Bill of Rights

When the U.S. Constitution was first proposed, there were objections to it because it did not contain explicit protection of the rights of the people. On the basis of their experiences in England, critics of the Constitution were aware of ways that the government can abuse its authority. As a result, the first U.S. Congress proposed a set of 12 amendments defining the powers of the government and the rights of the people. With issues of state sovereignty and individual liberty in mind, the first U.S. Congress adopted 12 amendments to the Constitution.

By 1791, the states had adopted ten of these, which became known as the **Bill of Rights**. The first eight amendments contain several guarantees of individual rights, including both procedural safeguards and a listing of specific individual liberties that should not be interfered with by the government without just cause. When originally adopted, the guarantees of the Bill of Rights protected the individual only against the possibility of prosecution by the federal government, not state government. The Supreme Court confirmed this in 1833, and it remained that way in the United States until the 1960s.[3]

Bill of Rights The first ten amendments, especially that portion of them that guarantees fundamental individual rights to the citizens of the United States vis-a-vis government.

With the enactment of the Fourteenth Amendment and subsequent decisions by the Supreme Court, the provisions of the Bill of Rights came to apply to the states as well. The only two exceptions are the Fifth Amendment's provision for prosecution of serious crimes only by indictment and the Eighth Amendment's ban on excessive bail.

Check your answers at
cl.glencoe.com.

How does the U.S. Constitution influence federal and state law?

3.2 Procedural Criminal Law

procedural criminal law
The rules governing how the criminal law is administered.

Procedural criminal law outlines the official mechanisms through which substantive criminal law is enforced. For example, criminal procedure sets forth the rules and laws to be followed from the investigative stage of a crime to the arrest, trial, and sentencing of the defendant. The following section will first discuss procedural criminal law. The next section will discuss substantive criminal law and specific individual due process rights enumerated in the Bill of Rights.

The sources of procedural criminal law include Article I of the Constitution and the Fourth, Fifth, Sixth, and Fourteenth Amendments. These four amendments provide for the following:

- The Fourth Amendment prohibits unreasonable searches and seizures.
- The Fifth Amendment provides due process protection, protection from double jeopardy and self-incrimination, and requires grand jury indictment in federal cases.
- The Sixth Amendment establishes the right to counsel, the right to a trial by an impartial jury, the right to a speedy and public trial, the right to confront opposing witnesses, the right to compel the attendance of witnesses favorable to the defendant, and the right to notice of the nature and cause of the accusation.
- The Fourteenth Amendment provides for due process and equal protection under the law.

ON THE JOB

Campus Police Officer

Description and Duties: Patrol campus to ensure safety and security of student population, which may involve hazardous and/or dangerous situations. Use tactful communications skills and ability to interact effectively with large & diverse constituency. Be physically capable of duty as bicycle patrol officer. Demonstrate a strong customer service orientation, which includes presenting self in professional manner.

Salary: Salaries range from approximately $25,000 to over $40,000. Higher-range salaries are often for people who have been promoted to sergeant or another supervisory role.

Other Information: Since many First Amendment issues arise on campuses, such as freedom of assembly, freedom of speech, and issues regarding locker searches, campus police officers should have a keen understanding of constitutional rights. Like other police, campus police must be prepared to work overtime on short notice and to work regardless of weather conditions or other factors. In addition, they sometimes must work on holidays and other nonstandard times.

Critical Thinking What qualities do you think a campus police officer ought to possess?

SOURCE: Palomar College (CA), http://www.palomar.edu; Southwest Texas State University, http://www.swt.edu/ police; Arizona State University, http://www.asu.edu/hr/jobs/.

Due Process and Equal Protection

As you can see, due process clauses appear in both the Fifth and Fourteenth Amendments to the U.S. Constitution. The Fifth Amendment states that no person shall be "deprived of life, liberty, or property, without due process of law." The Fourteenth Amendment to the U. S. Constitution provides that "no state shall deprive any person of life, liberty, or property, without due process of law. Over time, **due process** has been interpreted by the courts to encompass the multiple procedures and processes that must be followed before a person can be legally deprived of his or her life, liberty, or property.

The Fourteenth Amendment to the U. S. Constitution provides that no state shall "deny to any person . . . the equal protection of the laws." A law that distinguishes between two classes of persons (e.g., men and women, wealthy and poor, minorities and non-minorities)

due process The multiple criminal justice procedures and processes that must be followed before a person can be legally deprived of his or her life, liberty, or property.

is subject to attack if it does not provide **equal protection** to persons who should be treated equally with respect to the practice dealt with by the law.

For example, until the civil rights movement of the 1950s and 1960s, several states maintained laws that provided different rights for black and white residents under the "separate but equal doctrine" announced by the U.S. Supreme Court decision in the 1896 case *Plessy v. Ferguson*. Then, in *Loving v. Virginia* (1967), the Supreme Court struck down a Virginia statute that criminalized interracial marriage, relying on the equal protection clause. Similarly, in *Craig v. Boren* (1976), the Court declared invalid on equal protection grounds an Oklahoma law that prohibited the sale of beer to females under the age of 18 and males under the age of 21.[4]

Today, all laws that make a distinction between persons based on race, ethnicity, gender, religion, sexual orientation, or national origin are subject to constitutional scrutiny, even when they are designed to rectify the discrimination of the past.

The Americans with Disabilities Act In 1990, the U.S. Congress passed the Americans with Disabilities Act, which requires that businesses, public transportation, public accommodations, and telecommunications be made accessible to persons with disabilities. Since the passage of the law, the courts have interpreted these requirements in a variety of ways to provide equal protection to people with disabilities, such as the following:

- In 2001, the 9th Circuit Court of Appeals ruled that the PGA Tour must allow disabled professional golfer Casey Martin to use a golf cart, enabling him to pursue his career as a professional golfer. (The PGA has filed an appeal with the U.S. Supreme Court.)
- Jenine Stanley is blind and uses a guide dog. The State of Hawaii requires that all dogs be quarantined for 120 days in a state facility, so she would have had to travel without her dog or stay home. The Department of Justice intervened and reached an agreement with the state allowing individuals with guide dogs to travel without the quarantine, as long as they can demonstrate that the dog is free from rabies through documentation of rabies vaccination and testing.
- Denver, Colorado, police officer Jack Davoll suffered severe back injuries on the job. When he asked for reassignment to one of several vacant civilian jobs in the city, his transfers were denied. He filed a complaint with the U.S. Department,

which found that the City of Denver had violated the ADA. They required that Davoll be reassigned, and he was also awarded compensatory damages and lost wages. Subsequently, the city agreed to implement a written policy allowing officers with disabilities to be reassigned to civilian posts for which they are qualified.

- Wally Itrich, a wheelchair user and resident of Dickinson, South Dakota, filed a complaint with the Department of Justice because plans for a city hall did not include adequate wheelchair access. As a result, the city erected a new city hall that allowed citizens access to all municipal services, including courtrooms and elections.

- Jeremy Alvarez has asthma and takes medicine twice a day at home and carries an inhaler with him at all times. The Fountainhead Child Care Center refused to allow Jeremy to attend because of a "no medications" policy, even though Jeremy was able to use the inhaler with minimal supervision. A district court required that Fountainhead modify its policy and allow Jeremy to attend and to provide one-hour training sessions for its staff on the nature of asthma and how to supervise children who use inhalers.[5]

Bills of Attainder and *Ex Post Facto* Laws

As we saw in the discussion of the principle of legality in Chapter 1, conduct cannot be punished retroactively. In order to be consistent with this principle, the U.S. Constitution prohibits legislatures from enacting bills of attainder and *ex post facto* laws. A **bill of attainder** is a legislative enactment that declares individuals or members of a group guilty of a crime and subject to punishment without a trial. If an act imposes capital punishment on those supposed to be guilty of important crimes such as treason or felony, it is a bill of attainder. If it inflicts as lesser punishment, it is called a "bill of pains and penalties." Such laws are prohibited by Article I, Section 9 of the Constitution. An *ex post facto* **law** is one that:

- makes criminal an act done before passage of the law and punishes such action.
- aggravates a crime, making it more serious than it had been when it was committed.
- inflicts a greater punishment than the law imposed when the crime was committed, or alters the legal rules of evidence,

bill of attainder A special legislative enactment that declares a person or group of persons guilty of a crime and subject to punishment without a trial.

ex post facto law A law that: (1) makes an act done before passage of the law, and which was innocent when done, criminal; and punishes such action; or (2) aggravates a crime, or makes it greater than it was, when committed; (3) changes the punishment, and inflicts a greater punishment, than the law imposed upon the crime, when committed; or (4) alters the legal rules of evidence, allowing evidence of guilt that is lesser or different from what the law required at the time of the commission of the offense.

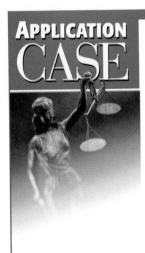
Carmell v. Texas

In *Carmell v. Texas* (2000), the court held that altering the rules of evidence in a trial for offenses that were committed before the effective date of the amendment was a violation of the prohibition against *ex post facto* laws. In 1996, the defendant was convicted of 15 counts of committing sexual offenses against his stepdaughter during a period from 1991 to 1995, when the victim was 12 to 16 years old. Under the Texas Criminal Code, a victim's testimony about a sexual offense could not support a conviction unless there was corroborating evidence or the victim informed another person of the offense within six months of the act. However, under a 1993 amendment to this law, the victim's testimony alone could support a conviction if the victim was under 14 at the time of the offense.

The defendant argued that the convictions for those offenses committed after the victim reached the age of 14 in July 1992 should be reversed, on the grounds that they were based solely on her testimony and there was no corroborating evidence. In agreement, the court was forced to hold that retroactive application of the 1993 amendment violated the federal constitutional prohibition against *ex post facto* laws.

Critical Thinking Do you think laws like this one and sex offender registry laws violate the federal prohibition against *ex post facto* laws?

SOURCE: *Carmell v. Texas*, 529 U.S. 513 (2000).

allowing evidence of guilt that is lesser or different from what the law required at the time of the commission of the offense.[6]

For example, although the courts have failed to accept their claims, many previously convicted sex offenders argue that new state laws requiring them to register with the local police, who can then notify the community of their presence, amount to *ex post facto* punishment, because such requirements did not exist at the time that they pled or were found guilty. They also claim that such requirements continue to punish them even though they have already served their time. With few exceptions, the courts have rejected these claims, noting that the requirements of registration and community notification are not punishments but regulatory measures aimed at protecting the public.

Criminal Law and the Criminal Justice System

Fair Notice and Vagueness

The due process clauses of the Fifth and Fourteenth Amendments require that the law provide **fair notice**. The right to "fair notice" means that the law must clearly define the precise conduct that is prohibited. Thus, statutes that are written ambiguously or in which the words are vague (subject to different interpretations by different people) also violate the constitutional requirement of due process.

Under the due process clause of the Fourteenth Amendment, criminal statutes cannot be vague, ambiguous, or overly broad. Criminal statutes lacking clarity violate the fair notice requirement that people are entitled to know what they are forbidden to do, so that they may shape their conduct accordingly. In addition, criminal statutes lacking in clarity are susceptible to enforcement in an arbitrary or discriminatory manner within the discretion of the police, prosecutors, and judges and juries.[7]

An example of a statute found to be unconstitutionally vague is a Jacksonville, Florida, city ordinance that prohibited various forms of vagrancy.[8] Other statutes that have been found unconstitutionally vague include:

fair notice The due process requirement that people are entitled to know what they are forbidden to do so that they may shape their conduct accordingly.

◄ **Vagueness and Overbreadth in the Law** Certain laws, such as those outlawing vagrancy, are overly vague and do not offer any specific guidelines for their enforcement. Therefore, they can be overly used or discriminatorily used. *How can such laws promote overuse or discriminatory behavior?*

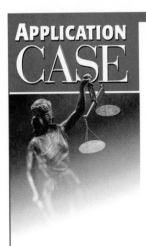

APPLICATION CASE

Fair Notice

Fair Notice

The law requires fair notice that certain conduct is criminal before anyone can be convicted of such conduct. In addition, the law does not allow *ex post facto* declaration of crimes not previously declared to be a violation of the law. Despite this, everyone is "presumed" to know the law, even if they do not actually have knowledge of it. No one can claim ignorance of the law as a defense, excuse, or justification for violating a validly existing criminal law.

People v. Maness

In *People v. Maness* (2000), the Illinois Supreme Court affirmed a trial court's invalidation of a state statute. The defendant was charged with permitting the sexual abuse of the child, an offense created by the Wrongs to Children Act of 1992. The act provided that a parent or stepparent who "knowingly allows an act of criminal sexual abuse or criminal sexual assault on his or her minor child and fails to take reasonable steps to prevent its commission or future occurrences of such acts commits the offense of permitting the sexual abuse of a child."

The defendant's 13-year-old daughter was dating and having intercourse with a 17-year-old male. During the relationship, the defendant learned of the sexual conduct between her daughter and her boyfriend; although she disapproved of it, she obtained birth control for her daughter and allowed the boyfriend to spend the night at their home.

In a report from the Department of Children and Family Services, the defendant stated that she did not know what steps to take to prevent the sexual relationship her daughter was having. The defendant argued that the statute was unconstitutionally vague because it failed to define "reasonable steps" to prevent future acts of sexual abuse. The court agreed with the defendant, in that the statute is unconstitutionally vague if its terms are so indefinite that people of common intelligence must guess at its meaning. In addition, the court held that a statute must adequately define the offense in order to prevent its arbitrary and discriminatory enforcement, and it must provide explicit standards to regulate the discretion of governmental authorities.

Critical Thinking How did the Wrongs to Children Act fail to give fair notice?

SOURCE: *People v. Maness* 732 N.E. 2d 545 (Il. 2000).

- One that punished a person who "publicly treats contemptuously the flag of the United States"
- An ordinance stating that "no person shall loiter . . . in or upon any street, park or public place, or in any public building," with no definition of the term "loiter"
- A harassment statute prohibiting conduct that "alarms or seriously annoys" another person

City of Chicago v. Morales

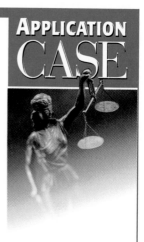

In *City of Chicago v. Morales* (1999), in response to an increase in gang-related murders that also intimidated law-abiding citizens, Chicago enacted an ordinance that criminalized loitering. In sum, the Anti-Gang Loitering Ordinance stated that if "a police officer observes a person whom he reasonably believes to be a criminal street gang member loitering in any public place with one or more other persons, he shall order all such persons to disperse and remove themselves from the area. Any person who does not promptly obey such an order is in violation of this section."

Over a three-year period following an enactment of the statute, 89,000 dispersal orders were given and 42,000 people were arrested. In *Morales*, each defendant was alleged to have been in the presence of a gang member; each was arrested when he failed to disperse as directed by the police. The Court of Appeals held that the ordinance was unconstitutional because it violated freedom of association, congregation, and expression protected by the First Amendment.

Vagueness

In addition, the court held that the ordinance was unconstitutionally vague under the Illinois Constitution, which ensures the right to assemble in a peaceful manner. The court also stated that since the statute was intended to address the behavior of gang members, but an innocent bystander could also be convicted, the statute failed to specify a standard of conduct and failed to provide minimal guidance to limit the discretion given to police officers to enforce the law.

Critical Thinking How could this law be rewritten to be less vague and more constitutional?

SOURCE: *City of Chicago v. Morales*, 527 U.S. 41 (1999).

All of the preceding statutes were also invalidated because they were overly broad, meaning that they could result in the punishment of individuals for engaging in conduct that is constitutionally protected.

Self Check

1. Why are *ex post facto* laws considered unconstitutional? Do you agree? Why or why not?
2. How do due process and equal protection protect people's rights?

CRIMINAL LAW *Online*

Check your answers at cl.glencoe.com.

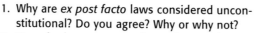

3.3 Substantive Criminal Law and Individual Due Process Rights

substantive criminal law
The law defining acts that are criminal.

Substantive criminal law differs from procedural criminal law in that substantive criminal law defines criminal conduct and prescribes the punishment to be imposed for such conduct. That is, substantive law defines what actions are criminal. For example, the homicide section of a state's criminal code defines the elements of the offense of murder and states the punishment that can be imposed for the offense.

The number of individual liberties, or due process rights, specifically enumerated within the Bill of Rights include:

- The freedom of religion, speech, and assembly
- The right to bring grievances against the government
- The right to keep and bear arms
- Protection against cruel and unusual punishment
- The right to personal privacy

With the exception of the right to privacy, each of these individual liberties is expressly guaranteed within the Bill of Rights. (See Figure 3–1 for a more complete listing of liberties granted by the Bill of Rights.)

These rights affect the ability of both federal and state authorities to prohibit and punish individual conduct that falls within the protection of the Bill of Rights. This means that no state or federal agency can legally enact or enforce criminal statutes that unnecessarily inhibit the substantive rights identified in the amendments. Typically, criminal statutes may run afoul of the specific dictates of the First or Second Amendments or the somewhat broader prohibitions in the Eighth Amendment, or they may interfere with the general exercise of liberty mentioned in both the Fifth and Fourteenth Amendments.

First Amendment Rights

The First Amendment provides that Congress shall make no law prohibiting the free exercise of religion or abridging the rights of free speech and peaceable assembly. Those guarantees of free exercise of religion, freedom of speech, and freedom of assembly are among

Criminal Law and the Criminal Justice System

FIGURE 3-1

Liberties Granted by the Bill of Rights

First Amendment

Free speech

Free exercise of religion

Freedom of assembly

Second Amendment

Right to bear arms

Fourth Amendment

Freedom from unreasonable searches and seizures

Fifth Amendment

Grand jury indictment in felony cases

No double jeopardy

No compelled self-incrimination

Sixth Amendment

Speedy and public trial

Impartial jury of the state and district where crime occurred

Notice of nature and cause of accusation

Confront opposing witnesses

Compulsory process for obtaining favorable witnesses

Right to counsel

Eighth Amendment

No excessive bail and fines

Prohibition of "cruel and unusual punishment"

the most protected. Freedom of religion and speech are sometimes grouped together and referred to as "freedom of expression."

Free Speech   In general, Americans can say what they like and are free to criticize the government without fearing punishment. However, the guarantee of free speech is not absolute. In order to protect the public, government can regulate certain kinds of speech. Such restrictions "must be evaluated by the Court in light of the government's responsibility to meet the public's interest, as well as the individual's First Amendment guarantee of free speech."

In the area of free speech, the **clear and present danger test** is one of those limiting principles. Justice Oliver Wendell Holmes expressed the test in memorable terms, in the 1919 case of *Schenck v. United States*:

clear and present danger test A test to determine whether a defendant's words created a clear and present danger that would bring about substantive evils that Congress has the right (and duty) to prevent.

Evolving First Amendment Rights

Despite the protection of the First Amendment, the government did not always recognize rights as the U.S. Supreme Court has elucidated them in its decisions over the years. For example, in 1912, feminist Margaret Sanger was arrested for giving a lecture on birth control. Meetings held by trade unions were banned, and persons violating court orders prohibiting strikes and labor protests were sentenced to prison. Individuals peacefully protesting American involvement in World War I were jailed for expressing their opinion. The display of red or black flags, symbols of communism and anarchism, was outlawed in many states in the early 1920s. Author Upton Sinclair was arrested in 1923 for attempting to read the text of the First Amendment at a union rally.

SOURCE: ACLU Briefing Paper, Freedom of Expression at www.aclu.org

The most stringent protection of free speech would not protect a man in falsely shouting fire in a theater and causing a panic. It does not even protect a man from an injunction against uttering words that may have all the effect of force. The question in every case is whether the words used are used in such circumstances and are of such a nature as to create a clear and present danger that they will bring about the substantive evils that Congress has the right (and duty) to prevent. It is a question of proximity and degree. When a nation is at war many things that might be said in time of peace are such a hindrance to the war effort that their utterance will not be endured so long as men fight and . . . no Court could regard them as protected by any constitutional right.[9]

In the case from which the quote is taken, the defendant was convicted of interfering with the draft during wartime and of urging insubordination in the military. Justice Holmes's language suggests that the advocacy of unlawful conduct and of fighting words can also be limited in order to protect public welfare. However, not every urging to violate the law satisfies the clear and present danger test, which was redefined by the Supreme Court to require advocacy of "imminent lawless action."[10] Given this redefinition, it is unlikely that the conduct and speech in the very case in which Justice Holmes announced the clear and present danger test would be considered criminal by the Supreme Court today.

Fighting words are another subcategory of unprotected speech that poses a clear and present danger. The Supreme Court has defined "fighting words" as "those which by their very utterance inflict injury or tend to incite an immediate breach of the peace."[11] Such speech threatens public peace or order by being so provocative that it is too likely to induce a violent reaction.

Other areas of potentially unprotected speech include hate speech, profanity, libelous utterances, and obscenity. (Obscenity is discussed more fully in Chapter 13.) Questions relating to these types of speech present complex questions of balancing that yield no clear rule for determining how far the government may go to regulate such speech, if at all. For example, in *R.A.V. v. St. Paul*, the U.S. Supreme Court held unconstitutional a city ordinance banning the burning of a cross and the display of symbols such as swastikas.[12] Finally, with the advent of the Internet and other modern technologies, courts are

Myth	Fact
The Bill of Rights gives citizens the absolute right to gather in public areas for the purpose of picketing, demonstrations, and meetings.	This right is not absolute. It can be regulated by statutes imposing reasonable restraints on the time, place, and manner of speech in public areas.

faced with new challenges to the First Amendment, and they must evaluate statutes seeking to regulate the information that is transmitted in cyberspace.

The notion that the government has the power and obligation to provide for the common defense and promote the welfare of the general public by enacting laws is expressly written into the federal Constitution. Still, this concern for collective society must be addressed while also recognizing the rights of individuals. Under what has come to be known as the "police powers," federal, state, and local governments may enact laws and authorize enforcement activities that regulate the time, place, and manner in which an individual can exercise constitutionally protected rights, but these rights cannot be completely taken away (or banned) in the interest of the general public. They are balanced against the potential harm that might be caused to others in society.

Free Exercise of Religion   American courts will invalidate criminal statutes that are viewed as thinly veiled attempts to restrict the freedom of religion. For example:

- The U.S. Supreme Court struck down a state statute criminalizing door-to-door solicitation for religious purposes without prior approval from state officials, where the statute had been applied to Jehovah's Witnesses.
- The Court also struck down an ordinance of the City of Hialeah, Florida, banning ritualistic animal sacrifice aimed at a particular religion's practice.[13]

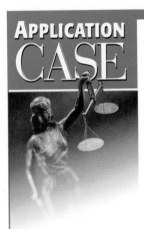

APPLICATION CASE

The First Amendment and the Internet

Hatch v. Superior Court

In *Hatch v. Superior Court* (2000), the defendant was convicted pursuant to the California Penal Code for using the Internet to send harmful matter to a minor in an attempt to seduce her. In *Hatch*, Fox Television hired 20-year-old Jennifer Hersey to pose as a 13-year-old girl involved in Internet chats with persons interested in having sexual encounters with underaged girls.

The defendant made contact with Hersey, then engaged in a series of communications wherein she posed as girls named "Stacie" and "Lisa." He also sent Hersey pictures of nude girls and of young girls having sex with men. The defendant then attempted to arrange meetings for sexual encounters, and discussed via e-mail his plans to have sex with "Stacie" and "Lisa." Hersey agreed to meet the defendant at a hotel, and also forwarded her communication with the defendant to the police. The defendant was then convicted of attempting to seduce a minor by means of the Internet.

The defendant argued that the statute violated his First Amendment rights, but the Court of Appeals held that such communication did not enjoy First Amendment privileges. In addition, the statute was not seeking to prohibit forum communication (such as in chat rooms), but only adults seeking to seduce a child. Finally, the court stated that the statute is directed more toward an activity or conduct than toward communication.

Critical Thinking Do you think the defendant should still be found guilty even though he was actually sending harmful matter to an adult?

SOURCE: *Hatch v. Superior Court*, 94 Cal. Rptr. 2d 453 (Cal. Ct. App. 2000).

On the other hand, religious freedom claims have been rejected in upholding criminal convictions for:

- Polygamy
- A Christian Scientist parent's withholding medical treatment for a child
- Handling poisonous snakes in religious ceremonies
- The use of peyote as part of a religious practice [14]

Clearly, not all claims based upon the free exercise of religion will exempt a defendant from criminal liability. (See Chapter 14 for a discussion of legislation on the use of peyote.)

Criminal Law and the Criminal Justice System

Freedom of Assembly   The right of the people to assemble publicly is not absolute. Because public assembly may threaten public safety, peace, and order, the government has the right to impose reasonable restrictions on the time, place, and manner of assembly. In addition, there are specific statutes that curtail the right to assemble under specific circumstances. For example, the Freedom of Access to Clinic Entrances Act (FACE), criminalizes "physical obstruction, intentionally . . . interfer[ing] with or attempt[ing] to . . . interfere with any person" who is or has been "obtaining or providing reproductive health services." In other words, although individuals can demonstrate in front of an abortion clinic, they cannot physically prevent individuals from going into the clinic.

Other state statutes that prohibit loitering also affect the right to assemble. Anti-loitering statutes have always been part of the United States criminal legal system. However, these laws are subject to scrutiny by the court and may be unconstitutional if they are found to be vague. The statutes must also reasonably promote identifiable public interests in order to justify the interference with individual liberty.

Constitutional Law on the Web

Visit **Findlaw.com**'s section on Constitutional law by accessing the link at **cl.glencoe.com**. Read the current articles on the front page, then write a half-page report explaining the breadth of issues you read about, and how they are covered under constitutional law. Don't forget to include the amendments to which these issues pertain.

Second Amendment Rights

The right to keep and bear arms provided in the Second Amendment is not absolute and has been the source of much litigation in recent years. While various organizations such as the National Rifle Association (NRA) contend that the right to bear arms is an individual one, the U.S. Supreme Court has held that this provision must be read in conjunction with the other, less-known clause of the Second Amendment, which requires a "well regulated militia."

Typical federal and state gun control statutes impose licensing requirements such as background checks and waiting periods; restrict carrying, concealing, and purchasing of firearms; and prohibit firearm ownership by convicted felons. Under the Brady Bill, criminal offenses committed with a firearm carry more severe penalties than those committed without one.[15]

Eighth Amendment Rights

proportionality The constitutional principle that the punishment should fit the crime expressed in the Eighth Amendment's cruel and unusual punishment clause.

The Eighth Amendment to the U.S. Constitution prohibits the infliction of "cruel and unusual punishments." The Supreme Court has interpreted the Eighth Amendment requirement of **proportionality** to mean that the punishment inflicted for a criminal violation should not be grossly disproportionate to the crime committed. This proportionality requirement affects:

- The grading of offenses
- The imposition of the death penalty
- The assessment of the validity of terms of imprisonment

Non-Capital Cases In the area of disproportionate sentences in non-capital cases, the Supreme Court's jurisprudence "has not been a model of clarity." For example:

- In one case, a defendant with two previous convictions for theft was sentenced to life imprisonment for obtaining a check for $120.75 under false pretenses and cashing it. The Supreme Court upheld the defendant's sentence.
- In another case three years later, a defendant with seven prior felony convictions was sentenced to life imprisonment for a check-cashing violation. The Court held that this sentence was invalid.[16]

Why did this disparity occur? In the first case, the state had a liberal parole policy; in the second case, the defendant had been sentenced to life without the possibility of parole. The Court distinguished the two cases on those grounds.

Finally, in a third case, a defendant was sentenced to life imprisonment without the possibility of parole for a first-offense possession of 672 grams of cocaine. The Supreme Court upheld the sentence, concluding that the sentence did not violate the Eighth Amendment.[17] The decision in all three cases was by a vote of 5-4. Because of this, proportionality is still an unresolved issue that can lead to controversial decisions.

Capital Cases Whether the death penalty itself constitutes cruel and unusual punishment is another area of disagreement among Supreme Court justices, legislators, and citizens in general. The death penalty has been used since the early years of the nation, for example, in the Salem Witch Trials. The U.S. Supreme Court has placed limits on the circumstances under which the death penalty may be imposed under this clause.

- In *Coker v. Georgia* (1977), the Court held that death was an excessive penalty for the rape of an adult woman.
- The Court has also ruled that the death penalty cannot be imposed upon a defendant who was less than 16 years old at the time of the killing offense.

Furman v. Georgia In the 1972 case of *Furman v. Georgia*, the U.S. Supreme Court examined the imposition of the death penalty in three cases. Each of the three petitioners had been convicted in a state court and sentenced to death after a trial by jury, in which the jury had the discretion to determine whether to impose the death penalty. The Supreme Court analyzed in detail the constitutional issues raised by capital punishment.

In this landmark 5-4 decision, each of the nine justices wrote a separate opinion. Five of the justices in the majority believed that the death penalty was cruel and unusual because it was being implemented in a discriminatory manner toward the poor and minorities. However, only three (Justices Brennan, Marshall, and Douglas) held that capital punishment was in itself cruel and unusual. The effect of this decision was an "informal moratorium" until the execution of Gary Gilmore in 1977.[18]

In subsequent years, the Court issued a number of decisions that established the constitutionality of the death penalty for specific

Cruel and Unusual Punishment?

For a brief time between 1972 and 1974, the United States made the death penalty illegal. With the 5-4 decision in *Furman v. Georgia* (1972), the U.S. Supreme Court held that the death penalty was cruel and unusual. This was partly because of the discriminatory way in which it was implemented at the time, but three of the five justices in the majority also felt that it was in and of itself cruel and unusual. Despite this finding, the death penalty resumed in 30 states in 1974 because of strong public opinion supporting it.

crimes. For example, *Gregg v. Georgia* (1976) recognized the legitimacy of the death penalty for murder. In *Coker v. Georgia* (1977), the Court held that it was an excessive punishment for rape. In the next two decades, executions were resumed with growing approval from the public.[19] Most recently, however, concerns about the inequity in imposition of the death penalty and about the execution of innocent persons has again arisen, as is illustrated by the decision of the governor of Illinois to halt executions pending a review of these issues.

The Right to Privacy

Although the Constitution does not expressly mention a right of privacy, the U.S. Supreme Court has held that it is implied by the following constitutional provisions:

- The First Amendment right of free association
- The Third Amendment dealing with the quartering of soldiers in private homes
- The Fourth Amendment ban on unreasonable searches and seizures

The right of privacy includes the right to be let alone, the right to be free from unwanted publicity, and the right to live without unwarranted interference. For example, the Court has recognized, within the concept of personal privacy, a person's right to "decide whether or not to beget a child." In various cases, the Court has held that government cannot interfere by statutory proscription with the availability of contraceptives and contraceptive devices for single and married persons.[20]

Myth	**Fact**
The U.S. Supreme Court has held that any sexual act between consenting adults is protected by a fundamental right to privacy.	The Court has not issued a finding that addresses this issue; therefore, states may continue to prohibit certain consensual sexual acts.

Abortion Rights Another area of privacy relating to childbirth is the right of a woman to choose to terminate her pregnancy through abortion. In 1973, in *Roe v. Wade*, the Supreme Court held that the right of privacy extended to protect a woman's right to abortion, and it invalidated the anti-abortion statute involved in that case. The Court vote in *Roe v. Wade* was 7–2. The Court reaffirmed this position on abortion in 1992 in the case of *Planned Parenthood v. Casey*. However, the vote in the 1992 case was 5–4, and the abortion issue continues to be a hotly debated one.[21]

Consensual Sodomy Interpersonal sexual conduct has also been recognized as an area protected by the right of privacy. In a 1986 decision, the U.S. Supreme Court refused to prevent the state of Georgia from punishing consensual homosexual acts committed by adults in private. This case raises questions about the right to privacy with respect to consensual sexual conduct that includes such acts as sodomy, adultery, and fornication.

In a 1998 decision, the Georgia Supreme Court changed its own law and reversed the conviction of a defendant charged with engaging in consensual sodomy with a 17-year-old girl. The court held that a statute criminalizing the private and unforced acts of sexual intimacy between consenting adults was unconstitutional. Because the U.S. Supreme Court has not held that the act of sodomy between consenting adults is protected by a fundamental right to privacy, other states may continue to prohibit consensual as well as nonconsensual sodomy, even though cases involving consent between adult parties (in private) are rarely prosecuted. In the case, the Georgia Supreme Court held that the Georgia constitutional right of privacy is more extensive than the federal right of privacy considered by the U.S. Supreme Court in *Hardwick v. Bowers*. As a result, the Georgia Supreme Court found the Georgia sodomy statute unconstitutional and reversed Powell's conviction under the statute. (For a more detailed discussion of *Powell v. State* and sodomy in other states, see Chapter 13.)[22]

Abortion Clinic Protections

Although the 1994 Freedom of Access to Clinic Entrances Act provides federal protection against unlawful tactics used by abortion opponents and has led to a decrease in some types of clinic violence, attacks at women's health care clinics remain a major concern. Since 1993, seven persons working or volunteering at clinics have been killed, and 16 attempted murders have occurred since 1991. From 1977 to 1999, women's health care clinics have experienced at least 40 bombings, 161 arsons, 77 attempted bombings and arsons, and 513 bomb threats.

SOURCE: National Abortion Rights and Action League (NARAL), http://www.naral.org/issues/issues _violence.html.

Self Check

1. Which Amendment of the Bill of Rights do you feel is most important to one's fundamental rights? Why?
2. Why is the right to privacy controversial in American society?

Check your answers at **cl.glencoe.com**.

Constitutional Limitations on the Criminal Law

SUMMARY BY CHAPTER OBJECTIVES

1. Identify who determines whether a legislative enactment violates a constitutional prohibition.

Both state and federal courts determine whether a legislative enactment violates a constitutional prohibition, but in different capacities. State courts can enforce both federal constitutional principles and state constitutional principles in state cases. Federal courts can enforce federal constitutional principles, which are principles relating to the U.S. Constitution.

2. List those areas of the Constitution that limit criminal law enactments.

Constitutional subjects relating to the substantive criminal law include:

- The principle of legality (which includes the prohibition of bills of attainder and *ex post facto* laws)
- A number of rights specifically enumerated in the Bill of Rights (including the freedoms of religion, speech, and assembly, the right to keep and bear arms, due process, and cruel and unusual punishment)
- The personal right of privacy and equal protection of the law

3. Identify the one crime defined in the U.S. Constitution.

The only crime defined in the U.S. Constitution is treason. It is defined in Article III, § 3, as consisting "only in levying war against [the United States], or in adhering to their enemies, giving them aid and comfort. No person can be convicted of treason except on the testimony of two witnesses or by confession in open court."

4. List the provisions of the Bill of Rights that limit the government's ability to prohibit and punish crimes.

The rights enumerated in the Bill of Rights that specifically limit the government's ability to prohibit and punish crimes are:

- Freedom of religion, speech, and assembly, as protected by the First Amendment
- Right to keep and bear arms, as protected by the Second Amendment
- The Fifth Amendment's due process clause, as it relates to the vagueness or over-reaching qualities of a criminal statute
- The Eighth Amendment's ban upon cruel and unusual punishment, as it relates to the death penalty

5. State three categories of unprotected speech.

Three categories of unprotected speech are:

- Speech that violates the clear and present danger test (as expressed by Justice Oliver Wendell Holmes in the 1919 case of *Schenck v. United States*)
- Speech advocating unlawful conduct
- Fighting words

6. Name three areas of personal privacy protected by the U. S. Constitution as it affects crimes.

Three areas of personal privacy that may be protected by the Constitution from statutory interference by the government are the availability of contraceptives and contraceptive devices for single and married persons, the right of a woman to choose to terminate her pregnancy through abortion, and interpersonal sexual conduct.

KEY TERMS

Bill of Rights, page 55
procedural criminal law, page 56
due process, page 57
equal protection, page 58

bill of attainder, page 59
ex post facto law, page 59
fair notice, page 61
substantive criminal law, page 64

clear and present danger test, page 65
proportionality, page 70

Why can falsely yelling "Fire!" in a crowded movie theatre result in criminal prosecution?
Find it on page 55.

QUESTIONS FOR REVIEW

1. What is the difference between substantive and procedural criminal law?
2. Name at least five constitutional subjects relating to procedural criminal law.
3. Name the three possible definitions of an *ex post facto* law.
4. What are two possible problems that can arise from vague criminal statutes?
5. Define the due process clause of the Fourteenth Amendment, and explain its relevance to criminal law.
6. Name some examples of limitations on the First Amendment, as applied by the courts.
7. What are fighting words? How do these legally differ from hate speech or profanity?
8. What does the Eighth Amendment address, and how is this applied to criminal justice?
9. How does proportionality affect the grading of offenses?
10. Explain what "equal protection under the law" means, and how it applies in criminal law.

PROBLEM-SOLVING EXERCISES

1. **Juvenile Rights** You are a police officer working in the city. You see a group of youths on the corner of a busy intersection in the downtown area. They are standing around talking. You suspect they are involved in a drug transaction, since you recognize one of them as a member of a drug ring. What constitutional rights of the youth you recognize might prohibit you from taking any police action against him at this time?
2. **False Alarm** While at a college football game, someone makes a loud noise like a banging gun and yells, "He has a gun!" In response, spectators in the immediate area panic and begin running for the exit. Six people are trampled, and two are seriously injured. During the investigation, campus police learn that nobody had a gun; the panic was the result of two young men playing a practical joke. Answer the following questions:
   a) Which test would you apply to determine if this speech was protected by the First Amendment?
   b) What if someone either made the gunshot sound or only shouted, "He has a gun!" but it produced the same result? Would this be protected?
   c) What other factors would you consider as you write your report for this case? What, if anything, would you recommend to your prosecutor?

3. **Anti-Loitering Ordinance** Your city has passed an anti-loitering ordinance, and you are a prosecutor who must deal with the arrests that result from the enforcement of these laws. Recently, local police have started arresting teenagers who seem rather scruffy and aggressive, but who have no apparent drug or gang involvement. The defendants were loitering around a local strip mall that has had numerous drug activities, but is also a popular hangout. Their arrests were legal under the current city ordinance.
   a) Is this ordinance constitutional or not? Why?
   b) How will you handle this case?

WORKPLACE APPLICATIONS

1. **Incitement to Riot** It is a hot night, and you are among a group of officers called into an inner-city neighborhood in response to a disturbance. You arrive at the scene and discover a group of angry citizens facing a line of officers, who are struggling to hold them back. One very angry citizen is yelling above the crowd, telling the others to attack the police. Some of his comments are very violent and very specific, and he appears to be making the crowd even angrier. Answer the following questions:
   a) Is this man violating any laws? If so, what are they?
   b) Can you arrest this citizen without violating his constitutional rights? Why or why not?
   c) If he succeeds in inciting others to riot, do you think that are there any additional charges for which he may be liable? Why or why not?

2. **The Bill of Rights** Interview three or four friends (not from this class) and ask them to name seven out of the ten amendments in the Bill of Rights. Tally their results, then answer the following questions:
   a) Did they seem to have a fairly complete understanding of the Bill of Rights? Why or why not?
   b) Were you surprised by the results? Why or why not?
   c) What do your survey results say about the average American's understanding of the Bill of Rights? How can this affect people when they are unexpectedly caught up in the criminal justice system?

3. **Illegal Assembly** You are a judge who is hearing a case regarding an illegal assembly on a state university campus. The defendants, who are mainly students, state that they were denied a

permit to protest because of political reasons, and thus were deprived their First Amendment rights to peaceful assembly; the university, they state, held back from issuing the permit so that they would have an excuse to arrest them. You examine the statutes regarding this and find that your state has a 1908 statute that requires student assemblies to have at least one "monitor or chaperone." In addition, the statute requires that the school approve all student activities.

a) Will you strike down this law, or apply it? Why?

b) If you apply it, in whose favor will you decide?

INTERNET APPLICATIONS

1. **Gay Rights** Pretend that you are an attorney defending a gay couple who wish to get married. Check out the Web site for Gay & Lesbian Advocates & Defenders (GLAD) by clicking the link at **cl.glencoe.com** and read their information on current gay marriage activism. When you are done, answer the following questions:

   a) For what reasons are gay marriages not allowed or even illegal in most states?

   b) Does this prohibition appear to have a religious basis? Why or why not?

   c) If so, how does it affect the constitutionality of such restrictions?

   d) If not, is it constitutional to limit or outlaw gay marriage?

   e) Do you think that this matter should be decided by individual state courts or by the U.S. Supreme Court? Why?

2. **Death Penalty** Read "Frontline: The Execution," an online feature covering a convicted Texas killer, available through a link at **cl.glencoe.com**. Read "The Story" and three selections from the list under "Who Was Boggess?" When you are done, answer the following questions:

   a) What is your general opinion of the death penalty, especially as it related to cruel and unusual punishment? Do you feel any different about it in this case?

   b) Do you feel that Boggess showed any genuine remorse? Why or why not? How would this affect his sentencing in court?

   c) Do you feel that the information provided on his personal life explained some of his behavior? Did it legally excuse it to any degree? Why or why not?

ETHICS ISSUES

1. **Ethnicity and the Law** You are a police investigator working in an ethnically diverse community. Over time, you confirm that young men from one ethnic group are most often involved in the criminal conduct that you investigate. You also notice that many of your colleagues make assumptions about the criminal behavior of all young men in that ethnic group. Answer the following questions:

   a) Is there anything improper in the way in which your colleagues take into account the ethnicity of a suspect when observing or investigating criminal activities? Why or why not?

   b) What can you do to make sure that your behavior is within constitutional limits?

   c) What can you do to influence or change your colleagues' behavior? What are some possible problems that may occur if they do not change?

   d) What other constitutional concerns might you have regarding this behavior?

2. **Domestic Violence** You are the mayor of a medium-sized city, which has an ordinance that requires arrest in domestic violence cases that "show evidence of physical injury." Unfortunately, the ordinance does not define physical injury. Most officers interpret this to mean any sign of physical injury, such as a black eye or bruised arm, but some officers choose to interpret it to mean only serious injuries such as fractures. As a result, some cases are ignored, and you have heard rumors that some of these women are considering a civil lawsuit against the police department.

   a) What can be done to remedy this problem?

   b) What additional efforts should you make with the police and to the public?

Review and Applications

ENDNOTES

1 *U.S. v. Place*, 462 U.S. 696 (1983).

2 *Commonwealth v. Johnston*, 530 A, 2d 74 (Pa 1987).

3 *Barron v. Baltimore*, 32 U.S. (7 Pet.) 243 (1833).

4 *Loving v. Virginia*, 388 U.S. 1 (1967); *Craig v. Boren*, 429 U.S. 190 (1976); and *Plessey v. Ferguson*, 163 U.S. 537 (1896).

5 Americans with Disabilities: http://www.usdoj.gov/crt/ada.

6 See *Calder v. Bull*, 3 U.S. (3 Dall.) 386, 390 (1798), as quoted in Joshua Dressler, *Understanding Criminal Law*, § 5.01 [c][1], p. 41 (3d ed. 2001).

7 Herbert L. Packer, *The Limits of the Criminal Sanction* at 80, note 5 (1968); Joshua Dressler, *Understanding Criminal Law*, § 5.03, p. 45 (3d ed. 2001).

8 *Papachristou v. Jacksonville*, 405 U.S. 156 (1972).

9 *Schenck v. United States*, 249 U.S. 47, 51 (1919).

10 *Brandenburg v. Ohio*, 395 U.S. 444, 447 (1969).

11 *Chaplinsky v. New Hampshire*, 315 U.S. 568, 571 (1942).

12 *R.A.V. v. St. Paul*, 505 U.S. 377 (1992).

13 *Cantwell v. Connecticut*, 310 U.S. 296 (1940); *Church of the Lukumi Babula Aye, Inc. v. City of Hialeah*, 508 U.S. 520 (1993).

14 *Reynolds v. United States*, 98 U.S. (8 Otto) 145 (1878); *Walker v. Superior Court*, 763 P.2d 852 (Cal. 1988); *Harden v. State*, 216 S.W.2d 708 (Tenn. 1949); and *Employment Division v. Smith*, 494 U.S. 872 (1990).

15 18 U.S.C. § 924 (c)(a)(A).

16 Joshua Dressler, *Understanding Criminal Law*, § 6.05[C], at p. 58 (3d ed. 2001); *Rummel v. Estelle*, 445 U.S. 263 (1980); and *Solem v. Helm*, 463 U.S. 277 (1983).

17 *Harmelin v. Michigan*, 501 U.S. 957 (1991).

18 *Furman v. Georgia*, 408 U.S. 238 (1972).

19 *Gregg v. Georgia*, 428 U.S. 153 (1976); and *Coker v. Georgia*, 433 U.S. 584 (1977).

20 *Eisenstat v. Baird*, 405 U.S. 438, 453 (1972); and *Griswold v. Connecticut*, 381 U.S. 479 (1965).

21 *Roe v. Wade*, 410 U.S. 113 (1973); *Planned Parenthood v. Casey*, 505 U.S. 833 (1992).

22 *Bowers v. Hardwick*, 478 U.S. 186 (1986); *Powell v. State*, 510 S.E. 2d 18 (Ga. 1998).

POLICE LINE DO NOT CROSS

Chapter Objectives

After reading this chapter, you will be able to:

1. Differentiate criminal, tort, and moral responsibility.
2. Explain the difference between felonies, misdemeanors, and petty offenses.
3. Describe the requirement of a physical act (*actus reus*).
4. Understand and define the requirement of *mens rea* (guilty mind).
5. Distinguish between specific intent and general intent crimes.
6. Distinguish cause-in-fact from the proximate cause of a crime.
7. Explain how a concurrence of events is needed for a crime to occur.

Chapter Outline

How can a person commit a crime without doing a thing?

Chapter 4

Classification of Crimes and Elements of Criminal Responsibility

4.1 Classification of Crimes

There are many ways to classify crimes, and the classification of specific conduct as criminal has significance for two reasons. First, only crimes can result in loss of liberty through incarceration; civil offenses, in contrast, may result in punitive damages but not incarceration. Also, in the United States, the U.S. Constitution and the constitutions of individual states require that special rights and protections be afforded to an accused criminal. This can be seen in several specific Amendments in the Bill of Rights, such as:

- The Fifth Amendment's protection against self-incrimination and double jeopardy, and right to a grand jury indictment
- The Sixth Amendment's rights to a speedy and public trial, trial by jury, confrontation and cross-examination of witnesses, and counsel
- The Eighth Amendment's protection against excessive bail, excessive fines, and cruel and unusual punishment
- The Fourteenth Amendment's right to due process of law, which means that the federal government must grant all of the aforementioned rights to every defendant and state governments must grant most of them

In short, criminal defendants have many more protections than those who commit civil or moral wrongs, because criminal defendants have considerably more to lose through criminal punishment. This is why the burden of proof in a criminal trial is "beyond a reasonable doubt," but in civil trials it is 50 percent plus a feather by a "preponderance of the evidence." For moral wrongs that are neither criminal nor civil offenses, no burden of proof is necessary because such wrongs are not heard or tried in the American court system.

Criminal, Civil, and Moral Responsibility

In order to understand the complexities of criminal law, it is not only important to distinguish different classifications under the criminal law. You must also be able to distinguish among crimes, civil offenses, and moral wrongs.

Crimes Most people informally define a crime as an act that is deeply wrong, that is worthy of strong community disapproval, and that calls for a punitive sanction. People might refer to certain legal conduct as criminal in everyday conversation, such as, "It's a crime that he got away with charging that much."

In contrast, formal definitions of crime result from the criminal law of federal, state, or local legal systems. What is truly a **crime** is any act or omission that is forbidden by the law (or penal code) as a violation of the public interest. Although the actual victim of a crime is often a person, legally the true victim is the community. By definition, therefore, a crime involves social harm and requires vindication through a public process. It is prosecuted by government attorneys who represent the community as a whole, not the individual or individuals who have been victimized by the specific offense. A victim may initiate the investigation that leads to prosecution by going to the police, and may aid the prosecution by testifying at the criminal trial, but does not actually prosecute a perpetrator for a criminal act. This is why criminal cases have names such as *State v. Jones* or *U.S. v. Smith*; this reflects that the defendant is accused of violating the laws of an entire society and must answer to that society in return.

American criminal law has developed from English common law, which recognized the importance of holding individuals accountable for immoral actions that deserve punishment. What is considered immoral and deserving of punishment, however, can vary considerably depending on the time and culture. Consider that acts such as breaking the Sabbath, smoking (for women), and interracial marriage were once illegal in some American jurisdictions. Consider also that today in Afghanistan, the education of women and girls, which only ten years ago was considered perfectly legal there, is now a crime. Therefore, definitions of "immoral" and "deserving of punishment" are extremely flexible, depending on who defines them and when.

An important aspect of crime is punishment. Whereas a person who commits a civil wrong may have to pay damages or do some specific act to compensate the wrong, a person convicted of a crime is punished. *Punishment* can take many forms, all of which carry one essential characteristic that distinguishes criminal from civil wrongdoing in Anglo-American law: the condemnation and stigma that accompanies the conviction of a crime. For example, even if a punishment is only a fine, such a fine serves a different purpose than an award of damages in a civil case. The criminal punishment (or *sanction*) of a fine expresses social disapproval and is not a method of compensating an individual. Such differences in the nature and aims

crime An act or omission that the law makes punishable, generally by fine, penalty, forfeiture, or confinement.

of civil judgments and criminal sanctions help to explain why they are handled though separate court systems.

Civil Wrongs A civil wrong can be classified as a **tort**, which is a wrongful act that results in injury and leaves the injured party entitled to compensation, or a breach of contract or trust. Although criminal and civil law both involve holding individuals accountable for actions that the law deems inappropriate, there are two significant differences between the consequences of criminal liability and civil liability.

First, a crime is committed against the community at large, but a tort is a wrong against specific individuals only. Therefore, the pursuit of a tort remedy (as through a lawsuit) involves not government action against individual defendants, but the action of private citizens against another individual or individuals who have violated civil law. For example, a lawsuit often involves one person seeking monetary damages against another person. A class action lawsuit involves several people taking legal action against a person or corporation who has wronged them.

Second, the consequences of tort liability are less than the consequences of criminal liability. This is because a party in a civil suit does not face the possibility of punishment, such as loss of liberty or life. Although many people would consider punitive damages a form of punishment, it is not considered equivalent to incarceration or the stigma of conviction.

An individual's single act may constitute both a crime and a tort and thus may be punishable under criminal and civil law. Suppose that a drunk driver kills a pedestrian. He can be prosecuted for vehicular homicide and sued in civil court for medical costs, funeral costs, and punitive damages. It is important to note that although the same general action (hitting a pedestrian while driving drunk) is being tried in different courts, it is for somewhat different reasons and aims. The criminal prosecution is to punish the driver for the harm caused to society, and the civil prosecution is to alleviate the expenses and suffering encountered by the individual's family.

Moral Wrongs If one commits an act that is morally bad, it may lead to both civil and criminal proceedings. For example, a murder can lead to criminal sanctions, civil action for wrongful death, and moral condemnation from others. However, not all morally wrongful conduct is classified as criminally or even civilly wrong. Because a foundation of American philosophy is individual freedom, the criminal law prohibits only extreme conduct, not all morally repre-

tort A civil wrong for which a remedy may be obtained, usually in the form of fines or punitive damages.

Federal Lawmaking

All federal criminal laws are statutorily based, and none are based on judicial decisions; in other words, there are no federal common law crimes.

The Elements of Crime

hensible conduct. Returning to the example of murder, this qualifies as extreme conduct and is considered criminal in every jurisdiction. On the other hand, standing by and watching while another person commits a robbery without offering assistance when one could easily do so could be considered morally reprehensible by some people, but is not extreme enough to require a civil or criminal remedy.

Furthermore, the criminal law does not seek to punish thoughts or moral character, only conduct such as actions and specific omissions that cause social harm. For example, thinking about a criminal act or writing stories about imagined criminal acts is not a crime. Possessing questionable moral character is not a crime, as long as it does not lead to criminal conduct. In contrast, committing an illegal act or an illegal omission (such as neglecting to take care of a sick child, leading to that child's death) is a crime.

Felonies, Misdemeanors, and Petty Offenses

Perhaps the most common way to classify crimes is according to their punishment. Crimes can be broken into three major categories: felonies, misdemeanors, and petty offenses. (See Figure 4–1 on page 88 for a comparison of these categories.)

Felonies   At common law, felonies were the most serious class of criminal offense and were uniformly punishable by death. All other offenses were considered misdemeanors and thus were not punishable by death. The modern definition of a **felony** is any serious crime that is punishable by more than a year of imprisonment or by death. Felonies include, but are not limited to, various degrees of homicide, rape, robbery, possession or distribution of illegal narcotics, and arson. It is important to understand that a crime does not have to be violent or even be perpetrated against a specific individual victim to constitute a felony. For example, *white-collar crime*, a term that covers several types of felonies relating to dishonesty in commercial matters, is generally nonviolent. Both federal and state legislatures have enacted laws that criminalize other nonviolent acts as well.

The majority of modern jurisdictions divide felonies into various categories or degrees, in order to treat some offenses as more serious than others. This can be seen in homicide cases, where a person may be charged with first-degree murder, second-degree murder, voluntary manslaughter, or involuntary manslaughter in jurisdictions that make these distinctions. One reason for these distinctions is the level of punishment: First-degree murder can be punishable by death, while other levels of homicide usually are not.

Common Law Felonies

The list of common law felonies, which were all punishable by death, was very short but contained a few offenses that may surprise modern readers:
- Murder
- Arson
- Mayhem, which is the disabling of an eye or a limb
- Rape
- Robbery
- Larceny, which is the theft of another's property for one's own use
- Burglary, which is the act of entering another's dwelling to steal their property
- Escape from prison
- Sodomy

felony A serious crime that is usually punishable by imprisonment for more than one year or by death.

misdemeanor A crime that is less serious then a felony and is usually punishable by fine, penalty, forfeiture, or confinement in a jail for less than one year.

Misdemeanors   The common law classified all crimes that were not felonies as misdemeanors. Similarly, modern law defines a **misdemeanor** as a crime that is less serious than a felony and is usually punishable by fines, penalties, or incarceration of less than one year. Examples of misdemeanors include shoplifting and disorderly conduct. A person who is convicted of a misdemeanor and incarcerated usually serves his or her sentence in a local or county jail. In contrast, a convicted felon serves his or her sentence in a state penitentiary and the term will exceed one year. Misdemeanor punishment may also include forms of incarceration other than a local or county jail; alternative options include boot camps and in-patient drug treatment programs.

CRIMINAL LAW Online

Definitions of Offenses

Check out **FreeAdvice. com**'s definitions of petty offenses, misdemeanors, and felonies through the link provided at **cl.glencoe.com**. How are petty offenses, misdemeanors, and felonies defined differently as offenses? How do their punishments differ?

FIGURE 4–1

Felonies, Misdemeanors, and Petty Offenses

Felonies →	*Examples include* • Serious crime • Punishable by more than a year of imprisonment or death • Sentences usually served in prison • Include homicide, rape, robbery, possession or distribution of illegal narcotics, and arson
Misdemeanors →	*Examples include* • Less serious than felonies • Punishable by fines, penalties, or incarceration of less than one year • Sentences usually served in local or county jail or alternative programs • Include shoplifting and disorderly conduct
Petty Offenses →	*Examples include* • Insignificant crime involving minor misconduct • Punishable by fines and community service • Include traffic violations and other infractions

In modern law, the line drawn between felonies and misdemeanors can be quite unclear. This is partly because many jurisdictions have enacted laws that allow a number of offenses to be prosecuted as felonies or misdemeanors, depending on the circumstances. Some factors that a prosecutor may consider in deciding whether to charge an offense as a felony or a misdemeanor can include:

- Prior offenses
- Seriousness of the offense
- The number of victims
- The age of the perpetrator.

In plea bargaining, a defense attorney will often attempt to reduce a felony to a misdemeanor when this option exists.

Petty Offenses   A **petty offense** is any insignificant crime involving very minor misconduct. Petty offenses often consist of violations that protect the public welfare. In fact, they are usually called violations or infractions rather than crimes; a common example of a petty offense is a traffic violation. Petty offenses are usually not punishable by incarceration, but by monetary fines or community service requirements. The stigma attached to a conviction for a petty offense is usually minimal; one possible exception occurs when a person commits enough traffic violations to have his or her license suspended or revoked.

Punishments

Since petty offenses carry such minimal punishments, defendants charged with petty crimes are not entitled to a trial by jury. This is because the maximum penalty for petty offenses is rarely six months' confinement, which is the minimum punishment required to justify a trial by jury.

petty offense A minor or insignificant crime.

◀ **Petty Offenses**
Most of us have committed petty offenses, such as jaywalking or speeding. *How are petty offenses usually punished?*

Although petty offenses may be technically classified under criminal codes, the Model Penal Code classifies them as noncriminal. It limits the sentence of a petty offense to a fine, fine and forfeiture, or other civil penalty such as the cancellation or suspension of a license. Since many citizens have suffered petty offense convictions, such as for speeding or jay walking, the position of the Code and the states that follow this procedure is that penal sanctions are justified only for conduct warranting the moral condemnation implicit in the concept of a crime.

CRIMINAL LAW *Online*

Check your answers at cl.glencoe.com.

Self Check

Give one example each of a felony, misdemeanor, and petty offense. In what important ways do these offenses differ?

4.2 Basic Elements of Criminal Culpability

You have just learned about the broad categories of liability and criminal liability as defined by modern law. However, before this book discusses the elements of any specific offense, you must first understand the basic requirements of criminal culpability. That is, you need to understand what actions and state of mind are required of an individual to hold that person criminally responsible for such acts. Under the general principles of American criminal law and its predecessor, English common law, criminal liability requires a concurrence, or unity, of two general criteria: An act or physical element, known as the *actus reus*, and a certain mental state or intent, known as the *mens rea*.

In addition, under the general principles of criminal responsibility developed from the common law tradition, the physical act must be voluntary and cause social harm. (For example, actions performed accidentally or those that do not cause harm are not considered crimes.) Criminal responsibility or liability, therefore, has five elements. Conversely, a person who commits an act that does not contain these five elements has not committed a crime. Unless a person who fulfills these five elements is justified or excused, he or she can be punished under the criminal law.

1. The *actus reus*
2. The *mens rea*
3. A unity of *actus reus* and *mens rea*
4. Causation
5. Resulting social harm

The next two sections will discuss the first two elements, the *actus reus* and the *mens rea*.

Explain why these five elements of criminal responsibility are required.

Check your answers at
cl.glencoe.com.

4.3 The Physical Act: *Actus Reus*

The **actus reus** is the physical action that a person must take in order to be responsible for a criminal offense. As will be discussed later, it is also possible for one to commit a crime by an omission rather than by an affirmative act. That is, a failure to do something may constitute the necessary *actus reus*. In this context, one may look at the *actus reus* element as any act or omission containing the ingredients of causation and social harm. Suppose that Rick shoots Allan in the leg, causing Allan serious injury. Rick committed the voluntary act of shooting Allan, which caused the social harm of Allan's serious injury. Suppose, also, that Amber neglects to file or pay income tax for five years. Amber's voluntary failure to perform the legally required act of filing and paying taxes causes the social harm of unpaid taxes.

In order to be responsible for a particular crime, a person must in some way perform the act legally required for that crime. For example, the *actus reus* required for burglary is that the defendant must *break* and *enter* into a structure or into a vehicle. There are many actions that would constitute this *actus reus*, such as pulling the trigger to shoot through a closed door or smashing a window to break into a car.

As you will read later in this section, the *actus reus* is different from hopes, desires, or wishes. A person may wish to commit a crime and may think about that crime often, but until he or she actually carries out that action, the crime has not been committed and the person cannot be held responsible.

actus reus The wrongful deed that comprises the physical components of a crime and that generally must be coupled with *mens rea* to establish criminal liability.

Voluntary Action

Actus reus usually consists of a voluntary action. That is, except for a few limited circumstances, a person is not responsible for an action over which he or she had no control. A good example of this would be a person who suffers from epilepsy and experiences uncontrolled seizures. If that person were at a grocery store shopping, went into seizures, and by doing so caused property damage, he or she probably would not be responsible for any criminal liability. On the other hand, if that same person were not allowed to drive a car because of an epileptic condition, but went out and did so anyway, he or she would be responsible for injuries or damage caused if he or she had a seizure and lost control of the car. (See Application Case *People v. Decina*.)

For the act to be voluntary, the defendant must have possessed sufficient free will to exercise choice and be responsible for his or her conduct. Even if a person who has acted voluntarily later regrets the act, he or she is still held responsible. This requirement is consistent with the fundamental principle of individuality upon which the Anglo-American legal system is based. For example, a person who is forced at gunpoint to steal a car will probably not have the same level of criminal responsibility as a person who single-handedly and voluntarily breaks into a car. Likewise, conditions such as mental infirmity or extreme youth can also diminish a person's criminal responsibility.

Thoughts Versus Acts

To fully understand *actus reus*, it is important to understand the difference between voluntary actions and mere thoughts. A person cannot be punished for thinking about committing a crime. On the other hand, if he or she actually acts on that thought and commits the physical acts connected to the thought, he or she will be liable for the crime committed. Everybody can think of times when they were angry at someone and wished that something bad happened to that person. However, even if something bad did happen to that person, you would not be criminally responsible if you have not acted upon the thought of doing harm.

Omissions as Acts

An *actus reus* usually involves a physical act. In certain circumstances, however, a person may be guilty of a crime by *failing to act*.

People v. Decina

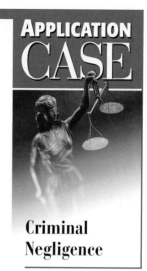

In the 1956 New York case of *People v. Decina*, the defendant, who suffered from epilepsy, killed four children when his car went out of control during a seizure. The defendant was convicted of criminal negligence because he knew that he was highly susceptible to seizures and failed to take proper precautions. Although the ultimate act that caused the deaths was involuntary, the act of driving a car under these circumstances constituted the necessary *actus reus*.

Critical Thinking What other involuntary acts can you think of that could result in a conviction for criminal negligence?

SOURCE: *People v. Decina*, 138 N.E.2d 799 (N.Y. 1956).

Criminal Negligence

In this sense, **omissions** are legally viewed as actions that can lead to criminal liability, usually in one of two situations. The first situation occurs where the definition of a crime specifically designates an omission as punishable. Examples of this include failure to register for the draft or failure to file an income tax return. The second situation occurs where a person has an affirmative duty to act in some way but fails to do so, and such failure causes a criminal result.

An example of this second situation is child neglect: Almost every jurisdiction has laws that require parents and legal guardians to take care of children in a way that will not injure them or threaten their well being. By failing to protect a child, a parent or guardian may be criminally liable without having engaged in any physical act, such as battering the child. If, for example, a parent stopped feeding a child and that child died from starvation, that parent would be criminally liable. The omission of necessary care for a child would constitute the *actus reus* of the crime.

A legal duty to act can arise from a relationship, such as those between a parent and a child or between a doctor and a patient. It can also be imposed by law, such as the requirement that a driver must stop and help if he or she is involved in an automobile accident. It can also arise from a contractual relationship, such as that imposed upon a lifeguard or nurse. However absent a relationship that is not defined as these are, a person usually does not have a duty to provide assistance in all situations. Even though most people would feel obligated to act if someone's life were in danger,

omissions Narrowly defined circumstances where a failure to act is viewed as a criminal act.

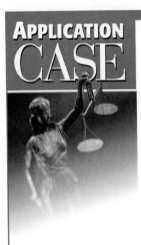

Omissions as Acts

Jones v. United States

The case of *Jones v. United States* (1962) states the basic principles upon which criminal responsibility may rest for omission to act. In the case, the accused was found guilty of involuntary manslaughter for the death of a ten-month-old child, the illegitimate baby of Shirley Green. The baby, Anthony Lee Green, died of lack of care while staying with the defendant. The defendant was a family friend of Shirley Green. Ms. Green lived in the house with the defendant. There was conflicting evidence on the question of whether the defendant was paid for taking care of the baby, but there was no conflict on the evidence that defendant had ample means to provide food and medical care, but she did not do so. The trial court had refused to instruct the jury that it had to find beyond a reasonable doubt as an element of the crime that the defendant was under a legal duty to supply food and necessities to the child.

The United States Court of Appeals for the District of Columbia Circuit reversed the conviction because of the trial court's failure to give this instruction. In doing so, the court stated:

> There are at least four situations in which the failure to act may constitute breach of a legal duty. One can be held criminally liable: first, where a statute imposes a duty to care for another; second, where one stands in a certain status relationship to another; third, where one has assumed a contractual duty to care for another; and fourth, where one has voluntarily assumed the care of another and so secluded the helpless person as to prevent others from rendering aid.

Critical Thinking Does Shirley Green have any liability in this case? If so, why?

SOURCE: *Jones v. United States*, 308 F.2d 307 (D.C. Cir. 1962).

there are numerous judicial decisions holding that there was no criminal liability when a person stood by and did nothing to help someone else in jeopardy.

The 1964 murder of Kitty Genovese is a notorious example of a failure to act that did not lead to criminal liability. Kitty Genovese was brutally attacked late one night outside her Queens, New York, home. She cried out for help for half an hour prior to being stabbed

People v. Beardsley

The court that decided the *Jones* case relied on another case, *People v. Beardsley* (1907), which is instructive of the law's view of the duty requirement before criminal liability will be imposed for an omission. In that case, Beardsley spent a weekend at his home with a female friend, Blanche Burns, while his wife was away. Ms. Burns took a fatal dose of morphine. Beardsley failed to call a physician to help her. She died, and Beardsley was charged and convicted of manslaughter. The Supreme Court of Michigan reversed the conviction on the ground that Beardsley owed no legal duty to help Ms. Burns, even though he may have had a moral duty.

Critical Thinking Does a person who does have a legal duty to protect another person have a responsibility to prevent that person's suicide?

SOURCE: *People v. Beardsley*, 113 N.W. 1128 (Mich. 1907).

**Legal Duty
Versus
Moral Duty**

to death. A reported 38 neighbors heard her screams and witnessed the attack, yet did nothing to help her. It was not simply that they refused to go outside and try to stop the assailant; they did not even call the police from the comfort of their homes. While the unwillingness of Genovese's neighbors to act is morally reprehensible, they were not prosecuted for their failure to act because they were under no legal duty to do so.

Another notorious case involving the question of the failure to act was the heinous killing of seven-year-old Sherrice Iverson by Jeremy Strohmeyer. Strohmeyer's friend David Cash watched the assailant haul the victim into a bathroom stall, begin to assault her, and threaten to kill her. Cash just turned away as she fought for her life. Strohmeyer plead guilty to murder and, in exchange for his plea, was sentenced to life imprisonment without the possibility of parole. Cash, who could have tried to stop the killing, went off to college and was never charged with any crime.

The law's failure to hold Cash responsible, or the neighbors who did not come to the aid of Kitty Genovese, raises difficult moral questions and leaves many Americans dissatisfied with this aspect of the American legal system. Jurisdictions have been reluctant to impose criminal liability in the absence of a legal duty, and lawmakers have been reluctant to enact statutes that create liability in such circumstances. In contrast, an Israeli court recently convicted Margalit Harshefi, a friend of the assassin of Prime Minister Rabin, under a law that holds a person criminally liable for having knowledge or full awareness of the possibility that another person is about to commit a felony. This law, which exists in Israel as a remnant of colonialism, has been rarely used and is generally unpopular. Nonetheless, after Rabin's assassination, there was no public objection to using the law against Ms. Harshefi.[1]

Words as Acts

In most cases, as has been discussed, the *actus reus* requirement for criminal liability is satisfied by overt, willed physical acts. In other cases, it is met by specific omissions. In still other cases, under certain circumstances, mere words can constitute the *actus reus*. Such words are so offensive that they can constitute a threat or cause further physical actions that society views as a social harm.

Where and how a person makes a statement has a lot to do with whether the statement could be considered a criminal act. Often, context alone can determine whether a statement counts as an *actus reus*. For example, yelling "Fire!" in a crowded theater can be criminally prosecuted. The effect of yelling such a statement would be to

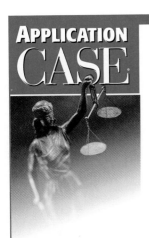

APPLICATION CASE

Omission and Legal Duty

Barber v. Superior Court

In *Barber v. Superior Court*, the California Court of Appeals held that doctors who turned off the life support equipment sustaining the life of Clarence Herbert, who had been in a coma, had not committed an unlawful act for which they could be charged with homicide. The doctors were acting with the permission of Mr. Herbert's family. In resolving the legal question, the court concluded that, even though physicians have a relationship from which a legal duty to act may result, the doctors' omission to act in this case did not constitute an unlawful failure to perform a legal duty.

Critical Thinking In what situations should a doctor, working under a patient's family's wishes, be charged with a crime?

SOURCE: *Barber v. Superior Court*, 195 Cal. Rptr. 484 (Ct. App. 1983).

cause such a panic among the crowd that the word itself meets the *actus reus* requirement. Another example is certain types of threats. Because of the high social value in preventing harm to the President, making a threat to harm the President of the United States is a criminal act. Even if a person has no intention of carrying out the threat, the words alone are enough to trigger the necessary *actus reus* requirement.

These definitions of mere words as criminal acts can create conflict with the First Amendment of the U.S. Constitution, which provides freedom of speech to every citizen. Free speech advocates argue that prosecuting people for self-expression directly violates the First Amendment. Those who support a legal distinction between free speech and criminal speech argue that words that have a very good possibility of causing physical criminal harm should be illegal. Ideally, the law should balance the interests of people wishing to protect their right to free speech and people who may be harmed by another's words.

Possession as an Act

Virtually all jurisdictions have statutes for **possessory offenses**, which criminalize the possession of certain items or substances. A person can be guilty of a crime requiring possession without any further act than possession of the prohibited article. For example, possession of illegal drugs and possession of criminal instruments such as burglar's tools both constitute criminal acts. Actual possession is usually required: A houseguest at a dwelling where illegal narcotics are found would not be in actual possession of the drugs, and thus would not be guilty of the crime of possession.

To prove a possessory offense, the prosecutor must prove that the accused person knowingly possessed the illegal item. The Model Penal Code states that possession is a criminal act if the possessor either knowingly obtained the object possessed, or knew he or she was in control of it for a sufficient period to have been able to terminate possession.[2]

Possessory offenses are limited to circumstances where it is likely that an individual will use what he or she possesses to ultimately commit a crime, and this explains the reason for their existence: to deter further criminal activity. By holding someone criminally liable for possessing the tools to commit a crime, further

Good Samaritan Laws

The following states require bystanders to report certain crimes: Florida, Massachusetts, Minnesota, Ohio, Rhode Island, Washington, and Wisconsin.

SOURCE: Natalie Perrin-Smith Vance, *My Brother's Keeper? The Criminalization of Nonfeasance*, 36 Cal. W. L. Rev. 135, 1999.

possessory offenses
Criminal offenses where the law defines possession as an act.

social harm is eliminated. By the same reasoning, however, a locksmith who possesses tools that burglars also use would not be criminally liable, because it would be clear that he or she plans to use the tools for a legitimate purpose.

Check your answers at cl.glencoe.com.

1. How can omissions legally be treated as the *actus reus*?
2. How can words legally be treated as the *actus reus*?

4.4 The Mental State: Mens Rea

mens rea The state of mind that the prosecution, to secure a conviction, must prove that a defendant had when committing a crime.

Actus reus makes up only one part of the criminal culpability requirement. Only in rare circumstances, however, can someone be convicted of a crime without both the physical act *and* the guilty mind. The guilty mind is known as the **mens rea**; it is also called *intent* or *culpability*. You will read about *mens rea* several times throughout this book.

Broadly speaking, *mens rea* is the mental state that a person has at the time that he or she does the acts that constitute the commission of a crime. For example, if the accused stabbed the victim with desire to cause the victim's death, then the accused had the *mens rea* of "specific intent to kill," which is one variety of *mens rea* that makes a person criminally liable for murder. You will learn more about different types of *mens rea* later in this section.

motive The emotion that prompts a person to act. It is not an element of a crime that is required to prove criminal liability, but it often may be shown in order to identify the perpetrator of a crime or explain his or her reason for acting.

Motive, which is a term sometimes used to mean intent, is actually slightly different and must be explained. **Motive** usually means the emotion prompting a person to act. For instance, the motive for a man killing his wife's lover would be jealousy. In this sense, motive is not a form of *mens rea* and is not an element of required proof for criminal culpability. In other words, the criminal actor is not liable for the jealousy that motivated him to commit this killing (although he may be liable for the killing in other ways). Nonetheless, motive is often important as a matter of proof because it may help to identify the perpetrator of a crime or explain *why* a suspect may have acted in a particular way.

As you will learn, there are different ways that *mens rea* may be satisfied for different crimes or even for the same crime. The *mens rea* requirement for murder in many jurisdictions is *malice afore-thought*, a form of *mens rea* that can exist in four different mental states:

1. A specific intent to kill
2. An intent to inflict serious bodily injury
3. A wanton disregard for human life
4. The commission of a dangerous felony[3]

For voluntary manslaughter, many jurisdictions require the *mens rea* of intent to kill, but in the sudden heat of passion. Involuntary manslaughter requires only the *mens rea* of negligence or the commission of an unlawful act not amounting to a felony. Although there may be a variety of mental states that will satisfy the requirement of *mens rea*, some form of it will be required. Thus, it is essential for prosecutors to understand *what* mental state is required for criminal culpability with respect to any particular crime.

Specific Intent and General Intent

Specific intent and general intent have been used in Anglo-American law for centuries, but have been confusing to many lawmakers and judges. To clarify these terms, **specific intent** can be any one of the following:

- The intention to do an act for the purpose of doing some additional future act

specific intent The intention to commit an act for the purpose of doing either some additional future act, to achieve some further consequences, or with the awareness of a statutory attendant circumstance.

Myth	Fact
The only form of *mens rea* that will lead to criminal culpability is intent.	There are numerous mental states that may satisfy the *mens rea* requirement for criminal liability of any particular crime. These include specific intent to cause the result, careless disregard of the consequences, and gross negligence.

- The intention to do an act to achieve some further consequences beyond the conduct or result that constitutes the *actus reus* of the offense
- The intention to do an act with the awareness of a statutory attendant circumstance[4]

In contrast, a crime that does not require any of these states of mind is a general intent crime. **General intent** is the intent only to do the *actus reus* of the crime.

For example, common law burglary is a specific intent crime. It requires that a person break and enter the dwelling of another at night, not merely knowingly or on purpose, but with the further purpose to commit a felony inside the dwelling. The *actus reus* of common law burglary, therefore, is the breaking and entering of a particular dwelling. If the perpetrator also plans the future act of committing a felony, then the requirement of *mens rea* is also satisfied. The crime is complete upon the entry and the accused can be convicted of burglary, even if he or she does not actually commit a felony inside.

Other examples of specific intent crimes are assault with intent to kill, larceny, and receiving stolen property with the knowledge that it is stolen. Each of these crimes consists of an *actus reus* that involves intentional acts, but each also requires either an additional purpose or knowledge of an attendant circumstance:

- Assault with intent to kill requires that a person commit a battery, which is the intentional application of unlawful force upon another, with the specific further purpose of killing that person.
- Larceny is the trespassory taking and carrying away of the personal property of another with the further specific purpose of permanently depriving the other person of that property.
- A person is guilty of receiving stolen property with knowledge that it is stolen only if the accused has knowledge that the property was stolen.

In contrast are the general intent crimes. A perpetrator who breaks and enters a dwelling is guilty of the general intent crime of trespass even if he or she had no additional intent to commit a felony inside. Similarly, a person who commits a battery but has no additional purpose to kill the victim would be guilty of the general intent crime of simple battery.

general intent The intent only to do the *actus reus* of the crime, without any additional intention to do some future act or to achieve some further consequences beyond the conduct or result that constitutes the *actus reus* of the offense, or in the absence of the awareness of a statutory attendant circumstance.

United States v. Melton

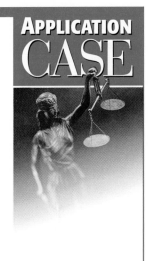

In *United States v. Melton*, Ms. Vessels was awakened by a loud noise. She went downstairs to investigate and found several pieces of plywood that had been stacked against a door that opened inward from an unheated sunroom. She went next door to a neighbor's house and called the police. When the police arrived, they found the door to the sunroom partially open and discovered the defendant lying on the floor. He was charged and convicted of first-degree burglary that required the unlawful breaking and entering into the dwelling of another with intent to commit a criminal offense, namely larceny, in the instant case.

The court reversed the defendant's conviction on the basis that there was insufficient evidence to sustain a conviction for burglary. The court reasoned that intent was the element that separated unlawful entry, or trespassing, from burglary. Unlike trespassing, burglary requires intent to commit a crime once unlawful entry is accomplished. What was lacking in this case was circumstantial evidence that showed a purpose other than unlawful entry. Such circumstantial evidence includes flight upon discovery, carrying or trying to conceal stolen goods, and an assault upon a resident. Since the defendant did not attempt to escape or resist arrest, even though there was an open window nearby; and since no stolen goods, weapons, or burglary tools were recovered from him, there was insufficient proof that the defendant was on the premises to commit larceny.

Intent

Critical Thinking What crimes do you think a person could be prosecuted for without an intent? Should there be more?

SOURCE: *United States v. Melton*, 491 F.2d 45 D.C. Cir.

The general intent crimes of bigamy and statutory rape provide further examples. The crime of bigamy is committed when a married person remarries while having a spouse living; since it does not require that the perpetrator specifically know that his or her spouse is living, it is therefore a general intent crime. In most jurisdictions, statutory rape requires sexual intercourse with a girl who is underage, but the perpetrator does not have to be shown to have specific knowledge that the girl was underage.

Transferred Intent

Transferred intent holds a person criminally liable even when the consequence of his or her action is not what the actor actually intended. If a person intends to harm one person, but with his or her harmful action mistakenly injures or kills another, the required criminal element of intent instead applies to the harm committed against the unintended victim. If a perpetrator fires a gun out of his car window with the intent of killing a rival gang member, but the bullet misses the gang member and kills a three-year-old girl, he is guilty under the doctrine of transferred intent. Even though the perpetrator had no intention of shooting the child, his intent to kill the gang member transfers to her. As a result, he will be found to have had the same *mens rea* as if he intended to kill the child.

Transferred intent is sometimes called a "legal fiction" because a prosecutor can not definitely prove that the actor had the necessary intent needed to punish him or her for the injury to the innocent bystander. The transferred intent doctrine exists to ensure that a person is punished for his or her criminal culpability, even though

➤ **Transferred Intent**
Under the doctrine of transferred intent, if this robber intended to kill a teller but instead shoots and kills any innocent bystanders, he or she is equally liable for murder charges.
How is transferred intent used by prosecutors?

the intended harm was directed at the wrong person accidentally. In other words, if a perpetrator is a lousy shot or burgles the wrong address, that should not make him or her free from guilt.

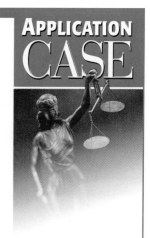

APPLICATION CASE

Transferred Intent

People v. Scott

In *People v. Scott* (1996), the defendants were convicted of murder in the second degree for the murder of an innocent bystander and attempted murders of the intended victims. As a result of a family vendetta, the defendants tried to kill Calvin Hughes, the ex-boyfriend of their mother, Elaine Scott. Following a physical altercation with Scott, Hughes returned to their apartment with a friend to remove his personal belongings. Scott refused to let him in, but Hughes forced his way in and removed his belongings. Scott threatened to page the defendants, who were her sons.

Hughes and his friend then went to a local park. They parked next to Nathan Kelly, whose teenaged son Jack Gibson was parked nearby. As Hughes stood beside Kelly's car, talking to him through the open window, three cars entered the park. The first vehicle contained the defendants, who sprayed the area with bullets. Hughes ran for cover behind the front bumper of Kelly's car, then sprinted toward the park and was immediately followed by a hail of gunfire. One bullet hit the heel of his shoe, and the shooting did not stop until Hughes took cover behind the gym. During the shooting, both Kelly's and Gibson's cars were riddled with bullets. Kelly was shot in the leg and buttocks, and his son Jack Gibson had been shot in the head and killed.

Following their conviction for one count of murder in the second degree and two counts of attempted murder, the defendants argued that the jury should not have been instructed to apply the doctrine of transferred intent to the unintended victim, since they were also charged with the attempted murder of an intended victim. The court rejected the appeal and affirmed the convictions, holding that intent is not capable of being "used up" once it is used to convict a defendant of the crime that he or she intended to commit. Hence, the prosecutor successfully used the doctrine of transferred intent to convict for both the intended and unintended crimes.

Critical Thinking If Jack Gibson had only been wounded in the shooting, would transferred intent still apply, considering the defendants' aim was to kill?

SOURCE: *People v. Scott*, 927P. 2d 288 (Cal. 1996). Citing *The Queen v. Saunders and Archer*, 75 Eng.Rep. 706 (1576).

Model Penal Code Classifications of Mental States

The Model Penal Code, which has greatly influenced modern American criminal law, designates four kinds of *mens rea* by which a person can be found criminally liable. The MPC provides that "a person is not guilty of an offense unless he acted purposely, knowingly, recklessly or negligently, as the law may require, with respect to each material element of the offense."[5] This makes a person criminally liable only if he or she possesses one of these specific states of mind, but not for mere immorality. This provision is an attempt to simplify the concept of *mens rea* by doing away with specific intent, general intent, and other older terms.

Under the MPC, a person acts with one of four types of mental states (see Figure 4.2), which are listed below. The first two are broken in two subcategories each.

purposely with respect to result or conduct The actor's conscious object to engage in conduct of that nature or to cause such a result.

purposely with respect to attendant circumstances When the actor is aware of the existence of such circumstances, or he or she believes or hopes that they exist.

Acting with Purpose When a perpetrator acts **purposely with respect to result or conduct**, it is his or her voluntary wish to act in a certain way or produce a certain result. A perpetrator who buys a gun and ammunition, points the gun at a victim, and fires the gun has manifested a purpose to kill the victim. When a person acts **purposely with respect to attendant circumstances**, he or she is aware of conditions that will make the intended crime possible, or believes or hopes that they exist. If a perpetrator enters an occupied dwelling in order to

---

FIGURE 4–2

Classifications of Mental States

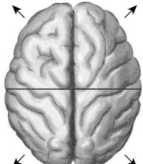

Acting with Purpose
Purposely with respect to result of conduct
- Perpetrator's voluntary wish is to act in a certain way or produce a certain result

Purposely with respect to attendant circumstances
- Perpetrator is aware of conditions that will make the intended crime possible

Acting Knowingly
Knowingly causes a result
- Perpetrator commits an act aware that it is practically certain that his or her conduct will cause a certain result

Knowingly with respect to conduct and attendant circumstances
- Perpetrator commits an act aware that his or her actions are criminal or that attendant circumstances made an otherwise legal act a criminal one

Acting Negligently
Perpetrator should be aware that a substantial and unjustifiable risk exists or will result from the negligent conduct

Acting Recklessly
Perpetrator voluntarily ignores a substantial and unjustified risk that a certain circumstance exists or will result from the reckless conduct

commit a felony inside, he or she has acted purposely with respect to the attendant circumstance that the dwelling was occupied—if he or she was aware it was occupied, believed it was, or hoped it was.

✗ Acting Knowingly

A person **knowingly causes a result** if he or she knows or is practically certain that his or her conduct will cause this result. If a perpetrator fires 50 rounds into a crowd of people and kills five persons, he or she knowingly killed the victims if aware or practically certain that firing the weapon would likely result in one or more deaths.

A person acts **knowingly with respect to conduct and attendant circumstances** if he or she knows that his or her actions are criminal, or that attendant circumstances made an otherwise legal act a criminal one. With regard to conduct, if the accused is charged with knowingly endangering the life of a person by shooting a gun at him, he would be guilty if he was aware that his conduct endangered that person's life. If he was unaware of the presence of the victim, he did not act knowingly, even if the victim's presence seemed obvious. With respect to knowledge of attendant circumstances, a person would be guilty of receiving stolen property if, at the time he received the property, he was aware that it had been stolen. Sometimes, people will engage in "willful blindness" by not asking questions in highly suspicious circumstances and then claiming a lack of *mens rea* due to a lack of knowledge. To avoid such manipulation, the MPC provides that knowledge is established if a person knows that there is a high probability that such an attendant circumstance exists.

✗ Acting Recklessly

The MPC states that a person acts **recklessly** if he or she voluntarily ignores a substantial and unjustified risk that a certain circumstance exists or will result from the reckless conduct. A risk is considered substantial and unjustified if a reasonable law-abiding citizen considers it a clear deviation from how a reasonable person would behave. Since this is rather vague, juries are required to look at the perspective of the defendant when determining whether the actions he or she took created a substantial and unjustified risk. Peculiar characteristics of the defendant may be taken into account when determining whether he or she acted recklessly. For example, physical traits such as blindness may compel a person to act differently than someone with sight, and a jury can be instructed to take that into account.

✗ Acting Negligently

Under the MPC, a person acts **negligently** if he or she should be aware that a substantial and unjustifiable risk

knowingly causes a result Committing an act in the awareness that it is practically certain that his or her conduct will cause such a result.

knowingly with respect to conduct and attendant circumstances Committing an act in the awareness that his or her conduct is of that nature or that such circumstances exist.

recklessly Committing an act that consciously disregards a substantial and unjustified risk that the material element exists or will result from his or her conduct.

negligently Committing an act when one should have been aware of a substantial and unjustifiable risk that the material element exists or will result from his or her conduct.

CRIMINAL LAW Online

Legal Definitions

Visit **XRefer.com** through the link provided at **cl.glencoe.com** and read the definition of *mens rea*. While on this page, read the five definitions to the right under "XReferences." (These are *actus reus*, intention, recklessness, strict liability, and *actus reus non facit reum nisi mens sit rea*.) How did these extended definitions help your understanding of these concepts?

Jury Coordinator

Salary: Salaries range from approximately $25,000 to $40,000.

Description and Duties: Responsible for the management and processing of jurors for superior, district, and municipal courts. Ensures that courts are supplied with adequate jurors in a timely manner. Use strong interpersonal skills in working with the jurors, either in person or on the phone, to ensure their needs and the needs of the courts are met. Coordinate the handling of juror excuse requests. Conduct juror orientation classes in any one of three trial court locations, as often as four times per week.

Other Information: Jury coordinators generally provide jurors with miscellaneous information, such as dress codes, a list of local restaurants for lunch break, and parking information.

> **Critical Thinking** List three things you would like about being a jury coordinator and three things you think you might not like.

SOURCE: Http://www.co.pinellas.fl.us/persnl/pay&clas/specs/18784.html.

---

exists or will result from the negligent conduct. As with recklessness, the risk involved for negligence must be substantial and unjustifiable. The difference between negligence and recklessness is that the reckless person consciously disregards the risk, but a negligent person does so unknowingly. It could, however, be said that the negligent person should have known that his or her actions would create the risk. A jury determines whether someone is negligent by deciding whether the risk taken would have been taken by a reasonable person in the actor's situation. If the risk would not have been taken, the actor is found to be negligent. As when determining recklessness, a jury is required to look at the perspective of the accused individual to decide whether he or she should have known that the actions created a substantial and unjustifiable risk.

CRIMINAL LAW *Online*

Check your answers at **cl.glencoe.com.**

Self Check

1. Explain the doctrine of transferred intent. Though a "legal fiction," is this doctrine valid? Why or why not?
2. How do purpose and knowledge differ in regard to liability?

4.5 Causation and Concurrence

Although causation is an ingredient of the *actus reus* requirement for all criminal culpability, it is only an issue in the case of *result crimes*, which are crimes that cause a specific result. There are two steps in determining whether an act caused a specific result:

1. The accused person's act must be the cause-in-fact of the result.
2. If it was, then the accused person's actions must also be the proximate cause of the result.

If both conditions are satisfied, the accused can be said to have caused the result. The best example of a result crime is homicide, where the defendant's conduct results in the death of another human being. Inchoate offenses and possessory offenses are not result crimes.

Cause-in-Fact and But-For Tests

To determine whether the defendant's actions were the **cause-in-fact** of the result, courts apply the **"but-for" test**. This test asks, "But for the defendant's conduct, would the social harm have occurred when it did?" In other words, would the result have occurred if the defendant had not acted?

Suppose that a defendant shoots a victim, causing only minor injuries. During surgery for these injuries, a doctor acts negligently and causes the victim's death. The defendant's act of shooting the victim is still the cause-in-fact of the death because "but for" the shooting, the victim would never have required surgery in the first place. With one limited exception, the prosecution must prove beyond a reasonable doubt that the accused was the but-for cause of the social harm in order to hold the accused criminally responsible. That single exception is where there are two independent causes that operate simultaneously, either of which could have caused the result. This can occur when two people independently shoot a victim at exactly the same time. In this case, both can be viewed as the cause-in-fact.[6]

cause-in-fact The cause of the social harm in a criminal act that is determined by the but-for test.

but-for test The test that asks the question whether the result would have occurred if the defendant had not acted.

Proximate and Intervening Causes

If the defendant's actions were the cause-in-fact of the social harm, the next step is to determine whether the action was the

proximate cause The cause, from among all of the causes-in-fact that may exist, that is the legal cause of the social harm.

proximate cause of the result. **Proximate cause** is the cause, from among all of the causes-in-fact that may exist, which is the *legally defined* cause of the social harm. Often, there is no question about proximate cause because the accused person's conduct is the direct cause of social harm. For example, if the accused shoots a victim who dies at the scene of the shooting, there is no other possible cause of the social harm of death. In such a case, the defendant's act is the direct cause and no other possible proximate causes need to be considered.

Sometimes, though, a case involves various types of intervening causes. An intervening cause is a cause other than the defendant's conduct that contributes to the defendant's social harm. For example, if a defendant recklessly hits a child with his car and then another driver runs over the child, this second action is an intervening cause. One way to deal with intervening causes is to ask, "Under what circumstances does the intervening conduct of a third party, the victim, or a natural force make it no longer seem fair to say that the social harm was caused by the defendant's conduct?"[7] The answer is generally that when an intervening cause relieves the accused of criminal responsibility, it is because the law has described the intervening event as a more important cause of the harm.

When there are competing causes that could qualify as the proximate cause, a court or jury must select one. Usually, proximate cause will be decided by distinguishing between dependent and independent intervening causes. *Dependent intervening causes* are intervening causes that are either largely foreseeable or related to the defendant's conduct, so their existence still makes the defendant liable for the resulting social harm. Returning to the earlier example of the shooting victim, if the accused shoots a victim who is then taken to a hospital and receives poor medical treatment, the accused's conduct will still be the proximate cause of the victim's death because the shooting is still the proximate cause of the social harm.

An *independent intervening cause* is one that is deemed separate enough from the defendant's actions so that it would be unfair to hold him or her responsible for its results. If this same shooting victim were taken to the hospital and, while recovering there from the non-fatal wound, was poisoned by another person, the conduct of the defendant who shot him would not be the proximate cause of the victim's death.[8]

Concurrence of Elements

In addition to the two elements of *actus reus* and *mens rea*, a crime also requires the concurrence of these two elements. In other words, a person cannot be convicted of a crime unless the prosecution proves beyond a reasonable doubt that the accused performed a voluntary act *accompanied by* the required mental state that actually and proximately caused the prohibited social harm. This requirement of concurrence has two components:

1. The *mens rea* must have been present at the same moment in time that the accused did the act (or omission) that caused the social harm.
2. The concurrence must be motivational as well.

The first requirement of concurrence, also called the *temporal requirement*, simply means that the accused must have had the required *mens rea* at the same time that he or she did the voluntary act or omission. The fact that the defendant had the requisite *mens rea* at another point in time does not satisfy the concurrence requirement. For example, it is not enough that the defendant had the intent to kill the victim but did not act upon it, then later accidentally kills the victim.

The second requirement of concurrence, known as the *motivational requirement*, holds that the motivation to commit a specific crime must be present. If, therefore, a defendant plans to kill someone and picks up a gun he believes to be unloaded to test the trigger, but then accidentally shoots the victim when he unexpectedly walks into the line of fire, the motivational requirement is not present. In this example, the temporal requirement was met since the intent to cause death was present, but the motivational concurrence was not present because the actuating force behind pulling the trigger was the desire to test the gun.

1. Explain how causation is tested.
2. What concurrence of elements is necessary to constitute a crime?

Check your answers at cl.glencoe.com.

Classification of Crimes and Elements of Criminal Responsibility

SUMMARY BY CHAPTER OBJECTIVES

1. **Differentiate criminal, tort, and moral responsibility.**

Criminal responsibility leads to the imposition of punishment, including the possibility of incarceration. Tort responsibility leads to monetary loss only, does not involve the stigma of being labeled a criminal, and involves a lawsuit by one party against another, not an action in the name of the public. Moral responsibility carries no legal consequences.

2. **Explain the difference between felonies, misdemeanors, and petty offenses.**

A felony is punishable by imprisonment for more than a year or by death. A misdemeanor is a crime usually less serious then a felony and is usually punishable by fine, penalty, forfeiture, or confinement in a place other than prison. A petty offense is a minor or insignificant crime.

3. **Describe the requirement of a physical act (*actus reus*).**

The *actus reus* is the requirement for criminal culpability that consists of a willed, voluntary act that causes proscribed social harm.

4. **Understand and define the requirement of *mens rea* (guilty mind).**

In order for a person to be criminally culpable he or she must do the proscribed act with an accompanying mental state as required for the crime, such as having the intent to do the acts.

5. **Distinguish between specific intent and general intent crimes.**

General intent usually means the intent to do the acts that constitute the *actus reus* of the crime. Specific intent usually means the intention to do an act for the purpose of doing some additional future act, or to achieve some further consequences beyond the conduct or result that constitutes the *actus reus* of the offense, or with the awareness of a statutory attendant circumstance.

6. **Distinguish cause-in-fact from the proximate cause of a crime.**

The cause-in-fact is that cause of the social harm in a criminal act that is determined by the but-for test. Proximate cause is that cause, from among all of the causes-in-fact that may exist, which is the legal cause of the social harm.

7. **Explain how a concurrence of events is needed for a crime to occur.**

A crime requires a concurrence of the two elements of *actus reus* and *mens rea*. In other words, a prosecutor must prove that a defendant performed a voluntary act accompanied by the required mental state that caused the social harm in order to convict. There are two elements to this requirement:

- The *mens rea* must have been present at the same moment in time that the accused did the act (or omission) that caused the social harm.
- The concurrence must be motivational as well.

KEY TERMS

crime, page 85
tort, page 86
felony, page 87
misdemeanor, page 88
petty offense, page 89
actus reus, page 91
omissions, page 93
possessory offenses, page 97
mens rea, page 98
motive, page 98

specific intent, page 100
general intent, page 100
transferred intent, page 102
purposely with respect to
    result or conduct, page 104
purposely with respect to
    attendant circumstances,
    page 104
knowingly causes a result,
    page 105

knowingly with respect to
    conduct and attendant
    circumstances, page 105
recklessly, page 105
negligently, page 105
cause-in-fact, page 107
but-for test, page 107
proximate cause, page 108

How can a person commit a crime without doing a thing?
Find it on page 92.

QUESTIONS FOR REVIEW

1. How can some actions be torts and crimes at the same time, and what is the essential difference between torts and crimes?
2. What is a voluntary, willed act?
3. What is the difference between thinking about committing an act and acting upon the thought?
4. How do *actus reus* and *mens rea* work together to create a criminal act?
5. Why must an act be voluntary to be a crime, and how does this work in situations where a person commits a voluntary act with involuntary consequences (such as drunk driving)?
6. When does an omission constitute an act for purposes of criminal responsibility?
7. When do words alone constitute a criminal act?
8. Explain the difference between motive and intent.
9. Explain the doctrine of transferred intent.
10. What is the difference between the MPC's definition of acting purposely and acting knowingly?
11. According to the MPC, when does a person act recklessly? What about negligently?

PROBLEM-SOLVING EXERCISES

1. **Hazardous Waste** Assume that negligent handling of hazardous waste is a strict liability crime and carries a penalty of up to a year in jail. Rollie Davis bought a manufacturing company, but had no intention of being involved in the operation of the business; he lives in a different part of the county from the business and lets the business' long-time managers handle the day-to-day operations. A year later, authorities discover that Davis's company has been illegally dumping hazardous waste for the past ten years, well before he bought the company. Can Davis be held criminally liable for the company's past conduct of illegal handling of hazardous waste? Why, or why not? What about for the last year of dumping? Why, or why not?

2. **Battery** Brittany and Josh were boyfriend and girlfriend for the past three years in high school. At the end of Josh's senior year, they had an amicable break-up, then both went off to college in different parts of the country. In the fall of the first year of college, both of them went to their high school reunion. They had not seen each other or spoken for more than six months. When Josh saw Brittany, he excitedly ran up to her, grabbed her, and kissed her in front of several of his friends. Brittany tried to push him away, but he did not let her go until after her third attempt to break free. She was not injured, but she was very angry and reported the incident to the police. You are the officer who receives the report.

You consider the possibility that Josh might be guilty of committing a battery, which is defined as the intentional application of unlawful force upon another. Josh claims he did not intend to commit a crime. Did Josh's conduct constitute the *actus reus* and *mens rea* of the offense of battery? Why or why not? Should he be charged with the crime? Why or why not?

WORKPLACE APPLICATIONS

1. **Deciding on Charges** You are a police officer who is writing up the paperwork for someone whom you caught in the act of attempting a burglary. He is armed with an unloaded handgun, but seems remorseful and is embarrassed for his family. This is his first offense. You have the option of charging him with attempted burglary as a misdemeanor, attempted burglary as a felony, or aggravated attempted burglary because he possessed a weapon—although he told you that he wasn't planning to use it, and you believe him because he appears naïve. In your jurisdiction, a felony charge carries a minimum of three years' imprisonment.
   a) How will you charge this suspect, and why?
   b) How would you charge him if he seemed aggressive and unremorseful? If this was not his first offense? Why?

2. **Deciding on Defense** You are a defense attorney whose client is charged with robbery. Your client states that she had formerly planned to rob the victim, her step-aunt, but was not thinking of it when she went to visit her on the day of the crime. That day, she visited to have lunch, they began to fight, and the fight ended when the defendant physically intimidated her step-aunt and then stole her jewelry, which was later recovered.
   a) Is the element of *actus reus* present? What about *mens rea*? What about a unity of the two factors?
   b) If the jewelry was recovered, is causation still a factor? Why or why not?

INTERNET APPLICATIONS

1. **Take the Role of the Prosecutor** Research online or at your library about the Exxon *Valdez* crash, which led to an enormous oil spill. Learn what circumstances led to the crash, how the crash and damage control were handled, how Exxon was punished, and how the oil clean up was managed. When you are done, assume that you are a federal prosecutor and ask the following questions:
   a) Based on the concepts you learned in this chapter, with what charges would you prosecute Exxon? The ship's captain? Anyone else involved?
   b) Would you prosecute the defendants criminally, civilly, or both ways?
   c) Would your approach differ from what was actually done? Why or why not?
   d) How would you make the defendants responsible for the clean-up cost and management?

2. **Research Liability Offenses** Learn more about potentially strict liability offenses through the link provided at **cl.glencoe.com**. Read the page, then assume that you are a federal prosecutor and answer the following questions:
   a) When would you be justified to impose criminal liability versus civil liability?
   b) Should you, on behalf of the government, impose strict liability in instances of oil pollution, where people who operate vessels cause spills that jeopardize lives and property?
   c) Should the person be guilty of a misdemeanor with the possibility of going to jail without the government having to prove negligence?

3. **The Kitty Genovese Case** Read "The Killing of Kitty Genovese" through the link provided at **cl.glencoe.com**. When you are done, answer the following questions:
   a) What were some of the responses of the neighbors to Kitty's struggle for help? Did anyone aid her in any way?
   b) What excuses did they give afterward? What is your opinion of these excuses?
   c) Should certain morally reprehensible acts be made into crimes? Why or why not?

ETHICS ISSUES

1. **Child Neglect** You are a prosecutor who is negotiating a plea bargain for a woman who is accused of child neglect. It is her third offense of child neglect, and this time the child nearly starved to death. You have the option of accepting a plea bargain that would give her five years' probation and allow her to continue to raise her child. If you decline the plea bargain, she can face a minimum of three years' imprisonment and the child will be taken into state care, and possibly a foster home. The child, who is eight, does not want to be separated from his mother. The mother, who has an IQ of 81, seems remorseful that the child has been harmed but does not appear to fully understand the charges against her.

   a) Which choice will you make? What else can you do in addition to this decision?

   b) Does the mother appear to possess the required *mens rea*? Does this matter regarding her sentence? Regarding the child's welfare?

ENDNOTES

1 The account of this case comes from an e-mail message distributed to the Crimprof Listserv, October 14, 1998, by Dr. Ron Shapira, Professor of Law, Tel Aviv University.

2 Model Penal Code § 2.01(4) (1985).

3 Cal. Penal Code § 188 (West 1998).

4 Joshua Dressler, *Understanding Criminal Law* § 10.06 at p. 136 & n.121 (3d ed. 2001), citing *People v. Hood*, 462 P.2d 370, 378 (Cal. 1969) and *Dorador v. State*, 573 P.2d 839, 843 (Wyo. 1978).

5 Model Penal Code § 2.02(1) (1985).

6 Peter W. Low, Criminal Law 75 (Revised 1st ed. 1990).

7 Joshua Dressler, *Understanding Criminal Law* § 14.03 [c][1] at p. 188 n.35, citing and quoting from *State v. Malone*, 819 P.2d 34, 37 (Alaska Ct. App. 1991).

8 Peter W. Low, *Criminal Law* 77 (Revised 1st ed. 1990).

Chapter Objectives

After reading this chapter, you should be able to:

1. Learn how an accomplice can aid and abet in a criminal activity.
2. Understand the difference between an accessory and a principal.
3. Know the difference between an affirmative act and an act of omission.
4. Explain how causation affects accomplice liability.
5. Understand the *mens rea* of accomplice liability.
6. Describe the natural and probable consequences doctrine.
7. Learn how justifications and excuses affect accomplice liability.
8. Explain the difference between accessorial and conspiratorial liability.

> **How can an accessory to a crime be found guilty when the principal actor is innocent?**

Chapter Outline

11:23:25

11:23:32

Chapter 5

Parties to a Crime

11:23:30

11:23:33

5.1 The Role of the Accomplice

accomplice Someone who knowingly and willingly associates with others in the commission of a criminal offense, and who intentionally assists another in the commission of a crime.

aid and abet To assist or facilitate a person in accomplishing a crime.

In the criminal law, people other than the principal criminal actor can be held accountable for criminal conduct. An **accomplice** is someone who knowingly and willingly associates with others in the commission of a criminal offense, and who intentionally assists another person in the commission of a crime. Accomplices are said to **aid and abet** another in the commission of a crime when they assist or facilitate that person in accomplishing the crime. Other ways that a person can act as an accomplice are by encouraging, soliciting, or advising. In other words, a person could be an accomplice to a crime through many actions that help or promote the crime's commission, including:

- Offering words of encouragement
- Providing a weapon to be used during the offense
- Being a lookout during the criminal act
- Driving the getaway car

As you can see, a person can be an accomplice to criminal acts committed by another without being present when the crime was committed.

accomplice liability The accountability of one individual for the criminal act or acts of another.

Accomplices are held criminally responsible for their actions. In essence, one who is an accomplice can be held liable for an underlying criminal act, even though he or she did not commit that underlying criminal act. This is known as **accomplice liability**, which is the accountability of one individual for the criminal act or acts of another. Accomplice liability, which is also referred to as *complicity*, does not constitute an independent criminal offense. Rather, it exists only when a person is held liable *as a result* of a criminal offense committed by another. Accomplice liability ensures that a person who is affiliated with criminal activity does not go unpunished.

Myth

Most criminals are quiet loners who commit their crimes without assistance.

Fact

The commission of a criminal offense often involves the conduct of two or more persons.

The criminal law holds an accomplice accountable to the same extent as a principal actor. This accountability is justified because an accomplice:

- Intentionally participates in the criminal goal
- Voluntarily identifies with the primary actor
- Willingly consents to the same liability

Moreover, the theory of moral culpability holds a person who is intimately connected with a crime responsible for the criminal act, even if he or she did not physically participate in its actual commission.

Common Law Distinctions

The common law rule separated accomplice liability into four categories. The first two categories cover the roles of the **principal**, who is present at the crime and participates in it in some way, or who uses an innocent agent (such as an insane person or a child) to commit the crime. (The role of the innocent agent or instrumentality will be discussed later in this chapter.) The second two categories cover the roles of the **accessory**, who aids in the commission of a crime without being present when the crime is committed. An accessory may furnish the principal actor with the gun and masks to be used in a robbery or plan the details of how to commit the crime.

principal One who is present at and participates in the crime charged or who procures an innocent agent to commit the crime.

accessory One who aids in the commission of a crime without being present when the crime is committed.

Principal in the First Degree
A **principal in the first degree** is usually the primary actor or perpetrator of the crime. A person may be a principal in the first degree if he or she physically commits the criminal act or commits the offense by use of an innocent instrumentality.

principal in the first degree Usually the primary actor or perpetrator of the crime.

Principal in the Second Degree
In contrast, a **principal in the second degree** is one who intentionally assists in the commission of a crime in his or her presence. This presence is either actual or constructive. Actual presence means physical presence at the scene of the crime. **Constructive presence** is satisfied if the individual is within the vicinity of the crime and is able to assist the primary actor if necessary. For example, one who waits in the getaway car, or who acts as a lookout, is constructively present at the scene of the crime and would be a principal in the second degree.

principal in the second degree One who intentionally assists in the commission of a crime in his or her presence; such presence is either actual or constructive.
constructive presence Where an individual is within the vicinity of the crime and is able to assist the primary actor if necessary.

↗ Not Present at the Crime

Accessory Before the Fact
An **accessory before the fact** is a person who intentionally counsels, solicits, or commands another in committing a criminal act. A person who "cases" a bank to determine

accessory before the fact One who intentionally counsels, solicits, or commands another in the commission of a crime.

where the vaults are and provides the layout of the bank, but does not physically participate in the robbery, is an accessory before the fact. The major difference between a principal in the second degree and an accessory before the fact is that the latter is not present *during* the commission of the crime.

Accessory After the Fact   An **accessory after the fact** is a person who intentionally aids another who he or she knows committed a felony, in order for the person assisted to avoid criminal prosecution and punishment. An accessory after the fact might provide the principal or accomplices with a place to hide, a plane ticket to leave the jurisdiction in which the crime was committed, or a car with which to escape.

Historically, the distinction between principals and accessories regarding accomplice liability has been of great importance. At one time, all felons were subject to the death sentence, and judges did not possess the discretion that today's law provides. Because accomplice liability did not originally distinguish between principals and accessories, accomplices faced prosecution and punishment for the same criminal offense as that perpetrated by the principal actor. This created the concern that the punishment did not always fit the crime—which, in the case of accomplices, is often determined by the individual's degree of culpability.

In response, the common law created a separate category of parties—*aiders and abettors*—that allowed judges to distinguish among different types of felons and thus punish accessories less severely than principals. In time, judges gradually acquired more authority in sentencing discretion; as a result, the distinction between principals and accessories became less crucial.

Modern Parties to a Crime

As you have learned, the Model Penal Code (MPC) functions as a model in the reform of principles of American criminal responsibility; the result of its initial publication in 1962 is that an overwhelming majority of the states have revised their criminal codes. Even before the development of the Model Penal Code (MPC), however, many state legislatures eliminated the distinction between principals and accessories, as recommended in the MPC.

The California Penal Code offers a typical example of this. It defines principals in the commission of a crime as anyone "concerned in the commission of a crime," whether directly or not, and whether as aiders, abettors, or accessories before the fact. It adds that

---

accessory after the fact One who intentionally aids another whom he or she knows committed a felony, in order for the person assisted to avoid criminal prosecution and punishment.

Bank Robber Guilt

A jury for the trial of an accomplice to a bank robbery would be instructed by the judge as follows: "For you to find someone guilty of bank robbery, it is not necessary that you find that he actually robbed the bank himself. It is enough if he intentionally helped someone rob the bank. To find the defendant guilty therefore you must be convinced that the government has proved each of these things beyond a reasonable doubt: a) that the defendant helped the principal rob the bank and, b) that the defendant intended to help the principal rob the bank."

SOURCE: *Modern Federal Jury Instructions*, Volume III, 47 A; Section 11.01

FIGURE 5–1

California Statute on the Definition of an Accomplice

30. The parties to crimes are classified as:
    1. Principals; and,
    2. Accessories.

31. All persons concerned in the commission of a crime, whether it be felony or misdemeanor, and whether they directly commit the act constituting the offense, or aid and abet in its commission, or, not being present, have advised and encouraged its commission, and all persons counseling, advising, or encouraging children under the age of fourteen years, lunatics or idiots, to commit any crime, or who, by fraud, contrivance, or force, occasion the drunkenness of another for the purpose of causing him to commit any crime, or who, by threats, menaces, command, or coercion, compel another to commit any crime, are principals in any crime so committed.

32. Every person who, after a felony has been committed, harbors, conceals or aids a principal in such felony, with the intent that said principal may avoid or escape from arrest, trial, conviction or punishment, having knowledge that said principal has committed such felony or has been charged with such felony or convicted thereof, is an accessory to such felony.

33. Except in cases where a different punishment is prescribed, an accessory is punishable by a fine not exceeding five thousand dollars ($5,000), or by imprisonment in the state prison, or in a county jail not exceeding one year, or by both such fine and imprisonment.

SOURCE: California Penal Code, § 30–33.

"[t]he distinction between an accessory before the fact and a principal, and between principals in the first and second degree is abrogated. . . .", which means that such former distinctions were put aside and ended.[1]

In other words, principals, aiders, abettors, and accessories are all prosecuted as principals under modern law. The sole exception is an accessory after the fact, who assists after the crime has been committed. Most modern statutes, including California's, classify an accessory after the fact as a separate crime and treat it as a less serious offense, carrying a lighter punishment. (See Figure 5–1 for California's definition of accessory.)

Punishments

Accessories after the fact are typically punished less severely than principals because their actions are most often directed at concealing the crime or shielding the perpetrator from apprehension and prosecution.

Self Check

1. What is the difference between a principal in the first degree and a principal in the second degree?
2. What is constructive presence? How is someone who is constructively present at a crime scene charged?

CRIMINAL LAW Online

Check your answers at cl.glencoe.com.

5.2 *Actus Reus* of Accomplice Liability

Accomplice liability may appear to be lacking in one of the law's basic prerequisites for criminal liability, which is the requirement of the *actus reus*, or act, of the crime. After all, if the accomplice did not actually commit the crime, how is he or she liable? The law responds to this by requiring, for accomplice liability, some act or conduct that *contributes* to the commission of a crime. This contribution may arise by either some affirmative act or by an omission.

Affirmative Acts

An *affirmative act* includes either physical assistance or psychological influence. Physical assistance in the commission of a crime is the clearest form of accomplice liability. This includes casing the scene of the crime, masterminding the crime, providing a weapon to use during the crime, preventing help from reaching an intended victim, and driving a getaway car. A person may also be an accomplice by exerting psychological influence in the form of words of encouragement, assurance by being present at the scene of a crime and being ready to offer assistance if necessary, or by provoking someone to commit a crime. A person who "blends in" with a crime scene by not physically assisting with the commission of a crime is still an accomplice if there is a prior understanding that his or her presence indicates a willingness to assist if necessary. Liability can also be inferred if the situation fits the criteria for conspiracy. This will be discussed in greater detail later in this chapter.

If a person aids another in the commission of a crime, there is no requirement of a certain level of aid. Any kind of aid, no matter how trivial, made toward the commission of an offense establishes accomplice liability. Even psychological support can be enough to establish accomplice liability if it aids or facilitates the commission of the crime. For example, Ted, who had aided Bob in a previous bank robbery, discovers that Bob is plotting to rob a bank. Since Ted does not want to get Bob in any trouble, he assures Bob that he will not inform the police of his illegal plan. Ted is liable as an accomplice because he provided psychological reassurance to Bob and, by doing this, possibly facilitated the commission of the crime. As another example, suppose that someone feeds a hearty meal to a perpetrator in order to give him the strength and stamina needed to complete the crime.

Although the act of preparing a meal seems insignificant, the person who prepared it is an accomplice if he or she acts with the intent that the perpetrator commits the crime and succeeds.

Acts of Omission

Failure to act to prevent another from committing a crime—known as an *omission*—can be a basis for complicity if the person has a legal duty to act or intervene. An accomplice must still act with the required *mens rea*; in other words, an omission must be accompanied with the *intent* to facilitate the actor in accomplishing the crime. For example, a police officer who fails to prevent a crime or stop a crime in progress is liable for the substantive crime on the basis of accomplice liability, because a law enforcement officer has a legal duty to act in such a situation.

Another common example, and one that can present legal obstacles, is a parent's failure to intervene to prevent a crime against his or her child. Although such an act of omission satisfies the *actus reus* of accomplice liability, the requisite *mens rea* (or required mental state) may appear to be lacking, especially if the accomplice is another parent and is a nonabuser. A North Carolina court made an attempt to resolve this *mens rea* issue in the case of *State v. Walden* (1982). The court held that "the failure of a parent who is present to

CRIMINAL LAW Online

Child Abuse

The problem of child abuse and the culpability of parents, including parents who expose their children to adults who abuse and sometimes kill them, is discussed at the Web site of the National Clearinghouse for Child Abuse and Neglect Information which can be accessed through the link at **cl.glencoe.com**. Explore this site and determine how child abuse laws and American society's awareness of child abuse is changing—and still needs to change.

People v. Stanciel

In the Illinois case *People v. Stanciel* (1992), Violetta Burgos was charged as an accomplice to murder when her boyfriend Elijah Stanciel beat her three-year-old daughter, Eleticia Asbury, to death. Burgos had violated a court order to keep Stanciel away from her child. Instead, she allowed Stanciel to discipline the child, which led to the child's death; an autopsy revealed approximately 130 bodily injuries and evidence of sexual abuse. Although Burgos did not aid or participate in the beating, the court found her liable as an accomplice for failing to prevent the beating and for not protecting her child in the situation where a legal duty existed for her to act.

Critical Thinking If there were no court order requiring Burgos to keep Stanciel away from her child, would she still be found liable as an accomplice? Why or why not?

SOURCE: *People v. Stanciel*, 606 N.E.2d 1201 (Ill. 1992).

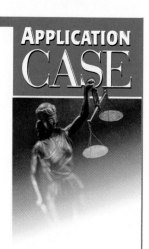

APPLICATION CASE

Acts of Omission

Mens Rea

Statements attributed to a defendant can often be used to establish the *mens rea* that he or she possessed at the time of the crime. Since many people who are arrested make some sort of statement, all parties to a criminal prosecution should carefully examine anything that the defendant may have said.

take all steps reasonably possible to protect that parent's child from an attack by another person constitutes an act of omission by the parent showing the parent's consent and contribution to the crime being committed." It suggested that the parent's "consent," regardless of the reason why it is given, satisfies the mental state of the criminal act; this establishes accomplice liability. However, in order for the nonabusing parent to be prosecuted as a primary actor, the omission must also be "an actual and proximate cause of the result."[2]

The MPC has stricter requirements regarding liability. It requires a person to act with the *purpose* of promoting or facilitating a crime in order to be held liable as an accomplice by an act of omission. Under the MPC, the outcome of the *Stanciel* case (see Application Case, page 123) would be different if the prosecution could not prove that the mother shared the same purpose as the actual perpetrator of the crime, her boyfriend. According to the MPC guidelines, in order to establish accomplice liability when someone fails to act when a legal duty is owed, mere knowledge of a criminal act and a failure to prevent or stop the crime is not enough. Purpose or intent to achieve the underlying crime is necessary for prosecution. The legal differences between knowledge and purpose will be discussed later in this chapter.

Accountability

Under the MPC, accomplice liability rests on accountability: "A person is guilty of an offense if it is committed by his own conduct, by the conduct of another person for which he is legally accountable, or both." The MPC provides that a person is an accomplice if he or she:

- Solicits another to commit a crime.
- "Aids or agrees or attempts to aid such other person in planning or committing" a crime.
- Has a legal duty to prevent the commission of a crime, but "fails to make proper effort to do so."[3]

Accomplice liability may appear to be lacking another one of the law's basic prerequisites for criminal liability, which is the causation of harm or injury. Although causation is a necessary element of a criminal offense, the assistance given does not have to cause the intended result for an accomplice to be liable. Even though the same result might have occurred without the assistance rendered by the accomplice, liability is established nonetheless if the assistance can be shown to facilitate the crime in any way.

The lack of a causation requirement makes sense because the liability of an accomplice is derived from the criminal act of the actor. An important principle to remember regarding accomplice liability is that an accomplice, "by [his or] her actions and state of mind, has chosen to adopt [the primary actor's] criminal act as [his or] her own."[4] Therefore, the prosecution needs only to prove that a criminal act was committed and the person being charged as an accomplice somehow assisted in the commission of the crime.

Sometimes assistance is not accepted, not needed, or not helpful to the perpetrator in the way he or she wants to commit the crime. This is known as *ineffectual assistance*. For example, suppose that a would-be accomplice provides a gun that is not used, or that malfunctions and cannot be used, during the crime. At common law, if assistance in a criminal activity was ineffective, the person who rendered the ineffective aid was not considered an accomplice. What this means today is that in order to be liable as an accomplice, one's conduct must in fact assist or facilitate the crime, and not merely attempt to do so.

A person's unpremeditated presence at a crime scene in order to provide assistance does not establish liability if that person is never called upon for assistance. Suppose that Leah walks into a liquor store as her friend Freddie is robbing it, but Leah did not know that Freddie was planning to rob the store and does not assist him in any way. Leah is not liable as an accomplice, even though it could be

◁ Actions and Accomplice Liability
By committing affirmative acts such as aiding or abetting a crime, accomplices make themselves criminally liable.
How do these two people demonstrate the actus reus *of committing a crime?*

proven that she would have helped her friend if he asked her. On the other hand, when one's presence at a crime scene is coupled with a previous conspiracy or agreement to be present and provide assistance if necessary, but assistance is never needed or called upon, liability could be based upon either accomplice liability or conspiracy principles. Therefore, if Leah arrived at the liquor store pretending to just be a customer, but actually had agreed in advance to work as a lookout for Freddie, she would be considered an accomplice.

Check your answers at cl.glencoe.com.

Under the MPC, what are the three factors that, individually or together, determine if a person is an accomplice?

5.3 Mens Rea of Accomplice Liability

The act of aiding or assisting must be accompanied with the requisite *mens rea*, also known as *intent* or *mental state*, in order to establish accomplice liability. A person is an accomplice only if he or she:

- Aids or assists another in the commission of a crime.
- Possesses the intent to support or encourage the commission of the crime.
- Intends that the primary party commit the underlying offense.

In the U.S. Supreme Court case *Hicks v. United States* (1893), John Hicks and Stand Rowe, who were both Native Americans, were jointly indicted for the murder of Andrew J. Colvard, a white American citizen. Colvard was married to a Cherokee woman and was friendly with both of the defendants.

One day, Colvard and Hicks were riding their horses when Rowe approached them. Rowe raised his rifle to Colvard twice, then lowered it. At that point, Hicks allegedly told Colvard to take off his hat and die like a man. When Colvard removed his hat, Rowe raised his rifle for a third time and fatally shot Colvard. Originally, Hicks was convicted as an accomplice, but the U.S. Supreme Court reversed Hicks's conviction. The Court held that absent proof of a "previous conspiracy" between Rowe and Hicks, there was no evidence that Hicks shared Rowe's intent to kill Colvard. Hicks's statement to Colvard about taking off his hat was ambiguous, and could not be clearly interpreted as encouragement to Rowe to kill Colvard. In addition, Hicks testified that he feared Rowe and left a few minutes after the shooting. With no evidence that Hicks had intended to encourage Rowe, Hicks could not be held to be an aider and abettor in Rowe's killing of Colvard. Although Rowe was convicted of murder, Hicks's conviction was reversed, and the case was remanded for a new trial.[5]

Purpose and Knowledge

The MPC is strict in its requirements defining intent, and it clearly distinguishes between purpose and knowledge for accomplice liability. This is necessary because the line between purpose and knowledge often seems to blur.

The most common example illustrating the thin line between the two concepts is where a person provides someone else with a critical item to be used for the commission of a crime. Purpose, which is the mental state of intent, makes one liable as an accomplice, Some examples of purpose are:

- A storeowner sells a gun or explosive to an individual whom he knows intends to use it in a criminal manner.
- A pharmacist sells prescription drugs to someone that he or she knows will illegally resell them to minors.
- A person provides an answering service to a prostitution ring.

All of these people are criminally liable for having provided a means for the criminal to achieve the criminal act. There may be an economic motive to provide these means, and proof of a continuous economic stake in an illegal operation can establish the requisite *mens rea*; however, this is not necessary. All that is necessary is the required purpose to advance the commission of the criminal offense.

Without the required mental state of purpose to advance the commission of the criminal offense, mere *knowledge* that one's act may facilitate a crime does not necessarily prove accomplice liability. For instance, the fact that a person sells a gun to someone who may use it for a criminal purpose does not make the gun seller an accessory to any crimes committed by the buyer. If such were the case, all gun sellers would be held liable for crimes committed with the weapons that they have sold. On the other hand, if someone sells a gun to someone who the gun seller knows clearly intends to use it in a criminal manner, that seller will be liable as an accessory.

Unwitting Involvement

In the case where a person unknowingly aids another in the commission of a crime, the individual is said to be an *innocent aider and abettor*, and is not held liable as an accomplice.

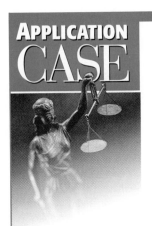
State v. Gladstone

The legal difference between purpose and knowledge is illustrated in *State v. Gladstone* (1980), where an undercover police officer approached the defendant seeking to buy marijuana. The defendant told the officer that he did not have any marijuana to sell, but directed him to another person, Kent, who the defendant said could provide the officer with the marijuana. The defendant had never communicated with Kent, nor did he have a business association with him. The court concluded that since the defendant had no interest in the sale (because he would not benefit from it in any way), he was therefore not liable as an accomplice.

Critical Thinking To what extent should people be liable to prevent crimes from occurring?

SOURCE: *State v. Gladstone*, 474 P2d 274 (Wash. 1980).

criminal facilitation
Where an individual knowingly aids another, but does not truly have a separate intent to aid in the commission of the underlying offense.

Some lawmakers believe that mere knowledge can make a person liable to a lesser degree. To address this concern, a few jurisdictions address the distinction between purpose and knowledge by making mere knowledge a crime with a lesser penalty than the penalty for one who aids with specific purpose. This crime is called **criminal facilitation**. For example, New York State has added criminal facilitation to its Penal Code. The statute provides that a person is guilty of this crime when "believing it probable that he is rendering aid . . . to a person who intends to commit a crime, he engages in conduct which provides such person with means or opportunity for the commission thereof and which in fact aids such person to commit a felony."[6]

In *United States v. Fountain* (1985), a court of appeals held that when the offense is serious, mere knowledge of a principal's purpose is enough to establish accomplice liability. If someone furnishes a gun knowing that it will be used for a murder or sells explosives knowing that they will be used in a terrorist attack, that person is liable. In *Fountain*, prison inmate Randy Gometz was found guilty of aiding and abetting fellow inmate Clayton Fountain to murder a corrections officer. Immediately before the attack, Fountain was being led down a hallway in handcuffs. He then thrust his manacled hands through the bars of Gometz's cell as he went by. Gometz immediately pulled up his shirt to reveal a knife in his waistband. Fountain got his hands free, seized the knife, and fatally stabbed the guard with it. In upholding Gometz's conviction, the court held that it was not necessary for

FIGURE 5–2

Requirements for Accomplice Culpability by State

States that require knowledge for accomplice culpability

States that require purpose for accomplice culpability

Other

the prosecution to prove that it was Gometz's purpose that Fountain should kill the officer. By providing Fountain with a contraband weapon, Gometz's knowledge was enough. Both Gometz and Fountain received sentences of imprisonment for 50 to 150 years.[7]

Agents Provocateurs and Entrapment

In rare cases, primary actors receive assistance from someone who actually wishes to set them up. Such an accomplice is known as an **agent provocateur** or *feigning accomplice*. An agent provocateur intends for the principal to fail in his or her illegal venture. Because of the causation factor, such an individual is not an accomplice: the individual has the requisite intent to assist, but does not have the additional intent that the underlying crime be completed successfully. This is similar to the lack of culpability seen when someone provides ineffectual assistance, except that here the lack of helpful

agent provocateur
Someone who intends for the principal to fail in his or her illegal venture and, because of this lack of causation, is not an accomplice.

assistance is deliberate, and the agent provocateur's actions may extend to helping police apprehend the principal.

The concept of the agent provocateur is especially important in police undercover activities, "when a police officer . . . joins a criminal endeavor as an 'accomplice' and feigns a criminal intent in order to obtain incriminating evidence against the primary party or in order to ensnare the other in criminal activity."[8] Sometimes, police officers have to use encouragement of some kind in order to detect criminal activity that occurs between private people. Encouragement by the police could come in several forms, such as:

- acting as the victim.
- encouraging the defendant to commit a crime either through actions or words.
- influencing the commission of the crime.[9]

In normal circumstances, such psychological aid would create accomplice liability. In these circumstances, however, a police officer may act as a feigning accomplice in order to detect and expose criminal activity.

The difficult aspect of this concept is in differentiating between an officer who acts as an agent provocateur (which is legal) and an officer who goes too far and engages in entrapment (which is not legal). **Entrapment** is a defense that exists when the acts of officers or agents of the government, for the purpose of instituting a criminal prosecution against a person, induce that person to commit a crime that he or she had not contemplated. The U.S. Supreme Court has stated that the "function of law enforcement is the prevention of crime and the apprehension of criminals. Manifestly, that function does not include the manufacturing of crime."[10] If any court finds that a defendant was entrapped into committing a crime, the defendant will not be convicted of that crime.

The MPC states that there are two forms of entrapment:

1. When an officer knowingly makes false representations to citizens that are designed to make them believe that certain criminal conduct is actually legal. For instance, an undercover agent could lead somebody to believe that it is legal to possess marijuana as long as one does not smoke it, then arrest that person for possession.
2. When an officer employs methods of persuasion or inducement that create a substantial risk that such an offense will be committed by persons other than those who are ready to commit it. In other words, entrapment

Wilson v. People

A classic case of an agent provocateur is *Wilson v. People* (1939). Wilson and Pierce were drinking together one night, and Wilson accused Pierce of stealing his watch. After the argument appeared to die out, the pair agreed to burglarize a drug store. Wilson boosted Pierce through a transom into the store, then telephoned the police while Pierce was inside the drug store. Wilson returned to the drug store and the police arrived; after the police discovered Pierce had escaped, Wilson directed them to Pierce's hotel room. After Pierce's arrest, Wilson told the police that he had been involved in the burglary for the purpose of getting even with Pierce for taking his watch, which he hoped to recover (but never did).

Wilson was convicted of the burglary, but the Colorado Supreme Court reversed his conviction on appeal. The court reasoned that Wilson's actions were similar to those of a detective who enters into criminal activity in order to expose it. This reasoning is questionable because Wilson specifically planned this crime to set up Pierce and because he did aid Pierce with illegally breaking in and entering the drug store. However, by calling the police, his actions demonstrated that he did not have the requisite intent to permanently deprive the drug store of its property and therefore was not guilty of burglary.

Agents Provocateurs

Critical Thinking Should private citizens be allowed to use the defense of agent provocateur if they are trying to "get even" with someone?

SOURCE: *Wilson v. People*, 87 P.2d 5 (Colo. 1939).

---

occurs when people who had not previously considered committing a particular crime are talked into doing so.

One way to think of the difference between the agent provocateur and the entrapper is that an agent provocateur will get involved with the criminal actions of a suspect who would have carried on his or her criminal activity even if the agent provocateur had never been involved, but an entrapper will induce a person to commit a crime that this person would not have or could not have commited without the officer's aid or involvement.

Ignorance of the law is generally not accepted as an excuse for accomplice liability. If a person encourages or aids another person in committing a crime, the aider is guilty as an accomplice even if he or she did not know the act was criminal. But what if the aider is merely reckless or negligent regarding the circumstances that make

entrapment When officers or agents of the government, for the purpose of instituting a criminal prosecution against a person, induce an otherwise innocent person to commit a crime that he or she had not contemplated.

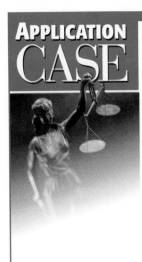

Entrapment

United States v. Twigg

In *United States v. Twigg* (1978), the defendant Henry Neville was convicted of conspiracy to manufacture methamphetamines. A government informant, Robert Kubica, had proposed to Neville that he construct a meth lab. Neville raised all the money for the operation and handled the distribution of the drugs. The informant supplied the equipment, raw materials, and lab site, and worked completely alone in the lab when making the drugs; in fact, he was the only one who knew how to make the drugs.

Because Neville could not demonstrate that he was not predisposed to join Kubica in the criminal enterprise, the court concluded that there was no basis for an entrapment defense. However, the court reversed Neville's conviction. As the court put it: "although proof of predisposition to commit the crime will bar application of the entrapment defense, fundamental fairness will not permit any defendant to be convicted of a crime in which police conduct was "outrageous." The court found that the police conduct was sufficiently outrageous to prevent the prosecution on due process grounds given that:

- At the behest of the Drug Enforcement Agency, Kubica, a convicted felon striving to reduce the severity of his sentence, communicated with Neville and suggested the establishment of a speed laboratory.
- The government gratuitously supplied about 20 percent of the glassware and the indispensable ingredient, phenyl-2-propanone.
- The DEA made arrangements with chemical supply houses to facilitate the purchase of the rest of the materials.
- Kubica, operating under the business name "Chem Kleen" supplied by the DEA, actually purchased all of the supplies with the exception of a separatory funnel.
- When problems were encountered in locating an adequate production site, the government found the solution by providing an isolated farmhouse well-suited for the location of an illegally operated laboratory.
- At all times during the production process, Kubica was completely in charge and furnished all of the laboratory expertise.
- The only evidence that Neville was predisposed to commit the crime was his receptivity to Kubica's proposal to engage in the venture and the testimony of Kubica that he had worked with Neville in a similar laboratory four years earlier.

Critical Thinking What implications does the *Twigg* decision have for law enforcement?

SOURCE: *United States v. Twigg*, 588 F.2d 373 (3d Cir. 1978).

FIGURE 5-3

Kentucky Statute on Entrapment

505.010   Entrapment

(1) A person is not guilty of an offense arising out of proscribed conduct when:

    (a) He was induced or encouraged to engage in that conduct by a public servant seeking to obtain evidence against him for the purpose of criminal prosecution; and

    (b) At the time of the inducement or encouragement, he was not otherwise disposed to engage in such conduct

(2) The relief afforded by subsection (1) is unavailable when:

    (a) The public servant or the person acting in cooperation with a public servant merely affords the defendant an opportunity to commit an offense; or

    (b) The offense charged has physical injury or the threat of physical injury as one (1) of its elements and the prosecution is based on conduct causing or threatening such injury to a person other than the person perpetrating the entrapment.

(3) The relief provided a defendant by subsection (1) is a defense.

SOURCE: www.lrc.state.Ky.us/statutes/505%2D00/010.pdf

the underlying act criminal? For example, Mark encourages his friend Rick to have sexual relations with a female who he does not know is underage. If the crime of statutory rape only requires that Rick, the primary actor, be negligent as to the age of the victim, can Mark be liable as an accomplice based on negligence, or must he have known for certain the victim was underage? [11]

In the absence of a statute that covers cases such as these, the aider could be held liable if he or she has a state of mind with respect to the attendant circumstances sufficient to be convicted as principal. In other words, if Mark was negligent about the age of the victims, he could have liability as an accomplice. In such a case, it may appear that intent is lacking; however, if intent exists in relation to the general act, ignorance that the act is criminal (in this case, ignorance of the girl's age) should not allow an individual to escape liability as an accomplice.

Self Check

1. What is the difference between purpose and knowledge?
2. Define an agent provocateur, and explain how an agent provocateur differs from one who commits entrapment.

CRIMINAL LAW *Online*

Check your answers at **cl.glencoe.com.**

5.4 Extent of Accomplice Liability

Because accomplice liability requires a specific intent relating to the accomplishment of a target crime, and because it allows liability to extend to one person for the criminal acts of another, the *extent* of liability attributed to an accomplice is an important factor. As stated above, most states hold an accomplice liable only for the crime or crimes of the principal actor that the accomplice intended to aid or encourage. In contrast, some jurisdictions hold accomplices to greater responsibility and apply the **natural and probable consequences doctrine**. This doctrine holds an accomplice liable "not only of the offense he intended to facilitate or encourage, but also of any reasonably foreseeable offense committed by the person he aids and abets." Liability not only extends to the actual crime contemplated by the accomplice, but may also reach beyond the crime planned or intended.[12] The reasoning of the natural and probable consequences doctrine is based upon the belief that an aider and abetter should be held "responsible for the criminal harms they have naturally, probably and foreseeably put in motion."

natural and probable consequences doctrine A doctrine that holds an accomplice liable not only of the offense he intended to facilitate or encourage, but also of any natural and foreseeable additional offenses committed by the principal to whom he or she is an accomplice.

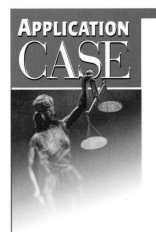

APPLICATION CASE

Accomplice Liability

People v. Luparello

In *People v. Luparello* (1987), the defendant Thomas Luparello's ex-girlfriend, Terri Cosak had left him to marry someone else, and he wanted to know her whereabouts "at any cost." A few of Luparello's friends visited Mark Martin, a friend of the ex-girlfriend's husband, to find out where she was. Because Martin failed to provide the information needed, Luparello's friends returned the next day, and one of them shot and killed Martin. Although Luparello was not present at the murder and did not intend for Martin to be killed, he was charged with and convicted of the murder and conspiracy along with one of his friends.. The court held that Luparello was responsible for the actions he put in motion and for all reasonably foreseeable crimes committed. This case illustrates the principle that liability can extend beyond the crime planned or intended.

Critical Thinking In this case, of what crime is the murder a "natural and probable consequence"?

SOURCE: *People v. Luparello*, 231 Cal Rptr. 832 (1987).

Natural and Foreseeable Consequences

In applying the natural and probable consequences doctrine, there may be some difficulty in defining what exactly is natural and foreseeable. Generally, any additional criminal act that is necessary to accomplish the criminal goal will be considered a natural and foreseeable consequence. This legal question is initially decided by the judge, and once he or she concludes that the defendant can be held legally accountable, the question goes to the jury.

An accomplice will not usually be held liable for an act that is not in furtherance of the target crime, or for an act motivated by a separate and independent intent from that of the ultimate criminal goal. For example, a person who aids another in a bank robbery will be liable as an accomplice for the robbery. This accomplice will also be liable for any kidnapping of patrons, security guards, or employees, as well as for any injuries or deaths that result in furtherance of the robbery. The accomplice will not be held liable for crimes committed during the robbery that are not in furtherance of that crime or of any other to which the accomplice has agreed.

Suppose that David, the primary actor, is committing a bank robbery with two accomplices when he sees his wife in the bank with her lover. In a rage, he shoots and kills his wife. As the primary actor, he will be charged with both the robbery and for killing his wife. Because the killing was independent of the robbery, personally motivated, and in no way related to the goal of furthering the robbery, his two accomplices would probably not be held liable for her murder. On the other hand, suppose that David kills his wife because she is jeopardizing the success of the robbery; for example, she could be trying to prevent the robbery by calling the police on her cell phone. In this case, David's two accomplices would be liable for the murder because the act was done in furtherance of the criminal goal, and thus was a natural and foreseeable consequence.

The MPC does not follow the natural and probable consequences doctrine; it does not extend accomplice liability to crimes that were not agreed to, or to crimes the accomplice did not aid or intend. Under the MPC, an accomplice is not liable for crimes that follow as a natural extension of the target crime and are necessary to the success of the intended crime to which he is an aider and abetter. In the bank robbery example, the two accomplices would only be liable for the robbery and not the individual acts of David during the course of the robbery.

Negligent Acts

Liability as an accomplice can also extend to negligent and reckless conduct on the part of the primary actor that results in a criminal offense. Since a person who commits a negligent or reckless crime automatically lacks specific intent, it seems logical that one could not be an accomplice to a crime involving negligence or recklessness. Accomplice liability is, after all, founded upon the theory that the accomplice *wants* the primary party to commit the crime. One who acts negligently or recklessly does not intend the consequences, so therefore one who aids a negligent or reckless actor cannot know that the criminal result will be achieved.

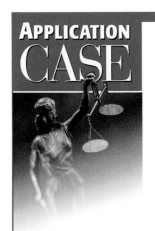

APPLICATION CASE

Liability Without Intent

Echols v. State

In *Echols v. State*, the defendant Arthur W. Echols allowed her husband, Melvin Echols, to beat their child repeatedly with an extension cord. When the child reported the abuse at school, she was permanently removed from the home and both parents faced trial. Melvin Echols was tried and convicted as the principal, and Arthur was tried as an accomplice because she woke up Melvin to punish their daughter, which started the string of beatings.

It was clear that Arthur showed reckless disregard toward her husband's abuse of the daughter; at one point, she washed dishes while Melvin beat their child in the kitchen. However, because common law and the statutes of the state of Alaska require that a principal possess intent that a specific crime be committed, an appellate court reversed Arthur's original conviction of assault in the first degree, a class A felony. It found that the jury at the original trial had been given incorrect instructions regarding intent, and that Arthur did not have the intent required for such a conviction.

Ironically, the more severe charge of principal would likely have sustained a conviction for Arthur because "proof of specific intent would not have been necessary. Echols would have been subject to conviction if the jury found that she recklessly caused serious physical injury to T.E. [the child] by means of a dangerous instrument."

Critical Thinking Why do you think the prosecutor chose to charge Arthur as an accomplice if she could have been convicted as a principal?

SOURCE: *Echols v. State* 818 P.2d 691 (Alaska Ct. App. 1991); James B. Gottstein, http://touchngo.com/ap/html/ap-1164.htm.

Some jurisdictions refuse to extend accomplice liability to those who encourage negligent or reckless behavior because there is no intent for the criminal outcome. Under the MPC, an accomplice is judged by the same *mens rea* as would be required for the conviction of the perpetrator of the offense; a core requirement of accomplice liability under the MPC is acting with purpose to commit a *specific* crime. On the other hand, a majority of jurisdictions do allow prosecution of an accomplice for aiding a negligent or reckless act. Most of these jurisdictions require that the accomplice have intent to aid or encourage the general behavior that negligently or recklessly caused harm, but do not require intent that the principal commit the specific crime.

A clear example of this occurred in *State v. McVay* (1926), where the defendant, Kelley, ordered the captain and engineer of a steamer carrying several hundred passengers to fire the boiler of the vessel although he knew that it was dangerous to do so. The boiler burst and several people died as a result. Kelley was charged as an accessory before the fact of the captain's and engineer's felonious manslaughter. Kelley claimed that since the principals' crime was unintentional, it would be contradictory to hold him as an accessory. The Supreme Court of Rhode Island disagreed, stating that since it was possible for Kelley to "intentionally direct and counsel the grossly negligent" acts of the principals, he could be culpable. The court further stated, "There is no inherent reason why, prior to the commission of such a crime, one may not aid, abet, counsel, command, or procure the doing of the unlawful act or of the lawful act in a negligent manner."[13]

A classic case of accomplice liability for a crime committed by negligent conduct is one involving two or more persons who are drag racing, where each encourages the other to participate in reckless conduct. Liability as an accessory is established in such a case because the negligent conduct is deliberate, even though any criminal results (other than reckless driving) are not intended. At least one court has found a drag racer guilty on an accomplice theory based on this reasoning.[14]

Self Check

1. For what does the natural and probable consequences doctrine hold an accomplice liable?
2. What is a natural and foreseeable consequence?

CRIMINAL LAW Online

Check your answers at **cl.glencoe.com**.

5.5 Relationship Between the Principal Actor and the Accomplice

This section will discuss three complex situations that affect the actor/accomplice relationship. The first is the primary actor's use of an innocent agent or instrumentality, in which the primary actor is considered to be a principal (and not an accomplice) because the innocent agent could not form intent. The second issue is accomplice liability when the principal actor is acquitted; contrary to popular belief, accomplices can still be liable for a crime even when the principal actor is acquitted for individual reasons. The third issue is accomplice liability when the principal is a feigning primary party, which means that he or she is not culpable for his or her involvement in the crime.

Innocent Agent or Instrumentality

innocent agent or instrumentality An object, animal, or person who cannot be culpable under the law, such as an insane person or a child, that is used by a principal to commit a crime.

An **innocent agent or instrumentality** is a person, animal, or inanimate object that cannot be culpable under the law because of an inability to form intent, but who is used by a principal to commit a crime. When the innocent agent is a person, that person physically commits the criminal act but does not act with criminal intent because he or she was coerced, forced, or tricked into committing the act.

An innocent agent can be a non-responsible person such as an insane person or a child, or even a normally functioning adult who simply does not know that he or she is participating in a crime. For example, if a messenger takes a package from a customer and delivers it, the messenger is an innocent agent if he or she was unaware that the package contains an illegal substance such as drugs. The messenger, lacking guilty knowledge, was tricked into carrying the package and does not have the mental state required to be guilty of the crime. Instead, the sender of the package will be treated as the principal actor.

The person who is used as an innocent agent and who has any of the following excuses will not be held liable for a criminal offense:

- Insanity.
- Infancy, or being younger than the minimum age at which one is considered able to form intent. At common law and many current laws, children under the age of seven are considered unable to form intent. Under today's juvenile laws,

children under the ages of 16 to 18 (the age varies depending on the states) are considered unable to form the same intent as adults, but can be prosecuted through the juvenile justice system.

- Duress. To commit an act "under duress" is to commit it against one's will.

As mentioned earlier, an innocent, nonhuman object or instrumentality (such as an animal or a mechanical object) may also be used to commit a crime. Such objects cannot formulate the mental state required to commit the crime. Thus, if a person trains a dog or programs a robot to place an explosive device in a building, that person will be treated as if he or she physically placed the explosive.

A person who uses an innocent agent to commit a crime is considered a principal, not an accomplice, because the innocent agent is not liable for the crime. Current law treats an individual who uses an innocent agent to commit a crime with the same level of culpability as if the user had physically committed the crime himself or herself. Thus, a person who manipulates and takes advantage of an unsuspecting individual, using him or her to achieve a criminal goal, will be prosecuted as if he or she actually committed the crime.

The Model Penal Code explicitly states what is required of a person to be prosecuted as a principal when the crime is committed by an innocent agent:

- A person who "causes an innocent or irresponsible person to engage in [criminal] conduct" is liable for that conduct or act.[15]
- The accused must cause the agent to commit the criminal act. In other words, the innocent agent must be manipulated, forced, or coerced to commit the act, and it must be proven that the agent would not have committed the offense otherwise.
- The defendant must act with the intent to commit the crime. For example, the messenger who unknowingly delivers a package full of cocaine is not liable for the drug offense; the customer who sent the package is.

The concept of intent, and of being an innocent instrumentality, can go both ways. If that same messenger knowingly plants an explosive in the same package and it results in injury or death to the recipient, the sender of the package will not be liable for this act because he or she only intended to deliver drugs, not to cause physical harm or death by an explosive.

Sometimes the doctrine of innocent instrumentality is difficult to apply, even when it is clear that the accused possessed the intent to accomplish the criminal goal and that the innocent agent is not culpable. The doctrine runs into technical problems in two cases:

1. Where a statute only applies to a certain class of people by definition. This arises where a statute defines a particular group of persons who can be liable for a crime. A person who intended the crime but who is not a member of the specified class cannot be held liable as an accomplice when he or she uses an innocent agent from this specific group to commit the crime. This does not include only the underaged or mentally infirm: For example, if a statute prohibits any officer or employee of a bank from entering false records of transactions, then a person who is not an officer or employee cannot commit the offense. If a person who is not an officer or employee dupes an innocent employee or officer into entering a false record, "the absence of a guilty principal precludes accomplice liability."

2. Where the crime can only be performed by the person him- or herself and not through an agent. Such a crime is called a **nonproxyable offense**. Problems that arise with

nonproxyable offense
A crime which can only be committed through the actor's own conduct and cannot be committed by an agent.

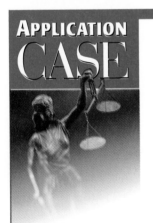

APPLICATION CASE

Nonproxyable Offenses

United States v. Walser

One example of a nonproxyable action is perjury, which can only be committed by the person who testifies falsely under oath. However, a federal appellate court affirmed a defendant's perjury conviction even though she did not personally give false testimony under oath. In *United States v. Walser* (1993), the defendant Virginia Walser was charged with defrauding an insurance company. She called an insurance specialist to testify about two documents that supported her claim of innocence and was acquitted of the fraud charges in part due to the specialist's testimony. However, Walser had falsified one of the documents to which the specialist had testified, causing him to give false testimony under oath.

Critical Thinking What are some other scenarios where a person can be charged with another actor's nonproxyable offense?

SOURCE: *United States v. Walser*, 3 F.3d 380 (11th Cir. 1993).

these offenses derive from the nature of the prohibited action. For example, a sober defendant may cause a disorderly drunk to appear in a public place by physically placing the drunk in public. However, it could not be said that the sober person has, through the instrumentality of the drunk person, him- or herself committed the crime of being drunk and disorderly in public.[16]

Federal prosecutors have found ways around the statute and class problems in innocent actor cases. Usually, they will find a loophole and interpret the federal aiding and abetting statute to include these unusual cases. Also, some courts interpret accomplice liability to apply to those perpetrators who cause another to commit the criminal act even though a statute may not include the accomplice as a member capable of committing the crime.[17] Usually, though, many jurisdictions will not allow convictions for nonproxyable crimes.

The application of the innocent agent doctrine varies from jurisdiction to jurisdiction, and good examples of these variations can be seen in the way that rape cases are handled. In *Dusenbery v. Commonwealth* (1980), a Virginia court refused to uphold a conviction of rape against an armed guard who coerced a teenage couple to have sex while he watched, threatening to tell their parents if they did not comply. The court held that the theory of innocent agency did not apply because an element of rape was not met (penetration of the female organ by the defendant).[18] However, in *People v. Hernandez* (1971), a California court upheld a conviction of rape against a woman, as a principal actor, who compelled her husband to have sexual intercourse with an unwilling woman. Although the act of rape is generally considered nonproxyable, the court applied the doctrine of innocent agency.[19]

Where a crime has been committed through an innocent instrumentality, the courts aim to punish the perpetrator who possessed the intent to accomplish the crime. The principal who induces an innocent agent to commit a crime on his or her behalf is, to many, the most morally reprehensible of all perpetrators. This is why many courts apply a liberal and somewhat flexible interpretation of this doctrine: "If a defendant may fairly be held liable when he aids or encourages a *guilty* principal to commit the crime (even where the defendant is not within the defined class or where the criminal action is nonproxyable)," wrote one commentator, "there are no moral or policy reasons why he should not be similarly treated if he causes the prohibited actions of an *unwitting* primary actor."[20]

Feigning Primary Party

The *feigning primary party* is the converse of the agent provocateur, who is also known as a feigning accomplice. In this situation, the principal pretends to have the required intent to be culpable of a crime, but does not actually possess this intent. In the case of undercover police work, a feigning primary party can set up willing accomplices for arrest by pretending to commit any type of crime. Since the accomplice's liability derives from the acts of the principal, and the principal is not sincere in his or her intent, the question is: How can the accomplice be criminally liable if the principal is not?

The answer usually lies in the specific actions of each party. For example, if an accomplice carries through with every element necessary to be culpable of a crime, he or she may be convicted regardless of whether the primary party has the requisite mental state. "Where each of the overt acts going to make up the crime charged is personally done by the defendant, and with criminal intent," stated one judge, "his guilt is complete, no matter what motives may prompt or what acts be done by the party who is with him, and apparently assisting him."[21] On the other hand, if a feigning party such as an undercover police officer or a private person carries out some act that

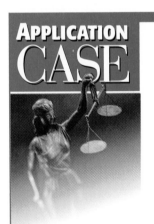

APPLICATION CASE

Accomplice Liability Without Principal Actor Liability

Vaden v. State

In *Vaden v. State* (1989), Department of Fish and Wildlife officers in Alaska received information that Vaden, a local guide, was facilitating illegal hunting practices by his customers. An undercover officer posed as a hunter and hired Vaden as a guide. Vaden then navigated a small airplane so that the undercover officer could illegally shoot and kill four foxes. Even though the officer was not criminally liable, Vaden was convicted as an accomplice. On appeal, Vaden argued that he could not be guilty as an accomplice because the officer's actions were justified as a "public authority justification." The Supreme Court of Alaska disagreed with him, reasoning that the justification that excused the officer from criminal liability was individual; it could not vicariously apply to Vaden. Although the officer carried out the actual shooting, Vaden's actions of guiding the officer to do so were enough for him to be convicted.

Critical Thinking Did the Department of Fish and Wildlife officer commit entrapment? Why or why not?

SOURCE: *Vaden v. State*, 768 P.2d 1102 (Alaska 1989).

is essential to the commission of a crime and the accomplice was not involved in that aspect, the feigning party's actions cannot be imputed to the accomplice and the accomplice cannot be guilty of the crime. As you recall from earlier, any attempt to prosecute accomplices in cases such as that would not succeed because entrapment has taken place.

Indeed, an accomplice will likely raise the defense of entrapment when charged with an offense that was perpetrated by a feigning principal party. In cases involving a feigning primary party, the individual steps each person took in committing the crime will be critical in determining whether an accomplice may be criminally culpable.

Entrapment When a police officer or someone acting on behalf of the police (such as an informant) induces someone to commit a crime that he or she would not have otherwise committed.
Is this undercover officer, who is posing here as a drug dealer, guilty of entrapment if he succeeds in selling drugs to this person? Why or why not?

Additionally, the entrapment defense is only available when the conduct in question was that of either a law enforcement officer or an agent of a law enforcement officer, such as an informant. If a private person working solely for his or her own motives induces someone to commit a criminal act, the accused will not be able to raise a successful entrapment defense.

To help determine if entrapment has occurred, the *Sherman-Sorrells* test has been adopted by many jurisdictions. With this test, the first inquiry determines whether the offense was induced by a government agent. The second inquiry determines whether the defendant was predisposed to commit the offense. Next, the court looks at whether the defendant was ready and willing to commit the crime at any time prior to or after being encouraged by the officer or agent. Under this test, the court will look at the defendant's willingness to commit the crime rather than the officer's wrongdoing. If a defendant raises the entrapment defense in a jurisdiction that follows the *Sherman-Sorrells* test, evidence that normally may not be admitted in a trial will be allowed if the defense is raised. For example, the prosecutor can introduce the defendant's criminal history and reputation to demonstrate the required propensity to commit the act.

Other jurisidictions use a different approach, the objective test of the Model Penal Code, to determine whether an entrapment defense is valid. The objective test focuses on the officer's actions, and asks

Myth	Fact
As long as an accomplice stops his or her participation in a criminal activity, criminal culpability is eliminated.	In most jurisdictions, an accomplice will have to do more than simply abandon a criminal activity in order to avoid prosecution. They should also retrieve tools they provided and inform other participants of their intentions.

whether that officer or agent "employ[ed] methods of persuasion or inducement which create a substantial risk that such an offense will be commited by persons other than those who are ready to commit it."[22] The reason for using the objective test is to deter police from engaging in wrongdoing by encouraging defendants to commit crimes that they would not otherwise have committed.

When the Principal Actor is Acquitted

At common law, an accomplice could not be convicted of a crime unless the primary actor was also convicted. Because accomplice liability is derivative, it made logical sense that the accomplice's liability depended on the conviction of the person whom he or she aided. Sometimes, though, the primary party escaped liability and punishment when evidence against the principal was insufficient, when a technicality prevented prosecution, or when the primary actor used an excuse that justified his or her conduct. Eventually, this old common law rule was ended. In its place, various jurisdictions created statutes enabling prosecution of individuals for aiding and abetting another in the commission of a crime as long as the prosecutor could prove that a crime was actually committed. In jurisdictions following this rule, an accomplice may be liable even when the principal is not identified or when a principal is acquitted.[23]

Still, if the court finds that a wrongful act was not committed by the principal, the accomplice will usually escape liability. If the criminal conduct of the primary actor is justified, the implication is that no wrongful act was committed and therefore there is no criminal liability. In addition, although justification of a criminal act is often personal, some courts will allow a defense of justification to be raised by an accomplice as well as by a principal. For example, Stephanie and Julie get in a fight at a bar. Stephanie is heavily intoxicated and threatens Julie's life with a pocket knife. Fearing for Julie's safety, Julie's boyfriend Chris throws her his pocket knife to defend herself against the unlawful attack. In the course of the fight, Julie stabs and kills Stephanie in self-defense. Julie's action is justified based on a claim of self-defense, and therefore Chris will also likely avoid liability as an accomplice.

Sometimes, the principal has a legal excuse that allows him or her to avoid liability by virtue of a condition that the accomplice lacks. A principal who commits a criminal offense may avoid culpability if he or she is entitled to such a legal defense, which would prove a lack of capacity, but one who acts as an accomplice to a criminal act does not escape liability if he or she is not personally entitled to such an excuse. This is because although the principal avoids punishment because of incapacity, he or she is still regarded as guilty of a crime. It is important to remember that the accomplice

ON THE JOB

Undercover Police Investigator

Description and Duties: Investigate and regulate all vice, liquor, tobacco, gambling, and other vice-related criminal activities. Obtain physical evidence that others are committing crimes and obtain arrest warrants. Make large numbers of arrests by maximizing contacts in a crime ring, or by convincing a number of contacts to become informants. Undercover work can also include surveillance, eavesdropping, and espionage.

Average Salary: For undercover work in police departments, salaries can range from approximately $35,000 to $60,000, depending on the jurisdiction. Since undercover police are experienced, their salaries are somewhat higher than that of a rookie officer.

Private undercover investigator salaries range more widely, but an average estimate is $30,000 to $40,000.

Other Information: Undercover officers are experienced police officers who have generally served in their departments in other capacities (such as patrol) before going undercover. Ethical issues in undercover work include entrapment, corruption, and the ethical management of informants.

> **Critical Thinking** What kind of special training should undercover officers receive?

SOURCE: "Police Undercover Work," http://faculty.ncwc.edu/toconnor/205/205lect08a.htm. City of Everett (WA) Police Department, http://www.ci.everett.wa.us/EVERETT/police/investigations/smart.htm

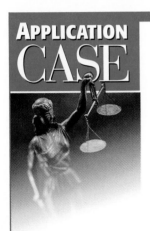
People v. Eberhardt

In *People v. Eberhardt* (1985), a husband and wife violated the California Fish and Game Code, which prohibited salmon net fishing and the sale of salmon harvested from California waters. The defendant's wife was Native American, and because of federal laws that protect Native Americans' extended rights to hunt and fish, she was immune from prosecution by the state. Her husband, however, was not Native American and therefore was not granted this immunity. Although the wife as the principal actor could not be convicted, her husband—who was the accessory and who was found guilty of assisting the crime—was prosecuted and convicted.

Critical Thinking Would the husband in this case have been found guilty as an accomplice under common law?

SOURCE: *People v. Eberhardt*, 215 Cal Rptr. 161 (Cal. Ct. App. 1985).

derives liability from the principal's *guilt* rather than from legal liability. Other personal defenses that enable the principal to escape liability while imposing criminal liability on the accomplice include duress, insanity, infancy, and involuntary intoxication. In some of these situations, the theory of an innocent agent could apply instead, thus turning the accomplice into the principal actor.

An acquittal of the principal does not morally excuse a criminal action, nor does it amount to a proclamation that the act is not wrongful. An excuse allows the principal to escape liability because:

- The law protects anyone who is part of a certain class from being prosecuted.
- The principal is not responsible for the conduct because he or she did not possess the requisite *mens rea*.
- The law provides a defense of some other excusing condition.

In summary, a person who intentionally assists in a crime and intends that the crime be completed, even where the principal is excused, is culpable and will face liability as an accomplice.

CRIMINAL LAW *Online*

Check your answers at
cl.glencoe.com.

Self Check

1. What is a feigning primary party?
2. Why have the laws changed for convicting accomplices in cases where, for whatever reason, the principal is acquitted?

5.6 Issues in Accomplice Liability

At common law, an accessory could not be convicted of a greater criminal offense than the offense for which the principal was convicted. The sole exception was for criminal homicide; in these cases, depending on the circumstances, the accomplice could receive either an equal or lesser sentence than that of the principal. Today, there is no obstacle that prevents a conviction of an accomplice for a more serious crime than that committed by the principal. At first glance, the common law rule seems appropriate due to the derivative nature of accomplice liablity. However, where individuals act in concert to achieve a common criminal goal, the courts look to the *actus reus* of the principal and the separate intent of each participant to assess individual culpability.

For example, a husband who discovers his wife is having an affair might, in a heat of passion and rage, solicit a hitman to kill his wife. In this case, the husband, as an accomplice, could be found guilty of manslaughter while the hitman, the principal, would be guilty of first-degree murder.[24] The reverse can also be true. Suppose that a spiteful friend purposefully and incorrectly informs a husband that his wife is

CRIMINAL LAW Online

Industry Liability

To better understand industry liability, you can examine the theories that plaintiffs are offering in support of their lawsuits against cigarette, pharmaceutical, and firearms manufacturers. One such organization is The Brady Campaign to Prevent Gun Violence. Explore this site by accessing it through **cl.glencoe.com**, then answer the question: Should accomplice liability be imposed on a company that sells a dangerous product if it can be proven that it is likely that that product will be used to injure or kill someone?

Regina v. Richards

In *Regina v. Richards* (1974), the defendant hired two men to beat her husband "enough to put him in the hospital for a month." The men found the husband and beat him up, but did not cause any serious injuries. The court assessed each party according to his or her own *mens rea*. The two men were acquitted of the felony assault and convicted only of a misdemeanor count, but Richards was convicted of felony assault. The court found that, because she had the greater intent to cause serious bodily harm, she could be convicted of the more serious charge if she possessed the mental intent required for the crime.

Critical Thinking If the two men had killed the husband, what crimes would each of the parties involved be charged with?

SOURCE: *Regina v. Richards*, [1974] Q.B. 776, cited in Sanford H. Kadish and Stephen J. Schulhofer, *Criminal Law and Its Processes: Cases and Materials* 679 (6th ed. 1995).

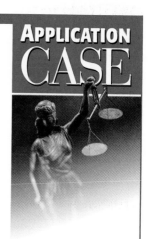

APPLICATION CASE

Accomplice Liability and Mens Rea

having an affair with another man. This causes the husband to beat his wife to death in a drunken rage. The husband will be charged with manslaughter. In contrast, if the spiteful friend intentionally set out to have the husband kill his wife by inciting and provoking him, he or she—as an accomplice—could be charged with first-degree murder.[25] In the scenarios above, the crime of murder is viewed as one act, and the degree of culpability of the primary and secondary parties is assessed by the accomplice's and primary actor's individual mental states.

Limitations and Defenses to Complicity: Abandonment

A person who aids and abets another in the commission of a crime might have a change of heart and wish to get out of the agreement to commit the planned offense. In order to end liability as an accomplice, the aider and abettor must abandon the agreement. However, it is not enough to silently renounce the criminal plot and relinquish responsibility. The accomplice must effectively inform the principal of his or her intent to withdraw support and communicate the lack of a shared common intent for the crime to be committed. Additionally, the accomplice must attempt to make ineffectual any aid given to the principal that facilitates the commission of the offense. Therefore, if the accomplice provided a critical instrument such as a weapon, he or she must attempt to reclaim possession or render it useless. If police have been notified, and if they think that the accomplice has already gone too far in the activity to avoid prosecution, this would be an appropriate time to contact the prosecutor, inform him or her of the situation and hopefully facilitate a plea bargain agreement to allow the officer to go forward in pursuing the other actors.

The Model Penal Code stipulates that termination of complicity must be made prior to the commission of the crime. The Code additionally requires that the accomplice either "wholly deprive [the aid] of effectiveness in the commission of the offense; or give timely warning to the law enforcement authorities or otherwise make proper effort to prevent the commission of the offense."[26]

Accomplice Liability versus Conspiracy: The *Pinkerton* Doctrine

A **conspiracy** is a partnership in crime, which means that it is an agreement between two or more people to achieve a criminal purpose or to achieve a lawful purpose using unlawful means. It is also called

conspiracy A partnership in crime that is an agreement between two or more people to achieve a criminal purpose or to achieve a lawful purpose using unlawful means. Also called a common criminal enterprise.

a common criminal enterprise. Generally, a conspiracy involves an ongoing, organized criminal activity, such as illegal gambling, distribution of drugs, or a series of robberies. Because conspiracy is continuous and open-ended, several crimes may be committed during the course of the activity in order to achieve the criminal goal.

Criminal liability based on a conspiracy theory differs from accomplice liability in that, to be guilty of conspiracy, the perpetrator must actually agree to the ongoing criminal enterprise, not only to single crimes. In turn, conspiracy liability can impose broader criminal responsiblity upon those involved in a criminal plot: A co-conspirator is liable for the acts of his or her partners in crime for any criminal conduct engaged in by any one of them that is perpetrated during the course of and in furtherance of the conspiracy. In addition, criminal culpability for conspiracy is itself a separate criminal offense. This extended conspiratorial liability is based upon **agency theory**, which holds that all conspirators act as the agent of (or represent) the other conspirators involved in the criminal scheme and are liable for all criminal acts committed by other co-conspirators.

One may be guilty of conspiracy even though he or she did nothing more than agree to the criminal enterprise, even if the underlying goal of the conspiracy is not accomplished, or sometimes even if the underlying criminal goal has not been attempted. In short, all that is necessary for conspiracy is an agreement and any overt act in pursuance of the conspiracy by any of its members. The conspiracy may involve several conspirators who are personally unknown to one another and are associated only through the principal. Still, someone who agrees to the conspiracy will be liable for the criminal acts of any co-conspirator even if he or she does not know that a crime was committed, does not agree to that particular crime, or does not know the other participants of the conspiracy.

Accomplice liability can derive from encouragement, assistance, or sometimes mere knowledge. In most situations, an accomplice will also be a co-conspirator with the primary actor, but one can be a conspirator without being an accomplice. Again, conspiratorial liability may impose liability for any and every criminal act committed by a co-conspirator in furtherance of the common criminal scheme. This theory of liability is derived from principles of conspiracy, not accessory, liability.

Under one doctrine of extended conspiracy liability, a conspirator is liable for *any* act, planned or unplanned, committed by a co-conspirator that is a forseeable consequence of the unlawful agreement. The ***Pinkerton* doctrine**, named after *Pinkerton v.*

agency theory The theory that all conspirators act as the agents of (and represent) their co-conspirators involved in the criminal scheme and are liable for all criminal acts committed by other co-conspirators.

***Pinkerton* doctrine** The doctrine that holds a person associated with a conspiracy responsible for any criminal act committed by a co-conspirator if the act is within the scope of the conspiracy and is a forseeable result of the criminal scheme.

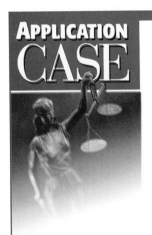
Pinkerton v. United States

In *Pinkerton v. United States* (1946), brothers Daniel and Walter Pinkerton were charged with violations of the Internal Revenue Code, including ten substantive offenses and one count of conspiracy. There was no evidence that Daniel directly participated in the substantive offenses because he was in the penitentiary when they occurred. There was sufficient evidence to prove that Walter committed the substantive offenses. Since the conspiracy between the two brothers was continuous and had never ended, Daniel could be (and was) charged with any act committed by his co-conspirator Walter in furtherance of the conspiracy.

Critical Thinking Should co-conspirators be charged for crimes that they have no knowledge of? Why or why not?

SOURCE: *Pinkerton v. United States*, 328 U.S. 640 (1946).

Accomplice Corroboration Rule

Many jurisdictions have enacted statutes that will not allow a person to be convicted of a crime based *solely* on the testimony of an accomplice. This is referred to as the *accomplice corroboration rule*. Because an accomplice may lie under oath to minimize his or her role and place blame on others, the law instructs jurors to look especially carefully at statements made by one party to a crime that implicate another.

United States (1946; see Application Case, page 150) holds a person associated with a conspiracy culpable for any criminal act committed by a co-conspirator if the act is within the scope of the conspiracy and is a foreseeable result of the criminal scheme. Under this doctrine, the principal actor and the conspirator have agreed to violate certain laws, then the principal commits the crimes while the conspirator is incarcerated in prison (for reasons having nothing to do with the conspiracy). The theory of prosecution is not based on a claim that the conspirator assisted the perpetrator in the planning or commission of the offenses; rather, the conspirator's liability is based on his prior agreement, as a conspirator, to the perpetrator's criminal activity.

Under *Pinkerton*, a conspirator may be liable for a crime he or she did not assist in, intend to commit, or wish to occur. For example, those involved in a common agreement to commit a series of bank robberies will be liable for grand theft of an automobile if a co-conspirator steals a car for a getaway during one of the robberies. Even where a person only aids the conspiracy by casing the bank, that conspirator is liable for any crimes committed in furtherance of the common scheme, even those the conspirator was not present for, did not agree to, or were unknown to him or her.

The Model Penal Code rejects the extended liability imposed by the *Pinkerton* doctrine, and requires an accomplice or conspirator to have an intent or purpose that the crime be committed. It will not allow liability for any and all crimes that extend from the agreed crime if an accomplice or conspirator did not participate in, aid, or encourage those additional crimes. Most state jurisidictions agree, and they require more than membership for someone to be guilty of conspiracy. Nonetheless, the *Pinkerton* doctrine has been adopted in the federal criminal justice system, where many defendants have been convicted of conspiracy for large-scale drug operations that fall under federal jurisdiction. Even though these defendants are not tried for the substantive offense (because prosecutors do not have enough evidence to convict on specific offenses), prosecutors can prove conspiracy under *Pinkerton*. Because criminal conspiracy is an important target of federal law enforcement and prosecutors, this approach can be seen as practical and appropriate.

How Far Should Accomplice Liability Reach?

As you have learned in this chapter, criminal liability can be extended to include individuals who play only seemingly minor roles in criminal conduct. This seems particularly true in the case of conspiracy, yet criminal conspiracies can have extremely dangerous and far-reaching consequences. Criminal liability for the actions of another raises important public policy questions that legislators and courts must face. If an individual can be liable for assisting in some small way in criminal conduct, what type of liability should be imposed on a conspiracy—or on an industry, such as those that sell prescription drugs or firearms? This has been a particularly controversial area that will continue to challenge lawmakers in the years to come.

Self Check

1. What must a person do to legally abandon an agreement to commit a crime and end his or her liability as an accomplice?
2. What is agency theory, and how does it relate to the *Pinkerton* doctrine?

CRIMINAL LAW *Online*
Check your answers at
cl.glencoe.com.

Parties to a Crime

SUMMARY BY CHAPTER OBJECTIVES

1. Learn how an accomplice can aid and abet in a criminal activity.

An accomplice can aid and abet another in the commission of a crime in a variety of ways:

- offering words of encouragement.
- providing a weapon to be used during the offense.
- being a lookout during the criminal act.
- driving the getaway car.

2. Understand the difference between an accessory and a principal.

At common law, all felons were subject to death. As the law changed, it developed accessory liability to allow gradation in the sentencing of felons and to permit judges to punish accessories less severely than principals. Today, a principal is someone who is present at the crime and participates in it in some way, or who uses an innocent agent (such as an insane person or a child) to commit the crime; and an accessory is someone who aids in the commission of a crime without being present when the crime is committed.

3. Know the difference between an affirmative act and an act of omission.

An affirmative act is any overt physical assistance, such as:

- providing a weapon to be used in the crime.
- casing the scene of the crime.
- masterminding the crime.
- providing information on the person or place to be attacked.
- preventing help from reaching an intended victim.

An act of omission is the failure to act to prevent another from committing a crime where the person has a legal duty to act or intervene. A common example of this is in child abuse cases, where one parent fails to report the abusive behavior of the other.

4. Explain how causation affects accomplice liability.

Causation is satisfied if the assistance facilitates the crime because an accomplice, by his or her actions (*actus reus*) and state of mind (*mens rea*), has chosen to adopt and share responsibility for the principal's criminal act.

5. Understand the *mens rea* of accomplice liability.

To be liable as an accomplice, one must act with the requisite *mens rea*, also known as *intent* or *mental state*. A person is an accomplice only if he or she:

- aids or assists another in the commission of a crime.
- possesses the intent to support or encourage the commission of the crime.
- intends that the primary party commit the underlying offense.

6. Describe the natural and probable consequences doctrine.

The natural and probable consequences doctrine holds an accomplice liable not only of the offense he intended to facilitate or encourage, but also of any natural and foreseeable offense committed by the person he aids and abets. Therefore, an accomplice to a bank robbery is liable for any kidnappings or murders that result during the commission of the robbery, even if all of these additional crimes were committed by the principal.

7. Learn how justifications and excuses affect accomplice liability.

When a primary party escapes liability due to being a member of a certain class (such as the underaged or mentally infirm), a technicality, or a privilege, the accomplice will still be held accountable if he or she can not also provide a personal excuse that will release him or her from liability. This is because the principal, although not punished, is still considered guilty and escaped punishment for a personal reason that cannot be transferred to someone else.

In other situations, however, when a principal is not held culpable, the accomplice will also be relieved of criminal liability. One example of this is in cases of self-defense, where a defendant helps another person defend him- or herself against an illegal attack.

8. Explain the difference between accessorial and conspiratorial liability.

Accessorial liability holds that accomplices are criminally responsible for their actions. One who is an accomplice can be held liable for an underlying criminal act, even though he or she did not commit that underlying criminal act.

Conspiratorial liability requires the additional intent to agree to an ongoing criminal enterprise, in which several crimes may be committed to achieve a particular lawful or unlawful goal. Conspiratorial liability extends farther than accessorial liability because a member of a conspiracy can be liable for crimes committed by co-conspirators that the member did not participate in, agree to, or even sometimes know about.

How can an accessory to a crime be found guilty when the principal actor is innocent?
Find it on page 142.

KEY TERMS

accomplice, page 118
aid and abet, page 118
accomplice liability, page 118
principal, page 119
accessory, page 119
principal in the first degree, page 119
principal in the second degree, page 119

constructive presence, page 119
accessory before the fact, page 119
accessory after the fact, page 120
criminal facilitation, page 128
agent provocateur, page 129
entrapment, page 131

natural and probable consequences doctrine, page 133
innocent agent or instrumentality, page 137
nonproxyable offense, page 139
conspiracy, page 148
agency theory, page 148
Pinkerton doctrine, page 149

QUESTIONS FOR REVIEW

1. What are the two categories of accessories and principals?
2. How are accessories after the fact treated differently than principals under modern law?
3. How significant must one's actions be for one to be culpable as an accomplice?
4. What is the difference between an agent provocateur and one who commits entrapment?
5. What is the nonproxyable offense theory of doctrine of innocent agency?
6. Can an accomplice still be convicted even when a principal is acquitted? Why or why not?
7. What is the difference between a feigning accomplice (agent provocateur) and a feigning primary party?
8. How can an accomplice abandon an agreement to aid a crime?
9. What is a conspiracy?
10. What are agency theory and the *Pinkerton* doctrine?

PROBLEM-SOLVING EXERCISES

1. **Accomplice or Not?** Ron has been selling cocaine and marijuana out of his apartment for several years. He is a notorious and ruthless drug dealer who the local authorities have been watching for several years. Marisol is Ron's live-in girlfriend. While she does not directly sell drugs, at times she will package the drugs when Ron is selling large quantities, take messages for Ron, and instruct buyers when to come by. Ron's operation ends when police execute a search warrant and discover large quantities of cocaine. They charge Marisol as an accessory after Ron informs them that she has been helping him by packaging the drugs and assisting buyers. Answer the following questions:

a) Can Marisol be convicted as an accomplice?

b) Why or why not?

c) Does it matter if Marisol was never in the house when the actual drug sales took place?

2. **An Abandoned Crime?** Paul is angry at his longtime friend Tim for abandoning a criminal plan at the last minute. A few days before the day on which they planned to rob a liquor store, Tim showed up at Paul's house. He stated clearly in front of Paul and Paul's girl-friend that he did not want to take part in the robbery, he retrieved some notes he had left with Paul about the liquor store's hours and employees. Paul com-mitted the robbery anyway, using an unregistered gun that Tim had given him several years ago. When questioned by police, he named Tim as an accom-plice, stating that Tim had given him the weapon he used to commit the robbery. Answer the following questions:

a) Is Tim an accomplice? Why or why not?

b) How does Tim's intent affect his liability as an accomplice?

c) Could Tim be charged with any-thing in this case? Why or why not?

3. **Guilty of Child Abuse?** You are a police officer who has taken into custody a married couple who is accused of child abuse. The mother physically abused the child while the father, who is a cocaine addict, sat in the other room and watched television. The father stated that he knew the abuse was going on and could hear his child crying, but said that he felt afraid to get involved because his wife is violent.

a) Is the husband guilty of any crime? Why or why not?

b) Is his excuse for not stopping the abuse adequate? Why or why not?

WORKPLACE APPLICATIONS

1. **Accomplice Liability** You are a police officer who is the first to arrive at the scene of a bank robbery in progress. You are able to catch and arrest the robbers. Once they are in custody and you begin interviewing witnesses for additional information, you discover that the teller who received the hold-up note person-ally knows two of the robbers. She informs you that several weeks ago she had been at a party where one of the robbers had questioned her about her job, asking how many security guards were present, where the cameras had been placed, and who knew the bank combination. The teller admits that she innocently discussed these facts, but did not intend to help faciliate a robbery. According to her, her intentions were only to brag about her important posi-tion at the bank. Consider the facts, then write a statement for the prosecutor recommending whether or not to charge her as an accomplice.

2. **Defining an Accomplice** Contact your local prosecutor's office and ask someone if your jurisdiction holds people respon-sible as accomplices when they possess knowledge, but not purpose, that a crime will be committed. You may ask them

the following questions, or use these questions as a basis for your interview.
a) Why did they make this choice, and what caused it?
b) How well is it working?
c) Do they see any need for modifications in the future?

Note: You may also ask them the same basic questions about whether or not they apply the *Pinkerton* doctrine.

3. **Principal in the Second Degree** You are a witness to the robbery of a school bookstore. While you were in line, the defendant came into the store and said,

"Hi, Recia," to your cashier. During the robbery that soon took place, the store manager frantically signaled Recia to press an alarm button under her cash register, but she did not. She later stated that she was afraid to get caught pressing the alarm. She admitted that she knew the defendant, but was not friends with him and had no knowledge of the robbery.
a) In your opinion, is Recia an accomplice? Why or why not?
b) What other information do you need to help decide whether or not to press charges against her?

INTERNET APPLICATION

1. **Work on Key Terms** Go to cl.glencoe.com for a link to the "nolo" Web site. Click on Criminal Law and search for reference materials using key terms from this chapter. When you have found material for three key terms, answer the following questions:
a) How did these reference materials help expand your knowledge of these key terms?

b) What new questions arose as you read this new material? What answers did you find?
c) As you read more about criminal law, do you find it more or less complex than you originally imagined? Why or why not?

ETHICS ISSUES

1. **Aiding and Abetting** Your nephew, who lives down the street with his mother, is accused of burglarizing several homes in the neighborhood. You know that he was severely abused by his father during his early childhood, and that his mother has struggled to bring him up on her own. Therefore, you know him well and feel sorry for him; you also feel that he can be rehabili-

tated. Your sister, who is his mother, calls you and asks you to lie to police that he visited your home last Wednesday night. If you don't, she tells you, he will be tried as an adult and face a felony sentence.
a) What will you tell your sister, and what will you do?
b) Is your sister aiding and abetting her son? Why or why not?

ENDNOTES

1 Cal. penal code § 971 (1997).

2 Joshua Dressler, *Understanding Criminal Law* § 30.04[B][4], at p. 469, n.56 (3d ed. 2001), citing *State v. Walden*, 293 S.E.2d 780, 786–87 (N.C. 1982)

3 Model Penal Code § 2.06(1) (1985); Model Penal Code § 2.06(2)(a)–(c) (1985); Model Penal Code §2.06(3)(a)(ii) (1980).

4 Sanford H. Kadish, *Complicity, Cause and Blame: A Study in the Interpretation of Doctrine*, 73 Calif. L. Rev. 323, 354–55 (1985).

5 *Hicks v. United States*, 150 U.S. 442 (1893).

6 N.Y. Penal Law § 115 (McKinney 1998). Kadish & Schulhofer, *id.*, note that Arizona, Kentucky, and North Dakota, have followed New York in enacting a law defining criminal facilitation as a crime.

7 *United States v. Fountain*, 768 F.2d 790 (7th Cir. 1985).

8 Joshua Dressler, *Understanding Criminal Law* § 30.04[B][1], at p. 440 (2d ed. 1995).

9 L. Tiffany, D. McIntyre, & D. Rotenberg, Detections of Crime 210 (1967), as cited in Wayne R. LaFave & Austin W. Scott, Jr., *Criminal Law* § 5.2, n.1 (Hornbook Series 2d Student ed. 1986).

10 *Sherman v. United States*, 356 U.S. 369, 372 (1958).

11 This hypothetical appears in Sanford H. Kadish and Stephen J. Schulhofer, *Criminal Law and Its Processes: Cases and Materials* 660 (6th ed. 1995) and in Joshua Dressler, *Understanding Criminal Law* § 30.05[B][4], at p. 442 (2d ed. 1995).

12 *People v. Luparello*, 231 Cal. Rptr. 832 (Cal. Ct. App.1987), quoting *People v. Croy*, 710 P.2d 392 (Cal. 1985).

13 *State v. McVay*, 132 A. 436 (R.I. 1926).

14 *People v. Abbott*, 445 N.Y.S.2d 344 (N.Y. App. Div. 1981).

15 Model Penal Code §2.06(2)(a) (1985).

16 Sanford H. Kadish and Stephen J. Schulhofer, *Criminal Law and Its Processes: Cases and Materials*, 6th edition, 1995; page 676. Quoting Sanford H. Kadish, *Blame and Punishment: Essays in the Criminal Law*, 1987; pages 171–72.

17 In addition to *Walser*, see *United States v. Ruffin*, 613 F.2d 408 (2d Cir. 1979)

18 *Dusenbery v. Commonwealth*, 263 S.E.2d 392, 394 (Va. 1980).

19 *People v. Hernandez*, 96 Cal. Rptr. 71, 74 (Cal. Ct. App. 1971).

20 Sanford H. Kadish, *Blame and Punishment: Essays in the Criminal Law* 173 (1987).

21 *State v. Hayes*, 16 S.W. 514, 515 (1891), quoting *State v. Jansen*, 22 Kan. 498 (1879).

22 Model Penal Code §2.13 (1985).

23 *Id.* at 340 citing *Standefer v. United States*, 447 U.S. 10 (1980)

24 Sanford H. Kadish and Stephen J. Schulhofer, *Criminal Law and Its Processes: Cases and Materials* 681 (6th ed. 1995), *Moore v. Lowe*, 180 S.E. 1 (Va. 1935).

25 Sanford H. Kadish, *Blame and Punishment: Essays in the Criminal Law* 182–83 (1987).

26 Model Penal Code §2.06(6)(c)(I)(ii)(1985).

Chapter Objectives

After reading this chapter, you will be able to:

1. Explain the purpose of defining attempt as a crime.
2. Explain how the Model Penal Code test for the *actus reus* of attempt differs from all the other tests.
3. State the elements of an attempt.
4. Name the two principal defenses to attempt.
5. Explain when the crime of solicitation can be charged.
6. Define the crime of conspiracy.
7. Define the *actus reus* element of conspiracy.
8. Explain the *mens rea* requirement for conspiracy.

Chapter Outline

When can someone who has intercourse with a corpse be convicted of rape?

Chapter 6

Incomplete Crimes

6.1 Attempted Crimes

inchoate crimes A crime that generally leads to another crime. The principal modern inchoate crimes are attempt, conspiracy, and solicitation.

This chapter discusses **inchoate crimes**, which are criminal acts that are detected and punished before the ultimate or intended crime actually occurs. The most common inchoate crimes are attempt, conspiracy, and solicitation. The word *inchoate* means imperfect or partial. Thus, inchoate crimes are defined by the fact that they are not completed, although they are intended to be.

For instance, an accused may intend to commit a crime but be unable to complete it because he or she is unexpectedly interrupted. Such an incomplete criminal scheme or plan is still punishable as a crime that is separate from the intended harm. In other words, the law punishes agreements to engage in criminal conduct, soliciting such conduct, and taking a substantial step toward engaging in such conduct. The focus is on anticipatory, preparatory, or unsuccessful conduct.

It should be noted that the three most common inchoate crimes—attempt, conspiracy, and solicitation—are not crimes in and of themselves. There are no crimes of attempt, conspiracy, or solicitation by themselves. They are criminal only when they occur in conjunction with other crimes or are defined by reference to other crimes, such as murder, robbery, and battery. For example, when attempt is combined with the target offense of murder, it becomes the crime of *attempted murder* or when two or more persons agree to commit a murder that becomes *conspiracy to commit murder*.

Lawmakers enact statutes that punish individuals for incomplete crimes in order to avoid the social harm that will result if the crime is actually carried out. Because society has an interest in preventing harm, such crimes are defined with a view toward punishing an individual before certain harms are completed. It would be unduly burdensome to require society to wait until someone is harmed before dispensing punishment for the intended act. In addition, failing to punish attempts would greatly hamper the ability of the police to prevent or intervene in the commission of a substantive crime. Therefore, the purpose of these crimes is to deter a greater harm than that which is involved in the conduct of the individual in connection with the incomplete crime.

On the other hand, if an unsuccessful attempt is criminalized too easily, innocent people might be punished. For instance, there is a risk that the individual's intention may have been misinterpreted as criminal or that the individual would have ultimately abandoned

The Elements of Crime

the plan. Premature punishment would result in punishing an individual for little more than an evil thought. The mere intent to commit a crime is not sufficient for attempt; the intent must be accompanied by some conduct on the part of the accused.

Several other crimes also have a large inchoate aspect:

- Larceny
- Forgery
- Kidnapping
- Arson
- Burglary
- Possession of burglary tools
- Stalking
- Drunk driving

As an example, the crime of drunk driving is preventive in nature since the law seeks to prevent accidents that would cause personal injury and property damage.

Inchoate crimes also have *actus reus* and *mens rea* requirements, which will be discussed later in this chapter. Defenses to inchoate crimes, such as legal impossibility and renunciation, will also be discussed later.

The Six Stages of Committing a Crime

In order to better understand the concept behind the law's treatment of the inchoate crimes of attempt, conspiracy, and solicitation, you need to understand the process by which a person intentionally commits a crime. It is a six-stage process in which the actor:

1. conceives of the idea of committing the crime.
2. evaluates the idea, considering whether or not to proceed.
3. forms the intention to go forward.
4. prepares to commit the crime, for example, by obtaining a gun.
5. commences commission of the offense.
6. completes his or her actions, achieving the goal.[1]

Only after the third stage is a person liable for criminal punishment under Anglo-American law.

Both a *mens rea* and an *actus reus* are necessary for criminal liability. As will be shown, the legal definitions of inchoate crimes such as attempt, conspiracy, and solicitation require that the perpetrator advance past the third stage described above.

Reasons to Prosecute Attempt

Reasons to prosecute attempt are numerous: to prevent crime, to prevent harm, to punish an individual even if he or she does not succeed in attempting a crime, to facilitate the police's ability to prevent crime, and as a deterrent to greater harm.

Inchoate Crimes and Modern Technology

You can learn more about the new types of inchoate crimes by accessing the link at **cl.glencoe.com**. What are the elements of stalking? What acts are punishable as cybercrimes?

Historical Development

The crime of attempt has caused confusion and controversy for centuries. Although almost all modern jurisdictions criminalize attempt, it was not recognized as a crime prior to the late 1700s. Before that time, the *mens rea* requirement for attempt was that the accused must have manifested his or her intent "by some open deed tending to the execution of his intent. So as if a man had compassed the death of another, and had uttered the same by words or writing, yet he should not have died for it, for there wanted an overt deed tending to the execution of his compassing."[2] Convictions for attempt prior to the late 1700s were rare. As long as a perpetrator did not actually carry out the offense, he or she was usually off the hook unless the crime was particularly heinous.

The crimes of attempt and solicitation were developed through case law, as the following two landmark cases illustrate.

Rex v. Scofield   In 1784, the English court in *Rex v. Scofield* first recognized the crime of attempt. In that case, the defendant was charged with placing a lighted candle and combustible material in a rented house with the intent to set it on fire. Although there was no allegation or proof that the house was burned, the court held that the defendant turned an otherwise innocent act into a criminal one. In addition, the court found that the completion of a criminal act was not necessary to constitute criminality.[3]

Rex v. Higgins   In 1801, the idea that attempt was itself a crime was recognized in the case of *Rex v. Higgins*. In that case, a British court upheld an indictment charging an unsuccessful attempt to steal, where the accused solicited a servant to steal his master's property. After *Higgins*, the common law adopted the widespread principle that an attempt to commit either a felony or a misdemeanor was itself an indictable crime, usually a misdemeanor. The common law treated all attempts as a misdemeanor, even an attempt to commit a felony.[4]

Today, according to the Model Penal Code (MPC), a person is guilty of **attempt** to commit a crime, if, acting with the kind of culpability otherwise required for commission of the crime, he or she:

- Purposely engages in conduct that would constitute the crime if the attendant circumstances were as he believes them to be.

attempt When a person, with the intent to commit an offense, performs any act that constitutes a substantial step toward the commission of that offense.

◄ The Crime of Attempt
When all of the elements of a crime are in place and a person is near completing a criminal act, but does not succeed, he or she is still liable for the crime of attempt.
Can anyone considering a criminal plan be liable for this crime?

- When causing a particular result is an element of the crime, does or omits to do anything with the purpose of causing or with the belief that it will cause such result without further conduct on his part.
- Purposely does or omits to do anything that, under the circumstances as he believes them to be, is an act or omission constituting a substantial step in a course of conduct planned to culminate in his commission of the crime

Under modern law, an attempt to commit a substantive crime is usually classified as a lesser crime than the target or object offense. An attempt to commit a felony is usually treated as a felony but is punishable to a lesser degree than the underlying substantive offense. An attempt to commit a capital crime or a crime punishable by life imprisonment is usually punishable by a specific number of years of imprisonment.

Mens Rea of Attempt

The crime of attempt requires the specific *mens rea*, or intent, to commit an act that, if carried out, would have resulted in a completed substantive crime. It is not enough that the defendant intended to commit some other innocent or even criminal act. For example, if the actor lit a match with the intent to set fire to a building, the actor would be guilty of attempted arson. However, if the actor intended only to light a cigarette, then he or she would not be guilty of attempted arson even though he or she intentionally lit the match, because he lacked the specific intent to burn a building. In short, attempt is a specific intent crime, even if the underlying substantive offense is a general intent crime.

For crimes that are defined by prohibiting a certain result, the defendant must have had the intent to cause that result. For example, if a person randomly shot a gun in the air on New Year's Eve, almost hitting an innocent victim, but did not have the specific intent to kill someone, he or she would not be guilty of attempted murder. The specific intent requirement for attempt crimes makes sense, because the concept of attempt encompasses the idea that a person is trying to do something specific. Without that specific goal, the actor could not be said to have tried to cause the result. A good example of an attempt statute is the Wisconsin law that requires "that the actor have intent to perform acts and attain a result which, if accomplished, would constitute such crime."[5]

Mens Rea and the MPC   The MPC takes a slightly different approach to the mental element of attempt. Section 5.01(1) provides that a person is guilty of attempt if it was his or her purpose to engage in the conduct or to cause the result that would constitute the substantive offense, with two exceptions:

1.   A person may be guilty of an attempt to cause a criminal result if he or she believes that the result will occur, even if it is not the actor's conscious object to cause the result.
2.   In holding a person culpable for attempt when he or she acts "with the kind of culpability otherwise required for the commission of the crime," the Code does not require that the *mens rea* of "purpose" or "belief" apply to the attendant circumstances.

For such attendant circumstance elements to be present, the actor can be guilty of attempt without specific intent to cause the result if the underlying crime could be committed by less than purposeful achievement of the result. For example, a perpetrator could be found guilty of attempted statutory rape if there was proof that he was reckless with respect to learning the girl's age.

Under the reasoning of the Model Penal Code, the intent requirement can be met even though a defendant may not have desired or wanted a particular result, *if* it can be shown that the defendant acted with a substantial certainty that a certain result would occur. For instance, a defendant who detonates a bomb, intending to destroy a building, with knowledge that the people inside will almost certainly be killed, can be convicted of attempted murder. This is because the defendant knew with substantial certainty that a certain result would occur, that people would be killed. He or she can be convicted of attempted murder even if the ultimate intent was only to destroy the building.

Actus Reus of Attempt

The conduct element, known as the *actus reus*, is essential to the crime of attempt. It is generally accepted that a defendant cannot be held liable for an attempt unless he or she has committed some act to further his or her plan to commit the substantive offense. This is because one of the basic principles of Anglo-American criminal law is that the law does not punish people for their thoughts or, in general, for their speech.

One of the biggest problems in imposing criminal responsibility for an attempt is determining *when* a suspect has crossed the line from mere preparation or planning. Only prohibited criminal conduct justifies prosecution for the crime of attempt. (See the discussion of First Amendment rights in Chapter 3.) Therefore, a prosecutor must prove that enough steps were taken by an accused to show that he or she would have carried out the substantive crime had the plans not been interrupted.

The law has created several tests to help measure when a person is actually guilty of the crime of attempt:

The Last Act Test   Under the **last act test**, which was established in England in the case of *Regina v. Eagleton* (see Application Case on page 166), an attempt occurs when a person has performed all of the acts that he or she believed were necessary to carry out the action that would constitute the underlying offense.

According to the last act test, an attempted murder would not occur until the trigger had been pulled and an attempted arson would not occur until the fire had been set. This test is no longer utilized because most lawmakers believe that a person does not have to take the very last step to be criminally culpable. Opponents of this

last act test The test that determines that an attempt has occurred when a person has performed all of the acts that he or she believed were necessary to commit the underlying offense.

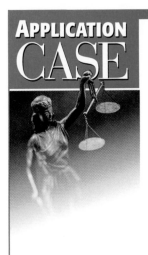

Regina v. Eagleton

In this English case, a welfare office hired the defendant to provide bread to the poor. In turn, each poor person would provide him with a ticket that he later turned in to the welfare office. Following the submission of the ticket to the office, the defendant would receive credit for a payment to be made by the welfare office at a later date. The defendant delivered underweight loaves, but received tickets for the credit he should have received for loaves of full weight, then turned in these tickets. He was charged with the attempt to obtain money by false pretenses from the welfare office. The defendant argued that because he had not yet received any money, he was not guilty. However, the court held that the defendant was still liable for attempting to obtain the money by false pretenses based on the fact that there were no other acts required to complete the crime. Hence, turning in the tickets was the last act towards obtaining the money and was therefore sufficient for attempt liability.

Critical Thinking Do you think the last act test is a good way to determine attempt liability? Why or why not?

SOURCE: *Regina v. Eagleton*, 6 Cox Crim. Cas. 559, 571 (1855), as cited in Joshua Dressler, *Understanding Criminal Law*, § 27.06[B][2] at 391 n.98 (3d ed. 2001).

test point out that it defeats the policy of making attempt a separate crime, because such a test prohibits arrest of a suspect until it is too late to prevent the harm.

The Physical Proximity Test Some courts follow the **physical proximity test**. Under this test, the perpetrator need not have advanced so far as the last act, but the conduct must be "proximate" to, or very near, the completed crime. The accused's conduct must reflect either a first or later step in physically carrying out the crime *after* planning this particular crime. Under this approach, an attempt has not been committed unless the accused has the immediate power to actually carry through with the crime at the time of the intervention of the police. For example, under the physical proximity test, a person would not be convicted of attempted bank robbery unless he or she was approaching the bank, was armed, and was carrying a hold-up note.

physical proximity test
The test that determines that an attempt has occurred when the perpetrator's conduct, though not having advanced so far as the last act, approaches sufficiently near to the completed crime to equal a first or subsequent step in a direct movement toward the commission of the offense.

The Dangerous Proximity Test The **dangerous proximity test** incorporates the physical proximity test but is somewhat more flexible. Under this test, a person is guilty of attempt when his or her conduct is in "dangerous proximity" to succeeding at the crime. There is no clear point when a defendant has met this test's requirements, but factors used are closeness of the danger, significance of the harm, and the level of apprehension felt by a potential victim. In some cases, preparation may not be sufficient to sustain an attempt when there are circumstances outside the perpetrator's control that prevent the completion of the crime. In others, certain preparation may be enough depending on the degree and closeness of the preparation to completion of the act. Clearly, therefore, dangerous proximity is evaluated on a case-by-case basis.

dangerous proximity test
An attempt test that states that a person is guilty of attempt when his or her conduct is in dangerous proximity to success, or when an act is so near to the result that the danger of its success is very great.

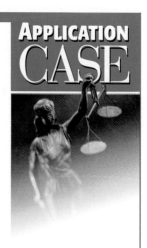

APPLICATION CASE

People v. Rizzo

In *People v. Rizzo*, the court adopted the dangerous proximity test, which led to the reversal of the defendant's conviction of attempted robbery. The defendant and three other armed men planned to rob an individual while he was carrying his company's payroll from the bank. The defendant and the other men drove around looking for a man who they believed would be withdrawing a large amount of money from a bank. They first went to the bank and entered various buildings, looking for the victim. They failed to find him or any other payroll messenger, but as they were searching the police became suspicious and arrested them.

The court found that the defendants were not dangerously close to success since they had never located the victim. Therefore, they were not guilty of attempted robbery. The court concluded the defendant could not be found guilty of attempted robbery prior to locating the victim. Neither could they be found guilty of attempted burglary if they were in the process of search for the building. It was at least necessary to locate the victim to be guilty of attempt robbery.

Dangerous Proximity Test

Critical Thinking What flaws and benefits can you find in the dangerous proximity test?

SOURCE: *People v. Rizzo*, 158 N.E. 888 (N.Y. 1927).

Courts have applied this test in a variety of different situations, with different results. As seen in the *Rizzo* decision (see Application Case on page 167) and also in *United States v. Harper* (1994), the court held that making an appointment with a potential victim does not constitute an attempt and is not a sufficient commitment to an intended crime even if it made a later attempt possible. Compare this to the California case *People v. Vizcarra*. Also, compare it to *People v. Parrish*, where the defendant was convicted of attempted murder for going to the home of his wife with a loaded gun and listening outside to be sure she was alone.[6]

indispensable element test A test that determines that no attempt has occurred when a suspect has not yet gained control over an indispensable instrumentality of the criminal plan.

The Indispensable Element Test Yet another aspect of proximity utilized in evaluating an attempt is the **indispensable element test**. Under this test, a suspect who has not yet gained control over an indispensable instrumentality of the criminal plan cannot be

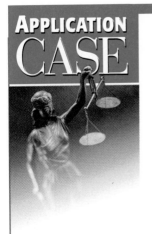

APPLICATION CASE

Attempted Robbery

People v. Vizcarra

In *People v. Vizcarra*, the defendant was observed standing in front of the liquor store at night, wearing a poncho, and carrying a rifle. He was standing on a walkway approximately four feet wide. When a customer came by on the walkway, the defendant turned away so that his nose was right up against the block wall. The customer observed the defendant's strange behavior and the butt of the rifle protruding from his poncho. The defendant then returned to the car that was parked across the street and drove past the liquor store.

In upholding the defendant's attempted robbery conviction, the court held that approaching the liquor store with the rifle and attempting to hide on the walkway when observed by a customer was a sufficient direct act toward the accomplishment of the robbery. The court reasoned that the proximate act need not be the final proximate act necessary to complete the crime. It is sufficient that the overt acts (acts in preparation) reached far enough for the accomplishment of the offense to amount to a beginning of the substantive act.

Critical Thinking Do you think that the defendant's actions met the requirements of the dangerous proximity test? Why or why not?

SOURCE: *People v. Vizcarra*, 168 Cal. Rptr. 257 (Cal. Ct. App. 1980).

guilty of attempt. For example, a person planning a killing by shooting who has not obtained a gun, or a person planning arson who has not yet acquired the incendiary material necessary to start the fire, could not be held for attempted arson under this test.

This test does not look into the actor's mental state or intent but, rather, focuses on whether he or she possesses the necessary instruments to carry out the offense. At times, the objectivity of this test could be unfair, for a defendant who may have had a change of heart or held the instrument for a different purpose could still be criminally culpable. On the other hand, when acts are dependent on other parties, the defendant may escape liability.

The Unequivocality Test The **unequivocality test** does not look at how close the defendant came to succeeding, but at whether the defendant's conduct was indicative of his or her criminal intent. Under this test, an attempt occurs when a person's conduct alone unambiguously manifests his or her criminal intent. Thus, the defendant's conduct must clearly indicate a criminal intent and not a possible innocent one.

The leading case supporting this test is *King v. Barker* (1924), which stated that buying a box of matches to burn a haystack was

unequivocality test A test that determines that an attempt has occurred when a person's conduct, standing alone, unambiguously manifests his or her criminal intent.

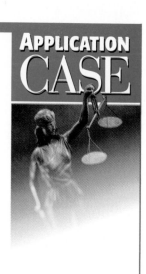

APPLICATION CASE

People v. Orndorff

In *People v. Orndorff*, the defendant was a professional con man engaged in a plan to steal money from the victim. The plan required the victim to go to a bank and withdraw her money, which the defendant planned to switch with counterfeit money. However, the defendant drove away while the victim was in the bank. He was later arrested and charged with attempted grand theft. The court held that the defendant did not go far enough to be liable for attempt, because the scheme required the victim to withdraw the money from the bank and give it to the defendant. It could not have succeeded without this step; hence, the act did not go beyond mere preparation.

Critical Thinking What substantial step was missing from the defendant's actions?

SOURCE: *People v. Orndorff*, 67 Cal. Rptr. 824 (Cal. Ct. App. 1968).

Substantial Step Test

too ambiguous to justify conviction for attempted arson, but that taking matches to a haystack and lighting one there is an unambiguous act.[7] This conclusion has been criticized, though, because even in the haystack example, the person who struck a match near the haystack may have intended only to light a pipe.

The Substantial Step Test   The MPC adopts an entirely different test for the *actus reus* of attempt—the **substantial step test**. This test requires that the suspect must have done or omitted to do something that constitutes a "substantial step" in plans to commit the substantive offense. In addition, conduct falling within the realm of a substantial step requires strong corroboration of the actor's criminal intent.

It may be easiest to convict a person for attempt under this test because a prosecutor only has to show that the defendant took a substantial step. For example, a person who purchases flammable materials and soaks rags in them could be convicted of attempted arson without doing anything else because the purchase, coupled with the act of soaking the rags, may be deemed a substantial step toward arson. With this test, close proximity is not required, and attempt liability may attach even if the actor does not get far along in consummating the crime.

The MPC provides several examples of conduct that would be considered a substantial step toward the commission of a crime. They include:

- lying in wait, searching for, or following the contemplated victim of the crime.
- enticing or seeking to entice the contemplated victim of the crime to go to the place contemplated for its commission.
- reconnoitering the place contemplated for the commission of the crime.
- unlawful entry of a structure, vehicle, or enclosure in which it is contemplated that the crime will be committed.
- possession of materials to be employed in the commission of the crime, that are specially designed for such unlawful use or that can serve no lawful purpose of the actor under the circumstances.
- possession, collection, or fabrication of materials to be employed in the commission of the crime, at or near the place contemplated for its commission, if such possession,

substantial step test The MPC's test to determine whether the *actus reus* of attempt has occurred, which requires that the suspect must have done or omitted to do something that constitutes "a substantial step" in the commission of the substantive offense.

collection, or fabrication serves no lawful purpose of the actor under the circumstances.

- soliciting an innocent agent to engage in conduct constituting an element of the crime.[8]

Handling Multiple Counts of Attempt Multiple counts of attempt can arise from a single act that goes beyond mere preparation. The issue in this type of case whether the particular act was sufficient to prove beyond a reasonable doubt that the accused had multiple purposes (intents) accompanying the single act. In other words, the act must be sufficient to support an attempt to commit each substantive offense. A simple case of a single act producing multiple counts of attempt would be a person firing a gun at two or more persons or in some other way attempting to injure multiple

---

FIGURE 6–1

A Comparison of the Various Tests for Attempt Liability

The Last Act Test

- Perpetrator has performed all of the acts that he or she believed necessary to commit the intended offense.

The Physical Proximity Test

- Perpetrator must be very close to completing all of the acts necessary to commit the intended offense.

The Dangerous Proximity Test

- Perpetrator is guilty of attempt when his or her actions are in dangerous proximity to success or when an act is so near the result that the danger of its success is very great.

The Indispensable Element Test

- Perpetrator is innocent until he or she gains control over an indispensable instrumentality of the criminal plan.

The Unequivocality Test

- Perpetrator's conduct, regardless of other factors, unambiguously manifests his or her criminal intent.

The Substantial Step Test

- Perpetrator must have done something or omitted to do something that constitutes a "substantial step" toward the commission of the substantive offense.

Tests to Determine Attempt

Regardless of the tests that different jurisdictions offer, a person will be guilty of attempt if he or she:

- has the specific intent to commit a substantive crime.
- takes steps that a jury would find sufficient to indicate that he or she was in the process of committing the act.

persons with a single act. In such a case, the defendant could be charged with the attempted murder of each victim. However, a more difficult application occurs when a single act by the defendant is taken to show the intent to commit several different substantive offenses.

In conclusion, courts in various jurisdictions determined the *actus reus* of attempt, based on the circumstances and utilizing one of the tests discussed above. Ultimately, it must be determined whether the actor went beyond mere preparation and can be held culpable for attempt. In some jurisdictions, the courts hold that the *actus reus* has been met if the actions of the defendant in preparing to commit a crime pose serious danger to the public that would warrant the involvement of the police. Depending on which test a particular jurisdiction adopts, a person can be guilty of attempt if he or she has the intent to commit the substantive crime and takes steps that a jury would find sufficient to indicate that he or she was in the process of committing the act.

Other Elements and Issues

Usually, attempt has been committed if an individual has the requisite intent to carry out the underlying offense but, for whatever reason, falls short of doing so. There are a number of reasons why a person may be stopped prior to completing the underlying crime and therefore be guilty only of attempt.

For example, Bob devises a plan to rob the First Bank of Westmoreland. He has observed the bank for several weeks and picks a time where the guard is out to lunch and there are few customers. He writes a hold-up note with a threat of harm, demanding all of the cashier's money. He purchases a semi-automatic machine gun, ski mask, and gloves. Bob arrives at the bank at the designated time, with the ski mask on, the hold-up note in his pocket, and the gun in his hand.

As he is walking into the bank, an armed off-duty police officer notices Bob, becomes suspicious, and stops him prior to his entering the bank. At this point, Bob could be arrested for attempted robbery because, but for the officer being there, Bob would have carried out the actual offense. At trial, Bob may argue that he was planning on abandoning the crime and not going through with it; however, Bob would likely be convicted and his abandonment argument would probably not be believed, because he was so close to carrying out the crime.

As in the case of Bob, a crime may never get beyond the level of attempt because the police may stop it before it happens. Other possible reasons could be that a defendant's plan to commit a crime did not work out, or a defendant could get concerned that the police were about to intercept his actions and stop out of fear of being caught.

Whatever the reason, attempt is a very common charge that is used to punish individuals who were going to commit an underlying crime, even if they didn't actually do so. The purpose of the law's defining attempt as a crime is to prevent the commission of crimes before they take place and to protect the safety of the public by allowing police officers to stop the continuance of criminal activity.

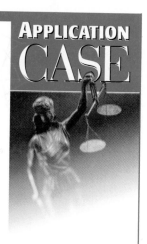

APPLICATION CASE

People v. Kraft

In *People v. Kraft*, the defendant forced the victim's car off of the road when the victim attempted to pass him. The victim later noticed the defendant's vehicle and pulled up next to it to say something to the defendant. Before the victim had a chance to speak, the defendant pulled out a gun and fired several shots, some going above the car and one hitting the back of it. The victim then notified police of the incident, and, as a police officer approached the defendant's car, the defendant pointed a gun at the officer and later shot at him.

At trial, the defendant testified that when the victim approached his car he was scared and was only trying to scare the victim away. He stated that when he shot at the officer, he was in shock and only wanted to kill himself. The trial court instructed the jury that the defendant could be found guilty of attempted murder if he did "any act which constitutes a substantial step toward the commission of the offense of murder" with the *mens rea* to commit murder. The trial court further instructed the jury that the *mens rea* for murder included doing acts that create "a strong probability of death." The appellate court held that the jury instructions given were wrong for the charge of attempt and that "[t]he offense of attempted murder requires the mental state of specific intent to commit murder, to kill someone . . . ." On this basis, the appellate court overturned the defendant's conviction.

Attempted Murder

Critical Thinking Do you think the defendant had the necessary *mens rea* to be convicted of attempted murder?

SOURCE: *People v. Kraft*, 478 N.E.2d 1154 (Ill. App. Ct. 1985).

Defining attempt as a crime makes sense because a person who has taken a substantial step towards the commission of a substantive offense with the intent to do so deserves punishment.

CRIMINAL LAW Online
Check your answers at cl.glencoe.com.

Self Check

1. Why are inchoate crimes considered criminal behavior?
2. In your own words, how does the MPC define attempt?
3. Why must the *actus reus* be accompanied by the *mens rea*?

6.2 Defenses to Attempt

A defendant may have done everything in his or her power to accomplish a specific result, but due to uncontrollable circumstances could not commit the substantive crime. Two examples of this are:

- A would-be pickpocket reaches into the pocket of another to remove money without that person's knowledge, but the defendant discovers that the pocket is empty. Was his reaching a case of attempted theft?
- A man smokes what he believes to be a marijuana cigarette, but is in fact a garden weed. Can he be convicted of attempted possession of marijuana?

These defendants may claim that they cannot be convicted of attempted crimes because the money and the marijuana were not present, so they could not have committed the crimes intended. This type of defense is called the impossibility defense, which you will learn about in the following section.

Impossibility

Under what circumstances can a defendant successfully claim impossibility as a defense? The point is whether the law should punish a person who has attempted to do what was not possible under the existing circumstances. There are two main types of impossibility: factual and legal. This discussion will explore circumstances under which impossibility can be a defense to the crime of attempt. At common law, the traditional answer to the impossibility question turned upon the distinction between legal impossibility on the one hand, and factual impossibility on the other. Legal impossibility could be a defense; factual impossibility could not. The problem, however, is that courts have great difficulty distinguishing between legal and factual impossibility.

Factual Impossibility   **Factual impossibility** is a defense used when a person's intended end constitutes a crime, but the actor does not complete the act that would have been a crime because an attendant circumstance is unknown to him or her or beyond his or her control. In factual impossibility cases, the defendant is mistaken regarding some fact that is critical to the success of the crime. A person who attempts to detonate a bomb containing no explosive material and an impotent man who tries to rape a woman are two examples of factual impossibility.

Under both common law and modern law, factual impossibility is not a defense that would bar conviction for attempt. In such cases, the actor had the mental state necessary to be guilty of the crime and by committing the acts has proven his or her dangerousness. The accused in each of these cases, therefore, is deserving of criminal punishment, and there is no policy reason for the law to treat the person otherwise. Therefore, the physical impossibility of accomplishing the crime will not prevent conviction.

In some cases, the sheer impossibility of committing certain crimes may establish that the defendant lacked the requisite mental state to be criminally culpable. To address this, some jurisdictions look to the defendant's *mens rea* in determining whether factual impossibility would justify an acquittal. For example, if a person "attempted to murder" someone by swatting them over the head

factual impossibility
When a person's intended end constitutes a crime, but he or she fails to consummate the offense because of an attendant circumstance that is unknown or beyond his or her control.

Myth	**Fact**
Factual impossibility is usually a complete defense to the crime of attempt.	Factual impossibility is not a defense to the crime of attempt.

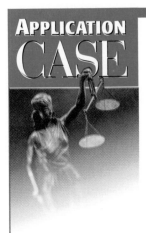
United States v. Thomas

In *United States v. Thomas*, three enlisted Naval men met a woman at a bar. While she was dancing with one of the defendants, she collapsed in his arms. Believing that she was drunk and had merely passed out, they placed her in the back seat of their car and drove home. One of the defendants suggested having sexual intercourse with her, since she appeared drunk and would not remember what happened. The three of them proceeded to have sexual intercourse with her. It was later discovered that she had not fainted, but had died of a heart attack (acute interstitial myocarditis); in this type of death, rigor mortis may not set in for hours. As a result, the defendants were not aware of the fact that she was dead.

While it was generally undisputed that the time of death was probably when she collapsed on the dance floor, the defendants were nevertheless tried and convicted of attempted rape and conspiracy to commit rape. The defendants argued that it was legally impossible to rape a corpse and hence they could not be guilty of attempted rape. An appeal court affirmed the conviction, following the Model Penal Code's position on the crime of attempt. The court reasoned that various legal authorities had addressed the difficult issues surrounding the crime of attempt, and that prior cases had established that physical impossibility is never a defense.

Critical Thinking Do you think factual impossibility should be a legal defense? Why or why not?

SOURCE: *United States v. Thomas*, 13 U.S.C.M.A. 278 (1962).

with a fly swatter, the defense would likely be able to prove that the defendant did not have the *mens rea* to murder, because it is impossible to kill someone in this manner.

legal impossibility When the intended acts, even if completed, would not amount to a crime. Legal impossibility is a common law defense to the crime of attempt.

Legal Impossibility Legal impossibility exists when the intended acts, even if completed, would not have amounted to a crime. For instance, if a defendant bribes a person because she wrongly believes that individual to be a juror, the defendant could not be convicted of attempting to bribe a juror. The classification of legal impossibility has been criticized because in most instances the case could just as easily be classified as one of factual impossibility.

United States v. Berrigan

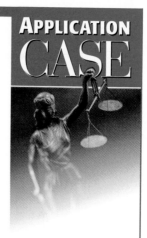

A classic example of legal impossibility is the case of *United States v. Berrigan*. In this case, federal prisoner Father Daniel Berrigan was charged with the federal offense of smuggling letters out of prison without the knowledge of the warden. The warden discovered the plot, although Berrigan was unaware of the warden's discovery.

The defendant was convicted of attempting to smuggle the letters, but the Court of Appeals treated the case as one of legal impossibility, reversing the defendant's conviction for attempt. In addition, the Court of Appeals acknowledged the varying views and opinions on the law of attempt and outlined the following criteria for legal impossibility:

"where,

1. the motive, desire and expectation is to perform an act in violation of the law;
2. there is intention to perform a physical act;
3. there is a performance of the intended physical act; and
4. the consequence resulting from the intended act does not amount to a crime."

The court held it was a legal impossibility to smuggle the letters, since the warden was aware of their existence. Incidentally, this case, like many others dealing with legal impossibility, could just as easily have been treated as one of factual impossibility.

Critical Thinking How does this case meet the requirements for the defense of legal impossibility?

SOURCE: *United States. v. Berrigan*, 482 F.2d 171, 188-189 (3rd Cir. 1973).

Legal Impossibility

"Hybrid" Legal Impossibility Some cases demonstrate that the distinction between legal and factual impossibility fails, because the reasons for punishing unsuccessful attempts apply equally to both acts in both categories. One commentator calls these cases of **"hybrid" legal impossibility**. Attempts to pick an empty pocket or to shoot a dead body believed to be alive have been treated as factual impossibility that resulted in liability for attempt, but these are equally capable of being classed as legal impossibility, which could possibly result in no liability. For an

"hybrid" legal impossibility A case of factual impossibility, as distinguished from cases of true legal impossibility.

example of another case that could have been defended either way, see Application Case *United States v. Berrigan* on page 177.

The true question is whether the suspect acted with the intent to commit the offense. If so, then the perpetrator's conduct would constitute the crime if the circumstances had been as he or she believed them to be. Such an actor would have demonstrated culpability and dangerousness to the same degree as a perpetrator who successfully completed the crime, and therefore he or she should be charged with attempt. A similar approach is taken by most modern statutes and by the MPC. In fact, with the exception of true legal impossibility, the MPC favors abolishing the defense of impossibility in all situations. True legal impossibility is defined in the next section.

Genuine Legal Impossibility   Another type of legal impossibility case that is distinguishable is referred to as a case of **genuine legal impossibility**, or "pure," or true, legal impossibility. Genuine legal impossibility exists when the law does not define as criminal the goal the defendant sought to achieve. In such an instance, the defense of impossibility is valid under any view. The defendant cannot be convicted because the result, if achieved, by definition could not be a crime. Genuine legal impossibility, therefore, is really just an application of the principle of legality (discussed in Chapter 1). Few cases justify the application of the principle of pure legal impossibility. If the defendant commits an act that he or she believes to be a crime and no such offense exists, there is no liability for attempt.

 Abandonment

What if a defendant has the required mental state and has taken the necessary step towards commission of the act, but changes his or her mind? Should the defendant be still guilty of an attempt to commit a crime? **Abandonment**, which is also called *renunciation* by the MPC, is an affirmative defense to the crime of attempt. It is used when the defendant claims to have freely and voluntarily abandoned a crime before it is completed. An accused may argue that he or she abandoned the criminal enterprise, did not intend to actually commit the crime, and, therefore cannot be charged with nor found guilty of attempt.

The MPC provides for this defense if the actor abandons his or her effort or otherwise prevents the commission of the crime, "under

genuine legal impossibility Where the law does not define as criminal the goal the defendant sought to achieve. This is a valid defense to the crime of attempt.

abandonment An affirmative defense to the crime of attempt that exists only if the defendant voluntarily and completely renounces his or her criminal purpose.

Wilson v. State

An example of genuine legal impossibility is the case of *Wilson v. State* (1905), in which the defendant was prosecuted for forgery. He had altered a check made out to him for "$2.50" to read "$12.50," by adding the number "1." However, the defendant did not alter the words "two dollars and fifty cents." Pursuant to the banking rules, when there is a conflict between figures and words on a check, only the words are legally operative. The trial judge instructed the jury that they could not convict him of forgery, but that they could convict him of attempted forgery. The jury did so.

The Supreme Court of Mississippi reversed the defendant's conviction on the basis that what he did was not a crime since he did not alter the words on the check. Therefore, the defendant's act did not amount to forgery as a matter of law.

Critical Thinking Under what tests for attempt liability do you think the defendant was originally convicted?

SOURCE: *Wilson v. State*, 38 So. 46 (Miss. 1905).

Genuine Legal Impossibility

circumstances manifesting a complete and voluntary renunciation of his or her criminal purpose." If a person truly abandons his or her purpose of committing a crime "it would be only just to interpret his or her previous intention where possible as only half-formed or provisional, and hold it to be insufficient *mens rea*."

Controversy over the Abandonment Defense Should abandonment be a defense? If considered a defense, under what circumstances should a defendant escape criminal liability? On the one hand, it is easy for a perpetrator, once detected, to claim that he or she did not mean to complete the job. For this reason, the common law did not consider abandonment a valid defense to attempt. On the other hand, an actor who truly has voluntarily terminated the criminal enterprise arguably should not be held criminally liable. As a result, some jurisdictions recognize a defense in such circumstances.

Abandonment is a valid defense only when the defendant has had a change of heart on his or her own because of a sincere belief that furtherance of the act is wrong, and not because he or she was

unable to carry out the attempt due to some logistical or technical reason, or because law enforcement intervened. Nor is abandonment a defense when the defendant ceases his or her action out of fear that the police are closing in, or if he or she postpones the project until a better time arises to carry out the crime.

Abandonment and the Common Law At common law, abandonment was not a defense. Jurisdictions that recognize abandonment as a defense to the crime of attempt do so for various reasons, such as:

- The defense may deter an actor from continuing the plan to commit a crime.
- By abandoning plans to commit a crime, a person has demonstrated that he or she does not threaten the safety of the public in the same way as someone who continues plans to carry out a crime.

On the other hand, one argument against the defense is that it allows an actor to undo criminal plans by renunciation and avoid punishment, a possibility that may encourage persons to take preliminary steps toward a crime. Some of the questions that are raised by this defense are:

- Should a defendant who sincerely abandons his or her plan escape liability?

People v. Kimball

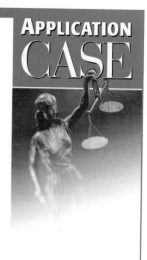

The defendant in *People v. Kimball* was convicted of attempted armed robbery. The factual allegations surrounding the events in issue were not in dispute, but the Court of Appeals determined that what was in dispute was whether the actions amounted to a criminal offense or merely a bad joke.

On the day in question the defendant, who had consumed some vodka and taken medication that morning, and his friend went to a store. The defendant went inside and according to the store clerk began talking and whistling to the Doberman Pincher, the guard dog. The clerk stated she gave the defendant a dirty look because she did not want him playing with the dog. The defendant then approached the cash register and demanded money. She thought he was joking and told him so until the defendant demanded money again. The clerk stated that when she began separating the checks from the 20-dollar bills, the defendant stated to her, "I won't do it to you; you're good-looking and I won't do it to you this time, but if you're here next time, it won't matter." He left, then returned again and repeated the same scenario with the clerk.

The defendant argued he was not guilty because he voluntarily abandoned his criminal enterprise before completing the offense. Pursuant to the Michigan statute, a person who voluntarily abandons a criminal scheme, without the intervention of outside forces, has not committed an attempt. The trial court rejected the defendant's arguments, holding that an attempt may still be shown even if the defendant fails to consummate the offense due to mere lack of perseverance.

Abandonment

The appellate court noted that the trial court should have considered the affirmative defense of abandonment. Abandonment required the defendant to establish by a preponderance of the evidence that he voluntarily and completely abandoned his criminal purpose. The abandonment is not voluntary only if the defendant fails to complete the attempted crime because of unanticipated difficulties, unexpected resistance, or circumstances that increase the probability of detection or apprehension, or deciding to postpone until another time. The appellate court reversed the defendant's conviction, then remanded the case for consideration of an affirmative defense of abandonment and to determine whether the abandonment was voluntary or involuntary.

Critical Thinking Do you think the defendant's abandonment was voluntary or involuntary? Why or why not?

SOURCE: *People v. Kimball*, 311 N.W.2d 343, (Mich. Ct. App. 1981).

Myth	**Fact**
Abandonment is a complete defense to an attempt charge, even if an accused ceases to carry out the crime because the police are about to arrest him or her.	Abandonment is only a valid defense when two circumstances are met: 1) The crime occurs in a jurisdiction that recognizes this defense, and 2) The accused has a genuine change of heart about committing the crime and clearly manifests the desire to abandon the criminal enterprise entirely.

FIGURE 6-2

Defenses to Attempt Liability

Factual Impossibility

- A person intends to commit a crime but is unaware of an attendant circumstance beyond his or her control

Legal Impossibility

- A person attempts to commit an act that would not amount to a crime if completed

"Hybrid" Legal Impossibility

- A case of factual impossibility, as distinguished from cases of true legal impossibility

Genuine Legal Impossibility

- The goal that the actor intended to achieve is not defined as criminal by law

Abandonment

- An actor voluntarily renounces his or her criminal purpose

- Is the timing of the abandonment relevant?
- If a thief who returns the stolen property is still guilty of larceny, should a defendant who has committed the offense of attempt (overt act beyond mere preparation) but later decides to abandon, be treated the same as the thief who returns the stolen property?
- Is the rationale for punishment the same in both in circumstances?

Clearly, abandonment is a complex issue, and the above questions will help juries and judges to determine the best approach in each different case.

Self Check

1. In your own words, what are the differences between factual and legal impossibility? Give an example of each.
2. What elements are generally required for a successful abandonment defense?

CRIMINAL LAW Online

Check your answers at cl.glencoe.com.

6.3 Solicitation

The crime of **solicitation**, also known as *incitement*, is the act of seeking to persuade someone else to commit a crime with the intent that the crime be committed. It is designated a crime because a deliberate inducement of another to commit a crime is sufficiently dangerous behavior to call for the imposition of criminal penalties. A person is guilty of solicitation when he or she advises, commands, counsels, encourages, entreats, hires, importunes, incites, instigates, invites, procures, requests, stimulates, or urges another to commit any felony, or to commit any misdemeanor relating to obstruction of justice or a breach of the peace.

Solicitation exists only if the crime solicited has not been completed, attempted, or agreed to. If the person solicited agrees to commit a crime, then both the solicitor and the party solicited are criminally liable for conspiracy. If the person solicited attempts to commit the crime, then both parties are criminally liable for attempt. If the person solicited completes the crime, then both parties are criminally liable for the completed crime, the solicitor being responsible on a theory of accomplice liability. A common example of solicitation is a person's hiring a "hit man" to kill another person.

solicitation (incitement)
The act of seeking to persuade someone else to commit a crime with the intent that the crime be committed.

Under the Model Penal Code, a person does not have to directly communicate his or her request to solicit as long as the conduct effects such communication.

The common law crime of solicitation, a misdemeanor, was first recognized in 1801, in the case of *Rex v. Higgins*. In that case, the court held that the solicitation of a servant to steal his master's goods was an offense even though the servant ignored the suggestion.[9] This case demonstrated that solicitation occurs when one requests or encourages another to engage in a criminal act, whether or not the person agrees to do so. Solicitation was a specific intent crime at common law, and is still one under current statutes that consider it a crime.

Solicitation has been criticized for various reasons:

- Since the crime requires an independent individual, who is capable of forming his or her own moral judgments, to act on behalf of the solicitor, it is always possible that the individual will refuse.
- It has also been argued that the solicitor manifests reluctance to commit the crime him- or herself, and thus is not "a significant menace."
- As with inchoate crimes in general, the ultimate criticism of solicitation is that an unsuccessful solicitation is so far removed from any actual societal harm that its punishment comes close to punishing evil thoughts or intentions alone, thus raising First Amendment issues.

Mens Rea of Solicitation

Common law solicitation is a specific intent crime. A person can be convicted only if he or she requests, encourages, or commands another to commit a crime, with the specific intent that the other person successfully complete the solicited crime. All modern jurisdictions similarly require that the solicitor have a mental state of desiring that the crime be carried out. Expressing a vague desire that an act be committed or hoping that someone else will decide on their own to commit a crime is usually not enough to prove the requisite mental state for this specific intent offense. When the specific intent exists at the same time as the solicitor's communication, the crime is complete. Therefore, even if the completion of the intended underlying crime is impossible, the actor is criminally liable for solicitation.

Intent by the solicitor can be established a number of ways. Usually, the mere speaking of words demonstrates the intent necessary to be culpable. Expressing the intent in writing is another way to prove the requisite intent. For example, if a man in jail writes to his friend and asks him to kill the person who is going to testify against him in his upcoming robbery trial, the letter will be enough to prove the inmate's criminal intent to solicit for murder.

Actus Reus of Solicitation

The physical act of solicitation occurs when the solicitor takes any action, whether verbal or otherwise, to urge another to commit a crime. Speaking or writing the words of solicitation is an act, and when that act is done with the intent that the person solicited commit the underlying crime, the crime of solicitation is complete.

If the solicitor attempts to solicit someone but fails because an intermediary did not reach the person or a letter was never received, most jurisdictions still consider the solicitation complete. Some juries would consider it to be only attempted solicitation. In *State v. Cotton*, however, a defendant in jail wrote to his wife soliciting certain criminal activities. There was no evidence that the wife received the letter, and the court held that the defendant could not be convicted of solicitation.[10]

Defenses to Solicitation

Although apparently not a defense at common law, abandonment is a defense under modern penal codes. The MPC, in Section 5.02(3), provides that "renunciation of criminal purpose" is a defense to solicitation when two actions occur:

1. The solicitor "completely and voluntarily renounces his criminal intent."
2. The solicitor "either persuades the solicited party not to commit the offense or otherwise prevents him from committing the crime."

Suppose that David hires a hit man to kill his wife. and pays him half of the money to carry out the murder. Then he realizes that he still loves his wife and does not want her to die. He calls the hit man and tells him about his change of heart, saying that he can keep the money already received, but that he will not be sending any more money and that he wants all plans to carry out the crime to stop.

If the hit man agrees at that point, then most likely David will not be charged with solicitation even if the police find out. However, if the hit man refuses to stop the plans as a form of blackmail to get the rest of the money, David can be charged with solicitation unless he goes to the police and informs them of everything. By doing so, he would be able to prevent the commission of the crime, which would be a valid defense.

CRIMINAL LAW *Online*

Check your answers at cl.glencoe.com.

Self Check

1. Why is solicitation considered a crime?
2. Briefly, what are the *actus reus* and *mens rea* required for a solicitation conviction?

6.4 Conspiracy

conspiracy An agreement between two or more people to commit an unlawful act or acts, or to do a lawful act unlawfully. It is a partnership in crime.

Conspiracy is an agreement between two or more people to commit an unlawful act or acts or to do a lawful act unlawfully. It is also called a *partnership in crime*. The gist of this offense is the agreement. To ensure that the law does not punish a person for his or her thoughts or intentions alone, most modern jurisdictions require that one of the parties to the conspiracy engage in an overt act.

For example, if Dick and Dan discuss a plan to rob a bank and reach an agreement to do so, and Dick then buys a gun and mask to be used in the robbery, both Dick and Dan are criminally liable for the crime of conspiracy to rob a bank. Furthermore, if the two of them carry out the robbery, each can be prosecuted and convicted for both robbery and the conspiracy to commit robbery.

Conspiracy has been the subject of longstanding criticism by legal scholars. Many people have called for reformation or abolition of the crime on the grounds that the law is vague and requires that a defendant do very little in order to be convicted of the crime. Conspiracy punishes people who come together and have a "meeting of the minds" with the purpose of formulating a criminal plan. The crime focuses primarily on the *mens rea* of the defendants, rather than the *actus reus*. The accused need not be charged with a substantive offense to be convicted of conspiracy. In fact, federal law imposes stiff penalties for conspiring to commit a number of offenses, and the punishment for conspiracy in some instances is greater than for the corresponding substantive offenses if committed absent the element of conspiracy.

On the other hand, the crime of conspiracy is said to exist as a necessary and important aid to law enforcement. Most criminal enterprises that involve more than one person are carried out in secret. Such secret enterprises threaten society and are extremely difficult to detect. Even if detected, proof of the conduct that constitutes the underlying crimes is extremely difficult. The dangerousness of crimes planned by groups justifies the law's definition of the agreement stage as being what constitutes the crime of conspiracy, even though the agreement has not ripened into the completed criminal plan. As the Supreme Court has stated, "The strength, opportunities and resources of many [are] obviously more dangerous and more difficult to police than the efforts of a lone wrongdoer."[11]

Modern penal law universally recognizes conspiracy, and it is more severely punished today than it was under the common law rule. In Section 5.03(1), the MPC provides that someone is guilty of conspiracy

ON THE JOB

FBI Special Agent

Description and Duties: Investigate "organized crime, white-collar crime, public corruption, financial crime, fraud against the government, bribery, copy-right matters, civil rights violations, bank robbery, extortion, kidnapping, air piracy, terrorism, foreign counterintelligence, interstate criminal activity, fugitive and drug-trafficking matters, and other violations of federal statutes." Work with other law enforcement agencies at the federal, state, or local level to investigate crime. Wear or have immediate access to a firearm at all times when on duty, and be prepared to use deadly force when needed.

Salary: Salaries are based on government salary scales, which change often. Most special agents start at the GS-10 level and can advance to GS-13.

Other Information: The application process is lengthy and requires a variety of tests and security checks. Applicants who are fluent in a foreign language, or who have a degree in law or accounting, can enter with a four-year degree. Others must have an advanced degree or work experience.

Critical Thinking What qualities do you think a good FBI Agent should possess?

SOURCE: FBI Web site, http://www.fbi.gov.

A law enforcement officer may be faced with a situation where he or she does not have enough evidence to charge a suspect with a substantive offense, but might be able to charge conspiracy. However, he or she should not jump the gun in these situations. The officer must remember to have enough evidence to: a) establish that there is an agreement between two or more people to commit a crime; and, usually, b) prove that the suspects have taken some overt act in furtherance of the conspiracy. In addition, the officer must make sure to have legally admissible evidence to support the conspiracy charge. Conspiracy can often be used as a tool for law enforcement to get a dangerous person off the street, but the elements of this offense must still be proved in court.

"if with the purpose of promoting or facilitating its commission he agrees with such other person or persons that they or one or more of them will engage in conduct that constitutes such crime or an attempt or solicitation to commit such crime; or agrees to aid such other person or persons in the planning or commission of such crime or of an attempt or solicitation to commit such crime."

Mens Rea of Conspiracy

The mental state required for conspiracy is two-tiered; the parties must have both the intent to agree and the specific intent that the object of the agreement be achieved. Both *mens rea* elements require that there be more than one person involved. The act of agreement is virtually indistinguishable from the first *mens rea* requirement. Therefore, proof of the *actus reus*, the existence of the agreement, will satisfy the first *mens rea* element as well. The specific intent requirement is in addition to the intent to agree. However, the question arises whether a showing of knowledge can satisfy this element, or whether the element requires proof of the actor's purpose to achieve the result.

The following three examples will help illustrate the point of whether a supplier should be held criminally liable for conspiracy, where that supplier furnishes goods or services to another person or group knowing that the goods or services will be used for illegal purposes:

- A woman goes to a gun dealer to buy a gun to kill her husband and the dealer knows the wife's plan but, nonetheless, sells her the gun.
- The defendant, a drug wholesaler, sells legal drugs to a person whom he knows will use them for unlawful purposes.
- The operator of a telephone answering service provides telephone messaging services for known prostitutes.[12]

The courts are divided on the issue of whether knowledge alone is enough, but they are consistent in concluding that if purpose is required it may "often" be inferred from the accused's knowledge of the recipient's plans. Under the MPC, a person cannot be guilty of conspiracy "unless the conspiratorial agreement was made with the purpose of promoting or facilitating the commission of the substantive offense."[13]

Actus Reus of Conspiracy

The *actus reus* of conspiracy is the act of reaching an agreement. Such an act constitutes a person's advancement of the intent to further the criminal purpose, and it is that advancement that justifies the law's intervention. An agreement can, of course, be proven by direct evidence, by either spoken or written words. On the other hand, most people do not form illegal agreements openly, and sometimes all participants may not know the identity of all conspirators. Therefore, proof of the existence of conspiracy can only be inferred from proof of conduct of the defendants, often in the form of proof of their cooperation. In other words, proof of conduct of one or more of the alleged co-conspirators often forms the basis of the prosecution's case in a conspiracy prosecution. But, the gist of the crime is still agreement, and the prosecution has the burden of convincing the jury, not only that the alleged co-conspirators acted towards the accomplishment of the conspiracy's goal, but also that they actually agreed to try to achieve the goal.

Although the common law and some modern jurisdictions require for the *actus reus* of conspiracy only that two or more persons agree to

CRIMINAL LAW Online

Conspiracies

Details regarding major multiple party conspiracies can be found by accessing the link at **cl.glencoe.com**. What offenses are most typical of large-scale conspiracies, and why?

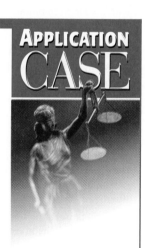

APPLICATION CASE

United States v. Alvarez

In *United States v. Alvarez*, the defendant was convicted of conspiracy to import marijuana. Others had arranged for the shipment of marijuana to be made to supposed buyers who were actually undercover agents. One of the persons who had arranged the shipment, in the presence of the defendant, told an undercover agent that the defendant would unload the shipment when it arrived in the United States. When the undercover agent asked the defendant if that were true, the defendant nodded.

The court of appeals reversed the defendant's conspiracy conviction, holding that the evidence, though sufficient to show defendant's knowledge that something illegal was transpiring, was not sufficient to show his knowledge of an agreement or his having joined in it.

Critical Thinking What kind of overt act do you think would have been necessary for the defendant's conviction to be upheld?

SOURCE: *United States v. Alvarez*, 610 F.2d 1250 (5th Cir. 1980), as cited in James A. Burke & Sanford H. Kadish, "Conspiracy" in 1 *Encyclopedia of Crime and Justice* 231, 233 (S.H. Kadish ed. 1983).

Conspiracy

engage in criminal conduct, most jurisdictions require that in addition to the agreement, the prosecutor must prove that some overt act was committed in furtherance of the conspiracy. The purpose of the requirement of an overt act is to prove that the conspiracy is actually alive and at work. This requirement does not pose a substantial hurdle in most prosecutions, however, since almost any act is applicable.

Defenses to Conspiracy

Impossibility, such a thorny problem in the area of attempt law, is dealt with more simply in the realm of conspiracy law. Most courts hold that impossibility of any kind is not a defense to a charge of conspiracy, though a few decisions exist that hold impossibility is

---

FIGURE 6–3

Alaska's Statute on Conspiracy

AS 11.31.120.   Conspiracy

(a)   An offender commits the crime of conspiracy if, with the intent to promote or facilitate a serious felony offense, the offender agrees with one or more persons to engage in or cause the performance of that activity and the offender or one of the persons does an overt act in furtherance of the conspiracy.

(b)   If an offender commits the crime of conspiracy and knows that a person with whom the offender conspires to commit a serious felony offense has conspired or will conspire with another person or persons to commit the same serious felony offense, the offender is guilty of conspiring with that other person or persons to commit that crime whether or not the offender knows their identities.

(c)   In a prosecution under this section, it is not a defense that a person with whom the defendant conspires could not be guilty of the crime that is the object of the conspiracy because of

(1)   lack of criminal responsibility or other legal incapacity or exemption;

(2)   belonging to a class of persons who by definition are legally incapable in an individual capacity of committing the crime that is the object of the conspiracy;

SOURCE: http://touchngo.com/lglcntr/akstats/Statutes/Title11/Chapter 31/Section120.htm

(3)   unawareness of the criminal nature of the conduct in question or of the criminal purpose of the defendant; or

(4)   any other factor precluding the culpable mental state required for the commission of the crime.

(d)   If the offense that the conspiracy is intended to promote or facilitate is actually committed, a defendant may not be convicted of conspiring to commit that offense with another person for whose conduct the defendant is not legally accountable under AS 11.16.120(b).

(e)   In a prosecution under this section, it is an affirmative defense that the defendant, under circumstances manifesting a voluntary and complete renunciation of the defendant's criminal intent, either (1) gave timely warning to law enforcement authorities; or (2) otherwise made proper effort that prevented the commission of the crime that was the object of the conspiracy. Renunciation by one conspirator does not affect the liability of another conspirator who does not join in the renunciation.

(f)   Notwithstanding AS 22.10.030, venue in actions in which the crime of conspiracy is alleged to have been committed may not be based solely on the location of overt acts done in furtherance of the conspiracy.

---

a defense. The MPC also does not recognize impossibility as a defense to conspiracy charges.

The crime of conspiracy is complete in some jurisdictions at the moment the agreement is reached, and, in other jurisdictions, upon commission of an overt act in furtherance of the conspiracy. Therefore, once the offense is complete, abandonment or withdrawal from the conspiracy cannot be a defense. However, abandonment or withdrawal has the effect of terminating the abandoning conspirator's liability for subsequent acts by other conspirators in furtherance of the conspiracy, and of starting the statute of limitations to run.

Where abandonment is provable, either to limit liability or to show the statute of limitations has run, courts have imposed strict requirements of proof of abandonment. Almost all jurisdictions have applied the same test in determining whether a participant in a conspiracy has withdrawn early enough not to be convicted. Courts look for an affirmative act that will prove that abandonment was timely and effective. "Effective" can be basically defined as an effort that would make a reasonable person understand that the conspirator is withdrawing. In addition, the conspirator who is withdrawing must give notice to everyone involved in order for it to be a valid withdrawal.

Some jurisdictions go even further and recognize withdrawal only if the defendant not only abandons the planned crime, but also talks his or her co-conspirators out of committing the act. The Model Penal Code provides "that withdrawal by an individual occurs only if and when he advises those with whom he conspired of his abandonment or he informs the law enforcement authorities of the existence of the conspiracy and of his participation therein." The MPC does allow withdrawal to be an affirmative defense to conspiracy but requires that the defendant "thwarted the success of the conspiracy, under circumstances manifesting a complete and voluntary renunciation of his criminal purpose."[14] In other words, a defendant may validly assert withdrawal as a defense if he or she was able to stop the other co-conspirators from continuing plans to commit a crime. Some jurisdictions that follow the MPC's approach provide that withdrawal is a valid defense if a conspirator notifies police of the criminal activity as a way to end the activity.

Self Check

1. How does this text's definition of conspiracy differ from your original conception of the crime? Why do you think that there is a frequent misunderstanding of it?
2. What factors help justify making conspiracy a crime?

Check your answers at cl.glencoe.com.

Incomplete Crimes

1. Explain the purpose of defining attempt as a crime.

Lawmakers created attempt crimes to prevent the commission of crimes before they took place. They were also created to protect the safety of the public by allowing police officers to stop the continuance of criminal activity.

2. Explain the how the Model Penal Code test for the *actus reus* of attempt differs from all the other tests.

Under the MPC test to determine whether an attempt has occurred, the only requirement is to show that the suspect has done (or omitted to do) something that constitutes a substantial step in a course of conduct, which must be planned for the commission of the underlying crime. The sole inquiry is into whether the accused person's conduct strongly matches his or her criminal intent. Therefore, any ambiguous factors, such as proximity or equivocality, are not considered.

3. State the elements of an attempt.

A person is guilty of the crime of attempt if he or she intentionally commits the act constituting the *actus reus* (either the last act, "proximity," or substantial step test), with the additional intent to commit the substantive crime or to cause the prohibited result that constitutes the underlying crime.

4. Name the two principal defenses to attempt.

The two principal defenses to attempt are impossibility and abandonment (renunciation). Abandonment is not recognized in some jurisdictions; where it is recognized, a defendant's abandonment must fit within certain guidelines to be considered a valid defense.

5. Explain when the crime of solicitation can be charged.

Solicitation is a crime only if the crime solicited has not been completed, attempted, or agreed to. This is because when any of these other three situations occur, the solicitor and solicited party become liable for other criminal acts instead, as shown below:

- If the person solicited agrees to commit a crime, then both the solicitor and the party solicited are criminally liable for conspiracy.
- If the person solicited attempts to commit the crime, then both parties are criminally liable for attempt.
- If the person solicited completes the crime, then both parties are criminally liable for the completed crime, the solicitor being responsible on a theory of accomplice liability.

6. **Define the crime of conspiracy.**

Conspiracy is a partnership in crime; it is an agreement between two or more people to commit an unlawful act or acts, or to do a lawful act unlawfully.

7. **Define the *actus reus* element of conspiracy.**

The *actus reus* element of conspiracy is the act of agreement. In addition, many jurisdictions require an overt act in furtherance of the conspiracy.

8. **Explain the *mens rea* requirement for conspiracy.**

The mental state required for conspiracy has two facets: the intent to agree and the specific intent that the object of the agreement be achieved. In addition, both of these *mens rea* elements require that there be more than one person involved, since the crime contemplates agreement between two or more persons.

KEY TERMS

inchoate crimes, page 160
attempt, page 162
last act test, page 165
physical proximity test,
    page 166
dangerous proximity test,
    page 167

indispensable element test,
    page 169
unequivocality test, page 169
substantial step test, page 170
factual impossibility,
    page 175
legal impossibility, page 176

"hybrid" legal impossibility,
    page 177
genuine legal impossibility,
    page 178
abandonment, page 178
solicitation (incitement),
    page 183
conspiracy, page 186

QUESTIONS FOR REVIEW

1. What is the six-stage process by which an actor commits a crime, and after what stage is a person liable for criminal punishment?
2. Explain the historical cases in which the crime of attempt was first recognized.
3. Your textbook names six of the various tests for the crime of attempt. How do they differ?
4. How does the MPC define the mental element of attempt, and how is this different from other definitions?
5. What are the similarities and differences between "hybrid" legal impossibility and pure legal impossibility?

6. What are some reasons why some jurisdictions recognize abandonment as a defense?
7. Why is solicitation designated as a crime, and what are some of the criticisms of this practice?
8. How does the treatment of conspiracy as a crime help law enforcement efforts?
9. What are all of the possible requirements to determine the *actus reus* of conspiracy?
10. How can the defenses of abandonment and impossibility apply to conspiracy?
11. What does the MPC allow in regard to defenses to conspiracy?

PROBLEM-SOLVING EXERCISES

1. **Prostitution** Sandy and Luisa are bored housewives who are sick of their menial household responsibilities and their bratty kids. In desperate need of excitement, they decide to start a brothel and operate it as co-madams. For several weeks, they devise a plan of action including: soliciting customers, hiring female employees, creating a price list, and decorating various theme rooms in Sandy's house, which is to be used as a brothel. When they are ready to start business, a man tells Luisa he is interested and sets a time to come to the house the next evening. When he arrives, he pays Sandy, chooses a girl, and then arrests everyone in the house. At this point, they realize that the man is an undercover vice detective. Answer the following questions:
   a) With what charges can Sandy and Luisa be charged? Explain your choices.
   b) With what charges, if any, could the other women be charged? Explain your choices.
   c) What do you think tipped off the detective to investigate their activities?

2. **Drug Trafficking** Fred and Raul are arrested for conspiracy to distribute cocaine by a police officer who had been tipped off by an informant. Fred and Raul are charged with distributing, but due to a technical error in the warrant, the evidence is inadmissible and the case is dismissed. In response, the prosecutor charges them with conspiracy to distribute marijuana. As you interview Fred in

the presence of his attorney, he begins to tell you that he has owed Raul $100,000 for the last two years as a result of a gambling loan. Fred believes that Raul will kill him unless he pays back the money somehow, but has had no way of repaying the loan. Raul had told Fred that instead of being murdered, Fred could work for Raul for five years by assisting him in his narcotics distribution. Fred agreed. Answer the following questions:
   a) Was there a meeting of the minds?
   b) Was there an agreement to commit a criminal act?
   c) Will the conspiracy charge hold up when this evidence is presented?

3. **Attempted Murder** You are a police investigator. A distraught wife appears at the local police station and states that her husband just informed her that he had been putting poison in her coffee for over a week. She also states that she had not been feeling well and went to the doctor, who advised her that she had indigestion. Her husband confesses to you that he hates her, wants her dead, and had been putting a poisonous substance in her coffee for the past week. Upon investigation, you obtain the substance from the husband. The lab analyzes the substance and you are advised that it is harmless.
   a) Do you trust that this is the substance that was used? What else will you do to determine this?
   b) If the substance was harmless and could not possibly poison the wife, with what crime(s), if any, will the husband be charged?

WORKPLACE APPLICATIONS

1. **Substantial Step Test** As a prosecutor, you are told that a man has been arrested for reckless driving through a crowded residential neighborhood at 3:00 P.M. in the afternoon. At the time of the accident, he was driving 90 miles per hour in a 25 mile-per-hour zone, then struck and killed a child crossing the street on her way home from school.
   a) Can the driver be charged with murder? With any other charges? Explain your choices.
   b) What are some of the considerations for applying murder based on a substantial certainty?
   c) What responses may the driver raise for his behavior? How will you respond?

2. **False Testimony** A defendant is charged with the attempted murder and robbery of Mrs. Gray, a 78-year-old woman, and you are the prosecutor for the case. In the middle of the trial, just before Mrs. Gray testifies, she tells you that she has a confession to make. She states that her original statement to the detective was slightly exaggerated. In this new statement, she tells you that the defendant attacked her in the parking lot and attempted to take her handbag, but was interrupted by someone walking by. Originally, Mrs. Gray said that the defendant pointed a gun at her head and said, "If you don't give me your bag, I'll kill you." Now Mrs. Gray states that the defendant only grabbed her bag and said he would kill her but did not have a gun. Mrs. Gray explains to you that at the time of the attempted robbery, she was very upset and angry and she embellished her story a little.
   a) As the prosecutor do you continue the trial and advise Mrs. Gray she must stick with her original statement? Why or why not?
   b) Do you continue with the trial with Mrs. Gray's true story and hope that the jury convicts the defendant of attempted murder based solely on his statement? Why or why not?
   c) Do you drop the attempted murder charges and prosecute only the attempted robbery? Why or why not?

3. **Last Act Test** While on duty as a municipal police officer, you observe a female and two males sitting in a vehicle parked across the street from a bank. You notice the female holding a handgun. As you are arresting the female for possession of a firearm, you observe a bank employee drive up with equipment to fix a broken ATM machine. Upon further investigation, you learn two things from the bank employee: 1) that the female is a former bank employee and 2) that someone had tampered with the machine, which guaranteed the arrival of a bank employee to fix it.
   a) Applying the last act test, is there sufficient evidence to charge the suspects with attempted robbery?
   b) Would the result be different if you applied the dangerous proximity test? Was the fact that the robbery did not take place a matter of chance, or is it possible that they may have changed their minds just as you, the officer, appeared?

INTERNET APPLICATIONS

1. **Incomplete Crimes** Visit Baker's Legal Pages, available through the link at **cl.glencoe.com**, and check out the Texas Penal Code's list of Inchoate Offenses. When you are done, complete the following exercises:
   a) Summarize each of the offenses covered in Chapters 15 and 16 in your own words, giving an example of each.
   b) Do all of these crimes have similar penalties? Why or why not?
   c) Which of these crimes do you think is most common? Least common? Why?

2. **Conspiracy** Visit Conspire.com by clicking the link at **cl.glencoe.com**, and click on the "JFK" link. Read "JFK: Conspiracy of Confusion" and

"Nomenclature of an Assassination Cabal" for some background information on this well-known, but still unsolved, conspiracy. Pretend that the assassination attempt did not succeed, and that you are a federal prosecutor with permission to prosecute all offenders in this case. Answer the following questions:
   a) Both articles provided several names and a wealth of information. Who and what did you find most relevant to this conspiracy?
   b) How would you charge these people, and on what grounds? Could you apply charges other than attempted murder and conspiracy? Why or why not?
   c) Explain how you would use the concept of *mens rea* to establish guilt.

ETHICS ISSUES

1. **Conspiracy to Commit Murder** Bill asks his two friends to help him kill his wife. They agree, and the three of them work out a plan. A few days later, Bill gets cold feet; he tells the others that he wants nothing further to do with the plan and specifically asks them to abandon it. Later that evening, Bill comes to the police department and tells you about the plan. You plan your next day's schedule around conducting interviews of his friends as a means of investigating the matter further. Unfortunately, the night Bill comes to see you, Bill's friends carry out the original plan to kill his wife. When the friends are apprehended,

they admit to killing Bill's wife but insist that Bill "planned the whole thing." The prosecutor is preparing to indict all three for conspiracy and first-degree murder.
   a) Should you tell the prosecutor about your meeting with Bill? Why or why not?
   b) What, if anything, should Bill be charged with?
   c) Does Bill have any legal liability in this case? Why or why not? What about his friends? Why or why not?

2. **Charge for an Incomplete Crime** Bob decided to rob the neighborhood store because he desperately needed money to pay his rent. He points the gun at the

cashier and demands the large bills. The cashier tells Bob that he needs to reconsider his actions and that he could go to jail for a long time. She tells him that she will not call the police if he simply leaves the store. Bob decides that she is right, that he might get caught and go

to jail. He immediately leaves the store, but is arrested while walking to his car.

a) Has Bob committed attempted robbery?

b) Did Bob abandon his plan? Was the abandonment voluntary or involuntary?

ENDNOTES

1 Model Penal Code, "Introduction to Article 5 (Inchoate Crimes)" (1985).

2 Ill. Comp. Stat. 5/8-4 (West 1998), formerly, Ill. Ann. Stat. ch. 38, § 8-4 (Smith-Hurd 1993 & Supp. 1994), as cited and quoted in Joshua Dressler, *Understanding Criminal Law*, § 27.02[B] at 348 (2nd. ed. 1995). Model Penal Code, "Introduction to Article 5 (Inchoate Crimes)" (1985).

3 *Rex v. Scofield*, Cald. 397 (1784), as cited in Wayne R. LaFave & Austin W. Scott, Jr., *Criminal Law* § 6.2, n.15 (Hornbook Series 2d Student ed. 1986).

4 *Rex v. Higgins*, 102 Eng. Rep. 269 (K.B. 1801), as cited in Ira P. Robbins, "Solicitation" in 4 *Encyclopedia of Crime and Justice* 1502, 1503 (S. H. Kadish ed. 1983).

5 Wis. Stat. Ann. § 939.32(3) (West 1996).

6 *People v. Parrish*, 87 Cal.App. 2d 853 (1948).

7 *King v. Barker*, [1924] N.Z.L.R. 865.

8 Model Penal Code § 5.01(a)-(c) (1985).

9 *Rex v. Higgins*, 102 Eng. Rep. 269 (K.B. 1801), as cited in Ira P. Robbins, "Solicitation" in 4 *Encyclopedia of Crime and Justice* 1502, 1503 (S. H. Kadish ed. 1983).

10 *State v. Cotton*, 790 P.2d 1050 (N.M. 1990).

11 *Krulewitch v. United States*, 336 U.S. 440, 448–49 (1949).

12 Joshua Dressler, *Understanding Criminal Law*, § 29.05[B] at 434 (3d. ed. 2001); *Direct Sales Co. v. United States*, 319 U.S. 703 (1943); and *People v. Lauria*, 59 Cal. Rptr. 628 (Cal. Ct. App. 1967).

13 Comment 1, Model Penal Code § 5.02 (1985), citing *State v. Davis*, 6 S.W.2d 609, 615 (Mo. 1928) (concurring opinion).

14 Model Penal Code § 5.03(7)(c) and § 5.03(6) (1985).

When can someone who has intercourse with a corpse be convicted of rape?

Find it on page 176.

Chapter Objectives

After reading this chapter, you will be able to:

1. List the three elements of self-defense.
2. Describe when deadly force may be used in self-defense.
3. Name two situations in which a first aggressor can claim self-defense.
4. Describe the circumstances in which a person can use force to defend property.
5. Explain when a police officer may use deadly force in effecting an arrest or preventing escape.
6. List five tests for determining insanity.

Chapter Outline

7.1 Types of Defenses

Failures of Proof Versus True Defenses

Burden of Proof

Mitigating Versus Complete Defenses

Justification Versus Excuse as the Basis of a Defense

7.2 Defenses Based on Justification

Self-Defense

Other Defenses Based on Justification

Defense of Others

Defense of Property and Habitation

Defenses Related to Crime Prevention and Law Enforcement

Necessity (Choice of Evils)

Consent

7.3 Defenses Based on Excuse

Age/Infancy

Duress

Intoxication

Insanity

Diminished Capacity (Partial Responsibility)

Mistake

Entrapment

Specialized Defenses

How can a first aggressor use a claim of self-defense?

Chapter 7

Defenses to Crimes

7.1 Types of Defenses

Once a defendant has been charged with a criminal offense, the prosecutor has the burden of producing evidence and proving beyond a reasonable doubt the existence of the five elements of criminal culpability:

1. *Actus reus*, i.e., the defendant's voluntary act (or omission when there was a duty to act)
2. The requisite *mens rea*
3. A unity of *actus reus* and *mens rea*
4. An actual and proximate causal connection between the *actus reus* and the social harm
5. The social harm resulting from the offense

Even if the prosecutor introduces evidence to prove all five elements, the defendant can and may raise a defense to the charge, which can lead to an acquittal. **Defense** "is commonly used, at least in a casual sense, to mean any set of identifiable conditions or circumstances which may prevent a conviction for an offense."[1] A defense may consist either of a failure of proof by the prosecution or of a statement by the defense of a reason why the prosecutor has no valid case against the defendant.

defense Either a failure of proof by the prosecution, or a defendant's statement of a reason why the prosecutor has no valid case against him or her.

Failures of Proof Versus True Defenses

Failure of proof occurs when the prosecution fails to prove the cause of action in its entire scope and meaning. The defendant may succeed in presenting a failure of proof defense in one of two ways. The defendant may "rest" after the prosecution's case-in-chief, make a motion for judgment of acquittal, and successfully argue that the prosecution has failed to introduce evidence on each element sufficient to sustain a jury finding of guilt beyond a reasonable doubt. More commonly, the defendant will introduce evidence to show that the prosecution's case does not provide sufficient basis for conviction. In a homicide prosecution, for example, the defendant might claim that he mistakenly believed the object at which he fired his gun was a tree stump rather than a human being; this would be a mistake of fact. Or, the defendant might claim that he was not at the scene when the crime was committed and therefore was misidentified as the offender; these would be the defenses of alibi and mistaken identity.[2]

failure of proof A defense in which the defense counsel either makes a successful motion for judgment of acquittal or the defendant introduces evidence that shows that the prosecution's case is lacking.

Contrasted with such failure of proof defenses are true defenses, also referred to as affirmative defenses. A **true defense**, if proved, results in the acquittal of a defendant, even though the prosecutor has proved the defendant's guilt beyond a reasonable doubt.

Burden of Proof

As noted in previous chapters, the prosecution bears the burden in all criminal cases of proving the defendant's guilt, and the standard of proof required is beyond a reasonable doubt. This standard is both a customary and constitutional requirement since the 1970 Supreme Court decision in *In re Winship*.[3] This **burden of proof** requires that the prosecution provide both factual evidence of the defendant's guilt and persuade the jury that the evidence presented establishes the defendant's guilt beyond a reasonable doubt. This means that the jury need not be absolutely certain of the defendant's guilt; absent a successful legal defense, reasonable certainty is sufficient to convict.

If the defense asserted falls into the "failure of proof" category, not only must the prosecution introduce its own evidence of the defendant's guilt, it must also disprove the defendant's failure of proof claim beyond a reasonable doubt. For example, if the defendant claims that he or she has an alibi and that the charges against him or her are based on mistaken identity, the prosecution must disprove both these claims beyond a reasonable doubt.

With respect to a true defense, criminal statutes sometimes require that the defendant (via his or her attorney) introduce evidence of the claimed defense and bear the burden of persuading the jury of the facts establishing the defense by a preponderance of the evidence (the same level of proof required in civil cases; see Chapter 1). Once the defendant has met that burden, it is the responsibility of the prosecutor to disprove the defense, beyond a reasonable doubt.

This shifting burden of proof has raised constitutional concerns in some cases (*Mullaney v. Wilbur*),[4] but it is generally recognized as the primary means of establishing an affirmative defense (*Patterson v. New York*).[5] An **affirmative defense** is one in which the defendant admits to the existence of all of the necessary legal elements for criminal liability but offers one or more legally recognized reasons (a true defense or defenses) why he or she should nonetheless be acquitted.

true defense A defense that, if proved, results in the acquittal of a defendant, even though the prosecutor has proved the defendant's guilt beyond a reasonable doubt.

burden of proof The onus of producing evidence and also of persuading the jury with the required level of proof, which in a criminal case is "beyond a reasonable doubt."

affirmative defense A defense in which the defendant admits to the existence of all of the necessary legal elements for criminal liability, but offers one or more legally recognized reasons why he or she should nonetheless be acquitted.

For example, in *Mullaney v. Wilbur*, the defendant was charged with murder under the laws of the state of Maine. The Maine statute defined murder as unlawful and intentional homicide. The defendant raised a "heat of passion or sudden provocation" defense, an excuse defense that, if successful, would mitigate the crime from murder to manslaughter. The U.S. Supreme Court ruled that once the defendant had introduced the heat of passion defense, the prosecution bore the burden of establishing that the defense did not exist. In contrast, in *Patterson v. New York*, Patterson was charged with murder under New York law, which defined the crime simply as a killing caused by the accused where the accused intended the result, rather than as a killing both intentional and unlawful. Patterson raised the affirmative defense of extreme emotional disturbance, which would have mitigated the crime from murder to manslaughter. In this case, the Supreme Court held that the defense had the burden of proving the existence of the defense. In contrast to the Maine statutory definitions in *Mullaney*, the New York law placed the burden of production and persuasion, with respect to the affirmative defense, on the defendant. The Supreme Court held that this was constitutionally permissible and consistent with the *Mullaney* decision.

Mitigating Versus Complete Defenses

Another way to classify defenses is as either mitigating or complete. A mitigating defense reduces the level of offense for which the defendant may legally be convicted—for example, from murder to manslaughter (this is covered in greater detail in Chapter 8). A complete defense, if successfully established by the defense and not disproved by the prosecution, results in an acquittal of any wrongdoing.

The bulk of this chapter consists of a discussion of complete or true defenses, but an example of a defendant's attempt to use a mitigating defense is *Patterson v. New York*. In the *Patterson* case noted above, although the defendant admitted to intentionally killing the victim, he sought to have the charge of second-degree murder reduced to manslaughter by raising the defense of extreme emotional disturbance. The jury rejected this defense and found the defendant guilty of murder as charged. The evidence of provocation presented by the defendant was not sufficient to convince the jury that he was guilty only of the lesser crime.

Justification Versus Excuse as the Basis of a Defense

The two most important categories of true defenses are justification and excuse. In early English legal history, there could be significant differences between the legal results of defenses based on justification versus defenses based on excuse. Today, however, justified and excused actors are treated the same by the criminal justice system. Criminal defendants who successfully assert either type of defense are acquitted of the offense and are not punished for their conduct. However, there is a difference between the two defenses in terms of the underlying theory of why their successful assertion should result in an actor's going unpunished. A defense based upon **justification** renders lawful conduct that would otherwise constitute a violation of the criminal law. In other words, a successful justification defense exempts the actor from criminal sanctions.

For example, if a person were to kill another who was an aggressor (i.e., the one who first displayed hostile force), and the killing was a necessary and reasonable response to prevent the aggressor from inflicting death or serious injury to the accused, killing the aggressor would be justifiable self-defense and therefore lawful. "Those who act in self-defense exercise a privilege and act in conformity with the law."[6] Even the early common law recognized justifiable homicide—based largely on a theory of necessity—such as a law enforcement officer who kills in the line of duty, an executioner carrying out a death sentence imposed by law, or a person who kills in order to prevent any "forcible and atrocious crime."[7]

A defense is based upon **excuse** when the actor has violated a criminal statue but there is a reason for not holding him or her personally accountable. An excuse defense thus frees the accused from criminal responsibility for his or her actions. For example, persons who kill another but who, because of psychological incapacity (mental illness/insanity), either do not realize that what they are doing is wrong or cannot prevent themselves from doing so, cannot be blamed for their violation of the law.

Although the common law distinction between excuse and justification defenses differed to some degree from the distinction today, with few exceptions, the contemporary impact of successfully establishing either category of offense is that the actor is not punished.

A few commentators have suggested that it is worthwhile to distinguish between justified and excused conduct in the criminal law for at least four reasons: for moral guidance, and to determine criminal

justification A defense that, because of the circumstances, renders criminal conduct lawful and therefore exempts the actor from criminal sanctions.

excuse A defense where the criminal actor has committed an unjustified crime, but there is a reason for not holding him or her personally accountable for it.

responsibility with respect to questions of retroactivity, accomplice liability, and third party conduct.[8] As for moral guidance, "people should take justifiable, rather than wrongful-but-excusable paths" whenever possible.[9] With respect to determining responsibility when there are questions of retroactivity, accomplice liability, and third party conduct, an actor's liability might exist if the defense were based on excuse, but not liable if the defense were based on justification.[10]

CRIMINAL LAW *Online*

Check your answers at
cl.glencoe.com.

Self Check

1. In your own words, distinguish between failure of proof and a true defense.
2. Explain the differences between mitigating and complete defenses.

7.2 Defenses Based on Justification

There are five major types of defenses based on justification:

- Self-defense
- Defense of others
- Defense of property or habitation
- Crime prevention and law enforcement
- Necessity

In specific situations, consent may also function as a defense. The following sections will discuss all of these defenses in greater detail.

Self-Defense

self-defense The justified use of reasonable force by one who is not an aggressor, when the actor reasonably believed it was necessary to defend against what he or she reasonably perceived to be an unlawful and imminent physical attack.

Self-defense is the justified use of reasonable force by one who is not an aggressor, when the actor-defendant reasonably believed it was necessary to defend against what the defendant reasonably perceived to be an unlawful and imminent attack upon the defendant's person. Self-defense is probably the most common of the affirmative defenses, certainly of the justification defenses. At early common law, it was not a complete defense; an accused who killed in self-defense would be convicted but pardoned by the king. By about 1535, the defense became a defense to conviction itself.[11] Self-defense is universally recognized in American criminal law—every jurisdiction now recognizes self-defense as a justification for committing a crime and even permits the use of deadly force if the defendant is able to prove the elements of the defense.

Usually, a defendant must prove three elements in order to be acquitted of a crime because of self-defense:

- The necessity of using force (including the use of deadly force only to prevent imminent and unlawful use of deadly force by the aggressor)
- The proportionality of the force to the threat (i.e., the level of force used in self-defense cannot be excessive in light of the level of force threatened)
- The reasonableness of the belief that force was necessary

An **aggressor** is one who first employs hostile force, by either threatening or striking another in such a way that justifies a similar response. With respect to the necessity of force, the defendant must show that he or she honestly and reasonably believed that there was no reasonable alternative to the use of force against an aggressor for self-protection. For example, if the defendant were threatened with a physical attack by an aggressor who was so ill or otherwise incapacitated that he or she could not carry out the threat, the defendant would be unable to show necessity for the use of force. With respect to the requirement of proportionality, the level of force used by an actor pleading self-defense must be warranted by the harm threatened by the aggressor. For example, use of deadly force to repel an attack by someone using a peashooter would not be justified.

Finally, both the necessity and proportionality requirements are subject to a reasonableness standard. A person may succeed in a self-

aggressor One who first employs hostile force, either by threatening or striking another, which justifies like response.

Myth	Fact
In order to raise the claim of self-defense, a defendant needs to have only an honest belief that the use and level of force used for self-protection was required.	In the overwhelming majority of states, a defendant must have both an honest and a reasonable belief that self-defense was required in order to avoid criminal culpability.

FIGURE 7–1

States That Allow an "Imperfect" Self-Defense Claim

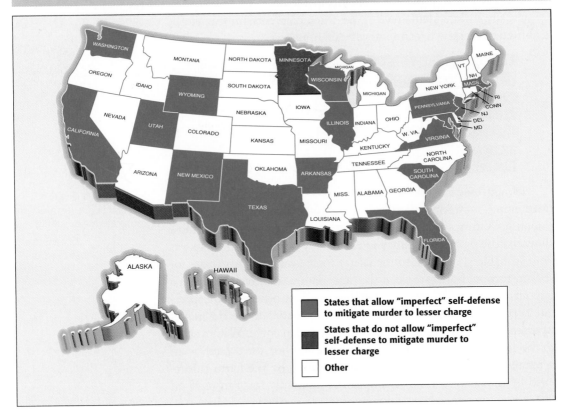

Legend:
- States that allow "imperfect" self-defense to mitigate murder to lesser charge
- States that do not allow "imperfect" self-defense to mitigate murder to lesser charge
- Other

defense claim only if he or she had an honest belief that the use of force was necessary and, in addition, there were reasonable grounds for that belief. A defendant who has an honest but unreasonable belief that he or she was required to use force or that a certain level of force was necessary for self-protection usually will not be able to use this defense and will be criminally culpable for his or her actions. A few states allow an unreasonably mistaken defendant to assert an "imperfect" self-defense claim, in which case a murder offense will be mitigated to manslaughter. (See Figure 7–1 to see which states allow this claim.)

Most frequently, self-defense is asserted in a homicide case, thus raising the question of when the use of deadly force is justified. As noted above, usually a non-aggressor (the person who does not initiate the situation in which the use of force becomes necessary) may use deadly force if he or she reasonably believes that such force is necessary to protect against imminent use of unlawful deadly force

People v. Goetz

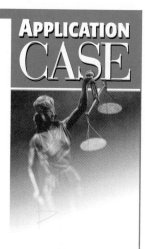

People v. Goetz (1984) was a notorious subway shooting in New York. Bernard Goetz, a previous mugging victim, shot four youths and claimed that he feared imminent attack. Allegedly, one of the youths approached Goetz and demanded that he hand over $5, but there was no evidence that any of the youths had weapons or threatened physical violence against Goetz. When the money demand was made, Goetz pulled out a handgun and fired four shots. He struck three of the youths, one of whom suffered permanent injuries. He then looked around and fired an additional shot at the youth who had demanded the $5.

When Goetz was arrested, he stated that he carried a weapon because he had been mugged on several occasions and that, based on these incidents, he was fearful of being maimed by the youths although he knew they had no weapons on them. He admitted that his intention in shooting was to kill the youths and to make them suffer as much as possible. In fact, he fired the additional round at the instigator, Darryl Cabey, when it appeared that he had not hurt him with the first shots. Goetz was convicted of carrying an unlicensed concealed weapon but acquitted of attempted murder.

A number of legal commentators expressed dissatisfaction with the verdict because they felt that the verdict was not based on the evidence presented. They thought that the evidence clearly showed that Goetz overstepped the bounds of self-defense. These critics thought the verdict resulted because the jury, like the general New York public, was tired of living with uncontrollable urban violence.

In 1996, the instigating youth, Darryl Cabey, who suffered paralysis and brain damage, sued Goetz for damages for reckless and deliberate infliction of emotional distress. The jury awarded Cabey millions of dollars in damages, both compensatory and punitive, making a poignant statement of disapproval of the use of excessive force by Goetz in this case.

Self-Defense

Critical Thinking Do you think Goetz was justified in his actions? Why or why not?

SOURCE: People v. Goetz, 497 N.E. 2d 41 (N.Y. Ct. App. 1986).

---

by the aggressor. **Deadly force** is defined as "force likely or intended to cause death or great bodily harm."

For example, John is dancing in a bar with a girl he just met. The girl's boyfriend, Dave, walks in and approaches the dancing couple. Dave becomes hostile and punches John. John initially

deadly force Force likely or intended to cause death or great bodily harm.

> **Valid Self-Defense Claims** A person is justified in a self-defense when he or she has reason to fear physical harm from the aggressor.
> *Under what circumstances is deadly force justified?*

responds by punching Dave back, and a fight ensues. John would not be justified in pulling out a gun and shooting Dave in the head. John would have a difficult time convincing a jury that it was necessary to shoot and kill Dave in order to protect himself from death or grievous bodily injury. On the other hand, suppose John has heard that Dave is a gun-carrying hothead who has previously shot another person. In this case, John has a good chance of escaping criminal culpability by raising the claim of self-defense, because it may have been reasonable for him to use deadly force against Dave in the circumstances. (See Figure 7–2 on page 209 for a typical state statute defining the use of deadly force.)

In most jurisdictions, a person who initiates the aggressive behavior—the first or initial aggressor—may not raise the self-defense claim in order to escape criminal culpability. However, there are two situations in which an aggressor may legitimately argue self-defense:

1. When a non-deadly aggressor is met with deadly force. For example, suppose a first aggressor initiates a dispute by calling someone a name or pushing someone lightly, and that person retaliates by pulling out a weapon that could kill the first aggressor. The first aggressor may then be justified in taking defensive action, because his or her conduct was not reasonably calculated to produce a fatal or seriously harmful response.

2. An aggressor may completely withdraw from any continued conflict with the other person. To effectively withdraw, the aggressor must take reasonable steps to notify the other person of his or her intention to withdraw from the conflict situation after the initial aggressive act.[12] If the other person continues to threaten harm to the initial aggressor, the initial aggressor is "purge[d] . . . of that status and regain[s] the right of self-defense."[13] However, deadly force can be used only if the initial non-aggressor is threatening fairly immediate harm of a serious physically harmful nature or death.

In order to succeed in a claim of self-defense, a person must show why it was necessary to use force for self-protection. In many circumstances, there may be an alternative to using force, such as avoiding the threatened harm by escaping or retreating. Almost all jurisdictions allow for self-defense in cases of non-deadly force, even if a person could have safely retreated.

In deadly force cases, some jurisdictions have adopted the no-retreat rule, which states that a non-aggressor is permitted to use deadly force when faced with deadly force, even if he or she has the

---

FIGURE 7–2

Alaska Statute Regarding Use of Deadly Force

AS 11.81.335. Justification: Use of Deadly Force in Defense of Self.

(a) Except as provided in (B) of this section, a person may use deadly force upon another person when and to the extent:

   (1) the use of nondeadly force is justified under AS 11.81.330; and

   (2) the person reasonably believes the use of deadly force is necessary for self-defense against death, serious physical injury, kidnapping, sexual assault in the first degree, sexual assault in the second degree, or robbery in any degree.

(b) A person may not use deadly force under this section if the person knows that, with complete personal safety and with complete safety as to others, the person can avoid the necessity of using deadly force by retreating, except there is no duty to retreat if the person is:

   (1) on premises which the person owns or leases and the person is not the initial aggressor; or

   (2) a peace officer acting within the scope and authority of the officer's employment or a person assisting a peace officer under AS 11.81.380.

SOURCE: http://touchngo.com/lglcntr/akstats/Statutes/titleII/Chapter81/Section335.htm

opportunity to escape to complete safety. At common law, this rule is typically limited to situations in which individuals are attacked in their own home. Modern case law has extended this no-retreat rule to cover situations in which an individual is attacked within his or her workplace or office. However, some states require a person threatened by deadly force to retreat if he or she is aware that retreat is possible and safe.

The common law rule, case law, and statutes concerning self-defense require that the defendant reasonably believe that his or her adversary's unlawful violence, especially deadly force, is imminent—that is, almost immediately forthcoming, or about to happen at once. The imminence requirement is also closely related to the reasonable belief requirement, imposing an objective standard upon the defendant. Both of these principles have been severely tested in recent years.

Another area in which imminence of the aggressor's attack and the reasonableness of the defendant's claimed perception of it arises is that of battered person syndrome, most commonly arising in the case of battered women. In recent years, self-defense claims have been made by persons who have killed an abuser after being subjected to a pattern of abuse over a period of months or years. Women who have been abused by their husbands or lovers have sought to assert the defense and to introduce evidence of "battered woman syndrome." Courts will generally allow evidence of the history of the man's abuse to support the woman's claim of self-defense.

Legal controversy surrounds how this evidence should be used. If the woman kills the man in midst of a battering incident, then traditional principles of imminence and reasonableness apply with little difficulty. However, if the woman kills her batterer when abuse is not at that time taking place, the traditional imminence requirement and reasonableness requirements may not be satisfied. Evidence of battered woman syndrome and of the battering behavior may be presented by an expert witness to explain a woman's belief that the threat of deadly harm is imminent. Such evidence may be presented as a justification for killing the batterer, even while he is sleeping.

Taking evidence of a battering syndrome into account requires a "subjectification" of the reasonableness test, an objective standard that all persons are expected to meet. Most courts are unwilling to change the universal notion of reasonableness into one that recognizes and accepts individual circumstances, temperaments, or peculiarities. Courts are divided on whether self-defense may be

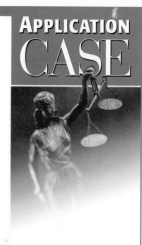

State v. Kelly

In *State v. Kelly* (1984), Gladys Kelly stabbed her husband to death with a pair of scissors, arguing that she did so in self-defense. Kelly's defense was that her husband had repeatedly and brutally beaten her over a seven-year period, and that he had threatened to kill her if she ever tried to leave him. On the day of the killing, Mr. Kelly became enraged and began beating his wife on a public street in front of a crowd of people. Some of the observers broke up the altercation, and the two were separated for a short time. Mrs. Kelly testified that at a later point that day, Mr. Kelly began running towards her with his hands raised. Unsure of whether he had a weapon, she took the scissors out of her purse and began stabbing him.

Mrs. Kelly called an expert witness to testify about battered woman's syndrome. Although the lower court denied this evidence, the Supreme Court of New Jersey reversed the decision and allowed the evidence to be introduced. In brief, battered woman's syndrome exists when someone is repeatedly subjected to physical brutality by her domestic partner and does not feel that she can leave the relationship out of fear that the domestic partner will kill her. As a result, this continued abuse creates the perception in the battered person that she must use physical force as protection or be killed. (You will read more about battered woman's syndrome in Chapter 9.) In the *Kelly* case, the expert was called to show the reasonableness of Mrs. Kelly's perception: that she believed she was in imminent danger of death or serious injury.

Battered Woman Syndrome

> **Critical Thinking** Do you believe that battered woman syndrome is a valid excuse to murder? Why or why not?

SOURCE: *State v. Kelly*, 478 A.2d 364 (N.J. 1984).

---

claimed when, reasonably or not, the woman believed that the threat of deadly harm was imminent.[14] In cases where the defendant has hired another to kill the claimed abuser, courts have not allowed the defense.[15]

Historically, the self-defense justification seems to have applied to two people of approximately equal fighting ability. Advocates for battered women have argued that their situations do not fit this model. Such women may have few options (e.g., no money, no car), and they may fear for their lives, knowing that they cannot win a physical fight with their stronger male partners. In fact, many battered women who leave are hunted down and killed by their abusers. On the other hand, some battered women do get away, often with the help of the staff at shelters for battered women.

Other Defenses Based on Justification

In addition to self-defense, the defense of others and the defense of property have been recognized as justification-based defenses. The use of force in order to prevent crime may also be added to justification defenses as may the necessity of an act or consent to it. In this section, we examine these five forms of justification defenses.

Defense of Others

Universally, the law recognizes a defense based on protection of another person from attack. The defense likely grew out of the right of persons to defend their property. It was extended to include the right to protect spouse, children, and servants, in whom the law recognized a property interest similar to that in personal property. However, as the defense developed, the persons who could be defended expanded to include others in the household and beyond—eventually even including strangers. Thus, in most jurisdictions, a person is justified in using reasonable force to defend someone else when that person reasonably believes that the other person is in imminent danger of bodily harm from an unlawful aggressor and that using force is necessary to avoid the harm. (For a map showing which states allow a defense of others defense, see Figure 7–3.)

Although the right to prevent harm to another is universally recognized as a defense, there are two problem areas. The first problem is determining the category of persons who can be assisted; the second is identifying situations in which the person defended had a legal right to act in self-defense. The early common law rule allowed force to be used to defend others only when they stood in a special relationship to their protector, such as that of spouse, child, parent, employer, or employee. Though a number of states retained this restriction, those states also adopted legal provisions allowing the use of force to prevent the commission of a crime. In effect, then, even strangers can be protected against criminal attack. However, some states still have laws that are intended to limit the use of force in defense of others to defending persons who are in a certain relationship to the defender.[16]

FIGURE 7–3

Defense of Others Laws by State

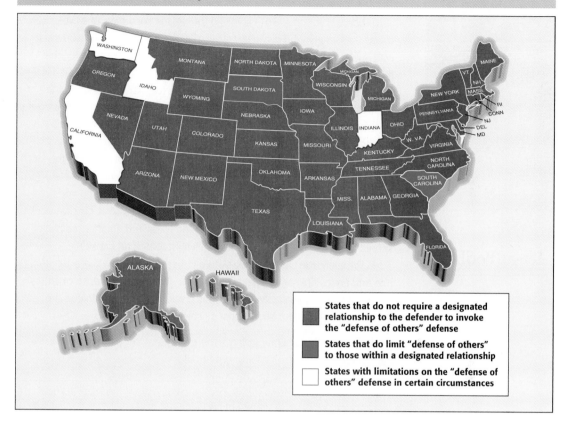

States that do not require a designated relationship to the defender to invoke the "defense of others" defense

States that do limit "defense of others" to those within a designated relationship

States with limitations on the "defense of others" defense in certain circumstances

The second problem concerning the applicability of the defense arises in situations such as the following. Al attacks Bill, and Bill uses force in self-defense. Dave, a stranger to both Al and Bill, comes upon the scene and, believing that Al is being attacked by Bill, uses force upon Bill to protect Al. From the point of view of justification, Dave's reasonable belief that Al is under attack from Bill justifies Dave's use of reasonable force to protect Al. However, since Bill was not engaged in criminal conduct (he was acting in justifiable self-defense), some courts would hold that Dave could not assert the defense of others in acting to protect Al.

If the defense were limited to the defense of loved ones (or others close to the actor), then the actor would be more likely to know whether the situation of the person defended justified intervention. In other words, to minimize the possibility of error, we should act at our peril when we attempt to protect a stranger. Some states retain this act-at-peril rule, but, under the influence of the MPC, most

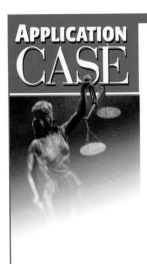

APPLICATION CASE

Act-at-Peril

People v. Young

People v. Young (1961) involved the assault conviction of a Western Union messenger who came upon two middle-aged white men struggling with an 18-year-old African-American youth. The defendant believed that the youth was the victim of an unlawful assault. When he intervened, his leg locked with the leg of one of the men and the two fell. The weight of the fall broke the other man's leg at the kneecap. As it turned out, the two men were plainclothes detectives making a lawful arrest of the youth for disorderly conduct.

Initially, a lower appellate court reversed the conviction, due to the fact that the defendant had acted reasonably when he intervened. The New York Court of Appeals reversed that reversal, upholding the conviction and holding that one who goes to the aid of a third person does so at his own peril. According to this court, the "right of a person to defend another ordinarily should not be greater than such person's right to defend himself."

Ultimately, the New York legislature chose not to follow the act-at-peril rule and enacted a statute that allows for the justification defense of others if the defendant reasonably believed force was necessary to defend the third person. This is the law in most jurisdictions today.

Critical Thinking Do you think the defendant should have been acquitted in this case? Why or why not?

SOURCE: *People v. Young*, 210 N.Y.S.2d 358 (N.Y. App. Div. 1961), *rev'd.*, 183 N.E.2d 319 (N.Y. 1962); see *People v. Melendez*, 588 N.Y.S.2d 718 (N.Y. Sup. Ct. 1992), referring to New York Penal Law § 35.15(1)(b), added in 1968.

states have adopted a reasonable appearance rule. Under the latter rule, the actor can claim the defense as long as he or she uses force based on what reasonably appears necessary.

Subject to retreat provisions, the MPC establishes three conditions that must be met for the defense of another to be asserted in situations involving third-party protection:

1. The actor must use such force as he or she would be entitled to use in his or her own self-defense, based on the circumstances as he or she believes them to be.
2. Under the circumstances as the actor believes them to be, the third person must be legally justified in using such protective force.

3. The actor must believe that his or her action is necessary for the protection of the third person.

Focusing on the second condition, for example, if the person protected were resisting arrest by a known police officer, or if he or she were using excessive force in making an arrest, the person protected would have no defense. If the third-party actor knew those circumstances, he or she would have no defense either.

With respect to retreat, the MPC adapts the requirements for self-defense of oneself to apply to the defense of others. The actor need not retreat before using force to protect a third person unless he or she knows that doing so is possible while still assuring the complete safety of that person. For example, if a child is attacked, the actor must, if possible, pick up the child and retreat with the child, rather than use fatal force in the child's defense. The actor must attempt to secure the retreat of the person needing protection in those situations where retreat would be required under the rules of self-defense.

Defense of Property and Habitation

A person is justified in the use of force to protect his or her property from encroachment. However, unless the threat is against habitation (a person's residence), the actor is not justified in the use of deadly force. In short, the law generally values life over property. A person may use force to prevent another from dispossessing him or her of real or personal property or to regain possession of property immediately after dispossession. However, the actor can never use deadly force solely to protect property. Nonetheless, the notion that "every Englishman's home was his last retreat from a hostile world" was at the root of the common law rule that deadly force could be used in "defense of the home that sheltered life."[17] Thus, when there is a threat of unlawful entry into a home, the dweller inside may, under some circumstances, use deadly force to defend his or her dwelling.

The earliest common law rule on the use of deadly force to defend one's home was that, under the category of crime prevention, a homicide to prevent breaking into a house at night was justifiable. The rule subsequently evolved to allow a dweller to use deadly force if he or she reasonably believes it necessary to do so to prevent an imminent, unlawful entry of his or her dwelling. Some jurisdictions have taken a narrower approach to the defense of habitation, allowing the use of deadly force only when the actor believes that the intruder intends to

Good Samaritan Laws

Although there is usually no legal responsibility to provide first aid to another person, there is a very clear responsibility to continue such care once you start. You cannot start first aid and then stop unless the victim no longer needs your attention, others take over the responsibility from you, or you are physically unable to continue. Most states have passed Good Samaritan laws that protect you from liability when you render emergency aid. Such laws require only that you provide the level and type of care that would be given in those circumstances by a reasonable person with the same training as you.

injure the actor or another occupant and deadly force is necessary to repel the intruder. (See Figure 7–4 for an example of a modern-day statute on the use of force in defense of habitation.)

Other jurisdictions have imposed an even narrower rule, requiring that:

- The actor reasonably believes that the intruder intends to commit a forcible felony in the dwelling or to kill or seriously injure an occupant.
- Deadly force is necessary to repel the intrusion.

The MPC limits the use of deadly force to instances in which there is a substantial risk to the person.

In contrast to the defense of habitation, a person may use reasonable, but not deadly, force in the defense of property from trespass or theft when the actor reasonably believes that the property

---

FIGURE 7–4

Utah Statute on the Use of Force in Defense of Habitation

76-2-405.   Force in defense of habitation.

(1) A person is justified in using force against another when and to the extent that he reasonably believes that the force is necessary to prevent or terminate the other's unlawful entry into or attack upon his habitation; however, he is justified in the use of force which is intended or likely to cause death or serious bodily injury only if:

(a) the entry is made or attempted in a violent and tumultuous manner, surreptitiously, or by stealth, and he reasonably believes that the entry is attempted or made for the purpose of assaulting or offering personal violence to any person, dwelling, or being in the habitation and he reasonably believes that the force is necessary to prevent the assault or offer of personal violence; or

(b) he reasonably believes that the entry is made or attempted for the purpose of committing a felony in the habitation and that the force is necessary to prevent the commission of the felony.

(2) The person using force or deadly force in defense of habitation is presumed for the purpose of both civil and criminal cases to have acted reasonably and had a reasonable fear of imminent peril of death or serious bodily injury if the entry or attempted entry is unlawful and is made or attempted by use of force, or in a violent and tumultuous manner, or surreptitiously or by stealth, or for the purpose of committing a felony.

SOURCE: http://www.le.state.ut.us/~code/TITLE76/htm/76_02024.htm

---

is in immediate danger of unlawful interference and that force is necessary to prevent the interference. Only if the interference with the property is accompanied by a threat of deadly force would the actor be justified in defending with deadly force. But in this case, the use of such deadly force would really be based upon self-defense, as described in an earlier section of this chapter.

The amount of force used in protecting the property must be proportional to what is needed to protect the property. If the property can be protected without resorting to physical force, the owner must do so. Most jurisdictions require an owner to ask the perpetrator to refrain from taking the property before resorting to physical force, unless it is clear from the circumstances that a request to desist would be useless or would put the owner in a more dangerous situation. As a policy consideration, the protection of property is not thought to be as important as the protection of a human life; therefore, the law requires that steps be taken to avoid any physical harm to persons when protecting one's property.

The MPC provides that an individual can use non-deadly force to protect his or her property if three conditions are met:

1. The other person's interference with the property must be unlawful.
2. The property owner must have possession of the property in question or must be acting on behalf of someone who is in possession of the property.
3. Force must be immediately necessary to protect the property, or the actor must believe that the person against whom he or she uses force has no rightful claim to the property and, in the case of land, the circumstances must be such that it would be an exceptional hardship to postpone the entry or re-entry until a court order is obtained.

A property owner is forbidden to use any mechanical device, such as a spring gun, that would cause disproportional harm, such as a severe injury or death, to protect the property from trespass or theft.[18] Use of a device that kills someone for trespassing would be justified only if the person who employed the device would have been justified in killing the trespasser had he been present to physically carry out the act him- or herself.

Under the MPC, however, the use of devices that kill is not justifiable under any circumstances.[19] Mechanical devices such as warning alarms or electric fences may be used if they are reasonable and give adequate warning to the intruder that they exist. The MPC

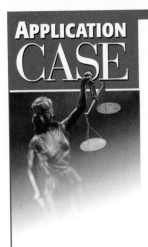

Defense of Property

People v. Caballos

In *People v. Caballos*, the defendant was convicted of assault with a deadly weapon for rigging a loaded .22 caliber pistol to go off when the door of his dwelling opened. The defendant had been robbed of expensive equipment on previous occasions and rigged the gun as a way of catching any future perpetrators. Two teenaged boys, who had been the perpetrators in the previous break-in, tried to break in again. One of them was shot in the face.

The defendant argued that he should not have been convicted because had he been physically present he would have been justified in shooting the two boys. The court disagreed stating that "where the character and manner of the burglary do not reasonably create a fear of great bodily harm, there is no cause for exaction of human life . . . or for the use of deadly force. The character . . . of the burglary could not reasonably create such a fear unless the burglary threatened, or was reasonably believed to threaten, death or serious bodily harm."

The court reached this decision partly because it believed that to allow people to employ deadly mechanical devices in the defense of property would imperil the lives of children, as well as firefighters, police officers, and others acting within the scope of their employment. The court also stated that even when one is home when intruders enter, the dweller might resort to other options besides exerting deadly force or serious injury.

Critical Thinking To what degree should a person be allowed to use force to protect his or her property?

SOURCE: *People v. Caballos*, 526 P.2d 241 (Cal. 1974).

requires three things in order to maintain non-deadly mechanical devices:

1. The device must not be designed to cause or create a substantial risk of death or serious injury.
2. Use of the device must be reasonable under the circumstances.
3. The device must be one that is customarily used for the purpose of protection, and reasonable care must be taken to make probable intruders aware that the device is being used.

Defenses Related to Crime Prevention and Law Enforcement

There is some overlap among justifications in the areas of defense of others and crime prevention or law enforcement. Although private citizens and private security agencies can act in a law enforcement capacity, their powers to do so are not as broad as those of sworn police officers. The rules for private citizens have been covered in the section on defense of others. A few additional points will be made here. However, the primary purpose of this section is to discuss the justification defense as it applies to sworn police officers in the exercise of their duties.

A category of defense that may be called a **law enforcement defense** authorizes the use of force by law enforcement officers in various circumstances. Law enforcement officers are allowed to use non-deadly force:

- to stop and arrest someone who is committing or who has committed a crime.
- to prevent an escape from custody by someone subject to arrest or who has been arrested.
- to prevent the commission of a crime.
- to suppress riots and disorders.[20]

Because of the nature of their jobs, police officers are at times compelled to use lawful force in order to prevent criminals from causing further harm to society. A police officer must always act reasonably when using force and must not deprive suspects of important constitutional rights. For example, a police officer who wrongfully arrests an individual for a crime the arrested person did not commit and then physically restrains the person when he or she attempts to flee might be charged with false imprisonment or some other offense. Therefore, it is very important for a police officer and anyone acting as a law enforcement agent to understand when it is appropriate to use force on a person and what degree of force is considered reasonable.

Private citizens can make arrests under the common law rule. Such a citizen's arrest can be made for a felony or for a misdemeanor involving a breach of the peace, if the crime actually occurred and the citizen reasonably believed the suspect committed the offense. A citizen's arrest for other misdemeanors in the citizen's presence is also authorized.

A police officer making a lawful arrest may be met with resistance and may reasonably believe that using force on the arrestee is

law enforcement defense
Authorizes the use of force by law enforcement officers in various circumstances.

the only way to stop a suspect from physically harming the police officer, or some other innocent person. A law enforcement officer or private citizen authorized to arrest may use non-deadly force in making an arrest when it is necessary to prevent the commission of a crime, to prevent the escape of an arrestee, or to complete an arrest.[21] When a person who has been arrested flees, an officer may use the degree of force necessary to make the arrest. This does not mean that an officer can always use deadly force in such cases; the requirements governing the use of deadly force are much more rigorous.

As Blackstone noted, early common law permitted the use of deadly force "where a man by the commandment of the law is bound to arrest another for any capital offense or to disperse a riot, and resistance is made to his authority: it is here justifiable and even necessary to beat, to wound, or perhaps to kill the offenders, rather than permit the murderer to escape or the riot to continue."[22] The common law rule permitted a law enforcement officer to use deadly force to effect an arrest or even a detention. Incorporating an element of necessity modified that rule.

Under the modified common law rule, a law enforcement officer is justified in using deadly force upon another if the officer reasonably believes that the suspect committed a felony and that such force is necessary (that is, the legal objective of arrest cannot be achieved without such action, or, without such force, the suspect will escape). Beginning in the late nineteenth century, some states modified this rule to allow the use of deadly force to effect an arrest for a forcible or atrocious felony.[23] The use of deadly force by a law enforcement officer is also subject to constitutional limitations, which will be discussed below.

Use of deadly force by a private citizen is more restricted than for police officers, in part to prevent vigilantism. Although the law is not uniform throughout the states, private citizens may use deadly force in effecting a felony arrest only when the offense is a forcible felony, the arresting citizen gives notice of the intent to make an arrest, and the citizen correctly believes that the person committed the felony. However, constitutional limitations that apply to law enforcement officers, such as probable cause and warrants, do not apply to private citizens.

The MPC's provisions with respect to the use of deadly force are also much narrower than the common law rule. An officer or private citizen may not use deadly force to prevent the commission of a crime unless he or she believes:

- that there is a substantial risk that the suspect will cause the death or serious bodily injury to another person unless prevented from doing so.
- that the use of deadly force presents no substantial risk to bystanders.[24]

Deadly force cannot be used by a private citizen acting on his or her own to effect an arrest or prevent an escape. A law enforcement officer or a citizen assisting someone believed to be a police officer may use deadly force to make an arrest or prevent an escape only under the following conditions:

- When the arrest is for a felony
- When the actor believes force is necessary
- When the actor makes known to the suspect the purpose of the arrest
- When the actor believes that the use of deadly force creates no substantial risk of harm to innocent bystanders
- When the actor believes either that the crime for which the arrest is made involved the use or threatened use of deadly force, or that there is a substantial risk that the suspect will kill or seriously injure someone if the arrest is delayed or the suspect escapes

(See Application Case *Tennessee v. Garner* on page 222 for a detailed discussion of the constitutional limits of the use of deadly force by law enforcement.)

Necessity (Choice of Evils)

Sometimes a person is faced with a choice between two courses of action, both of which will cause harm. If the actor chooses the lesser of the evils, he or she can claim the defense of **necessity**. The defense of necessity, therefore, is also known as the choice of evils, or the choice of lesser evils. It is a justification-based defense, in that if it applies, the actor is not held criminally liable at all. It overlaps with other defenses; for example, self-defense is grounded in part on the necessity of using force to prevent harm to oneself. Blackstone listed self-defense as one of the situations where the actor cannot be convicted of a crime due to necessity: "in such a case [where an actor kills an assailant] he is permitted to kill the assailant; for there the law of nature, and self-defense [its] primary [canon], have made him his own protector."[25]

necessity A defense where a person, under the pressure of circumstances, commits a justifiable crime, as long as the harm produced is less than the harm that would have occurred without the action.

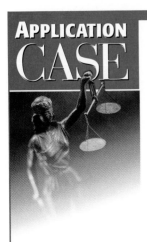

APPLICATION CASE

Deadly Force

Tennessee v. Garner

The final limitation on the use of deadly force by a law enforcement officer in effecting an arrest is the constitutional limitation imposed by the U.S. Supreme Court in its decision in *Tennessee v. Garner*. In that case, police officers responded to a call at night that there was a prowler inside a home. One of the investigating officers saw someone running in the back-yard of the house that was being burglarized. The suspect was a 15-year-old boy who ran to a six-foot chain-link fence in the back of the yard. The officer shone his flashlight on the boy and did not see a weapon. In fact, the officer stated that he was 'reasonably sure' that the boy did not have a weapon. The boy began climbing the fence, and as he did so, the officer yelled "Police, halt!" When the boy did not stop, the officer shot him in the back of the head, killing him.

Under Tennessee law, the officer's actions were justified because he was permitted to use deadly force to arrest a suspect for any felony. However, the suspect's father brought a federal action seeking damages for violations of the boy's constitutional rights. In this case, the Supreme Court held that an officer using deadly force violates a suspect's Fourth Amendment right to be free from unreasonable search and seizure unless the officer has probable cause to believe "that the suspect poses a signifi-cant threat of death or serious physical injury to the officer or others, and such force is necessary to make the arrest or prevent escape. In regard to the necessity element, a warning, if feasible, must be given to the suspect before deadly force is employed."

The Court held that an arrest constitutes a "seizure" that is unrea-sonable when deadly force is disproportionate to a suspect's actions. Furthermore, the Court said that "[w]here the suspect poses no immedi-ate threat to the officer and no threat to others, the harm resulting from failing to apprehend [the nonviolent felon] does not justify the use of deadly force." The gist of the Court's decision is summed up in this statement: "it is not better that all felony suspects die than that they escape."

Critical Thinking Do you agree with the Supreme Court's decision regarding the use of deadly force by law enforcement? Why or why not?

SOURCE: *Tennessee v. Garner*, 471 U.S. 1 (1985).

When, under the pressure of circumstances, a person commits what would otherwise be a crime, he or she is considered legally justified in acting if his or her actions were a necessity designed to prevent some greater harm. Necessity as a defense can be successful in producing an acquittal as long as the harm produced is less than the harm that would have occurred without the action.[26] The defense has been recognized in a variety of situations.

With respect to necessity as a defense to a charge of homicide, the law has not been so clear. The MPC "choice of evils" defense has influenced many American states to adopt statutes recognizing the defense.[27] More than half have done so. But in other jurisdictions, the common law definition of the defense still prevails. According to common law, a person is justified in violating a criminal law if the following six elements are present:

1. The actor must be faced with a clear and imminent danger.
2. The actor must expect, as a reasonable person, that his or her action will be effective in abating the danger sought to be avoided.
3. The actor may not successfully claim the defense if there is an effective legal alternative available.
4. The harm caused must be less than the harm avoided.
5. The legislature in the state must not have decided the balancing of the choice and legislated against it. For example, if the legislature considered approving marijuana use for medical reasons and rejected the choice, a person cannot claim that choosing to use marijuana for this purpose was a lesser evil than not treating the condition for which it was used. If the legislature has defined the circumstances under which abortion is legal, the actor cannot claim that necessity justified an abortion under circumstances not authorized by law.
6. The actor must not have wrongfully placed him- or herself in the situation that requires the choice of evils.

In addition to these elements, the defense may also be subject to three limitations:

1. Some states limit the defense to situations created by natural forces.
2. The defense may not apply in homicide cases.
3. A person may not act merely to protect his or her reputation or economic interests.[28]

CRIMINAL LAW Online

Use of Force by Law Enforcement

You can learn how often law enforcement personnel use force in the line of duty by visiting the National Criminal Justice Reference Service Web site by clicking the link at **cl.glencoe.com**. As part of the Violent Crime Control and Law Enforcement Act of 1994, the National Institute of Justice and the Bureau of Statistics have combined efforts to collect data and research police-citizen contact. Is the use of force in police-citizen contacts rare or prevalent? Is it usually accompanied by provocative behavior on the part of suspects?

FIGURE 7–5

States that Define the Necessity Defense and Those that Do Not

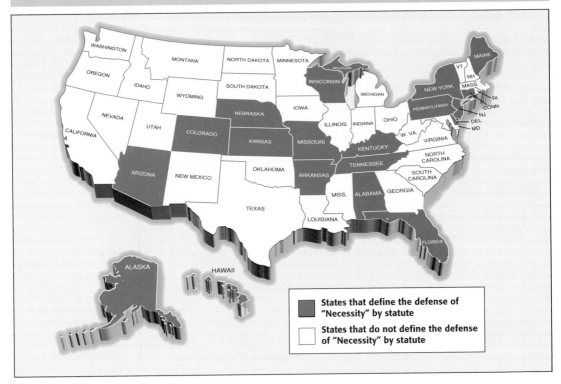

States that define the defense of "Necessity" by statute

States that do not define the defense of "Necessity" by statute

As noted above, the MPC's choice of evils defense broadened the common law rule. First, with respect to defense in a homicide case, the examples given in the comments accompanying the MPC are illuminating. First, the comment recognizes the sanctity of human life but then notes that conduct resulting in the taking of life may promote the very value that the law against homicide seeks to protect. The comment then presents two examples to illustrate this possibility:

1. An actor who makes a breach in a dike, knowing that doing so will flood a nearby farm, but that this is the only course available to save a entire town. If charged with homicide, the accused could rightly point to the net saving of innocent lives and "the numerical preponderance in the lives saved compared to those sacrificed surely should establish legal justification for the act."

2. A mountain climber, "roped to a companion who has fallen over a precipice, who holds on as long as possible, but

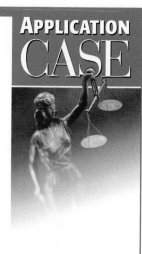
Regina v. Dudley and Stephens

In the English case *Regina v. Dudley and Stephens* (1884), three sea-men and a 17-year-old boy were stranded in the open sea for 20 days after their ship sank. They were without food for the last nine days and without water the last seven days. The boy was seriously ill, and all were very weak. Two of the men killed the boy in order to eat his flesh and drink his blood for survival. Four days later they were saved, and the two men were charged with the boy's murder.

The men raised the defense of necessity, arguing that had they not killed the victim, all of them would have died. The court rejected their claim, holding that they were not justified in taking another's life to save their own unless acting in self-defense against the other person. The defendants were convicted of murder, but their sentences were commuted to six months' imprisonment.

Critical Thinking Do you think the defendants should have been acquitted? Why or why not?

SOURCE: *Regina v. Dudley and Stephens*, L.R. 14 Q.B.D. 273 (1884).

eventually cuts the rope." According to the comment, the actor "must certainly be granted the defense that he accelerated one death slightly but avoided the only alternative, the certain death of both."[29]

It should be noted that the MPC defense still would not apply to the situation where the actor killed one person to save one other, or where a person acts to save him- or herself at the expense of another. These are choices of equal, not lesser, evils, and the defense of necessity would not be available under the common law or the MPC in those situations.

Necessity is related to the defense of duress. The major difference is that duress involves coercive threats from human beings rather than from physical or natural circumstances. Duress is considered primarily an excuse rather than a justification defense and is discussed in the following section on excuse-based defenses.

Finally, with respect to the defense of necessity, it is worthwhile to mention its use in cases involving political protests. From time to time, a person charged with violating some law as a matter of civil disobedience or protest raises the claim of necessity as a defense. For

| A person who kills to save his or her own life or the life of another can successfully assert the defense of necessity. | The defense of necessity is not available to one who kills another to save his or her life, or the life of another. |

example, during the Vietnam War, protests against the draft system involved illegal acts against the government and led to prosecutions. More recently, protesters of American policies in Nicaragua and El Salvador have raised the defense. Most appellate courts have "consistently" rejected it.[30]

consent A defense where, in certain circumstances, the victim agrees to the actor's conduct. The consent negates an element of the offense or precludes infliction of the harm to be prevented by the law defining the offense.

Consent

Consent is normally not a defense in criminal cases. However, in some circumstances when the victim agrees to the actor's conduct, the defense of **consent** may be raised when it negates an element of

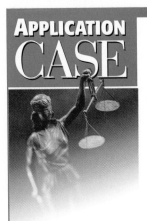

APPLICATION CASE

Choice of Evils

United States v. Holmes

In *United States v. Holmes* (1842), nine seamen and 32 passengers were in an overloaded lifeboat after a shipwreck. A storm threatened to sink the lifeboat, and, in order to lighten the boat to ride out the storm, the crew members, including the defendant, threw 14 male passengers overboard. The passengers, as expected, died. The lightened boat survived the storm and the defendant was charged and convicted of manslaughter, a conviction that was upheld on appeal. The trial court instructed the jury that the crew not necessary to man the boat should have been sacrificed before the passengers and that between those in an equal situation, those to be sacrificed should have been determined by lot.

Critical Thinking Should the defendant have been acquitted based on the necessity defense? Why or why not?

SOURCE: *United States v. Holmes*, 26 F.Cas. 360 (No. 15,383) (C.C.E.D.Pa. 1842).

the offense or prevents the harm addressed by the law defining the offense. In this sense, it is more appropriately classed as a defense that negates an element of the offense, rather than a true defense. The reason that consent is rarely accepted as a defense is that crimes are viewed as perpetrated against society as a whole and not just against the individual victim. Consent is not a defense even if the victim contributes to the negligence or somehow aided the defendant in the commission of the crime. However, certain crimes do make lack of consent an element of the crime, explicitly or implicitly, and in those situations, a defendant can assert consent as a complete defense. Hence, it is appropriate to discuss the defense under the heading of a justification defense.

For example, a defendant may be convicted of rape only if the sexual act against the victim was nonconsensual. The prosecutor normally must prove the victim's lack of consent to the sexual act as an essential element of the crime. If the defendant can show that he knew the victim and that, in fact, the sexual relationship with the victim was consensual, he will be acquitted. The defendant must still show that the victim consented to the particular sexual act in question.

Consent is normally not a valid defense in statutory rape cases, where the defendant is charged with having sexual relations with a minor. Even if the minor expressed a willingness to engage in sex, the law does not accept this as actual consent because the minor is deemed incapable of making a valid choice.

The MPC provides that consent is a defense "if such consent negates an element of the offense or precludes the infliction of the harm or evil sought to be prevented by the law defining such an offense."[31] The MPC also provides that consent is not effective if the victim is legally incompetent to authorize consent, consent is given by a person who is unable to make a reasonable judgment, consent is given by someone "whose improvident consent is sought to be prevented by the law defining the offense," or the consent is induced "by force, duress or deception of a kind sought to be prevented by the law defining the offense."

FYI

The Necessity Defense

The defense has been recognized in a variety of situations:

- A parent who keeps a child home from school due to long-term illness is not guilty of violating the law compelling school attendance.
- A person who drives on a suspended license to take a loved one to the hospital in a dire emergency would not be guilty of driving without a license.
- A police officer who plays cards to catch and arrest a gambler would not be guilty of violating the gambling laws.
- A person who kills one person in order to save two or more would not be guilty of homicide.

Self Check

1. How can self-defense be used as a complete defense? As a mitigating defense?
2. What are the two problem areas that arise from a defense based on the protection of another person?

CRIMINAL LAW *Online*

Check your answers at cl.glencoe.com.

7.3 Defenses Based on Excuse

As previously stated, an excuse defense is one establishing that even though an actor's conduct was criminal, he or she is not legally culpable. While justification defenses tend to focus on the act, excuse defenses focus on the actor. An actor is able to offer a valid excuse for his or her behavior, and society chooses not to punish the actor for the conduct. The major legal excuses are:

- Age/infancy of the actor
- Duress
- Intoxication
- Insanity
- Diminished capacity

Other excuses include mistake, entrapment, and various specialized defenses.

Age/Infancy

At common law, children under the age of seven were considered conclusively incapable of realistically forming the "evil" state of mind necessary for legal (and moral) culpability. With respect to persons between the ages of 7 and 14, a prosecutor could introduce evidence that although the defendant was young, he or she was mature enough to recognize the difference between right and wrong and the consequences of his or her voluntary actions. Any person age 14 or older was considered criminally responsible. Today, by statute, most jurisdictions have written some variation of this age scheme into their criminal code. Based on an approximate 20-year upswing in the number of crimes committed by juveniles, the current trend in criminal law is to reduce rather than increase the age at which children can be held criminally responsible. In New York, for example, juveniles as young as age 13 can be tried as adults if they commit a serious felony offense. However, for youth below the common law or statutory age of criminal responsibility, age is a complete defense to the charge, regardless of the harm caused by their conduct.

Duress

A person who commits an unlawful act because of a threat of imminent death or serious bodily injury to self or to another is entitled to assert the common law defense of **duress**, or coercion, unless the actor intentionally kills an innocent third person. This statement of the defense is generally accurate, but it requires some refinement and explanation to be complete. The modern statutory versions of the defense are generally the same as the common law rule, although both the harm threatened and the crimes committed have been broadened by the MPC and many state enactments. Duress is a form of choice of evils and, in that respect, is similar to the defense of necessity. As the U.S. Supreme Court said in 1980, "Modern cases have tended to blur the distinction between duress and necessity."[32]

The simple distinction that necessity is a choice of evils created by natural threats or physical circumstances, while duress is a choice of evils created by human threats, is not the only distinction. For example, if Tom threatened to cut off Don's arm unless Don cut off Vince's arm, the harms are of equal severity, but Don could assert the defense of duress (but not necessity) if he complied with Tom's demand.[33]

The reason for the defense of duress has been explained as a circumstance where the "will of the accused is . . . 'neutralized' or 'destroyed' so that the behavior is no longer the voluntary act of the accused."[34] According to this view, the defense is one that negates the mental state required as an essential element of the crime charged. However, this rationale is generally rejected, and duress is more likely to be viewed as reducing the range of choice of the accused. In other words, a person acting under duress does act voluntarily, even if the act is contrary to his or her own true wishes.

Although jurisdictions vary in the requirements for the defense, a person will usually be acquitted of any offense (except intentional killing) based on the defense of duress, if the following circumstances exist:

- Another person must threaten to seriously injure or kill the actor or a third person (especially a close relative) unless the actor commits the crime.
- The actor must reasonably believe that the threat is real.

duress A defense that arises when a person commits an unlawful act because of a threat of imminent death or serious bodily injury to self or another, unless the actor intentionally kills an innocent third person.

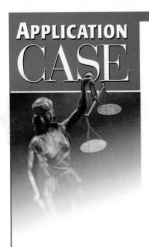

People v. Unger

In *People v. Unger* (1975), the defendant was charged with escape after he walked away from a minimum-security prison farm. He claimed that he left the camp after having been sexually assaulted by a group of inmates, then receiving a threatening telephone call saying that he would be killed because the caller had heard that he planned to go to the authorities about the incident.

When Unger was apprehended, he claimed that he was in fear of his life if he remained at the prison farm. His conviction for escape was reversed when the appellate court held that is was legal error for the trial court judge to instruct the jury that the reason given for the escape was immaterial and not to be considered as justifying *or* excusing the escape.

Critical Thinking Do you think duress should be a valid excuse to prison escape? Why or why not?

SOURCE: See *People v. Unger*, 33 Ill.App3d 770 (1975).

- The threat must be immediate or imminent at the time the actor commits the crime.
- There must be no reasonable means of escape from or avoidance of the threat other than for the actor to commit the crime.
- The actor must not be at fault in exposing him- or herself to the threat.

Some jurisdictions that do not recognize duress as a complete defense for intentional killing will allow it to reduce the crime from murder to manslaughter.

The MPC has broadened the defense in a number of ways. The defense can be asserted if "a person of reasonable firmness in his [or her] situation would have been unable to resist" the threat.[35] Thus, the MPC eliminates the requirements that the threat involve deadly force (the use of force need only be unlawful) and that the threat be imminent. It does not bar the defense in the case of certain offenses (including intentional homicide) and does not place restrictions on the category of imperiled persons (e.g., that the threat be to harm a member of the actor's family). Since the MPC requires that the

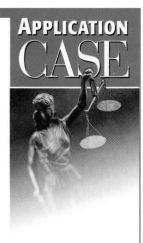

State v. Toscano

In *State v. Toscano* (1977), the defendant, a chiropractor, was convicted at trial of conspiring to obtain money by false pretenses. The defendant claimed that he had aided in the preparation of false insurance claims as a result of threats against him by the ringleader of a criminal conspiracy, to whom Toscano owed gambling debts. The ringleader said to Toscano, after he initially refused to aid in the conspiracy, "Remember, you just moved into a place that has a very dark entrance and you live there with your wife . . . You and your wife are going to jump at shadows when you leave that dark entrance." The defendant argued that he was forced to prepare the claims in order to protect himself and his wife. As the threats continued, the defendant moved to a new address and changed his telephone number to an unlisted number.

The trial court instructed the jury that duress was not an available defense for Toscano because the harm threatened was not "imminent, present, and pending." At the time this case came before the New Jersey Supreme Court, there was no statute on duress, but the MPC had been adopted. The Court, adopting a revision to the common law rule, reversed the conviction and held that "duress shall be a defense to a crime other than murder if the defendant engaged in conduct because he was coerced to do so by the use of, or threat to use, unlawful force against his person or the person of another, which a person of reasonable firmness in his situation would have been unable to resist. . . ." Thereafter, the New Jersey legislature adopted a duress statute patterned after the MPC.

Duress

Critical Thinking Should duress be a defense when danger is not imminent? Why or why not?

SOURCE: *State v. Toscano*, 378 A.2d 755 (N.J. 1977).

threat be one of "unlawful force," duress is an affirmative defense only to threats made by persons, not to threats arising from natural sources. The MPC continues the common law restriction of the defense to threats to the actor or another person; threats to property or reputation cannot be the basis for the defense.

There are some other noteworthy situations that would lead to a valid assertion of the duress defense under the MPC but not at common law:

- A person who is "brainwashed" or "coerced" over time into committing an illegal act by responding to earlier threats that have rendered the actor submissive. The MPC would allow the defense of duress in such a situation; because of the immediacy and imminence requirements of the common law rule, the defense would not be available under the latter.
- An escape from prison to avoid an intolerable condition or circumstance. The drafters of the MPC give an example of a prisoner, threatened with a homosexual assault, who escapes from prison to avoid the assault. The drafters note that this is a situation where the accused could assert both the necessity defense and the duress defense, even though the crime committed by the coerced actor is different from the one that the person making the threats demanded. (See Application Case *People v. Unger* on page 230 for an example of this use of the duress defense.)

The last situation in which the MPC might allow assertion of the duress defense, **coercion**, arises when a battered woman "commits a crime at the 'suggestion' of her abusive partner." Though it may be argued that such a person could possibly raise the defense under the modern statutes in some states, the defense is more likely available under the MPC version of the duress defense. However, the MPC does specify in section 2.09(3) that, "It is not a defense that a woman acted on the command of her husband, unless she acted under such coercion as would establish a defense under this Section." At common law, there was a legal presumption that a woman acting in the presence of her husband is coerced by him. The MPC abolishes that rule, placing wives and husbands on par with any other pairs claiming that their actions were coerced or coercive.

As noted earlier, some jurisdictions consider duress to be a justification defense, others consider it as both a justification and an excuse defense, and some jurisdictions choose not to differentiate between excuse and justification when duress is raised. Those who regard duress as a justification defense argue that one will always commit the lesser of two evils in avoiding a greater harm. Those who regard duress as an excuse defense argue that the actor should not be punished because he or she had no choice but to act—having no freedom of choice because of the limitations created by circumstances. The requirements of the duress defense are the same regardless of whether a jurisdiction defines it as an excuse or as a justification.

Intoxication

Although "it is a maxim of the common law that 'intoxication is no excuse,' . . . [s]ince the mid-nineteenth century . . . courts have developed a doctrine that . . . allows intoxication to serve as a partial defense." The MPC defines intoxication as "a disturbance of mental or physical capacities resulting from the introduction of substances into the body."[36] Although **intoxication** most commonly results from the ingestion of alcohol, any substance that causes a distortion of the senses and judgment can cause intoxication. A person accused of a crime can claim that, due to intoxication, he or she should not be held to blame for the crime. Intoxication as a defense can take the form of a failure of proof claim. That is, it can be used to show an element of the crime, such as *mens rea*, was lacking, or that the act was not voluntary (because the accused was unconscious).

Or, the claim of intoxication might be closer to a claim of insanity, either temporary or long-term, based on the effects of the intoxicant. Voluntary intoxication is rarely a basis for a defendant's acquittal of criminal charges, under the common law rule, modern statutes, or the MPC. Involuntary intoxication, far less common, may negate an element of the offense or may even constitute an affirmative defense.

Voluntary intoxication is a person's willful act of introducing substances into the body that a person knows or should know are likely to have intoxicating effects. Intoxication usually arises as a defense when the defendant voluntarily drank alcohol or took drugs. As long as the defendant is the one responsible for getting intoxicated, he or she has acted voluntarily. Intoxication can be considered voluntarily even if the defendant is physically addicted to drugs or alcohol.

Usually, a defendant may not raise the intoxication defense when he or she voluntarily became intoxicated. There are, however, a few circumstances where a person may be acquitted: first, if a defendant did not have the specific state of mind that is required to be criminally culpable for that crime; second, if long-term intoxication caused permanent brain damage that made the defendant incapacitated during the criminal act.

Voluntary intoxication is never a defense to a general intent crime. As long as the actor voluntarily ingested the drugs or alcohol, the law treats this act as the *mens rea* required for general intent crimes. Usually voluntary intoxication constitutes recklessness for *mens rea* purposes, because the law assumes that a person

intoxication A disturbance of mental or physical capacities resulting from the introduction of any substance into the body.

voluntary intoxication A person's self-willed act to introduce substances into the body that a person knows or should know are likely to have intoxicating effects.

who voluntarily intoxicates him- or herself knows of the risk associated with doing so.

The defense is valid for specific intent crimes. If a person, at the time the crime was committed, was incapable of forming the specific intent to commit the act, he or she will be acquitted of the crime. The defendant may introduce evidence, such as a blood test that produces a positive result for drugs or alcohol, to prove that he or she was so intoxicated at the time of the offense that he or she could not have had the specific intent to act.

Usually a defendant must be severely intoxicated for this to be a valid excuse. If the legislature has designated a particular state of mind as a material element of the crime, evidence of intoxication to the point of being unable to form the required intent will be a valid defense. In murder cases, a defendant can usually introduce evidence of intoxication to show that he or she was incapable of forming the premeditated intent required for a conviction of first-degree murder. The crime may be reduced to second-degree murder or manslaughter.

Involuntary intoxication occurs when the actor does not consume drugs or alcohol voluntarily or when the actor is not to blame for becoming intoxicated because, for example, he or she has an unanticipated reaction to drugs or alcohol. Four different kinds of involuntary intoxication have been recognized:

1. Coerced intoxication, which is intoxication that is involuntarily induced by duress or coercion
2. Pathological intoxication, which is grossly excessive intoxication given the amount of the intoxicant, to which the actor does not know he or she is susceptible[37]
3. Intoxication by innocent mistake, which occurs where the actor is mistaken about the character of the substance taken, as when another person tricks him or her into taking the substance
4. Unexpected intoxication resulting from the ingestion of a medically prescribed drug[38]

If a person can show one of the four types of involuntary intoxication, he or she is usually entitled to an acquittal for both specific intent and general intent offenses. Furthermore, one who suffers from a temporary involuntary intoxication-induced mental condition that satisfies the jurisdiction's definition of insanity is excused for his or her criminal conduct.

The MPC distinguishes three types of intoxication: self-induced, pathological, and involuntary (not self-induced).[39] Under the MPC,

involuntary intoxication
Intoxication that occurs when the actor does not consume drugs or alcohol voluntarily or if the actor is not to blame for becoming intoxicated, such as where he or she has an unanticipated reaction to drugs or alcohol.

Types of Involuntary Intoxication

As pointed out in the case *City of Minneapolis v. Altimus*, "Four different kinds of involuntary intoxication have been recognized: Coerced intoxication, pathological intoxication, intoxication by innocent mistake, and unexpected intoxication resulting from the ingestion of a medically prescribed drug."

SOURCE: *City of Minneapolis v. Altimus*, 238 N.W.2d 851, 856 (Minn. 1976).

Myth	**Fact**
Voluntary intoxication is a possible defense to any crime.	Voluntary intoxication is a possible defense only to crimes requiring specific intent.

any form of intoxication can operate as a defense if it negates an element of the offense, and both pathological and involuntary intoxication are affirmative defenses if the intoxication caused the actor to suffer from a mental condition comparable to that which constitutes insanity under the MPC.

Insanity

Beginning with English common law and continuing to the present, the law has recognized that a person accused of a crime who is suffering from mental disease when the crime occurred may be relieved of criminal responsibility by asserting the defense of **insanity**.[40] Although the defense of insanity receives a lot of coverage in the media, it is rarely asserted, probably because even if done successfully, it does not lead to the freedom of the accused. Instead, a defendant who is found not guilty by reason of insanity will be committed to a mental hospital for a determination of whether he or she should be institutionalized until such time as he or she is no longer dangerous.

Because of this indeterminate nature of a "sentence" resulting from an insanity plea, a defendant is more likely to seek alternatives other than insanity as a defense, even where it can be asserted. For instance, the defendant may seek a plea bargain according to which he or she receives a reduced sentence because of the claimed mental problem. Or, in some states, the defendant may argue for a finding of "diminished capacity" or "partial responsibility."

Another factor limits the actual use of the insanity defense. If a person is suffering from a mental defect and is accused of committing a crime, that person must be mentally competent to stand trial. **Incompetency** is a person's inability to consult rationally with an attorney or to understand the nature of the proceedings against him or her. The issue of competency can be raised by the prosecution or the court, as well as by the accused. When the question of

3 time 2 b insane

B 4 trial ''
During ''
After ''

insanity A defense wherein the law recognizes that the accused is suffering from mental disease when the crime occurred, and thus may be relieved of criminal responsibility.

incompetency The lack of capacity to rationally consult with an attorney, or the accused person's inability to understand the nature of the proceedings against him or her.

competency is raised, the trial court will decide the issue on the basis of a psychiatric examination. If an accused is found incompetent to stand trial, he or she will be committed to a mental hospital until such time, if ever, as the actor has regained the mental health to stand trial. If that time comes, the defendant still may opt for the more certain alternatives of ordinary criminal conviction rather than asserting an insanity defense.

If the insanity defense is raised, a jury is usually responsible for determining whether a defendant should be acquitted. In most jurisdictions, a jury may give one of three verdicts: guilty, not guilty, or not guilty by reason of insanity. In some jurisdictions, however, a court will bifurcate a criminal trial when the insanity defense is raised. A **bifurcated trial** is a division of the criminal trial into two parts:

1. First, a jury decides whether the defendant is guilty or not guilty. If the verdict is not guilty, the person is acquitted and the proceedings end. If the defendant is found guilty but asserts the insanity defense, the fact finder (whether that be a judge or jury) will hold a separate trial after the verdict to determine whether to enter an additional verdict of not guilty by reason of insanity.

2. In the second trial, the evidence introduced, principally expert psychiatric testimony, will relate solely to issue of the defendant's mental health. (A bifurcated trial is also used to determine the penalty that will be imposed when a defendant is convicted of a crime for which the death sentence can be imposed.)

Since insanity is an affirmative defense, the prosecution need not disprove the defense until the accused introduces evidence of it. Until the 1980s, most American jurisdictions followed this procedure. It is constitutional for the legislature to require the defendant to bear the burden of persuasion on the defense of insanity, and currently most jurisdictions require the defendant to prove by a preponderance of evidence that he or she was insane at the time of the offense. A preponderance of evidence is not as high of a burden as beyond a reasonable doubt. In the federal system, however, a defendant asserting the defense of insanity must prove by clear and convincing evidence that he or she was insane at the time of the offense. This is a higher burden than a preponderance of evidence. The burden of proof of "clear and convincing evidence" is not as rigorous as "beyond a reasonable doubt," however.

bifurcated trial The division of the criminal trial into two parts, the first part leading to a verdict of guilty or not guilty and the second relating to another issue such as the sanity of the accused (the death penalty is another).

Clinical Social Worker

Salary: Salaries range from approximately $25,000 to $45,000, depending on location and experience.

Description and Duties: Determine client needs for basic social services for children and adults. Perform social services requiring a high level of expertise and application of advanced techniques related to the provision of protective services for children and adults. Interview clients. Periodically reassess client needs and refer clients to community resources or other agency personnel.

Other Information: Social worker positions tend to require a strong education. Many positions require a master's degree in social work or an equivalent, or completion of all requirements for a Marriage, Family and Child Counseling (MFCC) state registration number.

Critical Thinking What qualities do you think a good clinical social worker should have?

There are four legal tests, or rules, that have been adopted by jurisdictions in the United States to determine the sanity of an accused:

1. The *M'Naghten* (right-wrong) test
2. The irresistible impulse test
3. The MPC test
4. The federal test

A fifth test, the product test, based on the *Durham* case and applied only in the District of Columbia, is no longer used even there. Depending on the jurisdiction, the defendant must meet one of these tests in order to be found not guilty by reason of insanity.

The *M'Naghten* Test The *M'Naghten* (or right-wrong) **test** comes from the 1843 English House of Lords case in which case Daniel M'Naghten shot and killed the secretary of a high-ranking government official, believing that the official was heading a conspiracy to kill him. M'Naghten claimed insanity because he was delusional. A jury agreed and found him not guilty. The verdict created controversy in England, and, as a result, the House of Lords

IN 16 states

M'Naghten **test** The rule that is used to establish an insanity defense. Under this rule, it must be clearly proved that, at the time of the offense, the accused was laboring under such a mental illness as not to know the nature and quality of what he or she was doing. Alternately, if he or she did know it, it was without knowing what was wrong.

Substantial

Defining the M'Naghten Rule

The *M'Naghten* Rule provides that "every man is to be presumed to be sane, and . . . to establish a defense on the ground of insanity, it must be clearly proved that, at the time of the committing of the act, the party accused was laboring under such a defect of reason, from disease of the mind, as not to know the nature and quality of the act he was doing; or if he did know it, that he did not know what he was doing was wrong."

SOURCE: *M'Naghten's Case*, 8 Eng. Rep. 718 (1843), 722, as cited and quoted in Abraham S. Goldstein, "Excuse: Insanity" in 2 *Encyclopedia of Crime and Justice* 736 (S.H. Kadish ed. 1983).

irresistible impulse test
A test for insanity that permits a verdict of not guilty by reason of insanity if the fact-finder concludes that the accused had a mental disease that kept him or her from controlling his or her conduct.

debated the issue of insanity. The majority concluded that a defendant could be found not guilty by reason of insanity only if his mental disorder made him unable to understand the nature of the act or the fact that it was wrong. The *M'Naghten* test tells the jury simply:

> that every man is to be presumed to be sane, and . . . that to establish a defense on the ground of insanity, it must be clearly proved that, at the time of the committing of the act, the party accused was laboring under such a defect of reason, from disease of the mind, as not to know the nature and quality of the act he was doing; or if he did know it, that he did not know what he was doing was wrong.[41]

The right-wrong test is used by a majority of jurisdictions in the United States. There are many varying mental disorders that could fall within the definition of this test, but the defendant must always show that a disease of the mind caused him or her to act in the way that he or she did. There is no clear definition as to what a disease of the mind is; however, some examples are psychosis, neurosis, and brain disorder.

When a person does not know the nature of the act he or she is committing under the *M'Naghten* test, many legal scholars interpret this to mean that the defendant does not know the difference between right and wrong. In other words, the actor does not understand the consequences of the act that he or she is committing. For example, if a person starts a fire in a home without understanding that this act will burn the house down and instead believes that the fire will ward off evil spirits, the actor may be found not guilty by reason of insanity. Because this person does not understand the consequences of his or her actions, he or she will not realize the action is wrong.

Sometimes, however, a person will understand the nature of the act but still not understand that it is wrong. For example, a delusional person may kill someone whom he or she mistakenly believes is going to kill him or her. The killer understands that he or she is killing someone but thinks that this action is justified. The delusional actor does not know that, at the time of the murder, he or she was acting wrongly. Under this test, the actor could be found not guilty by reason of insanity under the *M'Naghten* rule.

The *M'Naghten* test of insanity is still followed in a number of American states. In some of those states, an additional test has also been adopted—the irresistible impulse, or control test. This **irresistible impulse**[42] **test** requires a verdict of not guilty by reason of insanity if the fact-finder concludes that the accused had a men-

tal disease that kept him or her from controlling his or her conduct. Under this test, generally, a defendant is insane if, at the time of the offense, he or she acted as a result of an uncontrollable impulse, lost the power to choose between right and wrong and to avoid doing the act in question, or did not have the will necessary to control his or her actions. Under the irresistible impulse test, the focus is on the defendant's ability to control his or her actions, not on his or her understanding of the criminal act. By losing total control, the defendant is said to have lost his or her ability to act voluntarily and is therefore excused from criminal punishment.

Modal Peanal Code ✓

Under the **MPC test**,[43] an actor is not responsible for his or her criminal conduct if he or she lacked substantial capacity to appreciate the criminality or the wrongfulness of his or her conduct or to conform his or her conduct to the requirements of the law. The MPC test is a modified version of the *M'Naghten* and irresistible impulse tests, containing the second, cognitive prong of the *M'Naghten* test and the volitional aspects of the irresistible impulse test. The test differs from the *M'Naghten* test in that it uses the term "appreciate" rather than "know," and, unlike the irresistible impulse

MPC test A test for insanity that provides that an actor is not responsible for his or her criminal conduct if found to lack substantial capacity to appreciate the criminality of his or her conduct, or to conform his or her conduct to the requirements of the law.

test, does not use the word "impulse" at all. Both prongs of the test are modified by the words "lacks substantial capacity," thus allowing an accused use of the insanity defense with a showing of less than total incapacity.

The **federal test** is the result of a statutory enactment in 1984 when Congress defined insanity.[44] The statute stating the federal test for insanity provides that a person is excused by reason of insanity if he or she proves by clear and convincing evidence that at the time of the offense, as a result of a severe mental disease or defect, he or she was unable to appreciate the nature and quality of his or her act, or the wrongfulness of his or her conduct. This law, unlike previous rules, requires that the accused show that he or she suffered from a "severe" mental disorder. Like the *M'Naghten* test, but unlike the MPC test, this law requires total cognitive incapacity. Finally, like the MPC test, the federal test uses the word "appreciate" rather than "know," making the test broader than the *M'Naghten* test in this respect.

Finally, the short-lived *Durham* test[45] stated that a person is excused by reason of insanity if the actor's unlawful act was the product of a mental disease or defect. Under this test, the fact-finder merely determines whether the defendant suffered from a mental disease or defect and, if so, whether the criminal conduct would have occurred but for the condition. The test was adopted only by the District of Columbia and was abandoned there in 1972.

There has been much criticism of the insanity defense, especially in high-profile cases where the public has witnessed the effect of the defense. As a result, some states have abolished the defense completely, while others have reformed their laws to make it more difficult to avoid criminal punishment. For example, 13 states have reformed their law to include a guilty but mentally ill verdict. If a defendant is found guilty but mentally ill, he or she will still be sentenced to prison but will receive psychiatric care while there. For those who oppose the insanity defense because people do not receive punishment for their actions, the guilty but mentally ill verdict is a way to punish people while still offering mental health treatment.

Diminished Capacity (Partial Responsibility)

Accused persons who, at the time of the act charged, were suffering from a mental condition insufficient to support a successful

federal test The federal statutory definition of insanity, which provides that a person is excused by reason of insanity if he or she proves by clear and convincing evidence that at the time of the offense, as a result of a severe mental disease or defect, he or she was unable to appreciate the nature and quality of his or her act, or the wrongfulness of his or her conduct.

State v. Cameron

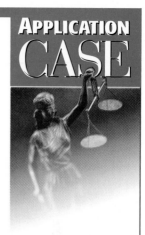

In *State v. Cameron*, the defendant stabbed his stepmother to death, leaving the knife in her heart. The defendant left the scene without making any attempt to hide the body or any evidence. He was later picked up hitch-hiking, wearing women's clothing and only one shoe. He confessed to the killing and claimed that he did it because his stepmother was an evil woman. A psychologist testified that the defendant had a delusional belief at the time of the killing that his stepmother was an agent of Satan. The defendant testified that he believed he was killing an agent of Satan at the direction of God and that at the time he believed that he was the Messiah.

The trial court gave a jury instruction stating that if the defendant knew that his actions were against the law of man, he was not insane. The Supreme Court of Washington agreed, holding that a person will not be found insane if he knew that the act was prohibited by the law of man. The Court, however, held in this case that the defendant suffered from a mental disease and that because of it, it was impossible for the defendant to realize that his actions were wrong. The Court therefore reversed the trial court's decision, finding that the jury instructions were incorrect.

Insanity

Here in Some Jurisdiction they select a lower grade.

Critical Thinking Do you think the defendant in this case deserved the verdict not guilty by reason of insanity? Why or why not?

SOURCE: *State v. Cameron*, 674 P.2d 650 (Wash. 1983).

---

insanity defense under the test applicable in the jurisdiction might nonetheless be able to introduce evidence of their mental condition on the question of whether they had the mental state required for conviction of the crime charged. The so-called **diminished capacity defense**, or the partial responsibility defense, may be available in such a circumstance.

"Diminished capacity" is a misleading and potentially confusing term. It can be used to describe two circumstances in which a mental condition short of insanity will exonerate the accused or lessen the crime for which he or she is convicted. The first circumstance is where the accused raises the condition as a failure of proof defense, negating an element of the crime, a *mens rea* use of the defense. The second circumstance is a true partial defense where the crime of murder can be mitigated by the defense to manslaughter.

> **diminished capacity defense** A term used to describe two circumstances in which a mental condition short of insanity will lead to an acquittal or lessened charges: 1) where the accused raises the condition as a failure of proof defense, and 2) a true partial defense, where the crime of murder can be mitigated by the defense to manslaughter.

The MPC and a few states allow the defendant to introduce evidence of mental illness when it is relevant to prove that the defendant lacked a mental state that is an element of the charged offense. For example, a child-like, retarded defendant facing a burglary charge could introduce evidence that his condition did not allow him to form the requisite *mens rea* to commit a felony after he entered the building where the act took place.

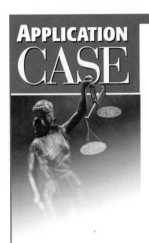

APPLICATION CASE

Guilty but Mentally Ill

United States v. John Hinckley, Jr.

On March 30, 1981, John Hinckley, Jr. attempted to kill President Ronald Reagan at the Washington Hilton hotel. While he failed to assassinate the President, he did wound Reagan along with a police officer, a Secret Service agent, and Press Secretary James Brady.

During the trial, it was revealed that Hinckley had been stalking Reagan and, before him, President Jimmy Carter. Hinckley's obsession with the film *Taxi Driver* and one of its stars, Jodie Foster, was also brought to light as his defense team tried to prove that he was insane at the time of the shooting. Expert witnesses for both the prosecution and the defense stated that Hinckley suffered from "narcissistic personality disorder."

The prosecution attempted to show that Hinckley was sane and had premeditated the assassination attempt. He had purchased bullets and guns ahead of time. A short while before the incident, he wrote a letter to Jodie Foster saying that he was about to kill Reagan.

In the end, the jury returned a verdict of not guilty by reason of insanity. Hinckley was committed to St. Elizabeth's Mental Hospital in Washington, D.C. The public outrage over the verdict caused changes across the country. In the three years after his acquittal, Congress and half of the states made it more difficult to use the insanity defense. Twelve states created a new verdict of guilty but mentally ill. And Utah did away with the defense all together.

Critical Thinking Do you agree with those states that implemented the "guilty but mentally ill" verdict? Why or why not?

SOURCE: http://www.law.umkc.edu/faculty/projects/ftrials/hinckley, http://www.pbs.org/wgbh/amex/reagan/peopleevents/pande02.html

Other jurisdictions limit the introduction of mental illness evidence to murder cases only. In these jurisdictions, a defendant can introduce evidence that would either reduce murder charges to a lesser offense or lead to an acquittal of the defendant. Many jurisdictions allow a defendant to introduce mental illness evidence that will negate the specific intent for specific intent crimes. A defendant using his condition to negate specific intent usually will not escape complete criminal punishment, because there is usually a lesser charge involving general intent for which he can be convicted.

The diminished capacity doctrine used as a true partial responsibility defense is recognized in the MPC and in only a few states, and it is limited to use as a basis for mitigating the offense from murder to manslaughter. The California Supreme Court adopted a partial responsibility defense by redefining *mens rea*. However, the defense was abolished by the state legislature and the electorate in the 1980s.[46] The MPC adopted this defense in its provision that mitigates murder to manslaughter due to "extreme mental or emotional disturbance for which there is a reasonable explanation or excuse."[47]

A person who is not entitled to a complete acquittal in these cases because he or she has not met the requirements for the insanity defense is entitled to mitigate the offense to a lesser charge because of his or her condition. As with the insanity defense, the defendant must first show that he or she was in fact suffering from a mental illness and that the illness had a direct effect on the actions of the defendant.

Mistake

Under mistake as an excuse negating moral culpability, the defendant acts without an "evil" state of mind because of his or her erroneous belief as to either the facts or the law applicable in a particular situation. While it is true that "ignorance of the law is not an excuse" in limited circumstance, people may avail themselves of a "mistake of law" defense and avoid criminal responsibility. An example would be when the law is written so imprecisely that a reasonable person cannot be certain whether his or her conduct falls within or outside of that defined in the statute, a defendant may make an inaccurate interpretation that his or her conduct is not prohibited.

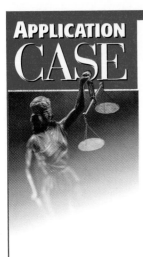

Mistake

People v. Evans

In *People v. Evans*, the 37-year-old defendant approached a female college student who was departing from a plane at a New York airport. The woman was from a small town and was fairly naïve. The defendant told the woman that he was a prominent psychologist doing a study for a magazine in which he observed the reactions of men and women in singles bars. He convinced the woman to ride with him into the city and took her to a bar where he was supposedly observing her interaction.

He then convinced the woman to come up to his apartment, which he pretended to be one of his five offices. The defendant approached the woman in his apartment, and when she resisted his advances he informed her that she had failed the test, and that in fact his advances were part of his research. He then proceeded to intimidate her by explaining that she was in a stranger's apartment and could easily be killed or raped.

The woman testified that at this point she became frightened of the man and therefore engaged in sexual activity that lasted throughout the evening. She left the next morning. The defendant, who was prosecuted for rape, argued that he was only culpable of seducing the woman into having sex, because he did not force her to do anything and therefore was not guilty of the crime.

The court found that the defendant's statements regarding his intimidation of the victim were ambiguous and could not be construed beyond a reasonable doubt as constituting force by threats. The court held that the defendant was therefore not guilty of rape, but did note that the defendant's actions were morally reprehensible and predatory.

Critical Thinking Should the defendant in this case have been convicted? Why or why not?

SOURCE: *People v. Evans*, 379 N.Y.S.2d 912 (N.Y. Sup. Ct.1975).

Entrapment

The defense of entrapment may be somewhat complicated in its variations from state to state, but the general idea is that the defendant is tricked or otherwise induced by law enforcement agents to commit an illegal act that he or she would not otherwise have committed. In a couple of recent cases, involving sentencing entrapment, federal agents insisted that the defendant "cook up" the powdered cocaine the agents were buying into crack cocaine, in order to charge the defendant with a more serious offense.[48] (For further discussion of entrapment, see Chapter 5.)

Specialized Defenses

There are some specialized defenses that apply only to certain crimes—for example, the defense of legal impossibility (a defense to attempt) and abandonment (a defense, in some states, to attempt and conspiracy; see Chapter 6). Other so-called extrinsic defenses are those that are not related to the nature of the crime or the defendant but are based on public policy concerns.

These defenses include the statute of limitations (a time period beyond which prosecution in certain types of offense cannot be pursued), diplomatic immunity (which shields certain government agents or foreign officials/dignitaries from prosecution for crimes), and the defendant's incompetence to stand trial (discussed earlier in this chapter).

Self Check

1. Explain the differences between insanity and diminished capacity.
2. Explain the elements that must be in place for entrapment to occur.

CRIMINAL LAW Online

Check your answers at cl.glencoe.com.

Defenses to Crimes

SUMMARY BY CHAPTER OBJECTIVES

1. List the three elements of self-defense.

The three elements of self-defense are:

- The necessity to use force, including the use of deadly force only "to prevent imminent and unlawful use of deadly force by the aggressor"
- The proportionality of the force to the threat
- The reasonableness of the belief that force was necessary

2. Describe when deadly force may be used in self-defense.

A non-aggressor may use deadly force if he or she reasonably believes that such force is necessary to protect against imminent use of unlawful deadly force by the aggressor.

3. Name two situations in which a first aggressor can claim self-defense.

The first is where a non-deadly aggressor is met with deadly force. The second is where an aggressor completely withdraws from any continued conflict with the other person by taking reasonable steps to notify the other person of his or her intentions, but the other person continues to instigate harm.

4. Describe the circumstances in which a person can use force to defend property.

In the defense of property from trespass or theft, the actor may use reasonable, but not deadly, force when he or she reasonably believes: 1) that his or her property is in immediate danger of such an unlawful interference and 2) that the use of such force is necessary to avoid that danger.

5. Explain when a police officer may use deadly force in effecting an arrest or preventing escape.

A police officer can use deadly force only if the officer has probable cause to believe that the suspect poses a significant threat of death or serious physical injury to the officer or others, and that such force is necessary to make the arrest or prevent escape. If feasible, a warning must be given to the suspect before deadly force is employed.

How can a first aggressor use a claim of self-defense?
Find it on page 208.

when h/she has reason to fear physical attack or harm from the aggressor

6. **List five tests for determining insanity.**

The five tests for determining insanity are:

- The *M'Naghten* (right-wrong) test
- The irresistible impulse test
- The MPC test
- The federal test
- The product test based on the *Durham* case

KEY TERMS

defense, page 200
failure of proof, page 200
true defense, page 201
burden of proof, page 201
affirmative defense, page 201
justification, page 203
excuse, page 203
self-defense, page 204
aggressor, page 205
deadly force, page 207

law enforcement defense, page 219
necessity, page 221
consent, page 226
duress, page 229
coercion, page 232
intoxication, page 233
voluntary intoxication, page 233
involuntary intoxication, page 234

insanity, page 235
incompetency, page 235
bifurcated trial, page 236
M'Naghten test, page 237
irresistible impulse test, page 238
MPC test, page 239
federal test, page 240
diminished capacity defense, page 241

QUESTIONS FOR REVIEW

1. Explain how the burden of proof defines the prosecutor's task, and how defenses shift the burden of proof to the defendant.
2. What is considered to be a reasonable defense of habitation and property? When can deadly force be used?
3. What are the MPC's three requirements in order to maintain non-deadly mechanical security devices?
4. Under what four conditions may police officers use non-deadly force?
5. Are citizen's arrests legal? If so, under what circumstances? If not, why?

6. Give some examples of cases in which the necessity defense would be valid.
7. Compare the MPC's choice of evils defense with the common law necessity defense.
8. Under what noteworthy situations does the MPC, but not the common law, allow the duress defense?
9. What is a bifurcated trial, and how is it used in a trial where the insanity defense is raised?
10. Explain the two ways in which the diminished capacity defense may be used, and give an example of each.

PROBLEM-SOLVING EXERCISES

1. **Duress Defense** A police officer has just arrested a male defendant for armed bank robbery. At the station, he agrees to speak to the officer without a lawyer present. He confesses to the offense but claims that he was under duress, stating that if he did not carry out the robbery he would be killed. The defendant goes on to say that an old enemy of his from Ecuador wrote him a letter and sent it to his home. The letter stated that the old friend desperately needed $5,000 for an operation and if the defendant did not rob a bank, he would find a way to travel to New York and kill the defendant and his entire family. Answer the following questions:
   a) What are the problems that the defendant will have with the duress defense in this case?
   b) What are some additional questions the officer should ask him to find out whether or not he has a chance at a defense?
   c) How might different circumstances in the facts affect the defendant's chances of getting acquitted by arguing duress?

2. **Voluntary Intoxication** Mark is on trial for double homicide, committed with the specific intent to kill. He maintains that extreme intoxication rendered him physically incapable of committing the murders and also accounted for his inability to recall the events on the night in question. The jury was instructed that the intoxicated condition was not a legitimate factor in considering the existence of the specific intent to kill, an element of the offenses charged. Answer the following questions:
   a) Assuming defendant is held in a common law state, can the defendant's voluntary intoxication provide either an excuse or justification for his crimes?
   b) Can the defendant even present such evidence to a jury?
   c) Does the due process clause give the defendant the right to present and have the jury consider all relevant elements to rebut the state's evidence?

3. **Insanity Defense** A local business owner has been arrested for the nonfatal shooting of a competitor, who he said taunted him and destroyed his business' reputation. The defendant is from a culture in which people who commit social wrongs make public apologies; in some cases, they commit suicide to show remorse. The defendant stated that his competitor slandered him to vendors and to customers. In addition, he refused to apologize when confronted, and only laughed at the defendant. The defendant said that he was "out of his mind" with rage when he pulled the trigger.
   a) Can the defendant use any affirmative defenses? Why or why not?
   b) Should the defendant be charged with any crime? Why or why not? What crime?

WORKPLACE APPLICATIONS

1. **Involuntary Intoxication** You are a patrol officer who has just arrested a defendant for vehicular manslaughter. He was driving his car when he drove off the road, hitting and killing a pedestrian. The defendant is clearly under the influence of some substance, although you do not know what it is. Later that evening, when the defendant sobers up, he tells the officer that he was at a party and drank only one soda the entire night. He claims that he does not drink alcohol or take drugs, and that the only possible explanation he can give is that someone drugged his soda. Answer the following questions:
   a) What steps should you take at the crime scene to secure a conviction?
   b) How should you carry on this investigation?
   c) What information do you need from the defendant to find out whether or not there is any validity to his story?

2. **Diminished Capacity** You are a juror hearing a case in which a young man is being tried for several counts of aggravated battery and one count of murder. One night, he consumed alcohol and violently attacked his co-residents in the group home in which he lives. The defense raises the diminished capacity defense for all charges, stating that his I.Q. is 83, he has Fetal Alcohol Syndrome, and he functions at the emotional level of an 11-year-old. You live in a state in which the diminished capacity defense can be used as a true partial responsibility defense. Can he use this defense? If so, in what specific way? If not, specifically explain why?

3. **Self-defense** You are a police detective investigating a homicide case in which the defendant shot and killed a man who had broken into her apartment and threatened to rape her. He was eight inches taller and 60 pounds heavier than she was, and she stated that she feared for her life.
   a) In such a case, is lethal force justified for self-defense? Why or why not?
   b) What other factors would you consider in a case such as this?

INTERNET APPLICATIONS

1. **Necessity Defense** Prison escapees have been successful in using defenses to justify their flight. To find out what defenses have worked in recent cases, visit APB Online by clicking on the link at **cl.glencoe.com**. When you are done, answer the following questions:
   a) In your opinion, do these various claimed defenses represent valid justifications or excuses for the inmates' conduct? Why or why not?
   b) Which defense seemed the most valid? Why?
   c) Which defense seemed the least valid? Why?

2. **Strategizing a Defense** To find out how defense strategies are formulated or to develop a strategy of your own, visit the Nolo.com Web site through the link at **cl.glencoe.com**. Using an example contained in this site, assume that you are an attorney for a defendant who has been charged with a series of violent crimes, and who wishes to develop an ingenuous defense. Answer the following questions:
   a) What information do you see as vital to a defense?
   b) What kind of defense will you use? Why?
   c) How will you present it?
   d) Under what circumstances regarding the jury, prosecution, and judge do you expect success? Under what circumstances do you expect to lose the case?

ETHICS ISSUES

1. **Defense of Habitation** You are a detective in charge of investigating a homicide that involves a homeowner who shot and killed an alleged burglar. During an in office interview, the homeowner gave you an oral and written statement indicating that he shot the burglar when he came at him with a knife once the homeowner discovered him in the kitchen. The homeowner states that he was afraid for his own safety and for that of his family, who were also at home during this time. You discover from the state data bank that the deceased victim has an extensive record for committing burglaries and fencing stolen property, but no record for violent crime.

   The day before the case against the homeowner is about to be presented to the grand jury with a possible recommendation for dismissal, you receive some startling information. Apparently the homeowner lied because his family was not present in the house on the night of the burglary and the deceased's fingerprints were not on the knife that he allegedly brandished in his bare hands on the night of the alleged attempted burglary. Do you bring this information to the attention of the district attorney, or let the case go to the grand jury without it? Why?

2. **Defense of Duress** A defendant, who has been charged with embezzlement, is using the affirmative defense of duress to justify her actions. She states that her boyfriend, who was also her supervisor, blackmailed her and threatened to show people pornographic photographs of her if she did not steal cash from the company safe on a regular basis. They split the money, which she spent to pay off a credit card, buy clothing, and have her car painted.

   a) Can she claim a defense of duress? Why or why not?

   b) Does it matter that she kept half of the money and spent it on nonessential items?

ENDNOTES

1 Paul H. Robinson, *Criminal Law Defenses A Systematic Analysis*, 82 Colum. L. Rev. 199, 203 (1982).

2 These examples, for the most part come from Joshua Dressler, *Understanding Criminal Law* § 16.02, at 202 (3d ed. 2001).

3 *In Re Winship*, 397 U.S. 358 (1970).

4 *Mullaney v. Wilbur*, 421 U.S. 684 (1975).

5 *Patterson v. New York*, 432 U.S. 197 (1977).

6 George P. Fletcher, Justification: Theory in 3 *Encyclopedia of Crime and Justice* 941 (S. H. Kadish ed. 1983)

7 4 William Blackstone, *Commentaries* *180.

8 See Joshua Dressler, *Understanding Criminal Law* § 17.05, at 216, n.41 (3d ed. 2001); Dressler relies upon his own works and works by George P. Fletcher in describing the reasons for distinguishing between justification and excuse defense, particularly George P. Fletcher, *Rethinking Criminal Law* 664-70, 759-69 (1978).

9 Joshua Dressler, *Understanding Criminal Law* § 17.05[B], at 217 (3d ed. 2001).

10 See authorities cited in notes 8 and 9 above.

11 George E. Dix, Justification: Self-Defense in 3 *Encyclopedia of Crime and Justice* 946-47 (S. H. Kadish ed. 1983).

12 Wayne R. Lafave & Austin W. Scott, Jr., *Criminal Law* § 5.7(e), at p. 460, n.50 (Hornbook Series 2d Student ed. 1986), citing *Rowe v. United States*, 164 U.S. 546 (1896).

13 Joshua Dressler, *Understanding Criminal Law* § 18.0[B][2], at p. 225 (3d ed. 2001).

14 See Joshua Dressler, *Understanding Criminal Law* § 18.06[B][2], at p. 241 (3d ed. 2001).

15 *Id.* n.127, citing *People v. Yaklich*, 833 P.2d 758 (Colo. Ct. App. 1991).

16 Model Penal Code § 3.05, comment 1 (1985)

17 Model Penal Code § 3.06 comment 7(c)(i) (1985).

18 Wayne R. Lafave & Austin W. Scott, Jr., *Criminal Law* § 5.9, at p. 468 (Hornbook Series 2d Student ed. 1986), citing *State v. Barr*, 39 P. 1080 (Wash. 1895).

19 Model Penal Code §3.06(5) (1985).

20 Ronald N. Boyce, Justification: Law Enforcement in 3 *Encyclopedia of Crime and Justice* 954–55 (S. H. Kadish ed. 1983).

21 Joshua Dressler, *Understanding Criminal Law* § 21.03[A], at p. 275 (3d ed. 2001).

22 4 William Blackstone, *Commentaries* *31.

23 *Id.* at § 21.03[B][2], pp. 275–76.

24 *Id.* at § 21.05[B][2], at p. 258, citing Model Penal Code § 3.07(5)(a)(ii)(A) (1985).

25 4 William Blackstone, *Commentaries* *30. See also, Glanville Williams, *Criminal Law: The General Part* § 234, at p. 733 (2d ed. 1961) ("Self-defense can be regarded as a part of necessity that has attained relatively fixed rules.").

26 This definition, though a distillation of many sources is paraphrase of language appearing in Wayne R. Lafave & Austin W. Scott, Jr., *Criminal Law* § 5.4(a) at p. 441 (Hornbook Series 2d Student ed. 1986).

27 Model Penal Code § 3.02 (1985).

28 Joshua Dressler, *Understanding Criminal Law* § 22.02, pp. 287–89, (3d ed. 2001).

29 Model Penal Code § 3.02, comment 3 (1985).

30 See Joshua Dressler, *Understanding Criminal Law* § 22.03, at p. 291 (3d ed. 2001).

31 Model Penal Code § 2.11(1) (1985).

32 *United States v. Bailey*, 444 U.S. 394, 410 (1980).

33 This example comes from Joshua Dressler, *Understanding Criminal Law* § 23.01[C], at p. 299 (3d ed. 2001).

34 Martin Lyon Levine, Excuse: Duress in 2 *Encyclopedia of Crime and Justice* 730 (S. H. Kadish ed. 1983), citing and quoting from *Regina v. Hudson*, [1971] 2 Q.B. 202 (C.A.).

35 Model Penal Code § 2.09(1) (1985).

36 Herbert Fingarette & Ann Fingarette Hasse, Excuse: Intoxication in 2 *Encyclopedia of Crime and Justice* 742 (S.H. Kadish ed. 1983).

37 *Altimus*, at p. 856, citing Model Penal Code § 2.08(5)(c) (1985).

38 *City of Minneapolis v. Altimus*, 238 N.W.2d 851, 856 (Minn. 1976), cited and quoted in *Id.* § 24.06[A], at p. 304,

39 Model Penal Code § 2.09(4) & (5) (1985).

40 Abraham S. Goldstein, Excuse: Insanity in 2 *Encyclopedia of Crime and Justice* 735 (S. H. Kadish ed. 1983).

41 *M'Naghten's Case*, 8 Eng. Rep. 718 (1843).

42 Wayne R. Lafave & Austin W. Scott, Jr., *Criminal Law* Sec. 4.2(d) at p. 320 (Hornbook Series 2nd Student ed. 1986).

43 Model Penal Code § 4.01(1) (1985).

44 18 U.S.C. § 17(a) (1988), as cited, *id.*, § 25.04[C][5], at p. 324.

45 *Durham v. United States*, 214 F.2d 862 (D.C. Cir. 1954), overruled by *United States v. Brawner*, 471 F.2d 969 (D.C. Cir. 1972).

46 Joshua Dressler, *Understanding Criminal Law* § 26.03[A][3], pp. 367–68 (3d ed. 2001).

47 Model Penal Code § 210.3(1)(b) (1985).

48 See *United States v. Walls*, 70 F.3d 1323 (D.C. Dir. 1995), and *United States v. Shepherd*, 857 F. Supp. 105 (D.D.C. 1994).

PART 3
Types of Crime

CHAPTER 8
Criminal Homicide

CHAPTER 9
Crimes Against Persons: Other Offenses

Chapter Objectives

After reading this chapter, you will be able to:

1. Distinguish between homicide and criminal homicide.
2. List the rules defining when life begins and ends for criminal homicide.
3. List the essential elements of murder.
4. Explain the felony murder rule.
5. Distinguish between first-degree and second-degree murder.
6. Describe the Model Penal Code's definition of murder.
7. Explain the difference between justification and excuse defenses.
8. Describe the differences in voluntary manslaughter, involuntary manslaughter, and murder.

Why Is Dr. Kevorkian called Dr. Death?

Chapter 8

Criminal Homicide

8.1 Homicide

homicide The killing of one human being by another human being.

criminal homicide Any act that causes the death of another with criminal intent and without lawful justification or excuse.

[handwritten: NoN-Criminal Homicide · justifiable · excusable I. Accidental II. insanity]

The law defines **homicide** as the killing of one human being by an act, procurement, or omission of another.[1] Not all killings are considered criminal and not all mandate punishment and criminal liability. A **criminal homicide**, however, is any act that causes the death of another person with criminally culpable *mens rea* and without a lawful justification or excuse. To illustrate the difference, consider the following examples of homicides:

- A death intentionally caused by a serial killer *[handwritten: ← Criminal]*
- An accidental death caused by an automobile driver striking a pedestrian on a rainy day
- A state's execution of a convicted serial killer

Of these examples, only the first could clearly be considered criminal. In the first example, the actor has a criminally culpable *mens rea* and would be criminally responsible for the killings unless he or she can provide a legal excuse. In the second example, if the driver was exercising caution while driving in the wet road conditions, his or her criminal *mens rea* is lacking with reference to the death. In the final example, in those states that have enacted a death penalty statute, the government is justified under the law to execute any defendant convicted of a capital crime.

At early common law, criminal homicide consisted of two types: murder and manslaughter. In modern times, criminal homicide is generally divided into three categories: murder, voluntary manslaughter, and involuntary manslaughter. An essential element distinguishing murder from the two types of manslaughter is **malice aforethought**, which is the *mens rea* (or mental state) of the accused at the time of the act. Within these categories, some states further distinguish and divide criminal homicide into varying levels of seriousness based on the circumstances under which the death occurred. For instance, in various states murder is divided by degrees, including first-degree and second-degree; this practice is known as *gradation of offenses*. These types of criminal homicide, as well as *mens rea* and the gradation of offenses, will be discussed in detail later in this chapter. Remember that all of the general principles of criminal liability that were discussed and analyzed in the previous chapters also apply to the offense of criminal homicide.

malice aforethought Under modern law, any one of four mental states that reveal the intent to: 1) kill; 2) inflict grievous bodily injury; 3) show extreme reckless disregard for human life; or 4) commit a felony that results in another's death.

The Beginning of Life

A basic requirement for assessing liability for criminal homicide is that the victim was alive at the time the act was committed. This requirement raises issues about when life legally begins, such as in the case of an unborn child, and when it legally ends. If, by definition, a criminal homicide requires the killing of a human being, the critical question becomes, "What constitutes a human being?"

Feticide and Criminal Abortions   Is the killing of an unborn fetus legally considered a homicide? The answer is *sometimes* and *in some places*: Some states allow prosecution for homicide for the killing of an unborn fetus (with or without the consent of the mother) under certain circumstances. Thus, the definition of a human being is not *always* limited to a child born alive.

At common law, an unborn child could not be the subject or victim of criminal homicide.[2] Neither a fetus *in utero* (within the mother's uterus, or womb) nor a stillborn child was considered alive for legal purposes. Only a person who caused the death of a child "born alive" could be guilty of criminal homicide. Under the **born-alive rule**, a child would have to be physically separated from the mother in order to be considered a human being. In other words, the fetus would have to be outside of the mother's body with the umbilical cord severed, showing clear signs of independent respiration and heartbeat. Although many states have abolished various common law rules, some states have maintained the born-alive rule by writing it into their current statutes.

born-alive rule The common law rule defining the beginning of life for purposes of criminal homicide, which states that human life begins with the birth of a live child.

Modern statutes that allow prosecution for the death of fetuses generally include four primary types of fetal homicide. These are defined by the stage of fetal development at which the death occurs. (For feticide definition by state, see Figure 8–1 on page 260.) These four stages are:

1. Viability, when the fetus is developed enough to survive outside the womb; usually about five to six months after conception
2. Quickening, or the first movement, of the fetus; usually about four to five months after conception
3. Seven to eight weeks after conception, or when an embryo (an earlier stage of pregnancy) becomes a fetus
4. Conception[3]

Fetus Viability

Currently, a few states impose criminal liability for abortions without the mother's consent that are performed any time from the moment of conception.

feticide The killing of a fetus.

With the development of modern medical technology, a medical professional can tell whether a fetus *in utero* is alive by evidence of heartbeat and blood circulation. By using ultrasound or other techniques, a medical professional can detect the presence and condition of the fetus far earlier and more accurately than ever before.

To adapt to these technological advances, many states have developed alternative legal definitions of when life begins in relation to criminal homicide. After the decision in *Keeler v. Superior Court* (see Application Case), the state of California specifically modified the wording of its penal code to include the death of fetuses as criminal homicide.[4] Under this revised statute, the purposeful killing of a fetus without the mother's consent is murder, and this criminal liability is in effect for the entire fetal stage of pregnancy. In *People v. Davis* (1994), a California court held that a fetus could be the victim of murder if it has progressed beyond the embryonic stage of seven to eight weeks.[5]

In other states, such as Iowa, killing a fetus is a criminal homicide that is called a **feticide**. It is important to understand the distinction between a legal abortion and a feticide. Legal abortion is generally protected by the mother's right to privacy until the fetus is viable,[6] so a mother's consent to such an abortion prior to viability is *not* a criminal act. In certain circumstances, state law also permits abortions after viability and with the mother's consent. These typically involve a medical emergency to protect the life of the mother. On the other hand, a feticide may be defined as an abortion performed after viability and when the mother's health is not at risk. Again, a feticide can be prosecuted as a criminal homicide, depending on the developmental stage of the fetus at the time of the act.

Criminal homicide liability may also apply in cases where the fetus is not yet viable. A Minnesota court held in *State v. Merrill* (1980) that the legislature can create liability and punish as murder the killing of a non-viable fetus.[7]

Infanticide   In cases involving the death of newborns, particularly in settings other than hospitals, officials always question whether the child was born alive during the act (or omission) that caused his or her death. In cases such as these, both prosecutors and defense attorneys must collect and examine all of the evidence related to the child's condition. Most of this evidence will be of a medical nature, and will help to establish or disestablish: 1) whether the child was born alive and thus physically separated from the mother's womb, and 2) whether the child showed independent

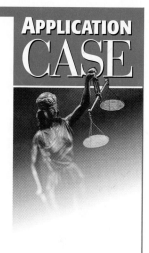

Keeler v. Superior Court

In the 1970 case of *Keeler v. Superior Court*, the Supreme Court of California held that the defendant could not be convicted of murder for the intentional killing of a fetus. Keeler physically attacked his recently divorced wife, who was pregnant by another man. During the attack, Keeler stated to his wife, "I'm going to stomp it out of you," and then proceeded to shove his knee into her abdomen. Shortly after the attack, the fetus was examined in utero, which revealed that its skull was severely fractured. The child, a five-pound girl, was delivered stillborn by Caesarian section. It was determined by medical evidence that prior to the attack, the fetus was viable; the viability of the fetus was terminated by the skull fracture and consequent cerebral hemorrhaging. The medical examiner concluded further that the skull fracture was as a result of force applied to the mother's abdomen.

Given the defendant's obvious intent to harm the fetus and given the fact that the fetus was conclusively harmed by the defendant's actions, the prosecution charged and convicted Keeler of criminal homicide. The indictment charged that Keeler did "unlawfully kill a human being." Keller appealed his conviction, claiming that since the child was stillborn, he had only caused harm to a fetus, not to a human being as required by the statute. The Supreme Court of California reversed Keeler's conviction for murder. It noted that at the time Keeler attacked his ex-wife, California law defined a "human being" in the same way as common law did, under the born-alive rule. The court reasoned that when the legislature passed the law in 1850, there was no intent to include a fetus within the meaning of human being. Therefore, in order for Keeler to be guilty for the death of the infant, under the criminal homicide statute charged, she would have had to be born alive. Although the California legislature subsequently reworded the statute to include the death of a fetus as a criminal homicide, the change in the law could not be applied retroactively to Keeler.

Feticide

Critical Thinking How do you think this case would be tried today in California? In Iowa?

SOURCE: *Keeler v. Superior Court*, 470 P.2d. 617 (Cal. 1970).

respiration and heartbeat at the time of death. Evidence of this nature is particularly important in states where killing a fetus is not considered criminal homicide. This is because *all* states consider the

FIGURE 8–1

Definition of Person by State for Purposes of Homicide

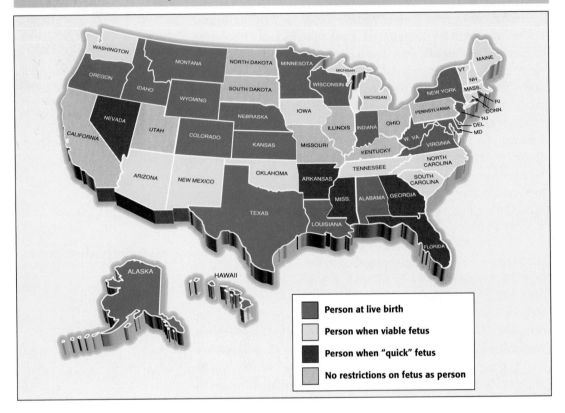

Person at live birth

Person when viable fetus

Person when "quick" fetus

No restrictions on fetus as person

killing of a newborn child, which is known as an *infanticide*, a homicide. Even in states that prosecute the illegal killing of a fetus as a criminal homicide or feticide, close examination of medical evidence to determine the victim's stage of development is still required for correct prosecution.

The End of Life

In order to consider an act a homicide, the defendant's conduct must have *caused* the death of somebody who was alive at the time of the act. It is important to determine whether death has occurred and that it occurred as the result of the defendant's conduct. For example, if the victim was already dead at the time of the defendant's conduct, the defendant cannot be prosecuted for criminal homicide with reference to the death.

At common law, a person was considered dead when there was a permanent cessation of respiration and heartbeat. However, in light of advancements in technology, including life-support systems, it has been argued that the common law definition may no longer be appropriate. If the lungs, heart, and circulatory system of a human being only function because of a machine, is that human life or mechanical life? Given this question, states have modernized their laws and developed other ways of measuring the end of life. Instead of adhering to common law standards, they have begun to define death as complete **brain death syndrome**.

brain death syndrome
The modern rule for defining death, which is characterized by absence of receptivity, absence of spontaneous movements or breathing, and absence of reflex activity.

FIGURE 8–2
Definition of Death by State

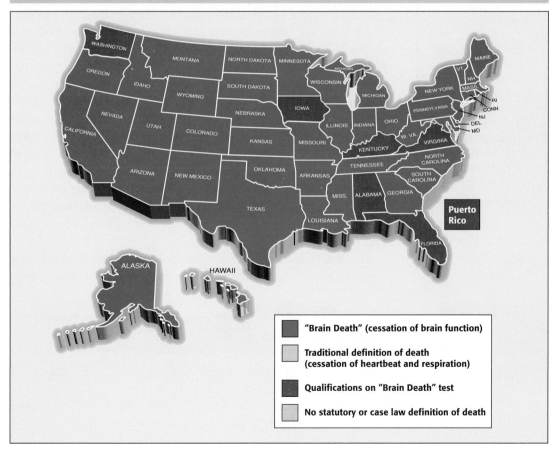

"Brain Death" (cessation of brain function)

Traditional definition of death (cessation of heartbeat and respiration)

Qualifications on "Brain Death" test

No statutory or case law definition of death

Brain death consists of:

- Absence of receptivity and unresponsiveness to externally applied stimuli and internal needs
- Absence of spontaneous movements or breathing
- Absence of reflex activity
- A flat electroencephalograph reading after a 24-hour period of observation[8]

Some states impose certain conditions on the brain death test and require a certain number of physicians or qualified persons to certify the death.

Right to Die

As courts expand individual rights to privacy and autonomy, the question arises whether an individual has the right to end his or her life. This issue has been the basis of great legal, moral, and ethical debate. At common law, suicide was a felony that was punishable by forfeiture, which is legal seizure by the government, of the deceased's property.[9] Under modern American law, neither suicide nor attempted suicide is a crime as these acts do not involve the killing of another. On the other hand, assisted suicide—the act of aiding or abetting another to commit suicide—has been made criminal by statute in 39 states, and it is still punishable as a common law crime in approximately six states.[10] While a small number of states have not affirmatively addressed the issue, Oregon is the only state that has legalized physician-assisted suicide in certain circumstances.[11] Other states have no such protection from prosecution for physicians who engage in assisted suicide of terminally ill patients.

It is important to note the distinction between euthanasia—the act or practice of painlessly putting to death persons suffering from

Myth	Fact
Under modern law, suicide is a form of criminal homicide.	Since suicide does not involve the killing of another, it does not fit the criminal homicide definition under modern law.

incurable and distressing disease as an act of mercy[12]—and physician-assisted suicide. In physician-assisted suicide, a medical doctor provides the necessary means, information, or both to enable the patient to accomplish death. The physician cannot administer the medication, or he or she can be found guilty of criminal homicide. The patient must get and use the physician's prescription, then self-administer it. In cases where the patient is too weak to self-administer, serious legal issues may arise if someone other than the physician becomes involved in the suicide attempt. If a medical assistant is aware of the nature and purpose of the medication and administers it nonetheless, he or she runs the risk of criminal prosecution because, legally, a homicide has occurred. Given that the actor specifically intends to bring about death, a murder prosecution is likely.

For example, in *People v. Cleave* (1991), the defendant was found guilty of murder in the second degree for participating in the death of a friend suffering from AIDS.[13] Similarly, in *People v. Hearn* (1998), the defendant was sentenced to one and a half to four years in prison for shooting her terminally ill husband in a murder-suicide pact.[14]

Dr. Jack Kevorkian, the well-known advocate of euthanasia who admittedly performed over 100 assisted suicides, was convicted following a televised *60 Minutes* recording of him administering a lethal injection to a terminally ill patient in Michigan. Prior to 1998, Dr. Kevorkian had been acquitted of murder several times. However, in 1996, the Michigan legislature enacted laws that affirmatively banned assisted suicide. A few days following the televised recording, Dr. Kevorkian was charged with first-degree murder. He was subsequently convicted of second-degree murder for the death of Thomas Youk, a terminally ill patient suffering from Lou Gehrig's disease. Dr. Kevorkian was sentenced to 10 to 25 years' imprisonment for causing the death and 3 to 7 years' imprisonment for delivery of a controlled substance.[15] Cases such as these reveal the ongoing controversy associated with assisted suicide, an issue that is not likely to be resolved in the near future.

FYI

Physician-Assisted Suicide

Oregon is the only state to expressly legalize physician-assisted suicide, and the Netherlands is the only country where euthanasia and physician-assisted suicide are legal.

Self Check

1. Why are the definitions of the beginning and end of life so important in criminal homicide cases?
2. If you could change one or two elements of the current definitions, what would be the legal consequences of such changes? Why?

CRIMINAL LAW *Online*

Check your answers at cl.glencoe.com.

Review the Murder

Felony Doctorant

8.2 Elements of Criminal Homicide

As noted previously, the offense of criminal homicide can be understood as consisting of five basic elements:

1. an act or omission
2. that causes the death
3. of another human being
4. with criminally culpable *mens rea*, and
5. without lawful justification or excuse.

As with all criminal offenses, all of the elements that constitute criminal homicide must be proven beyond a reasonable doubt by the prosecution. It must be proven that a person committed an act or failed to perform an act that he or she was legally required to perform, and that the accused person's act or failure to act was the legal or *proximate cause* of a death other than his or her own. There must also be proof that at the time of the killing, the accused had a criminally culpable *mens rea* regarding the death or the acts leading to the death and cannot offer a reason for the killing that the law would recognize as justifying or excusing his or her conduct. If these are not proven, the prosecution will not be able to gain a conviction.

The highest level of culpability in criminal homicide is reserved for killings where the actor specifically intends to cause death and achieves that goal through **premeditation and deliberation**. Despite this, a killing can still be charged as a criminal homicide even if the actor does *not* have the specific intent to kill. Those whose extremely reckless behavior indicates a *depraved indifference* (or a *depraved heart*) to the well-being of others, and those who commit a killing during the commission of another felony such as a rape or robbery, are traditionally also believed to deserve the most severe punishment. Because of the seriousness of these crimes, legislatures and courts have attempted to define their elements very carefully and comprehensively.

Corpus Delicti Requirement

A basic requirement for a homicide prosecution under American law is that of the ***corpus delicti***, which means the body or substance of the crime. The *corpus delicti* requirement exists for every crime, but in homicide it is especially important. It has two parts:

premeditation and deliberation The mental state that raises second-degree murder to first-degree murder in jurisdictions that classify murder into two or more levels. It implies a cold-blooded killing, in which the intent can be achieved in numerous ways.

corpus delicti The requirement of proof for any crime. In homicide cases, this usually means the corpse of the victim.

◄ **Evidence of Criminal Homicide** In the prosecution of a criminal homicide case, a defendant's testimony is not enough. Investigators must be able to find corroborating evidence that proves that a murder did take place, and that a particular person murdered a particular victim.

Why is a defendant's testimony not enough?

1. The prosecution cannot use statements of the defendant, or his or her confession alone, to prove that a crime has been committed. As unbelievable as it may sound, some people confess to crimes that they have not committed for a variety of reasons, including mental infirmity.

2. There must be proof that the victim died as a result of the accused person's criminal act. The prosecution does not have to produce a corpse to obtain a murder conviction: If no body is recovered a prosecution for murder is still possible and the fact of death can be proven circumstantially.

There are occasional exceptions to these strict requirements. The 1969 California case of *People v. Scott* was the first to hold that a murder conviction could be upheld when the evidence disclosed only the unexplained disappearance of the victim. In the *Scott* case, circumstantial evidence pointed to the defendant's husband as the perpetrator. Although the victim's body was not recovered, the U.S. Supreme Court refused to reverse Scott's murder conviction. As a result, its principle has become part of American jurisprudence.[16]

Actus Reus

As with all criminal offenses, in order to create liability for criminal homicide, the act that produces death must be voluntary. Deaths to others that occur while the actor is unconscious (for instance, suffering from a heart attack or epileptic seizure) or

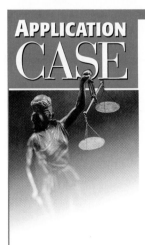
People v. Kimes and Kimes

On July 5, 1998, an 82-year-old millionaire vanished less than a month after renting an apartment in her mansion to Kenneth Kimes. Although the victim's body had not been recovered, prosecutors were successful in proving that Kenneth Kimes and his mother Sante Kimes had murdered Irene Silverman to steal her Manhattan townhouse worth $10 million. During a 15-week trial that included 130 witnesses, the prosecutors presented a trail of evidence that provided a roadmap of the detailed plans to kill the victim and dispose of her body. It was alleged that the victim had been strangled, wrapped with duct tape in a shower curtain and garbage bags, and placed in the trunk of the defendants' vehicle.

During the trial, prosecutors presented dozens of notebooks with incriminating entries of the defendants' plans and references made to the items used in the killing. Kenneth Kimes's fingerprints were recovered from tangled duct tape found in the apartment he rented from the victim. A critical piece of evidence was the deed to the mansion containing the forged signature of the victim. The forged deed transferred ownership of the mansion to a company controlled by the Kimeses.

Following their convictions of second-degree murder, fraud, and conspiracy, Kenneth Kimes, 25, was sentenced to 125 years' imprisonment. His mother Sante Kimes, 66, received 120 years. Approximately six months following his conviction, Kenneth Kimes confessed to killing Irene Silverman and to throwing her body into "a ditch at a New Jersey construction site."

Critical Thinking Suppose no evidence had been recovered but Kenneth Kimes had simply confessed to the crime upon the suspicions of a neighbor. How would the case be different? Why?

SOURCE: Barbara Ross and Alice McQuillian, *Missing Body of Evidence*, *Daily News*, May 14, 2000; Alice McQuillian, *Kimes Admits to Killing*, *Daily News*, November 16, 2000.

during a genuine case of sleepwalking would therefore be excluded unless the actor somehow caused the involuntary condition. Examples of how an actor may cause such an involuntary condition include:

- Knowingly driving while sleepy
- Knowingly drinking to the point of passing out
- Disregarding advice from doctors by driving or operating dangerous equipment knowing that he or she is subject to heart failure or epilepsy

- Driving or operating dangerous equipment while knowingly on any kind of psychoactive substance

In these cases, although the actor may not be acting voluntarily at the actual time of the victim's death, he or she can still be held liable for placing him- or herself in the position where his or her involuntary conduct might be dangerous to others.

Finally, an accused can also be held criminally liable for failure to act. In the case of criminal homicide, if the accused has a legal duty to act on behalf of another but fails to do so, and death results, the accused can be prosecuted.

Mens Rea

Determining a defendant's state of mind at the time of a killing is a critical element in criminal homicide prosecutions. Not every criminal homicide is a murder, and it is the element of *mens rea*, or state of mind, that distinguishes murder from lesser forms of criminal homicide. Consequently, it also determines the amount of potential punishment to which a defendant may be sentenced.

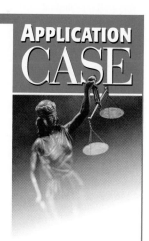

APPLICATION CASE

People v. Newton

An example of a non-volitional killing is the case of *People v. Newton*, in which the defendant Huey Newton, a reputed member of the Black Panther organization, was involved in an altercation with police officers during a traffic stop. During the altercation, the defendant was shot in the midsection, and immediately thereafter the defendant shot and killed a police office at point-blank range. The defense was successful on appeal in arguing that his loss of consciousness, as a result of being shot in the midsection, could have made his conduct involuntary. In that case, if the jury believed his act was non-volitional, he could not be held responsible for the shooting. The California Court of Appeal agreed, reversed his conviction, and held that Newton was entitled to a jury instruction on the subject of unconsciousness.

Critical Thinking Pretend you are the first investigator to have arrived at the scene, and now the defense attorney is hearing your testimony in court. What questions do you think he or she might ask of you?

SOURCE: *People v. Newton*, 8, 87 Cal. Rptr. 394 (Cal. Ct. App. 1970).

Non-Volitional Killing

Mens Rea

The *mens rea* for criminal culpability is sometimes referred to as "criminal intent." Use of the term criminal intent can be confusing when applied to criminal homicide. That is because the state of mind required for criminal culpability for homicide is not just the intent to kill. A perpetrator who has any one of five different mental states may be held guilty of criminal homicide and the specific intent to kill is just one of those states of mind. Intent to do some act may still be required for criminal homicide liability, but it can be just the intent to do the act that caused the death.

murder The killing of another *with* the mental element of malice aforethought.

manslaughter The killing of another *without* the mental element of malice aforethought.

The determination of a defendant's mental state at the time of the killing act is sometimes difficult to establish for two main reasons: The determination must be made at some later point, and state of mind can only be established by circumstantial evidence (that is, facts outside of the defendant's mind). Hence, inferences (logical deductions) must be made about the defendant's thoughts based on statements, events, or both that occurred before, during, and after the killing act.

As mentioned previously, not all forms of criminal homicide require intent to kill. Even murder, which is considered the most serious form of criminal homicide, can be committed intentionally or unintentionally. Given this fact, legislatures and courts have developed highly refined principles concerning the mental state required to prove a specific criminal homicide charge.

Generally, criminal homicides are divided into the two categories of murder and manslaughter. Under the common law definitions, **murder** is the killing of another *with* malice aforethought and **manslaughter** is the killing of another *without* malice aforethought. The specific elements of murder and manslaughter, and the various forms of malice aforethought, will be discussed later in this chapter. For now, it is important to note that under the revised common law, under which some felonies ceased to be punishable by death, the presence or absence of malice aforethought affected punishment. It became the sole determinant of whether one was guilty of murder, which remained a capital offense and thus was punishable by death, or the non-capital offense of manslaughter.

Model Penal Code   The MPC has adopted a different method of classifying criminal homicides, but still uses the important *mens rea* element. The mental states specified in the MPC are designed to be more concise and understandable than the vague common law term "malice." Under the MPC, a person is guilty of criminal homicide if he or she purposely, knowingly, recklessly, or negligently causes the death of another human being.[17] Therefore, the MPC names three categories of criminal homicide: murder, manslaughter, and negligent homicide. In addition, the MPC holds a person guilty of criminal homicide if she or he purposely caused a suicide by force, duress, or deception. The MPC also makes aiding or soliciting suicide (but not assisted suicides, which were discussed earlier) punishable as an independent second-degree felony if one's conduct causes a suicide or suicide attempt.[18]

Forensic Scientist

Description and Duties: Work in a crime laboratory, where duties usually include performing routine analytical and experimental work, participating in the search and collection of physical evidence, and preparing reports of findings. Work with evidence can include analyzing blood specimens collected from convicted offenders for DNA identification; comparing footwear, tool, and tire impressions; identifying gunshot residue from subjects and victims; and identifying and grouping blood and seminal stains.

Average Salary: Salaries range from approximately $24,000 to $60,000, depending on the level of experience.

Other Information: Education requirements include graduation from an accredited 4-year college with a major in criminalistics, biology, chemistry, biochemistry, or a related field. Some positions will substitute work experience for college education, and previous work experience is either preferred or required for all positions. In addition, most employers prefer some graduate work, such as a master's degree in criminalistics, and recommend that forensic scientists make an effort to keep updated on developments in this field.

Critical Thinking What qualities do you think a forensic scientist should possess?

SOURCE: Northeastern Association of Forensic Scientists, http://www.geocities.com/CapeCanaveral/Lab/5122/employ. html; Southern Association of Forensic Scientists, http://www. southernforensic.org/employment_opportunities.html

Inference of *Mens Rea* from Circumstantial Evidence

Rarely will an accused person admit to intentionally or purposely causing someone's death. And, even if he or she does make such a confession, that evidence alone is legally insufficient to bring about a conviction. In order to secure a homicide conviction, a prosecutor must introduce evidence of the circumstances surrounding the death. Such circumstances might include the actor's presence at the scene of the killing, conduct in relation to the killing, or statements made about the killing to the police, friends, or others.

Other forms of circumstantial evidence of *mens rea* may be more difficult for the prosecution to argue, but may certainly be just as effective as a confession. The act of pointing a gun and shooting someone dead is evidence of an intent to kill. Such a circumstance, known as the deadly weapon doctrine, allows the jury

CRIMINAL LAW Online

Homicide Trends

You can learn more about trends in criminal homicide including statistical information about victims, perpetrators, types of homicides, arrest rates, and more by visiting the Bureau of Justice Statistics Web site by clicking the link at **cl.glencoe.com**. Review statistics and descriptive information on crimes, victims, and criminal offenders. Are homicide victims most likely to be killed by someone known or unknown to them? What are the implications of the correct answer?

to conclude that the intent to kill was present. This is circumstantial evidence of a mental state through conduct. Another example is the accused stalking the victim prior to the crime, where there are witnesses who are called to testify to the accused's behavior. The mutilated photograph of the victim in the defendant's possession is also a form of circumstantial evidence of mental intent. A motive to kill is frequently used to prove intent. If the prosecution can trace back evidence of a disagreement or "bad blood" between the victim and the accused, this fact can lend itself to the inference of an intent to kill.

Although a motive (or reason) for committing the crime is not an essential legal requirement for any charge of criminal homicide, identifying a particular reason why a particular defendant would kill a particular victim is extremely useful to the prosecution, who needs to convince a jury of guilt beyond a reasonable doubt. Investigators working on homicide cases should always be on the lookout for the possibility that someone has a motive to kill the victim. Typical criminal homicide motives include revenge, jealousy, financial gain, or concealment of damaging information. Investigators should also consider the possibility that someone may have made some incriminating statement implicating him- or herself in the killings, indicating whether the killing was intentional or unintentional, or both. Confessions or partial admissions of guilt might be made to friends or family members of either the accused or the victim. Confessions are also overheard at police stations or courtrooms, or the accused may make statements to cellmates while in a jail or holding facility. It is important to investigate each of these avenues. If any of these are successful, any witness who has information about the motive or confession should be asked to give a formal (preferably written) statement and called as a witness at the trial.

Causation

As noted earlier in this chapter, in order for a defendant to be held criminally responsible for causing the death of another human being, the victim must be alive at the time of the defendant's actions. If, at the time of the defendant's actions, the victim is not yet alive or has already died, the defendant cannot be prosecuted for criminal homicide. Except in jurisdictions that consider "abuse of corpse" a crime, a defendant is not guilty of a crime if he or she inflicts injury on a victim who is already dead.

Determining death might appear to be a simple proposition. In fact, with the wide differences in the various definitions of death,

FIGURE 8-3

Elements of Criminal Homicide Crimes

Act or Actus Reus	Mental State or Mens Rea	Concurrence	Causation	Injury or Social Harm
The voluntary act or omission	Mental state of the perpetrator required by law for the individual crime	The concurrence of *actus reus* and *mens rea*	Acts setting in motion a chain of events that are the causes in fact and in law of the death of another	Death of another human being

such as brain death syndrome versus the permanent cessation of respiration and heartbeat, legal issues surrounding what constitutes death may produce varying criminal law outcomes from state to state. In the following sections, you will examine some of the different rules that are used.

Year-and-a-Day Rule   With advances in medical science, a victim might not die immediately following fatal injuries. Death may not occur until months or even years after the injury. At common law, in order to prevent a prolonged and uncertain threat of prosecution, and in order to prevent the potential for an unjust conviction, the year-and-a-day rule was created. The **year-and-a-day rule** holds that if the victim does not die within a year and a day of the time that the injury was inflicted by the defendant, the defendant cannot be convicted of being the legal cause of the victim's death. This time limit is an *absolute rule* of criminal liability. If a victim dies after this specified period of time, the defendant cannot be prosecuted for any form of criminal homicide in relation to that death. However, depending upon the circumstances under which the injuries occurred, the accused may still be charged with and convicted of attempted murder.

Although this common law rule currently remains in effect in a number of states, other states have extended the time period to three years and a day. The change has occurred for the same reason that the definition of the end of life has—advancements in medical technology. Figure 8–4 on page 272 indicates the current status of the year-and-a-day rule by state.

The "But for" Test and Multiple Causes   Questions of causation arise even if a long period of time does not pass between infliction of injury by the defendant and the victim's death. In the ordinary course of events, a defendant will be held criminally liable for a death if the other elements of criminal homicide are met *and* if

year-and-a-day rule The causation rule that requires that, in order to classify a killing as a homicide, the victim must die within a year and a day after the act causing death occurred.

FIGURE 8-4
Current Status of the Year-and-a-Day Rule by State

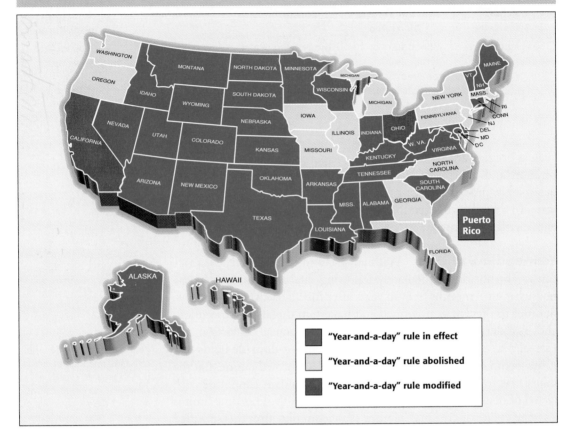

"Year-and-a-day" rule in effect

"Year-and-a-day" rule abolished

"Year-and-a-day" rule modified

without the defendant's conduct the victim would not have died at that point in time. If the defendant's conduct shortened the victim's life even by a minute, that defendant is guilty of criminal homicide. Put another way, "but for" the actions of the defendant, the victim would not be dead.

In modern times, even this seemingly simple test has become difficult to apply in cases where the defendant's conduct is not the direct cause of the victim's death. Events that occur after the defendant's conduct but before the victim's death, and which directly contribute to the death, have raised special concerns. These events, legally termed *intervening acts*, may or may not terminate the original defendant's criminal liability for the death. Over time, the courts have determined that in situations involving intervening acts, the defendant will be considered the initial actor and will not be relieved

Kibbe v. Henderson

Two defendants met the victim in a bar and decided to rob him. Although the victim was already so drunk that two bartenders refused to serve him, the defendants took him to yet another bar where they were all served drinks. The defendants then drove the victim to a rural area, stole his money, and left him on the side of an unlit highway. The victim was left without his eyeglasses and with his trousers down around his ankles. Shortly thereafter, a college student struck and killed the victim, who by that time was sitting in the middle of the road waving his arms in a drunken stupor. The surprised driver never applied his brakes before running the victim over.

Despite the defendants' objections, the Court of Appeals confirmed murder convictions against the two of them. The court found sufficient evidence to support a jury's conclusion that but for their actions that put the victim in harm's way, the victim would not have been killed. The intervening act of the student (striking the victim with his truck) was not sufficient to terminate their liability.

Foreseeable Consequences

Critical Thinking What do you think the student was charged with? What would his defense be?

SOURCE: *Kibbe v. Henderson*, 534 F.2d 493 (2d Cir. 1976).

of legal responsibility for causing the death. An exception to this rule is when the intervening act was totally unforeseeable, highly abnormal, completely independent of the defendant's actions, or any combination of these circumstances.

Through case law, courts have determined that complications such as medical malpractice and the intervening criminal acts of others are foreseeable consequences of subjecting an innocent victim to injury. These courts hold the initial perpetrator responsible for all subsequent injuries, including death, which occur to the victim at the hands of third parties. Other courts use a fairness analysis. The jury is instructed to decide whether, in light of the intervening act, it is still fair to hold the initial actor liable for the death. (See Application Case *Kibbe v. Henderson*). If an intervening actor meets the five required elements of criminal homicide, that person can also be held responsible for the death. Hence, a single death can create criminal liability for multiple perpetrators.

Causation may become a critical issue when the *actus reus* of the criminal homicide is an omission, which means that a death is caused by the defendant's failure to act. Assume, for example, that the victim's grandson, who is heir to his grandmother's fortune, purposely withholds his grandmother's medication and causes her to die of a heart attack. A critical issue for the prosecution is to prove that the victim died due to the absence of the heart medication and not of natural causes.

Another important factor is any individual characteristic of the victim that contributes to his or her death. Although some of these are the victim's choice, the defendant must accept the risk that a selected victim may have such characteristics. In the English case *Regina v. Blaue* (1975), the defendant sexually attacked a woman who was a Jehovah's Witness. During the attack, the woman was stabbed and subsequently died when she refused to accept a blood transfusion. Her refusal of the transfusion did not relieve the defendant of responsibility for criminal homicide.[19]

The "Substantial Factor" Test   On relatively rare occasions, two or more forces sufficient to cause death may occur simultaneously. In this instance, the "but for" test of causation fails. Even if one of the perpetrators had not acted, the victim would still be dead at that moment in time. To avoid fruitless finger-pointing and to insure that equally guilty people are subject to punishment, the substantial factor test was devised. An applicable example is a drive-by shooting in which three perpetrators shoot the same victim. If medical records demonstrate that bullets from all three guns struck vital organs while the victim was still alive, the law does not require that the medical examiner also determine how much blood was lost from each wound. If the medical examination establishes that each

Myth	Fact
Homicide is the least accurately and precisely measured crime.	Although many people believe that a large number of homicides go undetected or unresolved, homicide is actually the most accurately and precisely measured crime.

SOURCE: U.S. Department of Justice, Bureau of Justice Statistics.

shooter's conduct was a "substantial factor" in bringing about the victim's death, each may be held liable for causing the victim's death. As an alternative, these co-defendants may also be held liable for the death under accomplice liability, which you read about in Chapter 5.

Without Lawful Justification or Excuse

Under the law, if a killing occurs under circumstances that are legally justified, the actor is not guilty of criminal homicide. *Justification*, as a defense to a criminal homicide charge, means that the actor had a right or privilege to engage in conduct that otherwise would have been criminal. Usually, the defense of justification focuses on the circumstances of the incident, including the conduct of the accused and the victim. An example of a justifiable homicide includes a situation where a person kills someone whom he or she reasonably believes poses an imminent threat of serious physical injury or death to him- or herself, or to another individual. The rules regarding the use of force in self-defense, defense of others, and in the prevention of a crime are somewhat complex and tend to vary from state to state. In general, it is accepted that lethal force is justified in the defense of human life, but not for the purpose of protecting property only.

A person can have a legal *excuse* as a defense to a criminal homicide charge when the death occurs under circumstances that the law recognizes as lacking moral culpability, which you learned about in Chapter 4. This defense focuses on the status or condition of the defendant. For example, a person who is too young to understand the consequences of his or her actions, as well as an individual suffering from mental illness or involuntary intoxication, may be excused from liability for acts that cause death.

In most states, evidence to support the justification or excuse must be presented by the defense. If the jury accepts such evidence, the defendant will be acquitted. These complete defenses that result in acquittal should not be confused with partial or mitigating defenses, which are discussed later in this chapter. Partial or mitigating defenses only reduce murder to voluntary manslaughter, and still carry a penalty.

Self Check

1. Why is the concept of *actus reus* or voluntary action crucial in proving criminal homicide?
2. If the *actus reus* of a crime can also prove *mens rea*, have you then proven criminal homicide? Why or why not?

CRIMINAL LAW *Online*

Check your answers at cl.glencoe.com.

8.3 Types and Degrees of Criminal Homicide

At early common law, the commission of any felony was punishable by death. Since criminal homicide was a felony, degrees of criminal homicide were unnecessary. As punishment for crimes became more graduated, it became necessary to distinguish between crimes that warranted the death penalty and those that did not. Quite simply, the common law definition of criminal homicide provides that, unless there are circumstances that excuse or justify the killing, all killings with malice are murder and all killings without malice are manslaughter.

Today, many states have decided that there are many factors, primarily related to the actor's mental state, which can be used to distinguish between different levels of culpability (and the punishment deserved) in homicide cases. The various types and degrees of homicide include murder, voluntary manslaughter, and involuntary manslaughter. The distinctions among these different kinds of homicide, as well as the applicable defenses, are explained throughout the next two sections.

CRIMINAL LAW *Online*

Check your answers at cl.glencoe.com.

Self Check

How do common law and modern laws differ in regard to criminal homicide?

8.4 Murder

The crime of murder requires the five basic elements of all criminal homicides: *actus reus*, *mens rea*, causation, death of the victim, and a lack of lawful justification or excuse. Under both common law and modern American law, any killing done with the intent to kill is murder, and any killing accomplished when the actor intends to maim or seriously injure the victim is also murder, even if the accused did not intend to kill the victim. An example of this would be a killing that resulted from a bar fight when the accused attacked the victim with a broken bottle, intending to hurt him badly.

Any killing that results from extreme reckless conduct is also murder, even if the accused did not intend to kill but was aware that someone's death would be likely. As an example, a workman who throws a heavy beam from the top of a skyscraper onto the busy street below is culpable of murder if the beam strikes and kills a passing pedestrian. The fact that the workman did not specifically desire to cause anyone's death is irrelevant.

Finally, if the accused causes a death in the course of committing a felony (or, at common law, in an attempt to resist a legal arrest), the law implies that the *mens rea* for murder is present from the intent to commit the felony. This form of implied malice, which is discussed in the next section, gives rise to a prosecution for murder under the felony murder rule, which is also discussed later in this section.

Malice Aforethought

Malice aforethought, as you have already learned in this chapter, is a special legal term that refers to the *mens rea* element of murder under common law. As previously noted, this element distinguishes murder from the lesser homicides of voluntary and involuntary manslaughter. Contrary to popular belief, malice is *not* synonymous with intent. The term **malice** connotes an *abandoned and malignant heart* and is not limited to intentional killings, since even a wanton or reckless state of mind may constitute malice. Moreover, the word *aforethought* is misleading, since the mental state required for murder can be formed at the moment of the action causing death, or at least immediately beforehand. For example, a defendant can be found to have killed with malice aforethought without having planned the killing or taking any other previous action.

Malice aforethought is not a single state of mind, but five distinct states of mind that sometimes overlap. Each form existing alone is sufficient to support a murder conviction. The common

malice A state of mind connoting an "abandoned and malignant heart" that is not limited to the specific intent to kill, since even a wanton or reckless state of mind may constitute malice.

Myth	Fact
To prove malice aforethought, the accused must have either hatred or ill will toward the victim.	The accused does not have to have either hatred or ill will toward the victim. Malice connotes that the defendant has an *abandoned and malignant heart*, regardless of the victim.

law defines malice aforethought as any one of the following five mental states:

1. The specific intent to kill another human being
2. The intent to inflict grievous bodily injury or harm upon another
3. The intent to act in a manner that shows extreme reckless disregard for the value of human life
4. The intent to commit a felony that results in the death of another human being
5. The intent to resist a known lawful arrest

Causing a death with the specific intent to kill constitutes *express malice*, but malice aforethought may be express or implied. In the five states of mind listed above, only the first defines express malice; the other four define different types of implied malice. Under common law definitions and the current laws of many states, *implied malice* occurs when the actor causes death without intending to kill, but with a state of mind that is extremely dangerous to other persons.

The Felony Murder Rule

At common law, a person was guilty of murder if he or she killed another person, even accidentally, during an attempt or perpetration of a felony or while in flight from the perpetration of the felony. Since all murders and felonies were punishable by death, it was unnecessary to distinguish between intentional killings and those caused unintentionally. Since most felonies and many types of murder are no longer punishable by death under modern criminal law, modern felony murder statutes vary considerably from the original common law.

felony murder rule The rule that when the accused kills in the course of committing a felony, the *mens rea* for murder is present from the intent to commit the felony and therefore murder has been committed.

The common law **felony murder rule** originally created murder liability for all deaths that occurred as a result of the felony participants perpetrating, attempting, or fleeing the felony. Potential victims of felony murder included:

- The intended victim of the underlying felony
- Innocent bystanders
- Law enforcement officers
- Non-law enforcement persons attempting to rescue the victim
- All co-felons

Deterrence, which you learned about in Chapter 1, is the primary purpose behind the application of the felony murder rule.

Deterrence is seen as justifying the most severe punishment. In those states that divide murder into degrees, even if an individual's death was unintentional and unforeseeable, the law may authorize imposition of the death penalty for deaths resulting from the commission of certain felonies.

Whether or not the felony murder rule acts as a deterrent, it does lessen the burden on the prosecution by requiring only proof of the defendant's intent to commit the underlying felony that resulted in the death. Under this rule, the prosecution does not have the burden of proving specific intent to kill. It must only prove that the accused intended to commit a felony, such as a robbery, and that a person died as a consequence of the robbery, the attempted robbery, or flight from having attempted or committed the robbery.

The felony murder rule imposes a form of strict liability: It applies as long as there was intent to commit the felony and a death resulted.[20] The rule is applicable whether the victim is killed accidentally, negligently, or recklessly. Again, no *specific* intent to cause death is necessary.

Given the severity of the potential punishment and given that most felonies are no longer punishable by death, modern statutes have placed some limitations on the felony murder rule. For example, most states restrict the application of the rule to **inherently dangerous felonies**, also known as *forcible felonies*, which are those that pose a significant threat to human life. These felonies typically include

inherently dangerous felonies Felonies that require conduct that is inherently dangerous to human life, such as rape, arson, and armed robbery.

People v. Stamp

During a robbery, one defendant remained in the car outside, while the other two felons forcibly robbed the victims. During the robbery, the victims were forced to lie down on the floor and were ordered by the felons to stay in that position until after they left the location. A short time after the felons left, one of the victims died of a heart attack as a result of shock. All three defendants were convicted and sentenced to life imprisonment. The court of appeals reasoned that under the felony murder rule, the defendants were responsible for "all killing committed by him or his accomplices in the course of the felony."

Critical Thinking Imagine that you are the first police officer to arrive at the robbery scene. Write your report.

SOURCE: *People v. Stamp*, 2 Cal. App 3rd 203 (Cal. Ct. App. 1969).

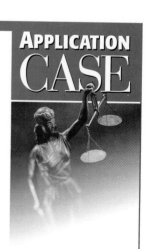

APPLICATION CASE

Felony Murder Rule

Felony Murder Rule Restrictions

Some courts have extended limitation to the felony murder rule even further, holding that the felony murder rule will only apply if the victim was innocent and killed by one of the felons.

residential burglary, arson, rape, robbery, kidnapping, and forcible sodomy. In states such as California and Pennsylvania, where murder is divided into degrees, killings that occur as a result of these enumerated (or specified) felonies often constitute first-degree murder, while killings that occur during the commission of other dangerous felonies constitute second-degree murder. In short, although felony murder liability was limited to unintentional killings under common law, in a number of modern jurisdictions the felony murder rule can be applied to both intentional and unintentional killings, even if the death was unforeseeable, unintended, or accidental.

Another major distinction between the felony murder rule at common law and its modern-day variations is the scope of vicarious liability for participating co-felons. As originally formulated, under agency theory, a person driving the getaway car for an armed bank robbery where a teller is shot and killed by one of the robbers, would have the same liability as the shooter. Even co-felons who are not present at the bank but who participated in the planning of the robbery could be held liable for the death. In addition, co-felons shot by the police during the course of the attempt, commission, or flight from the robbery could be seen as victims of felony murder and their deaths charged against the surviving felons as murder.

Several states, Pennsylvania being among the first, were troubled by the fact that a single death could be both a murder and justifiable homicide. In response, they began excluding from felony murder liability the deaths of co-felons killed by police during the felony attempt, commission, or flight. In *Commonwealth v. Redline* (1958), the court held that the felony murder rule did not apply to the death of a co-defendant who was shot by a police officer during an attempt to apprehend the defendants.[21]

In virtually all cases, courts will find felony murder liability if death was a foreseeable outcome in carrying out the felony. For example, the courts have held that an accused who intentionally sets fire to a building can be convicted of murder on the basis of felony murder if a firefighter dies while trying to put out the blaze. Similarly, courts have found felony murder liability in cases where the victim is killed as a result of being shot during an armed robbery.

Under modern law, there is much controversy surrounding the application of the felony murder rule. Some states evaluate the facts of the particular case to determine the dangerousness of the felony and apply the felony murder rule on a case-by-case basis. Common forms of inherently dangerous felonies include escape from lawful custody and sexual abuse of children. On the other hand, the Michigan Supreme Court has abolished the rule,[22] and the MPC

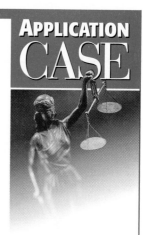
Taylor v. Superior Court

In *Taylor v. Superior Court*, the defendant was charged with first-degree murder when a botched robbery caused the death of one his accomplices. The defendant was waiting in a getaway car while two other accomplices robbed a liquor store. During the robbery, the other two accomplices acted in a reckless manner by provoking and repeatedly threatening to execute the storeowner they held at gunpoint. The storeowner shot and killed one of the robbers in self-defense. While the defendant was unaware at the time of what transpired in the liquor store, under accomplice liability, he was held liable for the natural and probable consequences of the acts of the other accomplices. The defendant was charged with first-degree murder instead of second-degree murder because the conduct of his accomplices was so extreme as to constitute aggravating circumstances.

Critical Thinking Explain why the accomplice was charged with first-degree murder.

SOURCE: *Taylor v. Superior Court*, 477 P.2d 131 (Cal. 1970)

Accomplice Liability

originally proposed its elimination. Instead, the drafters of the MPC decided to propose that the felony murder rule should not apply if the defendant can establish that he did not cause an unintentional killing with an "indifference to the value of human life."[23]

Reckless Disregard for the Value of Human Life

In the absence of felony murder liability, prosecution for murder can still be pursued on the theory of reckless indifference for the value of human life. As noted earlier, even when the defendant does not intend to kill, his or her actions may be so outrageous that they provide evidence of a strong disregard for the well-being of others. A defendant acts *recklessly* when he or she consciously disregards a substantial and unjustifiable risk that criminal harm will occur. In situations evidencing inherent danger, the charge of killing by wanton recklessness or depraved indifference is commonly pursued in place of the charge of felony murder.

Examples of conduct that the courts have recognized as wantonly reckless include drag racing on public streets and games of Russian roulette. Because these activities create a high risk of death and are not legally justifiable, defendants involved in them may face

Reckless Disregard

Reckless disregard has been referred to by various phrases, including *wanton recklessness*, *depraved indifference*, and having a *depraved heart*.

murder convictions. Like the rationale behind the felony murder rule, the high level of potential punishment is expected to deter such behaviors. Any dangerous behavior that results in an unintended death can be evaluated to see if it fits a wantonly reckless standard. The determination of whether the defendant's conduct is merely reckless, and thus liable for a conviction for involuntary manslaughter, or is wantonly reckless and liable for a murder conviction, is a question of fact for a jury.

The Division of Murder into Degrees

Many states assign first-degree and second-degree levels for the offense of murder, and others have divided the degrees even further. In both cases, they divide murder into degrees based on the level of culpability of the accused, the severity of the crime, or special circumstances under which the killing was committed. Other states follow the Model Penal Code.

Where the death penalty is allowed, first-degree murder is usually a capital offense. **Capital murder** is a charge of murder with the maximum punishment of death, which is usually only applicable to murder in the first degree. Murder in the first degree is committed under the following circumstances:

capital murder A charge of murder with the maximum punishment of death, often called murder in the first degree.

- An intentional killing that is aggravated by premeditation and deliberation
- Unintentional killing committed by poison, torture, ambush, or bomb
- A killing occurring during the commission of specifically enumerated or inherently dangerous felonies (felony murder rule)

In those states that distinguish between first and second-degree murder, second-degree murder is any form of murder committed with malice aforethought, either express or implied, which does not amount to murder in the first degree. The following statutes provide some specific examples of how to determine whether a murder is in the first degree.

Pennsylvania   In Pennsylvania, a person is guilty of criminal homicide if he or she intentionally, knowingly, recklessly, or negligently causes the death of another human being. There are three ways in which a killing can constitute murder in the first degree:

1. Willful, deliberate, and premeditated killings
2. Killings perpetrated in one of a number of specific ways, such as by means of poison or torture
3. Killings that occur during the perpetration or attempt of an enumerated felony

All other unlawful killings are considered second-degree murder.[24]

California Current California law defines murder as the unlawful killing of a human being or fetus with malice aforethought.[25] First-degree murder is any murder committed in a specific manner, such as by poisoning, lying in wait, or any other kind of willful, deliberate, and premeditated killing, or any killing committed while in the act of certain enumerated felonies.[26]

In *People v. Anderson* (1968), the California Supreme Court developed three elements that would show deliberation. The court concluded that proof of any one, or any combination, of the following elements was necessary:

1. Planning activity prior to the killing
2. Evidence of a motive

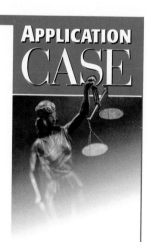

APPLICATION CASE

People v. Anderson

The defendant killed the ten-year-old daughter of his live-in girlfriend, and the victim's body was found with 60 stab wounds. There was evidence that the defendant had been drinking and may have been drunk at the time of the murder. In addition, the defendant had told conflicting stories to the victim's mother and brother about her whereabouts. The court found that the facts surrounding the murder were insufficient to support first-degree murder on the question of premeditation and deliberation, since there was no evidence of any planning activity by the defendant. In addition, there was no evidence of a motive, nor was the stabbing committed in such a way that would indicate a "preconceived design."

Critical Thinking Do you feel that this charge was appropriate, or was there evidence to support a first-degree charge? Is a preconceived design or motive necessary for such a charge? Why or why not?

SOURCE: *People v. Anderson*, 447 P.2d 942 (Cal. 1968).

First-Degree Murder

3. A manner of killing "so particular and exacting that the defendant must have intentionally killed according to a 'preconceived design.'"

In California, as in Pennsylvania, all unlawful, unjustified, and unexcused killings that are not first-degree murder are considered second-degree murder.

Elevation to First-Degree Murder One way that second-degree murder can be elevated to first-degree murder is by premeditation and deliberation, which implies the cold-blooded killer who plans and plots to end the life of another. The law simply seeks to separate the individual who kills spontaneously or impulsively from the individual who kills after deliberation or reflection. The length of time required for the accused to have thought about, and reflected on, the killing varies from state to state.

There is no particular time needed to establish premeditation and deliberation. Some courts have held that premeditation can be accomplished by a brief moment of thought and that the term does not imply any particular duration of thought or consideration.[27] Others have held that premeditation and deliberation require more than a momentary consideration. Many modern courts require a reasonable period of time of deliberation, but some require a significant period of actual reflection.

It has been suggested that jurors evaluating prior calculation and design should consider the following important factors:

- Whether the accused knew the victim before the killing
- Whether the accused and the victim were on bad terms with each other, or had a strained relationship
- Whether the accused gave careful thought and preparation to the weapon used, and to the place where the killing occurred[28]

The elevation of murder in the second degree to murder in the first degree focuses on the manner or method of killing and assesses a higher level of criminal culpability. For example, California Penal Code § 188 specifies that murder perpetrated by means of "destructive device or explosive, knowing use of ammunition designed primarily to penetrate metal or armor, poison, lying in wait, torture . . ." is murder in the first degree. In addition, as previously discussed under the felony murder rule, the laws of some states designate specific felonies (including inherently dangerous felonies) considered so likely to endanger human life, that a killing committed during the perpetration of such felony constitutes murder in the first degree. Finally, numerous states consider a killing committed under any of the following circumstances murder in the first degree:

- A killing that occurred during an attempt to escape lawful custody
- The person killed was a police officer or prison guard
- The killer was serving a life sentence in prison

Degrees of Murder under the Model Penal Code   As you know, the MPC specifies the mental states or *mens rea* of criminal conduct as purposeful, knowing, reckless, or negligent. Consistent with this classification, killing done purposely, knowingly, or with extreme recklessness is murder; killing done negligently is manslaughter, which is discussed in the next section. In addition, murder is any killing accomplished during the perpetration of typical enumerated felonies, such as robbery and rape.

The MPC does not distinguish between first-degree and second-degree murder. It simply notes that "murder is a felony of the first degree," and specifies the circumstances under which a person convicted of murder may be sentenced to death.[29]

Defenses to Murder

As previously stated, not all homicides are criminal. A killing done with a justification or excuse, which you read about earlier, releases the individual from criminal liability. Both justifications and excuses are affirmative defenses to murder, which means that the accused person who raises the defense is required to prove it. The standard of proof of a defense is usually a *preponderance of the evidence*, which is considerably lower than *beyond a reasonable doubt*. On the other hand, the prosecution has the burden of proving all of the elements of the crime beyond a reasonable doubt *and* disproving the existence of the accused person's defense.

As noted earlier in this chapter, some killings can be justified and some actions can be excused through circumstances. Although it may seem that all killings should result in criminal punishment, there are many common exceptions:

- Soldiers who kill enemies during wartime
- A warden who approves the lawful electrocution of a convicted serial killer

- A person who kills an armed assailant in self-defense, if he or she is rightfully protecting self or family

In certain instances, the existence of a mitigating factor (partial defense) may justify a reduction of the charge from murder to voluntary manslaughter, which you will read about in the following discussion.

CRIMINAL LAW Online

Check your answers at cl.glencoe.com.

Self Check

1. Why do you think provocation can be a mitigating factor in a case of voluntary manslaughter?
2. Do you think that the felony murder rule should be used in all states or rejected by them (as in Michigan)? Why or why not?

8.5 Manslaughter

Voluntary manslaughter is an intentional, unlawful killing of a human being without malice aforethought. Although early common law did not distinguish between voluntary and involuntary manslaughter, and only intentional killings were mitigated to manslaughter at common law, many states have modified the common law rule. Today, many provide for involuntary manslaughter to include killings that are unintentional.

Voluntary Manslaughter

voluntary manslaughter
An intentional, unlawful killing of a human being without malice aforethought.

At common law, there was only one form of manslaughter, which is now often referred to as voluntary manslaughter. **Voluntary manslaughter** is, by definition, killing committed *without malice aforethought.* This means that the killing would ordinarily be considered murder, but because of some mitigating factor the actor did not have the requisite state of mind for murder. The absence of malice aforethought thus makes manslaughter a lesser offense of murder. It is therefore considered one of the partial defenses, or mitigating defenses, to the charge of murder.

A person is guilty of voluntary manslaughter if the accused had intent to kill or cause great bodily harm, under any one (or any combination) of the following circumstances. Although the accused in these cases had intent to kill or cause great bodily harm, the law recognizes the three following circumstances as negating (taking away) those guilty states of mind.

Provocation   At common law, before a killing could be downgraded from murder to manslaughter, the actor must have been provoked in a way that caused him or her to act in the *heat of passion*. Many modern statutes allow similar mitigation if the defendant acts in a state of *extreme emotional distress* or disturbance. Under the common law rule, which still exists in some jurisdictions, in order to successfully make a provocation defense, the accused is required to show that at the time of the killing he or she:

- acted in the *heat of passion*
- caused by *legally sufficient provocation*
- of such a degree as would cause a person of *reasonable ordinary temperament*
- to lose normal self-control.

In addition, the accused must not have had sufficient time to cool off before engaging in the killing act.

Under any provocation claim, in order for a killing to be mitigated from murder to manslaughter, the provocation must involve a sudden and intense passion, and the defendant must have been in a state of passion when the killing occurred. The common law requirement for such **mitigation** is very strict, and it limits the situations in which a killer can claim heat of passion.

mitigation The reduction, or lessening, of a penalty or punishment imposed by law.

At common law, an accused could claim a heat of passion defense only if he or she had legally sufficient provocation. Legally sufficient provocation was limited to the following categories:

- Harmful battery
- An assault with the intent to kill or seriously injure
- Infidelity of a spouse
- Serious injury to a close relative
- A known illegal arrest

Claims of provocation that fell outside of these categories were unlikely to be successful.

It is important to note these additional provocation issues:

- In states that continue to follow the common law today, category five no longer has legal relevance.
- At common law, verbal insults alone, no matter how vile or abusive, were not considered legally sufficient provocation.
- At common law, an accused person who was not present at the provoking event could still claim a heat of passion defense. For instance, somebody who knew from a reliable

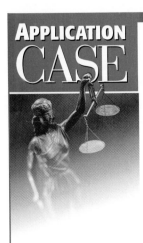

Provocation

State v. Gounagias
People v. Berry

In *State v. Gounagias*, the victim had committed sodomy on the defendant while the defendant was unconscious. For nearly a month, the victim bragged about the incident to others, and the defendant finally killed the victim because of the severe humiliation. The appellate court held that too much time had elapsed between the provocation and the killing and denied the defendant the legal right to take the provocation issue to the jury.

In contrast to *Gounagias*, the defendant in *People v. Berry*, who strangled his wife with a telephone cord after waiting 20 hours in the apartment for her to return, was still allowed to claim heat of passion. The defendant appealed his conviction of murder in the first degree. The California Supreme Court stated that there was sufficient evidence of a two-week period of provocation by the defendant's wife who had taunted him with her infidelity, possible pregnancy by the person she claimed to be in love with, and demands for a divorce. The court found that, although the defendant had waited in the apartment 20 hours, because of the long course of provocation, he did not have time to cool off and killed in an uncontrolled rage when his wife returned to the apartment and started screaming. In short, the defendant's passions were rekindled by the victim's behavior when she returned to the apartment.

Critical Thinking What do you think about the contrast between the decisions for these two cases? If you were the judge, how would you have handled each claim of provocation?

SOURCE: *State v. Gounagias*, 88 Wash. 304, 153 (1915); *People v. Berry*, 556 P.2d 777 (1976)

source that an enemy had shot his or her mother, then in turn shot and killed this enemy, could claim this defense.
• No single emotion constitutes the state of passion. Many emotions can be involved, such as fear, jealousy, severe humiliation, or some other intense emotion.

The trend in modern criminal law is to make the heat of passion less restrictive. In fact, in order to claim heat of passion as a defense, specific circumstances of provocation are no longer required. For instance, under the MPC and New York state law, killing can be downgraded to voluntary manslaughter if it was the result of extreme emotional disturbance for which there is reasonable explanation or excuse. Hence, an accused can claim a provocation defense under any set of circumstances, as long as there is a reasonable explanation or excuse for his or her emotional state at the time of the killing. A jury will ultimately weigh the reasoning of the defendant's response to the provoking event.

At common law, a heat of passion claim was assessed by an *objective test*, which showed that the defendant suffered adequate provocation before committing the act. **Adequate provocation** means that the acts or conduct of the person killed would be sufficient to cause a person of reasonable, ordinary temperament to lose self-control. Obviously, an accused person with a short temper cannot use this personal trait as part of his or her heat of passion claim. Today, the test used by New York and the MPC allows for the consideration of both objective and subjective factors when a claim of provocation is made.[30]

The accused cannot claim heat of passion if he or she had sufficient time to cool off. Again, the objective "reasonable person" standard is used to determine whether a reasonable person could have cooled off from the intense passion in the time span between the provocation and killing. Unlike the provocation element, which may be subjectively measured to assess a defendant's mental state, the cooling-off period is measured from an objective standpoint. Therefore, it does not take into account the defendant's peculiar mental state or characteristics; the time period is strictly measured by the time it would take the ordinary person to cool off. In addition, some courts have allowed a provocation claim where original passions had cooled off, but were rekindled by subsequent actions by the victim.

In summary, the courts have determined that the cooling-off period for a heat of passion defense should be evaluated on a case-by-case basis under the circumstances presented by each individual case, measured by an objective standard.

adequate provocation
When the acts or conduct of the person killed would be sufficient to cause a person of reasonable, ordinary temperament to lose self-control.

Mistaken Justification (Imperfect Self-Defense)
In some states, a private citizen who mistakenly uses deadly force can be held criminally liable for the death of the victim. For instance, Melanie is killed by Nino when Nino believed that Melanie was about to rob him. If Nino was wrong in his assessment of the facts, and it is later determined that Melanie was not justified in the use of deadly force, Nino can be held criminally liable. A few states will not hold an individual liable if his or her belief that a felony was being committed is reasonable. In contrast, if the accused unreasonably believed that deadly force was necessary in self-defense or defense of others,

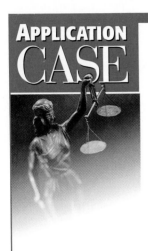
State v. Law

The defendant was convicted for mistakenly shooting and killing a police officer who he believed to be a burglar. The defendant, who was black, had had his home burglarized soon after moving into a predominately white neighborhood. Following the first break-in, the defendant purchased a shotgun. Shortly thereafter, a neighbor called the police believing that a second break-in was in progress. The police attempted to enter the house from where they believed the burglar had gained entrance. The defendant heard the sounds made by the police officers and thought that they were burglars. He shot through the closed door twice, killing one of the responding police officers. On appeal from his conviction for murder, the defendant argued that he was allowed to use deadly force to defend his home. The court disagreed and held that, even defending one's own home, the use of deadly force must be necessary under the circumstances.

Critical Thinking What type of evidence would have allowed the defendant to be found guilty of voluntary manslaughter as opposed to murder? Explain why and give examples.

SOURCE: *State v. Law*, 318 A.2d 859 (Md. 1974).

---

the accused will not be charged with murder but may still be charged with voluntary manslaughter. However the individual state statute is drafted, an **imperfect self-defense** claim such as this is sufficient to reduce murder to manslaughter. In light of the potential exposure to some criminal liability, private citizens who use deadly force to protect themselves or to prevent a crime do so at their own risk.

imperfect self-defense
A partial self-defense that reduces a murder charge to voluntary manslaughter, where the claim of self-defense fails because it is not objectively reasonable, but is honestly believed by the accused.

Diminished Mental Capacity Finally, if an accused is suffering from *diminished capacity* at the time of the killing, he or she may be entitled to have a murder charge reduced to voluntary manslaughter. Diminished capacity can be demonstrated by evidence of extreme voluntary intoxication, such as from drugs or alcohol, or it may be due to mental illness that does not rise to the level of insanity. In the case of voluntary intoxication, because the defendant is willfully in a situation where his or her conduct is harmful to others, he or she cannot completely escape criminal liability. On the other hand, since the effects of the drugs or alcohol may impede a person's ability to form the clear-minded intent to kill, the intoxication negates the higher level of intent. One type of

Montana v. Egelhoff

In *Montana v. Egelhoff*, the state prosecuted the defendant for murder, but the defendant Egelhoff claimed that he was too intoxicated to have formed the necessary mental state to be guilty of murder. Since Montana's statute prohibited a criminal defense based on voluntary intoxication, the defendant argued that he had a constitutional right to present this defense to the jury. The state court disagreed and refused his request to present a defense of intoxication to the jury. He was convicted of murder.

On appeal, the U.S. Supreme Court held that submitting the defense of voluntary intoxication to the jury is not a "fundamental principle of justice." Therefore, the Court upheld Montana's statutory ban on the basis that such evidence did not violate the U.S. Constitution. This decision by the Supreme Court substantially impacts on an accused person's ability to claim intoxication as a defense to murder, since any state can employ the same type of statutory ban as Montana's on voluntary intoxication as a defense.

Voluntary Intoxication

Critical Thinking What type of evidence and statements do you think were excluded from consideration by the Montana court?

SOURCE: *Montana v. Egelhoff*, 518 U.S. 37 (1996).

exception to this is that some courts will allow a murder conviction anyway, if the level of intoxication and the conduct accompanying it evidences a reckless disregard for life.

Involuntary Manslaughter

Some states divide manslaughter into involuntary and voluntary manslaughter. An actor is guilty of **involuntary manslaughter** if he or she causes an unintentional killing while acting in a criminally negligent or non-wantonly reckless manner, which is defined as creating a high and unreasonable risk of death or great bodily harm. Criminally negligent conduct is also referred to as *culpable negligence* or *gross negligence*. Mere negligence, or carelessness, is sufficient to create civil liability, which could result in a lawsuit, but insufficient to create criminal liability. For criminal negligence, the defendant's conduct must be so different from that of the ordinary careful person that it shows an indifference to the consequences. This is different from recklessness as a *mens rea*, which requires that the defendant must be aware of the risk of harm but nonetheless disre-

involuntary manslaughter
A criminal homicide that encompasses a killing done without intent to kill, and without such indifference to human life as to constitute implied malice, as a result of criminally negligent conduct on the part of the defendant.

gard it. Rather, a defendant can be held liable under a gross negligence *mens rea* standard even if he or she did not specifically consider the possible harm that would result from his or her conduct—if an ordinarily careful person would have, under the same circumstances. Therefore, like provocation, criminal negligence is measured against an objective standard.

There are sometimes fine lines separating criminally wantonly reckless, negligent, and merely reckless behavior. The following two examples will be helpful in distinguishing between the degrees of recklessness necessary, as this will help determine whether the charge shall be murder, manslaughter, or civil negligence:

Commonwealth v. Welansky

In *Commonwealth v. Welansky* (1944), the defendant owned a nightclub. While the defendant was hospitalized, a 16-year-old employee used a lighted match to view a burned-out lightbulb in the nightclub, but accidentally set fire to some flammable decorations. The fire spread throughout the nightclub, killing several hundred patrons. The defendant was convicted of manslaughter for allowing dangerous conditions (overcrowding,

> **Criminal Negligence Behind the Wheel**
Drivers with or without passengers have a special duty to make sure that their driving is safe to themselves and to others. *If the driver of this car is intoxicated and crashes the car, with what crime should he or she be charged? Why?*

faulty wiring, and insufficient exits) to exist in his nightclub, and his conviction was upheld on appeal.[31]

Commonwealth v. Malone   In this 1946 case, the defendant and his friend agreed to play Russian roulette. Exercising his turn at the game, the defendant shot and killed his friend. The 17-year-old defendant was convicted of murder, which was affirmed on appeal on the ground that his pulling the trigger manifested such extreme recklessness that malice may be implied. In short, drawing the line between the level of recklessness that warrants a charge of murder and that which justifies a lesser charge of manslaughter can be very difficult.[32]

An accused can also be convicted of involuntary manslaughter if an unintentional death occurs from the commission of a misdemeanor or non-forcible felony. This basis of involuntary manslaughter liability is often referred to as the *misdemeanor-manslaughter rule*. It can be thought of as a lesser form of the felony murder rule. An example of the application of this rule would be a defendant who is charged with involuntary manslaughter when he intentionally pushes the victim and the victim accidentally falls, striking his head on a hard object. The blow to his head causes his death. "But for" the push (the misdemeanor charge of simple assault), the victim would not have hit his head. Thus, the defendant is guilty of causing his death and can be charged with involuntary manslaughter under the misdemeanor-manslaughter rule. The fact that the death was not intended is legally irrelevant.

Some states have a category separate from involuntary manslaughter called **negligent homicide**. One who is guilty of negligent homicide is said to have acted in such a manner that he or she did not exercise the degree of care that an ordinary person would have exercised under the same circumstances. In addition, some states have also created a separate category of homicide termed **vehicular manslaughter**, which imposes criminal sanctions for causing a death while operating a motor vehicle in either a grossly negligent manner, or while under the influence of alcohol or other drugs.

[handwritten marginal note: not letting a person have this medium when they need it ! ▽]

negligent homicide A criminal homicide committed by a person who has neglected to exercise the degree of care that an ordinary person would have exercised under the same circumstances.

vehicular manslaughter A criminal homicide in which the perpetrator caused a death while operating a motor vehicle either grossly negligently or while under the influence of alcohol or other drugs.

Self Check

1. What elements of the *mens rea* of criminal liability apply to voluntary manslaughter? To involuntary manslaughter?
2. How do you differentiate wanton recklessness, negligence, and mere recklessness?

CRIMINAL LAW *Online*

Check your answers at **cl.glencoe.com**.

Criminal Homicide

SUMMARY BY CHAPTER OBJECTIVES

1. Distinguish between homicide and criminal homicide.

Homicide is the killing of one human being by another, and criminal homicide is the unlawful killing of one human being by another (that is, without justification or excuse). Criminal homicide has been classified into three categories: murder, voluntary manslaughter, and involuntary manslaughter. In addition, some states also have statutes for negligent homicide and vehicular manslaughter.

2. List the rules defining when life begins and ends for criminal homicide.

Common law provides that life begins with the birth of a live child. Many modern laws provide that life begins at different times of pregnancy, depending on the jurisdiction. For example, California law provides that life begins when a fetus has reached seven or eight weeks of gestation.

Common law provides that life ends with the cessation of circulatory and respiratory functions, but the modern rule is that brain death syndrome marks the end of life.

3. List the essential elements of murder.

The essential elements of murder are:

- The killing of one human being by another
- without justification or excuse

- by doing a voluntary act (or omitting an act when under a legal duty to act)
- when the act is accompanied by the mental state of malice aforethought and
- the death of the human being is caused by the act.

4. Explain the felony murder rule.

There are actually two felony murder rules:

- The first-degree felony murder rule, in those states that have graded murder. This rule provides that any act that causes death while committing an enumerated felony (such as rape, robbery, or arson) constitutes murder in the first degree, whether or not the perpetrator intended to kill.
- The common law felony murder rule, which is the second-degree felony murder rule in states that grade murder. This rule provides that any act that causes death while committing any felony, or any dangerous felony, constitutes murder whether or not the perpetrator intended to kill.

5. Distinguish between first-degree and second-degree murder.

First-degree murder is either an intentional killing that is accomplished with premeditation and deliberation, any killing perpetrated by certain means (such as poison, lying in wait, or torture), or any killing that occurs during the perpetration of certain, enumerated, highly dangerous felonies, such as arson, rape, or robbery. In states with a grading system, second-degree murder is killing with malice aforethought.

6. Describe the Model Penal Code's definition of murder.

Under the Model Penal Code, murder is a killing done purposely, knowingly, with extreme recklessness, or during the perpetration of certain enumerated felonies, such as robbery or rape. This does not cover negligent killings, which are a form of manslaughter.

7. Explain the difference between justification and excuse defenses.

Justification defenses focus on the victim's conduct. Excuse defenses focus on the status or condition of the defendant.

8. Describe the differences in voluntary manslaughter, involuntary manslaughter, and murder.

Voluntary manslaughter is the intentional killing of another without malice aforethought or killing in the heat of passion on sudden provocation. Involuntary manslaughter is an unintentional killing in which the killer has been reckless or negligent enough to be charged with criminal homicide. Murder is the killing of another with malice aforethought, and, in the case of intentional murder, that means with intent to kill.

KEY TERMS

homicide, page 256
criminal homicide, page 256
malice aforethought,
    page 256
born-alive rule, page 257
feticide, page 258
brain death syndrome,
    page 261
premeditation and deliberation, page 264
corpus delicti, page 264

murder, page 268
manslaughter, page 268
year-and-a-day rule,
    page 271
malice, page 277
felony murder rule, page 278
inherently dangerous
    felonies, page 279
capital murder, page 282
voluntary manslaughter,
    page 286

mitigation, page 287
adequate provocation,
    page 289
imperfect self-defense,
    page 290
involuntary manslaughter,
    page 291
negligent homicide, page 293
vehicular manslaughter,
    page 293

Why Is Dr. Kevorkian called Dr. Death?
Find it on page 263.

QUESTIONS FOR REVIEW

1. What is malice aforethought, and how does it distinguish murder from manslaughter?
2. What is feticide?
3. What is the difference between the common law and modern definitions of death?
4. What is the difference between express and implied malice?
5. Explain the difference between the felony murder rule and the misdemeanor-manslaughter rule.
6. What is the Model Penal Code's definition of murder?
7. What is a capital offense, and are all murders capital offenses?
8. What are the possible defenses to murder?
9. What role does negligence play in determining whether a killing is voluntary or involuntary manslaughter?
10. What are negligent homicide and vehicular manslaughter?

PROBLEM-SOLVING EXERCISES

1. **Prom Mom: Criminal Homicide?** On June 6, 1997, high school senior Melissa Drexler gave birth to a healthy baby boy in the bathroom of the catering hall of her prom. Melissa admitted that after giving birth, she removed the baby from the toilet and cut the umbilical cord, thus separating herself from the baby. She wrapped the baby in a series of garbage bags, then placed the baby into another garbage bag and tied that bag closed. This bag was thrown into a trash can and Melissa returned to the dance floor. The baby's body was later discovered by a janitor, but efforts to resuscitate him were unsuccessful. The medical examiner's autopsy revealed that there was air in one of his lungs and blood on one of his feet, indicating possible circulatory function. Answer the following questions:
   a) Should Drexler be charged with criminal homicide? Why or why not?
   b) What are some possible mitigating and aggravating circumstances in this case that could affect Drexler's conviction and sentence?
   c) What excuse, if any, could Drexler offer for this act?

2. **Evidence of a Crime?** Peter is suspected of killing David, who was found bludgeoned to death in his home. In Peter's residence, the police discover a love letter from David to Peter's girlfriend. In addition to the love letter, a floor plan of David's home was found lying next to a crowbar that was apparently used to gain entry to David's home. You are the prosecutor preparing to present the case to the grand jury. Answer the following questions:
   a) What crime or crimes will you ask them to consider in the indictment against Peter?
   b) What facts will you use to support the various charges?
   c) Will you need a confession from Peter in order to prove your case? Why or why not?

3. **School Violence** Joshua has repeatedly teased and harassed Colin at their high school. On one occasion, Joshua and some other people abducted Colin and tied him to the flag post, partially nude, for everyone to see. Colin wanted to get even, so he decided to scare Joshua. One morning before school, Colin drove his car at a high speed directly at Joshua, intending to stop just before hitting him. Colin couldn't stop in time, however, and Joshua was killed instantly.

a) Could Colin be charged with murder, voluntary manslaughter, or involuntary manslaughter? Why?

b) Suppose that this occurred in a state where Colin is still considered a minor, but can be transferred to adult court if the offense is serious enough to warrant it. Is Colin's age a mitigating factor, or should he be treated as an adult?

c) Could the length of time between the ongoing provocation and Joshua's killing be a factor in this? Why or why not?

WORKPLACE APPLICATIONS

1. **Police Investigation** You are a police officer called to investigate a reported gunshot. When you arrive at the scene, inside a residence you find a dead body with a gunshot wound to the head. It appears that the victim was shot while she was sleeping. In addition, there are several valuable items missing from the residence, such as a VCR, stereo system, and television. Write a report indicating what charges could be brought against the perpetrator. If you conclude that the perpetrator could be charged with first-degree murder, explain the primary basis on such a charge could be brought.

2. **Decisive Factors** In the preceding exercise, assume the perpetrator is apprehended. Further, assume that the victim and the perpetrator were married and living together before the victim had a restraining order issued against the perpetrator. The perpetrator, while in custody, tells an officer that if he couldn't have the victim, then no one else would. Under these facts, would your conclusion change from the previous example? If so, explain why and state what charges you would choose to bring against this perpetrator.

INTERNET APPLICATIONS

1. **Homicide on the Internet** Go to cl.glencoe.com for links to the Bureau of Justice Statistics and *The Sourcebook of Criminal Justice Statistics* online. Locate tables that present data on homicides in the United States. Are there different ways of measuring homicide? Explain.

2. **American Bar Association** Go to cl.glencoe.com for a link to the American Bar Association. Research victim rights in your particular state. What are the rights of victims of violent crimes? Are any important rights missing?

ETHICS ISSUES

1. **Infanticide, Feticide, or Neither?** You are the prosecutor in *People v. Grossberg and Petersen*. In the case, an 18-year-old female gave birth to a full-term baby boy in a Delaware motel room. The 18-year-old father of the child was also present at the time the baby was born. Sometime after the baby was delivered, it was wrapped in a garbage bag and thrown into a dumpster behind the motel. The baby's body was not discovered until more than 12 hours later. Medical examination revealed that the umbilical cord had been severed prior to the baby being placed in the dumpster. The baby's head showed signs of two skull fractures and some brain injury. The medical examiner concluded that the baby had died from being shaken, from multiple skull fractures from blunt trauma, or perhaps from both. She also noted that the baby might have sustained the injuries postmortem (after death) from the force of being thrown into the dumpster; also, the brain abnormalities might have developed while the child was still in the uterus. Answer the following questions:

   a) Must you consider all of the medical examiner's findings in determining whether to prosecute the teen parents for criminal homicide? Why or why not?

   b) What is the minimum amount of information that the medical examiner must find to determine criminal homicide? What else can she find in addition to this?

   c) As a matter of professional ethics, are you obligated to share all of the medical examiner's statements with the defense?

ENDNOTES

1 *Black's Law Dictionary*, 661 (5th ed.1990).

2 Wayne R. LaFave, *Modern Criminal Law*, 2ed (West,1988).

3 See Bicka A. Barlow, *Severe Penalties for the Destruction of "Potential Life"—Cruel and Unusual Punishment?*, 29 U.S.F.L. Rev. 463 (1995).

4 Cal. Penal Code §187 (a) (West 1988).

5 *People v. Davis*, 872 P.2d 591 (Cal. 1994).

6 *Roe v. Wade*, 410 U.S. 113 (1973).

7 *State v. Merrill*, 450 N.W.2d 318 (Minn. 1990).

8 *Black's Law Dictionary* (6th ed. 1996), citing *Commonwealth v. Golston*, 373 Mass. 249, 368 N. E. 2d 744 (1977).

9 David A. Pratt, *Too Many Physicians: Physician-Assisted Suicide after Glucksberg/Quill*, 9 Alb.L.J.Sci & Tech. 161.

10 *Ibid.*

11 Oregon Rev. Stat 127.805 (1997).

12 *Black's Law Dictionary*, 497 (5th ed. 1990).

13 *People v. Cleave*, 280 Cal. Rptr. 146, 151 (Cal. Ct. App. 1991).

14 *People v. Hearn*, 248 A.D.2d 889, 669 N.Y.S.2d 984 (1998).

15 Dirk Johnson, "Kevorkian Sentenced to 10 to 25 Years in Prison," *N.Y. Times*, Apr.14, 1999 at A1.

16 *People v. Scott*, 176 Cal. App.2d 458, 1 Cal. Rptr. 600 (1959).

17 ALI, Model Penal Code §§ 210 (American Law Institute 1985).

18 ALI, Model Penal Code §§ 210.5(2) (American Law Institute 1985).

19 *Regina v. Blaue*, 1 W.L.R. 1411, 3 All E.R. 446 (C.A.) (Ct. of App. England, 1975).

20 Rudolph J. Gerber, *The Felony Murder Rule: Conundrum Without Punishment*, 31 Ariz. St. L.J. 763, 770.

21 *Commonwealth v. Redline*, 137 A.2d 472 (Pa. 1958).

22 *People v. Aaron*, 299 N.W.2d 304 (Mich.1980).

23 ALI, Model Penal Code §§ 210.(1)(b) (American Law Institute 1985).

24 Pennsylvania Consolidated Statutes, Title 18, Section 2502 (1996).

25 Cal. Penal Code §187 (a) (West 1988).

26 Cal. Penal Code § 188 (1996).

27 *United States v. Brown*, 518 F.2d 821 (1975).

28 Lafave, note 2, at 271.

29 MPC, (sec. 210.2(2)) and sec. 210.6.

30 See MPC section 210.3 (1)(b).

31 *Commonwealth v. Welansky*, 316 Mass. 383, 55 N.E. 2d 902 (1944).

32 *Commonwealth v. Malone*, 354 Pa. 180, 47 A.2d 445 (1946).

Chapter Objectives

After reading this chapter, you will be able to:

1. State the elements of battery.
2. List the elements of assault.
3. State the elements of mayhem.
4. State the elements of rape, and understand the difference between rape and statutory rape.
5. Describe Megan's Law.
6. Define child abuse.
7. Distinguish between the elements of false imprisonment and kidnapping.

Where and how did Megan's Law originate?

Chapter 9

Crimes Against Persons: Other Offenses

intent to comit a battery
attempt to

battery : common law

9.1 Physical Crimes

This section will cover the crimes of assault, battery, and mayhem. Often, the terms assault and battery are used in conjunction with one another. Both were common law misdemeanors, and both exist today as statutory crimes in every American jurisdiction. Legally, however, the terms apply to separate and distinct crimes, distinguishable by the presence or absence of physical injury or offensive physical contact. The common law felony of mayhem is less well known than assault and battery, perhaps because it applies to specialized injuries. It exists in fewer jurisdictions than the other two crimes— many jurisdictions do not carry it in their statutes and prefer to charge defendants with aggravated assault instead.

Battery

> **battery** A misdemeanor consisting of the unlawful application of force that actually and intentionally causes the touching of another person against his or her will.

Battery is the unlawful application of force that actually and intentionally causes the touching of another person against his or her will. "Touching," in this context, refers to any physical contact that either directly or indirectly causes bodily injury or is offensive to the victim. Assault is an attempted battery and a battery is a completed assault. This close relationship explains why the terms are often used together. Thus, the elements of battery are:

- The actor's conduct of touching or applying force to the victim
- The actor's mental state (either intent to injure, with criminal negligence, or while committing an unlawful act, in some jurisdictions)
- The harm done to the victim (bodily injury or offensive touching)

Direct application of force is clearly battery: For example, shoving another person would be enough to constitute battery. The minimum conduct required for a battery conviction is simply the direct touching or the indirect application of force upon another person. The defendant may set in motion a force that indirectly causes bodily injury or is offensive to the victim. For example, if the defendant places some kind of poison in the victim's drink, resulting in injury to the victim, the defendant is guilty of battery. The act of placing poison in the victim's drink resulted in injury. The fact that no actual contact occurred between the defendant and the victim is immaterial.

A defendant will be culpable for battery if he or she possessed the intent to inflict injury by touching the victim. However, the accused does not have to possess a specific intent to inflict bodily injury or an offensive touching in order to be guilty of battery. In many jurisdictions, battery only requires that the defendant act with criminal negligence; in some, the defendant will be guilty of battery if he or she commits an unlawful act while engaged in the conduct, regardless of mental state. The defendant only needs to know that his or her actions could cause the application of force upon another; therefore, the defendant need not batter the person he or she intended to batter in order to be guilty. For example, if a man swung his arm at an enemy with the intention of striking him, but accidentally punched an innocent bystander, the accused could still be guilty of battery.

If the defendant's culpability for battery is based on criminal negligence, the negligence required must be distinguished from negligence in non-criminal settings. Criminal negligence in general, which also applies to the case of battery, requires that the actor create an unreasonable and high risk of harm to others by his or her actions.

In order for a defendant to be guilty of battery, not only must he or she intend to cause harmful or offensive touching, he or she must actually cause such a result to the victim. The result could be something obvious, such as broken bones, stab wounds, or a bullet wound. It could also be pain without physical signs of a wounding; spitting in another's face; or touching a member of the opposite sex in an inappropriate manner, such as touching a woman on her breast or kissing her without her consent. The conduct does not have to cause pain in order for a person to be guilty of battery. Currently, however, most jurisdictions follow the MPC guidelines, which limit battery offenses to physical injuries. Unwanted sexual touching is usually addressed in other statutes covering sexual offenses.[1]

Aggravated battery is a felony in many states. This crime is usually reserved for conduct accompanied by intent to kill or rape. Therefore, it is usually a specific intent crime and carries greater penalties. Even in states where it is not a felony, it is classified in a different category of misdemeanors than simple battery is.

aggravated battery A battery accompanied by an intent to kill or rape—thus, usually a specific intent crime. A felony in many states.

Assault

Assault has two definitions: 1) attempted battery or 2) the intentional frightening of another person. Any willful attempt or threat to inflict injury upon the person of another, when coupled with an apparent present ability to do so, or any intentional display of force that would give the victim reason to be fearful of immediate bodily harm constitutes an assault.

The elements of the crime of assault are: An attempt to batter, or conduct that is threatening, menacing, or otherwise designed to frighten the victim intentionally, with the intent to commit a battery upon the victim or to frighten the victim and that in fact does frighten the victim and would reasonably cause the average person to fear physical injury.

The first type of assault is *attempted battery*, in which the actor actually intends to commit a battery. Attempted battery is committed by any gesture or movement that threatens future physical harm to a victim. In most jurisdictions, assault can also be committed by *intentional frightening*. Any conduct that is designed to frighten another will suffice—a menacing movement or pointing a gun, for example. Words alone are usually not enough to constitute the required conduct to sustain the charge; however, in some situations words may meet the requirement. Usually, the *actus reus* is satisfied when a defendant makes a movement with his or her body or with a weapon that indicates future harm. In some states an assault committed by attempted battery must be accompanied by the actor's present ability to commit a battery.[2]

An assault may be committed without actually touching, striking, or doing bodily harm to the person of another. Nonetheless, an essential element of the crime in most states, which must be proven by the prosecution, is that the defendant intended to use force on the victim or intended to put the victim in fear of actual harm. A negligent but inadvertent imposition of fear—that is, when the defendant's behavior unintentionally frightens a victim—usually will not suffice for a charge of assault. If the defendant is wildly flailing his or her arms and nearly strikes the victim, but does nothing to indicate that he or she intends to cause harm to the victim, the defendant is not guilty of assault. His or her actions, although perhaps reckless, were not intended to cause harm to another. Therefore, an assault charge would not be warranted.

The second type of assault is the intentional frightening of another person. A victim of the threat must reasonably fear immediate personal harm, or must view the defendant's actions as a threat that could cause such harm. If the defendant intended to put the victim in fear, and the victim experienced an apprehension of immediate harm, most jurisdictions would hold the defendant culpable for assault. At the time of the act, the victim must fear that a physical injury will result from the defendant's actions.

On the other hand, where intent is present, the defendant's movement does not need to cause an actual harm to the victim in order for him or her to be criminally culpable of assault. The defendant only needs to take some action that will bring him or her reasonably close to successfully completing the injury or harm, such as making a fist and waving an arm while walking toward a victim. From the victim's perspective, it is likely that the defendant will take a punch at him; therefore, this could constitute assault. This victim has actually been assaulted because there was a physical act by the defendant, which was a movement toward the victim likely to result in physical harm. In addition, all other elements of the crime were present.

Although mere words are usually not enough to charge a person with assault, words accompanied by some movement may be sufficient. If a defendant approaches a victim from behind and whispers in his ear, "Don't turn around or I'll shoot you," and the victim then feels a gun-like object shoved into his back, the victim has reason to believe that the defendant does have a gun, or some other deadly weapon, and can fulfill his threat. It is likely that this defendant would be charged with the crime of assault.

A prosecutor must prove that the victim was aware of the assault and was placed in fear or apprehension of immediate danger. This must be determined by sight or by another sense, such as hearing or touch. If a defendant approached a blind man from behind and pointed a gun at him without saying anything, the defendant would not be guilty of assault because the victim would be unaware—and therefore not fearful—of any intent on the part of the defendant to harm him.

Another form of assault is **conditional assault**, where the actor threatens harm only under certain conditions, such as the failure of the victim to act a certain way demanded by the actor. If a defendant threatens to shoot the victim unless the victim leaves, this would be a conditional assault. In most instances, the defendant will be guilty of assault, even though the victim complied with the condition. Still another form is **aggravated assault**, which like aggravated battery is a felony in most

Assault

A person commits an assault when he or she threatens harm upon a condition. If a man points a gun at someone and says, "I will shoot you if you don't raise your hands," the actor is guilty of assault, even though the victim complies and the condition is satisfied.

On the other hand, if the same actor says, "If it weren't Christmas, I would shoot you," he or she is using language that disclaims a threat and probably would not be guilty of assault.

SOURCE: *See* Wayne R. LaFave & Austin W. Scott, Jr., *Criminal Law* § 7.16(c), at p. 695, nn. 34 & 35 (Hornbook Series 2d Student ed. 1986).

conditional assault An assault where the actor threatens harm only under certain conditions, such as the failure of the victim to act a certain way demanded by the actor.

aggravated assault Assault with intent to kill, rob, or rape, and assaults with specified deadly weapons. A felony in most states.

jurisdictions. Assault with intent to kill, rob, or rape, and assaults with specified deadly weapons qualify as aggravated assault under most of these laws.

Mayhem

mayhem A felony defined as "violently depriving another of the use of such of his members, as may render him the less able in fighting, either to defend himself, or to annoy his adversary."

Mayhem is a common law felony that is defined by historical legal commentator William Blackstone as "violently depriving another of the use of such of his members, as may render him the less able in fighting, either to defend himself, or to annoy his adversary."[3] This crime was created to deter acts that tended to make one of the king's subjects less able to render the king "aid and assistance."

The law of mayhem in the United States developed to protect the physical integrity of the person. The injuries prohibited by the crime of mayhem can be characterized as "dismemberment, disablement, or disfigurement."[4] Although state laws vary, those that designate the specific crime of mayhem generally define it by types of prohibited injury. Uniformly, state laws on mayhem prohibit the infliction of a permanent injury upon a victim that disables a limb or an eye. Some states also define mayhem as an injury that causes "grievous bodily harm," and a number include specific types of disfigurement within a prohibited injury. The most prevalent of these is the slitting of an ear or nose; scarring may also be included.

The elements of the crime of mayhem are subject to variation, even among those states that still have it as a separate crime. Still, they may be stated generally as the infliction of a specified injury constituting dismemberment, disablement, or disfigurement; and the intent to maim or disfigure. Though it is possible for an actor to be held culpable for mayhem when the injury was inflicted by accident or with negligence, in the absence of specific statutory provision, it is not likely.

The *actus reus* of mayhem is that the defendant caused the victim bodily injury that permanently dismembered, disabled, or disfigured the victim:

- Dismemberment means the severing of a body part.
- Disablement requires the loss of use of a major part of the body, such as an arm, leg, eye, or testicle, although the part need not be actually removed. Disablement must cause permanent injury to the victim to constitute mayhem. If a defendant jams his finger in the victim's eye, causing the victim to be permanently blind in that eye, the victim's eye is disabled.
- Disfigurement requires an alteration of the victim's face or body that changes its normal appearance. Like disablement, disfigurement must cause permanent injury to the victim to constitute mayhem. If the defendant slashes a victim's lip and the victim's lip is unable to be restored to what it was prior to the incident, the victim's lip has been permanently disfigured. If, however, the lip is stitched and heals, leaving no mark, the defendant most likely will not be convicted of mayhem but will be charged with another offense, such as battery or attempted murder.

The *mens rea* for mayhem depends on the particular statute in a jurisdiction. Some states only require that the defendant intended to commit harm, and this intent resulted in the maiming. Others require that the defendant specifically intended to cause the particular type of disfigurement or disablement that he or she did in fact cause. Should a defendant intend to maim in one way and cause a different maiming through his actions, however, he or she will still be culpable of this crime. If a defendant jabs a knife at a victim attempting to slash his face, but instead gouges his eye, he or she will still be guilty of mayhem.

Defining Mayhem

In its earlier form, the crime of mayhem prohibited an actor from "cutting off, or disabling, or weakening a man's hand or finger, or striking out his eye or foretooth, or depriving him of those parts" because those acts would tend to abate his courage. In contrast, such acts as cutting off an ear, or nose, or any other cutting that caused scarring would not be mayhem because they only disfigured and did not weaken.

SOURCE: William Blackstone, *Commentaries*, p. 205–206.

FIGURE 9–1

States That Consider Mayhem a Crime

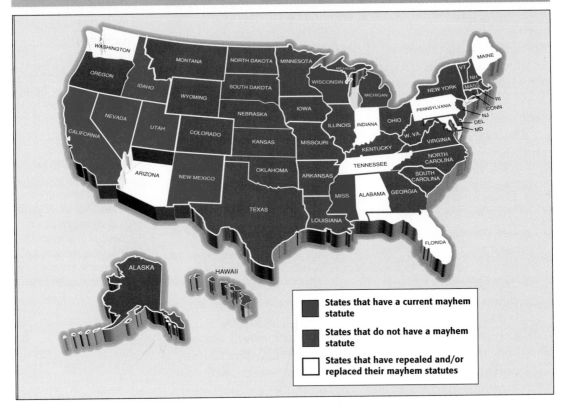

States that have a current mayhem statute

States that do not have a mayhem statute

States that have repealed and/or replaced their mayhem statutes

Because of this crime's origins, it has outlived its purpose and is being gradually eliminated from American criminal law. Today many jurisdictions, as well as the MPC, have eliminated mayhem and treat it as aggravated battery. The trend to eliminate mayhem as a separate crime continues. At present, there are only a few states that treat the crime separately. (See Figure 9–1.)

CRIMINAL LAW *Online*

Check your answers at cl.glencoe.com.

Self Check

1. What is the difference between assault and battery, and why are the two sometimes confused with each other?
2. Describe the trend to eliminate mayhem.

People v. Keenan

In *People v. Keenan* (1991), the defendant entered the apartment of a woman at night. He tied her up and burned both of her breasts with a lit cigarette, leaving permanent scars. He also raped and sodomized her, stole property from her home, then left the apartment. In addition to other charges, the defendant was convicted of mayhem for permanently scarring the victim's breasts with the lit cigarette. On appeal, he challenged the mayhem conviction by arguing that mayhem is only an appropriate charge for the most disfiguring or disabling attacks, and by claiming that the harm to the victim was minor.

The appellate court upheld the mayhem conviction. It concluded that the disfigurement of the victim's breasts was within the definition of the mayhem statute, and although the scars could not be seen by others, the impact they had on the victim was as serious as if the scars had been on her face.

Critical Thinking Do you believe that a person is disfigured only if it can be publicly seen? Explain.

SOURCE: *People v. Keenan*, 227 Cal.App.3d 26 (Cal. Ct. App. 1991).

What Constitutes Mayhem?

9.2 Sex Crimes

This section will cover four sexual offenses: rape, statutory rape, spousal rape, and child molestation. Child molestation will also receive some coverage in the following section, under the section covering child abuse. You will also learn about effective ways in which you, as a criminal justice professional, can deal with victims of the highly personal crime of rape.

Rape

Rape is a common law felony that is defined as "the carnal knowledge [i.e., sexual intercourse] of a woman forcibly and against her will."[5] Sexual penetration by the penis of the vulva is necessary to constitute rape. Sexual emission, or ejaculation, is neither sufficient nor necessary. Therefore, a man who ejaculates

rape A felony defined as "the carnal knowledge of a woman forcibly and against her will."

without penetration has not committed rape, but a man who penetrates someone without ejaculation has.

Today the crime of rape, which is one part of the broader criminal conduct classified as sexual assault, continues to be a widespread problem. According to the 1999 National Crime Victimization Survey (NCVS), the total number of rapes, attempted rapes, and sexual assaults increased to 383,000 last year, up 50,000 from 1998's 333,000 total attacks. Overall totals increased by 13.3%.[6]

In general, rape is sexual intercourse by a male defendant with a female victim that is committed in one of these ways:

- Forcibly
- By means of some specific forms of deception
- While the victim was asleep or unconscious
- Under circumstances in which the victim was not competent to give consent (e.g., under the influence of drugs, mental disability, or being too young)

These definitions do not include sexual offenses committed by a man against his wife. A new category of statutes covers *spousal rape*, which is discussed later in this chapter.

The most prevalent form of rape is forcible rape. Although the law is changing in this area, forcible rape traditionally requires proof that the victim did not consent *and* "that the sexual act was 'by force' or 'against her will.'"[7] The problem with this requirement is that it appears self-contradictory: When force is used, consent is typically not an issue for two reasons:

1. Any consent could be coerced through the use of such force.
2. If the defendant had to use force to carry out the rape, the victim was obviously not a willing or consensual participant.

Traditionally, the victim must physically "resist to the utmost," "resist until exhausted or overpowered," or "resist the attack in every way possible." She was expected to continue such resistance until she was overcome by force, insensible through fright, or ceased resistance out of exhaustion or fear of death or great bodily harm."[8] Alternately, she must have been prevented from physically resisting by threats for her safety.

When a victim does not resist out of fear that she will be physically harmed, the trier of fact will look at both the victim's belief that she faces harm as well as the defendant's conduct in determining whether the defendant can be convicted of forcible rape.[9] For example, suppose that Raelene is five feet tall and weighs 105 pounds. As she is walking alone at night, a six-foot-tall man weighing 250 pounds grabs her and tells her that if she does not allow him to have sexual intercourse with her, he will kill her. Raelene does not see a weapon, nor does the perpetrator tell her he has a weapon, but she chooses not to fight and allows the perpetrator to have sexual intercourse with her. Under these circumstances, the defendant would still be guilty of forcible rape. It is reasonable for a small woman who is alone at night to fear harm from a large man who grabs her. Raelene most likely felt that if she didn't allow the sex to occur, the perpetrator would be able to kill her even without a weapon. Therefore, forcible rape has occurred.

Rapes that are the product of non-consent, yet do not occur because of force, threat, or bodily injury, are still punishable as rape but receive a lesser penalty. In addition, some jurisdictions have expanded their forcible rape statutes to include acts where force is inferred through the circumstances, or where a rape has occurred solely because the victim did not give permission. For example, the New Jersey Supreme Court has held "that a person is guilty of forcible rape if he commits an act of sexual penetration of another person in the absence of affirmative and freely given permission, either express or implied, for the specific act of penetration. Without such permission, any force used, even the force inherent in the sexual act itself, justifies a forcible rape prosecution."[10]

Rape is a general-intent offense. The defendant does not have to have the specific intent to have non-consensual sex in order to be guilty of rape, but is guilty "if he possessed a morally blameworthy state of mind regarding the victim's lack of consent."[11] This also means that a defendant is not guilty of rape if he had a reasonable and genuine belief that the victim consented. A reasonable and genuine belief of consent is hard to argue where the defendant used some type of force to achieve his goal, but it does arise in date-rape cases, especially where the victim and the defendant had prior sexual relations.

Rape and the Law Traditionally, rape statutes have only addressed the scenario where a male is the perpetrator and the female is the victim. That is why the language "against her will" still exists in many rape statutes. Recently, some states have expanded their rape statutes to provide for same-sex rape, as well as rape by a female against a male. Statutes involving nonconsensual sex against

CRIMINAL LAW Online

Rape Awareness at RAINN

Visit the Web site for RAINN (Rape, Abuse, and Incest National Network) through the link provided at **cl.glencoe.com**. Read their home page and the sections entitled "Counseling Centers" and "What Should I Do?" How does this information and the 800 number help victims? How could criminal justice and medical professionals benefit from such information?

FIGURE 9–2

Wyoming Statute on Sexual Assault

6-2-302. Sexual assault in the first degree.

(a)   Any actor who inflicts sexual intrusion on a victim commits a sexual assault in the first degree if:

   (i)   The actor causes submission of the victim through the actual application, reasonably calculated to cause submission of the victim, of physical force or forcible confinement;

   (ii)   The actor causes submission of the victim by threat of death, serious bodily injury, extreme physical pain or kidnapping to be inflicted on anyone and the victim reasonably believes that the actor has the present ability to execute these threats;

   (iii)   The victim is physically helpless, and the actor knows or reasonably should know that the victim is physically helpless and that the victim has not consented; or

   (iv)   The actor knows or reasonably should know that the victim through a mental illness, mental deficiency or developmental disability is incapable of appraising the nature of the victim's conduct.

SOURCE: http://legisweb.state.wy.us/statutes/titles/title06/c02a03.htm

a grown woman or a child are sometimes divided into categories depending on the circumstances of the case. For example, a man who rapes while holding a loaded gun to a woman's head may be punished more severely than a man who rapes without a weapon.

Because the men who created rape laws feared that women could falsely claim rape too easily, the common law crime was predicated on the fact that rape was a capital offense and an inordinate burden of proof was placed upon the victim. For the successful prosecution of rape, the common law required proof that the victim made fresh complaint, was of chaste character, and could provide corroboration, among other things. For centuries, the prosecution of a rape case involved grave difficulties for the victim, who often was on trial as much or more so than the accused. This was because the victim, while on the witness stand, was subject to intrusive personal interrogations because of her reputation, personal characteristics, and frequently her race and economic class. As a result, women today still fear reporting rape. Unfortunately, rape is still the most underreported violent crime. 28.3 percent of rape victims reported the crime to police in 1999, compared to 44 percent of victims of all violent crimes.[12]

Recently, to deal with the problems faced by sexual assault victims, including their low report rates, legislators enacted *rape-shield statutes* that offered rape victims protection of their privacy. These statutes deny a defendant the opportunity to cross-examine the victim with respect to her sexual history and general moral character. One exception is that a victim's past sexual history *with the defendant* may be allowed into evidence, but only to the extent it may relate to the defense of consent.

Statutory Rape At common law, sexual intercourse between a man and a "woman child under the age of ten years" was considered rape regardless of whether consent was given. Today, the age of the victim has generally been raised to 17 and under, with some variation

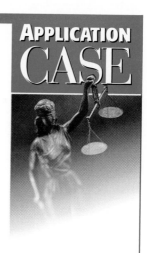

statutory rape A form of rape involving sexual intercourse between an adult and a child, usually between the ages of 13 and 17.

from state-to-state, and is known as **statutory rape**. Many states divide statutory rape offenses into two categories, and statutory rape involving a very young girl usually carries a stiffer penalty than cases involving girls in their late teens. (See Figure 9–3 to see the age of consent in every state.)

Spousal Rape   The common law did not consider sexual intercourse forced upon a wife by her husband to be rape. Recently, laws have been passed prohibiting **spousal rape**, which can be defined as "non-consensual sexual acts between a woman and her husband, former husband or long term partner, and . . . any unwanted, humiliating and painful sexual activity."[13] Lack of consent can be determined by the use of intimidation or threats. Spousal rape is a serious problem: Approximately 28 percent of all rape victims are raped by husbands or boyfriends.[14]

spousal rape Nonconsensual sex between a woman and her husband, ex-husband, or partner.

Currently, all 50 states and federal territories have passed laws that make spousal rape a crime. In most places, it is a crime only when accompanied by force. As another legal option, a wife may also sue her husband in civil court for pain, suffering, and medical and other costs incurred as a result of spousal rape.[15]

Dealing with Rape Victims   Because rape is an extremely intrusive offense, it is crucial that a rape victim is treated with sensitivity, compassion, and respect regardless of the circumstances. Due to the intrusive nature of the offense, victims will react differently ranging from an extremely subdued state–almost a state of shock–to an excited and animated state. If possible, when a police department receives a call for help from a rape victim, female personnel should be designated to speak to the victim. This is because rape victims often feel more comfortable confiding in a woman.

Often, victims will want to shower immediately because they feel dirty. It is *critical* that they do not shower until they have been properly examined by medical personnel. Showering will remove fingerprints, semen, and other physical evidence that is needed to ensure conviction of a perpetrator. Usually, medical personnel will perform a series of exams on the victim, and will collect evidence using a rape kit, which contains sealable plastic bags and other items to help preserve evidence.

Police or medical personnel should find out if there is someone close to the victim who she would like to be with her during this time. Nearly always, a familiar face will make the process more comfortable. They should also provide the victim with resources that can assist in her recovery, such as rape hotlines, counseling centers, and rape survivor support groups that can assist the victim during this difficult period. Again, it is important that, regardless of one's personal impression about the victim, the victim should always be treated with respect.

Rape Trauma Syndrome   In recent years, an ailment unique to rape victims has become noticeable in the prosecution of rape cases in the United States. **Rape trauma syndrome** is a condition observed in some rape victims. Immediately after an attack, the victim exhibits behavior such as appearing calm and subdued; over time, the victim will exhibit physical symptoms such as tension headaches, fatigue, and sleeplessness, which lead to the development of phobias related to the circumstances of the rape.[16] Increasingly, courts in various states are allowing expert testimony in rape trials to explain the behavior of a rape victim based upon rape trauma syndrome. Such a move is intended to allow juries to better understand the long-term physical and psychological damage caused to rape victims.

rape trauma syndrome A condition observed in some rape victims, in which the victim develops phobias and physical problems as a result of having been raped.

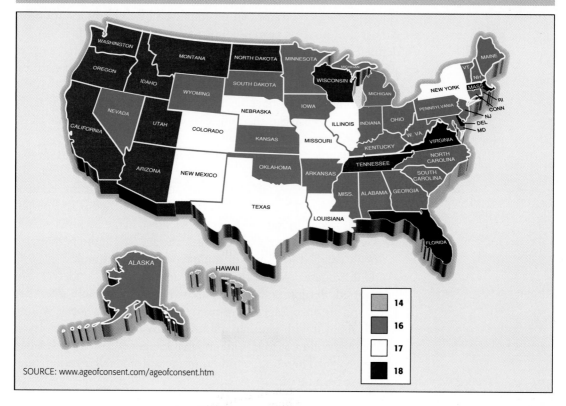

FIGURE 9-3

Age of Consent by State

SOURCE: www.ageofconsent.com/ageofconsent.htm

	14
	16
	17
	18

Child Molestation

According to the U.S. Department of Justice, four million child molesters reside in the United States. The average molester will abuse between 30 and 60 children before an arrest occurs, and may molest as many as 360 children during his or her lifetime.[17] Child molesters will often seek employment where they will have the most contact with children. They may work at summer camps, day care centers, and schools, as these jobs provide the easiest opportunities to target children.

child molestation Any sexual conduct by an adult with a child.

Generally, an adult person is guilty of **child molestation** if he or she engages in any sexual conduct with a child. This includes, but is not limited to:

- Exposing the genitals to a child
- Having a child touch the perpetrator's genitals
- Removing the child's clothing
- Taking nude pictures of a child
- Having a child touch the perpetrator or another child in an inappropriate fashion

Many jurisdictions have general child molestation statutes providing that a perpetrator can be convicted of child molestation for almost any kind of sexual contact with a child, which is usually defined as an individual under the age of 13. In some states, such as Arizona, the age can be as high as 15. With almost all state statutes, the *mens rea* for child molestation is established by showing that the molester intended to have sexual contact with a child. This is fairly easy to prove because if the molestation occurred, the intent to cause the act or harm is usually a given.

Child molestation statutes are often divided between first-degree and second-degree offenses, depending on the age of the victim. In Missouri, first-degree child molestation occurs where the child is under the age of 12 and the contact between the victim and perpetrator was sexual in nature. A second-degree charge involves a child who is 12 or 13. When a child is over the age of 13, the perpetrator is usually charged with rape or some type of sexual assault.[18]

Unfortunately, sexual abuse of children often goes undetected or unreported. Because so many children are abused by adults who they know and are encouraged to respect, the children may not be willing to talk about it with another adult. In many instances, the molester will tell the child not to talk about what happened and may threaten further harm. Therefore, children often will not tell anyone about the abuse because of:

- A desire to protect the molester, who is often a family member or close family friend
- A feeling that they were at fault, especially if they have been taught to look up to the molester
- Fear of punishment
- Difficulty in verbally expressing what has occurred

Another possible problem is that once a non-offending parent does learn of the events, that parent may not be inclined to push the issue because of the relation to the molester.

A serious issue in dealing with sexual abuse of children is the recidivist nature of the offender—in other words, offenders usually continue to molest each time they are released from prison. Upon release from prison, they move to communities in which their neighbors are unaware of their past history. In July 1994, convicted sex offender Jesse K. Timmendequas sexually assaulted and murdered seven-year-old Megan Kanka, who lived across the

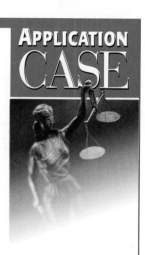

APPLICATION CASE

Buckey v. County of Los Angeles

One of the most publicized and time-consuming criminal trials in the United States involved teachers at the McMartin Preschool in Manhattan Beach, California. Virginia McMartin, several of her family members (including Peggy McMartin Buckey) who taught at the school, and other caregivers were charged with several counts of child molestation. In 1993, a parent who was known to be paranoid and mentally ill alleged to the police that her child had been sexually molested at the school. The police sent letters to all McMartin parents, which resulted in a wave of allegations regarding atrocious sexual acts against the children. In addition, a therapist who interviewed many of the children used manipulative tactics to get the children to say they had been molested. As a result, children fabricated their testimony at trial.

All charges that were made ultimately were either dropped or the defendant was acquitted. The irresponsible tactics used by therapists and law enforcement officers demonstrates the strong animosity that many people have toward child molesters. Unfortunately, in this case the well-meaning outrage of the police and therapist backfired.

Child Molestation

Critical Thinking What types of safeguards can help prevent slanderous accusations from damaging people's reputations?

SOURCE: *Buckey v. County of Los Angeles*, 968 F.2d 791 (7th Cir. 1992).

street from him in Hamilton Township, New Jersey. Megan's family was completely unaware of his prior record of sexual offending. As a result, Megan's Law was enacted in New Jersey later that year. **Megan's Law** requires community notification by authorities when a convicted sex offender is released from prison. The identities of these offenders are placed in a database, to which parents and other concerned community members have access. This database can perform a search by zip code to determine if convicted molesters reside in a given community. Many states have enacted their own version of Megan's Law. See Figure 9-4 for a list of those that have or have not adopted this law.

In California, all residents over the age of 18 who are not registered sex offenders have access to the database, and only must state their reason for viewing it in order to do so. The information provided

FIGURE 9–4
States with Megan's Law

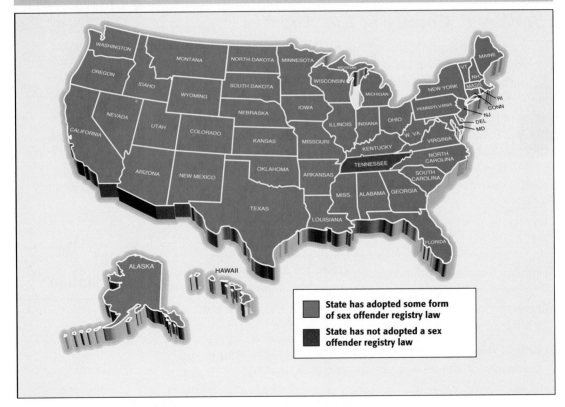

State has adopted some form of sex offender registry law

State has not adopted a sex offender registry law

includes the names of sex offenders in a particular zip code (but not addresses), the crime committed, and (if available) a photograph of the perpetrator. Sexual offenders are added to the database for the following crimes: sexual abuse of a child, penetration of a genital or anal opening by a foreign object, kidnapping for purposes of lewd conduct, and sodomy.[19]

1. How have recent laws changed the ways in which rape victims are treated at trials?
2. How does Megan's Law protect a community from recidivism among sexual offenders?

Check your answers at cl.glencoe.com.

9.3 Crimes Against the Person in the Home

This section will discuss historical and current issues regarding:

- Criminal abortion, which continues the discussion of feticide that began in Chapter 8
- Child abuse, which can be physical, emotional, sexual, or the result of neglect
- Spousal abuse, problems with prosecuting spousal abuse cases, and ways in which criminal justice personnel can learn to effectively deal with these cases
- Elder abuse, which only recently has gained attention as a widespread form of family violence

Criminal Abortion

Abortion is defined "as the spontaneous or artificially-induced expulsion of an embryo or fetus."[20] Before 1973, abortion was a crime at common law, but the killing of an unborn child was a different offense than homicide. Early American criminal statutes included the crime of abortion, most of them punishing only the person performing the abortion. Later American laws in the mid- to late-nineteenth century made abortion a felony. These new laws punished the pregnant woman as well as the abortionist, and criminalized attempted abortion to eliminate the former legal necessity of proving pregnancy.

Defining Feticide

No state laws define feticide as the killing of an embryo. For the purposes of the law defining feticide, the dividing line between embryo and fetus has been held to be the seventh or eighth week of pregnancy.

criminal abortion The artificially induced expulsion of a fetus by illegal means, such as spousal abuse.

feticide The killing of a fetus other than by legal abortion.

viability The point at which a fetus can reasonably live outside its mother's womb, with or without artificial support.

In *Roe v. Wade* (1973), the U.S. Supreme Court recognized the right to a legal abortion if the woman had not yet reached the third trimester of pregnancy. The decision in *Roe v. Wade* and in companion cases largely ended the criminal law of abortion as stated in the MPC and many state penal statutes. Current laws governing criminal abortion are enforceable only with respect to requirements that abortions must be performed by licensed physicians, and to abortions during the final trimester of pregnancy, when the fetus is usually viable. The law relating to abortion continues to be an area of considerable controversy in the United States.

Criminal abortion is something very different than legal abortion. It involves the act of **feticide**, which is the killing of a fetus, or unborn child, other than by legal abortion. In any jurisdiction where feticide is not defined as homicide, the terms criminal abortion and feticide can be used interchangeably. In other jurisdictions whose definitions of a person, for purposes of homicide, include fetuses, anyone who kills a fetus with the requisite intent of murder may be charged with feticide as the criminal homicide of a fetus. In that case, the killer must commit the act with malice, but whether the fetus was the intended victim is irrelevant because transferred intent is sufficient to meet the *mens rea* requirement. This means that if the defendant intended to kill another, such as a pregnant woman carrying the fetus, but killed the fetus instead, he or she can still be criminally liable for murder. (See Figure 9–5 on page 321 for an example of a criminal abortion statute.)

Although some states, such as California, will charge a person with feticide long before the fetus has reached viability, most states require that the fetus reaches the point of viability before a person can be charged with the offense. **Viability** is the point at which a fetus can reasonably live outside its mother's womb, with or without artificial support. The point of viability is often reached at 20 weeks (a little less than five months) of development. At this point, tests can

Myth	Fact
To be convicted of feticide, the perpetrator must have intended to kill the fetus.	A perpetrator does not need to have specific intent to kill the fetus. If the perpetrator had intended to kill another but accidentally kills the fetus, he or she could still be charged with feticide.

FIGURE 9-5

Tennessee Criminal Abortion Statute

Title 39 Criminal Offenses
Chapter 15 Offenses Against the Family
Part 2 Abortion

39-15-201. Criminal abortion and attempt to procure criminal miscarriage—Penalties—Lawful abortions and attempts to procure miscarriage—Requirements.

(a) For the purpose of this section:

(1) "Abortion" means the administration to any woman pregnant with child, whether such child be quick or not, of any medicine, drug, or substance whatever, or the use or employment of any instrument, or other means whatever, with the intent to destroy such child, thereby destroying such child before the child's birth; and

(2) "Attempt to procure a miscarriage" means the administration of any substance with the intention to procure the miscarriage of a woman or the use or employment of any instrument or other means with such intent.

(b) (1) Every person who performs an abortion commits the crime of criminal abortion, unless such abortion is performed in compliance with the requirements of subsection (c). Criminal abortion is a Class C felony.

(2) Every person who attempts to procure a miscarriage commits the crime of attempt to procure criminal miscarriage, unless such attempt to procure a miscarriage is performed in compliance with the requirements of subsection (c). Attempt to procure a criminal miscarriage is a Class E felony.

(3) Every person who compels, coerces, or exercises duress in any form with regard to any other person in order to obtain or procure an abortion on any female commits a misdemeanor. A violation of this section is a Class A misdemeanor.

SOURCE: http://www.state.tn.us/tccy/Tnchild/39/39-15-201.htm

be used to determine whether the fetus is actually viable. For example, suppose that a man accosts a woman who is three months pregnant at gunpoint, beats her until she is unconscious, and rapes her. As a result of the trauma from the attack, she suffers a miscarriage. Most likely, the fetus was not viable at the time of the miscarriage and could not survive outside of the womb. As a result, the perpetrator would not be charged with feticide in states that require the viability test. However, if the attack took place in a state where viability is not a necessary element, the man would be charged with feticide in addition to the crimes against the woman.

Child Abuse

Child abuse is an intentional or neglectful physical or emotional injury imposed on a child. This includes sexual molestation, which you have learned about earlier in this chapter. According to

child abuse An intentional or neglectful physical or emotional injury imposed on a child, including sexual molestation.

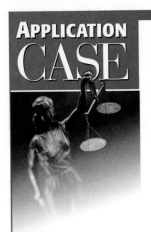
State v. Horne

In *State v. Horne*, a man violently beat his wife, which not only resulted in serious injuries to her but caused the death of their nine-month-old fetus. Following the beating, the woman was rushed to the hospital, but the fetus had already suffocated due to the fact that during the beating, his mother's blood supply had been cut off to him. The child, therefore, was born dead.

The prosecution was able to prove beyond a reasonable doubt that 1) the defendant had the requisite malice because he beat his wife, which transferred to the fetus, and 2) the fetus was viable at the time of the beating. As a result, the defendant was charged and convicted of feticide.

Critical Thinking In this case, how is the *mens rea* requirement fulfilled for feticide?

SOURCE: *State v. Horne*, 319 S.E. 2d 703 (N.C. 1984).

the National Committee to Prevent Child Abuse, 3,126,000 incidents of child abuse were reported to state child protective agencies in 1997 alone.[21] In addition, it is estimated that millions more cases go unreported each year. Moreover, 68 percent of all abuse occurs at the hands of the child's father or stepfather.[22] Child abuse can range from a failure to supervise a child that results in harm to actual physical abuse. In other words, a parent or guardian does not need to hit a child to be guilty of child abuse, but hitting can be considered child abuse in certain circumstances.

Child abuse often takes place in the home; whether the abuse is an action or an omission, parents are usually the perpetrators. Like many states, Maryland requires that in order to be convicted of felony child abuse in the first degree, the abuser must be either a parent, a person acting as the parent (a legal responsibility referred to as *in loco parentis*), or another person responsible for the supervision of the minor child.[23] Parents and guardians have an inherent duty that no other person has to care for, protect, and provide for their child. If the parent is the abuser, an observer of the abuse, or knows that the child is being abused but fails to intervene, that parent will be punished by the child abuse laws of any state.

A person who does not have a special duty as a parent or guardian is still culpable for actual abuse, but does not have the same obligations if he or she is only a witness to abuse or someone who is aware that abuse is occurring. If a child is being beaten continually by his father, and his live-in mother and next-door neighbor are both aware of the abuse, the mother must intervene or face punishment. On the other hand, the neighbor arguably has a moral obligation to intervene, but will not be criminally prosecuted should he or she fail to do so. One exception is that in almost all states, professionals who perform guardian-like roles, such as teachers and school nurses are required to report the possible abuse of a child.

There are four general types of child abuse:

Neglect

Neglect of a child could come in various forms, such as:

- Denying a child proper nutrition
- Failing to enroll a child at school
- Leaving a young child alone
- Residing with a child in an unsanitary home

For example, Colorado's child abuse statute provides that "a person commits child abuse if such person [among other things] . . . engages in a continued pattern of conduct which results in malnourishment, [or] lack of proper medical care."[24] Suppose that a married couple has two children aged six and eight. They reside together in a one-bedroom apartment that has not been cleaned for several months. It is infested with cockroaches due to the unwashed dishes and food scraps left throughout the house. Both parents work at night, and they leave the children at home for up to ten hours by themselves. At times, there is no food in the house for the children to eat. There is no telephone so that if there is an emergency, the children cannot call for help.

In such a situation, a social worker who visited the house and discovered the situation would most likely remove the children from the home because the parents' neglect could have serious consequences. Still, when neglect does result in an injury to a child, the punishment may not be as severe as if the parent directly injured the child. If a child who is left alone were hospitalized for malnutrition, the parent may only be charged with a misdemeanor, whereas if the parent physically harms the child, they may be charged with a felony.

Physical Abuse

Physical abuse is another form of child abuse. It normally involves hitting, striking, beating, or in some way injuring the child, either by direct or indirect physical force. Indirect physical force includes the use of a belt or throwing an object with the intent to cause injury to a child. Direct physical abuse involves extreme forms of corporal punishment. Often, a parent will attempt to justify his or her actions by stating that the punishment was for the good of the child. California's child abuse statute provides that "'child abuse' means a physical injury which is inflicted by other than accidental means on a child by another person."[25]

Occasionally, it is hard to distinguish between child abuse, which is unlawful, and punishment by the parent, which is not. For example, many parents believe that spanking is an effective disciplinary tool, and spanking is normally not a criminal offense; however, a social worker may feel that a parent's use of spanking is excessive and beyond the bounds of reasonable parenting. To determine whether the action was excessive, a social worker will typically look for the following criteria:

- Permanent injuries, such as scarring
- The amount of physical force used
- How often the child is spanked
- The age of the child when the incident occurs

Sexual Abuse   Sexual abuse includes rape and child molestation. It ranges from improper touching of the child's genitalia to sexual intercourse. Although sexual abuse is often repetitive and ongoing, after one incident an abuser can be charged with child abuse. California's child abuse statute, for example, provides that sexual abuse of a child is considered child abuse.

Emotional Maltreatment   Emotional maltreatment involves what is often referred to as *verbal abuse*, which may include berating the child for his or her appearance, intelligence, or what a disappointment he or she is. Verbal abuse is not normally included in child abuse statutes, but a social worker may determine that the excessive verbal attacks create an unhealthy environment for a child and remove the child from the home. In addition, a parent may be ordered by a court to attend parenting classes, where he or she learns how to parent without the verbal abuse.

Spousal Abuse

spousal abuse Long-term physical abuse by the victim's spouse or partner.

Spousal abuse usually involves long-term physical abuse by a man against his wife or girlfriend, although occasionally it involves abuse of a man by a woman and can also happen in homosexual relationships. Spousal abuse raises different concerns than other types of abuse because of the pre-existing relationships involved. In spousal abuse cases, the person being abused often does not feel free to leave

State v. Williams

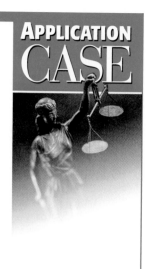

In *State v. Williams*, a husband and wife breached their duty of care to their 17-month-old baby by failing to get medical help when the baby became ill. An abscessed tooth had gone untreated and developed into an infection of the mouth and cheeks, which eventually became gangrenous. This condition left the child unable to eat, which caused malnutrition and lowered the child's resistance until the child contracted pneumonia, which was the actual cause of death. The couple had neglected to seek medical help because they were afraid that when a doctor saw the child's swollen cheeks, the child would be removed from the home. By the time they finally sought help, it was too late.

Although the parents were not well-educated, the court found no evidence that they were either physically or financially unable to take the child to a doctor. The autopsy surgeon testified that the odor from the gangrene would have been noticeable ten days prior to the child's death, so the parents had considerable warning that their child was in grave danger. As a result, both parents were convicted of manslaughter.

Neglect

Critical Thinking Do you think the conviction of manslaughter is too severe? Why or why not?

SOURCE: *State v. Williams*, 484 P.2d 1167 (Wash. Ct. App.1971).

the relationship because he or she fears for his or her physical safety, or because he or she feels financial and emotional dependence on the abuser.

In recent years, psychologists have recognized a pattern exhibited by many abused women who endure long-term abuse. **Battered woman's syndrome**, where the victim of abuse eventually "snaps" and kills the abuser, is now recognized as a valid defense in many jurisdictions. A victim of domestic abuse may raise the defense of battered woman's syndrome if charged with the death of her husband or boyfriend. The defense is usually only allowed in a very particular set of circumstances, which is where a woman kills her spouse because she believes that if she does not kill him, he will kill her. This unique form of self-defense also creates unique problems because usually when a defendant claims self-defense, he or she must show that there were no reasonable alternatives. Often, battered women stay in abusive relationships long after the beating

battered woman's syndrome A defense in many jurisdictions where the victim of abuse eventually "snaps" and kills the abuser.

CRIMINAL LAW Online

Children's Defense Fund

Go to the Web site for the Children's Defense Fund by clicking the link at **cl.glencoe.com**. Place your cursor over the list in the center of the page that begins with, "A Healthy Start" and read the different boxes that will appear, highlighting the goals of the CDF. When you are done, answer the following questions: What does CDF mean by "A Healthy Start," "A Head Start," and the other items that you see listed on the main page? Overall, what is the goal of the CDF?

Battered Woman's Syndrome

If the battered woman's syndrome defense is raised in court, the defense counsel will usually bring in an expert witness to explain the syndrome and to show the jury why the defendant thought she was about to be killed.

begins and are physically capable of escaping, but do not for complex psychological reasons.

The following provides a brief overview of the battering cycle:

- **Phase one** is the tension-building stage, where the batterer engages in minor incidents of verbal abuse or physical incidents. At this stage, the victim begins to have fear that she will be harmed. Often, she tries to be as passive as possible to avoid further abuse, but by not taking action she is actually setting herself up for the next phase.
- **Phase two** is the acute battering incident, where something provokes the perpetrator and he acts out physically.
- **Phase three** is where the abuser regrets his actions and promises to get help in stopping the abuse, whether that is by refraining from alcohol use or seeking out anger management assistance. This phase is what gets women to stay because they believe the abuser's remorse and think that the abuse has ended. This cycle repeats indefinitely for months or years, until either the victim is killed or leaves.[26]

Even if a woman kills her abuser while he sleeps or several hours after he abused her, experts in the field believe that a woman suffering from the syndrome reasonably believes that her life is in jeopardy at the time she commits the killing. Therefore, in these cases, this defense can be used successfully.

Dealing with Domestic Violence Victims Unfortunately, law enforcement officers see countless incidents of domestic violence. Often, the batterers are drunk; equally often, victims of domestic violence may call the police when being beaten, but will refuse to press charges or testify in court. This may become a frustrating process for officers who respond to these calls for service because their efforts to help the victim can go nowhere.

The officer should always try to be sympathetic, regardless of the situation or the history of the couple's behavior. Even if the woman refuses to press charges, the officer should try to separate the couple for the time being so that the abuse will not continue at that time. The officer should see if there is a friend or relative of the victim who the officer can call for assistance for the victim. The officer should refer the victim to the emergency shelters in her community and any hotline numbers available for her to call when being abused. Depending on the jurisdiction, the officer may be able to arrest and even gain a conviction of the perpetrator without the assistance of the victim. In addition, to facilitate convictions for domestic violence, some states are using expert witnesses to testify to abuse when victims refuse to do so.

Elder Abuse

Abuse of the elderly may bring to mind news stories of horrific conditions in nursing homes: residents left for days in their bed, laying in their own urine, and enduring physical abuse from caregivers or nurses. In reality, **elder abuse**, which is the abuse or neglect of elderly persons, usually occurs in the home. Furthermore, the perpetrators are frequently the victim's spouse or children. When an older person requires another to take care of him or her, he or she is at the mercy of the caregiver; all too often, the burden is overwhelming and the elder does not get the care and attention he or she needs.

Because elder abuse often occurs after the victim has become incapacitated and requires the assistance of another person for basic living, reporting the abuse can be difficult. The victim may not have access to a telephone, may be unable to communicate, or may not know who to contact. Because the abuse is usually committed by a family member, the victim may not want to report the abuse or may hope that it will eventually end on its own.

Financial exploitation is a common form of elder abuse. A common action is for the abuser to take advantage of the victim's possible memory loss or inability to organize and manage his or her own possessions and assets. Often, a victim will request help in managing finances, and this leads to manipulation or outright theft by the perpetrator.

elder abuse The abuse, mistreatment, or financial exploitation of elderly persons.

◄ **Elder Abuse**
Although most elder abuse occurs in the home, it can also occur in nursing homes like this.
How prevalent do you think elder abuse is in nursing homes?

Myth	**Fact**
Elder abuse is generally always physical, never financial.	There are many cases of elder abuse in which the elderly are coerced or tricked out of their money or possessions.

Females represent 52 percent of abusers, which is quite different from other abuse profiles, and 62 percent of those who suffer from elder abuse are female.[27] As medical progress makes it possible for people to live longer despite chronic health conditions and overall deterioration, older adults will continue to need assistance for longer periods of time. As a result, family members may experience additional emotional and financial pressures, and this may continue to trigger elder abuse.

CRIMINAL LAW *Online*

Check your answers at cl.glencoe.com.

Self Check

1. How does viability affect the prosecution of feticide cases?
2. What are the differences in how social workers and prosecutors treat emotional abuse, physical abuse, sexual abuse, and neglect of children?

9.4 False Imprisonment and Kidnapping

False imprisonment and kidnapping are discussed together in this chapter because most jurisdictions currently view them similarly. Although there is a correlation between the two offenses, it is important for you to recognize that the elements of these crimes are different. These elements are discussed throughout this section.

False Imprisonment

false imprisonment
Knowingly and unlawfully restraining a person so as to substantially interfere with his or her liberty.

False imprisonment is defined as knowingly and unlawfully restraining a person and thus substantially interfering with his or her liberty. Therefore, the elements of the crime are 1) the act of unlawfully restraining a person, so as to substantially interfere with his or her liberty, and 2) the specific intent to restrain that person. Prior to the adoption of the MPC in the 1960s, few states considered false imprisonment a crime. After the introduction of the MPC, many states revised their penal codes; a majority of them included the offense for the first time.

Most false imprisonment statutes punish the crime as a misdemeanor, but a felony charge is possible where aggravated circumstances are involved. An example of false imprisonment would be a situation where two friends are arguing over money that one friend owes another. Suppose the person owing the money is at the other friend's residence and wants to leave without paying. If the person who lives at the residence blocks the exit and refuses to allow his friend to leave unless he pays the money, he may be charged with false imprisonment regardless of whether he was rightly owed the money. There are other courses of action he could take to get the money back, such as suing his friend in civil court, but he does not have the right to hold his friend against his will.

The *actus reus* requirement of false imprisonment is that the defendant compel the victim to remain in a place he or she does not want to remain or compel the victim to go where he or she does not want to go. There is no requirement that the defendant make threats of physical injury or harm. The defendant need only confine the person in some place against his or her will and without his or her consent. The place of confinement may be as small as a closet or as large as a house, or may even be on a public street. The length of time required can be as short as a few seconds or as long as days or weeks.

What determines whether actual confinement has taken place is whether the victim had alternate ways of leaving. Suppose that a man traps a woman in a room with only one locked door and no windows. Since there is no alternate way for the woman to leave the room, and assuming that she did not consent to being in the room, she has been falsely imprisoned. If there were a window through which the woman could safely escape without harm, the woman would be obligated to do so and the defendant would likely not be found guilty of false imprisonment. If, however, the woman were 80 years old, in poor health, and with little mobility, the defendant would probably not be able to defend his actions by arguing that she had an alternate means of escape. In determining whether a victim had a safe alternate way of escape, a fact-finder must determine whether the average reasonable person in the same situation would feel that they could escape safely. A reasonable 80-year-old woman would probably not be able to crawl out of a window and jump to safety.

Most jurisdictions require a showing of specific intent in order for someone to be guilty of false imprisonment. This means that the defendant must have intended to confine the victim. Suppose that Jim invites his female friend Bonnie to his house to watch a movie. As he leaves the house to go rent the movie, he accidentally locks a door that can only be opened from the outside. When Bonnie attempts to go outside to get something from her car, she cannot get out; in a panic, she calls 911. In most jurisdictions, Jim would not be guilty of false imprisonment because he had no intention of restraining Bonnie.

There are some unique situations where a person may be held by lawful restraint, and there are two main lawful restraint categories:

Lawful Restraint: The Shopkeeper's Rule
The first category is known as the **shopkeeper's rule**. It provides that a shopkeeper, who is defined as an owner or manager of a store or restaurant, may restrain a person if the shopkeeper possesses a reasonable belief that the customer has not paid a bill or has shoplifted an item. In this situation, a

shopkeeper's rule An exception to false imprisonment laws that provides a shopkeeper with the right to restrain a person if the shopkeeper possesses a reasonable belief that the customer has not paid a bill or has shoplifted an item.

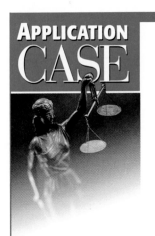

APPLICATION CASE

False Imprisonment

In the Matter of the Welfare of R.W.C.

In the Minnesota case *In the Matter of the Welfare of R.W.C.* (1997), the defendant was a high school student who, with three of his friends, wrapped duct tape around another student until he was unable to move. Before leaving the student in an isolated stairwell, the defendant shoved the student, causing him to fall and sustain injuries. The defendant argued that he did not know he was not allowed to engage in "taping" because it was a tradition at his high school.

The court interpreted the *mens rea* requirement of Minnesota's false imprisonment statute only as acting with intent to produce a specific *result;* it did not require acting with knowledge that the conduct was wrongful. Whether or not the defendant knew he was not allowed to tape the other student had no bearing on the defendant's guilt because he acted to produce a specific result—to restrain the student by taping him and leaving him immobile. The appellate court affirmed the defendant's conviction for false imprisonment.

Critical Thinking Is the "tradition" defense a viable one? What other traditions can lead to criminal prosecution?

SOURCE: *In the Matter of the Welfare of R.W.C.*, 1997 WL 3366 (Minn. Ct. App. 1997).

shopkeeper may be able to restrain the customer in order to ascertain whether the bill or item was paid for. As long as the restraint does not last an inordinate amount of time and no physical force is used, the owner will not be charged or convicted of false imprisonment even if the customer has actually paid the bill or paid for the item.

Lawful Restraint by Law Enforcement The second and most common type of lawful restraint involves restraint by law enforcement. If a police officer lawfully detains or arrests a person, such imprisonment is not against the law. If a driver is speeding, the police officer is within his or her lawful right to sound the siren, flash the lights, and force the driver to pull over. The time the driver spends waiting for the officer to check for registration and write a ticket is a form of restraint because the driver has to remain in his or her car, but the restraint is lawful. If an officer restrains a person unlawfully, the officer could be charged with false imprisonment. Suppose that a male officer notices an attractive female driver and pulls her over without any legal cause to do so. Once he pulls her over, he makes up a reason for doing so, asks for her license, and goes to his car to run a computer check on it. He then returns to her car and admits that the only reason he pulled her over was to ask for her phone number. In this situation, an officer can be charged with and convicted of false imprisonment.

Kidnapping

At common law, kidnapping was a rather obscure misdemeanor defined as "the unlawful confinement and transportation of another out of the country."[28] Today, **kidnapping** is a serious major felony, defined as "[t]he act or an instance of taking or carrying away a person without consent, by force or fraud, and without lawful excuse—and often with a demand for ransom."[29] The common law requirement of transporting the victim out of the country, which was also known as *asportation*, established the basic element of removing the victim from the protection of the law. Modern kidnapping statutes retain this element to some extent. They usually involve the forcible movement of a person from one place to another, or, in the alternative, confining the victim secretly.

For example, Illinois' kidnapping statute provides that: Kidnapping occurs when a person knowingly: (1) and secretly confines another against his [or her] will, or (2) by force or threat of imminent force carries another from one place to another with intent

kidnapping A felony defined as "[t]he act or an instance of taking or carrying away a person without consent, by force or fraud, and without lawful excuse—and often with a demand for ransom."

ON THE JOB

Certified Victim Assistance Specialist

Job Description and Duties: Provide victim assistance and advocacy immediately following the crisis and for several months following. Provide telephone support. Provide referral assistance to crime victims in their homes. Develop and update resource and referral contacts files. In some positions, dispatch locksmiths to secure the homes of victims of domestic violence, robbery, burglary, sexual assault, harassment, and other types of crimes.

Salary: Many specialist positions are filled by volunteers, and a typical specialist does not make more than $30,000.

Other Information: Victim assistance specialists must complete certification training, which can include the following elements:
- One year experience in trauma-related field
- Associate's degree or two years trauma services or crisis response training or two years trauma services or support work
- Letters of recommendation from one supervisor and one colleague
- Current resume with documented experience in trauma service field
- Recertification required every three years
- 30 hours of continuing education
- Six days of training designed to enhance the knowledge, skills, and effectiveness of victim assistance

Critical Thinking What issues do you think certified victim assistance specialists must deal with in their jobs?

SOURCE: The Association of Traumatic Stress Specialists (ATSS), http://www.atss-hq.com; The Victim Assistance Institute at the University of South Carolina, http://www.sc.edu/cosw/center/vai.html; and Safe Horizon, http://www.safehorizon.org/LLMAIN.html.

secretly to confine him [or her] against his [or her] will, or (3) by deceit or enticement induces another to go from one place to another with intent secretly to confine him [or her] against his [or her] will.[30]

Most jurisdictions require that a person specifically intend to move a person from a particular locale and confine that person for some period of time against his or her will. Kidnapping is often committed in tandem with another, usually violent crime. In some instances, it is incidental to the commission of another crime. Suppose that Gerry walks into a liquor store to rob it. The store

Myth	Fact
Kidnapping involves the forcible abduction and removal of a person from his country to another.	Although the common law required such drastic movement, under modern law a kidnapping can occur simply by removing a person from one place to another in the same general area.

clerk hits the alarm and Gerry hears police sirens coming closer while he is still in the store. He panics and holds a gun to the clerk's head, demanding that she come with him. He then drives her to his house, where he holds her for 12 hours while deciding what to do. Gerry would be guilty of kidnapping in addition to the robbery.

Parental Kidnapping and Child Abduction   According to the American Bar Association, more than 300,000 children are abducted each year. About half of these cases involve parents kidnapping their own children and taking them out of state—usually because the kidnappers are unhappy with child custody decisions. In response to the growing numbers of children being abducted by their parents, Congress enacted legislation that responds to the specific crime of parental kidnapping and child abduction. The Parental Kidnapping Prevention Act requires states to enforce child custody decisions entered by a court of another state if the custody decision is consistent with provisions of the act.

The other federal law involving child kidnapping is the Lindbergh Act. Although this act is not specific to children, it was passed in 1934 in response to the kidnapping and murder of Charles Lindbergh Jr., the 20-month-old son of aviator Charles Lindbergh. This law specifically addresses kidnapping for ransom or reward when the victim is transported to another state or to a foreign country.[31]

Self Check

1. How have laws changed regarding kidnapping?
2. Explain the Parental Kidnapping Prevention Act.

CRIMINAL LAW *Online*

Check your answers at cl.glencoe.com.

Crimes Against Persons: Other Offenses

SUMMARY BY CHAPTER OBJECTIVES

1. State the elements of battery.

The three elements of battery are:

- The actor's conduct of touching or applying force to the victim
- The actor's mental state (either intent to injure, with criminal negligence, or while committing an unlawful act, in some jurisdictions)
- The harm done to the victim (bodily injury or offensive touching)

2. List the elements of assault.

The three elements of the crime of assault are:

- An attempt to batter or conduct that is threatening, menacing, or otherwise designed to frighten the victim (intentional scaring)
- The intent to commit a battery upon the victim or to frighten the victim
- The result that the conduct in fact does frighten the victim and would "arouse a reasonable apprehension of bodily harm in the average person"

3. State the elements of mayhem.

The elements of mayhem are the infliction of a specified injury constituting dismemberment, disablement, or disfigurement; and the intent to maim or disfigure.

4. State the elements of rape, and understand the difference between rape and statutory rape.

In general, rape is sexual intercourse by a male defendant with a female victim that is committed in any one of the four following ways:

- Forcibly
- By means of some specific forms of deception
- While the victim was asleep or unconscious
- Under circumstances in which the victim was not competent to give consent (e.g., under the influence of drugs, mental disability, or being too young)

Rape is sexual intercourse without consent. Statutory rape consists of sexual contact, with or without consent, between an adult and a minor. In most states, the age range for statutory rape is from 13 to 17. An individual who has reached the age of sexual consent, which is often 18, is considered an adult, and an individual below the minimum age is considered a child; an adult that has sexual contact with anyone below this minimum age will be tried for child molestation.

5. **Describe Megan's Law.**

Megan's Law is a statute that requires community notification by authorities when a convicted sex offenders is released from prison and moves into that community. It originated in New Jersey in 1994, but has since been adopted in many other states.

6. **Define child abuse.**

Child abuse is any intentional or neglectful harm done to a child; in other words, child abuse can be inflicted either by an action or by an omission. The four main categories of child abuse are neglect, physical abuse, sexual abuse, and emotional maltreatment. Prosecution varies depending on the nature and the extent of the abuse, but all states have laws that make parents and legal guardians for committing, witnessing, or even knowing about the abuse of their child without notifying authorities.

7. **Distinguish between the elements of false imprisonment and kidnapping.**

The elements of false imprisonment are the act of unlawfully restraining a person, so as to substantially interfere with his or her liberty, and the specific intent to restrain that person. Modern elements of kidnapping usually involve the forcible movement of a person from one place to another, or, in the alternative, confining the victim secretly.

KEY TERMS

battery, page 302
aggravated battery, page 303
assault, page 304
conditional assault, page 305
aggravated assault, page 305
mayhem, page 306
rape, page 309
statutory rape, page 314
spousal rape, page 314
rape trauma syndrome, page 315
child molestation, page 316

Megan's Law, page 318
criminal abortion, page 320
feticide, page 320
viability, page 320
child abuse, page 321
spousal abuse, page 324
battered woman's syndrome, page 325
elder abuse, page 327
false imprisonment, page 328
shopkeeper's rule, page 330
kidnapping, page 331

Where and how did Megan's Law originate?
Find it on page 318.

QUESTIONS FOR REVIEW

1. Name some ways in which assault and battery differ from mayhem.
2. How do aggravated assault and aggravated battery differ from simple assault and simple battery?
3. Why is rape considered a general-intent offense?
4. Explain how the laws regarding statutory rape have changed over time.
5. Define spousal rape and explain recent legislation to outlaw it.
6. Name some reasons why child molestation frequently goes unreported.
7. Why are parents and guardians more liable for child abuse than others?
8. What are some ways that social workers can respond to child neglect? To child physical abuse? To child emotional maltreatment?
9. Who is usually the perpetrator in elder abuse cases, and why?
10. How did the MPC affect laws regarding false imprisonment?
11. Explain how the shopkeeper's rule works. What are its limitations?
12. Name and define the two legal responses to child abduction that are discussed in this chapter.

PROBLEM-SOLVING EXERCISES

1. **Assault and Battery** A police officer responds to a call to a park late at night and finds eight young men huddled around one 18-year-old male, who is lying on the ground. He is bleeding from his nose and mouth and is cupping his right eye, screaming, "I can't see, I can't see!" From what the officer learns, there had apparently been a "meeting" of two rival gangs, and one member from each gang fought each other. The victim lying on the ground had taken the first punch, but threw the last punch. Answer the following questions:
   a) What crimes have been committed against the young man lying on the ground?

   b) What crimes has the young man committed?
   c) How would you recommend that the prosecutor handle the case?

2. **Spousal Abuse** An officer responds to a 911 dispatcher's call that a man has been bludgeoned to death with a shovel. When the officer arrives on the scene, the officer finds a woman on the ground, holding her husband's lifeless body in her arms 100 yards from their home. After speaking to a neighbor who witnessed the events leading up to the man's death, the officer learns that the couple had been married three years, and almost from the beginning, they had a very tumultuous relationship. The police had

been called to the house twice before, both times for domestic disturbances. On this particular day, the couple had fought for approximately an hour–both screaming at the top of their lungs. The man apparently chased his wife out of their home and down the street. He then turned around and began walking home, as though nothing had happened. The wife picked up a shovel lying on another neighbor's front lawn, charged at her husband from behind, and hit him over the head. He immediately dropped to the ground, and although his wife tried to resuscitate him, he had obviously died the moment he was hit with the shovel. At the wife's trial, could the battered woman's syndrome be successfully used as a defense? Why or why not? Based on what you have read in this and the previous chapter, could another defense be used successfully?

3. **Sex Crimes and False Imprisonment** A man and woman are set up on a blind dinner date, and arrive at the restaurant in their own cars. During the dinner, the woman is totally turned off by the man's sick sense of humor and bad eating habits, but the man finds the woman extremely entertaining and attractive. When they finish dinner, the woman intends to leave, but the man insists that she goes for a ride in his car to the beach, which is just a mile away. The woman really doesn't want to go and tells the man this, but he repeatedly asks her and she finally gives in, only because she really loves the beach and hasn't been in a long time. They get into his car, begin a conversation, and arrive at the beach parking lot. The woman begins to unbuckle her seatbelt, but the man grabs her hands, holds her down, and eventually forces the woman to have sexual intercourse against her will. Can the man be charged with kidnapping? False imprisonment? Rape?

4. **Assault** You are a parole officer. One of your clients has been arrested for waving around a large cattle bone, which he said that he found in the trash of a nearby meat packing plant. He was arrested when he waved around the bone in a crowded public place and the bone brushed against someone's head. At the time of his arrest, he was heavily intoxicated.

   a) Should your client's parole be revoked? Why or why not?

   b) Was the arrest of the client justified? Why or why not? With what crimes could he be charged?

WORKPLACE APPLICATIONS

1. **Child Abuse** You are a social worker responding to a report of an anonymous call, which stated that the three children next door have not been seen in ten days. When you arrive, you meet a woman who is apparently the mother. You tell her the station received an anonymous call and wanted to make sure everything was okay. The woman invites you to come in, where you see children's toys on the floor. When you ask if her children are home, she responds that they are in their rooms and have been punished for being bad. She goes on to tell you that they are not good in school, so she has pulled them from their school and is thinking about home-schooling them. Answer the following questions:
   a) What questions should you ask the mother to determine if abuse is occurring?
   b) What evidence should you look for?
   c) Could the mother be charged with child abuse?
   d) What other facts might be helpful in making this determination?

2. **Domestic Violence** Contact your local domestic violence shelter and ask to speak to someone who works as a counselor or in a counseling role (most of the employees at these shelters are volunteers). Ask him or her to describe the services that the shelter provides, as well as the typical outcome for women who come to this shelter. Do many return to their husbands, or do they stay separated? How many of them have children, and how does this impact a woman's decision to leave an abuser? Write your findings in a one-page report.

3. **Crime on Campus** You are a police officer answering a service call near the local university. A woman comes out of her apartment crying, and states that her roommate intimidated her and wouldn't let her leave the bedroom until she gave her money. When the woman gave her roommate $40 in cash, the roommate shoved her onto the bed and ran out of the room.
   a) With what crimes could the roommate be charged?
   b) Do you need other information before you make an arrest? Why or why not?

INTERNET APPLICATIONS

1. **Learn About Elder Abuse** Access the site of the Association for Protection of the Elderly through **cl.glencoe.com**. Read their front-page story, "About APE," "Action Alert," and any other sections that interest you. When you are done, answer the following questions:
   a) What is the goal of this organization?
   b) What kind of abuses do elderly people risk facing in today's nursing homes?
   c) How can people get involved to improve conditions for elderly relatives who are in nursing homes?

2. **The Lindbergh Case** Read the FBI's coverage of the crime that prompted the passage of the Lindbergh Act of 1934. "The Lindbergh Kidnapping" can be accessed through the link at **cl.glencoe.com**. When you are done, answer the following questions:
   a) How did the FBI determine that Bruno Hauptmann was the kidnapper?
   b) What evidence did they look for, and was it enough to convict?
   c) Was there anything that you, as an investigator or prosecutor, would have done differently?
   d) Do you agree with the charge(s) that were eventually filed? Why or why not?

ETHICS ISSUES

1. **Abuse** A young homeless woman and her baby arrive at a church for shelter. An older woman who lives alone and is a member of the church offers to take them in and provide them with food and shelter until the young mother can find a job and get back on her feet. After about one week, the young woman begins to act strangely and tells the old woman that she is possessed by the devil. The old woman starts to be concerned, but assumes that her head is just "a little messed up from living on the streets." During the next week, the old woman hears the young girl chanting in her room while the baby is crying. Two days after that, she hears what sounds like the woman beating the baby, and the baby crying continually. The old woman questions the young woman, who replies, "I have to beat the Devil, I can't let him take over my life. Those who are bad must be punished." Answer the following questions:
   a) What kind of abuse seems to be occurring?
   b) If physical abuse is occurring, what legal options could she exercise?
   c) Does the woman have a duty to protect the child from further abuse, as she was giving food and shelter to the mother and baby?
   d) Could she be charged for the abuse that has already occurred? What about the mother?

ENDNOTES

1 *Id.* at 685 n.5 citing Model Penal Code § 211.1 and comment (1985).

2 Wayne R. LaFave & Austin W. Scott, Jr., *Criminal Law* § 7.16(b), at p. 694, nn. 26 & 28 (Hornbook Series 2d Student ed. 1986).

3 William Blackstone, *Commentaries,** p. 205.

4 Wayne R. LaFave & Austin W. Scott, Jr., Criminal Law § 7.17(c), at p. 697 (Hornbook Series 2d Student ed. 1986).

5 William Blackstone, p. 210.

6 Bureau of Justice Statistics, National Crime Victimization Survey (1999). From *RAINNews*, "Rape and Sexual Assault Up Again in 1999, Continue to Buck National Crime Trend," http://www.rainn.org/stat(61).html.

7 *Id.*, § 33.04[B][1][a], at 538 n.39 citing *Commonwealth v. Berkowitz*, 641 A.2d 1161, 1164 (Pa. 1994); *State v. Alston*, 312 S.E.2d 470 (N.C. 1984).

8 *Id.* at p. 539 n. 45 citing *People v. Dohring*, 59 N.Y. 374, 386 (1874).

9 *Id.* n. 46 citing *King v. State*, 357 S.W.2d 42, 45 (Tenn. 1962).

10 *Id.*, § 33.04[B][2][b], at p. 542, nn. 59–61, citing and quoting State in the Interest of M.T.S., 609 A.2d 1266 (N.J. 1992).

11 *Id.*

12 Ibid.

13 Flora Guillory, *The Trap of Marital Rape.* http://suite101.com/article.cfm/rape_prevention_survival/51294.

14 *Violence against Women.* Bureau of Justice Statistics, U.S. Dept. of Justice, 1994. From http://www.rainn.org/stats.html.

15 The Sexual Harassment and Rape Prevention Program [SHARPP], *The Wife Rape Information*

Page. http://www.unh.edu/student-life/sharpp/Stats%20and%20Facts/marital.htm.

16 *Id.*

17 *Child Abduction Statistics: How Safe is Your Child?,* http://www.yellodyno.com/html/stats.html.

18 Mo. Ann. Stat. §566.068 (West 1998).

19 Cal. Penal Code § 290.4 (West 1999). For an explanation of the law available on the World Wide Web go to http://sexoffenders.net.

20 *Black's Law Dictionary* 2 (Pocket Edition 1996)

21 Wang, Ching-Tung and Deborah Daro (1997). *Current Trends in Child Abuse Reporting and Fatalities: The Results of the 1996 Annual Fifty State Survey.* Chicago, IL: National Center on Child Abuse Prevention Research, National Committee to Prevent Child Abuse.

22 Roesler, Thoman and Tiffany Weissman Wind (1994). "Telling the Secret: Adult Woman Describe their Disclosures of Incest." *Journal of Interpersonal Violence,* 9(3): 327–338.

23 Md. Code Ann., Fam. Law § 5-701(b)(1) (1998).

24 Colo. Rev. Stat. Ann. §18-6-401(1) (West 1998).

25 Cal. Penal Code §11165.6 (West 1999).

26 Joshua Dressler, *Understanding Criminal Law* § 18.05[B][3][6], at p. 242 (3d ed. 2001), citing Lenore Walker, Battered Woman 32–51 (1979).

27 Bureau of Justice Statistics. (1994). *Elder Crime Victims.* Washington, D.C.: U.S. Department of Justice, Bureau of Justice Statistics.

28 Model Penal Code § 212.1, comment 1 (1985).

29 *Black's Law Dictionary* (Pocket Edition 1996)

30 720 Ill. Comp. Stat. § 5/10-1(a) (West 1999).

31 18 U.S.C. § 1201 (West 1999).

341

Chapter Objectives

After reading this chapter, you will be able to:

1. Understand the difference between common and modern law arson.
2. Explain the difference between specific intent and general intent arson.
3. List the three elements of burglary.
4. Explain how a burglary can be committed without actual entry by the perpetrator.
5. Understand the intent required to commit a burglary.
6. Explain the difference between simple and aggravated burglary.
7. State the difference between burglary and breaking and entering.
8. Name the elements of the crime of possession of burglar's tools.

Chapter Outline

How can a person commit burglary without entering a building?

Chapter 10

Crimes Against Habitation

10.1 Arson

This chapter categorizes arson and burglary not as crimes against property, but by their common law distinction of being crimes against habitation. At common law, the felonies of arson and burglary developed to provide special protection and security to people's dwellings. This distinction existed for several reasons, one of the most important being that crimes against dwellings could lead to serious violent crimes against the residents of the house. Although modern statutes do not retain the same strict dwelling requirements as before and have broadened their scope considerably, it is still useful to categorize arson and burglary separately, as we have done here.

Common law arson was the malicious, voluntary, or willful burning of another's house or outbuilding within the curtilage. A house was defined as the dwelling of the occupant and any buildings located in the **curtilage**—the land immediately surrounding and associated with the home, such as a barn, outhouse, or milk house. Arson was considered a crime against habitation only, and not a crime against property. Therefore, the burning of an unoccupied house or dwelling was not considered arson.

For the burning of the dwelling to constitute arson, charring of the wood, no matter how minor, was required. Scorching, discoloration, or smoking of the wood did not constitute arson unless charring also occurred. The law also required that the burning be malicious and willful. **Malice**, as you have learned in previous chapters, is the desire to injure the victim by means of a crime. **Will** was a separate element that required proof that the arsonist set the fire intentionally.

Under modern law, most jurisdictions consider arson to be a violent crime against *both* habitation and property. **Modern arson** is generally defined as the malicious, willful burning, or attempted burning, of one's own or another individual's property. The Model Penal Code, for example, provides that a person is guilty of arson:

> "[I]f he starts a fire or causes an explosion with the purpose of:
> (a) destroying a building or occupied structure of another; or
> (b) destroying or damaging any property, whether his own or another's, to collect insurance for such loss."[1]

Prior to the Model Penal Code, there was a "vast legislative development" in the United States that changed the definition of

---

common law arson The malicious and willful burning of the house of another by day or by night.

curtilage The land immediately surrounding and associated with the home, such as a barn, outhouse, or milk house.

malice A desire to injure the victim of the unlawful act, readily inferred from the nature of the act or the circumstances surrounding it.

will A separate element of arson that requires proof that the arsonist set the fire intentionally.

modern arson The malicious, willful burning of, or attempted burning of a dwelling house.

arson to include the burning of almost any property. At the time the MPC was drafted, its drafters noted that there were three legislative patterns that had developed in the United States:

- Classifying the offense in relation to the types of property involved
- Classifying the offense in relation to the danger to persons involved
- Following the influence of the Model Arson Law proposed by the National Board of Fire Underwriters in 1953. This proposal introduced the definition of arson as the burning of any property of any type, no matter by whom owned, for the purpose of defrauding an insurer.

States are still divided on how property is defined. Generally speaking, most states have expanded the definition of property from the limited "dwelling house" definition under the common law rule, to include virtually any structure and, in some instances, personal property. The definition of a dwelling house has been expanded to include structures that people do not use regularly as a place to sleep. For example, Florida statutes define arson in the first degree as the willful and unlawful damage by fire or explosion of:

- Any dwelling, whether occupied or not, or its contents
- Any structure where persons are normally present, such as jails, hospitals, department stores, office buildings, or churches
- Any other structure that the arsonist knew or had reasonable grounds to believe was occupied by a human being[2]

Moreover, this statute defines structure "as any building of any kind, any enclosed area with a roof over it, any real property and appurtenances thereto, any tent or other portable building, and any vehicle, vessel, watercraft, or aircraft."[3]

Some states, on the other hand, still follow the narrow common law definition of arson as a crime against habitation only, especially when defining more serious levels of arson. For example, Maryland law provides that arson in the first degree is the burning of an inhabited structure, but the burning of any other structure constitutes arson in the second degree. This statute did not, however, define dwelling house; this was defined by judicial decision in the case of *Poff v. State* (1968) (see Application Case on page 347).

CRIMINAL LAW Online

International Association of Arson Investigators

Check out the International Association of Arson Investigators (IAAI) by accessing their Web site through the link at **cl.glencoe.com**. What is their focus, and how do they educate the public about arson?

FIGURE 10–1

Vermont Statutes Defining Arson

§ 502. First degree arson

A person who wilfully and maliciously sets fire to or burns or causes to be burned, or who wilfully and maliciously aids, counsels or procures the burning of any dwelling house, whether occupied, unoccupied or vacant, or any kitchen, shop, barn, stable or other outhouse that is parcel thereof, or belonging, or adjoining thereto, whether the property of himself or of another, shall be guilty of arson in the first degree, and shall be imprisoned not more than ten years nor less than two years or fined not more than $2,000.00, or both. (Amended 1971, No. 199 (Adj. Sess.), § 15; 1981, No. 223 (Adj. Sess.), § 23.)

§ 503. Second degree arson

A person who wilfully and maliciously sets fire to or burns or causes to be burned, or who wilfully and maliciously aids, counsels or procures the burning of any building or structure of whatsoever class or character, whether the property of himself or of another, not included or described in section 502 of this title, shall be guilty of arson in the second degree, and shall be imprisoned not more than five years nor less than one year or fined not more than $1,000.00, or both. (Amended 1971, No. 199 (Adj. Sess.), § 15; 1981, No. 223 (Adj. Sess.), § 23.)

§ 504. Third degree arson

A person who wilfully and maliciously sets fire to or burns or causes to be burned, or who wilfully and maliciously aids, counsels or procures the burning of any personal property of whatsoever class or character, not less than $25.00 in value and the property of another person, shall be guilty of arson in the third degree, and shall be imprisoned not more than three years nor less than one year, or fined not more than $500.00, or both. (Amended 1971, No. 199 (Adj. Sess.), §15; 1981, No. 223 (Adj. Sess.), § 23.

§ 505. Fourth degree arson

A person who wilfully and maliciously attempts to set fire to or willfully and maliciously attempts to burn or to aid, counsel or procure the burning of any of the buildings or property mentioned in sections 502–504 of this title, or who wilfully and maliciously commits any act preliminary thereto, or in furtherance thereof, shall be guilty of arson in the fourth degree, and shall be imprisoned not more than two years nor less than one year or fined not more than $500.00, or both. (Amended 1971, No. 199 (Adj. Sess.), § 15; 1981, No. 223 (Adj. Sess.), § 23.)

SOURCE: http://www.leg.state.vt.us/statutes/title13/CHAP011.HTM

Intent Required for Arson

At common law, and almost universally today, arson is a general intent crime. In other words, only the intent to commit arson is required for guilt, even though some forms of the crime require specific intent. For example, arson statutes that require only general intent define the crime as the voluntary or "willful" setting of a fire. As previously explained in Chapter 4, when a crime requires a *mens rea* of general intent, a person can be culpable if he or she voluntarily commits the underlying criminal act or acts without accident, mistake, or negligence, but not necessarily with the purpose of achieving any particular result. When a crime requires a *mens rea* of specific intent, a person is culpable only if he or she voluntarily commits the underlying criminal act or acts without accident, mistake, or negligence, *and in addition* has the intent to achieve a particular result.

Poff v. State

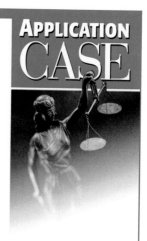

This case applies to both crimes discussed in this chapter: Although it involved the definition of *dwelling house* for the purposes of the laws relating to burglary, the same definition is applicable to the crime of arson.

In *Poff v. State* (1968), a Maryland court stated that the test for determining whether a structure is a *dwelling house* is whether it is used "regularly as a place to sleep." In *Poff*, an apartment was rented by police officers, and personal property was moved there for the purpose of enticing burglars. The officers occupied the apartment only during the daytime. The court held that the defendant, who was apprehended while breaking into the apartment, could be properly convicted only of breaking into a storehouse rather than a dwelling.

Critical Thinking Would a summer home, which is only used seasonally as a place to sleep, be considered a dwelling house? Why or why not?

**Defining
Dwelling House**

SOURCE: *Poff v. State*, 241 A.2d 898 (Md. 1968).

The California arson statutes provide a good example of this distinction. Under the statutes, a person commits the felony of arson who "willfully and maliciously sets fire to or burns [. . .] any structure or property." This provision requires only a general intent for the

◄ **Accidental Fire or Arson?** Investigators look for several different clues to determine if a fire is accidental or intentional. *What are some of the clues that are listed in your textbook?*

crime of arson to be committed. It is, of course, a more serious felony if it results in any level of bodily injury to any person.

Another provision of the California statute specifies that arson may also be committed with specific intent when a person "willfully, maliciously, deliberately, with premeditation, and with intent to cause injury to one or more persons [. . .] sets fire to [. . .] any residence [or] structure." This form of the crime requires two types of intent simultaneously:

1. The general intent to set fire to or burn property.
2. The additional intent to cause injury to one or more persons. This is a felony of a higher degree than that defined above and constitutes the crime of aggravated arson.

Elements and Degrees of Arson

Many states have degrees, or levels of severity, of arson in their statutes. Each different level of arson ranges in severity of punishment, and each includes elements that are not included in other levels. For example, Alaskan law provides for arson in the first and second degree.

- Arson in the first degree is defined as when a "person intentionally damages any property by starting a fire or causing an explosion and by that act recklessly places another person in danger or serious physical injury."
- Arson in the second degree occurs "if the person intentionally damages a building by starting a fire or causing an explosion."[4]

States include different requirements in their arson statutes, such as:

- The type of building burned
- The location of the fire (such as within the curtilage)
- The value of the building
- Any attempts to commit arson while other people are present inside the building[5]

A rash of racially motivated church fires, primarily targeting southern African-American churches, in the last few years have led federal lawmakers to enact arson statutes that carry much greater penalties for those people convicted of setting such church fires. In 1997, three white defendants were the first to be prosecuted and convicted under the new federal arson statute. They were convicted of the

FIGURE 10–2

States that Define Arson as a "Crime Against Habitation" and States that Define Arson as a "Crime Against Property"

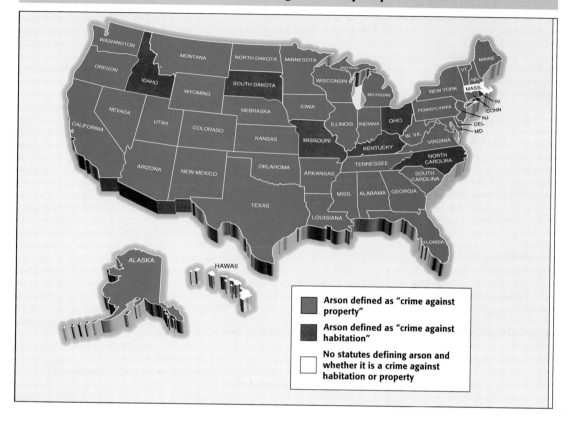

Legend:

- Arson defined as "crime against property"
- Arson defined as "crime against habitation"
- No statutes defining arson and whether it is a crime against habitation or property

racially motivated burning of a predominately black church, the St. Joe Baptist Church in Alabama, and did receive the harsher penalties.[6]

Usually, fire departments have an arson investigator who will respond to a burning building call to determine whether the fire was accidental or intentional. In addition, when an officer responds to the scene of a fire, there are several things he or she can do to help determine the fire's origin:

- The officer should look for incendiary devices, fuel cans, broken door locks, or any other signs of forced entry.
- The officer should also interview all available witnesses at the scene, asking questions that will help to determine the financial stability of the building owner or occupants. Any financial instability might indicate a motive to collect on an insurance policy.

ON THE JOB

Fire/Arson Investigator

Description and Duties: Investigate fire origins and causes; determine arson cases and provide reports. Determine accidental and intentional fires. Work with law enforcement and insurers in cases of arson. Enforce compliance with city and state fire prevention codes.

Salary: Salaries range from approximately $35,000 to $48,000.

Other Information: Requires state inspection certificate, as well as any accreditation

from state firefighter standards councils. Also usually requires a two-year degree in fire science, criminal justice, public administration, or related area; and three to five years experience in local or state government fire inspections.

Critical Thinking What special skills or traits do you think a fire/arson investigator must have?

SOURCE: Florida Fire Marshals and Inspectors Association, http://www.ffma.org/employment.html.

- The officer should also seek to learn of any enemies of the owner or occupant, who might have set the fire for revenge.
- Finally, the officer should scan the crowd for any known firebugs, or known arsonists. Many arsonists get a psychological rush by watching the fires that they have set and often are present at the fire.

These early efforts, coupled with the work of an arson investigator, will provide valuable aid in catching the arsonist.

CRIMINAL LAW *Online*

Check your answers at cl.glencoe.com.

Self Check

1. How have laws regarding arson changed since common law?
2. What are the steps that officers need to take to investigate a fire, in order to determine if it was accidental or intentional?

10.2 Burglary

At common law, burglary was viewed as a forcible invasion and disturbance of a person's right of habitation, and had a high risk of being punished by death. The law comes to the aid of the inhabitant and designates the acts against habitation as a crime. Thus, **common law burglary** was defined as the breaking and entering, in the nighttime, of the mansion or dwelling house or curtilage of another, with the intent to commit a felony.[7]

The purpose of the burglary laws was not to protect persons merely against unlawful trespass (also called breaking and entering), which does not require the intent to commit a crime beyond the actual trespass or entering. Rather, their purpose was to protect the habitation.

Today, this common law perspective of burglary has been statutorily expanded beyond the dwelling house and its curtilage to include other places that are susceptible to burglary. The modern definition of burglary, brought about by judicial decision and legislation, has substantially enlarged the scope of the offense. Under the most comprehensive definitions of **modern burglary**, the offense can be committed by entry alone; in the daytime as well as night; in any building, structure, or vehicle; with the intent to commit any criminal offense. The MPC defines burglary as the entry of a "building or occupied structure, or separately secured or occupied portion thereof," with the purpose to commit a crime, "unless the premises are at the time open to the public or if the actor is licensed or privileged to enter."[8]

common law burglary
Breaking and entering, in the nighttime, of the mansion or dwelling house or curtilage of another, with the intent to commit a felony.

modern burglary Entry alone, in the daytime as well as night, in any building, structure, or vehicle, with the intent to commit any criminal offense.

Elements of Burglary

Generally, burglary requires three elements:

1. An entry,
2. Of a dwelling or building,
3. With intent to commit a crime inside.

In addition, some statutes differentiate between burglaries committed during the daytime and those committed at nighttime, with the latter carrying a heavier penalty.

Entry An entry into a structure of some sort, no matter how slight, is required for there to be a burglary. Entry can be accomplished through many different means, such as forcing open a door

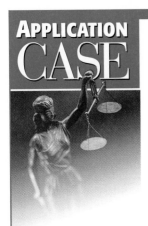
Youthful Burglars

In 1986, two nine-year-old California boys were arrested and later convicted of several residential burglaries. They were caught when one of them got stuck in a chimney as he was attempting to enter a house. The chimney had been the point of entry for all of the burglaries and unfortunately for the boy, this particular chimney was too small for him to slip through. Entry through the chimney met the necessary breaking and entering element requirement to constitute burglary.

Critical Thinking Do you think the boys in this case should be prosecuted? If you were a prosecutor, how would you handle this case?

SOURCE: Patricia Klein, "Boy Pulled from Chimney, Friends are Charged in Home Burglaries," *Los Angeles Times*, January 1, 1986, Valley Edition p. 6.

CRIMINAL LAW Online

The Burgled Helpline

Visit this UK-based site by clicking the link at **cl.glencoe.com** and read "Recently been burgled?" and "Making your home safer." Which of these suggestions have you already implemented? Which should you implement to increase your safety?

or window, entering through a partially opened door or window, or entering through a closed inner door. Contrary to popular belief, entries with consent can also satisfy the entry element of burglary.

Some states follow the common law definition of burglary and require that the entry occur "at night." Today, though, the distinction between commission of the offense at night (as opposed to the daytime) is most frequently a matter of defining the degree of the crime, rather than defining the basic offense. For example, under the MPC, burglary is a felony of the second degree if it is committed at night in the dwelling of another.

The usual method of gaining entry of a structure is to break open a closed door or window. From this comes the term breaking and entering, which you will learn more about later in this chapter. Many jurisdictions have eliminated the burglary requirement of a breaking, and others have changed their statutes to read "breaking *or* entering." If there is no requirement for a breaking, burglary can occur when a person enters an open business with the intent to commit a crime inside, even if the entry is not trespassory in nature. In these jurisdictions, a person is guilty of burglary if he or she walks into a store open for business with the intent to steal.[9] In contrast, the MPC does not classify such an entry into a public place as a burglary.

In those jurisdictions where the requirement of "breaking" remains, the further opening of an already partially opened door or

FIGURE 10-3

States That Impose a More Severe Penalty for Burglary When It Is Committed at Nighttime vs. States That Have Entirely Discarded the Nighttime Requirement

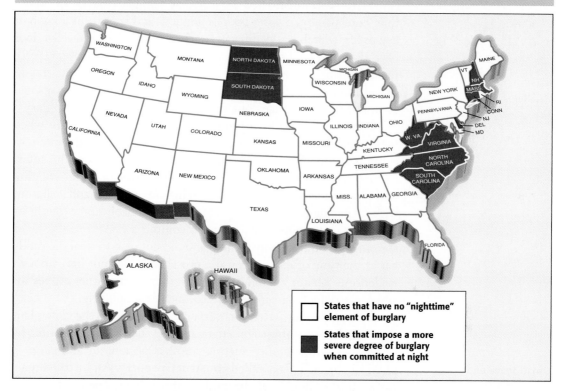

States that have no "nighttime" element of burglary

States that impose a more severe degree of burglary when committed at night

window is sufficient to constitute a burglary. The slightest removal of an obstruction to the burglar's entry into the dwelling is enough for a breaking—in other words, the amount of force needed to remove an obstacle to the entry is immaterial. Therefore, raising a partially opened bedroom window or pushing open a hotel room door that was ajar three to four inches is considered a "breaking."[10]

In *Green v. Commonwealth* (1972), for example, an on-duty police officer was found guilty of a storehouse-breaking when he entered an unlocked back door of a barber shop. Other officers had "staked out" the shop prior to the officer's entry and observed Green take a bottle of shampoo, some pocket combs, $25 in cash, and a bottle of hair oil. The court held that Green had a right to be in the store for purposes of protecting the owner's property, but if he entered with the intent to steal, he "shed his official immunity at the door" and therefore broke and entered feloniously.[11]

An **inner door** is any door that is inside a building but does not lead directly outside; one must already be inside to gain entry. Such

inner door A door inside the building that does not lead directly to the outside of such building.

Crimes Against Habitation   **CHAPTER 10**   **353**

doors could be bedroom, bathroom, suite, or office doors. Even if one achieved entry through an open outer door with consent, breaking into an inner door of a building is still burglary. In *State v. Edell* (1935), the court instructed the jury that a burglary has occurred if a thief enters an open outer door or window, and later turns a knob or key, or lifts a latch.[12] Opening an attached garage door and cellar door have also been held to constitute burglary. In *People v. Davis* (1959), the defendant entered a service station and hid until after the station closed and was locked up for the evening. The defendant then opened an unlocked inner office door, and this act made the entry burglary.[13]

It may be difficult to prosecute defendants for burglary when they enter a business that is open to the public, but have the intent to commit a crime. For example, how do you charge a person who enters a grocery store and buys $100 worth of groceries, but after entering the store decides to put a candy bar in his or her pocket and walks out without paying for it? Such a person would probably argue that he or she never had the requisite intent to commit a crime because he or she entered the store only to shop and did not plan to steal the candy bar at the time of entry. Even if a prosecutor does not have enough evidence to obtain a burglary conviction, there are other crimes for which the defendant can be charged, such as shoplifting.

To commit an entry for purposes of burglary, the defendant does not have to physically enter. Instead, he or she can enter by using an instrumentality—such as another person, an animal, or a physical object. This is called **constructive entry**. An instrumentality, such as a hook, can be pushed through an open window to retrieve an item inside the structure. Also, a trained monkey or dog can be used to make the entry for the defendant.

Consent can be a valid defense to a burglary charge in jurisdictions where a breaking is required, either under the common law

constructive entry An entry effected by using an instrumentality—either another person, an animal, or a physical object.

Myth	Fact
Almost all burglaries occur at night primarily in residences, not businesses.	One-third of reported burglaries involve stores, offices, and other structures. About one-half of all residential burglaries, and about one-quarter of commercial burglaries, take place during the day.

SOURCE: Floyd Feeney, "Burglary," in *Encyclopedia of Crime and Justice* 131 (S.H. Kadish ed. 1983).

State v. Cochran

This case and the two Application Cases on page 356 demonstrate that entry with consent will not preclude a burglary prosecution in many instances.

In *State v. Cochran*, Cochran spent the night at his niece's house, which she shared with two other women. The next morning, he entered the locked room of one of the women, and stole several items. In affirming Cochran's burglary conviction, the court found that the locked bedroom was a "building" and that, although Cochran had permission from his niece to be within the house, no consent was given to enter the locked bedroom.

Critical Thinking Would Cochran have been convicted if the bedroom had been unlocked? What if he had entered a closet?

SOURCE: *State v. Cochran*, 463 A2d 618 (Conn. 1983).

rule or under a statute. For example, in *People v. Carstensen* (1966), the defendant could not be found guilty of burglary where he had permission to enter an apartment to paint it, and was still engaged in painting when he stole a television set from the apartment. Therefore, there was no breaking or entering.[14]

Here is another example: Carol and Victor plan to burglarize a jewelry store. Carol breaks open the back door and enters the store. Victor goes to the roof and lowers down a basket on a string through an open skylight. Victor has committed burglary by constructive entry, even though he has not entered the store. He has, in fact, effected constructive entry in two ways: 1) Carol made entry on Victor's behalf to steal the jewelry, and 2) Victor used an instrumentality under his control to effectuate the entry into the building.

Time of Day Requirements The common law and many current state laws require that for an entry to be a burglary, the act must be committed at nighttime. **Nighttime** was defined at common law as the period between sunset and sunrise where there is not enough daylight to discern a man's face. For states following this common law definition, the time of day, amount of sunlight, and use of sunlight to see becomes important in establishing whether it is nighttime. The existence of moonlight, streetlights, or building lights does not count as "sunlight." Alternatively, many states define burglary without a time requirement, so that it can occur during the day or night. (See

nighttime The period between sunset and sunrise where there is not enough daylight to discern a man's face.

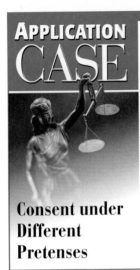

People v. Czerminski

In *People v. Czerminski*, a police officer was convicted of burglary when he stole several items while investigating a warehouse break-in. The court upheld the conviction on the grounds that the consent for the officer to be on the premises was to perform a public duty only, and when the officer remained on the property to commit a theft, he exceeded the scope of that consent.

Critical Thinking Should police officers be held to a higher standard of conduct? Should they be punished more harshly when they commit crimes?

SOURCE: *People v. Czerminski*, 464 N.Y.S.2d 83 (App. Div. 1983).

Figure 10–3 on page 353 to see how various states use the nighttime requirement.) The jury has the right to apply common sense and knowledge to determine when the burglary occurred.

Dwelling or Building Requirements Burglary requires the entering of a dwelling, building, or structure. The absence or presence of an occupant from a structure may make a difference in whether a structure is considered a "dwelling." Some jurisdictions require for the highest degree of burglary not only that the structure must be used as a dwelling, but also that a person must be physically present in the dwelling at the time the burglary occurred. In other jurisdictions, a person does not have to be physically present in the home at the time of the burglary, but to be a dwelling the structure must be considered "inhabited." A temporary absence does not necessarily make the dwelling uninhabited. In *State v. Hicks* (1973), the court upheld a conviction of aggravated burglary of an inhabited dwelling where the defendant entered a dwelling with no one home and fled when he heard the occupants return.[15]

sleep test Whether the dwelling is used regularly as a place to sleep determines whether a dwelling is occupied.

Some states apply a **sleep test** in determining whether a dwelling is occupied. According to this test, if a dwelling is used regularly as a place to sleep, it is inhabited. Occasional sleeping on the premises is usually not enough to satisfy the sleep test. Nonetheless, in one case, a summer vacation home in Maine that was entered in the winter was held to be a "dwelling place," even though the house did not have heat or other utilities and was therefore uninhabitable during the winter months.[16] Usually, residences that are under con-

Myth	Fact
A person cannot commit burglary by breaking into his or her own residence.	If a person shares his or her residence with other people such as a roommate, it is possible for that person to commit burglary by entering that portion of the residence in which the others have exclusive dominion or control.

struction and have never been occupied are held to be uninhabited. If the sole owner and occupant of the dwelling was deceased or in a mental hospital at the time of the burglary, most jurisdictions would consider the house uninhabited.

The Model Penal Code states that a person commits burglary who "enters a building, occupied structure, or separately secured or occupied portion thereof with [the] purpose to commit a crime therein, unless the premises are at the time open to the public or the actor is licensed or privileged to enter." The MPC defines "occupied structure" as "any structure, vehicle, or place adapted for overnight accommodation of persons, or for carrying on business therein, whether or not a person is actually present." A person does not have to be physically present in the dwelling for the crime to be burglary, because it is only a coincidence that the burglar happened to miss the residents at that particular time.[17]

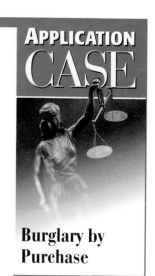

APPLICATION CASE

K.P.M. v. State

In *K.P.M. v. State*, the defendant made an agreement with a store clerk to pay the clerk to receive groceries with a retail value of more than the amount he paid the clerk. The court upheld the defendant's conviction for burglary and rejected the defendant's argument that the clerk had consented to the agreement. The court reasoned that the clerk had no authority to give such consent and the defendant could not in good faith have reasonably believed the transaction was legal.

Critical Thinking How does this case meet the requirements of burglary?

SOURCE: *K.P.M. v. State*, 446 So. 2d 723 (Fla. Dist. Ct. App. 1984).

Burglary by Purchase

FIGURE 10–4

Minnesota Statute on Burglary

609.582 Burglary

Subdivision 1. **Burglary in the first degree.**
Whoever enters a building without consent and
with intent to commit a crime, or enters a building
without consent and commits a crime while in the
building, either directly or as an accomplice, commits burglary in the first degree and may be sentenced to imprisonment for not more than 20
years or to payment of a fine of not more than
$35,000, or both, if:

(a) the building is a dwelling and another person,
not an accomplice, is present in it when the burglar
enters or at any time while the burglar is in the
building;

(b) the burglar possesses, when entering or at any
time while in the building, any of the following: a
dangerous weapon, any article used or fashioned
in a manner to lead the victim to reasonably
believe it to be a dangerous weapon, or an explosive; or

(c) the burglar assaults a person within the building or on the building's appurtenant property.

Subd. 1a. **Mandatory minimum sentence for
burglary of occupied dwelling.** A person convicted of committing burglary of an occupied

dwelling, as defined in subdivision 1, clause (a),
must be committed to the commissioner of corrections or county workhouse for not less than six
months.

Subd. 2. **Burglary in the second degree.** Whoever
enters a building without consent and with intent to
commit a crime, or enters a building without consent and commits a crime while in the building,
either directly or as an accomplice, commits burglary
in the second degree and may be sentenced to
imprisonment for not more than ten years or to payment of a fine of not more than $20,000, or both, if:

(a) the building is a dwelling;

(b) the portion of the building entered contains a
banking business or other business of receiving
securities or other valuable papers for deposit or
safekeeping and the entry is with force or threat
of force;

(c) the portion of the building entered contains a
pharmacy or other lawful business or practice in
which controlled substances are routinely held or
stored, and the entry is forcible; or

(d) when entering or while in the building, the burglar possesses a tool to gain access to money or
property.

SOURCE: http://pigseye.revisor.leg.state.mn.us/stats/609/582.html

To assist the investigation, a burglary report taken from a victim
should state how the crime was committed. The reporting officer
should look for the burglar's *modus operandi* (mode of operation), as
well as any other details that will assist in ultimately identifying and
convicting the perpetrator. The list and description of stolen property should be as detailed as possible, including information such as
serial and model numbers, initials, or noticeable scratches.

Here is a sample narrative of a burglary report:

Between 7 A.M. and 5 P.M. on 5-29-97, one or more unknown
suspects obtained entry from the northwest window of 123
Westmoreland Avenue, 2-story house, by using approximately a ½″ pry tool, possibly a flat head screwdriver. The sus-
pect(s) popped open the latch on the window and slid the

window open. Fresh sneaker marks were found on the dirt outside the window, and the dust on the windowsill had been disturbed. The suspect(s) then proceeded to ransack the bedroom, living room, and dining room, taking the items listed in the attached property report. The suspect(s) exited out the living room patio door, leaving it slightly ajar. Latent prints were discernable on both the window and sliding door, and were lifted and sent to the crime laboratory under the above property number for analysis. The victim was interviewed and stated that she left the house secured and she was not present during the burglary.

The report should also have a list of the items taken, make, model, and serial numbers, and approximate value.

When is "Nighttime"?

The common law definition of burglary in the "nighttime" has been modified. Although it still defines the time between sunset and sunrise, this is often set by statute, such as between 6 P.M. and 6 A.M.

Intent   In most jurisdictions, the specific intent to commit a crime must be present at the time of entry in order for the crime to be a burglary. The burglar does not actually have to remove or even touch an item from the structure to be guilty of burglary. If the intent is formed after the entry is made, or there is no intent to commit a crime at all, the crimes of theft or trespass may have been committed, but not burglary.

The intent to commit a crime can be inferred from the circumstances surrounding the entry. Examples include:

- If the defendant enters a business open to the public with a shopping bag that is lined with aluminum foil, it is reasonable to infer that the suspect intended to place stolen merchandise in the bag and avoid detection from the electronic security devices at the store's entrance.
- Intent can also be inferred from the time of entry. For instance, if one enters a stranger's residence or a closed place of business at midnight, intent to steal could be reasonably inferred.
- The type of building entered, such as a warehouse not open to the public, can imply intent.
- Possession of a weapon or burglar tools can determine intent.
- When applied to the crime of shoplifting, specific intent can also be shown if the suspect went shopping and selected items with no money or credit cards in his or her possession, possessed a shopping bag with a false bottom, or wore baggy clothes to hide stolen items.

Thus, the elements and the crime of burglary are complete when the entry is made with the requisite intent.

➤ Breaking and Entering
Breaking and entering does not require the specific intent to commit a felony that burglary does.
Do you think this person is committing burglary or breaking and entering?

Breaking and Entering

Breaking and entering, or unlawful forced entry, is very similar to burglary, except it is lacking one element—the specific intent to commit a theft or felony inside the structure. Therefore, if a homeless person breaks into a structure to get out of the rain and forms the intent to steal after entry, or never even steals, he or she has not committed burglary, but rather the lesser crime of breaking and entering. The breaking and entering offense can be an effective tool for prosecutors to use because they may offer this charge to a defendant, rather than burglary, in the hopes of a plea bargain.

Degrees of Burglary

There are two ways in which burglary is divided into degrees. Some states divide burglary offenses into simple and aggravated burglary. For example, Louisiana defines **simple burglary** as "the unauthorized entering of any dwelling, vehicle, water craft, or other structure, movable or immovable, with the intent to commit a felony or any theft therein." Simple burglary is a lesser included offense of **aggravated burglary**, which consists of the added elements of entering an inhabited dwelling, or any structure or vehicle, while armed with a dangerous weapon, or by committing a battery after or upon the entry.[18]

simple burglary The unauthorized entering of any dwelling, vehicle, water craft, or other structure, movable or immovable, with the intent to commit a felony or any theft therein.

aggravated burglary Simple burglary with the added elements of entering an inhabited dwelling, or any structure or vehicle, while armed with a dangerous weapon, or by committing a battery after or upon the entry.

Other states classify burglary offenses into degrees or grades. California has two degrees of burglary: first and second degree. Under the California classification, "every burglary of an inhabited dwelling house, trailer coach as defined by the Vehicle Code, or inhabited portion of any other building, is burglary of the first degree. All other kinds of burglary are of the second degree."[19]

Arizona divides burglary into three categories:

1. First-degree burglary occurs when a person or accomplice commits second- or third-degree burglary "and knowingly possesses explosives, a deadly weapon or a dangerous instrument in the course of committing any theft or any felony."

2. Second-degree burglary is committed when a person enters or remains unlawfully "in or on a residential structure with the intent to commit any theft or any felony therein."

3. A person commits third-degree burglary "by entering or remaining unlawfully in or on a nonresidential structure or in a fenced commercial or residential yard with the intent to commit any theft or any felony therein."[20]

Furthermore, whether a structure is residential or nonresidential will affect the degree of burglary in Arizona.

Possession of Burglar's Tools

Most states make it illegal to possess **burglar's tools**, which are tools and instruments that are designed, adapted, or commonly used to commit burglaries. The possession of burglar's tools is a separate crime, not an element of the crime of burglary. Therefore, a person can be convicted of burglary, even though he or she is not in possession of these tools, and a person can be convicted of possession of burglar's tools even if he or she is nowhere near a structure to burglarize. The typical elements of this crime are:

- Possession of the burglar's tools, or instruments that are adapted, designed, or commonly used for committing any burglary
- The intent to use the tool in the commission of a burglary[21]

A person does not have to own the burglar's tools to be criminally culpable; the person need only possess the tools with the requisite intent.

There must also be the intent to burglarize to be convicted of possession of burglar's tools. The prosecution does not need to establish

Burglar's Tools or Not?

When investigating the crime of possession of burglar's tools, an officer must determine the suspect's purpose or motive, and explore all of the circumstances surrounding the possession.

Questions to ask may include:

- What reason does the person have for possessing the tools?
- Is he or she a locksmith, or someone who needs these tools for a business purpose, or is there really no legitimate reason for their possession?
- For example, where was the person when caught with the tools?

burglar's tools Tools and instruments that are designed, adapted, or commonly used to commit burglaries.

that the defendant intended to commit a particular burglary, only that he or she intended to commit some burglary. Intent can be established by the time of day, location of possession, employment of the possessor, or the possessor trying to get rid of the tools when confronted by police.

All of the items that could be burglar's tools can have legitimate uses. For example, even if a tool is commonly used or originally designed for a lawful purpose, it can still be a burglar's tool. Lug wrenches, lock-picking devices, screwdrivers, slim jims, bolt cutters, porcelain chips from spark plugs, crowbars, wire, and nitroglycerin or other explosives all have legitimate uses—but can still be burglar's tools.

Remember, possessing such tools is just one part of this crime. A person must also have the requisite intent to commit burglary. Some states, therefore, require that there be a lack of a lawful excuse for the possession of the tools to be illegal. This would be satisfied if the defendant could not give a legitimate explanation for what the tools were used for or why he or she was in possession of them. A law enforcement officer has to use discretion to determine if the suspect has a lawful reason for possessing these items. If someone was discovered outside of a closed business, late at night, wearing black, inference of the requisite intent would probably be justified.

Vehicular Burglary

The basic burglary statute of many states creates the crime of vehicular burglary by defining vehicles as a type of structure that can be the subject of breaking and entering. The definition of breaking, for purposes of committing the crime of vehicular burglary, is adapted for the nature of vehicles. For example, using the slightest force to turn a vehicle's unlocked door handle, or using a coat hanger to open the trunk, may be sufficient to constitute a breaking. Additionally, the slightest intrusion or entry into the vehicle by a body part or instrument is sufficient to constitute burglary. Some states, like California, require that the vehicle be locked, although case law does not require the state to prove that every door was locked—the owner's testimony that the doors were locked is usually sufficient.[22]

A **motor vehicle** is generally defined as "a vehicle proceeding on land by means of its own power plant and free of rails, tracks, or overhead wires."[23] Each state defines vehicle and motor vehicle for burglary and for breaking and entering. For example, a van that has flat tires and is used for storage is considered a vehicle under the breaking and entering statute in Michigan. Under this statute, "vehicle" includes all vehicles that could be moved on the state's public highway with mechanical power.[24] The court reasoned that the van could be easily repaired and that thousands of vehicles in need of repair sit in repair lots, yards, and garages, yet are still considered vehicles. In *Trevino v. State* (1985), a vehicle sitting in a car lot without an engine was still a vehicle under Texas statutory language, which defines vehicle as any device that could be moved, propelled, or drawn by a person in the normal course of commerce or transportation. The court found that the temporary condition of the vehicle was less important than its mechanism, design, and construction.[25]

There are only a few crimes that a person might intend to commit when he or she breaks and enters a vehicle: stealing the vehicle, stealing something out of the vehicle, or joyriding. **Joyriding** is defined as the illegal removal and driving of someone else's car, but with the intention of keeping it only temporarily. Although joyriding is a felony in many jurisdictions, it is not considered as serious as burglary and may be the tool necessary for a defendant to accept a plea bargain and not go to trial. Sometimes, and under certain circumstances, a prosecutor may reduce the original charge of vehicular burglary to joyriding. For example, if a very young person steals a car and uses it to drive around with friends, then returns the car unharmed, the prosecutor might not charge burglary.

motor vehicle A vehicle proceeding on land by means of its own power plant and free of rails, tracks, or overhead wires.

joyriding The illegal driving of someone else's automobile without permission, but with no intent to deprive the owner of it permanently.

Self Check

1. What are the differences between burglary and breaking and entering?
2. What are the three general purposes of vehicular burglary?

CRIMINAL LAW Online

Check your answers at cl.glencoe.com.

Crimes Against Habitation

SUMMARY BY CHAPTER OBJECTIVES

1. Understand the difference between common law and modern law arson.

Common law arson required that the burning occur at night and the dwelling be occupied. The common law definition of dwelling was narrowly defined, to include only the dwelling of the occupant and any buildings located in the curtilage surrounding the dwelling. Under the definition of modern law arson, most structures qualify as a dwelling, arson does not have to occur at night, and the dwelling need not be occupied. Another modern element concerning arson, which is covered under many statutes, is the intent to defraud insurers through arson.

2. Explain the difference between specific intent and general intent arson.

Specific intent arson statutes include the lesser intent requirement of general intent and go one step further by requiring an additional intent of a definite and actual purpose to accomplish some particular thing. Specific intent statutes usually include the specific words 'with intent to' effect a certain result. One example of this is the intent to defraud insurers by making a fire appear accidental.

3. List the three elements of burglary.

The three elements are:

- The entry,
- of a dwelling,
- with intent to commit a crime inside.

4. Explain how a burglary can be committed without actual entry by the perpetrator.

Entry can be made *constructively*, which means that the burglar uses an instrumentality—such as another person, an animal, a robot, or a physical object such as a tool—to actually break into the structure.

5. Understand the intent required to commit a burglary.

The specific intent to commit a crime must be present at the time of entry in order for it to constitute a burglary. If the intent is formed after the entry is made, or there is no intent to commit a crime at all, the crimes of theft or trespass may have been committed, but not burglary. The crime of breaking and entering, or unlawful forced entry, is similar to burglary, but it does not require the specific intent to commit a theft or felony inside the structure.

6. Explain the difference between simple and aggravated burglary.

A simple burglary is the unauthorized entering of any dwelling with the intent to commit a felony or any theft therein. Simple burglary is a lesser offense than aggravated burglary, which adds the elements of entering an inhabited dwelling, or any structure or vehicle, while armed with a dangerous weapon, or by committing a battery upon or after entry.

7. State the difference between burglary and breaking and entering.

A breaking and entering, or unlawful forced entry, is very similar to burglary, except that it is lacking the specific intent to commit a theft or felony inside the structure.

8. Name the elements of the crime of possession of burglar's tools.

The typical elements to this crime are possession of the burglar's tools or instruments that are adapted, designed, or commonly used for committing any burglary, and the intent to use the tool in the commission of a burglary. Although all burglar's tools can be used for legal purposes, police look at the totality of circumstances—including the suspect's explanation for possessing such tools—to determine whether a crime has taken place. This allows people like locksmiths to possess burglar's tools without being arrested.

KEY TERMS

common law arson, page 344
curtilage, page 344
malice, page 344
will, page 344
modern arson, page 344
common law burglary, page 351
modern burglary, page 351
inner door, page 353

constructive entry, page 354
nighttime, page 355
sleep test, page 357
simple burglary, page 360
aggravated burglary, page 360
burglar's tools, page 361
motor vehicle, page 363
joyriding, page 363

How can a person commit burglary without entering a building?
Find it on page 354.

QUESTIONS FOR REVIEW

1. What level of burning is required to constitute arson? What levels of burning do not constitute arson?
2. Under modern law, what is the definition of dwelling structure in most jurisdictions?
3. What are some of the differences between first-degree and second-degree arson?
4. State the common law purpose of the burglary law.
5. What is an inner door, and what is its meaning in relation to burglary?
6. What is the difference between the common law and modern definitions of nighttime, and its relevance to the crime of burglary?
7. What is the sleep test?
8. How can the offense of breaking and entering be used as a prosecutor's tool, and why?
9. What are some general and specific definitions of a motor vehicle, as given in your text?
10. What is joyriding, and how can this offense be used as a prosecutor's tool?

PROBLEM-SOLVING EXERCISES

1. **Burglar's Tools** It is five P.M. on a Saturday night and an officer pulls over a vehicle for a missing taillight. The officer notices some tools on the passenger floorboard. The officer gets permission from the driver to inspect the tools and inventory the items. There are two large flat-head screwdrivers, a small pry bar, a flashlight, a knife, a large crescent wrench, and a pair of plastic gloves. The officer runs the driver's name on the computer database and discovers that he has been convicted of burglary, breaking and entering, and theft. The driver says he was coming from his contracting job, where he was laying some carpet. He says he cannot remember the address where he was working because he followed his boss there.

   a) Does he appear to be telling the truth regarding carpet tools? Why or why not?
   b) What else can you ask him to gain pertinent information?
   c) Should the officer arrest the driver for possession of burglar's tools? Why, or why not?

2. **Arson Investigation** You are investigating a fire at a hardware store that has been in your community for nearly 40 years. It is located in a neighborhood that, because of a growing industrial presence, receives little business. When you arrive at the scene, you see in front of the

building the owner, his wife, some neighbors, and a small group. Among those in the group is a young man who is talking excitedly about the fire and is apparently oblivious to the owner's obvious grief. Answer the following questions:

a) Who do you question first, and whom do you question afterward? Why?
b) Who appears to be a suspect? Why?
c) What else can you do to investigate this fire properly?

WORKPLACE APPLICATIONS

1. **Burglary Statutes** Look up the burglary statute in your jurisdiction. Under the statute, which of the following are dwellings:
   a) A motorcycle
   b) A dog house
   c) An empty house that is for sale
   d) A tool shed next to a house
   e) A corn crib
   Why or why not? What additional information do you need to know in order to determine if they are dwellings?

2. **Theft or Burglary?** On a Saturday morning, an officer responds to a burglary call. When he arrives, he finds beer cans and bottles strewn all over the living room. The victim denies having a party the night before and says he and his roommate are bad housekeepers. The victim claims that he keeps the back door closed, but unlocked, because he and his roommate often forget their keys. He reports some jewelry and cash was stolen the night before, while he was at the movies. The officer suspects the victim had a party and one of the guests took the items. The officer also knows that the victim's roommate has a history of thefts and may have taken the property. Answer the following questions:

   a) Should the officer take the victim's word at face value, or should he question the validity of the report?
   b) If the officer believes the victim is lying, should he still make a report of the crime as stated by the victim? Why or why not?
   c) What other information should the officer gather from the victim, roommates, and from investigatory activities?

INTERNET APPLICATIONS

1. **Arson Prevention** Visit the "Arson Prevention for America's Churches and Synagogues" Web site by clicking the link at **cl.glencoe.com**. Read the suggestions, then answer the following questions:
   a) What are some suggestions listed here that any church could follow to prevent arson?
   b) If a church faced arson or attempted arson, what measures should it take to prevent this in the future?
   c) How can involvement with the local fire department help prevent arson?

2. **Burglary Cases** Visit a "Burglary" Web site through the link at **cl.glencoe.com**. Read one of the cases listed on this page, then pretend that you are an investigator for this case. Answer the following questions:
   a) What are the circumstances of the case you chose?
   b) What helpful information has been provided?
   c) What additional information will you need to crack this case?
   d) From whom do you think you can get this information?

ETHICS ISSUES

1. **Blue Wall of Silence** Assume that you are a newly assigned police officer and you respond to a burglary call with your training officer. No one is at the house when you get there, and the back door is wide open. The house is totally ransacked, and it is immediately apparent that the television, VCR, and stereo are missing. In addition, a jewelry case in one of the bedrooms is almost empty. You glance at the jewelry case and see that a woman's gold watch and some rings were left behind by the burglars. After you clear the house for suspects, you go back to take pictures of all of the rooms for your report. As you take a picture of the jewelry case, you notice the watch is missing.
   a) What do you do first?
   b) Who do you speak to about this?
   c) What possible repercussions concern you?

ENDNOTES

1 Model Penal Code § 220.1(1) (1985).

2 Fla. Stat. Ann. § 806.01(1) (West 1997).

3 Fla. Stat. Ann. § 806.01(1) (West 1997).

4 Cal. Penal Code § 451, 457 (West 2001).

5 Ariz. Rev. Stat. Ann. §13-1701 (1997).

6 Church Arson Prevention Act of 1996, amending 18 U.S.C. § 241 (1998). See also "Whites Convicted of Burning Church," *L.A. Times*, November 4, 1997, at A11.

7 4 William Blackstone, *Commentaries* 224.

8 Model Penal Code § 221.1 cmt. 1 (1985); § 221.1(1) (1985).

9 Emile F. Short, Annotation, *Breaking and Entering of Inner Door of Building as Burglary*, 43 A.L.R. 3d 1147 (1996).

10 *State v. Rosencranz*, 167 P.2d 170 (Wash. 1946)

11 *Green v. Commonwealth*, 488 SW2d 339 (Ky. 1972).

12 *State v. Edell*, 183 A. 630 (Del. 1935), as cited in Emile F. Short, Annotation, Breaking and Entering of Inner Door of Building as Burglary, 43 A.L.R. 3d 1147 at § 9(a) (1996).

13 *People v. Davis*, 346 P2d 248 (Cal. App. 1959), as cited in Emile F. Short, Annotation, *Breaking and Entering of Inner Door of Building as Burglary*, 43 A.L.R. 3d 1147 at § 10 (1996).

14 *People v. Carstensen*, 420 P.2d 820 (Col. 1966).

15 *State v. Hicks*, 286 So 2d 331 (La. 1973).

16 *State v. Albeert*, 426 A.2d 1370 (Me. 1981).

17 Model Penal Code § 221.1 (1985), § 221.0(1), and § 221.0(1) cmt. 2.

18 La. Rev. Stat. § 14:62 and § 14:60 (West 1998).

19 Cal. Penal Code § 460 (West 1998).

20 Ariz. Rev. Stat. § 13-1506, § 13-1507, and § 13-1508 (West 1998).

21 *E.g., People v. Pesce*, 239 N.Y.S.2d 651 (N.Y. App. Div. 1963); Ariz. Rev. Stat. § 13-1505 (West 1998).

22 *People v. Blalock*, 98 Cal. Rptr. 231 (Cal. Ct. App. 1971); People v. Lombardi, 23 Cal. Rptr. 35 (Cal. Ct. App. 1962).

23 Jeffrey F. Ghent, *Annotation; Burglary, Breaking, or Entering of Motor Vehicle*, 72 A.L.R. 4th 710 § 1(a) (1990).

24 *People v. Matusik*, 234 N.W.2d 517 (Mich. Ct. App. 1975).

25 697 S.W.2d 476 (Tex. Ct. App. 1985).

Chapter Objectives

After reading this chapter, you will be able to:

1. List the elements of larceny.
2. Explain the difference between larceny from the person and robbery.
3. List the elements of embezzlement.
4. State the difference between embezzlement and larceny.
5. List the essential elements of robbery.
6. Differentiate between extortion, blackmail, and bribery.
7. State the essential elements of forgery.

Chapter Outline

What is the difference between larceny and robbery?

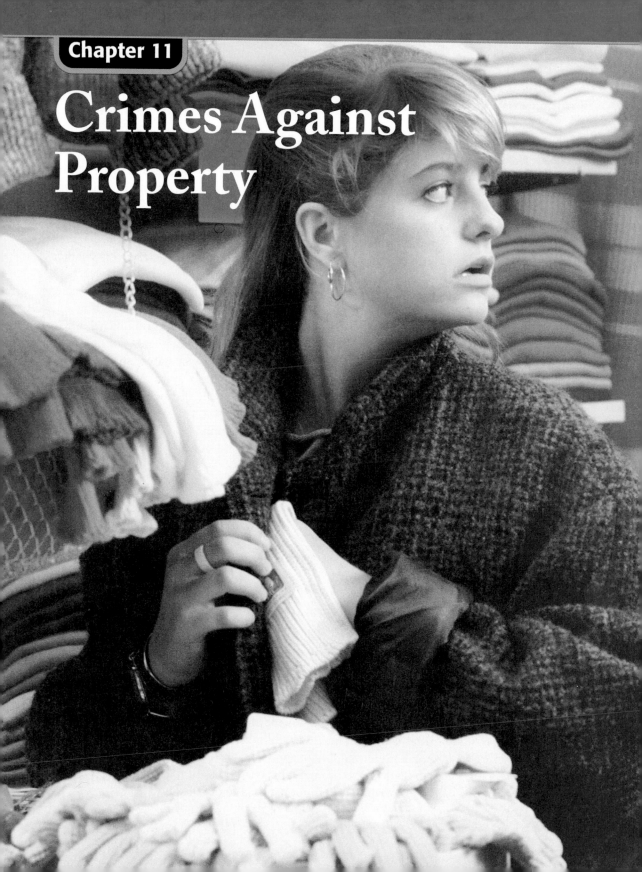

Crimes Against Property

11.1 Forms and Variations of Theft

It is often confusing to officers, prosecutors, defense attorneys, and even judges to determine if a theft is larceny, stealing, shoplifting, or something else. The common law definitions of all of the crimes under the broad category of theft are very narrowly drawn, but still can be difficult to distinguish. To remedy this, many states have eliminated these common law distinctions and have instead created a single term to cover everything. For example, Maine's criminal code states, "Conduct denominated theft in this chapter constitutes a single crime embracing the separate crimes such as those heretofore known as larceny, larceny by trick, larceny by bailee, embezzlement, false pretenses, extortion, blackmail, shoplifting and receiving stolen property."[1] Similarly, the California Penal Code says: "Wherever any law or statute of this state refers to or mentions larceny, embezzlement, or stealing, said law or statute shall hereafter be read and interpreted as if the word "theft" were substituted therefor."[2] However, many states have kept the distinctions between the different crimes of theft. For that reason, you will learn about each type and variation of theft in more detail.

Theft

theft A broad category of misconduct against property that includes the crimes of larceny, embezzlement, theft by false pretenses, shoplifting, robbery, and receiving stolen goods.

grand theft Theft that is usually defined by statute to be the felonious taking of property valued above a set monetary amount, or the theft of a motor vehicle. More serious than petty theft.

petty theft Theft that is usually defined by statute to be the misdemeanor taking of property under a set monetary amount. Less serious than grand theft.

thief The person who commits an act of larceny or theft, who is principal in the original taking of property and not merely a subsequent receiver of the property.

Theft is a broad category of crimes against property that includes:

- Larceny
- Embezzlement
- Theft by false pretenses
- Shoplifting
- Robbery
- Receiving stolen goods

Theft can be divided into **grand theft**, a felony charge for thefts of property worth greater than a statutorily determined amount of money (such as $1,000); and **petty theft**, a misdemeanor charge for thefts of property worth less than the minimum required for grand theft.

The common ingredient among all theft crimes is a thief. A **thief** is the original unlawful taker of the property of another person. This term does not apply to persons who are merely subsequent receivers of the property; hence, the intent to deprive the owner of his or her property is not required for all of theft crimes.

FIGURE 11–1

States That Have Eliminated the Common Law Distinction Between Various Theft Crimes and Those That Have Not

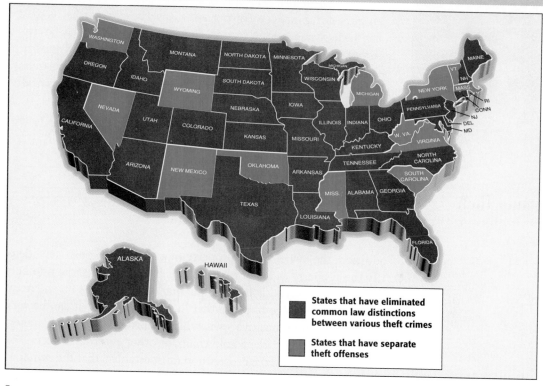

States that have eliminated common law distinctions between various theft crimes

States that have separate theft offenses

Larceny

Larceny has four elements:

1. The taking and carrying away
2. of the property of another
3. without consent
4. and with the purpose of stealing or permanently depriving the owner of possession.[3]

The first element, of taking and carrying away, occurs when a thief exercises control over the property. The thief must begin to move, or actually move, the property for at least a brief period of time. Only the slightest movement of the property is required for the thief to exercise dominion and control over it. Therefore, a person who slides a computer monitor across the top of a computer desk has satisfied the taking and carrying element of larceny.

The property taken 1) must be tangible, or concrete, such as a ring or a check; 2) must have value; and 3) must have an owner. In

larceny The taking and carrying away of property of another, without consent, with the purpose of stealing or permanently depriving the owner of possession.

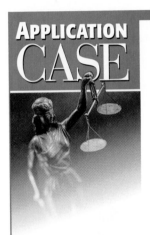

Quarterman v. State

In *Quarterman v. State* (1981), a reporter once parked his vehicle on an interstate highway in anticipation that it would be stolen so that he could film the theft in progress. A court found that this did not mean that he consented to having his vehicle stolen. Since the reporter neither suggested the theft to anybody nor urged the defendant to commit it, and since the criminal plan originated with the defendant, the court considering this case held that the car was indeed stolen.

Critical Thinking Should the media be allowed to set up "bait" as the reporter in this case did? Should the police be allowed to?

SOURCE: *Quarterman v. State*, 401 So. 2d 1159 (Fla. Dist. Ct. App. 1981).

Auto Theft

CRIMINAL LAW *Online*

What Exactly is Larceny?

Visit Butterworth's Legal Words by clicking the link at cl.glencoe.com and read about larceny. Next, read and compare their definitions for larceny by finding, larceny by mistake, petty larceny, and theft. What are the key differences, and by what criteria are they determined?

---

addition, the owner of the property must be able to positively identify the property as his or hers, such as by providing serial numbers for stolen property, identify unique marks or scratches on the item, or otherwise be able to prove that he or she owns it. It can be very difficult to prove positive ownership of property such as money, nondescript jewelry like a gold chain, or other everyday objects.

In larceny cases, the prosecution must establish that the owner of the property did not give the defendant permission to take the item. This is usually easily accomplished by having the owner testify to that fact. In addition, the prosecution must show that the defendant possessed the specific intent to permanently deprive the owner of the property, not merely intend to borrow it temporarily. This can be proven through direct evidence, such as the defendant stating that he or she intended to keep the property. It can also be proven through circumstantial evidence, such as the length of time the defendant had possession of the item, or if the defendant tried to scratch out the owner's name on the property or replace it with his own name.

As with theft and other offenses, many jurisdictions classify larceny along degrees of seriousness of the offense. For example, West Virginia law divides charges into grand larceny and petty larceny. The distinction is simple: If the loss of goods is less than $1,000, it is the misdemeanor offense of petty larceny. If the loss is greater than $1,000, it is the felony offense of grand larceny.[4]

There are two types of larceny that deserve special attention: larceny from a person, which is the offense of taking property from the person of another; and shoplifting, which is defined by a specific theft statute to address thefts of merchandise, concealment of merchandise, altering price tags, and retail theft.

Larceny from the Person   Some states have a statutory offense called **larceny from the person**. Larceny from the person differs from robbery in that robbery requires the additional element of taking by fear or force. The rationale for larceny from the person statutes is to prevent crimes like pickpocketing, purse snatching, and similar offenses where there is a greater risk of the victim being injured because of the close contact between the victim and the perpetrator. The penalties for taking property from the person of another are usually greater than those provided for a simple larceny.

Essentially, two different definitions of this offense have been adopted by different states, depending on their definition of "from the person." Some states define the term to mean that the victim must have had actual possession of the property on their person when the larceny occurred, but other states require only that the property be within the person's immediate presence.

Property that is "on" a person must be actually on the person, attached to the person, or held or carried by the person. This would include items such as jewelry, clothing, purses, wallets, and shopping bags that a person is actually touching. Courts in Colorado and Texas have found that larceny from the person was committed when a purse was taken from a shopping cart that the victim was pushing.[5] In a California case, two perpetrators fought with a victim while trying to take his wallet from his pocket. During the struggle, the victim's pants were torn off and his wallet fell to the ground. Although the perpetrators picked up the wallet and pants from the ground, not directly from the victim's person, the perpetrator's actions caused those items to fall to the ground in the first place. Therefore, they were guilty of larceny from the person.[6] On the other hand, larceny from the person did not occur in a case where the defendant took $250 worth of gaming chips from a craps table rack that was immediately in front of the victim.[7]

To constitute larceny from the person in other states, the only requirement is that property lie within a person's "actual and immediate physical control," but not necessarily attached to or on the person. For example, purses that are taken from car seats next to victims, or from beneath the victims' car seats, are within the immediate control of the victim. Therefore, the offenses constituted larceny from the person. Larceny from the person was also committed where the perpetrator took $350 from a wallet that was placed under the sleeping victim's pillow.[8]

larceny from the person
Statutory offense of taking property from the person of another; the penalty is usually greater than that of simple larceny.

➤ **Larceny from the Person** Larceny from the person occurs when an object is taken either from the victim's immediate person or the area within his or her immediate control. *How does this differ from mere larceny?*

T

shoplifting A crime defined by a specific theft statute to address thefts of merchandise, concealment of merchandise, altering price tags, and retail theft.

Shoplifting Most states have created specific theft statutes for thefts of merchandise, concealment of merchandise, altering price tags, and retail theft. All of these offenses are otherwise known as **shoplifting**. The essential elements of shoplifting are the willful taking of possession of merchandise of another

- Without consent of the seller
- With the intention of converting the goods and without paying for the goods

In addition, some shoplifting statutes do not require that the shoplifter intend to permanently deprive the store of its merchandise.

Since larceny covers many types of theft, it is also important to understand what larceny does not usually cover. Two common examples are 1) lost and abandoned property and 2) the crime of joyriding.

abandoned property Property over which a person voluntarily gives up permanent possession or ownership.

Lost or Abandoned Property If property is lost or abandoned, the issue becomes who owns the property. An object becomes **abandoned property** when the person who owns it voluntarily gives up permanent possession or ownership of it, such as by throwing it away. To prevent thieves from claiming that every item that they "found" was lost or abandoned and that they are entitled to it by right of "finders keepers," courts generally hold that the

Fingerprint Technician

Other Information: High school diploma required. Some positions require one to two years' experience; others require experience in classifying fingerprints with the Henry system, the Modified Henry System, and/or the Automated Fingerprint Identification System (AFIS).

Description and Duties: Enter fingerprints and information such as case identification number, race, sex, and birth date into automated information system for examination and retention. Initiate computer searches for suspects. Compare new finger, palm, and footprints with prints on file for points of identification to determine a match. Verify positive identification through comparisons of recidivist (second or more) prints to existing prints in criminal's folders. Work with local, state, and federal police.

Salary: Trainee salaries range from approximately $18,000 to $23,000. Technician salaries range from $23,000 to $35,000.

> **Critical Thinking** What skills and talents do you think a person needs to be a fingerprint technician?

SOURCE Delaware State Police, http://www.state.de.us/dsp/recruiting/fptrain.htm; Hillsborough County Sheriff's Office (Tampa, FL), http://www.crime-scene-investigator.net/JOB01028.html; and State of Virginia, http://www.dpt.state.va.us/services/compens/70000/descrip/71091.html.

"finder" has an obligation to give the item back to the owner if three conditions are met:

1. The owner of the property can be identified
2. The item can be easily given back to the owner
3. The item has substantial value

Failure to give back the item under these conditions can result in the "finder" being found to be guilty of some form of theft.

For example, the Maryland code, § 342(d) states:

A person commits the offense of theft when he obtains control over property of another which he knows to have been lost or mislaid . . . if he (1) Knows or learns the identity of the owner or knows, or is aware of, or learns of a reasonable method of identifying the owner; and (2) Fails to take reasonable measures to restore the property to the owner; and

Shoplifting

Some states view shoplifting as a separate offense, others view it as a type of theft or larceny, and still others consider larceny a type of shoplifting. States that view shoplifting as a type of theft typically do so because shoplifting is listed under the jurisdiction's theft statutes or codes.

joyriding The unlawful taking, using, or operating of a motor vehicle without the consent of the owner.

(3) Has the purpose of depriving the owner permanently of the use or benefit of the property either when he obtains the property, or at any later time.[9]

Thus, although a $20 bill found lying on the sidewalk has substantial value, the owner cannot be easily identified and the finder may keep the money. In contrast, if a person found a purse lying on the sidewalk containing cash and a driver's license, the finder would be required to return all of the property because the owner could easily be identified. (See Figure 11–2 for another state statute on theft.)

Joyriding If a defendant merely borrows an item and intends to return it to the owner, then larceny has not occurred even if the borrowing was without permission. A common example of this is **joyriding**, which is the unlawful taking, using, or operating of a motor vehicle without the consent of the owner. Joyriding is usually committed by juveniles, who take a car without permission and drive it for a short period of time before abandoning it.

The exact definition of joyriding depends on the exact words of each state's statutes. In some states, joyriding is a lesser-included offense of larceny, having all the elements of larceny except the intent to permanently deprive the owner of the vehicle. Other states have separate statutes for joyriding and unauthorized use. Under these statutes, joyriding requires the taking of the vehicle without the owner's permission. Unauthorized use would occur if the defendant were given consent to drive the vehicle, but exceeded that

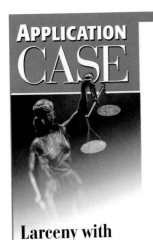

APPLICATION CASE

Fussell v. United States

If the owner of the property gives the possessor permission to use the property and the possessor misappropriates or steals it, the crime is not larceny. In the case of *Fussell v. United States* (1986), a plainclothes police officer was approached by the defendant, who offered to sell the officer a fake subway pass. Although the officer gave the defendant $10 for the pass, the defendant could not be convicted of larceny because the $10 was taken by the defendant with the officer's consent.

Critical Thinking What crimes could the defendant be charged with in this case?

SOURCE: *Fussell v. United States*, 505 A.2d 72 (D.C. 1986).

Larceny with Consent

consent; or if the defendant was not driving the vehicle at the time, such as by being a passenger.

Unauthorized use of a motor vehicle generally requires that a person:

- Knowingly takes control
- without authority
- of another person's vehicle.

The state does not need to prove the defendant took the property "without intent to permanently deprive." In addition, the motor of the vehicle does not have to be running nor does the car have to be in motion to satisfy this element. For example, in *People v. Roby* (1976),[10] the defendant was convicted of unauthorized use when he sat in the front passenger seat of a stolen car and his companion sat behind the driver's seat, attempting to put a key in the ignition.

FIGURE 11–2

Wisconsin Statute Concerning Theft

943.20 Theft

(1) Acts. Whoever does any of the following may be penalized as provided in sub. (3):

943.20(1)(a)

(a) Intentionally takes and carries away, uses, transfers, conceals, or retains possession of movable property of another without the other's consent and with intent to deprive the owner permanently of possession of such property.

943.20(1)(b)

(b) By virtue of his or her office, business or employment, or as trustee or bailee, having possession or custody of money or of a negotiable security, instrument, paper or other negotiable writing of another intentionally uses, transfers, conceals, or retains possession of such money, security, instrument, paper or writing without the owner's consent, contrary to his or her authority, and with intent to convert to his or her own use or to the use of any other person except the owner. A refusal to deliver any money or a negotiable security, instrument, paper or other negotiable writing, which is in his or her possession or custody by virtue of his or her office, business or employment, or as trustee or

bailee, upon demand of the person entitled to receive it, or as required by law, is prima facie evidence of an intent to convert to his or her own use within the meaning of this paragraph.

943.20(1)(c)

(c) Having a legal interest in movable property, intentionally and without consent, takes such property out of the possession of a pledgee or other person having a superior right of possession, with intent thereby to deprive the pledgee or other person permanently of the possession of such property.

943.20(1)(d)

(d) Obtains title to property of another person by intentionally deceiving the person with a false representation which is known to be false, made with intent to defraud, and which does defraud the person to whom it is made. "False representation" includes a promise made with intent not to perform it if it is a part of a false and fraudulent scheme.

943.20(1)(e)

(e) Intentionally fails to return any personal property which is in his or her possession or under his or her control by virtue of a written lease or written rental agreement, within 10 days after the lease or rental agreement has expired.

SOURCE: http://folio.legis.state.wi.us/cgi-bin/om_isapi.dll?clientID=95305&infobase=stats.nfo&jump=ch.%20943

Embezzlement

The crime of **embezzlement** consists of two elements: 1) the misappropriation 2) of the property of another. The element of theft that the perpetrator have the intent to permanently deprive the owner is not an element of embezzlement. Therefore, an employee who fraudulently "borrows" property entrusted to him or her, but does so with the intent to return it, can still be found guilty of embezzlement.

Embezzlement is not a common law crime, but a statutory crime created to resolve common law inadequacies. Since embezzlers do not meet the theft or larceny requirement of wrongfully obtaining the property, their misdeeds were not covered in the common law definitions of larceny. As a solution, the crime of embezzlement was created to deal with people, typically employees, who lawfully come into possession of property and then take it for their own use. Unlike the crime of theft by initial wrongful taking, embezzlement involves a violation of trust. Today, some states include embezzlement under their theft or larceny statutes, and others have separate statutes.

Misappropriation is the key element of embezzlement, just as taking is the key element of a larceny. **Misappropriation** is the wrongful misuse or taking of another's property that has been entrusted to the embezzler. The property of another can include real or personal property; securities; or negotiable instruments, such as notes that are promises to pay, drafts that are an order to pay, checks that are payable on demand, and certificates of deposit. The same issues that arise in connection with larceny also arise in connection with embezzlement, such as proving that the property actually belongs to someone else, was not lost or abandoned, and can be positively identified.

In the embezzlement case of *Gwaltney v. Commonwealth* (1995), the defendant was a bank teller who took $1,000 from another teller's cash drawer. The defendant claimed that since she was not placed in a position of trust of the other teller's drawer, she did not misappropriate the bank's property and thus was not guilty of embezzlement. She argued that she could only be found guilty of larceny. The court rejected this argument, finding that the defendant was in fact in a position of trust even though she was only indirectly responsible for the cash drawer not assigned to her.[11]

False Pretenses

The theft crimes discussed so far deal only with crimes where property is taken or misappropriated from the owner. The crime of

People v. Lorenzo

Theft by false pretenses did not occur in *People v. Lorenzo* (1976), where a market manager observed the defendant switch price tags on merchandise, pay less for the items than they were previously marked, and leave the store. The court found that false pretenses was not committed because the market manager was aware that the defendant switched the price tags and did not rely upon the defendant's conduct.

Critical Thinking Of what crime could the defendant in this case be convicted?

SOURCE: *People v. Lorenzo*, 135 Cal. Rptr. 337 (Cal. App. Dept Super. Ct. 1976).

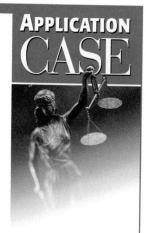

APPLICATION CASE

False Pretenses

false pretenses, on the other hand, deals with the owner being tricked by misrepresentation into voluntarily transferring title to the property. Technically, there is no *taking* of the property from the owner, but the owner is nonetheless deprived by illegal means. As with embezzlement, the common law did not consider obtaining property by false pretenses to be a crime. Therefore, the crime of false pretenses is also strictly a statutory offense.

The elements of false pretenses are:

- The making of a material misrepresentation of fact
- with intent to defraud the owner of the property
- and thereby inducing the owner to part with both possession of and title to his or her property.

false pretenses A crime that occurs when title or ownership of the property is passed to the defendant in reliance of the defendant's misrepresentation.

Myth	**Fact**
False pretenses is basically the same crime as larceny.	False pretenses differs from larceny because in larceny, the property is taken and the defendant has possession of the property, but title of the property is not passed to the defendant. In the crime of false pretenses, both possession and title are passed to the defendant.

Note that false pretenses is not committed if the defendant only obtains possession of the property and not title. When the perpetrator gains *possession* alone of the property, the similar crime of *larceny by trick* has been completed.

Receiving Stolen Property

Receiving stolen goods or property is a separate and distinct offense from theft, although it is sometimes included in the same statute. Theft is not an element of receiving stolen goods, nor does the prosecution usually have to prove that the defendant did not steal the goods. **Receiving** means acquiring the goods or property that have been stolen. A fence is a professional receiver of stolen property.

receiving Acquiring possession, control, or title, or lending on the security of the property.

The essential elements of the offense of receiving stolen property are that the accused:

- Bought, received, or otherwise came into possession of the property
- which property was stolen
- and at the time of possession of the property, the accused knew the property had been stolen.

Some jurisdictions do not require that a person other than the accused steal the property. This provision allows a thief to be prosecuted for receiving his or her own stolen goods when the prosecution does not have sufficient evidence to prove that the defendant stole the goods, but only enough to prove that he or she possessed them.

Possession is easily shown when the perpetrator is caught in actual physical possession of the property. A person need not be in actual physical control of stolen property to be guilty of receiving it as long as he or she has constructive possession. **Constructive possession** is a relationship between the defendant and the stolen goods, where, because of this relationship, it is reasonable to treat the extent of the defendant's dominion and control over the property as if it were actual possession. In *Nelson v. State* (1981), one male defendant and one female defendant were convicted of receiving stolen property, even though only one defendant was present in the trailer when the police discovered stolen property inside of it. Although the court did not find any evidence that the defendants had actual, physical control over the property, the

constructive possession

A relationship between the defendant and the stolen goods such that it is reasonable to treat the extent of the defendant's dominion and control over the property as if it were actual possession.

Crimes Against Property

court held that there was ample evidence that constructive possession existed because letters and other items had the defendants' names on them, both male and female clothes were located in the trailer, and there was testimony that both defendants lived in the trailer.[12]

Constructive possession can also exist when stolen property is in close proximity to the accused. The defendant in *State v. Bozeyowski* (1962) was seen by police on top of a stolen truck, attempting to unload stolen cases of beer from the truck. The court stated that there was enough evidence of the defendant's actions to infer the defendant's intentional control over the stolen truck, which satisfied the requirement of possession.[13]

Mere possession or unexplained possession of stolen property is not enough to constitute the crime of receiving stolen property; the crime also requires that the perpetrator knows that the property was stolen. Knowledge can be shown by actual knowledge, such as the defendant saying, "I knew it was stolen." It can also be shown by knowledge of circumstances that would alert any reasonable person that goods were stolen, such as the defendant buying the property for a price greatly below its real value. Other circumstances could also show knowledge. In one case, contradictory statements made by the defendant as to where he got a stolen car, from whom, and other circumstances surrounding obtaining the vehicle were sufficient evidence to prove that the defendant knew the vehicle was stolen.[14] In *Hurston v. State* (1991), the defendant was found guilty of receiving a stolen car when he rode in a recently stolen vehicle for two hours as a passenger. The car was being driven without keys and had steering wheel damage, and the defendant attempted to flee from the police. All of these factors clearly indicated that the defendant had knowledge that the car was stolen.[15]

Receiving Stolen Property

West Virginia has a typical statute for receiving stolen property. Under that statute, receiving stolen property is defined as follows:

If any person buy or receive from another person, or aid in concealing, or transfer to a person other than the owner thereof, any stolen goods or other thing of value, which he knows or has reason to believe has been stolen, he shall be deemed guilty of the larceny thereof, and may be prosecuted although the principal offender be not convicted.

SOURCE: W. Va. Code § 61-3-18 (1998).

Self Check

1. What is larceny, and how is it distinguished from the other types of theft discussed here?
2. How is receiving stolen goods related to, but not a part of, theft?

Check your answers at cl.glencoe.com.

11.2 Robbery, Extortion, Blackmail, and Bribery

robbery A common law crime that consists of larceny committed by the use of force or fear, where the property taken is either taken from the person of the victim or within his or her immediate presence.

Robbery is a common law crime that consists of the taking of property by the use of force or fear, where property is either taken from the person of the victim or within his or her immediate presence. Extortion, blackmail, and bribery are related crimes, and modern statutes frequently use the terms interchangeably. Today, many states' laws do not even use the terms extortion or blackmail, but describe and call them criminal coercion (or just theft).

Robbery

Although the wording of the elements of robbery may vary from jurisdiction to jurisdiction, the essential elements of Florida's statute are typical: The taking of property from a person or the person's custody with the intent to either permanently or temporarily deprive the person or the owner of the property when in the course of the taking there is the use of force, violence, assault, or putting in fear.[16]

If force or fear is missing, a theft or larceny has taken place. (See Figure 11–3 on page 386 for another robbery statute.) These elements are explained in greater detail as follows:

Taking of Property   The taking of property element of robbery is the same element found in larceny: the taking and carrying away of property of another, without consent, with the purpose of stealing or permanently depriving the owner of possession.

Taking from a Person   The crime of robbery requires that the property either be taken from the person or from the person's immediate presence. The victim's immediate presence is considered to be the area within his or her immediate control; therefore, the property may not be at some distance away in order for robbery to occur. If a threat of force were used to cause a victim to telephone another location to have property delivered to the perpetrator, the property would not be sufficiently within the victim's presence to satisfy the traditional definition of robbery.

Intent to Deprive the Owner   One difference between robbery and larceny is that in modern robbery statutes, such as the Florida statute listed above, the intent of the perpetrator to deprive the owner temporarily, rather than permanently, is enough to create criminal liability.

Use of Force or Fear   The element of the use of force or fear is the primary distinction between robbery and larceny. If a larceny from a person occurred with force or fear, then a robbery has taken place. **Force** is the actual use of physical power to aid in obtaining the money or property from the victim. The use of **fear or intimidation** is the use of threats to do immediate bodily injury or harm to the victim, a family member, or to someone else who is present. Threats can be implied or explicit, and they can be verbal or nonverbal. When force, fear, or intimidation are used, the victim is not required to actually be scared as long as he or she is aware of the impending force or threat.

Whether the force, fear, or intimidation occurred in order to take property or merely in an attempt to retain or escape with it, makes a difference in some states and determines whether the crime is robbery rather than merely larceny. In some states, there is a question of whether a robbery occurs when the property is obtained peacefully but force or fear is subsequently used to retain possession or allow escape. Some jurisdictions rationalize that if force or fear is used only subsequent to the taking, it does not satisfy the robbery element. In one case, the court stated that the test was whether or not the defendant had completed the taking of the property by the time he used the force or fear.[17]

On the other hand, the Model Penal Code and some states define robbery as using force or fear at any time during the attempt or commission of theft, including the escape after committing the

force   The actual use of physical power against the victim to aid in obtaining the money or property.

fear or intimidation   The use of threat, either implied or explicit, verbal or nonverbal, to do immediate bodily injury or harm to the victim, family member, or to someone else who is present.

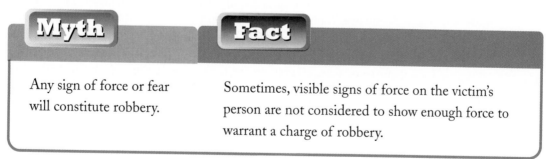

Myth	Fact
Any sign of force or fear will constitute robbery.	Sometimes, visible signs of force on the victim's person are not considered to show enough force to warrant a charge of robbery.

FIGURE 11-3

Missouri Statute Concerning Robbery

**Missouri Revised Statutes
Chapter 569
Robbery, Arson, Burglary and Related Offenses**

Robbery in the first degree

Section 569.020.

1. A person commits the crime of robbery in the first degree when he forcibly steals property and in the course thereof he, or another participant in the crime,

   (1) Causes serious physical injury to any person; or

   (2) Is armed with a deadly weapon; or

   (3) Uses or threatens the immediate use of a dangerous instrument against any person; or

   (4) Displays or threatens the use of what appears to be a deadly weapon or dangerous instrument.

2. Robbery in the first degree is a class A felony.

Robbery in the second degree

Section 569.030

1. A person commits the crime of robbery in the second degree when he forcibly steals property.

2. Robbery in the second degree is a class B felony.

SOURCE: http://mega.state.mo.us/statutes/C500-599/5690020.HTM

---

theft. In *Santilli v. State* (1990), the court held that robbery had occurred, and the element of force or fear was satisfied, when the perpetrator hit a police officer with his car as he attempted to flee after completing the act of shoplifting a greeting card.[18]

Purse snatching is a crime that can be considered either a larceny or a robbery, depending on two factors: the circumstances and the jurisdiction. As with other takings of property, if the purse snatching includes the use of force or fear, it is robbery; absent the force or fear, it is larceny or larceny from the person. Several states make purse snatching a robbery, but the majority of jurisdictions consider it to be larceny or larceny from the person if the snatching in itself does not involve enough force or fear. Some statutes draw fine lines. For example, if the taking is unnoticed and accomplished by stealth, with no resistance, it will be classified as larceny from the person. However, if the victim resists, even slightly, then the crime will be considered a robbery. For example, robberies occurred in cases where the defendant grabbed money from the victim's hands and beat the victim before leaving with the money,[19] and where the victim struggled with the defendant to retain possession of her purse.[20] In another case, where a victim testified that she was very scared when her purse was taken at gunpoint, the crime of robbery by fear from threat of force was shown.[21]

There is one common circumstance that affects punishment for robbery: the use of a weapon. Another less common circumstance affecting punishment is the act of robbing persons over the age of 65.

Armed Robbery   Most robbery statutes are divided into different degrees based on one important factor–whether the defendant was armed with a dangerous or deadly weapon. The actual amount of force used is not relevant. **Armed robbery** has different meanings in different jurisdictions, but usually is defined as robbery accomplished by means of a dangerous or deadly weapon. It is often classified as robbery in the first degree or aggravated robbery. Armed robbery cases are always treated as more serious offenses than unarmed robbery cases.

Whether an instrumentality is a dangerous weapon for purposes of armed robbery is a question for the jury to decide. Numerous cases have determined that a wide variety of instrumentalities other than a loaded gun can be dangerous weapons. A toy gun or a simulated gun, such as an object in a coat pocket intended to look like a gun, may be a dangerous weapon. Pepper spray, BB guns, pocket knives, hands, feet, a car, scissors, and a bottle are all objects that can be dangerous or deadly weapons if used in a manner to intimidate and evoke fear. Even an unloaded gun can qualify as a dangerous weapon because it can still evoke considerable fear in the victim or can be used as a bludgeon to inflict serious bodily injury. Few jurisdictions require that a weapon must be loaded, or that the prosecution must prove that the gun was loaded at the time of the robbery.

Robbing the Elderly   Robbing the elderly is not a separate or more serious offense than the same type of robbery committed against a younger person, but in at least one jurisdiction it carries sentence enhancements that will make the minimum punishment considerably greater. For example, Georgia recognizes that persons over the age of 65 are more likely to be robbed and are more likely to have serious bodily injuries as a result of the robbery. To address

The Debate about Force

Courts have given widely varying opinions on what is sufficient force to constitute a robbery. For example, in *People v. Thomas* (1983), the court concluded that a robbery did not occur when the defendant snatched the victim's purse from her, leaving a red streak on her arm. However, another court in *Raiford v. State* (1982) found that a robbery did occur when the defendant ripped the victim's purse from her shoulder, even though the victim herself did not resist and the only resistance was by reason of the attachment of the strap of the bag to the victim's shoulder.

SOURCE: *People v. Thomas*, 456 N.E.2d 684 (Ill. App. Ct. 1983); *Raiford v. State*, 477 A.2d 496 (Md. Ct. Spec. App. 1982).

armed robbery Armed robbery usually means robbery accomplished by means of a dangerous or deadly weapon, robbery in the first degree, or aggravated robbery.

extortion At common law, the gaining of property by threat of physical harm to a person or property by a public official by color of his or her office.

this, Georgia created a statute that enhances the penalty for robbery of a person age 65 or older. The punishment for robbery of a person over the age of 65 is at least five years of imprisonment, whereas robbery of a person under 65 years of age begins at one year.[22]

Extortion, Blackmail, and Bribery

As stated earlier, these three crimes are related. The common law treated extortion and blackmail as separate crimes, whereas modern statutes frequently use the terms interchangeably. You will note in the following separate discussions that many issues relating to extortion also relate to blackmail and bribery.

Extortion The common law crime of **extortion** is the gaining of property by threat of physical harm to a person or property by a public official by color of his or her office. The common law crime of extortion had five elements: 1) Seeking an unlawful fee, 2) by a public officer, 3) collected under color of office, 4) where the fee is actually received, and 5) where the fee was taken corruptly.[23] A good example of modern extortion laws can be found in the current New Jersey statute, which provides:

A person is guilty of theft by extortion if he purposely and unlawfully obtains property of another by extortion. A person extorts if he purposely threatens to:

- Inflict bodily injury on or physically confine or restrain anyone or commit any other criminal offense;
- Accuse anyone of an offense or cause charges of an offense to be instituted against any person;
- Expose or publicize any secret or any asserted fact, whether true or false, tending to subject any person to hatred, contempt or ridicule, or to impair his credit or business repute;
- Take or withhold action as an official, or cause an official to take or withhold action;
- Bring about or continue a strike, boycott or other collective action, if the property is not demanded or received for the benefit of the group in whose interest the actor purports to act;
- Testify or provide information or withhold testimony or information with respect to another's legal claim or defense;
- Inflict any other harm which would not substantially benefit the actor but which is calculated to materially harm another person.[24]

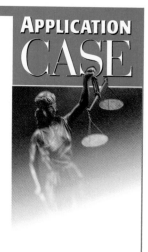
United States v. Jackson

A high profile case example of extortion was the conviction of Autumn Jackson for scheming to extort $40 million from the actor Bill Cosby. She threatened to tell the tabloids that she was Cosby's illegitimate daughter unless Cosby gave her the money. Jackson had the right to tell her story to the media. However, the element that made her action extortion was her demand of the money in return for not telling the "secret" to the media, which would harm Cosby's reputation and publicly disgrace the famous TV father.

Critical Thinking Which of the seven threats in the New Jersey statute did Jackson make? If she had told the "secret" to the media, what would have happened?

SOURCE: *United States v. Jackson*, 196 F.3d 383 (2d Cir. 1999).

Extortion

A defendant can claim an affirmative defense by stating that the property obtained was honestly claimed as restitution or indemnification, either for harm done or as lawful compensation for property or services.

Where the crime of extortion is based upon the acts of a public official, one of the elements usually is that the perpetrator act **under color of authority or office**. This element requires that the action taken by the perpetrator be in his or her capacity as a public official; therefore, services performed in a private capacity usually will not amount to extortion. Public officials are forbidden from misusing their title and position to obtain services or property to which they are not otherwise entitled. In *United States v. Tillem* (1990), health department officials were guilty of extortion under federal law for exchanging favorable health inspections for money or free food from restauranteurs.[25]

The definition of property for purposes of committing modern extortion (and blackmail) is very broad, and includes both tangible and intangible property. The property does not need to have actual cash value to be extorted; it can be a particular right belonging to the individual victim. In one case, a defendant was found guilty of grand larceny by means of extortion when he threatened the victim with bodily harm if the victim did not give up a business customer to the defendant. The victim gave up the customer, who the court

under color of authority or office The requirement for the crime of extortion that the action taken by the perpetrator be in his or her capacity as a public official.

FIGURE 11–4

District of Columbia Code on Extortion

District of Columbia Code

§ 22-3851. Extortion.

(a) A person commits the offense of **extortion** if:

(1) That person obtains or attempts to obtain the property of another with the other's consent which was induced by wrongful use of actual or threatened force or violence or by wrongful threat of economic injury; or

(2) That person obtains or attempts to obtain property of another with the other's consent which was obtained under color or pretense of official right.

(b) Any person convicted of **extortion** shall be fined not more than $10,000 or imprisoned for not more than 10 years, or both.

SOURCE: D.C. Law 4-1164 § 151,29 DCR 3976.

determined was "property" that was delivered to the defendant under threat of physical harm.[26] In another case, a real estate agent was found guilty of extortion for refusing to honestly testify in a malpractice lawsuit against an attorney unless the victim paid her for appearing at the deposition and trial. The court determined that the "property" was her interest in the malpractice lawsuit.[27]

Extortion and blackmail are also related to robbery. The distinction is that robbery is committed by a threat to do immediate bodily harm, whereas extortion (or blackmail) is committed by a threat to do harm in the future. Whereas a robber merely seeks to gain money by physical threat or intimidation, extortion and blackmail usually involve a threat to expose the victim's involvement in a crime or a shameful act unless the victim pays money or does some other act.[28]

blackmail A threat by a private citizen seeking *hush money*, which is payment to remain silent about a crime or a shameful act.

Blackmail   The crime of **blackmail** is a threat by a private citizen seeking *hush money*, which is payment to remain silent about a crime or a shameful act. Although it is easy to see the moral reprehensibility of blackmail, the fact that it is a crime presents a legal paradox. This is because blackmail involves the threat to do something that the threatener has a legal right to do. For example, if one threatens to expose a businessman's tax evasion unless he gives the threatener a lucrative contract, the threatener has committed blackmail. Yet the blackmailer

◁ **Key Elements of Bribery** Bribers attempt to use payoffs to illegally pass inspections, avoid criminal liability, and otherwise avoid legal responsibilities. *What can happen if an official refuses to accept a bribe?*

has a legal right to expose and to threaten to expose the tax evasion, and a legal right to seek a lucrative contract. Nonetheless, combining the two legal rights constitutes a crime.[29] This specific combination of elements—of using the threat of public shame to obtain something desirable—is what constitutes the crime of blackmail.

Bribery The crime of **bribery** is the payment by a person to a public official in order to gain an advantage that the person is not otherwise entitled to, in which case both parties are guilty of the crime. The aforementioned case of *United States v. Tillem*, in which the defendant was found guilty of extortion, involved circumstances similar to bribery.

bribery Payment by a person to a public official in order to gain an advantage that the person is not otherwise entitled to; both parties are guilty of the crime.

Self Check

1. How do you determine whether enough force or fear was used to justify a robbery, as opposed to a larceny or larceny from a person, charge?
2. In your own words, how are extortion, blackmail, and bribery similar? How are they different?

Check your answers at **cl.glencoe.com**.

11.3 Forgery and Uttering

Forgery is a common law crime that has been codified in most states. Generally speaking, a person who, with the purpose of deceiving or injuring, makes or alters a writing in such a way as to convey a false impression concerning its authenticity, is guilty of **forgery**. The Indiana forgery statute is a typical example of the modern statement of the essential elements of forgery:

A person commits forgery who, with intent to defraud, makes or utters a written instrument in such a manner that it purports to have been made:

- By another person
- At another time
- With different provisions
- By authority of one who did not give authority[30]

Forgery can occur when a person signs a name other than his or her own on a writing and claims that the signature belongs to another person. It can also occur by signing a writing using a fictitious or assumed name, by falsely signing a credit charge or sales slip, or by falsifying a money order. In some states, a person who uses trick, artifice, or other fraudulent devices to procure a genuine signature on a writing that has legal significance is guilty of forgery.

Falsifying another person's name on a credit charge or sales slip is forgery. It is immaterial whether the writings are orders for merchandise, or merely receipts for delivery, as long as the writing, if taken as genuine, would have the effect to defraud. In one case, the defendant signed his "guest check" at an oyster bar with the name of another person. The court rejected the defendant's argument that a "guest check" was not subject to forgery, stating that the person whose name had been forged would have been obligated to pay for the amount of the "guest check" had it been genuine.[31]

The subject matter of forgery under the law in most jurisdictions must be a writing; therefore, contrary to popular belief, there cannot be a forgery of an object such as a work of art. The writing in a forgery needs to appear sufficiently convincing to be used to fool others. A forgery cannot occur if the writing does not deceive an ordinary, prudent person with ordinary observational skills.[32] Thus, a $3 bill that is larger than an authentic paper bill, made from a different shade of green, and with the face of Jim Carrey on it, would

forgery A person who, with the purpose of deceiving or injuring, makes or alters a writing in such a way as to convey a false impression concerning its authenticity is guilty of forgery.

Defining a "Writing"

For purposes of forgery, a writing is usually given a broad definition, as this New York statutory definition demonstrates:
[A]ny instrument or article, including computer data or a computer program, containing written or printed matter or the equivalent thereof, used for purposes of reciting, embodying, conveying or recording information, or constituting a symbol or evidence of value, right, privilege or identification, which is capable of being used to the advantage or disadvantage of some person.

SOURCE: N.Y. Penal Law - § 3-K-170(1) (Consol. 1997).

◄ **Elements of Forgery**
Forgery involves the use of writing instruments, printing and photo techniques to alter documents and pass them off as authentic. *How is forgery different from fraudulent making?*

not deceive an ordinary, prudent person with ordinary observation skills and, thus, could not be the subject of a forgery.

In addition, a person who merely has a forged writing in his or her possession is not guilty of forgery until he or she "utters" it, or attempts to pass it off. **Uttering** occurs when a person presents the writing and attempts to use it. The intent required for forgery is the intent to defraud, or with the "purpose to deceive or cheat another person or entity out of his or its legal due."[33] The intended act does not need to be successfully completed for the intent element to be satisfied.

Forgery is different from **fraudulent making**, which is defined as the creation of documents that are not authentic. If a writing is full of false statements, the author is not guilty of forgery but of fraudulent making. In contrast, if a document is full of truths, but is signed by a person using another person's name without permission, the writing is a forgery.

uttering When a person presents a forged writing and attempts to use it.

fraudulent making Creating a document that is not authentic.

Self Check

1. What, in your opinion, is the most common type of forgery? Why?
2. Give an example of the crime of fraudulent making, and explain why this behavior satisfies the elements of a crime.

CRIMINAL LAW *Online*

Check your answers at **cl.glencoe.com**.

Crimes Against Property

1. List the elements of larceny.

Larceny is:

- The taking and carrying away
- of the property of another
- without consent
- but with the purpose of stealing or permanently depriving the owner of possession.

2. Explain the difference between larceny from the person and robbery.

Larceny from the person differs from robbery in that robbery requires the additional element of a taking by fear or force.

3. List the elements of embezzlement.

There are two elements to the crime of embezzlement:

- Misappropriation
- of the property of another.

4. State the difference between embezzlement and larceny.

Embezzlement is the taking of property by persons, typically employees, who have the property lawfully put in their possession by the owner, and therefore do not meet the theft or larceny requirement of wrongfully obtaining the property. Embezzlement occurs when the accused was given considerable control over the property and violated that trust by appropriating the property.

5. List the essential elements of robbery.

- The taking of property
- from a person or the person's custody
- with the intent to either permanently or temporarily deprive the person or the owner of the property
- when in the course of the taking there is the use of force, violence, assault, or putting in fear.

6. Differentiate between extortion, blackmail, and bribery.

Extortion is the gaining of property by threat of physical harm to a person or property by a public official by color of his or her office. Blackmail is a threat by a private citizen seeking hush money. Bribery is the payment by a person to a public official in order to gain an advantage that the person is not otherwise entitled to, in which case both parties are guilty of the crime.

7. State the essential elements of forgery.

A person commits forgery who, with intent to defraud, makes or utters a written instrument in such a manner that it purports to have been made:

- By another person
- At another time
- With different provisions
- By authority of one who did not give authority

KEY TERMS

theft, page 372
grand theft, page 372
petty theft, page 372
thief, page 372
larceny, page 373
larceny from the person,
   page 375
shoplifting, page 376
abandoned property,
   page 376
joyriding, page 378

embezzlement, page 380
misappropriation, page 380
false pretenses, page 381
receiving, page 382
constructive possession,
   page 382
robbery, page 384
force, page 385
fear or intimidation,
   page 385
armed robbery, page 387

extortion, page 388
under color of authority or
   office, page 389
blackmail, page 390
bribery, page 391
forgery, page 392
uttering, page 393
fraudulent making, page 393

QUESTIONS FOR REVIEW

1. Name the different crimes listed under theft, and explain why there is so much confusion in distinguishing among these different crimes.
2. What are the elements of shoplifting?
3. How can a person be convicted of larceny of "found" property?
4. What is the difference between joyriding and larceny?
5. State the difference between false pretenses and larceny.

6. List the essential elements of receiving stolen property.
7. How can a purse snatching be either a larceny or a robbery?
8. Explain the difference between robbery and extortion (or blackmail).
9. What is uttering, and how does it relate to the crime of forgery?
10. What are the differences between forgery and fraudulent making?

PROBLEM-SOLVING EXERCISES

1. **Shoplifting** A woman looking at cosmetics in a drug store was noticed by the store manager because she was not carrying a purse. She was pushing a shopping cart and put several cosmetic items into the cart. She went to the checkout stand and paid for all the items but one lipstick, which remained in the shopping cart. The manager noticed the lipstick in the cart and followed the woman to her car. As the manager approached her, she was picking the lipstick up from the cart. When the manager told her he was arresting her for shoplifting, she said that she did not see the lipstick in the cart until she got to her car and picked it up to return it to the store. The lipstick cost $5.99 and

the woman had $1.09 on her person. Answer the following questions:

a) Was there any responsibility on the part of the clerk or manager to ensure that all items were paid for because she left the store? Why or why not?

b) Should she be arrested? If so, on what charges and why? If not, why?

c) Write a statement reflecting your decision as though you were filling out a police report.

2. **Embezzlement** A jail guard is working on the night shift all alone. He locks himself out of his office, leaving all the jail keys in the office. He remembers an inmate brought in earlier in the day, who had lock-picking devices in his possession when he was booked. He goes to the evidence locker, retrieves the lock-picking devices, opens the locked door, and returns the devices to the locker. The lock-picking devices were gone for less than five minutes. Answer the following questions:

a) Has he embezzled the devices?

b) Does it make a difference that he put the property back within five minutes?

c) If you were his supervisor, how would you handle this situation?

WORKPLACE APPLICATIONS

1. **Burglary** A homeowner entered her home and saw a burglar unplugging her television. The burglar ran off without the television, but grabbed the homeowner's purse from her as he left. The woman tried holding onto the purse, but did not succeed. The purse contained credit cards, a box of new checks from her bank, and $80 cash. Answer the following questions:

a) What crime(s) has the burglar committed? What crime(s) has the burglar attempted?

b) Regarding the television, has the burglar committed a sufficient act for the taking and carrying away element of larceny?

c) How can the monetary value of the checks and credit cards be ascertained to determine the degree of the crime?

2. **Shoplifting without Larceny** Your state has a law that provides that a person can commit shoplifting without committing larceny. Remember that for larceny, only the slightest movement is required to satisfy the taking and carrying away element. Answer the following questions:

a) How can this law justify the fact that shoplifters move items when they conceal them on their person?

b) Does it have anything to do with proving intent to permanently deprive the owners of the property?

c) Would you change this law if you could? If so, how and why? If not, why, and how would you address this current apparent contradiction?

INTERNET APPLICATIONS

1. **False Pretenses** Read "Obtaining Information Under False Pretenses," available through the link at **cl.glencoe.com**. When you are done, answer the following questions:
   a) What are the types of false pretenses that can be used for obtaining personal or classified information?
   b) What clues may indicate that information is being gathered under false pretenses?
   c) How can businesses protect themselves from these practices?

2 **Work a Robbery Case** Visit "The Brinks Robbery" at the FBI's Web site by clicking the link at **cl.glencoe.com**. As you read this article, pretend that you are one of the investigators assigned to this case from the beginning and answer the following questions:
   a) What evidence and leads were available to you at the beginning?
   b) What would you be able to turn up after preliminary investigations?
   c) What were the main obstacles in solving this case?
   d) How did FBI investigators assemble clues to determine all of the suspects? Would you do anything differently? Why or why not?

ETHICS ISSUES

1. **Cheeseburger Bribes?** Janene, a volunteer for her suburban town's Police Explorer program, takes a break from her shift to eat lunch at Burgerland, a fast food restaurant. When the Burgerland manager sees her in full uniform, he groans and says, "You Explorers and cops are always coming in here, at least a dozen times a day. I know if I don't feed you I won't get adequate police responses the next time we get robbed again. I'll do it, but I'm sick of it." Janene is surprised and insists on paying for her meal, but the manager refuses to take the money. She finally agrees to accept the free meal. Answer the following questions:
   a) Is the Explorer extorting the restaurant or manager for food for police protection, even if she accepted the meal reluctantly? Why or why not?
   b) Does it matter that no threats were ever made by anyone?
   c) If the manager has reason to believe that police protection will be withheld if free food is not given, what is a better course of action for him to take?

ENDNOTES

1 Me. Rev. Stat. Ann. tit. 17-A, § 351 (West 1996).

2 Cal. Penal Code § 490a (West 1998).

3 Louis B. Schwartz, *Theft*, 4 *Encyclopedia of Crime and Justice*, 1538 (Sanford H. Kadish ed. 1983).

4 W. Va. Code § 61-3-13 (1997).

5 *People v. Evans*, 612 P.2d 1153 (Colo. App. 1980); *Mack v. State*, 465 S.W.2d 941 (Tex. 1971).

6 *People v. Smith*, 73 Cal. Rptr. 859 (1968).

7 *Terral v. State*, 442 P.2d 465 (Nev. 1968).

8 *Banks v. State*, 40 S.E.2d 103 (Ga. App. 1946).

9 Md. Code Ann. Code of 1957, art. 27, §342(d) (Michie 1997).

10 346 N.E. 2d 540 (N.Y. 1976).

11 *Gwaltney v. Commonwealth*, 452 S.E.2d 687 (Va. 1995).

12 *Nelson v. State*, 628 P.2d 884 (Alaska 1981).

13 *State v. Bozeyowski*, 185 A.2d 393 (N.J. Super. 1962), *cert. denied*, 374 U.S. 851 (1963).

14 *Austin v. State*, 81 S.E.2d 508 (Ga. Ct. App. 1954).

15 *Hurston v. State*, 414 S.E.2d 303 (Ga. Ct. App. 1991).

16 Fla. Stat. Ann. § 812.13(1) (West 1997).

17 *State v. Aldershof*, 556 P.2d 371, 375 (Kan. 1976). The principle stated in that case was reconsidered and reaffirmed in *State v. Bateson*, 1998 WL 857274 (Kan. 1998).

18 *Santilli v. State*, 570 So.2d 400 (Fla. Dst. Ct. App. 1990).

19 *Andre v. State*, 431 So.2d 1042 (Fla. Dist. Ct. App. 1983).

20 *Jefferson v. State*, 840 P.2d 1234 (Nev. 1992).

21 *People v. Freeman*, 157 Cal. Rptr. 454 (Cal. Ct. App. 1979).

22 Ga. Code Ann. §16-8-40(b), (c) (1997).

23 James Lindgren, *Blackmail and Extortion*, 1 *Encyclopedia of Crime and Justice*, 115, 116 (Sanford H. Kadish ed. 1983).

24 N.J. Stat. Ann. § 2C:20-5 (West 1998).

25 *United States v. Tillem*, 906 F.2d 814 (2d Cir. 1990).

26 *People v. Spatarella*, 313 N.E.2d 38 (N.Y. 1974).

27 *State v. Manthey*, 487 N.W.2d 44 (Wis. Ct. App. 1992).

28 Floyd Feeney, *Robbery*, 4 *Encyclopedia of Crime and Justice*, 1398,1400 (Sanford H. Kadish ed. 1983).

29 This hypothetical comes from James Lindgren, *Blackmail and Extortion*, 1 *Encyclopedia of Crime and Justice*, 115, 118 (Sanford H. Kadish ed. 1983).

30 Ind. Code Ann. § 35-43-5-2 (Burns 1996).

31 People ex rel. *Arter v. Foster*, 104 N.Y.S.2d 39 (N.Y. Sup. Ct. 1951).

32 Peter Goldberger, *Forgery*, 2 *Encyclopedia of Crime and Justice*, 795 (Sanford H. Kadish ed. 1983).

33 *Id.* at 796.

What is the difference between larceny and robbery?
Find it on page 385.

PART 5

Crimes Against the Community and Institutions

Chapter Objectives

After reading this chapter, you will be able to:

1. Define white-collar crime.
2. List the elements of tax evasion.
3. List the elements for a civil action for false advertising.
4. List the elements of mail fraud.
5. List the elements of securities fraud.
6. List the elements of an FDCA action.
7. List the main federal antitrust acts and the elements of an antitrust action.
8. Explain a monopoly.

Why couldn't corporations be prosecuted for crimes at common law?

Chapter 12

White-Collar Crimes

12.1 Understanding White-Collar Crime

white-collar crime A broad category of nonviolent misconduct involving commercial and financial fraud.

White-collar crime is a term that describes a broad category of nonviolent misconduct involving commercial and financial fraud. Examples of it are:

- Tax evasion
- False advertising
- Mail fraud
- Securities fraud
- Crimes against the Food and Drug Act
- Monopolies and antitrust crimes

White-collar crimes are more often perpetrated by corporations than by individuals. At common law, however, a corporation could not be held liable for any criminal activity. This is because most crimes required the element of *mens rea* at the time of commission or omission; since corporations do not have minds, it was virtually impossible at common law to hold corporations accountable for their misdeed. Instead, individuals acting on behalf of the corporation were indicted. Recently, however, legislatures began passing statutes that allow corporations to be penalized for white-collar criminality.

CRIMINAL LAW *Online*

Check your answers at cl.glencoe.com.

Self Check

What issues arise when the government or consumers try to prosecute corporations for white-collar crimes?

12.2 Tax Evasion

tax evasion The willful attempt to avoid paying legally due taxes; a specific intent crime. Also called *tax fraud*.

Tax evasion, also *tax fraud*, is the willful attempt to avoid paying legally due taxes. One can evade paying federal, state, or local taxes. However, because evasion of federal taxes is the most commonly prosecuted tax offense, this part of the chapter will focus on it.

Tax evasion generally involves three elements. To obtain a conviction for tax evasion, the government must prove *all three elements* of the tax offense beyond a reasonable doubt:

1. The existence of a tax deficiency
2. An affirmative act constituting an evasion or attempted evasion of a tax
3. Willfulness in the doing of the affirmative act

The element of willfulness in this context makes tax evasion a specific intent crime.

The following three sections will examine each of these three elements in detail.

Existence and Proof of a Tax Deficiency

A **tax deficiency** exists when the proper amount of tax to be paid is greater than the amount shown on a taxpayer's tax return. For example, if a taxpayer owes $5,000 in taxes but manipulates his or her tax return to state that he should pay only $4,000, a $1,000 tax deficiency exists. Most courts require proof of deficiencies of any size, but others require that the deficiency be substantial. What is "substantial" is a question of fact to be determined by the fact-finder (jury or judge).

To prove the existence of a tax deficiency, the government must show the following:

- The defendant received income in addition to what was reported.
- The unreported income was taxable.

The burden of the second element does not fall on the prosecution if it can prove a deficiency with direct evidence.

The government can utilize several methods to prove a tax deficiency, involving direct and circumstantial evidence:

Direct Evidence The government's burden of proof is much lighter if it is able to prove a tax deficiency by way of the "specific items" method. Using direct evidence involves examining and searching through the defendant's records for all taxable income, then comparing it to the tax return filed. This procedure is commonly known as the "specific items" method because it requires the government to produce evidence of specific items of reportable income by the defendant that do not appear, or appear in a diminished amount, on income tax returns. Examples of this include evidence of taxable income from checks the defendant received for services rendered; or checks made out to the defendant from the defendant's corporation, to him- or herself for personal use, which were not reported. In such

tax deficiency When the proper amount of tax to be paid is greater than the amount shown on a taxpayer's tax return.

Then and Now

Sociologist Edwin H. Sutherland first coined the term "white collar crime" in 1940. He defined it as a crime committed 1) by a person of respectability and high social status, 2) while in the course of his occupation. This original definition focused on the characteristics of the offender, rather than on the actual offenses committed. Modern definitions of white-collar crime instead focus on the criminal offense, regardless of the social status of the offender.

cases, the checks themselves would be considered the specific items of taxable income.

Although the use of direct evidence is the ideal way to prove a tax deficiency, it is often extremely difficult to obtain such evidence in criminal tax offense trials. Obtaining direct evidence is dependent upon the taxpayer retaining all records of income; if a defendant intended to evade paying income taxes, he or she will aim to conceal the existence of any unreported income, not retain it.

Circumstantial/Indirect Evidence As an alternative to direct evidence, the prosecution may opt instead to use circumstantial or indirect evidence to establish a tax deficiency. There are three main indirect methods of proving a tax deficiency:

1. *Net worth method*, which requires the government to establish that during the year for which the defendant is accused of evading taxes, his or her net worth increased by more than what is reflected on his or her income tax return for that year. A person's *net worth* is the value of everything owned (assets), less the total amount owed (debts).
2. *Cash expenditures method*, which involves the prosecution establishing to a reasonable certainty that all the expenditures the defendant made within the fiscal year under examination exceed the amount of income reported on the taxpayer's return.
3. *Bank deposits method*, in which the prosecution merely examines the deposits the defendant made into a bank account within the relevant year. If the total amount of the deposits exceeds the amount reported on the income tax return, the excess is presumed to be unreported income.

Affirmative Act

The second element that generally must be satisfied to obtain a conviction of tax evasion is that the accused must have performed an affirmative act towards the evasion or attempted evasion of taxes. This is a critical element because it can make the difference between a conviction of a felony and a misdemeanor. Although performing an affirmative act toward the evasion of taxes constitutes a felony, mere neglect to file a tax return or pay required taxes results in a misdemeanor conviction.

What are considered affirmative acts for purposes of tax evasion? There are several examples, including:

Net Worth and Cash Expenditures

The net worth method and the cash expenditures method apply very similar procedures to discover a tax deficiency. Why then, does the government choose to employ one method rather than the other? It all depends on the defendant's spending habits. In a case where the defendant spends or consumes all of his or her unreported income during the year in question, the net worth method is unhelpful but the cash expenditures method becomes useful. The more the defendant spends, the more the cash expenditures method will implicate him or her, because it is based on the discrepancy between one's spending and reported income.

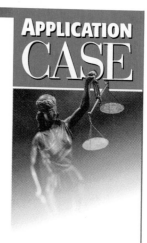

Friedberg v. United States

In *Friedberg v. United States* (1954), the defendant claimed that he had been saving cash over the course of several years, and accordingly his net worth was much higher than reported on income tax returns. Cash held over from previous years had already been taxed, and therefore, it need not be reported (see "cash hoard defense" below). Although the government, in this case, was unable to establish with complete certainty whether this cash on hand existed, it showed that it was unlikely. The government showed that (1) the defendant's property was foreclosed upon because he could not make minimum payments of $30 a month; (2) he lost his business because of inability to pay basic bills; and (3) the defendant claimed to have only $150 in cash in a loan application. The evidence was sufficient to satisfy the government's burden of negating alternative sources of non-taxable income.

"Cash Hoard" Defense

Critical Thinking In what ways can a person defend him- or herself against tax evasion charges?

SOURCE: *Friedberg v. United States*, 348 U.S. 142 (1954).

- Filing false tax returns
- Keeping a double set of books
- Concealing assets
- Placing assets in the name of a third party
- Lying to IRS agents

Many courts, including the U.S. Supreme Court, have held that any practice designed to mislead the government, or to conceal funds or income, can be categorized as an affirmative act. Additionally, some courts hold that if the government can show a pattern of failure to file tax returns, this pattern of omissions might be collectively viewed as an affirmative act in an attempt to evade taxes.

Willfulness

The third and final element that the government must prove for a tax evasion conviction is willfulness. **Willfulness**, for tax evasion purposes, is the voluntary, intentional violation of a known legal duty regarding a taxpayer's knowledge that he or she should have reported more income than he or she actually did. It is required for

willfulness For tax evasion purposes, the voluntary, intentional violation of a known legal duty regarding a taxpayer's knowledge that he or she should have reported more income than he or she actually did.

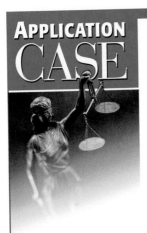

Spies v. United States

In the landmark case of *Spies v. United States* (1943), the defendant simply did not file his tax return, nor did he pay the required taxes. The Supreme Court held that for a felony conviction of tax evasion, the defendant must have willfully failed to file and pay the required taxes with the willful attempt to evade or defeat the tax. On the other hand, the Court concluded that a willful failure to file a tax return or pay taxes due, without the added purpose of evading or defeating that tax will only result in a misdemeanor, even if this omission is willful. Therefore, the defendant's behavior constituted only a misdemeanor offense. The Court held that for a felony conviction, the government must prove that the taxpayer did not merely neglect to file a return, but that he affirmatively attempted to evade paying the tax.

Critical Thinking What is the difference between a willful omission and an affirmative act?

SOURCE: *Spies v. United States*, 317 U.S. 492 (1943).

both the felony and misdemeanor tax statutes, and there is no difference in the definition of the word "willful" when it is used in either statute. The main issue at stake is what state of mind, or *mens rea*, must be shown to satisfy this willfulness requirement. Based on this, the government must show:

- The law imposed a duty on the defendant
- The defendant knew of this duty
- The defendant voluntarily and intentionally violated that duty

In other words, if the government can establish that the defendant was aware of his or her legal duty as a taxpayer, the willfulness requirement is satisfied. Conversely, if the defendant was unaware of his or her duty, then the willfulness requirement is not satisfied. However, to sustain a conviction for felony tax evasion, the government must show that the defendant willfully attempted to evade or defeat the tax.

Unlike other crimes, the Supreme Court has established that ignorance of the law is a defense when it comes to tax evasion. The Court stated that tax laws are extremely complex and difficult to understand. Therefore, several tax evasion offenses, including both felonies and misdemeanors, require a specific intent. This has the result of making the government's burden of proving willfulness much more difficult.

Myth	**Fact**
Ignorance of the law is an acceptable defense for tax evasion *only* if the defendant offers evidence of a reasonable good faith belief.	Willfulness to commit tax evasion is negated even if the defendant's good faith belief is unreasonable.

Defenses Against Tax Evasion

There are several defenses that a taxpayer can offer to negate one or more of the three elements discussed above:

"Cash Hoard" Defense   This defense attacks the showing of a tax deficiency and basically asserts that although there may seem to be a tax deficiency (i.e., unreported income), in actuality the alleged unreported income is not taxable for whatever reason. For example, taxpayers often claim that they had saved-up cash on hand.

Defense Against the Element of Willfulness   A second defense attacks the "willfulness" element. Remember that the government must show that the act or omission of tax evasion was done with an awareness of the illegality. Therefore, even if the defendant's good faith lack of knowledge or awareness is objectively unreasonable, the government's burden of proof is not satisfied.

Third Party Defense: Defense Against the Element of Affirmative Act   This defense shifts the blame of the alleged evasion to a third party, such as an accountant or attorney.

Self Check

1. What is the difference between willfulness for a felony versus a misdemeanor tax evasion charge?
2. What are some common defenses against charges of tax evasion?

CRIMINAL LAW *Online*
Check your answers at cl.glencoe.com.

12.3 False Advertising

Like tax evasion, false advertisement can be a violation of both state and federal laws. The following section examines both the federal and state laws in detail.

False Advertising Under Federal Law

Under federal law, there are two main laws that target false advertisement—the Trademark Law Revision Act (Lanham Act) and the Federal Trade Commission Act.

Trademark Law Revision Act of 1988 (Lanham Act) This statute allows any one who "is or is likely to be damaged" by a false advertisement to sue the advertiser. The courts have interpreted this provision to cover the rights of competitors, but consumers and other non-competitors are not considered to fall within the category of those "likely to be damaged." Under the provisions of the Trademark Act, originally enacted in the early 1900s, a plaintiff was only able to bring a false advertisement claim alleging that the defendant misrepresented the defendant's own product, injuring the plaintiff.[1]

Now, under the more recent Trademark Law Revision Act of 1988, liability falls on *anyone* who makes a false or misleading advertisement regarding his or her own goods, services, or commercial activities, as well as advertisements regarding someone else's goods, services, or commercial activities. This act only imposes civil liability, not criminal penalty; therefore, only plaintiffs can bring legal action, not prosecutors.

There are five showings that a plaintiff must make to succeed in a suit based on this act:

1. The advertiser made a false or misleading statement or representation about his or her or another person's goods, services, or commercial activity.
2. The statement or representation actually deceived, or has the capacity to deceive, a substantial segment of the targeted audience.
3. The deception is material, in that it is likely to influence purchasing decisions.
4. The advertising is made in connection with goods or services that traveled in interstate commerce.
5. The deception has resulted or is likely to result in injury to the plaintiff.

As stated above, the defendant must have made a *representation* or an *advertisement*. Hence, the first task is to understand what constitutes a representation or advertisement. A representation or advertisement can be in either words or pictures, and it must be about a product or service. For example, if a company advertises to sell shelves and displays a picture of a shelf on a brochure, a representation has been made about the shelves for sale. If the company then subsequently sells a shelf of inferior quality than the one pictured, the representation may be deemed to be false.[2]

An important issue regarding the nature of a representation is the question of whether the "representation" must always be in the affirmative, or does the Act also include omissions or non-disclosures that may mislead? Originally, it was proposed that such an omission of

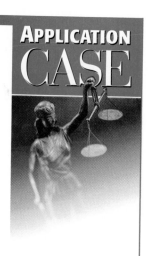

Truck Components, Inc. v. K-H Corp.

There have been cases where a plaintiff has tried to sue under the Trademark/Lanham Act, but the court held that the defendant's representation was not made about any good or service. In *Truck Components, Inc. v. K-H Corp.* (1991), the defendant agreed not to compete with the plaintiff in the sale of certain truck components. When the defendant breached this agreement, the plaintiff sued under the Trademark Act. The plaintiff claimed that the defendant's promotions were misleading because they "constitute representations that defendants are legally entitled and empowered to design, manufacture and market such products," when in fact, under the agreement, the defendant was not "legally entitled" to sell such products.

The court, however, disagreed with the plaintiff and held that the defendant's alleged representation did not fall within the Act. The court stated that the Act was limited to representations about "nature, characteristics, qualities, or geographic origin of his or her or another person's goods." In this case, the debate focused on the defendant's legal right to sell or manufacture the components. This is not enough to constitute legal liability, as the representation must be made about an actual good or service, and no representation regarding the production or quality of the goods in question (i.e., the components) were made.

APPLICATION CASE

False Advertising

Critical Thinking Do you think companies should be allowed to advertise products they are not "legally entitled" to sell?

SOURCE: *Truck Components, Inc. v. K-H Corp.*, 776 F.Supp. 405 (ND Ill. 1991).

material information should be actionable. However, this proposed amendment was deleted and the answer was left to the courts. The reason for its deletion was to prevent the likely misreading that an advertisement must contain every single material fact that may or may not influence a consumer's decision to buy a service or product.[3] As of now, there is a split in the courts as to whether a representation, as used in the Trademark/Lanham Act, includes omissions or non-disclosures. (See Application Case *American Home Products Corporation v. Johnson & Johnson* for an example of this ongoing and complex debate.)

Federal Trade Commission Act   This Act provides that it is illegal for any person or business to create or cause to be created any false advertisement that:

- By the U.S. Mail or by any means, is used for the purpose of inducing, or is likely to directly or indirectly induce the purchase of food, drugs, devices, services, or cosmetics
- By any means that is used for the purpose of inducing, or is likely to directly or indirectly induce, the purchase or

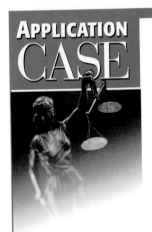

APPLICATION CASE

Omissions of Information

American Home Products Corporation v. Johnson & Johnson

This 1987 case is a good example of how a failure to disclose certain material may render the representation misleading. The defendant, the makers of Tylenol, made a list as part of its marketing scheme that compared the side effects of its drug to those of Advil, manufactured by the plaintiff. The plaintiff claimed that the defendant omitted one negative effect that the defendant's drug had, but that the plaintiff's drug did not. The court held in favor of the plaintiff, although it recognized the idea that the Lanham Act does not require that all facts be disclosed. It also held, however, that a caption used in the advertisement implied that the list was comprehensive, which would mislead the targeted audience. In addition, because the defendant is in an industry that can pose many risks to consumers, policy considerations motivated the court to decide that the defendants were held to a higher standard of care.

Critical Thinking Should advertisers be required to include all the information available about their products?

SOURCE: *American Home Products Corporation v. Johnson & Johnson*, 654 F.Supp 568 (SDNY 1987).

Crimes Against the Community and Institutions

commerce relating to food, drugs, devices, services, or cosmetics.

- The creation of, or the causing to be created, any false advertisement within the provisions of this section shall be an unfair or deceptive act or practice in or affecting commerce . . ."[4]

The Federal Trade Commission Act will be briefly covered again later, under Antitrust Laws.

False Advertising Under State Law

A defendant may be civilly or criminally liable under state laws prohibiting any false or misleading advertisements. Unlike the federal acts, however, these laws are mainly passed to protect consumers from being misled regarding products or services offered for sale. Although the laws vary from state to state, the falsity generally must be material and proof of an actual intent to sell the product is necessary. Many times in criminal false advertisement cases, however, it is not necessary for the prosecution to show that there has been an actual victim who made a purchase based on the deceptive ad.

For example, under California's false advertisement laws, a criminal violation is found by satisfying four elements:

1. A statement
2. made by the disseminator in connection with the sale or disposition of goods or services
3. which is untrue or misleading
4. and which statement is known, or should have been known, to be untrue or misleading.[5]

California courts have employed a "capacity to deceive" test: As long as the ad has the capability of deceiving the public, a violation can be established. Further, it is the general, overall impression of the ad that determines the violation. Finally, the *mens rea* requirement is negligence: The California law states that the defendant know, or with reasonable care should have known, the ad to be false.

When bringing charges of false advertising, what legally constitutes a representation or advertisement?

Check your answers at cl.glencoe.com.

12.4 Mail Fraud

Mail fraud is a form of fraud that uses a mail service to disseminate materials that deceive people. To obtain a conviction for mail fraud, the government must establish four basic elements all beyond a reasonable doubt:

1. A scheme to defraud
2. With the intent to defraud
3. While using the U.S. Postal Service, or any private interstate commercial carrier
4. In furtherance of that scheme

This statute has a very broad reach. Furthermore, it is an offense often charged in conjunction with other crimes. In the landmark case *United States v. Weatherspoon* (1978), a conviction of both mail fraud and false statements was upheld.[6] The majority of courts also allow a mail fraud conviction for mailing a fraudulent tax return, and mail fraud is also often charged together with securities fraud.

The next three sections will discuss the four elements of mail fraud in detail.

CRIMINAL LAW Online

Mail Fraud Tips

Read "What you need to know about mail fraud" by clicking the link at **cl.glencoe.com**. How can mail fraud affect you? How can you protect yourself from mail fraud?

➤ **Mail Fraud** Mail fraud can be committed with either the U.S. Postal Service or through private carriers.
What is the main difference in Congress' legal authority over the U.S. Postal Service and over private carriers?

Scheme to Defraud

Of all the elements of mail fraud, this one has resulted in the most litigation because the federal statute neither defines what constitutes a "scheme" nor what types of schemes fall within the purview of the statute. Thus, courts are given wide discretion in shaping this element. It is understood, though, that the government need not show that the scheme or plan was successful or completed. In other words, it is not necessary that the government show that an individual has actually suffered an economic loss or deprivation of property.

Originally, the statute was used only to prosecute "schemes" that consisted of traditional common law fraud, i.e., defrauding one of some tangible property or interest in property. Later, it was interpreted to prosecute schemes defrauding individuals out of intangible property as well. A congressional statute now expressly allows mail fraud to encompass fraudulent schemes involving intangible property rights.

Schemes involving traditional fraud deprive one of money or other tangible property through misrepresentations, including omissions, which are reasonably calculated to deceive. The courts apply an objective standard in determining whether a reasonable person would rely upon the representations made. Some examples of traditional fraud cases involving mail fraud are false loan applications and fraudulent investment schemes.

The **intangible rights theory** covers a type of prosecution for mail fraud that was primarily used to protect citizens from dishonest public officials. A public official using the mail as part of a scheme to "deprive the citizenry of the right to good government" was actionable under the mail fraud statute. This theory, however, has undergone some testing over the years. (See Application Case *McNally v. United States* on page 419 for an example.)

intangible rights theory
A type of prosecution for mail fraud that was primarily used to protect citizens from dishonest public officials.

Intent to Defraud

This element of mail fraud is the same as any fraud case: that the defendant intended to defraud the victim through the defendant's scheme. Some courts have found intent if the defendant was merely reckless. Therefore, the defendant is criminally liable even with only a reckless disregard for the truth.

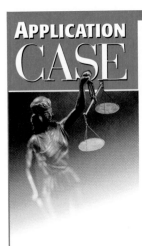
McNally v. United States

This 1987 Supreme Court case restricted the reach of the federal mail fraud statute. The Court found that this statute was no longer applicable to individuals engaged in political corruption because the interest or right involved did not fall within the definition of "scheme to defraud."

In this case, the chairman of the Democratic Party of Kentucky, Howard Hunt, was given the authority to select the insurance companies that were to provide the Commonwealth with its workmen's compensation policy. Hunt chose a certain insurance agent on condition that this agency share its commissions with other specified insurance agencies, one of them owned by McNally. The selected insurance company mailed commission checks to the other specified agencies, which served as the basis for one of the mail fraud counts: that a "scheme" was devised "to defraud the citizens of Kentucky of their right to have the Commonwealth's affairs conducted honestly."

The prosecution argued that the Commonwealth's public officials owe a fiduciary duty to the public, and to "misuse . . . [the public] office for private gain is a fraud." The Court held, however, that although the statute protects property rights, a "scheme to defraud" does not include protection of intangible rights to honest government.

In any case, Congress subsequently completely overturned the *McNally* decision in 1988 through passage of 18 U.S.C. § 1346, by defining "scheme to defraud" to include "a scheme or artifice to deprive another of the intangible right of honest services." In addition, when the prosecution is trying to establish a "scheme" dealing with the intangible rights doctrine (as distinguished from a traditional fraud scheme), there must be a fiduciary duty between the parties.

Critical Thinking Should mail fraud laws protect the intangible rights to honest government? Why or why not?

SOURCE: *McNally v. United States*, 483 U.S. 350 (1987); 18 U.S.C. § 1346.

Use of the Post Office or Private Interstate Carrier

Originally, the federal mail fraud statute only applied to cases in which the defendant used the U.S. Post Office to carry out his scheme to defraud. As can be seen from the modern mail fraud

Myth	**Fact**
To be guilty of mail fraud, the defendant must insert the item to be mailed into a mailbox, or deliver it to a post office.	The U.S. Supreme Court has determined that it is enough if the defendant *caused* the mailing.

SOURCE: *United States v. Pereira*, 347 US 1 (1954).

statute, however, a violation can occur from use of *any* private carrier. With regard to private carrier use, it must be an *interstate* carrier, whereas if the defendant is using the U.S. Post Office, it is enough if the defendant merely mailed something down the block. This is because Congress has complete power over Post Offices as granted by the Constitution, whereas Congress's control over private carriers is limited to power to regulate interstate commerce.[7]

Furtherance of the Scheme to Defraud

To support a conviction of mail fraud, the prosecution must prove that the use of mail was "in furtherance," or for the purpose, of executing or completing the scheme to defraud. Using the mail must be part of at least one key element of the mail fraud scheme.

Additionally, if the mailing occurred after the scheme was completed, the mailing element is usually not satisfied. In *United States v. Maze* (1974), the defendant used a stolen credit card. Thereafter, several mailings occurred between the bank and the vendor. The government argued that this was enough to satisfy the mailing element. The U.S. Supreme Court rejected this argument, because the scheme was complete once the defendant used the stolen credit card.[8] Nonetheless, the Court has also held that there are certain times when the mailing could occur even after the defendant defrauded the victim of his or her money and still satisfy the "in furtherance" element.

A defendant has two main defenses to a mail fraud charge:

1. A good faith defense, which is merely an assertion that there was no fraud intended
2. A statute of limitations defense. The statute of limitations is generally five years on a mail fraud charge, and ten years if it involves a financial institution. The statute of limitations begins at the time of the final overt act made in furtherance of the scheme to defraud.

Check your answers at cl.glencoe.com.

1. What are some schemes to defraud, and why has there been difficulty in defining a "scheme"?
2. What is the intangible rights doctrine, and how has the debate surrounding it been resolved?

12.5 Securities Fraud

With the crash of the stock market in 1929, Congress enacted the Securities Act of 1933 and the Securities Exchange Act of 1934 to promote integrity in the stock market. Although other statutes were passed since then, these two are the most important. The Securities Exchange Act is most widely used to prosecute defendants for securities fraud. It protects both purchasers and sellers of securities, whereas the Securities Act of 1933 protects only the purchaser.

A **securities fraud** offense can be criminal, civil, or administrative. There are four main elements for every type of securities fraud action:

securities fraud A criminal, civil, or administrative offense with the following elements: substantive fraud that is found in the offer, purchase, or sale of a security or in connection therewith; the use of interstate commerce or the mails; and willfulness.

1. Substantive fraud—including material omissions and misrepresentations, insider trading, parking, and broker-dealer fraud, each of which has its own elements
2. Such fraud is found in the offer, purchase, or sale of a security or in connection therewith
3. The use of interstate commerce or the mails
4. Willfulness[9]

The following sections will discuss the first three of these four elements in greater detail. The last, willfulness, has already been covered in previous discussions that can generally apply here as well.

Substantive Fraud

As shown above, there are four different ways this element can be satisfied, each with elements unique to that particular type of fraud:

Material Omissions and Misrepresentations

Liability for this most common type of securities fraud stems from the Securities Exchange Act of 1934. The Act states that it is illegal for anyone "to make any untrue statement of a material fact or to omit to state a material fact necessary in order to make the statements made . . . in connection with the purchase or sale of any security." To prove this crime, the government must prove four (sometimes five) of the following elements:

1. The defendant made a false statement or omission
2. that is material
3. that is made with knowledge
4. and that caused the injured party's damages
5. (in the case of an omission only) and the defendant had a duty to disclose the information.[10]

Insider Trading

Insider trading is a type of substantive fraud that involves the purchase and sale of securities based on material, nonpublic information. Insider trading usually deals with cases in which one insider, quasi-insider, or misappropriator has inside information and tips off another individual regarding certain material, nonpublic information. At times the tipper is liable, and at other times the tippee is liable. The Securities Exchange Act of 1934 prohibits certain trades by corporate officers, directors, and majority shareholders. It also prohibits misrepresentations and other "fraudulent, deceptive, or manipulative acts or practices" specifically with regard to tender offers.

An important question in regard to insider trading is who qualifies as an *insider*. Many different individuals have been classified as insiders, including directors, officers, major shareholders, lower-level employees obtaining information because of their jobs, outside professionals and advisors (e.g., accountants and lawyers), press, companies and firms of the above-mentioned individuals, and even their families.

Parking

A third method of securities fraud is known as parking. **Parking** can be defined as any sale of securities that are purchased with the understanding that they will be repurchased by the seller at

Causation and Reliance

In a securities fraud case, the government or plaintiff must establish both cause in fact ("transaction causation") and proximate cause ("loss causation"). Simply put, *transaction causation* requires a showing that but for the fraud, the victim/plaintiff would not have purchased, sold, or undergone any transaction with the security, whereas *loss causation* requires a showing that the fraud is proximately responsible for any injuries.

insider trading A type of substantive fraud that involves the purchase and sale of securities based on material, nonpublic information.

parking Any sale of securities that are purchased with the understanding that they will be repurchased by the seller at a later time, to manipulate stock prices or avoid reporting requirements.

a later time. Although parking is a criminal violation in and of itself, it is often part of a larger scheme. Parking is used to:

- "Manipulate the supply and demand of stock, which will affect its price
- Circumvent margin rules and minimum net capital requirements
- Avoid the reporting requirements . . . of the 1934 Act."[11]

Broker-Dealer Fraud   A final practice found under the substantive fraud element of a securities fraud action is a type of broker-dealer fraud known as churning. **Churning** occurs when a stockbroker excessively purchases and sells securities for a client without regard or concern for the client's investment objectives, but rather to advance his own interests, usually that of generating commissions.

For a conviction, the government (or investor) must establish that:

- The broker exercised control over the trading in the account.
- The trading was excessive in light of the character of the account.
- The broker showed an intent to defraud or showed willful and reckless disregard for the investor's interests.

churning When a stockbroker excessively purchases and sells securities for a client without regard or concern for the client's investment objectives, but rather to advance his own interests, usually that of generating commissions.

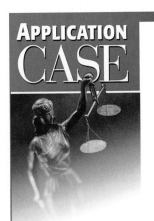

APPLICATION CASE

Insider Trading

Dirks v. SEC

In *Dirks v. SEC* (1983), a financial analyst discovered that an insurance company was involved in a major fraud resulting in an overstatement of the company's assets. Prior to the information becoming public, the analyst disseminated this information to his clients, who subsequently sold their shares in the insurance company based on this information.

The Court held that the analyst could not be held liable as a tippee, one who receives the information regarding the fraud from the tipper, because liability requires that the tipper breach a fiduciary duty. In other words, a tippee does not invariably inherit the insider's duty. The Court held that the analyst's tipper breached no duty, but was merely reporting a fraud.

Critical Thinking Do you think the defendant in this case had a duty to make information about the fraud public? Why or why not?

SOURCE: *Dirks v. SEC*, 463 US 646 (1983).

Offer, Purchase, or Sale of a Security

The 1933 and 1934 Acts require that the substantive fraud discussed above be "in the *offer or sale*" or "in connection with the *purchase or sale*" of a security. The 1933 Act defines an offer for sale, or offer, as "every attempt of offer to dispose of, or solicitation of an offer to buy, a security or interest in a security, for value." A transfer of title is not required for a sale to occur. The 1934 Act defines purchase as "any contract to buy, purchase or otherwise acquire" a security. A sale includes "any contracts to sell or otherwise dispose of" a security. These definitions include a corporation's purchase or sale of its own securities, mergers, and acquisitions.[12]

Use of Interstate Commerce or Mails

This third element of the crime requires that a securities fraud scheme include the "use of any means or instrumentality of interstate commerce or of the mails, or of any facility of any national securities exchange."[13] In some situations, an intrastate use of an interstate means of communication is sufficient, such as the use of a telephone to call someone within the same state. Further, use of interstate commerce or mails need only be incidental, so long as they were in furtherance of the fraud (similar to the mail fraud requirement).

Defenses

There are three common defenses to securities fraud:

1. *No Knowledge:* The defendant can argue that he or she did not have knowledge of the substantive law. This does not mean that the defendant asserts that he or she was not aware of the applicable securities laws, but rather did not know that his or her actions were contrary to the laws. Note that this is not a complete defense; it only lessens the penalties.
2. *Good Faith:* In a case where the substantive fraud entails a misstatement or omission, the defendant can claim that he or she had a good faith belief that the statement was true and accurate, or that the omission was not intentional or immaterial.
3. *Reliance on Counsel:* The defendant can also assert that his or her actions were a result of a good faith reliance on the advice of counsel. This defense requires the defendant to

show: (a) a request for counsel's advice regarding the legality of the proposed action, (b) full disclosure to counsel of all relevant facts, (c) counsel's assurance that the action is legal, and (d) good faith reliance on counsel's advice. This defense is not available if counsel is an interested party.[14]

Check your answers at
cl.glencoe.com.

1. What is insider trading, and who qualifies as an "insider"?
2. What are common defenses against charges of security fraud?

12.6 Crimes Against the Food and Drug Act

According to the Federal Food, Drug, and Cosmetic Act (FDCA), committing or causing the following acts are prohibited:

- The introduction, or delivery for introduction, into interstate commerce of any food, drug, device, or cosmetic that is adulterated or misbranded
- The adulteration or misbranding of any food, drug, device, or cosmetic in interstate commerce
- The receipt in interstate commerce of any food, drug, device, or cosmetic that is adulterated or misbranded, and the delivery or proffered delivery thereof for pay or otherwise
- The refusal to permit entry or inspection
- The manufacture within any territory of any food, drug, device, or cosmetic that is adulterated or misbranded

The underlying purpose of this act is to protect the health and safety of the public by prohibiting all adulterated and misbranded goods from entering the stream of interstate commerce. Any violation of the FDCA can be either a misdemeanor or a felony, and can result in criminal liability, injunctions, or seizure of the illegal merchandise.

The elements of FDCA violations differ depending on the level of criminality and on who the defendant is. For a *misdemeanor* conviction, three or four elements must be satisfied:

1. There must be a "food," "drug," "cosmetic," or "device."
2. The object must be "adulterated" or "misbranded."

3. The object must be introduced into interstate commerce.

4. (When defendant is a corporate officer only) The officer must bear a "responsible relation" to the violation.

To obtain a *felony* conviction, the above three or four misdemeanor elements must be shown as well as either intent or evidence of a prior FDCA violation.

The following sections will discuss the exact definitions of the key terms of the FDCA.

Definitions

The FDCA statutes define food, drugs, cosmetics, and devices as follows:

Food   The definition of food includes:

- Articles used for food or drink for man or other animals
- Chewing gum
- Articles used for components of any such article.

Drug   A drug includes any "articles intended for use in the diagnosis, cure, mitigation, treatment, or prevention of disease in man or other animals."

Cosmetic   Cosmetics include "articles intended to be rubbed, poured, sprinkled, or sprayed on, introduced into, or otherwise applied to the human body or any part thereof for cleansing, beautifying, promoting attractiveness, or altering the appearance."

Device   Devices include any "instrument, apparatus, implement, machine, contrivance, implant, in vitro reagent, or other similar or related article, including any component, part, or accessory, which is:

- Recognized in the official National Formulary
- Intended for use in the diagnosis of disease or other conditions, or in the cure, mitigation, treatment, or prevention of disease
- Intended to affect the structure or any function of the body.[15]

In addition, the FDCA defines adulterated, misbranded, interstate commerce, and the relevance of intent or prior violations as follows:

Adulterated Goods

An item has been subject to **adulteration** when its ingredients are poisonous, filthy, putrid, otherwise unsanitary, or have been contaminated.[16] In *United States v. Park* (1975), the Court held that food coming into contact with rodents can be considered "adulterated."[17] Some courts have held that a food can be labeled "adulterated" if there is a reasonable possibility that the method or where it is stored and/or processed may result in contamination.

Misbranding

For each article discussed above, **misbranding** means any branding of an item that includes the use of false or misleading information, labels, packaging, or containers. An example includes labeling an article as "sterile" when it is actually "not sterile."

Interstate Commerce

FDCA violations require that the adulterated or misbranded food, drug, cosmetic, or device be introduced into interstate commerce. Such interstate commerce is not limited "to the actual transportation of articles across state lines, but includes the whole transaction of which such transportation is a part."[18]

Felony: Intent or Prior Violation

For a felony conviction under the FDCA, the government has an additional burden of proving one of either situations:

- That the defendant had the intent to ship adulterated or misbranded foods, drugs, cosmetics, or devices into interstate commerce

> **Food Adulteration**
> Food adulteration occurs when food is contaminated in any way, such as improper handling, improper storage, or outside contaminants.
> *Does food need to come in direct contact with outside contaminants in order to be considered adulterated?*

- That the defendant has done this in the past and he is now being prosecuted again

Defenses

Two main defenses have been asserted in connection with FDCA violations: the Fourth Amendment and impossibility.

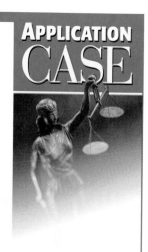

APPLICATION CASE

United States v. Dotterweich
United States v. Park

In *United States v. Dotterweich* (1943), a company purchased drugs from their manufacturer, re-labeled them, and shipped them out into interstate commerce. Dotterweich was found guilty of violating the FDCA. They took no part in shipping the misbranded and adulterated goods into interstate commerce, but because they had the "responsible share in the furtherance of the transaction," they were found liable.

Over 30 years later, the U.S. Supreme Court clarified this finding in *United States v. Park* (1975). In *Park*, the president of a national retail food chain was held strictly criminally liable under the FDCA for failing to prevent his company from storing food in an area where rodent contamination was a reasonable possibility. In other words, the *Dotterweich* strict liability standard was still upheld, i.e., no intent is required for a misdemeanor conviction.

FDCA Violations

A "responsible relation" test had been used in *Dotterweich*, but there were some questions about its application. This test was used again in *Park*, but to prevent any controversy it was articulated as such: In addition to the usual elements, it must be established with "evidence sufficient to warrant a finding by the trier that the defendant had, by reason of his position in the corporation, responsibility and authority either to prevent in the first instance, or promptly correct, the violation complained of, and that he failed to do so." In sum, the Court stated that strict liability will be applied to any individual who fails to prevent, detect, or correct the adulteration or mis-branding when the authority or power to do so is available to them.

Critical Thinking Does it seem that the president in the *Park* case had intent or was he negligent? Explain your answer.

SOURCE: *United States v. Dotterweich* 320 US 277, 281 (1943); *United States v. Park*, 421 US 658 (1975).

Fourth Amendment The Fourth Amendment protects the people against unreasonable searches and seizures. This provision applies to administrative searches as well. Administrative searches, however, may be valid without a warrant if:

- The inspection is made pursuant to a regulatory scheme for which there is a substantial government interest.
- The owner of the premises is aware of the periodic inspections, the inspection furthers this regulatory scheme.
- The scheme's predictable regularity leads the owner to inspect it, which creates an awareness that substitutes for a warrant.[19]

Impossibility The U.S. Supreme Court requires the government to show that a corporate officer whose business violated the FDCA also had the authority or power to prevent or correct the FDCA violation. If it was objectively impossible for the officer to do so, then liability cannot be found. Therefore, many defendants assert an

ON THE JOB

Food and Drug Inspector

Description and Duties: Investigate and inspect facilities, procedures, and products to ensure that they comply with required standards. Collect and evaluate evidence. Enforce restrictions on unacceptable products to prevent their sale or distribution. Supervise the destruction or reconditioning of restrained products. Investigate, evaluate, and take appropriate action on consumer complaints and illegal or fraudulent practices in the advertisement, manufacture, or sale of products.

Salary: Salaries for federal inspector are by federal government pay grades and vary depending on experience and supervisory level. State jobs are similar. Starting pay is approximately $35,000 and can reach $65,000.

Other Information: Generally requires a B.S. degree in bacteriology, biology, chemistry, food technology, pharmacology, environmental health, biomedical engineering, or other biological or chemical science. Job experience and at least 30 semester hours of college courses in an appropriate field can also be combined to substitute.

Critical Thinking What qualities do you think make a good food and drug inspector?

SOURCE: California State Personnel Board, http://www.dpa.ca.gov/textdocs/specs/s1/s1589.txt.

"impossibility" defense, which is a claim that the defendant did not have the authority to prevent or rectify the violative situation, and therefore had no liability. If such a defense is made, the government then has the burden of establishing that the defendant did in fact have the necessary control or authority to prevent or correct the situation.

Self Check

For a felony conviction under the FDCA, one of two requirements must be satisfied. Name these.

CRIMINAL LAW *Online*

Check your answers at
cl.glencoe.com.

12.7 Antitrust Crimes and Monopoly

Antitrust laws protect trade and commerce from restraints, monopolies, price-fixing, and price discrimination. These laws were designed to ensure and preserve a competitive economy to allow free enterprise to prosper and to allow everyone an equal opportunity to engage in business, trade, and commerce.

antitrust laws Laws that protect trade and commerce from restraints, monopolies, price-fixing, and price discrimination, to ensure and preserve a competitive economy.

Key Federal Acts

Both the federal government and the state governments have their own antitrust laws with which companies must comply. This section will focus on the four main federal antitrust laws—the Sherman Act, Clayton Act, Robinson-Patman Act, and Federal Trade Commission Act—mainly because many of the state laws follow the same outline as these federal ones.

Conspiracy in Antitrust Violations

To find guilt under the Sherman Act, the government must establish that a conspiracy existed between at least two competitors. A *conspiracy* requires "an agreement, understanding or meeting of the minds between at least two competitors, for the purpose of, or with the effect of, unreasonably restraining trade." For example, two corporations can conspire to illegally fix prices. The key is that there must be an agreement: "In the absence of an agreement or mutual understanding or meeting of the minds, there can be no conspiracy." Therefore, if the same actions were taken independently, by two separate businesses, without any agreement, no conspiracy could be found.

SOURCE: 15 USC section 1 (1994); *United States v. Continental Group, Inc.*, 603 F.2d 444, 465 (3d Cir. 1979) (Jury Instructions), cert. denied, 444 US 1032, (1980). *See also* Federal Jury Practice and Instructions, Devitt section 51A.06 (1998).

The Sherman Act The Sherman Act is the primary statute used to prosecute antitrust cases. Section 1 generally criminalizes unreasonable restraints on interstate commerce. It specifically makes illegal "[e]very contract, combination in the form of trust or otherwise, or conspiracy, in restraint of trade or commerce among the several States, or with foreign nations." A violation can result in a felony conviction. Section 2 criminalizes monopolizing, attempting to monopolize, or conspiring to monopolize a market through unfair practices.[20]

Under Section 1 of the Sherman Act, the government must satisfy three elements for a civil judgment and four for a criminal conviction:

1. Two or more entities formed a combination or conspiracy
2. The combination or conspiracy produces, or potentially produces, an unreasonable restraint of trade or commerce
3. The restraint is on interstate trade or commerce
4. (For criminal charges only) General intent

Penalties for violations of the various antitrust laws can be severe, including a three-year prison sentence for *each* offense, several millions of dollars in fines imposed on both the corporation and the individuals involved, injunctions, and other various fees and damages.

The Robinson-Patman Act Under the Robinson-Patman Price Discrimination Act, one "engaged in commerce" can be subjected to criminal liability if he or she is involved in any sale of goods "at unreasonably low prices for the purpose of destroying competition or eliminating a competitor."[21] This practice, known as *pricing*, creates a high risk of being sued. Nevertheless, because this seems to negate the underlying purpose of the antitrust laws—to preserve a competitive economy—the government usually does not bring criminal charges for it.

The Clayton Act This Act prohibits certain types of activities that harm competition, such as exclusive dealing arrangements and mergers damaging competition. Furthermore, this Act provides a private citizen's right to sue for injury caused by violation of the antitrust laws.

The Federal Trade Commission Act The FTCA, which you have already learned about in the section on false advertising, is mainly used to prosecute unfair and deceptive practices. In that capacity, it has provisions that apply to antitrust and monopoly issues as well. Specifically, it prohibits similar practices mentioned in the Sherman and Clayton Act that relate to harm done to competition.

Other Issues

Price-Fixing In general, price-fixing refers to an agreement formed in order to raise, lower, fix, peg, or stabilize commodity prices entering interstate commerce. There are two main types of price-fixing. **Horizontal price-fixing** agreements are direct or indirect agreements made between market participants at the *same level* within a given market, regarding the prices they will charge for a similar product they both sell. **Vertical price-fixing** agreements, on the other hand, are direct or indirect agreements made between market participants at *different levels* within a given market, regarding the price at which their product will be resold.

Market Allocation Agreements Agreements involving market allocation are those made between competitors within a given market to divide up markets by territory, product line, or customers. Such an agreement is usually done to minimize competition, and is thus an automatic violation of the antitrust laws.

Boycotts In *Klor's, Inc. v. Broadway-Hale Stores* (1959), the U.S. Supreme Court defined *boycotts* as "concerted refusals by traders to deal with other traders." As an anti-competitive measure, such boycotts are considered illegal.[22]

Tying Arrangement A **tying arrangement** is an agreement that a purchaser must buy additional (or tied) products along with the one product that he or she desires. At the very least, the purchaser must agree to not buy this tied product from any other supplier. Tying arrangements have the anti-competitive effect of denying competitors "free access to the market for the tied product, not because the party imposing the tying requirements has a better product or lower price, but because of his power or leverage in another market. At the same time buyers are forced to forego their free choice between competing products."[23]

Tying is illegal if: (1) there are actually two separate products, and (2) the seller has a substantial market share in one of the products and, thus, has "leverage" to force the purchase of the second

Defenses

There are several defenses a defendant can assert in an antitrust action, including:

- Withdrawal from the conspiracy
- Statute of limitations
- Double jeopardy
- Regulated industry
- Foreign commerce

SOURCE: *See* Alec Koch, Carrie B. Mahan & John Woykovsky, "Antitrust," 33 *Am. Crim. L. Rev.* 511, 520-32 (Spring 1996).

horizontal price-fixing Direct or indirect agreements made between market participants at the *same level* within a given market, regarding the prices they will charge for a similar product they both sell.

vertical price-fixing Direct or indirect agreements made between market participants at *different levels* within a given market, regarding the price at which their product will be resold.

tying arrangement An agreement that a purchaser must buy additional (or tied) products along with the one product that he or she desires; at the very least, the purchaser must agree not to buy this tied product from any other supplier.

product. If it is economically impractical to sell two items separately, there is no tying violation. Additionally, some tying arrangements actually have pro-competitive effects, in which case the agreement will only be found unlawful under the "rule of reason" analysis.

Recent government actions against Microsoft in *United States v. Microsoft Corp.* (1998) involve both federal and state claims for antitrust violations. The federal government found a violation of both sections 1 and 2 of the Sherman Act. The section 1 violation, which is not the main claim, is that Microsoft engaged in a tying arrangement by tying their Internet Explorer to Windows 95 and to Windows 98—two separate offenses.

Price Discrimination (Robinson-Patman Act) As stated above, the Robinson-Patman Act generally deals with pricing. It also prohibits other practices, such as discriminatory promotional allowances, unlawful brokerage payments, and the unlawful inducement of a discriminatory price. More specifically, it prohibits *price discrimination* that:

- Unfairly eliminates competition by another manufacturer.
- Unfairly causes one or more customers to go out of business.[24]

The first arrangement is intended to drive the defendant's competitors out of business, whereas the second is intended to drive competitors of the defendant's customer out of business. In both scenarios, the idea is basically the same: The idea is for a business to charge one distributor a lower price than that of another, in order to drive either the business's competition out of business, or the distributor's competition out of business.

monopolize To obtain the joint acquisition and maintenance of the power to control and dominate interstate trade and commerce.

attempt to monopolize Engaging in behavior and business practices that, if successful, would create a monopoly and come close enough to doing so to create a dangerous probability that it would have occurred.

Monopolies Obtaining or attempting to obtain a monopoly are both prohibited under the antitrust laws. To **monopolize** means to obtain the joint acquisition and maintenance "of the power to control and dominate interstate trade and commerce in a commodity to such an extent that they are able, as a group, to exclude actual or potential competitors from the field, accompanied with the intention and purpose to exercise such power."[25] An **attempt to monopolize** means engaging in behavior and business practices that, if successful, would create a monopoly and come close enough to doing so to create a dangerous probability that it would have occurred.

A monopolization conviction requires satisfaction of two elements:

1. The possession of a monopoly power, which includes the power to control or fix prices and unreasonably restrict or exclude competition in a relevant market
2. The willful acquisition or maintenance of such power through unlawful means, and not from fair competitive practices such as high quality products, business acumen, or historical accident[26]

Thus, if a company achieves a monopoly share of a market through lawful, pro-competitive means, there is no antitrust violation. In certain circumstances, however, a company can equally lower prices to all its customers subject to the laws of monopolization and attempted monopolization.

An attempted monopoly conviction requires satisfaction of three elements:

1. Specific intent to obtain a monopoly power in a given market
2. Use of unlawful means to increase market share
3. Dangerous probability that a monopoly will be obtained

As discussed earlier under tying arrangements, in *United States v. Microsoft Corp.* (1998), the U.S. government's lawsuit against Microsoft alleged violations of both sections 1 and 2 of the Sherman Act. The section 2 violation, which was the government's main claim, is that of monopolization and attempted monopolization, with the aforementioned tying allegations playing a role in the monopolization charges. The monopolization counts alleged that Microsoft abused its monopoly power in the market for PC-compatible computers, for the purpose of maintaining its monopoly power in that market. It also alleged that Microsoft attempted to monopolize the Internet browsers market through several anti-competitive means.[27]

Self Check

1. How does price-fixing harm competition? Do vertical price-fixing and horizontal price-fixing affect it differently?
2. Why is an attempt to monopolize a crime?

CRIMINAL LAW Online

Check your answers at cl.glencoe.com.

White Collar Crimes

SUMMARY BY CHAPTER OBJECTIVES

1. Define white-collar crime.

White-collar crime is a term that describes a broad category of nonviolent misconduct involving commercial and financial fraud. Examples of it are tax evasion, false advertising, mail fraud, securities fraud, crimes against the Food and Drug Act, and monopolies and antitrust crimes. White-collar crimes are more often perpetrated by corporations rather than by individuals.

2. List the elements of tax evasion.

To obtain a conviction for tax evasion, the government must prove *all three elements* of the tax offense beyond a reasonable doubt:

- The existence of a tax deficiency
- An affirmative act constituting an evasion or attempted evasion of a tax
- Willfulness

Remember that the element of willfulness indicates that felony tax evasion is a specific intent crime.

3. List the elements for a civil action for false advertising.

There are five showings that a plaintiff must make to succeed in a suit based on this act:

- The advertiser made a false or misleading statement or representation about his or her or another person's goods, services, or commercial activity.

- The statement or representation actually deceived, or has the capacity to deceive, a substantial segment of the targeted audience.
- The deception is material, in that it is likely to influence purchasing decisions.
- The advertising is made in connection with goods or services that traveled in interstate commerce.
- The deception has resulted or is likely to result in injury to the plaintiff.

4. List the elements of mail fraud.

To obtain a conviction for mail fraud, the government must establish four basic elements all beyond a reasonable doubt:

- A scheme to defraud
- With the intent to defraud
- While using the U.S. Postal Service, or any private interstate commercial carrier
- In furtherance of that scheme

5. List the elements of securities fraud.

There are four main elements for every type of securities fraud action:

- Substantive fraud—including material omissions/misrepresentations, insider trading, parking, and broker-dealer fraud, each of which has its own elements

- Such fraud is found in the offer, purchase, or sale of a security or in connection therewith
- The use of interstate commerce or the mails
- Willfulness

6. List the elements of an FDCA action.

For a *misdemeanor* conviction, three elements must be satisfied (four when the defendant is a corporate officer):

- There must be a "food," "drug," "cosmetic," or "device."
- The object must be "adulterated" or "misbranded."
- The object must be introduced into interstate commerce.
- (When the defendant is a corporate officer only) The officer must bear a "responsible relation" to the violation.

To obtain a *felony* conviction, the above three (or four) misdemeanor elements must be shown, *as well as* either intent or evidence of a prior FDCA violation.

7. List the main federal antitrust acts and the elements of an antitrust action.

The four main federal antitrust laws are the Sherman Act, Clayton Act, Robinson-Patman Act, and the Federal Trade Commission Act. Under the Sherman Act, the government must satisfy three elements for a civil judgment and four for a criminal conviction:

- Two or more entities formed a combination or conspiracy
- The combination or conspiracy produces, or potentially produces, an unreasonable restraint of trade or commerce
- The restraint is on interstate trade or commerce
- (For criminal charges only) General intent

8. Explain a monopoly.

To monopolize means to obtain the joint acquisition and maintenance "of the power to control and dominate interstate trade and commerce in a commodity to such an extent that they are able, as a group, to exclude actual or potential competitors from the field, accompanied with the intention and purpose to exercise such power."

Why couldn't corporations be prosecuted for crimes at common law?
Find it on page 402.

KEY TERMS

QUESTIONS FOR REVIEW

1. Define tax deficiency and give an example.
2. What are the various defenses for tax evasion?
3. What are the different methods, direct and indirect, of proving a tax deficiency?
4. What is the difference between a misdemeanor violation and a felony violation for tax evasion?
5. When is an act in furtherance of a scheme to defraud?

6. Explain the role of material omissions and misrepresentations according to the Securities Exchange Act of 1934.
7. Why is the crime of "parking" committed?
8. List and explain the elements of "churning."
9. Define the terms order, purchase, and sale as they relate to securities transactions.
10. What is the difference between horizontal and vertical price-fixing?

PROBLEM-SOLVING EXERCISES

1. **Mail Fraud** You are in charge of investigating mail fraud for the U.S. Post Office. You are handling a case that involves several cases of mail fraud using the U.S. Mail, UPS, and Federal Express. Some of the shipping was interstate and some was intrastate. With prosecutors, you must establish what qualifies as mail fraud under federal laws. Answer the following questions:
   a) What is the difference in the requirements for interstate shipping for the U.S. Mail and for private carriers? Why?
   b) Which intrastate mail can be used as evidence, and what intrastate mail cannot? Why?
   c) Suppose that international shipping was involved, too. Based on what you have learned, do you think that it could be used as evidence? Do you think that it would be used? Why or why not?

2. **Drug Inspection** You are a food and drug inspector working with a large pharmaceutical company that produces several types of drugs for children with "behavioral" problems. They are an extremely successful company, but lately they have been riddled with lawsuits from parents claiming that their children were given drugs unnecessarily. While eating at the company lunchroom, you overhear some salespeople talking. Evidently, they are paying doctors and psychiatrists kickbacks (illegal payments) in exchange for their promise to stop prescribing drugs from other manufacturers. They are also paying doctors to falsify information that can be used in marketing and advertising materials, as well as in journal articles read by other members of the medical community. Answer the following questions:
   a) What crimes appear to be taking place? How?
   b) Although you are a food and drug inspector, can you get involved in this legal issue? Why or why not? If so, how? If not, how can it be resolved?

c) What additional consumer or public health issues should be addressed?

3. **Tax Deficiency** You are a federal judge who is hearing the case of a defendant who is being charged with tax evasion. The defendant is a musician who has earned a large amount of money over the last two years and who has paid some taxes, but not enough to cover her total income. She pleads ignorance of the tax laws and explains that she had hired an inept accountant who misinformed her about her total income. She provides proof that the accountant told her she would have to pay a much smaller amount than what she actually owed. She is willing to pay what she owes, but does not feel that she should be penalized in any way.

   a) Is ignorance of tax law an adequate defense? Why or why not?

b) Is the accountant liable in any way, and does his inefficiency contribute to her defense? Why or why not?

4. **False Advertising** You are a judge in a trial in which the defendant is accused of false advertising. According to prosecutors, he gave misleading information about a free CD that he was offering people who visited his store. The CD was advertised as containing popular dance songs by famous artists, but in fact contained versions of these songs sung by a rather unpopular local band. The CD was given away during a weekend sale, and many customers who got a copy of the CD also made purchases within the store.

   a) Does the fact that the CD was free matter in this case? Why or why not?

   b) How could the CD giveaway be said to influence people's purchasing decisions in this case?

WORKPLACE APPLICATIONS

1. **Food Inspection** You are a restaurant inspector who is conducting a regular inspection of a new, popular restaurant. You are concerned because you have received three phone calls from customers who reported cases of food poisoning over the last two weeks. As you examine the dry goods storage area, you notice a long pink tail coming from behind a bag of rice. You move the bag and find a dead rat. Answer the following questions:

   a) What Act is being violated by this dead rat's presence?

   b) In what exact way is it being violated?

c) Is all of the food in the area affected, or just the bag of rice? Why?

2. **Tying Arrangements** You are a federal prosecutor who is part of a team that is bringing charges against a large software company. Over the years, this company is alleged to have forced distributors to buy their products in quantities that are dictated by the company, refuse to buy from other companies, and install only their products on computers that they sell. As a result, countless other companies have gone bankrupt, and many others are suffering irreparable damage. In its defense, this company states that it is only "winning

fairly" and that it charges everyone a uniform low price. Answer the following questions:

a) What specific laws are being violated by this company?

b) In what way are these laws being violated?

c) Does the fact that the company is charging uniform low prices have any legal bearing on the case?

INTERNET APPLICATIONS

1. **FDCA** Read "The Federal Food, Drug, and Cosmetic Act (FDCA)" by accessing it through **cl.glencoe.com**, then answer the following questions:

   a) What is the case referral process, and what are the different options within this process?

   b) Which process seems best for consumers seeking civil damages? The government seeking criminal punishment? Why?

   c) How does the Office of Consumer Litigation (OCL) differentiate between fraud on consumers and fraud on the FDA? Why does this distinction exist?

2. **Antitrust Laws** Visit "The Local 3 Antitrust" available through the link at **cl.glencoe.com**. Read the summary and pleading. Pretend that you are one of the plaintiffs in this case, and answer the following questions:

   a) What are the complaints against this union?

   b) On what evidence do the plaintiffs base these complaints?

   c) How does this violate the Sherman Antitrust Act? Why?

ETHICS ISSUES

1. **Insider Trading** You are a broker and financial consultant who works with both large businesses in your community and first-time investors. Many of the first-time investors in your community are elderly people who are interested in supplementing their income with low to moderate risk. A client comes in and asks your opinion about whether he should purchase stock in a local company that manufacturers parts for industrial vehicles. From all appearances, the company seems to be thriving and is a good investment. However, you know from a friend who works in their accounting department that their CEO is very close to being indicted for embezzlement, and that the company is in serious financial trouble as a result of the CEO's actions. When this becomes public, stock values are expected to dip sharply. Answer the following questions:

   a) Should you advise your client to not purchase this stock? Why or why not?

   b) How much can you tell your client about the situation regarding this company? Why?

c) Would you be liable if you, knowing this information, advised your client to purchase this stock and then it dropped? Why or why not?

2. **FDA Searches** You are an FDA inspector making a routine semiannual inspection of a pharmaceutical laboratory. Upon arrival, you are surprised at the disarray. The supervisor has just quit and the employees are being extremely careless in their handling and preparation of drug mixtures. You write them up for several violations, which the pharmaceutical company promptly rejects. They take the FDA to court and accuse you of violating their Fourth Amendment rights, since you did not contact the interim supervisor to make her aware of your visit.

a) Does this company have a case? Why or why not?

b) What would be the best way for the company to handle this situation?

ENDNOTES

1 15 U.S.C. § 1125(a)/Lanham Act §43(a). See also Bruce P. Keller & Tiffany D. Trunko, "Consumer Use of RICO to Challenge False Advertising Claims," C674 *ALI-ABA* 51, (1991).

2 *Professional Product Research, Inc. v. LTD Commodities*, No. 90-C-2078, 1991 US Dist. LEXIS 1876.

3 Senate Report Number 515, 100th Congress, 2d Session 41 (1988), Reprinted in 1988 USCCAN 5577, 5603.

4 Federal Trade Commission Act, Section 52(a).

5 California Business and Professions Code §17500. See also Thomas A. Papageorge, *State Regulations—California; The False Advertising Statute*, etc., 1010 PLI/Corp 97, 105 (1997).

6 *United States v. Weatherspoon*, 581 F.2d 595 (7th Cir. 1978).

7 U.S. Constitution, Article I, section 8.

8 *United States v. Maze*, 414 U.S. 395, 402 (1974).

9 James J. Armstrong, Deidre Corkery, E. Michael Karol, Kevin Lombardi, and Paul Secunda, "Securities Fraud," 33 *Am. Crim. L. Rev.* 973, 975 (1996).

10 Scott J. Davis, *Liability Under Sections 10, 18 and 20 of the Securities Exchange Act of 1934*, 1073 PLI/Corp 179, 189 (1998).

11 Armstrong, et. al., "Securities Fraud," 33 Am. Crim. L. Rev. 973, 989; quoting Kenneth J. Bialkin et al., *Counseling the Client in Enforcement*

Inquiries: The Criminalization of "Parking," 15 UC San Diego Sec.. Reg. Inst. 2 (1988).

12 Armstrong, et. al., 33 *Am. Crim. L. Rev.* at 1003.

13 15 USC section 78j (1994).

14 *C.E. Calson, Inc. v. SEC*, 859 F.2d 1429, 1436 (10th Cir. 1988).

15 21 USC §321(f), §321(g)(1)(B), §321(I)(1), and §321(h) (1998).

16 Erica L. Niezgoda & Maureen M. Richardson, "Federal Food and Drug Act Violations," 35 *Am. Crim. L. Rev.* 767, 770 (1998).

17 *United States v. Park*, 421 US 658, 660 (1975).

18 21 USC §§331(a), 331(k) (1998).b

19 *New York v. Burger*, 482 US 691, 702 (1987).

20 15 USC §1 and §2 (1994).

21 15 USC §13a (1994).

22 *Klor's, Inc. v. Broadway-Hale Stores*, 359 US 207, 212 (1959).

23 *Northern Pacific Ry. v. United States*, 356 US 1, 5–6 (1958).

24 See Kirk S. Jordan, "Model Antitrust Compliance Manual," C900 *ALI-ABA* 283, 299 (1994).

25 *American Tobacco Co. v. United States*, 328 US 781, 785 (1946).

26 *United States v. Grinnell Corp.*, 384 US 563 (1966).

27 *See* generally *United States v. Microsoft Corp.* and *State of New York v. Microsoft Corp.*, Transcripts from Microsoft trial, 1998 WL 735825 (D.D.C. Trans).

Chapter Objectives

After reading this chapter, you will be able to:

1. Define the crimes that encompass breaching the peace.
2. State the purpose and elements of nuisance crimes.
3. Understand the various traffic offenses and explain their distinctions.
4. Name typical circumstances that could constitute a weapons offense.
5. Explain and understand obscenity offenses.
6. Understand the crime of prostitution and the parties involved.
7. Explain the crime of sodomy.
8. Distinguish and understand legal and illegal gambling.

Chapter Outline

Is vagrancy against the law?

Chapter 13

Crimes Against Public Order, Safety, and Morality

13.1 Public Order and Safety Offenses

public order and safety offenses Offenses designed to protect the general public by dealing with behavior that is not necessarily immoral, but nonetheless affects the peace and safety of the community.

mala prohibita Crimes defining conduct that is wrong only because the law says it is wrong, in order to protect the general public.

mala in se Crimes, such as rape and murder, that are inherently wrong.

Public order and safety offenses are designed to protect the general public by dealing with behavior that is not necessarily morally wrong, but nonetheless affects the peace and safety of the community. They are a modern outgrowth of common law crimes aimed at keeping the peace and evolved after the onset of the industrial revolution, when lawmakers found it necessary to update the legal approach to respond to such problems.

These offenses are considered to be *mala prohibita* crimes. This means that these acts are not inherently bad, but are considered crimes only because the law dictates them to be for various reasons. In contrast are *mala in se* crimes, a designation that covers conduct that is prohibited because it is inherently wrong. Common examples of *mala in se* crimes are murder, rape, and kidnapping.

Public order and safety offenses are distinguishable from other crimes because most of them do not require a particular *mens rea* in order for a defendant to be guilty. Rather, they are usually strict liability offenses, which means that if the defendant committed the *actus reus* of the crime, his or her *mens rea*, or intent, to cause harm is irrelevant. In short, if the act is committed, the defendant will be found guilty. This is because lawmakers generally believe that the need to protect the public from potentially harmful action outweighs the defendant's usual right to a higher standard of blame, especially since the penalties for such offenses are usually light.

Offenses that Create a Public Disturbance

At common law, any voluntary action that disturbed a community's peace without lawful justification or excuse was considered a crime. These actions were generally categorized under the offense of *breach of the peace*. Breach of the peace offenses included unlawful assembly, rout, riot, disorderly conduct, and vagrancy. Each of these offenses is discussed in detail below.

unlawful assembly A gathering together of three or more persons with the common intent to achieve a lawful or unlawful purpose but who part without doing it or making any motions toward it.

Unlawful Assembly An **unlawful assembly** is a gathering together of three or more persons with the common intent to achieve a lawful or unlawful purpose but who part without doing it or making any motions towards it. A common intent need not have been formed prior to the assembly. Therefore, a meeting could begin as a lawful assembly but develop into an unlawful one.

For example, suppose that a group of students have gathered in front of a government building to protest military action by the government. Initially, the students are peacefully holding signs and handing out literature to those passing by. As the day progresses, however, the students begin blocking the entrance to the government building so that the employees cannot leave work. This would constitute unlawful assembly, and the students could be arrested.

Rout The definition of **rout** is an unlawful assembly that is escalating toward, but does not reach, the level of a riot. In short, a rout is an attempted riot: It requires a specific intent to riot and conduct that falls short of a riot. Today, the crime of rout is usually not a separate crime. Instead, it has been either eliminated or merged with the crime of unlawful assembly.

Riot A **riot** is an unlawful assembly that fulfills the participants' common purpose of violently breaching the peace and terrorizing the public. Due to the number of people involved in a riot, the group behavior is potentially more dangerous to the public than other activity, thus posing special problems for law enforcement. Because of this, many police departments, especially those in large cities, have trained riot units and protective riot gear with which to handle such occurrences.

Disorderly Conduct and Vagrancy At common law, there was no offense known as disorderly conduct. The closest offense was *breach of the peace*, which covered many public disturbances. Modern **disorderly conduct** laws include behavior that disturbs the safety, health, or morals of others, or that is intended only to annoy another person.

The Model Penal Code (MPC) defines disorderly conduct rather narrowly, but its definition contains the essential elements of the crime:

A person is guilty of disorderly conduct if, with purpose to cause public inconvenience, annoyance or alarm, or recklessly creating a risk thereof:

- engages in fighting or threatening, or in violent or tumultuous behavior.
- makes unreasonable noise or offensively coarse utterance, gesture or display, or addresses abusive language to any person present.
- creates a hazardous or physically offensive condition by any act that serves no legitimate purpose of the actor.[1]

Unlawful Assembly
Modern unlawful assembly statutes are currently divided as to whether there must be intent to perform the planned activity in a violent manner. Some jurisdictions require the presence or threat of force or violence that disrupts the public order. Other jurisdictions consider the nature of the assembly. If the purpose of the assembly is unlawful, then there is an unlawful assembly.

rout An unlawful assembly that is escalating, but does not reach, the level of a riot; an attempted riot.

riot A tumultuous disturbance of the peace by three persons or more assembling together in the execution of a lawful or unlawful act and committing it in a violent and turbulent manner.

disorderly conduct A loosely defined offense addressing behavior that disturbs the safety, health, or morals of others, or that is intended only to annoy another person.

Vagrancy   The largely outdated crime of **vagrancy** was vaguely defined as being idle, or wandering, without a visible means of support. Although all states once had anti-vagrancy laws, many states today have repealed these laws because the U.S. Supreme Court has issued decisions that effectively rendered them unconstitutional.

In the 1972 case *Papachristou v. City of Jacksonville*, the Court struck down the defendants' convictions on charges that stemmed from a fairly typical vagrancy law. The Court based its decision upon two grounds: 1) the vagueness of the ordinance, and 2) the overly broad scope of the ordinance, which was shown in the way in which the ordinance criminalized many modern innocent activities. After the *Papachristou* case, many states repealed or revised their vagrancy and disorderly conduct laws. (See Application Case.)

Nuisances

A **nuisance** encompasses anything that endangers life or health, gives offense to the senses, violates laws of decency, or obstructs the reasonable and comfortable use of property. Although criminal prosecution is one remedy for a nuisance, the most common approach is by a civil action on behalf of the community, either for damages or to abate the nuisance. To illustrate this point, consider the California Penal Code, which defines a public nuisance as follows:

> Anything which is injurious to health, or is indecent, or offensive to the senses, or an obstruction to the free use of property, so as to interfere with the comfortable enjoyment of life or property by an entire community or neighborhood, or by any considerable number of persons, or unlawfully obstructs the free passage or use, in the customary manner, of any navigable lake, or river, bay, stream, canal, or basin, or any public park, square, street, or highway, is a public nuisance.[2]

Anyone who maintains, permits, or allows a public nuisance will receive a notice for **abatement**, which means ending or eliminating the nuisance. If the person fails to abate the nuisance, he or she is guilty of a misdemeanor.

The historical development of the public nuisance concept did not result from a desire to deal harshly with a nuisance offender. Instead, it was intended for the protection of both the public and the individual committing the nuisance. If every member of the community who was annoyed by a public nuisance could maintain an action, the result would be disastrous to the person who had

Papachristou v. City of Jacksonville

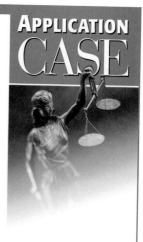

In *Papachristou v. City of Jacksonville* (1972), the following ordinance was declared unconstitutional by the U.S. Supreme Court:

Rogues and vagabonds, or dissolute persons who go about begging, common gamblers, persons who use juggling or unlawful games or plays, common drunkards, common night walkers, thieves, pilferers or pickpockets, traders in stolen property, lewd, wanton and lascivious persons, keepers of gambling places, common railers and brawlers, persons wandering or strolling around from place to place without any lawful purpose or object, habitual loafers, disorderly persons, persons neglecting all lawful business and habitually spending their time by frequenting houses of ill fame, gaming houses, or places where alcoholic beverages are sold or served, persons able to work but habitually living upon the earnings of their wives or minor children shall be deemed vagrants.

In striking down this ordinance, the Court found that this ordinance was void on account of vagueness for two reasons. First, it failed to give a person of ordinary intelligence fair notice that his contemplated conduct is forbidden. Secondly, it encouraged arbitrary and erratic arrests and convictions. The Court also noted that the ordinance imposed criminal sanctions on activities that by modern standards are lawful.

Vagrancy Statutes

Critical Thinking What changes do you think could be made to this statute to make it constitutional?

SOURCE: *Papachristou v. City of Jacksonville*, 405 U.S. 156 (1972).

CRIMINAL LAW Online

Vagrancy Laws

Visit **Louisiana Criminal Law.com** through the link provided at **cl.glencoe.com**. Read the current Louisiana law on vagrancy. Is this law constitutional? Are parts of it constitutional, and other parts not? Why or why not?

caused it. The king, therefore, would maintain one action on behalf of the community, and individuals could not bring a private action for public nuisance.

Today, even though criminal nuisance statutes still may exist in many jurisdictions, behavior that otherwise might be charged as a nuisance may also be the subject of action for disorderly conduct. Criminal prosecution may also be brought for other types of nuisances, such as for the maintenance of disorderly houses, the manufacture or storage of explosives, nuisances in streets or highways, liquor nuisances, and interference with the uses to which property has been dedicated. Nuisance statutes have also been used to close crack houses and other establishments used for drug use. In addition, courts also routinely find that massage parlors constitute a nuisance subject to abatement or other remedies. While administering massages is a legitimate occupation, massage parlors and similar establishments that specialize in sexually oriented massages administered to patrons by members of the opposite sex has led many municipalities to enact ordinances regulating or prohibiting massage parlors or by pursuing common law remedies.[3]

On the other hand, behavior with serious criminal implications is sometimes charged as a nuisance and prosecuted through civil courts, so that it can be prosecuted with the lowered burden of proof found in civil courts. In the case of *Gallo v. Acuna*, the city of San Jose, California, obtained an injunction against members of an alleged criminal street gang under the provisions of California's civil public nuisance statutes. The California Supreme Court upheld the injunction, rejecting claims that the court order violated the defendant's constitutional rights.[4]

Traffic Violations

Traffic violations are usually strict liability offenses that, in most jurisdictions, are criminal in nature. They usually carry light penalties, such as a fine, an order to attend traffic school, or possibly some jail time. If a person is sentenced to jail for a traffic violation, the time served is usually very short. The most common types of traffic offenses involve speeding, DUI, hit and run, and reckless driving.

Speeding   The traffic violation of speeding exists to ensure a safe and orderly flow of traffic on streets and highways. Drivers are provided with the speed laws by posted signs and by the local department of motor vehicles, to whom they must show an understanding of traffic laws before receiving a license to drive. Therefore, all drivers have received notice of the law. If they are speeding, they are usually guilty. Because of the strict liability of the offense, a defense that the car's speedometer was broken usually will have no effect on the outcome.

reckless driving Driving that involves the willful and wanton disregard for the safety of persons or property.

Reckless Driving   Another traffic violation is **reckless driving**, which is the voluntary and wanton disregard for the safety of persons or property. This offense requires a purpose or willfulness to commit an act as a free agent, but does not require an evil intent. It also includes the elements of:

- Consciousness of one's conduct
- The general intent to do or omit the act in question

- The realization of the probable injury to another
- Reckless disregard for the consequences

In a prosecution for reckless driving, the prosecution must prove that the defendant would have reasonably foreseen that death or injury might occur as a result of his or her driving. Suppose that Tom, a 19-year-old driver, has just bought his first car and is excited to take it out for a spin. Tom lives in Michigan, where snow and ice storms are frequent during the winter. Tom knows that the streets are covered with black ice, and he has heard radio warnings that motorists should avoid the roads unless absolutely necessary. Tom ignores the warnings, drives his car at 10 mph over the legal limit, spins out of control, and hits another vehicle. Tom would likely be charged with reckless driving, although in other circumstances, driving 10 mph over the speed limit alone would probably not warrant such a charge.

Failure to Stop   An individual violates the law if he or she is directed to stop by a duly authorized law enforcement officer, but willfully refuses or fails to do so. Another violation occurs when a driver stops in compliance with the direction of an officer, then willfully flees in an attempt to elude law enforcement. For example, if Lucy pulls over after being signaled by an officer, but gets frustrated because the officer takes so long looking up her registration and leaves without waiting for the officer to return to her vehicle, she will likely be guilty of fleeing a police officer.

Hit and Run   Leaving the scene of an accident involving death, personal injury, or property damage is more commonly referred to as *hit and run*. The elements of hit and run include:

- Involvement in an accident resulting in injury to, or death of a person, or damage to a vehicle
- Failure to stop and furnish information about one's identity and that of the vehicle
- Failure to render assistance to any persons injured and give immediate notice of the accident to the police

Hit and run statutes exist to ensure that people will stop, exchange information, and render aid (if necessary) in the event of an accident. These requirements usually exist regardless of who is at fault. Even if a driver is not to blame for an accident, by failing to stay at the scene, he or she prevents the other driver from getting insurance information, license information, and anything else needed to resolve any future problems.

Driving with a Suspended or Revoked License Another common traffic violation is driving on a suspended or revoked license. Most states require that their departments of motor vehicles notify drivers when their driving privileges have been revoked, suspended, or canceled. A person caught driving with a suspended license may receive an additional suspension or revocation period, or perhaps a stiffer penalty such as jail time or the impounding of the vehicle.

Driving Under the Influence The elements of **driving under the influence (DUI)** are the same in most jurisdictions:

- The defendant operated a motor vehicle upon a roadway within the jurisdiction of the court.
- The operation occurred while the defendant was either under the influence of an intoxicant, narcotic, or hallucinogenic to the extent that his or her normal faculties were impaired.
- The operation occurred while the defendant was driving with a blood or breath alcohol concentration above a prohibited level.

Even though the "D" in DUI stands for driving, a defendant does not have to actually drive the car in order to be convicted. Many statutes provide that DUI may be proved if the defendant is in actual physical control of the vehicle at the time it was stopped. *Actual physical control* can be defined as the legitimate inference that when a DUI defendant places him- or herself behind the wheel, he or she could start the car and drive away at any time.[5] This can be proven when an officer approaches a vehicle where the lights and ignition are on, but the driver has fallen asleep at the wheel. Therefore, the crime rests upon the defendant's readiness to operate the car while under the influence.

Although most traffic offenses are tried as summary offenses, which means that they are tried in front of a judge rather than a jury, almost every state specifically allows DUI cases to be tried before a jury of one's peers because of the seriousness of the penalties. (See Chapter 14 for a further discussion of DUI.)

DUI Manslaughter The crime of **DUI manslaughter** occurs when an individual is driving under the influence and, by reason of the operation of a motor vehicle, causes the death of any human being. Many statutes on DUI manslaughter declare that the defendant is guilty of manslaughter if:

CRIMINAL LAW *Online*

DUI Legal Advice

Visit "California DUI–A Drunk Driving Law Guide" through the link provided at **cl.glencoe.com**. Read the different answers to the list of questions in the center of the page. What kind of information is provided? How will this help somebody understand his or her liability for driving drunk?

Chemical Dependency Counselor

Description and Duties: Meet with residents individually and work out ways to combat reversion tendencies. Establish an understanding and cooperative relationship with residents. Arrange for released residents to join local Alcoholics Anonymous chapters or other appropriate aftercare resources. Meet with family or others close to the resident while he or she is in treatment to keep them informed of progress toward recovery.

Salary: $18,000 to $35,000, depending on location and experience.

Other Information: Should have considerable knowledge of the habits and actions of alcoholics and other drug abusers, the techniques employed in Alcoholics Anonymous type of recovery work, and comprehensive programs for recovery of alcoholics and other drug abusers. Many positions require at least a bachelor's degree, and some require a master's or doctorate degree in a mental health field.

Critical Thinking What characteristics do you think a good chemical dependency counselor should possess?

SOURCE: State of Kansas, http://da.state.ks.us/ps/documents/specs/4034D2.htm; State of Minnesota, http://www.doer.state.mn.us/stfcs-ac/cspcs-c/C-0212.HTML; and State of Wyoming, http://lmi.state.wy.us/98dirlic/14.html.

- Someone was killed by the defendant's vehicle
- While he or she was under the influence of alcohol
- Either his or her faculties were impaired or he or she had an unlawful blood alcohol level

Vehicular Manslaughter   The crime of **vehicular manslaughter** is the killing of a human being by the operation of a motor vehicle in a reckless manner likely to cause death or great bodily harm to another. Alternatively, vehicular manslaughter occurs when one drives a vehicle in the commission of an unlawful act, not amounting to a felony, and with gross negligence. In any event, this offense requires proof of death as a result of the operation of a motor vehicle in a reckless manner.

vehicular manslaughter
The killing of a human being by the operation of a motor vehicle in a reckless manner likely to cause death or great bodily harm to another.

Vehicular Homicide   If the required elements of the offense are present, a person can commit murder with a motor vehicle. These

➤ **DUI Dangers**
Individuals who choose to drive while intoxicated do not only risk the possibility of being pulled over and losing their licenses.
What is another, more serious offense that may result from driving under the influence?

elements are satisfied where the driver of a motor vehicle, with deliberation and premeditation and with malice aforethought, drives over or strikes a person with the specific intent of killing him. In the absence of any statute to the contrary effect, no degree of negligence, no matter how gross, will suffice to make the unlawful killing murder.

Weapons Offenses

In many circumstances, an adult is legally entitled to purchase and possess weapons, including firearms. However, a variety of circumstances could constitute a weapons offense. These include, but are not limited to:

- An underaged possessor
- The use of an illegal or legal but unregistered weapon
- The location where the weapon was discovered, such as in one's vehicle or on one's person, without permission to carry a weapon there
- The possession or transportation of an explosive, firearm, or ammunition, with intent that it be used or with knowledge that it may be used to commit a crime
- Placing another person in fear of a harmful weapon
- Offensive bodily contact with a weapon
- Use of a firearm as a weapon whether it is loaded or not

The case of *Figueroa v. Kirmayer* (1969) illustrates the different ways in which weapons offenses may be used to prosecute defendants. In this case, the defendant testified that he drew his pistol, pointed it at one victim, and fired one shot in the general direction of each of the victims. He also argued that he did not intend to shoot either of the two victims, and therefore was not guilty of assault. The court disagreed and established liability for both assault and battery.[6]

Unlike most assault or battery charges, an assault or battery with a dangerous or deadly weapon is usually classified as a felony. The charge will be higher or lower in degree depending upon whether the defendant acted intentionally, recklessly, or only negligently; whether serious physical injury or only physical injury resulted; and whether a deadly or only dangerous weapon was used.

In regard to weapons offenses, an unintended killing is one that results from the reckless or criminally negligent use of a firearm. Such a killing constitutes manslaughter. The following three examples show the variety of circumstances in which this may occur:

- A defendant points a gun that he or she believes to be unloaded at another person and pulls the trigger, causing the gun to be discharged and resulting in the other person's death.
- A hunter shoots and kills another person, believing him to be an animal.
- A defendant shoots at the occupants of a boat and so terrifies them that they overturn the boat and are drowned.

The following section will discuss the types of weapons that are most relevant to weapons offenses, followed by federal and state laws regulating the use of firearms and assault weapons.

Deadly or Dangerous Weapons   Due to the fact that some weapons are clearly lethal, it is the duty of the court to declare them to be such as a matter or law. The most obvious weapons in this class are guns, revolvers, pistols, swords, and the like, when used within striking distance of the victim. Objects that are considered deadly or dangerous weapons include bowie knives, pocket or folding knives, chisels (when used for stabbing), large stones or rocks, heavy iron weights, heavy pistols (when used for clubbing), and automobiles.

Firearms   A **firearm** is defined under federal law as:

- Any weapon, including a starter gun, that can, is designed to, or may readily be converted to expel a projectile by the action of an explosive

firearm Any weapon that can, is designed to, or may readily be converted to expel a projectile by the action of an explosive; in general, any destructive device excluding standard rifles, shotguns, and handguns.

- The frame or receiver of any such weapon
- Any firearm muffler or firearm silencer
- Any destructive device

This definition includes machine guns, along with certain other types of weaponry. It excludes the more common types of guns, such as most ordinary rifles, shotguns, and handguns.

Assault Weapons   The definition of **assault weapon** includes rifles with conspicuous pistol grips, pistols with shrouds, and shotguns with a higher ammunition capacity. Federal law has three basic definitions of assault weapons:

1. A list of specific assault weapon models
2. A list of duplicates
3. A generic, all-included category that covers certain assault weapon characteristics

assault weapon
Prohibited weapons named by federal legislation, such as rifles with conspicuous pistol grips, pistols with shrouds, and shotguns with a higher ammunition capacity.

Assault weapon legislation, which began with a 1989 California law and culminated in the Federal Crime Act of 1994, marked a new trend in firearms law. The federal assault weapon prohibition provided in this act stated that it was unlawful for a person to manufacture, transfer, or possess a semiautomatic assault weapon. However, this did not apply to any semiautomatic assault weapon otherwise lawfully possessed under federal law on the date of the enactment. (See Figure 13–1 for various states' laws on assault weapons.)

Firearms Owners Protection Act of 1986   The Firearms Owners Protection Act of 1986, also known as the National Firearms Act, comprehensively amended the Gun Control Act of 1968, which had been the first comprehensive federal statute regulating commerce in firearms. The 1986 Act regulates traditional firearms such as rifles, pistols, and shotguns. One section regulates defined firearms, including machine guns, short-barreled shotguns and rifles, destructive devices such as hand grenades and bazookas, silencers, and deceptive weapons. NFA firearms must be registered with the Bureau of Alcohol Tobacco and Firearms (BATF) and are subject to regulation.

To be convicted under the NFA, the prosecution must prove that the violation was willful or intentional. Thus, the government must prove that the defendant voluntarily and intentionally violated a known legal duty. The extent to which a weapon is or is not an NFA firearm and was known to be so by the defendant may determine whether the defendant has a defense, depending on the charges.

FIGURE 13–1

Various States' Assault Weapons Laws

	Texas	California	Montana	New York
Carrying Concealed Weapons Laws	Shall-issue; with restrictions	May-issue	Shall-issue; with restrictions	May-issue
Juvenile Possession Laws	None	Yes, age minor	Yes, age 14	Yes, age 21
Juvenile Sales Laws	Yes, age 18	Yes, age 18 for firearm, 21 for handgun	No	Yes, age 21
Permit to Puchase Required	No	No	No	Yes, background check required
One-Gun-per-Month Laws	No	Yes	No	No
Record of Sale Laws	No	Yes, sent to state agency	No	Yes, sent to state agency
Registration Laws	No	No	No	No
State-Wide Waiting Period	None	Yes	None	Yes

SOURCE: www.bradycampaign.org/facts/statelaws/viewstate

State Firearms Laws   Firearms laws greatly vary from state to state, but most states have constitutional provisions guaranteeing the right of its citizens to keep and bear arms. Almost all states restrict possession of firearms by convicted felons. More urbanized states such as New Jersey, Massachusetts, and California have stricter prohibitions, such as license or permit requirements for mere possession of a firearm. Southern and western states, with the exception of California, tend to regulate the carrying of concealed weapons but otherwise have few restrictions.

In California, it is unlawful for anyone convicted of a felony, a drug addict, a present or former mental patient, anyone ever committed for mental observation, or anyone ever acquitted of criminal charges by reason of insanity to own or possess any firearm. People with certain misdemeanor convictions involving force or violence may not possess or own any firearm within ten years of the conviction. A person who has been adjudicated as a juvenile offender or delinquent for any offense that would be classified as a felony or misdemeanor involving force or violence if committed by an adult may not own or possess any firearm until the age of 30. A minor may not possess a handgun except with written permission or under the supervision of a parent or guardian.

Check your answers at cl.glencoe.com.

Of the traffic offenses listed in the section above, which do you think is the most common and why?

13.2 Public Morality Offenses

This section covers a wide variety of offenses that are considered to be affronts to public morality. Some issues, such as what constitutes indecent exposure, change in the public's eyes over time; others, such as child pornography, do not. Some public morality offenses, such as prostitution and gambling, are geographically restricted to certain areas of the United States. There is considerable public debate about whether some of these offenses, such as gambling, prostitution, and sodomy, are victimless crimes and thus should be decriminalized. You will learn about the history of these laws, the changes to them that have occurred over time, and their current application by the courts.

Obscenity

The term pornography refers to sexually explicit material that is generally protected by First Amendment guarantees of freedom of speech and freedom of the press. Although the law may regulate pornography, it does not make the sale, possession, or distribution of it a crime. On the other hand, the law punishes the sale, possession, and distribution of obscene material. The term **obscenity** refers to the legal definition of certain materials that are not protected under the First Amendment. Obscenity may take the form of a book, magazine, newspaper, picture, drawing, photograph, motion picture, statue, or recording. Therefore, although obscenity is very similar to pornography, these terms are not legally synonymous.

Obscenity was first held to be an offense under English common law as early as 1729. In the United States, the first federal obscenity law resulted from the circulation of French postcards in the mid-nineteenth century. The Customs Law of 1842 barred the

obscenity Sexually explicit material that falls outside the protection of the First Amendment and therefore may be punished under a criminal statute.

importation of indecent and obscene prints, paintings, lithographs, engravings, and transparencies. Later, the Federal Comstock Act of 1873, named after the anti-vice crusader Anthony Comstock, prohibited the use of the mail to convey obscene material. The Comstock Act survives today with alterations and additions.

Federal Law and Obscenity Tests Through the early twentieth century, American courts applied the standard of obscenity articulated by an English court in the 1868 decision of *Regina v. Hicklin*. The *Hicklin* court made its decision based on the content of isolated passages of the book rather than as a whole, and this standard was known as the *Hicklin* test. In 1933, however, a federal district court rejected the "isolated passages" approach established in *Hicklin*. Instead, in determining whether the material was obscene, it focused on the dominant effect the entire book would have on an average person.[7]

In 1957, a new test evolved in determining whether material was obscene. That year, the U.S. Supreme Court held in *Roth v. United States* that while the First Amendment protected material with even the slightest redeeming social importance, obscenity was defined as material that is utterly without redeeming social importance. The Court established what has become known as the *tripartite test* for obscenity. In this three-part test, the Court focused on whether an average person, applying contemporary community standards, would think that the dominant theme of the material taken as a whole appeals to the *prurient interest*, which means that it has a tendency to excite lustful thoughts and its only appeal is to a shameful or morbid interest in sex.

This standard was the applicable law until 1966, when the Court was asked again to define obscenity. In *Memoirs v. Massachusetts*, the Court held that for a book or other publication to be outside the protection of the First Amendment, it must be utterly without redeeming social interest.[8]

In 1973, the Court overturned its previous decisions of 1957 and 1966 and abandoned its previous requirement of "utterly without redeeming social value." It established the test that is used today in determining whether material is obscene. The court provided these guidelines:

- Whether the average person, applying contemporary community standards would find that the work, taken as a whole, appeals to prurient interest

Obscenity and Literature

The first American conviction of obscenity occurred in *Commonwealth v. Holmes*, which involved the sale of the book *Fanny Hill*. In 1933, however, controversy over the sale of James Joyce's *Ulysses*, which is now considered a literary classic, led to the case *United States. v. One Book Called Ulysses*. In this case, the U.S. Supreme Court rejected former tests of obscenity and focused instead on the dominant effect of the entire work.

- Whether the work depicts or describes, in a patently offensive way, sexual conduct specifically defined by the applicable state law
- Whether the work taken as a whole, lacks serious literary, artistic, political, or scientific value[9]

The U.S. Supreme Court held that obscene material is an exception to the First Amendment, and the burden of deciding whether something is obscene rests upon the U.S. Supreme Court. Today, both the federal and state governments have enacted laws that make it a criminal offense to produce, distribute, or exhibit obscene material.

Obscenity and the Model Penal Code   Obscenity statutes cover many areas. The Model Penal Code (MPC) provides that material is obscene if its predominant appeal is to a shameful or morbid interest in nudity, sex, or excretion; and if, in addition, it goes substantially beyond customary limits of candor in describing or representing such matters. Undeveloped photographs, molds, printing plates, and other unfinished items are also deemed obscene, even though processing or other acts may be required to create and disseminate the finished product. Under the MPC, the concept of *predominant appeal* is judged with reference to ordinary adults. An exception occurs when material appears, from its character or the circumstances of its dissemination, to be designed for children or other especially susceptible audiences.

The MPC establishes an affirmative defense to a charge of obscenity if dissemination was restricted to noncommercial dissemination to personal associates of the actor. This is because the code attempts to prevent the commercial exploitation of ordinary members of society caught between normal sex drives and curiosities, while on the other hand providing powerful social and legal restraints on overt sexual behavior.

Obscenity and the Internet   Regulating indecent material on the Internet has proven a very difficult task. There is much concern over how to prevent children from encountering sexually explicit materials and discussions through their computers, yet still protect the First Amendment rights of adults to engage in constitutionally protected indecent speech. In 1996, President Clinton signed the Telecommunications Act of 1996, which was subsequently passed by Congress. This act, which was incorporated into the Communications Decency Act of 1996, bans the transmission of obscene materials to

Arcara v. Cloud Books, Inc.

Some laws provide that buildings may be declared as either public or private health nuisances. An example is the case of *Arcara v. Cloud Books, Inc.* (1986), where solicitation for prostitution was taking place in a New York adult bookstore and, under a court order, the premises were declared a nuisance and closed for one year. In affirming this action, the U.S. Supreme Court held that the nuisance law "sought to protect the environment of the community by directing the sanction at premises knowingly used for lawless activities." As a result, the nuisance statute was constitutionally permissible. The public good of eliminating the behavior that took place in the bookstore outweighed the need to protect the rights of the individuals running the bookstore.

Critical Thinking Should the owners and operators of a building be liable for crimes that, unknown to them, occur in their building?

SOURCE: *Arcara v. Cloud Books, Inc.*, 478 U.S. 697 (1986).

Nuisance Laws

minors via broadcast media, including the Internet. Such transmission is a crime that carries a maximum of two years in prison and $250,000 in fines. In 1996, however, a federal district court ruled that the CDA is unconstitutional on its face; in response, the Department of Justice appealed this ruling.

This case went to the U.S. Supreme Court, *Remo v. ACLU.* The Supreme Court held that: (1) provisions of the CDA prohibiting transmission of obscene or indecent communications by means of telecommunications device to persons under age 18, or sending patently offensive communications through use of an interactive computer service to persons under age 18, were content-based blanket restrictions on speech, and, as such, could not be properly analyzed on First Amendment challenge as a form of time, place, and manner regulation; (2) challenged provisions were facially overbroad in violation of the First Amendment; and (3) constitutionality of provision prohibiting transmission of obscene or indecent communications by means of telecommunications device to persons under age 18 would be saved from facial overbreadth challenge by severing term "or indecent" from statute pursuant to its severability clause.

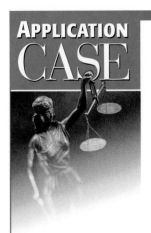
United States v. Thomas and United States v. Maxwell

In *United States v. Thomas* (1996), a couple living in California was convicted by a Tennessee jury for transmitting obscene computer-generated images to Tennessee via interstate commerce. In *United States v. Maxwell* (1995), the U.S. Air Force Court of Military Appeals ruled that the electronic transmission of visual images through an online computer service is a statutory violation. The court found it clear that Congress intended to stem the transportation of obscene material in interstate commerce, regardless of the means used to effect that end.

Critical Thinking Considering the Bill of Rights grants defendants a trial "by an impartial jury of the state and district wherein the crime shall have been committed," should a California couple be tried by a Tennessee jury?

SOURCE: Jonathon Rosenoer, *CyberLaw: The Law of the Internet* 182 (1997), citing *United States v. Thomas*, Nos. 94-6649, 1996 U.S. App. Lexis 1069 (6th Cir. 1996) and *United States v. Maxwell*, 42 M.J. 568 (A.F.C.C.A. 1995).

Currently, federal law prohibits the interstate and foreign transportation of obscene matters for sale or distribution by mail, importation, or transport via common carrier, broadcast, and private conveyance. In regard to the Internet, there have already been many obscenity prosecutions. (See above Application Case for two examples.)

Child Pornography   Child pornography is a highly organized, multi-million dollar industry. Its distribution operates on an international scale and is now making disturbing inroads on the Internet.

In 1977, Congress held hearings on child pornography. Witnesses told nightmarish tales about small children who were kidnapped by pornographers or sold to pornographers by their parents. After these hearings, Congress passed the Protection of Children from Sexual Exploitation Act of 1977. This act prohibited the production of any sexually explicit material using a child under the age of 16 if such material was destined for, or has already traveled in, interstate commerce. Violation of this act leads to penalties of up to ten years in prison and/or a $10,000 fine. The law is applicable to parents or other custodians who knowingly permit a child to participate in the production of sexually explicit material.

This act was revised under the Child Protection Act of 1984, which was enacted to extend criminal sanctions for child pornography. The 1984 Act did the following:

- Eliminated the requirement that child pornography distribution be undertaken for commerce, and criminalized distribution for any reason
- Eradicated former obscenity test requirements so that any pornography could be prosecuted
- Raised the age of protected persons to 18

In addition, current federal law prohibits employing, using, persuading, inducing, enticing, or coercing a minor to engage in any sexually explicit conduct for the purpose of producing any visual depiction of such conduct. Also barred is the knowing transmission or receipt by computer of visual depictions involving the use of a minor engaged in sexually explicit conduct, as well as the knowing publication of a notice or advertisement seeking or offering to receive, exchange, buy, produce, display, distribute, or reproduce such visual depictions. Possession with intent to sell visual depictions that have been transmitted by computer, or possession of three or more items containing such depictions that may have been transmitted by computer, is a criminal offense.[10]

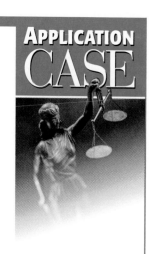

APPLICATION CASE

United States v. U.S. District Court

In 1989, several pornographic movie producers were charged with violating federal child pornography laws after law enforcement discovered that porn star Traci Lords was only 16 years old at the time that she made many adult movies. In the original trial, the defendants were denied the right to raise the defense and provide evidence that they had a reasonable belief that Lords was actually 18 at the time the movies were made. The Court of Appeals reversed this decision, stating that the defendants have an affirmative defense if they establish by clear and convincing evidence that they did not know, and could not know, she was not 18 years of age.

Critical Thinking Do you agree with the court's decision or should the producers have been held liable despite their lack of knowledge?

SOURCE: Sanford H. Kadish and Stephen J. Schulhofer, *Criminal Law and its Processes* 253–254 (6th ed. 1995) citing *United States v. U.S. District Court*, 858 F.2d 534 (9th Cir. 1988).

Child Pornography

Indecent Exposure

At common law and early statutes, indecent exposure was referred to as *lewdness*. The elements required to convict a person of lewdness were: 1) intentionally, indecently, and offensively exposing the sex organs, 2) in the presence of another. Prior to the drafting of the Model Penal Code, indecent exposure and related crimes were covered under a multitude of statutes and given widely varying titles, such as Lewd and Lascivious Behavior, Public Lewdness, and even Appearing on the Highway in Bathing Garb.

indecent exposure An offensive display of one's body in public, especially one's genitals or the female breasts.

Under modern law, **indecent exposure** involves the unlawful exposure of the human body, particularly a person's genitals or the female breasts. The purpose of indecent exposure statutes is to protect the public sensibilities and prevent public lewdness. Public exposure may occur on a street, building, beach, or even within a private location, provided that the exposure may be viewed from another public or private place.

Almost every jurisdiction recognizes indecent exposure as a criminal offense, and a general criminal intent is usually required to hold a person criminally liable for this offense. Some jurisdictions have adopted the common law approach of requiring that the conduct be committed in a public place, and others only require knowledge on the part of the defendant that his or her exposure is likely to cause affront or alarm.

Persons who practice this type of offense are often called exhibitionists. **Exhibitionism** is the repeated intentional act of exposing one's genitals to an unsuspecting stranger or strangers, for the purpose of achieving sexual excitement. Exhibitionists are intentional in what they do, and do not include people who occasionally and accidentally expose themselves, such as by undressing in their own homes and forgetting to close the blinds.

exhibitionism Repeated intentional acts of exposing the genitals to an unexpecting stranger for the purpose of achieving sexual excitement.

Many states have specific statutes dealing with exhibitionism, and others classify it as disorderly conduct. The Model Penal Code provides that a person commits a misdemeanor when, for the purpose of arousing or gratifying sexual desire of himself or herself or of any person other than his or her spouse, exposes his or her genitals under circumstances in which he or she knows his or her conduct is likely to cause affront or alarm. Under The Model Penal Code, a member of a nudist cult or a nude dancer who performs only for adults desiring such entertainment would not be in violation of the law.[11]

Similarly, many state laws and municipality ordinances contain provisions that permit exceptions to indecent exposure statutes, such

People v. Garrison

In *People v. Garrison* (1980), the defendant stood behind a storm door in his home, exposing his penis to a woman standing outside. The Supreme Court of Illinois held that this conduct was not private and that the defendant could not claim a right of privacy. It held that if a jury found that the defendant exposed his body with intent to arouse or to satisfy his sexual desire, the defendant could be found guilty of the Illinois Public Indecency Statute.

Critical Thinking If the defendant did not have the "intent to arouse or to satisfy his or her sexual desire," should he have been found guilty? Why or why not?

SOURCE: *People v. Garrison*, 412 N.E. 2d 483 (1980).

as partial or full nudity during public entertainment to which only adults are invited. Local communities usually set standards for what exceptions they will tolerate: One community might allow total nudity, whereas another may only allow topless dancing. Again, the distinction between this and indecent exposure is that indecent exposure crimes usually involve perpetrators exposing themselves for personal gratification, and without consent of the people witnessing the exposure. Where nudity is part of a form of entertainment between adults in a private place, indecent exposure usually won't be an issue.

Prostitution, Solicitation, and Pandering

Prostitution is committed when one person agrees to engage in sexual or deviate sexual intercourse in return for something of value, usually money. It is often referred to as the world's oldest profession and is described in history's earliest written records. Prostitution was not specifically a crime at common law, but when a woman solicited men on the street, her conduct was punishable as a public nuisance.

Today, prostitution is a statutory crime. Modern statutes forbid several types of sexual intercourse and sexual contact when done in exchange for money. It is important to note that the offense of prostitution does not consist of the sexual act itself; rather, it is the agreement to participate in sexual activity for compensation. Moreover, members of either sex may be convicted of prostitution,

prostitution A crime that is committed when one person agrees to engage in sexual or deviate sexual intercourse in return for something of value, usually money.

as distinguished from past laws that convicted only women. As long as there is agreement for pay, prostitution is criminal regardless of whether the agreement to perform sex is within a heterosexual or homosexual context.

Although state and local statutes generally prohibit prostitution, the crime also may be applicable in a federal context. The **Mann Act** is a federal statute that was originally enacted to prohibit:

- The interstate transportation of any woman or girl for purpose of prostitution, debauchery, or any other immoral purpose; or
- The interstate transportation of any woman or girl with the intent and purpose to induce, entice, or compel such woman or girl to become a prostitute or give herself up to debauchery or to engage in any other immoral practice.

A recent amendment to the act now prohibits the knowing transportation in interstate or foreign commerce of any individual, male or female, with the intent that such individual engage in prostitution or in any sexual activity for which any person can be charged with a criminal offense. The conduct constitutes a felony punishable by fine and/or imprisonment of not more than five years.[12] In addition, another federal statute prohibits travel in interstate or foreign commerce, or the use of the mails, in aid of state or federal prostitution offenses.

Efforts to decriminalize prostitution have met with limited success. Only one state, Nevada, has legalized prostitution under certain conditions. Nonetheless, prostitution and its related activities flourish and remain a nationwide public morality issue despite fears of AIDS. It probably will continue to flourish as long as customers are

Mann Act A federal act that prohibits the knowing transportation in interstate or foreign commerce of any individual, male or female, with the intent that such individual engage in prostitution or in any sexual activity.

Myth

A prostitute and patron will not be charged with any crime unless sexual activity actually took place in exchange for compensation.

Fact

A prostitute or a person who solicits a prostitute can be convicted of solicitation without sexual activity taking place.

willing to pay money for sexual favors and as long as there are persons willing to perform those favors in return for compensation.

Solicitation   Some jurisdictions make soliciting a prostitute an offense. A person is guilty of **solicitation** when he or she offers to pay another (as a customer) or to receive payment from another (as a prostitute) for sex. The purpose of statutes forbidding soliciting is to prevent prostitutes from standing in public places, trying to entice passersby into paying for sex. Since the crime of prostitution punishes both actors, the patron who solicits a prostitute is found guilty under these laws.

When a prospective patron propositions an undercover agent posing as a prostitute, this person is usually charged with soliciting. Indeed, most prostitution cases that go to court today involve police decoys that use solicitation as the basis of the criminal charge. Defendants in such cases are women who solicit male undercover officers, men who proposition female officers, and male prostitutes offering sex for a fee.[13]

Patronizing a Prostitute   If the prospective patron agrees to purchase sexual favors, he or she may bear the criminal responsibility for the separate offense known as *patronizing a prostitute*. Ordinarily, the offense of patronizing a prostitute is punishable to the same extent as prostitution, which is usually a misdemeanor.

As an example of laws covering this offense, a Connecticut statute provides that a person is guilty of patronizing a prostitute when pursuant to a prior understanding:

- The patron pays a fee to another person as compensation for such person or a third person having engaged in sexual conduct with him or her; or
- The patron pays or agrees to pay a fee to another person pursuant to an understanding that in return therefor such person or a third person will engage in sexual conduct with him or her; or
- The patron solicits or requests another person to engage in sexual conduct with him or her in return for a fee.

Pimping and Pandering   The real force behind prostitution is not the prostitute, but the person who promotes prostitution. Since the promoter makes prostitution a growing business, his or her activity is usually punished more severely than that of a prostitute. These promoters are commonly known as *pimps*, and their activity is

solicitation The act of offering to pay another, or receive payment from another, for sex.

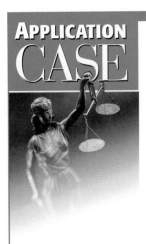

Prostitution

State v. Tookes

In *State v. Tookes* (1985), a civilian police volunteer engaged in sexual intercourse with women in order to obtain evidence for their prostitution convictions. The Supreme Court of Hawaii affirmed the convictions of the prostitutes, holding: "While we question whether the actions of [the volunteer] Fox and the police in this case comport to the ethical standards which law enforcement officials should be guided by, we cannot say that they constituted outrageous conduct in the constitutional sense. Neither are we able to find a due process violation because Fox's conduct, if undertaken by a police officer, would have violated an internal Department rule against engaging in sex with a prostitute in order to obtain evidence sufficient for a conviction."

Although this procedure might be legal, most law enforcement agencies and communities probably would not tolerate it in this day of AIDS and other diseases.

Critical Thinking Should the practice of allowing police and volunteers to engage in intercourse to obtain evidence be discontinued? Why or why not?

SOURCE: *State v. Tookes*, 699 P.2d 983 (Haw. 1985).

pimping Promoting prostitution, living off of the earnings of prostitutes, and in some cases coercing individuals to work as prostitutes.

pandering Either procuring a prostitute for a place of prostitution or procuring a place for a prostitute in which he or she can engage in prostitution.

called **pimping**. Pimps live off of the earnings of prostitutes, and the prostitute works for the pimp. Because of the financial gains, pimps have a motive to encourage and coerce young persons into prostitution. They increase the volume and extent to which prostitution is practiced, and often gain a strong emotional hold over the prostitute who works for them.

Pandering consists of either procuring a female for a place of prostitution or procuring a place for a prostitute in which she can ply her trade. If a person has engaged in either or these two activities, he or she is guilty of pandering even if no sexual activity has yet taken place. The principal difference between pimping and pandering is that a pimp solicits patrons for the prostitute and lives off her earnings, while a panderer recruits prostitutes and sets them up in business.

Promoting, pimping, and pandering are generally forbidden by state statutes. In California, a person is guilty of pimping when, knowing another person is a prostitute, he or she:

- Lives in whole or in part from the earnings or proceeds of the person's prostitution; or
- Lives from money loaned or advanced to or charged against that person by any keeper or manager or inmate of a house or other place where prostitution is practiced or allowed; or
- Solicits or receives compensation for soliciting for the person.

In Utah, there are three basic offenses: aiding prostitution, exploiting prostitution, and aggravated exploitation of prostitution. They are broken down as follows:

- A person is guilty of *aiding prostitution* when he solicits a patron for a prostitute, procures a prostitute for a patron, allows a place to be used for prostitution, or receives or agrees to receive a benefit for doing any of the acts prohibited.
- A person is guilty of *exploiting prostitution* when he procures an inmate for a house of prostitution, causes another person to become or remain a prostitute, transports or pays for the transportation of another person into or within this state for the purpose of prostitution, shares the proceeds of prostitution with a prostitute, or keeps a house of prostitution.
- A person is guilty of *aggravated exploitation of prostitution* when he, in committing an act of exploiting prostitution, uses any force, threat, or fear against any person; or when the person procured or transported, or with whom the proceeds of prostitution are shared, is under eighteen years of age or is the wife of the actor.[14]

Adultery, Fornication, and Illicit Cohabitation

At common law, adultery and fornication were not crimes unless the conduct was open and notorious, in which case it was punishable as a public nuisance. Today, **adultery** requires only a single act of sexual intercourse; each adulterous act constitutes a crime.[15] The elements of adultery are: 1) voluntary sexual intercourse, 2) by persons not married to each other, and 3) where one party is in a lawful marriage. **Fornication** is unlawful sexual intercourse that is consensual by both parties and is committed under circumstances not constituting adultery. To constitute intercourse, all that is necessary is that there be some penetration.

adultery Sexual relations with someone other than a spouse when the person is married.

fornication Voluntary, unlawful sexual intercourse, under circumstances not constituting adultery.

Myth	Fact
Adultery and fornication were serious common law offenses in both England and the United States.	Adultery and fornication were punished by church officials as *ecclesiastical offenses*, but were not recognized as common law crimes in England.

Today, these crimes are misdemeanors, if they are treated as crimes at all. In some states, fornication is no longer a recognized offense while adultery is. Here are a few examples of states that still carry such laws:

- In Utah, any unmarried person who shall voluntarily engage in sexual intercourse with another is guilty of fornication. If the other person is married, he or she is guilty of adultery.
- In Idaho, any unmarried person who has sexual intercourse with an unmarried person of the opposite sex is guilty of fornication.
- In Minnesota, sexual intercourse constitutes adultery only where the woman is the married party. If the woman is unmarried, neither party is guilty of adultery even if the man is married; instead, each party is guilty of fornication.[16]

Recognizing that many of the statutes against fornication and adultery that are still existing are no longer enforced, the Model Penal Code omitted any provisions relating to these offenses.

Sodomy and Related Sexual Offenses

sodomy The unlawful sexual penetration of the anus or mouth of one person by the penis of another.

The term **sodomy** has been defined in many ways and in many jurisdictions over many years. At common law, sodomy was much narrower in its scope, and was only committed when a male person penetrated his penis into the anus or mouth of another male or female person. In its broadest terms under modern law, sodomy requires an act of *deviate sexual intercourse*, which under most statutes occurs whenever a male penetrates his penis into the anus or mouth of another male or female person. Under most statutes, also, deviate sexual intercourse occurs whenever a male penetrates the vagina of a female animal or the anus of a male or female animal.

Bowers v. Hardwick

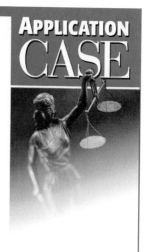

In *Bowers v. Hardwick*, the U.S. Supreme Court upheld a Georgia statute punishing sodomy between consenting adults. In that case, police officers in Atlanta were attempting to serve a warrant on Hardwick on an unrelated charge and followed him to his home. One of the officers was granted admission into the home and upon entering the bedroom, observed the act of sodomy between Hardwick and another male. The defendant filed an action in federal court, alleging that his right to privacy was being violated. He argued that the state statute prohibiting sodomy was unconstitutional because it punishes private consensual sexual activity. The Court held that homosexuals do not have a fundamental right of privacy to engage in consensual sodomy. Stating that such conduct was prohibited by common law and forbidden by the laws of the original 13 states, the Court declined to extend the right of privacy to consenting adults in their own bedroom.

The significance of *Bowers* goes well beyond homosexual sex. *Bowers* gives legislatures the right to punish victimless conduct. The Court also stated that a *presumed* belief, which is that the majority of the electorate consider that particular conduct immoral and unacceptable, provides sufficient justification for a state to prohibit behavior that is not otherwise constitutionally protected. The Court pointed out, however, that a fundamental right of privacy does exist.

As a result of the Court's decision, a number of legal authorities called for the abolition of statutes that prohibit consensual sexual activity between consenting adults. Today, a number of states have decriminalized private consensual sodomy among adults.

Sodomy

Critical Thinking Should consenting adults have the right to consensual sexual activity of any sort? Why or why not?

SOURCE: *Bowers v. Hardwick*, 106 S.Ct. 2841 (1986). *See also* Harvey Wallace and Cliff Roberson, *Principles of Criminal Law* (1996) p. 143 citing Gary Caplan, "Fourteenth Amendment—The Supreme Court Limits the Right to Privacy," 77 *Crim. L. & Criminology* 894 (1989).

Few sexual acts have created as much controversy throughout history as the act of sodomy, even when it applies only to consensual relations between adult humans. The term sodomy was derived from the ancient city of Sodom. According to some biblical interpretations, the residents of Sodom engaged in certain deviant sexual acts; in response, God allegedly destroyed their city. Early English statutes made sodomy a capital offense, and this act was considered

William Blackstone on Gambling

The renowned legal scholar William Blackstone said this about the corrupting influences of gambling: "It is an offense of the most alarming nature, tending by necessary consequence to promote public idleness, theft and debauchery among those of lower classes, and among persons of superior rank it hath frequently been attended with the sudden ruin and desolation of ancient and opulent families, an abandoned prostitution of every principle of honor and virtue, and too often hath ended in self murder."

SOURCE: Sir William Blackstone, *Commentaries on the Laws of England* (Book 4 Volume 2, 1916) 172.

gambling The act of staking or risking something of value on the outcome of a contest of chance, or on a future event of chance that is not under the gambler's control or influence.

so vile that the famous English legal commentator William Blackstone refused to name it.

Although it is no longer a capital offense, this early revulsion continued in American culture and some sodomy laws still exist today. Today, sodomy is defined as the unlawful sexual penetration of the anus or mouth of one person by the penis of another, committed by use of force or fear. Some states, however, punish sodomy even if it is a consensual act between consenting adults in the privacy of their bedroom.[17] See Application Case *Bowers v. Hardwick* on page 463 for an example of changing sodomy laws under Georgia state law.

Gambling

A person engages in **gambling** when he or she stakes or risks something of value on the outcome of a contest of chance, or on a future event of chance that is not under his or her control or influence. Gambling usually involves an agreement that a person will win something based on a certain outcome of events. There are many forms of gambling, including: track racing, state lotteries, video machines, commercial sweepstakes, gambling tournaments, charity, Indian bingo, and the rapid growth of legal card rooms, particularly for the game of poker.

Betting and wagering are used interchangeably, and they apply only to forms of gambling that are not lotteries. Betting or wagering is a promise to give something of value upon the determination of an uncertain event, whether or not skill is involved. A common example is horse racing. When people bet money at the races, they do so in the hope of increasing the amount if their horse wins. There is no guarantee that this will happen, and often someone who bets at the races will lose his or her money.

Gambling and the Law   At common law, gambling was not a crime unless it became a public nuisance. All games were considered legal and a loser had to pay off his debts. Courts would close down any gambling establishment only if it caused a breach of the peace or of public morals. Today, gambling is supported by a large segment of the population who enjoys it. Additionally, many states use lotteries as a legal form of gambling that is used to raise public revenues.

In order for gambling to be illegal, there must be a specific law or ordinance prohibiting it. In all states, there are at least some laws prohibiting gambling, and they vary by jurisdiction. Most forms of gambling are legal in Nevada; Atlantic City, New Jersey; and on

Indian reservations in several states. In these areas, gambling is legal only in licensed establishments, although the definition of "licensed establishments" can be quite broad. For example, some grocery stores surrounding Las Vegas offer slot machines for any member of the general public over the age of 21.

In most jurisdictions, the only forms of gambling that are lawful are state-operated lotteries, racing, and bingo or other contests sponsored on a nonprofit basis by social organizations. In jurisdictions such as these, gambling establishments will sometimes open on "off-shore" premises such as riverboats to circumvent laws about gambling on state land.

While state and local government regulate most gambling activities, there are several federal statutes that also limit gambling activities. Federal gambling statutes are similar to state statutes, but usually target large-scale operations where a significant amount of money is involved and there are many individuals working the operation. These statutes regulate gambling done through interstate transportation, wire communications, the U.S. Postal Service, or any other form where gambling is conducted between the states.

In contrast to the types of gambling discussed above, friendly gambling such as an office pool, a football pool, or a neighborhood poker game is generally legal. Friendly gambling can be distinguished from commercial gambling by factors such as where the game is played, who the players are, the size of the pot, and whether the house takes a percentage of each pot. Suppose that six friends who work together have a weekly poker game at one of their houses. They look at the game as a good social outlet and a way to have fun. They bet with pocket change and one-dollar bills, and no one ever loses or wins more than $20. It is unlikely that this type of gambling would be considered illegal under a statute.

Λ Illegal Gambling
Even where gambling is legal, some forms of betting and gambling are nonetheless prohibited. Most often this involves betting on animals that have been bred for aggressivity and are subjected to deadly fights.
How do you think illegal gambling can be tracked down and eradicated?

Self Check
Why do you think that adultery and fornication are no longer illegal in most jurisdictions?

Check your answers at
cl.glencoe.com.

Crimes Against Public Order, Safety, and Morality

SUMMARY BY CHAPTER OBJECTIVES

1. Define the crimes that encompass breaching the peace.

Crimes that breach the peace can be defined as follows:

- Unlawful assembly is the gathering of three or more persons with a common intent to achieve a purpose, unlawful or lawful, by committing disorderly acts.
- Rout is an attempted riot.
- Riot is an unlawful assembly in which people act in a violent and turbulent manner.
- Disorderly conduct is misconduct that constitutes a public nuisance.
- Vagrancy is idle wandering, or a variety of other vaguely defined acts.

Note that today, vagrancy laws have generally been declared unconstitutional.

2. State the purpose and elements of nuisance crimes.

Nuisance crimes exist in order to protect the public from acts or omissions that cause physical, emotional, or personal harm. The elements vary from jurisdiction to jurisdiction, but generally the laws criminalize any conduct that:

- Endangers life or health
- Gives offense to the senses
- Violates laws of decency

- Obstructs the reasonable and comfortable use of property

3. Understand the various traffic offenses and explain their distinctions.

The most common traffic offenses can be defined as follows:

- Speeding, which is driving faster than the posted speed limit
- Reckless driving, which is the voluntary and wanton disregard for the safety of persons or property
- Driving with a suspended or revoked license
- Leaving the scene of an accident, whether or not the individual is at fault
- Driving under the influence of an intoxicant

These offenses exist to protect drivers and passengers and to keep the roads and highways safe.

4. Name typical circumstances that could constitute a weapons offense.

Circumstances can include any of the following:

- An underaged possessor
- The use of an illegal or legal but unregistered weapon
- The location where the weapon was discovered, such as in one's vehicle or

on one's person, without permission to carry a weapon there

- The possession or transportation of an explosive, firearm, or ammunition, with intent that it be used or with knowledge that it may be used to commit a crime
- Placing another person in fear of a harmful weapon
- Offensive bodily contact with a weapon
- Using a firearm as a weapon (such as a club), whether it is loaded or not

5. Explain and understand obscenity offenses.

Obscenity offenses address certain materials that are not protected under the First Amendment. These materials may take the form of a book, magazine, newspaper, picture, drawing, photograph, motion picture, statue, or recording. Courts today use the following guidelines in determining whether material was obscene:

- Whether the average person, applying contemporary community standards would find that the work, taken as a whole, appeals to prurient interest
- Whether the work depicts or describes, in a patently offensive way, sexual conduct specifically defined by the applicable state law
- Whether the work taken as a whole lacks serious literary, artistic, political, or scientific value

6. Understand the crime of prostitution and the parties involved.

Prostitution is committed when one person agrees to engage in sexual or deviate sexual intercourse in return for something of value, usually money. The parties involved usually include:

- The prostitute
- The person paying for the sex
- (Usually) the person managing the activities of the prostitute, such as a pimp or a panderer

7. Explain the crime of sodomy.

Under its broadest modern definition, sodomy is defined as the unlawful sexual penetration of the anus or mouth of one person by the penis of another. Other sexual acts, such as bestiality, are often included in today's sodomy statutes. Sodomy has a history of controversy and was formerly a capital offense. Today, although it is still illegal in some American jurisdictions, these laws are often challenged.

8. Distinguish and understand legal and illegal gambling.

Legal gambling includes gambling in certain licensed establishments and in certain geographic areas, such as gambling establishments in Nevada or on some Indian reservations. It also includes activities that are regulated by the state, such as lotteries. Unlawful gambling is any gambling activity that is either specifically prohibited by statute or that does not fall under a validly recognized form of gambling in a particular jurisdiction.

Is vagrancy against the law?

Find it on page 440.

KEY TERMS

public order and safety
 offenses, page 438
mala prohibita, page 438
mala in se, page 438
unlawful assembly, page 438
rout, page 439
riot, page 439
disorderly conduct, page 439
vagrancy, page 440
nuisance, page 440
abatement, page 440

reckless driving, page 442
driving under the influence
 (DUI), page 444
DUI manslaughter, page 444
vehicular manslaughter,
 page 445
firearm, page 447
assault weapon, page 448
obscenity, page 450
indecent exposure, page 456
exhibitionism, page 456

prostitution, page 457
Mann Act, page 458
solicitation, page 459
pimping, page 460
pandering, page 460
adultery, page 461
fornication, page 461
sodomy, page 462
gambling, page 464

QUESTIONS FOR REVIEW

1. Why do public order offenses exist, and how do they differ from more serious crimes?
2. What is the history of vagrancy laws, and why are they no longer in common use today?
3. Why is speeding a strict liability offense?
4. What are the characteristics that define firearms, and what commonly used weapons do not qualify as firearms?
5. What is a DUI offense, and how is DUI manslaughter different from vehicular manslaughter?

6. What are the elements and required culpability for indecent exposure?
7. What are the differences between prostitution, solicitation, and patronizing a prostitute?
8. What is the difference between pimping and pandering?
9. For what reasons is sodomy still illegal in some jurisdictions?
10. What forms of legal gambling exist today, and under what circumstances?

PROBLEM-SOLVING EXERCISES

1. **Vagrancy Statutes** You work for the prosecutor's office in a fairly large, Midwestern city. A large political convention is coming to your city, and your police chief has been getting pressure from the mayor to "crack down" on homeless people and prostitutes. As a result, the police initiated a comprehensive sweep by using a vagrancy ordinance that prohibits, among other things,

"common night walkers, persons wandering or strolling around from place to place without any lawful purpose or object, and habitual loafers." Four people who were arrested are protesting that this ordinance is unconstitutional. Answer the following questions:
   a) Is this ordinance unconstitutional? Why or why not?

b) What are your options in dealing with these four defendants, and what would be the wisest move? The easiest move?

c) How should this situation be resolved to avoid similar future occurrences? Why?

2. **Consensual Sodomy** You are a state supreme court judge hearing a case in which an adult homosexual couple, who has been in a relationship for over 12 years, is being charged with state sodomy laws. They were arrested when police officers obtained arrest warrants based on probable cause that they were committing sodomy in their homes. They argue that their sexual relations are private and consensual, and that these charges violate their rights under the First and Fourth Amendment. Answer the following questions:

a) Are their First Amendment rights being violated? Why or why not?

b) What about their Fourth Amendment rights? Why or why not?

c) What are your options as a judge in your state's highest court? Which option will you pick, and why?

3. **Traffic Violations** You are a federal law enforcement officer who is testifying at an important trial today. Your alarm fails to go off and you are speeding to reach the courtroom when you are pulled over by the state highway patrol. The state officer does not care about who you are or why you were speeding, and is exceptionally slow in processing your ticket. You know that the judge in whose courtroom you are testifying is extremely impatient with people who are late or who fail to show up to testify. After waiting about 20 minutes, you start your car and leave.

a) Have you committed any violations? Why or why not?

b) Are any of the other factors relevant to your case? Why or why not?

WORKPLACE APPLICATIONS

1. **Unlawful Assembly** You are a municipal police officer working foot patrol in a public commons area during a large protest. The organizers of the protest obtained the necessary city permits to be there, and the police department received advanced notice that the event was going to happen. This particular protest involves the shooting of a young black woman by local officers. The woman was unarmed when she was shot and killed, and she had no criminal history; nonetheless, the officer involved in the shooting was acquitted. The protesters today are angry that he is not going to be punished. As the protest progresses, one speaker hollers, "If we are not going to get any justice, we've got to take justice into our own hands." The next three speakers urge the listeners to disobey the police. You are aware of the speakers' First Amendment rights, but because of their specific messages are concerned that the crowd will become violent and will direct their violence at you and fellow officers. Answer the following questions:

a) Do you allow the protest to continue or do you shut it down early?

b) What steps should you take to avoid the possibility of violence?

c) What other information do you need in making a decision?

2. **Indecent Exposure** You are a local prosecutor who receives a report filed by a homeowner, who is complaining that her next-door neighbors are sunbathing nude and violating public decency laws. Because the homeowner has small children, she wants her neighbors to stop doing this. To date, however, they have refused. Local police have spoken to the sunbathers, who responded that they are allowed to sunbathe naked on their own property in their backyard. They argue that it would be different if they were out on the street or in the front of the house. The only divider between the two homes is a four-foot picket fence. Answer the following questions:

a) Are the sunbathers guilty of indecent exposure? Why or why not?

b) Are there any other crimes for which they could be found guilty?

c) What are the various solutions available for this problem?

3. **Gang Nuisances** You are a city prosecutor whose city has cracked down on gang violence by issuing nuisance abatement orders to known gang members. Under these orders, these individuals are forbidden to sell drugs, congregate in public for longer than ten minutes, carry pagers, or engage in other activities that are related to gang and drug activities. As everyone knows, these orders forbid certain illegal actions, as well as certain actions that otherwise would be legal.

a) Are such orders constitutional? Why or why not?

b) Which is more important in this case: the good of the individuals or the good of the community?

INTERNET APPLICATIONS

1. **Internet Sex Offenders** You are a prosecutor in a small rural county that has little experience or resources in the area of Internet crimes. Now you are faced with a local resident who is believed to be using the Internet to initiate sexual relations with underaged boys. Visit the City of Keene (NH) Police Department through the link provided at **cl.glencoe.com**. In the left-hand menu, click on "Regional Task force on Internet Crimes Against Children." Read the main page of this section, as well as the section entitled "Sample Affidavit" and whatever other sections you feel would help your local judge,

police force, and yourself. When you are done, answer the following questions:

a) What resources here will help you identify this and other sex offenders? How?

b) What resources will help you bring charges against this suspect?

c) What information here will be of use to your local police department and judiciary?

2. **Online Gamblers Anonymous** Visit Gamblers Anonymous online through the link provided at **cl.glencoe.com**. Read "Q&A," "Recovery Program," and "20 Questions." When you are done, answer the following questions:

a) Is gambling a social evil or merely an activity that some people, because of their own personalities, cannot control? Why?

b) Is gambling, therefore, a "victimless" crime? Why or why not?

c) Should legislators regulate gambling? Why or why not?

ETHICS ISSUES

1. **Prostitution and Pandering** You are a parole officer, and one of your clients is a young woman with two small children. To make ends meet, she obtains a roommate who will watch her children while she works full-time during the day. After about a week, the roommate begins to lock the children in their bedroom and prostitute herself, bringing men into the living room to ply her trade. Your client catches on, but allows it to continue until she finds another babysitter that she can afford. About a week after your client catches on, her roommate is arrested. Your supervisor states that you should revoke her parole.

a) Of what crime is your client guilty?

b) Will you revoke her parole based on this violation? Why or why not?

ENDNOTES

1 Model Penal Code § 250.2(1) (1985).

2 Cal. Penal Code § 370 (West 1999).

3 Deborah Tussey, Annotation, "Massage Parlor As Nuisance," 80 *A.L.R.* 3d 1020 (1978).

4 *Gallo v. Acuna*, 929 P.2d 596 (1997).

5 *Griffin v. State*, 457 So. 2d 1070, 1072 (Fla. 2d Dist. Ct. App. 1984). See also *State v. Smeter*, 674 P.2d 690 (Wash. App. 1984).

6 *Figueroa v. Kirmayer*, 303 NYS2d 349 (App Div 1969).

7 Margaret C. Jasper, *The Law of Obscenity and Pornography* (1996) p. 3. See also *United States v. One Book Called Ulysses*, 5 F.Supp. 182 (1933).

8 Harvey Wallace and Cliff Roberson, *Principles of Criminal Law* (1996), p. 225, citing *Roth v. United States*, 354 U.S. 476 (1957) and *Memoirs v. Massachusetts*, 383 U.S. 413 (1966). See also Charles E. Torcia, *Wharton's Criminal Law* (15th ed. Volume 3, 1995) p. 138.

9 David A. Jones, *Crime and Criminal Responsibility* 359(1978).

10 Jonathon Rosenoer, *CyberLaw: The Law of the Internet* (1997) p. 179–80 citing 18 U.S.C. Section 2252 (a)(2), (a)(4).

11 John C. Klotter, *Criminal Law* (1983) p. 98 citing *People v. Conrad*, 334 N.Y. (2d) 180, 70 Misc. 2d 408 (1972).

12 Charles E. Torcia, *Wharton's Criminal Law* (15th ed. 1994) Section 271 citing 18 USCS Section 2421.

13 Thomas J. Gardner, *Criminal Law Principles and Cases* 477 (4th ed. 1989).

14 Charles E. Torcia, *Wharton's Criminal Law* (15th ed. 1994) Section 266 citing Utah Code Ann. Section 76-10-1305 (felony of third degree).

15 Charles E. Torcia, *Wharton's Criminal Law* (15th ed. Volume 2, 1995) p. 529 citing *Burns v. State* (1919) 17 Okla Crim 26, 182 P. 738 1919).

16 Charles E. Torcia, *Wharton's Criminal Law* (15th ed. Volume 2 1994) p. 536 citing *Miss Stats Ann*, Section 609.36.

17 Harvey Wallace and Cliff Roberson, *Principles of Criminal Law* (1996) p. 141 citing William Blackstone, 4 *Commentaries* 215, and *Phillips v. State*, 248 Ind.150, 222 N.E. 2d. 821 (1967).

Chapter Objectives

After reading this chapter, you will be able to:

1. Identify the five major categories of controlled substances.
2. State the purposes and effect of the Uniform Controlled Substances Act.
3. Recognize and describe the difference between actual and constructive possession of a controlled substance.
4. State the difference between the offense of possession versus the offense of possession with the intent to deliver.
5. Define the drug offenses of delivery, drug conspiracy, drug loitering, and possession of drug paraphernalia.
6. Understand when drug addiction is and is not a defense to drug offenses.
7. State the elements of driving under the influence.
8. Define the extent to which alcoholism can be a defense in a criminal case.

Chapter Outline

Can a police officer draw blood from an unconscious suspect to check for alcohol intoxication?

Chapter 14

Drug- and Alcohol-Related Crimes

14.1 Types of Psychoactive Drugs

In the United States, some drugs that affect mental states and behavior have been subject to little or no regulation, and others have been targets of extremely punitive legislation and a "war on drugs." There is disagreement about what substances are drugs, and which are harmful. Although nicotine and caffeine stimulate the central nervous system, many Americans do not consider smoking cigarettes or drinking alcohol to be drug use. Although Ritalin® and Valium® are clearly addictive and have controversial medical value, they are legally prescribed to thousands of people with little question.

controlled substances
Any substances that are strictly regulated or outlawed because of their potential for abuse or addiction.

Under the federal law, **controlled substances** are any *psychoactive* (affecting mind or behavior) or *bioactive* (affecting the body) chemical substances that are strictly regulated or made illegal because of their potential for abuse or addiction. Overall, drugs are classified as controlled substances based on medical use, potential for abuse, and probability of creating dependence.

psychoactive drugs Drugs that have the ability to alter mood, anxiety, behavior, cognitive processes, or mental tension.

From a biochemical standpoint, **psychoactive drugs** are drugs that have the ability to alter mood, anxiety, behavior, cognitive processes, or mental tension.[1] They are generally classified according to their principal or usual affects on human beings.

Stimulants   Stimulant drugs directly affect the central nervous system and tend to produce arousal, alertness, or excitation. They may also reduce fatigue. They include amphetamines, methamphetamines, cocaine, caffeine, nicotine, and the prescription drug Ritalin.

Depressants   Depressants are drugs that depress or slow down the activity of the central nervous system and tend to produce drowsiness, relaxation, or sleep. These are divided into narcotics (drugs derived from opium or opium-like compounds) and non-narcotic general depressants. Opiates are powerful pain-relieving depressant drugs that may induce sleep and that commonly become physically addictive after prolonged use. Opiates, including opium, morphine, heroin, and codeine, are derived from unripe poppy seed capsules. Synthetic narcotics include Percodan® and Demerol® (used for pain relief) and methadone (used to treat heroin addiction). Non-narcotic general depressants include alcohol, barbiturates, and tranquilizers such as Librium®, Valium®, and Xanax®.

Hallucinogens   Hallucinogenic drugs act on the central nervous system to cause visual or auditory hallucinations. They include LSD (lysergic acid diethylamide), PCP (phencyclidine), mescaline (derived from the peyote cactus), psilocybin (a mushroom), and numerous synthetic drugs.

Marijuana   Marijuana consists of the dried leaves and top of *cannabis sativa*, the common hemp plant. This drug has been classified as a hallucinogen, a stimulant, and a depressant. Some argue that it should be in a separate category because it does not closely resemble the other types of drugs. Hashish and hashish oil are derivatives of cannabis.

Inhalants   These drugs are classified by their method of use, rather than by the effects of their use. They have stimulating but very short-lived effects. They include amyl nitrite ("poppers") and nitrous oxide ("laughing gas"). Other household chemicals are used as inhalants but are not legally considered drugs.[2]

Designer Drugs   Designer drugs are synthetic drugs that mimic the effects of known illegal drugs, but are not specifically listed as controlled substances by the Drug Enforcement Administration. The best known designer drug, Ecstasy (3,4-methylenedioxy-N-methylamphetamine or MDMA), is chemically related to the family of amphetamines and also to mescaline. It was first synthesized in the early 1900s but was not used as a psychoactive drug until the 1970s. Some psychiatrists and psychologists began experimenting with it as a psychotherapeutic tool, claiming that it decreased anxiety, removed defenses, and facilitated communication between therapist and client. In the 1980s, it became popular at large, all-night dance parties, known as raves, in both England and the United States. The FDA classified it as a controlled substance in 1985, but it has continued to grow in popularity. Users say that it has amphetamine-like properties and produces positive feelings of relaxation, empathy, and confidence. Other designer drugs include Rohypnol (known as a "date rape" drug), China White, and New Heroin.

Self Check

Which categories of drugs seem the most dangerous? The most addictive? Why?

CRIMINAL LAW *Online*

Check your answers at cl.glencoe.com.

14.2 History of Drug Legislation in the United States

According to historians and archaeologists, marijuana and the opium poppy have been used as intoxicants and in rituals in many societies for thousands of years. The use of alcohol is, for the most part, "a human cultural universal."[3] World trade in such substances, however, began only after the European colonization of America.

Drug Use in Nineteenth-Century America

The classification of various drugs in the United States as legal or illegal has also changed over time.[4] Narcotics and cocaine are two good examples of this.

Narcotics During the nineteenth century, it was legal to distribute, promote, and sell narcotics. Opium was used to treat everything from teething pains to tuberculosis, and it also was a potent source of recreational pleasure. It had been used in home remedies and patent medicines since the latter part of the eighteenth century. Morphine was isolated in the early nineteenth century, and it became widely used as an anesthetic. After using it as a painkiller on the battlefields of the Civil War, tens of thousands of soldiers returned home addicted to the drug. By the end of the nineteenth century, both physicians and the general public became concerned about the addictive potential of opiates.[5] Heroin, a powerful derivative of morphine, was first introduced by the Bayer Company in 1898, as a cough medicine. It was also seen as a cure for morphine addiction and alcoholism.

Cocaine Cocaine, too, was widely used in the United States after it was chemically extracted from the coca leaf in 1844. Many patent medicines of the late nineteenth century contained cocaine, and until 1903, it was an ingredient in Coca-Cola®.[6] Its medical uses included the treatment of depression, narcolepsy (excessive sleepiness), and more mundane ailments such as hay fever, sinus troubles, and runny noses.

Other products that could be purchased over the counter at local drugstores and variety stores contained cocaine, opium, and morphine. During the 1800s, the use of opium, morphine, cocaine, and heroin was so extensive that by 1900, there were approximately

250,000 narcotics addicts in the United States. Some estimates put the number at as high as 8 million.[7] The widespread use of drugs gave rise to demands by the medical community, the media, and the general public for government regulation.

Drug Legislation from the 1800s to the Present

Drug legislation began at a local, rather than a national, level. In 1875, the City of San Francisco enacted the first drug law in the United States. The law did not outlaw the use of opium, but it prohibited smoking in opium dens. Whites used over-the-counter drugs containing opium in powder, liquid, and pill form, but opium smoking was associated with Chinese immigrants.

Beginnings of Federal Legislation In 1888, federal legislation placed certain restrictions on smoking opium. Smoking opium was banned in 1909, but drinking it remained legal. The law was one of the few restrictions on drug use in effect in the United States at the time. In 1906, in an attempt to control opiate addiction, Congress passed the Federal Pure Food and Drug Act. This law required that product labels specify the amount of drugs (opium, morphine, and heroin) in the product. The same was required for products containing alcohol, marijuana, and cocaine.

The Harrison Narcotics Act of 1914 In 1914, Congress passed the Harrison Narcotics Act of 1914, which took effect March 15, 1915. It was not intended to prohibit the use or sale of narcotics but, rather, was primarily an economic regulation. It required persons dealing in narcotics or cocaine to register with the government and pay a tax; however, anyone was allowed to engage in such trade. The Harrison Act was in part a response to international pressures to regulate opium trade; the law also provided revenue for the federal government. The Treasury Department was given the responsibility of enforcing the law.

Under the Harrison Act, it was still legal to use cough medicine that contained a restricted amount of heroin, and physicians could still prescribe opiates for medical treatment. However, in 1919, the United States Supreme Court held, in the case of *Webb v. United States*, that physicians could not maintain addicts on morphine. The Court ruled that such prescriptions prolonged addiction and thus could not be considered medical treatment.[8] As a result of the increased numbers of individuals addicted to drugs, the United States grew fearful and intolerant of recreational drug use.

The Marijuana Tax Act   The use and sale of marijuana was legal in the United States until the 1930s. Harry Anslinger, head of the Federal Bureau of Narcotics from its founding in 1930 until his retirement in 1962, led an anti-marijuana campaign that portrayed it as a "killer drug." With the aid of anti-marijuana stories run in mass-circulation newspapers and magazines, such as stories that claimed that marijuana would lead to the destruction of the youth of America, 46 of 48 states banned marijuana. The Women's Christian Temperance Union and the General Federation of Women's Clubs launched campaigns to ban marijuana.

At the federal level, the first law regulating marijuana was the Marijuana Tax Act of 1937. The law imposed taxes on marijuana, declared cannabis (hemp) a narcotic, and penalized its use and distribution. In 1951, Congress passed the Boggs Act, which made marijuana illegal and also removed heroin from the list of medically useful drugs.

Drug Use and Legislation in the 1950s and 1960s   During the 1950s, organized crime began to play a much larger role in the distribution and sale of drugs. Heroin addiction increased sharply during this time, especially among youth in the inner cities.[9] During the 1960s, drug use expanded from the cities to suburbia, and the use of heroin by U.S. soldiers in Vietnam became a national concern.

In addition, although legal in the 1950s, the drug LSD became illegal in 1967 because of its association with a generation whose values at the time were different from the general population. Laws were also created to regulate the availability and use of depressants.

The Uniform Controlled Substances Act of 1970   In 1970, the U.S. Congress enacted the Comprehensive Drug Abuse and Prevention Act, also called the Controlled Substances Act of 1970. It replaced the 1933 Uniform Narcotic Drug Act and the 1966 Model State Drug Abuse Control Act. The majority of the states enacted parallel legislation.

The goals of the Uniform Act were to achieve uniformity between the laws of the several states and those of the federal government and to complement the new federal narcotic and dangerous drug legislation.[10] Nevertheless, conflicts between federal and state laws sometimes arise, and there is significant variation among the state drug laws. For example, Minnesota treats marijuana possession in small amounts as a petty misdemeanor that may result in a maximum fine of $200 and participation in a drug education program. In contrast, Florida makes marijuana possession a first-degree misdemeanor, and possession of up to 20 grams can result in a fine of up to $1,000 and/or a prison term of up to one year.

The Uniform Controlled Substances Act forbids and makes it a crime to engage in the following conduct:

- Manufacture or deliver a controlled (forbidden) substance;
- Possess with the intent to manufacture or deliver a controlled substance;
- Create, deliver, or possess with intent to deliver a counterfeit substance;
- Offer or agree to deliver a controlled substance and deliver or dispense a controlled substance;
- Possess a controlled substance;
- Knowingly keep or maintain a store, dwelling, building, vehicle, boat, or aircraft, etc. resorted to by persons illegally using controlled substance; or
- Acquire or obtain possession of a controlled substance by misrepresentation, fraud, forgery, deception, or subterfuge.

The Uniform Controlled Substances Act divides controlled substances into five categories or "schedules" (See Figure 14–1 on page 480), graded according to their potential for abuse, relative physical danger to the abuser, and degree of accepted medical use. The drugs in Schedule I are the most tightly controlled, and possession of them results in the severest penalties.

The three criteria for placing a drug into Schedule I are that the drug must:

- Have a high potential for abuse.
- Have no currently accepted medical use.
- Lack safety even under medical supervision.

The War on Drugs Despite the enactment of anti-drug laws, drug use by Americans increased significantly from the 1960s until 1980. In response to this increase in drug usage, President Ronald Reagan launched the "War on Drugs" in the 1980s. Underlying this campaign was the belief that the nation should take a punitive approach to the possession and sale of illicit drugs. The War on Drugs was an attempt to create a uniform scheme for identifying, regulating, and prohibiting the use and possession of potentially dangerous drugs. Federal funds for drug treatment programs were sharply reduced, and tough mandatory sentencing laws were passed for possession of relatively small amounts of cocaine and other

The DC*MADS Drug Study

The DC*MADS was a study of drug abuse in one metropolitan area from 1989 to 1995. It was the first to focus on all types of people, including homeless people and institutionalized offenders. About 54 percent of adult offenders and 50 percent of juvenile offenders had used illicit drugs in the past year. More than 40 percent of violent crimes and 50 percent of the property crimes committed by adults were preceded by the use of a drug. Half of the adult drug users (i.e., approximately 20 percent of the convicted incarcerated population) reported that they would not have committed the crime if they had not taken the drug. The majority of these crimes, though, were not linked to involvement with drugs, which suggests that it will take more than reducing drug use to reduce high levels of crime in the United States.

SOURCE: Robert M. Bray and Mary Ellen Marsden, Eds., *Drug Use in Metropolitan America*. Thousand Oaks, CA: Sage, 1999, p. 301.

FIGURE 14–1

Schedule of Drugs Under the Controlled Substances Act of 1970

Schedule I: controlled substances that have no established medical usage; cannot be used safely, and have great potential for abuse:

> Heroin, LSD, mescaline, peyote, Quaaludes, psilocybin, marijuana, hashish, and some hallucinogens

Schedule II: drugs with a high potential for abuse (and addiction) but for which there is a currently accepted pharmacological or medical use:

> Opium, morphine, codeine, cocaine, phencyclidine (PCP), some stimulants such as methylphenidate (Ritalin®) and phenmetrazine (Preludin®), and some barbiturates

Schedule III: substances with some potential for abuse; with an accepted medical use; but which may lead to a high level of psychological dependence or a low to moderate level of physical dependence:

> Anabolic steroids (added in 1991), cold medicines, and pain relievers containing codeine

Schedule IV: substances with relatively low potential for abuse; useful in established medical treatment; involving only limited risk of psychological or physical dependency:

> Depressants and minor tranquilizers such as Valium®, Librium®, and Equanil® and some stimulants

Schedule V: prescription drugs with a low potential for abuse and a very limited possibility of psychological or physical dependence; cough medicines and antidiarrheals containing small amounts of opium, morphine, or codeine

---

drugs. Supporters of the War on Drugs advocate long prison sentences for users, dealers, suppliers, smugglers, and manufacturers of these drugs. The most extreme advocates of this view argue that harsher penalties are the only solution to the drug problem.

Current Drug Use

Although overall rates of illicit drug use leveled out in the late 1990s, Bureau of Justice data indicate that the rate of drug abuse violations remains high. According to FBI data for 1999, there were 1.53 million arrests for drug-related offenses, and 6.3 million persons were on probation, in jail, or in state or federal prison for these offenses. More than 80 percent of all drug arrests are for possession, with arrests for sales or manufacturing drugs constituting the remaining 20 percent of drug arrests.

While use of the majority of illicit drugs has decreased since the highs of the 1970s, the following drug trends are apparent:

- The use of inhalants and of the synthetic drug Ecstasy has increased among youth.
- Illicit use of prescription psychotherapeutics, especially pain relievers, for nonmedical purposes has also increased among adolescents. In 1990, there were 6.3 new users per 1,000 potential users in the 12–17 age group. By 1998, the number of new users of prescription pain relievers in that age group increased to 32.4 per 1,000 potential users.
- Illicit use of anabolic steroids has also increased.
- The increase in the rate of new users of marijuana between 1990 and 2000 seems due primarily to the increasing rate of new users among youths aged 12 to 17. In 1977, the rate of new users per 1,000 potential users was at a high of 3.4. It had declined to 1.4 by 1990, but reached 2.6 in 1996 and 2.3 in 1998.[11]

FYI

Saved by a Pardon

At age 19, Kemba Smith, a middle-class college student and mother of a small child, was sentenced to 24 and a half years in federal prison without the possibility of parole because of her minimal involvement with a drug dealer. She received a pardon from President Bill Clinton in December 2000.

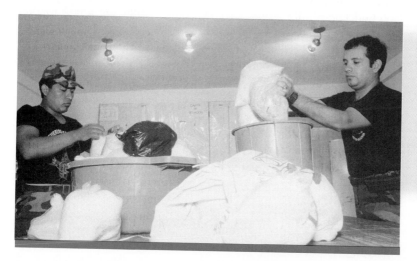

◄ **Possession with Intent to Deliver** Unlike mere possession, possession with intent to deliver carries severe penalties. *What evidence separates the person guilty of possession from the person guilty of possession with intent to deliver?*

Myth	Fact
Decriminalization of marijuana will lead to a substantial increase in use.	States that have decriminalized the use of marijuana have reported a minimal increase in consumption.

Current Drug Policy

Today, opponents of the War on Drugs argue that criminalization is not the solution to the drug problem. In their view, the 74 years of federal prohibition, the attempt to enforce zero tolerance for drugs in the 1980s, and the harsher penalties for drug violations have had limited success and have created important civil rights problems. They argue that drug laws and their implementation have been enormously expensive and served mainly to create enormous profits for drug dealers and traffickers, overcrowded jails, corruption among police and other government employees, a distorted foreign policy, and urban areas harassed by street-level drug dealers and terrorized by violent drug gangs.[12]

Some opponents of the War on Drugs say that the United States should emphasize medical and therapeutic approaches to the drug problem. Others believe that legalization would stop the violent crime associated with drug sales. Still others hold that the United States should remove all criminal penalties for the possession and sale of all psychoactive substances, allowing a free market to operate.[13]

By the dawn of the twenty-first century, however, many authorities on drug use had developed more complex proposals that recognize the many factors that affect an individual's choice to use drugs. Some advocate "harm reduction" not as a policy or program but as a principle suggesting that it is more reasonable to manage drug misuse rather than attempt to stop it altogether. Proposals for harm reduction can include any of the following:[14]

CRIMINAL LAW Online

Jailhouse Blues

Read "Jailhouse Blues" available through the link at **cl.glencoe.com**. Read the article, then write a half-page report discussing whether you think that incarceration is the correct response for non-violent drug offenders. Should they be punished? If so, why and how? If not, why?

Myth

If we could stop the traffic in illegal drugs, we would eliminate the bulk of the violent crime in the United States.

Fact

Alcohol is a factor in more crimes than is any other single drug, and there are more arrests for alcohol-related offenses than for all other drug offenses.

- Advocacy for changes in drug policies: legalization, reduction of criminal sanctions for drug-related crimes
- HIV/AIDS-related interventions: for example, needle exchange programs, HIV prevention programs
- Broader drug treatment options, including methadone maintenance by primary care physicians
- Drug abuse management for those who wish to continue using drugs
- Ancillary programs such as support and advocacy groups

Drugs and Religious Freedom

Peyote has been used in certain Native American rituals for at least 400 years. Until 1990, the First Amendment's guarantee of the free exercise of religion or its prohibition against the establishment of religion had been held to exclude the use of peyote in Native American religious ceremonies.[15]

In 1990, in *Employment Division, Department of Human Resources of Oregon v. Smith*,[16] the U.S. Supreme Court held that Native American religious use of peyote was not to be afforded First Amendment protection under the free exercise clause. The Court rejected the claim by the respondents that the religious basis for their use of peyote placed them beyond the reach of a criminal statute directed at use of peyote for non-religious purposes.

As the only Supreme Court decision on the issue, *Oregon v. Smith* was immediately accepted as controlling authority. This was to the dismay of the executive and legislative branches of the federal government, who had a well-established relationship with Native American tribes to protect their rights as dependent sovereign nations. In order to halt the impact of the *Smith* decision, Congress passed the American Indian Religious Freedom Act Amendments in October 1994. This bill stripped *Smith* of its authority over peyote use in Native American religious ceremonies.

This federal exemption served two important functions:

1. It provided uniformity in the varying state laws governing peyote use by Native Americans.
2. It exempted Native Americans from penalty under the federal Controlled Substances Act, as well as under any state statutes that criminalized peyote use.[17]

The Case for Decriminalization

Advocates for decriminalization of controlled substances put forth eight substantial benefits that could come from the legalization of currently controlled substances:

1. Savings of at least $200 billion per year to American tax payers
2. Reduced crime
3. Elimination of drug-related corruption and waste
4. Less crowded jails and more room in prisons for dangerous criminals
5. Improved public health
6. Restored civil liberties and respect for the law
7. Drug prosecutions would cease destroying the lives of otherwise productive citizens
8. The users of controlled substances would bear most of the cost for access and regulation

SOURCE: Steven B. Duke, *America's Longest War: Rethinking Our Tragic Crusade Against Drugs* 231–241 (1993).

Prior to the federal exemption, the diversity of state laws governing Native American peyote use caused fragmented treatment of Native Americans engaged in peyote use and transportation.

Check your answers at cl.glencoe.com.

Self Check

1. For what reasons was the Uniform Controlled Substances Act created?
2. In general, have efforts to fight and criminalize the use of psychoactive substances been successful in the United States? Why or why not?

14.3 Drug Offenses

Both federal and state systems have, in general, set up two penal categories for controlled substances: offenses involving possession and offenses involving the sale, distribution, and manufacture of controlled substances. The following section will first discuss possession, then will cover more serious drug offenses such as drug transportation and drug conspiracy.

Possession

The offense of (mere, simple, or straight) possession of a controlled substance is the most common criminal drug charge. The *actus reus* of the crime of criminal possession is the actual or constructive possession of a controlled substance.

actual possession When the controlled substance is on the defendant's person, or within an area of his or her immediate control and reach. Actual possession may also occur when the controlled substance is within a container that the defendant may be carrying or has within his or her reach.

Actual Possession   **Actual possession** is the charge when the controlled substance is recovered on the defendant's person. For example, a suspect who is apprehended while holding a marijuana joint in his or her hands, lips, or pocket will be charged with actual possession. This offense may also occur when the controlled substance is found in a container (e.g., bag) that the defendant is carrying.

constructive possession When illegal drugs are in a place immediately accessible to the accused and subject to his or her dominion and control.

Constructive Possession   **Constructive possession** of an illegal item (including controlled substances, guns, stolen goods, or other contraband) occurs when the item is in a place immediately accessible to the accused and he or she is able to exercise "dominion and control" over it. Hence, constructive possession does not require actual physical possession, but only that the accused be in a position

Wheeler v. United States

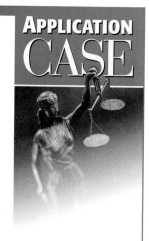

In *Wheeler v. United States*, the defendant was convicted of possession of heroin on the theory of constructive possession. Detectives executed a search warrant of a hotel room, based on information that female occupants had been selling heroin from the room. When the detectives knocked on the door, they received no response but could hear a lot of "scurrying" noises in the room. A minute later, after no one opened the door, the detectives broke the door down. They discovered the defendant and two other women coming out of the bathroom and leaving a toilet that had just been flushed. A fourth woman was sitting next to the bathroom in a chair. Two women were in regular street clothing, while the defendant and the other female were wearing sleeping attire.

Further examination of the room revealed luggage and clothing belonging to the defendant. The defendant and the other woman admitted to living in the room, but they gave aliases (false names) to the detectives. The other woman retrieved some slippers from under one of the two beds located in the room. At the opposite end of the room, where the other bed was located, the detectives recovered 3,550 milligrams of 2.7 percent heroin from under the pillow. Both the defendant and the other woman who admitted to living in the room were arrested. The charges against the other woman were later dismissed. However, following a bench trial, the defendant was convicted of possession of heroin. She appealed her conviction on the basis that the drugs were not recovered on her person, but in a room where three other female individuals were present at the time. The defendant argued that the drugs could have belonged to any one of the other women and could have been placed under the pillow by any one of them.

The court refused to reverse the defendant's conviction. It held that even though the evidence was circumstantial, it supported a finding of constructive possession. The defendant's mere presence in the room by itself might not have been sufficient; however, evidence of an ongoing criminal enterprise, the defendant's admission that she lived in the room, the fact that the heroin was recovered from the bed that the defendant appeared to have occupied, the defendant's giving an alias to the detective, and her failure to open the door for the detectives, requiring them to break it down while a toilet was being flushed, together permitted an inference that the defendant knew of the presence of the drugs and had a measure of control over the heroin. Thus, a finding of constructive possession was justified.

Constructive Possession

Critical Thinking Should the other inhabitants of the room be charged with constructive possession? Why or why not?

SOURCE: *Wheeler v. United States*, 494 A.2d 170, (D.C. 1995).

to move the illegal substance from one place or another or have a knowing ability and intent to do so ("guide its destiny"). Constructive possession is frequently proven by showing that the controlled substance was located in an area or container in the accused's house or car, backpack, or other container that was accessible to the accused. In addition, the prosecution can prove constructive possession even if more than one individual had the ability to exercise dominion and control over the illegal substance.

Knowing Possession   More than mere proximity to the illegal substance is required to prove constructive possession. Even when there is actual possession, most states require that a "knowing" state of mind (*mens rea*) accompany the act of possession. In order to be lawfully convicted, the accused must know (be consciously aware) that he or she is in possession of the substance and must know that the substance is of a contraband (illegal) nature. Even if the accused is not actually knowledgeable about the illegal character of the item, many states will uphold a conviction if there is sufficient circumstantial evidence indicating that the accused was aware of the presence of the contraband and knew or should have known that the item possessed was a controlled substance.

In particular, virtually every state allows suspects to be punished when there is proof that he or she "willfully blinded" him- or herself to actual knowledge of the illegal character of an item in his or her possession. (See *United States v. Civelli* on page 491 and *United States v. Jewell* on page 494.) However, under most state laws, a conviction will not result from situations in which a defendant has a white powdery substance on his or her person but honestly believes it to be sugar even though it is cocaine.

Irrelevance of Amount   In many states, a conviction for simple possession of a controlled substance does not require possession of any minimum amount of the drug. An accused person may be convicted of possession for even a minute amount of an illegal substance. Some states, such as New York, hold that possession of a controlled substance can be based on the presence of even a residue of a substance such as cocaine.

Other jurisdictions hold that a person can be convicted for the possession of a "trace" amount of a controlled substance. A trace amount is an amount that is so small it is unusable. What is required is that the trace amount of the controlled substance be "reflected in such form as reasonably imputes knowledge to the defendant."[18] In

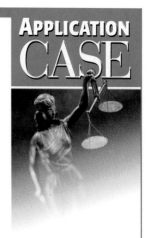

Jones v. State

In *Jones v. State*, the defendant was convicted of possession of a controlled substance. The basis for this conviction was an infinitesimal "residue" of cocaine on a small piece of metal ribbon, or screen, that is commonly used in smoking the drug. Because this screen was found in Jones's jacket pocket, he was convicted of possession of cocaine. The defendant contended that the cocaine, which was visible on the screen and detectable both by field and laboratory tests but was not "realistically weighable," was, as a matter of law, of insufficient quantity to justify a possession charge.

The appeal court disagreed and affirmed the conviction. It referred to the rule that one cannot be found guilty of possession when there are *only* trace amounts of *only* drug "lint" or "dust," but explained that this rule was inapplicable to this case. The reason was that the cocaine was found on an implement that is usable only for the obviously knowing use of the drug.

Irrelevance of Amount

Critical Thinking Should Jones have been convicted if he had only the cocaine, not the screen?

SOURCE: *Jones v. State*, 589 So.2d 1001 (Fla. Dst. Ct. App. 1991).

---

still other states, simple possession cannot be established when there are only minuscule amounts of drug amounting to "lint" or "dust" that often innocently adheres to commonly used objects in the environment. (See Application Case *Jones v. State*.)

Possession with Intent to Deliver Possession with intent to deliver is another prevalent drug-related offense. Possession with intent is referred to as "possession for sale" or "possession with intent to sell or distribute" in some jurisdictions. This offense may be shown circumstantially by evidence such as possession of a large quantity of drugs or a quantity of drugs worth a lot of money; possession of manufacturing or packaging equipment, such as measuring scales, large quantities of small glassine envelopes; or the activities or statements of the person or persons in possession of the substance. In contrast to crimes of simple "possession" of controlled substances, "possession with intent to deliver" is treated as a felony under both federal and state statutes. Due to the stiffer penalties imposed for "possession with intent" offenses, many states forbid the

possession with intent to deliver A drug offense that may be proven circumstantially by proof of a monetarily valuable quantity of drugs, possession of manufacturing or packaging implements, and the activities or statements of the person or persons in possession of the substance.

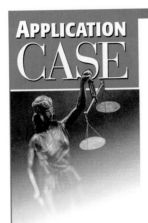
State v. Brown

In *State v. Brown*, the defendant, a young man, was found with a baggie containing 20 pieces of rock cocaine. There was no other evidence of intent to deliver, other than the quantity of the drug possessed. In reversing his conviction for possession with intent to deliver, the appellate court stated,

> The courts must be careful to preserve the distinction and not to turn every possession of a minimal amount of a controlled substance into a possession with intent to deliver without substantial evidence as to the possessor's intent above and beyond the possession itself. Convictions for possession with intent to deliver are highly fact specific and require substantial corroborating evidence in addition to the mere fact of possession.

Critical Thinking What additional evidence do you think should change a crime from possession to possession with intent to deliver? Why?

SOURCE: *State v. Brown*, 843 P.2d 1098 (Wash. Ct. App. 1995).

inference of intent to deliver merely on the basis of possession of a controlled substance.

In order to obtain a conviction for possession with the intent to deliver, the state must prove that the defendant(s) intended to deliver controlled substances to another person or persons, either immediately or at some time in the future. Evidence of intent to deliver must be sufficiently compelling that the specific criminal intent of the accused may be inferred from conduct where the intent to transfer the drug to others is a clearly indicated logical probability. However, in some cases, such proof may be no easy task for the prosecution, as the case of *State v. Davis* illustrates. (See Application Case on page 489.)

Other Drug Offenses

Other than possession, a person can be convicted for several other drug violations in the United States, including:

- Delivery of a controlled substance
- Drug conspiracy

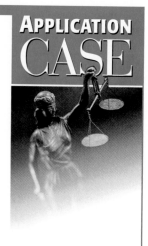

State v. Davis

In order to obtain a conviction for possession with the intent to deliver, the state must prove that the defendant(s) intended to deliver controlled substances, either presently or at some time in the future. Evidence of intent to deliver must be sufficiently compelling so that the specific criminal intent of the accused may be inferred from conduct where it is plainly indicated as a matter of logical probability. Understandably, this is no easy task for the prosecution, as the case of *State v. Davis* demonstrates.

In this case, Leroy Davis was convicted of possession of marijuana with the intent to deliver. The evidence against him included possession of a bread sack with six individually wrapped baggies of marijuana, two baggies of marijuana seeds, a film canister containing marijuana, a baggie with marijuana residue in it, a box of sandwich baggies, a pipe used for smoking marijuana, a number of knives, and a police officer's testimony that it was not customary for people who simply use marijuana to have that "quantity with that packaging." The question presented on appeal was whether the evidence presented by the state was sufficient to infer an intent to deliver marijuana.

The Court of Appeals of Washington found that it was not and reversed the conviction. It reasoned that there was no evidence Mr. Davis had bought or sold marijuana or was in the business of buying or selling. No quantity of money was found, nor were any weighing devices. The marijuana obtained from Mr. Davis totaled 19 grams, an amount which, the Court found, could certainly be consumed in the course of normal personal use. The packaging was also consistent with personal use. Therefore, the court found that there was not enough evidence to infer the specific criminal intent to deliver as required by statute. The intent to deliver did not follow as a matter of logical probability.

Intent to Deliver

Critical Thinking Do you think the Court of Appeals should have reversed this conviction? Why or why not?

SOURCE: *State v. Davis*, 904 P.2d 306 (Wash. Ct. App. 1995).

- Drug loitering
- Drug transportation
- Cultivation of marijuana
- Drug paraphernalia

delivery of a controlled substance The transfer of a controlled substance from one person to another person.

Delivery of a Controlled Substance

Delivery of a controlled substance is defined as the voluntary transfer of a controlled substance from one person to another person. Delivery, like possession, can be proven constructively, as well as through the actual delivery of the controlled substance. Delivery statutes are geared towards the suppliers of controlled substances. The Controlled Substances Act attaches the same felony penalties to delivery as it does to possession with intent to deliver.

simulated controlled substance A substance representing a controlled substance in its nature, packaging, or appearance, which would lead a reasonable person to believe it to be a controlled substance.

Some states also have statutes that make the delivery or possession of a **simulated controlled substance** a crime. A simulated controlled substance (or imitation) is a substance represented to be a controlled substance, which, because of its nature, packaging, or appearance, would lead a reasonable person to believe it to be a controlled substance.

Often a person engaged in selling controlled substances is also charged with the crimes of possession, possession with intent to deliver, and conspiracy, because there is a group effort to distribute the controlled substances. The case of *United States v. Civelli* illustrates the crimes of delivery of a controlled substance, drug conspiracy, and possession with intent to deliver. (See Application Case on page 491.)

drug conspiracy An agreement between two or more people to commit a criminal or unlawful drug-related act, or to commit a lawful drug-related act by criminal or unlawful means.

Drug Conspiracy

A **drug conspiracy** is an agreement between two or more persons with the intent to manufacture and/or distribute drugs. In order to establish this offense, the state must show that an agreement existed, that the defendant had knowledge of the agreement, and that the defendant voluntarily participated in the agreement. An agreement may be inferred from a concert of action, participation from a totality of the circumstances, and knowledge from surrounding circumstances. (See *United States v. Civelli* and *United States v. Eastman* on page 492.)

drug loitering When some public action is taken that manifests the intent to engage in illegal drug activity.

Drug Loitering

The crime of "drug loitering" or "loitering for the purposes of engaging in drug-related activity" is another category of drug-related offenses. The crime of **drug loitering** consists of an action done in public that manifests the intent to engage in illegal drug activity. Proof of the presence of a controlled substance, its possession, or its delivery is not required under most ordinances to support a charge of drug loitering; however, the action must occur in public.

drug transportation Transporting a controlled substance in a vehicle; a crime in every state.

Drug Transportation

Every state prohibits the transportation of a controlled substance in a vehicle, which is the offense of **drug transportation**. The case of *United States v. Jewell* demonstrates

Crimes Against the Community and Institutions

United States v. Civelli

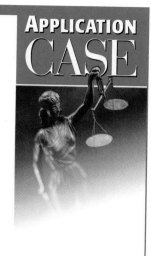
In *United States v. Civelli*, the defendant, Oscar Civelli, received a call from one Diego Bedoya, who asked the defendant to drive to Bedoya's home to make a delivery for him. Civelli was in the commercial delivery and moving business, and he had moved household items for Bedoya several times before. Civelli left his apartment and drove to Bedoya's home, which was under surveillance as a suspected center of narcotics distribution. Civelli was observed emerging from the house with four large tan envelopes.

Two officers followed Civelli as he drove away. After driving some distance, Civelli stopped to make a call from a public telephone. The officers approached the defendant and asked him what was in the packages in the van. He pulled one of the envelopes from the van to show the officers. The officers discovered 8.5 kilograms of cocaine in the four envelopes. Each envelope was folded shut but not sealed, and each had a name written on the outside. The officers also recovered from Civelli a beeper and a list of four names. The list was in his handwriting, and the names on the list corresponded to the names on the envelopes. There was a telephone number next to each name on the list, and a circled digit beside the name and number corresponded to the number of bricks of cocaine in one of the labeled envelopes.

Civelli was indicted for conspiracy to possess cocaine with intent to distribute and for possession of more than five kilograms of cocaine with intent to distribute. The key question at trial was whether the defendant knew he was carrying narcotics. The defendant testified that he never knew what was inside the envelopes until the officers opened them. He conceded that he had prepared the list of names, but he stated that he had transcribed the list verbatim at Bedoya's direction and that Bedoya was to pay him only $100 to deliver the packages. At trial, the judge instructed the jury that in order to find the defendant guilty on either the conspiracy or the substantive count, they had to find that the government had "prove[d] beyond a reasonable doubt that the defendant knew the packages in the van contained cocaine."

During deliberations, the jury sent the judge a note asking: "If Oscar Civelli suspected that he was carrying cocaine, but didn't look in the package, would that have constituted conspiracy?" The judge responded that a defendant's knowledge of a fact may be inferred from his willful blindness to the existence of the fact. The jury returned guilty verdicts on both counts. Civelli was sentenced to ten years imprisonment. The appellate court affirmed the conviction.

Critical Thinking Do you agree with Civelli's conviction? Why or why not?

SOURCE: *United States v. Civelli*, 883 F.2d 191 (2nd Cir. 1989).

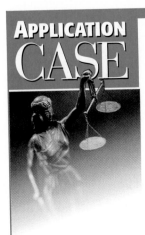

Conspiracy to Distribute

United States v. Eastman

A case that demonstrates a drug conspiracy is *United States v. Eastman* (1998), in which a jury convicted William Eastman of one count of conspiring to distribute cocaine and methamphetamine and two counts of conspiring to launder drug proceeds. In April 1990, one Lawrence Lawler in Minnesota began receiving cocaine and methamphetamine from his cousin, Joe Sakel, in California. For the next four years, Lawler periodically wired money to Sakel. Sakel and other suppliers shipped distribution quantities of drugs to Lawler by Federal Express. Lawler distributed about one-third of the drugs to a Robin Birk and two-thirds to the accused, William Eastman. Birk and Eastman supplied the money that Lawler wired for drugs. Over the course of the conspiracy, $250,000 was sent to California to purchase cocaine and methamphetamine for distribution in the Duluth area of Minnesota.

In June 1994, Lawler was arrested and agreed to cooperate with authorities. He arranged controlled buys from his sources in California and a controlled sale of two ounces of cocaine to Eastman in July 1994. Eastman was then arrested. At his trial, Lawler and Sakel testified against him for the government. Robin Birk also testified that she occasionally purchased drugs directly from Eastman.

To sustain Eastman's conviction for conspiracy to distribute drugs, the evidence had to establish that a conspiracy existed to distribute the drugs, and that Eastman knew of and intentionally joined the conspiracy. Eastman argued that he was a mere customer of the conspiracy. The Eighth Circuit Court disagreed and affirmed Eastman's conviction. It found the testimony of the other conspirators was sufficient for the jury to find that Eastman knowingly participated in a conspiracy.

Critical Thinking Should other members of a conspiracy be allowed to escape prosecution by testifying against a defendant? Why or why not?

SOURCE: *United States v. Eastman*, 149 F.3d 802 (8th Cir. 1998).

how the offense of transporting the controlled substance marijuana can be proven. (See Application Case on page 494.)

Cultivation of Marijuana   It is also a crime to cultivate or "dry" marijuana. Conviction of cultivating, drying, or processing mari-

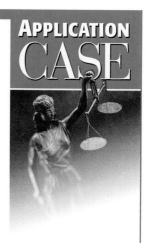
City of Tacoma v. Luvene

A case that illustrates the elements necessary to sustain a drug loitering conviction is *City of Tacoma v. Luvene* (1988). One Friday evening, a Tacoma (WA) police officer watched three men in their mid-twenties, including defendant Luvene, standing on a street corner. They were pacing two to three steps in all directions and continually surveying their surroundings. The men stood in the middle of the intersection waving at and trying to flag down vehicles, several of which stopped. The officer observed the defendant in the middle of the street and on the sidewalk for nearly one hour, in an area known to be one of drug trafficking. He was waving his arms at passing cars and standing by a car while another exchanged what looked to be rock cocaine for money.

After these observations, the officers approached and arrested five persons, including Luvene, for drug loitering. Glass tubing, commonly used to smoke crack cocaine, was found on one of the persons arrested. Although no drugs or drug paraphernalia were found on Luvene, the Supreme Court of Washington found there was sufficient evidence to sustain the conviction, considering the "totality of the circumstances."

Drug Loitering

Critical Thinking Do you agree with this conviction? Why or why not?

SOURCE: *City of Tacoma v. Luvene*, 827 P.2d 1374 (Wash. 1992).

juana is a felony punishable by a year or more in prison. In most states, in order to prove the crime of cultivating, drying, or processing marijuana the prosecution must prove that the person:

- knew plants were growing on his or her property.
- knew the plants were cannabis.

A person cannot be sentenced for both cultivation and possession of the same plants. The prosecution must elect one crime or the other.

Drug Paraphernalia The possession or sale of drug paraphernalia is another prevalent drug-related offense. **Drug paraphernalia** is defined as "any equipment, product or material of any kind that is primarily intended or designed for use with a controlled substance." Examples of drug paraphernalia include bongs, pipes, rolling papers,

drug paraphernalia Any equipment, product, or material that is primarily intended or designed for use with a controlled substance, such as bongs, pipes, rolling papers, scales, and hypodermic needles.

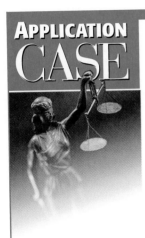

Drug Transportation

United States v. Jewell

In *Jewell*, the defendant was convicted of "knowingly" transporting marijuana in his car from Mexico to the United States. The defendant entered the United States driving an automobile in which 110 pounds of marijuana had been concealed in a secret compartment between the trunk and rear seat. The defendant testified that he did not know that the marijuana was present, although he knew of the presence of the secret compartment and had knowledge of facts indicating that it contained marijuana.

The court found that the defendant deliberately avoided positive knowledge (actual knowledge) of the presence of the marijuana in an attempt to avoid responsibility in the event of discovery. The court found the defendant's "deliberate ignorance" equally as culpable of the crime as positive knowledge of the presence of marijuana would have been. The court held that "[defendant's] narrow interpretation of 'knowingly' is inconsistent with the Drug Control Act's general purpose to deal more effectively 'with the growing menace of drug abuse in the United States.'"

Critical Thinking Do you think it is possible for a person to transport 110 pounds of marijuana and be unaware of its presence? Why or why not?

SOURCE: *United States v. Jewell*, 532 F.2d 697 (9th Cir. 1976).

scales, and hypodermic needles. Drug paraphernalia charges and convictions are most often obtained when the item or paraphernalia are seized at the same time that drugs such as marijuana or cocaine are seized. However, possessing drug paraphernalia is a crime without the possession of an illegal substance itself.

In response to the spread of AIDS, some cities, such as Baltimore, have amended paraphernalia laws to accommodate needle exchange programs. Under these programs, hypodermic needles are provided to addicts in an attempt to prevent the spread of the disease through needle sharing by intravenous drug users.

Narcotics or Drug Addiction as a Defense

Narcotics addiction is the repeated or uncontrolled use of controlled substances. While possession or use of controlled substances is a crime, being a drug addict is not. Addiction to drugs is a disease, which cannot be punished criminally under the cruel and

Chemical Dependency Manager

Description and Duties: Provide supportive counseling to adults (or youths, depending on the position) in a clinical setting and through community outreach. Act as advocate and coach in building daily living skills and in crisis prevention and intervention. Provide one-on-one counseling, assessments, treatment plans, and some group work. Some positions prefer previous experience with women, with youths, or in residential settings.

Salary: Salaries range from approximately $30,000 to $55,000.

Other Information: Many positions, especially full-time ones with benefits, require a bachelor's degree and certification as an alcohol and drug counselor. Most positions require or prefer one or two years of work experience.

Critical Thinking What qualities do you think a person should possess to be a good chemical dependency manager?

SOURCE: Community Psychiatric Clinic of Seattle, WA: Community Psychiatric Clinic of Seattle, WA: http://www.cpcwa.org/cnslgjob.html; Tualatin Valley Centers, http://www.tvcenters.org/hr.html; Loma Linda University Medical Center, Community Medical Center, and Children's Hospital, http://www.llu.edu/hrm/bmcnurse.html; NationJob.com, http://www.nationjob.com/.

◄ **Drug Loitering** Drug loitering occurs when individuals take public action, such as selling drugs from a street corner, which indicates the intent to engage in illegal drug activity. *Do police need to catch drug loiterers with drugs or paraphernalia in order to successfully prosecute them?*

Drug- and Alcohol-Related Crimes **CHAPTER 14** **495**

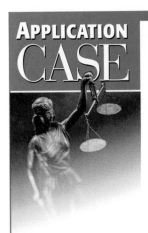

Addiction as a Defense

CRIMINAL LAW *Online*

Drug Court

Read "Drug Court, Part 1: A Court of Hope" available through the link at **cl.glencoe.com**.
Read this article and discuss your feelings about the future of drug courts. How do they operate differently from regular criminal courts? Do they seem to work? Why or why not?

Robinson v. California

In *Robinson*, the defendant was convicted of being a drug addict in violation of a municipal ordinance of the City of Los Angeles. The Court overturned the Los Angeles ordinance that made it a criminal offense for a person "to be addicted to the use of narcotics." It reversed the conviction, holding that a person cannot be punished criminally simply for having the status of drug addict. The Court noted that addiction is a "status" and not an "act," and that to punish an individual for the mere status was to inflict cruel and unusual punishment in violation of the Eighth and Fourteenth Amendments. However, the Court did emphasize that states were free to punish such crimes as the sale, purchase, or possession of narcotics.

On the other hand, an addict can be convicted for possession of a controlled substance, and addiction to drugs is not a defense to the possessory offenses or delivery offenses. In *United States v. Moore*, the U. S. Court of Appeals affirmed a heroin addict's conviction for possession of heroin noting that "particular nature of the problem of the heroin traffic makes certain policies necessary that should not be weakened by the creation of this defense."

Critical Thinking Do you think drug addicts should be allowed an addiction defense? Why or why not?

SOURCE: *Robinson v. California*, 370 U.S. 660 (1962); *United States v. Moore*, 486 F.2d 1139 (D.C. Cir. 1973).

---

unusual punishment clause of the Eighth Amendment to the Constitution of the United States, applicable to the states through the due process clause of the Fourteenth Amendment. This was the holding in the Supreme Court case of *Robinson v. California*. (See Application Case.)

CRIMINAL LAW *Online*

Check your answers at **cl.glencoe.com**.

Self Check

1. Why does possession with intent to deliver need more proof than mere possession?
2. How can police officers determine if people are drug loitering, or just loitering?

14.4 Alcohol Legislation and Offenses

Alcohol was widely used in early America; indeed, the per capita consumption has been estimated at five times that of today.[19] Until the eighteenth century, there were no attempts to prohibit the manufacture, sale, or consumption of alcohol, although there were regulatory fines, excise taxes, and license fees.

Temperance and Prohibition

Toward the end of the eighteenth century, a temperance movement began to develop, and during the early nineteenth century, religious leaders such as Cotton Mather and John Wesley galvanized public opinion against alcohol. The first prohibition law in America went into effect in 1843 in the territory of Oregon (it was repealed five years later), and in 1846, Maine became the first state to enact a prohibition statute. By 1855, twelve other states had followed suit. By the end of the Civil War, however, nine of these states had either repealed their laws or had them ruled unconstitutional. At the federal level, legislation continued to be regulatory in nature. In 1862, a federal tax on liquor and beer of 20 cents per gallon was imposed. The tax increased to $2 per gallon by 1868, but was decreased to 50 cents per gallon in 1869. [20]

With the end of the Civil War, the temperance movement gained momentum, and women assumed a prominent role with the founding of the Women's Christian Temperance Union (WCTU) in 1874. The National Prohibition Party was formed in 1869 and fielded its first presidential candidate in 1872. The Anti-Saloon League, formed in 1893, joined its efforts to the prohibition movement. In the late nineteenth century, there was a second wave of state prohibition laws. Kansas became the first state to incorporate prohibition into its constitution in 1880. By 1917, 13 states were totally dry, and another 13 had local option or other limited prohibition laws.[21]

With the entry of the United States into World War I, prohibitionists raised additional arguments that a ban on alcohol would stop the waste of grain and molasses and make workers more productive. In December 1917, Congress approved the Eighteenth Amendment prohibiting the manufacture, sale, and transportation of alcohol. Eleven months later, the amendment was ratified, and in

Drinking and Liability

Before 1983, Texas common law did not hold alcohol sellers or servers liable for harm their drunken customers caused to other people. Then, in 1983 and 1984, Texas instituted strict dram shop liability laws that significantly affected alcohol servers' practices. After a 1983 liability case was filed (and eventually proved successful), there were 6.5 percent fewer single-vehicle nighttime crashes. After a 1984 case was filed, the incidence of such crashes decreased by another 5.3 percent.

SOURCE: Alcohol-Related Injuries and Violence Program (ARIV), "Literature Summary on Dram Shop Liability Laws," http://www.tf.org/tf/alcohol/ariv/dram4.html. ARIV is a program of the Trauma Foundation at San Francisco General Hospital.

dram shop acts Legislative acts that impose strict liability upon the seller of intoxicating beverages when the sale results in harm to a third party's person, property, or means of support.

1919, Congress passed the Volstead Act, which contained the enforcement procedures needed to implement prohibition.

Prohibition was in part a response to high levels of alcohol production and consumption and to social problems related to drinking and alcoholism. However, in practice, "enforcement proved to be a national scandal that gave rise to bootleggers and gang wars, police corruption, "speakeasies," and general disrespect for law and order."[22]

With the outbreak of the Great Depression, a movement to repeal the Eighteenth Amendment gained strength, and in 1933, Congress passed the Twenty-First Amendment, repealing prohibition. Congress also established the Federal Alcohol Control Administration (FACA) to regulate the alcoholic beverage industry.

Changing Views on Alcohol Use and Abuse

Today FACA is an agency of the Department of the Treasury, responsible for enforcing laws concerning liquor taxes and penalties for unauthorized commerce in alcohol.[23] In addition, many states have passed **dram shop acts**, which hold alcohol servers responsible for harm that intoxicated or underage patrons cause to other people.[24] In American culture during the twentieth century, the concept of alcoholism gradually changed to focus on treatment and on the view that "the fault is in the man not the bottle," in that alcoholism afflicted individuals based on vulnerability, "genetic, biochemical, psychological, or social/cultural."

A great number of arrests were made, however, for alcohol-related offenses. According to Bureau of Justice data for 1999, 1,511,300 persons were arrested for drunk driving, 656,100 were arrested for drunkenness, and 657,900 were arrested for other liquor law violations, for a total of more than 2 million arrests for violating laws regulating alcohol use. Drug or alcohol treatment was a sentence condition for 41 percent of adults on probation, and 32 percent of adults on probation were subject to mandatory drug testing.

Alcohol is often associated with a wide range of criminal offenses. One of the most common is the offense of driving under the influence. Prior to 1980, drunk driving was seen not as a serious criminal problem, but as a behavior associated with drinking problems. In 1980, drunk driving was responsible for 28,000 fatalities and hundreds of thousands of injuries, raising awareness of the seriousness of drunk driving. As a result, federal and state legislatures have enacted laws with stiffer penalties.

Drunk Driving Offense
(Driving Under the Influence)

The **offense of drunk driving** is essentially the same in most states. Generally the offense is referred to as DWI (driving while intoxicated), DUI (driving under the influence, of alcohol or drugs), DWAI (driving while ability is impaired), or DUBAL (driving with an unlawful blood alcohol level). Some states distinguish between intoxication and impairment.

offense of drunk driving
The offense of driving while drunk, known as DWI, DUI, DWAI, or DUBAL.

Intoxication   Intoxication occurs when the accused has "consumed enough so that his physical and mental control are markedly diminished or that his judgment and ability to operate a motor vehicle are adversely affected to a substantial degree." A driver is impaired "after the consumption of sufficient alcohol to lessen or impair physical and mental control to any significant degree."

BAC Levels   The BAC (blood alcohol content) level that determines when a driver is legally drunk varies from state to state. In most jurisdictions, the BAC content is specified by statute to be 0.10 percent, or above, although in some, it is 0.08 percent or above. In addition, some states, such as Maine, have lowered the legal BAC level to .05 percent for drivers who were previously convicted of a DUI offense.

Finally, states have specifically lowered the BAC for drivers of commercial vehicles. For instance, the driver of a commercial vehicle in New York would be convicted of driving while intoxicated if he or she has a BAC of .04 or more. Meanwhile, the federal government is strongly urging states to lower their BAC from .10 to .08 percent, and it has threatened to withhold federal funding from those states that fail to comply. (See Figure 14–2 on page 500 to see how each state defines the allowable BAC level.)

Elements of a DUI Offense   The elements of the drunk driving offense are similar in every jurisdiction. Those elements are:

- The defendant operated a motor vehicle upon a roadway within the jurisdiction of the court.
- The operation occurred while the defendant was either under the influence of an intoxicant, narcotic, or hallucinogenic to the extent that his or her normal faculties were impaired, or

BAC Levels

Research indicates the ability to drive is affected with BAC levels as low as .02. Moreover, drivers with BAC levels between .02 and .04 have twice the risk of being in a fatal crash than sober drivers do.

FIGURE 14–2

Blood Alcohol Concentration Levels Allowed in Each State

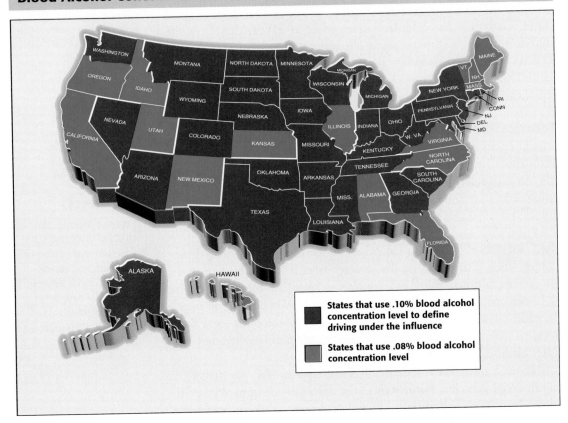

States that use .10% blood alcohol concentration level to define driving under the influence

States that use .08% blood alcohol concentration level

- The operation occurred while the defendant was driving with a blood or breath alcohol concentration above a prohibited level.

Operation, the first element of a DUI offense, is rarely at issue because operation is generally easy to establish. The arresting officer usually observes the operation. The arrest may have resulted from a sobriety checkpoint or an automobile accident that resulted in police intervention. In addition, the accused may have admitted operating the motor vehicle. Finally, a private citizen may have observed the incident and given consistent testimony.

DUI Traffic Stops The arresting officer's observations of the erratic operation of the vehicle or the behavior of a driver will often lead to a stop for investigation DUI/DWI. These observations serve as evidence of being under the influence, the second element of a DUI/DWI offense. After the stop, the officer will take note of the physical appearance of the driver to determine whether he or she may be intoxicated. For example, bloodshot or watery eyes, the smell of alcohol, and slurred speech are indicative of driving under the influence. In addition, during the investigation, the officer will ask the driver questions and observe the driver's demeanor.

If the officer is still suspicious, he or she will administer a series of field sobriety tests (FSTs). These consist of physical exercises, such as walking toe to heel and walking a straight line, and verbal exercises, such as counting backwards. All of the officer's observations may confirm his or her suspicion that the suspect is under the influence. This determination provides the constitutional foundation for a breath, blood, or urine test to determine the driver's BAC. The officer's right to demand that the suspect submit to such tests depends upon a valid Fourth Amendment justification for the search and seizure related to the activity.

DUI Statutes   DUI/DWI statutes in most states provide that a driver who is arrested for driving under the influence must submit to a blood, breath, or urine test to determine the blood alcohol level. Most states base this provision on the theory that by obtaining the privilege of driving, the driver can be "deemed to have given consent" to a chemical test of the level of alcohol when arrested for DUI.[25] Every state has laws specifying penalties for refusal to submit to a forensic test that detects the presence of a controlled substance. These include a fine and imprisonment, if convicted of DUI, and automatic suspension of driving privileges for one year.[26]

Variance in State Laws   The states vary greatly with respect to the specific test that is required and whether to provide an accused with his or her choice of tests. Some states give an accused the right to refuse to take a test for alcohol. Also, many states allow for an inference to be drawn against the accused if he or she refuses to submit to the required test. In these states, the jury can be told to draw that negative inference from the driver's refusal to be tested. Hence, if the driver refuses to submit to the test, he or she will be "presumed" to have been driving under the influence.

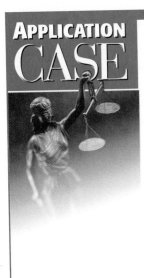
Schmerber v. California

In *Schmerber v. California* (1966), the defendant had been driving an automobile involved in an accident and was taken to the hospital for treatment of his injuries. A police officer arrested him while he was in the hospital and directed a physician to draw blood from the defendant to determine the level of alcohol in his blood. The evidence of the result of this blood test was admitted against Schmerber at his trial for DUI. He was convicted, but appealed to the Supreme Court of the United States, claiming that the removal of the blood from him without his permission violated his constitutional rights. Specifically, he argued that his right to due process, his privilege against self-incrimination, his right to counsel, and his right to be free from unreasonable search and seizure were all violated. The Court rejected all of these claims and affirmed Schmerber's conviction.

Critical Thinking Should a person have the right to refuse a blood or breath test without being presumed guilty? Why or why not?

SOURCE: *Schmerber v. California*, 384 U.S. 757 (1966).

Intoxication and Alcoholism as Defenses

Alcohol and drugs have been linked to violent crimes, including murder, rape, robbery, and domestic violence. They also play a role in other criminal offenses such as child abuse and neglect cases. In criminal law, voluntary intoxication is no defense against crimes of general intent, but may operate to disprove the existence of the *mens rea* necessary for crimes of specific intent.

For instance, an individual who is accused of larceny (a crime requiring specific intent) can use intoxication as a defense, arguing that intoxication rendered him or her unable to form the necessary intent. It should be noted, however, that although assault is a specific intent crime, intoxication may not be a defense to assault. Under the rationale that many assaults occur as a result of intoxication or drunkenness, some states have held that voluntary intoxication is not a defense to assault.

Since general intent crimes such as trespass do not require specific intent but can be committed recklessly or negligently, intoxication is not usually a defense to them. In addition, since *mens rea* is not an element of strict liability crimes, intoxication is not a defense to them. Hence, intoxication is not a defense to statutory rape or serving alcohol to a minor.

On the other hand, intoxication may be a mitigating factor reducing punishment for certain crimes. For instance, an individual accused of committing murder while intoxicated could not be convicted of murder with premeditation and deliberation, because his or her ability to deliberate may have been negated by the intoxication. In such cases, the defendant's criminal responsibility is diminished, though not eliminated, and the punishment will correspondingly be less serious. Involuntary intoxication, (e.g., being forced to ingest an intoxicating substance) will render an actor's conduct involuntary and thereby allow him or her to avoid criminal liability.

There are several ways in which an alcoholic's intoxication might be relevant to his or her criminal liability. The state of voluntary intoxication might be offered to show that the alcoholic defendant was so drunk that he or she was physically incapable of the crime charged. It could also demonstrate an absence of voluntary conduct. Finally, it might negate the mental state required for the crime. This subject is discussed in more detail in Chapter 7.

The question of whether alcoholics may be punished for certain acts attributable to their disease is often discussed in terms of the constitutional prohibition against cruel and unusual punishment as it applies to the voluntary act requirement. The foremost case on this issue is *Robinson v. California*, discussed earlier, in which the Supreme Court held that a minimal requirement of some voluntary behavior was constitutionally necessary as a basis for criminal liability. *Robinson*'s prohibition against prosecution for status crimes was soon extended to the prosecution of alcoholics. (See Application Case on page 496.)

Nevertheless, in 1968, in *Powell v. Texas*,[27] the U.S. Supreme Court refused to extend the holding of *Robinson* to public intoxication. The defendant, Powell, had been convicted of public intoxication. His attorneys, relying on the *Robinson* rationale, argued that Powell was afflicted with the disease of alcoholism, that his appearance in public while drunk was not of his own volition, and that to convict and punish him for that conduct would be cruel and unusual punishment in violation of the Eighth and Fourteenth Amendments.

A majority of the justices assented to the proposition that irresistible conduct caused by a condition not in itself punishable could

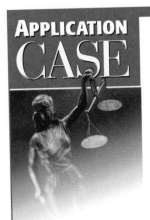

Driver v. Hinnant

In *Driver v. Hinnant*, the defendant appealed his most recent of (at least) two hundred convictions for public intoxication. The fourth circuit court agreed that he was a chronic alcoholic and classified alcoholism as a disease. Relying on a liberal interpretation of *Robinson v. California*, the court held that it was constitutionally prevented from convicting the defendant for behavior that was "compulsive as symptomatic of the disease." The court stated that "[t]he alcoholic's presence in public is not his act for he did not will it."

Critical Thinking Should alcoholism be allowed as a defense against certain crimes? Why or why not?

SOURCE: *Driver v. Hinnant*, 356 F.2d 761, 763 (4th Cir. 1966).

not constitutionally be subjected to criminal sanctions. However, only four of those Justices believed that the defendant actually suffered from the disease of alcoholism to such a degree as to be incapable of controlling his conduct. Therefore, Powell's conviction was permitted to stand, and the impact of the *Robinson* decision has since remained limited.

While alcoholics, like drug addicts, cannot be punished for their condition, they can legally be punished for appearing in public while they are in an intoxicated condition. Many local municipalities have ordinances prohibiting public drunkenness. However, as illustrated in the case *State ex rel. Harper v. Zegeer* (see Application Case on page 505), some states have opted to allow alcoholism as a defense to public intoxication charges under their own constitutions, despite the federal Court's decision in *Powell*.

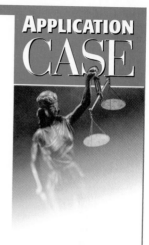
State ex rel. Harper v. Zegeer

An example of how the disease of alcoholism serves as a defense to the crime of public intoxication is illustrated by the case of *State ex rel. Harper v. Zegeer*. The defendant was arrested and incarcerated for public intoxication. He petitioned by *habeas corpus* to test the constitutionality of jailing chronic alcoholics who are intoxicated in public.

The Supreme Court of Appeals of West Virginia held that criminal punishment of chronic alcoholics for public intoxication violated the state constitutional prohibition against cruel and unusual punishment. The court in *Harper* agreed with medical experts and professional groups, including the World Health Organization, that alcoholism is a disease. The court reasoned that on the evidence presented, the defendant was no more able to make a free choice as to when or how much he would drink than a person would be who is forced to drink under threat of physical violence.

The *Harper* court specifically opposed two prevalent schools of thought that have been endorsed by other courts to uphold the convictions of alcoholics for public intoxication:

1. That drinking is a voluntary act
2. If alcoholism is allowed to be a defense to public intoxication charges, it might become a defense to other crimes.

The *Harper* court ruled that to hold that alcoholics can control their drinking and appearances in public contradicts all recognized medical evidence about alcoholics' overwhelming compulsion to drink. Further, alcoholism is only a defense to those acts which are compulsive and symptomatic of the disease, so the rationale that it will extend as a defense to other crimes is unfounded.

Public Intoxication

Critical Thinking Do you agree with the decision of the *Harper* court? Why or why not?

SOURCE: *State ex rel. Harper v. Zegeer*, 296 S.E.2d 873 (W. Va. 1982).

Self Check

1. What are some legal actions that can be taken against a drunk driver?
2. When can alcohol be used as a defense? When is it not an acceptable defense?

CRIMINAL LAW *Online*
Check your answers at
cl.glencoe.com.

Drug- and Alcohol-Related Crimes

SUMMARY BY CHAPTER OBJECTIVES

1. Identify the five major categories of controlled substances.

Classifications of controlled substances ordinarily fall into the following five categories:

- Narcotics: Opiates such as heroin, morphine, and cocaine; and non-opiate synthetics such as Demerol and Methadone
- Stimulants: Cocaine, amphetamine, methamphetamine, and others
- Depressants: Barbiturates and tranquilizers
- Cannabis: Marijuana and hashish
- Hallucinogens: Includes LSD, mescaline, and peyote.

2. State the purposes and effect of the Uniform Controlled Substances Act.

The Uniform Act was drafted to achieve uniformity between the drug laws of the several states and those of the federal government. It forbids the manufacture, delivery, possession, storage, or sale of controlled substances. It has five schedules of controlled substances, graded according to their potential for abuse, relative physical danger to the abuser, and degree of accepted medical use.

3. Recognize and describe the difference between actual and constructive possession of a controlled substance.

Actual possession is when the controlled substance is on the defendant's person, or within an area of his or her immediate control and reach. It may also occur when the controlled substance is within a container that the defendant may be carrying or has within his or her reach. Constructive possession occurs when illegal drugs are in a place immediately accessible to the accused and are subject to his or her dominion and control.

4. State the difference between the offense of possession versus the offense of possession with the intent to deliver.

In contrast to crimes of mere possession of controlled substances, possession with the intent to deliver is treated as a felony under both federal and state statutes. Due to the stiffer penalties imposed for possession with intent to deliver, many states forbid the inference of intent to deliver based on mere possession of controlled substances. Convictions for possession with the intent to deliver are highly fact-specific, and require substantial corroborating evidence in addition to the mere fact of possession.

5. Define the drug offenses of delivery, drug conspiracy, drug loitering, and possession of drug paraphernalia.

Delivery of controlled substances is defined as the voluntary transfer of a controlled substance from one person to another person. Drug loitering crimes require some action taken in public that manifests the intent to engage in illegal drug activity. Possession of drug paraphernalia is the possession of any equipment, product, or material of any kind that is primarily intended or designed for use with a controlled substance. Drug conspiracies are agreements between two or more persons that form a shared intent to manufacture and/or distribute drugs.

6. Understand when drug addiction is and is not a defense to drug offenses.

Drug addiction is a defense only against prosecution for the offense of being a drug user. On the other hand, an addict can be convicted for possession of a controlled substance, and addiction to the drug is not a defense to the possessory offenses or delivery offenses.

7. State the elements of driving under the influence.

The elements of DUI are:

- Operation of a motor vehicle on a public trafficway
- When such operation occurs while the driver is under the influence of any alcoholic beverage or drug

8. Define the extent to which alcoholism can be a defense in a criminal case.

Voluntary intoxication is no defense against crimes of general intent, but may operate to disprove the existence of *mens rea* for crimes of specific intent. Involuntary intoxication will render an actor's conduct involuntary and thereby allow him to avoid criminal liability.

KEY TERMS

controlled substances, page 474
psychoactive drugs, page 474
actual possession, page 484
constructive possession, page 484

possession with intent to deliver, page 487
delivery of a controlled substance, page 490
simulated controlled substance, page 490
drug conspiracy, page 490

drug loitering, page 490
drug transportation, page 490
drug paraphernalia, page 493
dram shop acts, page 498
offense of drunk driving, page 499

Can a police officer draw blood from an unconscious suspect to check for alcohol intoxication?
Find it on page 502.

QUESTIONS FOR REVIEW

1. Explain the differences between marijuana and hallucinogens.
2. Explain the Supreme Court's findings on the use of peyote in traditional Native American religious ceremonies.
3. Outline the history and outcome of the "War on Drugs."
4. What does the Uniform Controlled Substances Act forbid? Give at least five examples.
5. What is a simulated controlled substance? Is possession of this a crime?
6. What elements are required to convict a person of cultivating marijuana?
7. Define drug paraphernalia, and provide three examples.
8. What is narcotics addiction? Is it legal or illegal? What Amendment is relevant to this discussion, and why?
9. What procedures does an officer use after pulling over a suspect whom he or she believes is driving drunk?
10. What are dram shop acts?

PROBLEM-SOLVING EXERCISES

1. **Possession and Intent to Deliver** Due to the stiffer felony penalties imposed for possession with the intent to deliver versus mere possession, many states forbid prosecutors from assuming that there is an intent to deliver because of the defendant's mere possession of a controlled substance. If a suspected drug dealer is arrested with nine baggies of marijuana in his possession, a marijuana pipe, a bag of marijuana seeds, but only $20 in cash on his person, what are the chances that he could be charged with possession with the intent to deliver? Why?

2. **Drug Loitering** A police officer on patrol comes upon a group of six youths one night. They are gathered on a corner in a high-crime area known for its drug dealing and gang activities. The officer observes the youths for about ten minutes and sees a number of other persons approach the group, seeming to engage in some transactions involving the exchange of money for something in bags. Describe what other evidence, if any, the officer would need in order to arrest the youths for drug loitering.

3. **Probation and DUI** A defendant who is on probation for a drug-related offense is required to refrain from drug use during his probationary period. He is required to submit to a urine test once a month to determine whether he has used drugs within the last 30 days. During a casual conversation, prior to the test, the defendant tells his probation officer that he drove his car to the probation office. The test revealed traces of a controlled substance in the defendant's blood stream. Upon questioning by the probation officer, the defendant admitted to using crack cocaine a few hours prior to the visit.
   a) Should the defendant be charged with violating his probation? Why or why not?
   b) Should he be charged with driving under the influence? Why or why not?

WORKPLACE APPLICATIONS

1. **Peyote in Religious Ceremonies** As a state parole officer, you staunchly support your state's drug control laws. Any parolees on your caseload that test positive for any controlled dangerous substance is promptly taken into custody and set for a parole revocation hearing. Harold Running Bull, a Native American, has recently been assigned to you. His first urine sample tests positive for the presence of the hallucinogen peyote. You call the authorities and have Running Bull arrested when he reports to your office. As the police are taking him away, Running Bull shouts that he only uses peyote as part of his religious ceremonies. Answer the following questions:
   a) Do you investigate this claim? Why or why not?
   b) Do you ask the police to release him until you investigate the claim? Why or why not?
   c) Do you remain silent and let the police take him away? Why or why not?
   d) What are the ramifications if his assertions are correct?

2. **Pregnancy and Addiction** You are a nurse working at a county hospital, and in recent years you have noticed a surge in babies born with drug addictions, especially crack addiction. Your hospital is considering taking legal action against women who deliver babies born with drug or alcohol addiction, as well as the host of neurological and physical disorders that most addicted babies have. Answer the following questions:
   a) Should a pregnant woman who smoked crack cocaine hours before giving birth, be charged with delivery of narcotics to a newborn baby via the umbilical cord?
   b) Does the fact that the drug was taken five hours before birth constitute delivery, if she could not predict the exact time of birth enough to know that the drug would be delivered to the child?
   c) What other drug charges and child abuse charges could be used in such instances? What about any other charges?
   d) To what authorities could you report these crimes?

3. **Drug Transportation** You are a customs agent. During a routine search of a passenger's luggage, you recover a quantity of cocaine inside a small sealed package. The passenger tells the agent that the cocaine is not his. You have heard this before, but the passenger is adamant that he is equally shocked as you are and has never seen the package before in his life.
   a) Should the passenger be arrested immediately? What questions could you ask first?
   b) What issues may arise if the passenger was doing someone a favor by taking the package to a relative or friend?

INTERNET APPLICATIONS

1. **Medical Marijuana** Over the past several years, different states have legalized medical marijuana. The initiatives allow the use of marijuana for medical purposes when a licensed physician has found the use of marijuana to be medically necessary and recommends its use for the treatment of various chronic or long-term illnesses. In May 2001, the U.S. Supreme Court struck down this right and made any use of marijuana illegal. Several articles that cover this ongoing debate can be found through a link at **cl.glencoe.com**. When you are done, answer the following questions:
   a) What was the Court's finding, and how was it determined?
   b) How have those who used marijuana for medical reasons reacted to this finding?
   c) What is your personal opinion of this judgment, and why?

2. **DUI/DWI** You can learn more about criminal offenses caused by drugs and alcohol and the number of DUI/DWI arrests and fatalities in various states by visiting the Department of Justice web site by clicking the link at **cl.glencoe.com**. When you are done, answer the following questions:
   a) Do you think that alcohol plays a significant role in assaults and less so in rape, robbery, and burglary?
   b) Have the number of DUI/DWI fatalities decreased since new laws have been passed lowering the BAC?

ETHICS ISSUES

1. **Probation and Drug Use** You are a county probation officer, disturbed by the fact that more and more people on your caseload are on probation for drug offenses. Although you personally believe that marijuana is a harmless recreational drug, it continues to be outlawed in your state and can bring substantial terms in the county jail. One day, a probationer reports to your office. Up until now, he has been a model probationer: He is employed and has paid all of his fines. Today, however, he has very bloodshot eyes and smells like marijuana. It is at your discretion whether or not to request a urine sample from him. If he tests positive, he can be sent to jail. If you fail to report your observations about his physical appearance when he arrived at your office, you can be fired. The probationer reveals to you that he "may have smoked a little 'something'" because he was depressed about the death of this mother. He begs you not to ask for a urine sample because he has only one month remaining on probation.
   a) What are your options at this time? What should you do?
   b) How can you show him that you are serious about him committing no more offenses?
   c) Does this drug use seem like it will be a growing problem, or that it will end here?

2. **Medical Marijuana** You are a doctor who lives in a state where medical mari-

juana has been made legal, but a recent Supreme Court decision has declared your state's measure invalid. Nonetheless, the practice of prescribing medical marijuana has continued in your state as if nothing has happened. Several of your terminally ill patients are asking you to continue to prescribe it because it relieves their pain.

a) What decision will you make, and why?

b) What are the legal repercussions when people continue to follow a state measure that has been declared invalid at a federal level?

ENDNOTES

1 *Stedman's Medical Dictionary*, 23rd edition. Baltimore: William and Wilkins, p. 1164.

2 Duke, Steven B., & Albert C. Gross, *America's Longest War: Rethinking Our Tragic Crusade Against Drugs*. New York: G. P. Putnam's Sons, 1993, pp. 15–16.

3 Inciardi, pg. 3.

4 Courtright, Terry, & Pellens, Inciardi 1986, cited in Inciardi 1999, p. 3.

5 Benjamin, Daniel K., & Roger LeRoy Miller. *Undoing Drugs: Beyond Legalization*. New York: Basic Books, 1991, p. 254.

6 Benjamin & Miller, pp. 255–256. In 1903, the Coca-Cola Company began using caffeine as the main ingredient in its product.

7 Morgan, Terry, & Pellens, cited in Inciardi, p. 3.

8 Benjamin & Miller, pp. 93–94; *Webb v. United States*. (Source needs to be checked.)

9 Inciardi, p. 4.

10 Uniform Controlled Substances Act, 9 U.L.A. (1979).

11 Bureau of Justice data is available at www.usdoj.gov/dea/stats/overview.htm.

12 Inciardi, p. 16.

13 Erich Goode, cited in Inciardi, pp. 112–113.

14 Inciardi, pp. 6–7.

15 John T. Bannon, Jr., The Legality of the Religious Use of Peyote by the Native American Church: A Commentary on the Free Exercise, Equal Protection, and Establishment Issues Raised by the Peyote Way Church of God Case, 22 Am. Indian L. Rev. 475, 476 (1998).

16 *Employment Division, Department of Human Resources of Oregon v. Smith*, 494 U.S. 872 (1990).

17 Autumn Gray, Effects of the American Indian Religious Freedom Act Amendment on Criminal Law: Will Peyotism Eat Away at the Controlled Substances Act?, 22 *Am. J. Crim. L.* 769 (1995).

18 See *People v. Aguilar*, 35 Cal. Rptr. 516, 519 (Cal. Ct. App. 1964); more recently this principle was reaffirmed in *Thomas v. United States*, 540 A.2d 183, 196–97 (D.C. 1994) (citing *Aguilar*).

19 Benjamin and Miller, n5. p. 195.

20 Schaffer Library of Drug Policy, http://www.drug library.org/schaffer/LIBRARY/studies/nc/nc2a. htm. Retrieved from the World Wide Web Feb. 17, 2001.

21 Buenker, John D., "Prohibition and the Volstead Act," pp. 451–452 in Angela M. Howard and Frances M. Kavenik, *Handbook of American Women's History*, 2nd edition. Thousand Oaks, CA: Sage, 2000, p. 451.

22 Buenker, p. 452.

23 Shaffer Library of Drug Policy, www.druglibrary.org/schaffer/LIBRARY.

24 Alcohol-Related Injuries and Violence Program, "Literature Summaries on Dram Shop Liability Laws," http://www.tf.org/tf/alcohol/ariv/ dram4.html. Retrieved from the World Wide Web Feb. 17, 2001.

25 See, e.g., *People v. Selby*, 608 N.E.2d 961, 963 (Ill. App. Ct. 1993), relying upon what is now Ill. Comp. Stat. Ch. 625 § 5/11–501.1 (1999).

26 See, e.g., Cal. Vehicle Code § 23157(a)(1)(D) (1999); N.J. Stat. Ann. § 39:4–50.4a (1999).

27 *Powell v. Texas*, 392 U.S. 514, 517 (1968).

Chapter Objectives

After reading this chapter, you will be able to:

1. Recognize the difference between the offenses of bribery and commercial bribery.
2. Define the elements of perjury.
3. Define the offense of "obstruction of justice" and recognize the scope of crimes it covers.
4. Describe the crime of resisting arrest.
5. Recognize the offense of compounding a felony, and explain why it is different from the offense of misprision of a felony.
6. Define the elements of the crime of escape.
7. Recognize when constructive contempt takes place and how it differs from direct contempt.
8. Differentiate between the offenses and penalties for civil contempt and criminal contempt.

Chapter Outline

Is it legal to resist an unlawful arrest?

Chapter 15

Crimes Against the Administration of Justice

15.1 Crimes Against the Administration of Justice

This chapter covers two different types of offenses: 1) offenses that are committed by citizens who try to disrupt the legal system, and 2) offenses that are committed by those in positions of authority, such as government officials and law enforcement officers, who injure citizens by abusing their power. These offenses, also called crimes against the administration of justice, can also be defined as any offenses that hinder or prevent the effective operation of the criminal justice system, such as law enforcement, the civil and criminal court systems, and the corrections system.

At common law, the crimes of bribery, perjury, resisting arrest, and contempt of court were all recognized as offenses that threatened the administration of justice. Today, however, many of these crimes have been combined into the single crime of obstruction of justice. **Obstruction of justice** is the act by which one or more persons attempt to or actually prevent the execution of a lawful process. Crimes under this modern definition include:

obstruction of justice
The act by which one or more persons attempt to or actually prevent the execution of a lawful process

- Bribery and the attempt or conspiracy to commit bribery or extortion. An example of bribery would be paying off a police officer so as not to be arrested. An example of extortion would be threatening to accuse someone of a crime or to file criminal charges in exchange for money.
- Perjury, false testimony, and interfering with a law enforcement officer in the performance of his or her official duties. An example of this would be lying under oath.
- Tampering with the jury process, such as by threatening jurors, attempting to harm jurors, or actually causing harm to them or to their families.
- Suppressing or refusing to produce evidence relevant to a grand jury investigation, such as by destroying papers or other evidence after receiving notice of such an investigation.

In addition, these crimes must find a particular form of intent. The intent element of an obstruction of justice offense is referred to as the nexus requirement. The term nexus means a link or relationship; in legal terms, it refers to the way in which a defendant's obstruction of justice must have a relationship with the legal proceedings against him or her in order to show intent. In other words, the act must have an effect on interfering with the due administration of justice.[1]

Self Check

Which do you think are more serious: crimes that are committed by citizens who try to disrupt the legal system or crimes that are committed by those in positions of authority? Why?

CRIMINAL LAW *Online*

Check your answers at cl.glencoe.com.

15.2 Bribery

For the past 700 years in England and later in the United States, extortion was the most common public offense, but in recent years bribery prosecutions have become more prevalent. There is some overlap between the nature of the two offenses, for the principles that underlie extortion are similar to those of bribery.[2] Under common law, **bribery** was voluntarily giving or receiving anything of value as unlawful payment for the commission of an official act. In other words, if a private citizen who will be a defendant in an upcoming trial pays a prosecutor something of value, both are guilty of bribery.

According to the first English bribery statute in 1384, judges may not take "robe, fee, pension, girt, nor reward of any but the King, except reward of meat and drink, which shall be no great value."[3] Later, when the founders of the United States wrote the U.S. Constitution, they determined that bribery, along with treason, constituted serious grounds for the impeachment of a president or any civil officer of the United States.

bribery The voluntary giving or receiving of anything of value as unlawful payment for the commission of an official act.

Modern Bribery

Today, bribery exists in many forms. In general, the exploitation of public power for personal gain defines the modern concept of bribery. Modern statutes have extended the crime of bribery to include the party who offers the bribe, as well as the party who receives the bribe. For example, a prosecutor could commit bribery by receiving compensation in return for not filing or pressing charges, and the defendant who has paid the bribe is also guilty.

Modern statutes are balanced to fulfill their aim of controlling undue influence while avoiding a "chilling" or deterring effect on the right of private citizens to properly influence government action. An ideal bribery statute must distinguish between acts of undue influence, which constitute bribery, and appropriate acts that are intended to legally influence governmental action. In short, as the Supreme Court has stated, bribery laws should "deal with only the most blatant and specific attempts of those with money to influence governmental action."[4]

Some states have extended the crime of bribery to include people other than public officials, whose functions are nonetheless considered important to the public welfare. Such bribery is known as **quasi-bribery** because although it has the same essential effect as standard bribery, its recipients are private citizens. Officers of political conventions, officers or employees of public institutions, and representatives of labor organizations are considered positions important to the public that could be unduly influenced by quasi-bribery.

Under modern law, bribery forbids not just the results of influencing a public official, but also the act itself, whether the attempt to bribe is successful or not. In addition, the Model Penal Code forbids:

- Law enforcement and public officials to receive gifts from individuals subject to their jurisdiction
- A public servant who has the authority and discretion over contracts or transactions to accept or solicit gifts from any person "known to be interested or likely to become interested" in such contract or transaction[5]

quasi-bribery An extension of the crime of bribery, to include people other than public officials whose functions are considered important to the public.

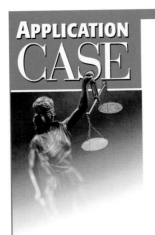

APPLICATION CASE

Bribery

Florida v. Saad

In *Florida v. Saad* (1983), the defendant attempted to deliver $1,000 each to two police officers to secure the return of $20,700 in cash, which had been taken from him in the course of a prior arrest. The defendant was charged with bribery. The trial judge granted a motion to dismiss the bribery charges on the grounds that the initial seizure had been unlawful and that the defendant was entitled to his $20,700 money in any case. An appeals court reversed this decision and found that the defendant was still guilty of bribery for unlawfully offering money to the police officers, regardless of whether he was entitled to have his money returned to him. The court stated, "In our system at least, the end does not justify the means. The effectuation of Saad's intent to get his money by short-circuiting and subverting that system may, and must, be held accountable to the criminal law."

Critical Thinking Do you agree with Saad's conviction for bribery? Why or why not?

SOURCE: *Florida v. Saad*, 429 So.2d 757 (Fla. App. 1983).

Crimes Against the Community and Institutions

Under the MPC, it is also forbidden to accept or agree to accept a gift from an individual in one's custody as a prisoner.

Sometimes bribery overlaps considerably with extortion. To compel or induce a person to provide a bribe, by means of instilling fear that criminal charges will be filed against that individual, is larceny by extortion.[6] In other words, threatening a person into paying someone to avoid criminal charges is always a crime.

On the other hand, should the law prevent individuals from entering into voluntary private agreements to avoid criminal prosecution where no threats or coercive actions are made? Suppose that Tom assaults Paul, then offers Paul money not to be a complainant against him. Should the law prevent this type of agreement? There are two things to consider before answering this question. On one hand, recall what you learned in Chapter 4, that while the person assaulted is a victim, criminal prosecutions are brought on behalf of the people of the state. Hence, the decision whether to prosecute belongs to the prosecutor, not to the complainant.[7]

On the other hand, an agreement by which a plaintiff or victim agrees to drop charges, whether criminal or civil, in exchange for money does not constitute receiving a bribe. This is because the plaintiff of a civil suit and the victim of a crime are not government officials with special responsibilities relating to their trials. In addition, they are not being asked to lie, alter their testimony, or avoid appearing at an action or proceeding, all of which are criminal actions that are generally *not* considered the same as the act of dropping charges. A plaintiff in a civil suit need not consult a prosecutor because civil suits are actions between private parties. A victim of a crime cannot determine whether or not a prosecutor files charges, but his or her unwillingness to help in the prosecution can create enough of a deterrent to the prosecutor so that charges will not be filed.

Commercial Bribery

Commercial bribery is a statutory expansion of the crime of bribery. The types of bribery that you have just learned about pertain to officials and private citizens who can influence official action in a way that gives the briber better treatment than he or she deserves. In contrast, **commercial bribery** entails the giving, receiving, or soliciting of anything of value to influence an employee or professional in the performance of his or her duties. The purpose is usually to influence the employee to breach his or her duty to his or her employer in order to give some undeserved or inappropriate

commercial bribery The giving, receiving, or soliciting of anything of value to influence an employee or professional in the performance of his or her duties.

benefit or information to the briber. This crime often occurs when business is conducted through agents. Unlike the principal in an agreement, an agent may have no direct interest or benefit in the contract and may be tempted to transact side deals for payments that are known as *kickbacks*. In large commercial cities such as New York, one out of every seven dollars exchanging hands involves or hints of commercial bribery.[8]

The following Alaska statute is an example of a commercial bribery statute:

> A person commits the crime of commercial bribery if, knowing that another is subject to a duty described in AS 11.46.660(a) and with intent to influence the other to violate that duty, the person confers, offers to confer, or agrees to confer a benefit on the other.

> A person commits the crime of commercial bribe receiving if the person solicits, accepts, or agrees to accept a benefit with intent to violate a duty to which that person is subject as:

> - an agent or employee of another;
> - a trustee, guardian, or other fiduciary;
> - a lawyer, physician, accountant, appraiser, or other professional advisor;
> - an officer, director, partner, manager, or other participant in the direction of the affairs of an organization, or;
> - an arbitrator or other purportedly disinterested adjudicator or referee.[9]

There is a distinction in the business community between legal favors and bribery. Most businesses today will give campaign contributions, gratuities, and entertainment of some sort to an entity, with the hope of the recipient favoring them over others. This practice is acceptable. However, it becomes bribery when there is an agreement between the payer and the recipient that there will be a *quid pro quo* payoff; in other words, "contributions" become bribery when the briber expects "something for something."

A number of states have created statutes to address various problems connected with commercial bribery.[10] In addition, courts today examine acts of commercial bribery under the Sherman Act to determine whether commercial bribery can be a combination, a conspiracy, and another illegal action with a negative effect on the restraint of trade.[11] To have a *combination* or *conspiracy*, which you learned about in Chapter 12, there must be an agreement between two or more independent companies in a bribery scheme.[12] Such a conspiracy negatively affects free trade if the briber creates a monopoly through payoffs.[13]

Many contracts have some semblance of this practice, but the companies who conduct it are rarely prosecuted. Therefore, this practice occurs often and is usually undetected. Courts will, however, impose liability if it creates an unreasonable restraint on competition sparked by this unfair trade practice.

Self Check

1. What are some ways in which bribery is different from quasi-bribery?
2. Should commercial bribery carry different penalties than regular bribery or quasi-bribery? Why or why not?

Check your answers at cl.glencoe.com.

15.3 Perjury

Perjury is the criminal offense of making false statements under oath or affirmation. At common law, perjury was considered a willfully corrupt sworn statement that was:

- Made without sincere belief in its truth,
- Made in a judicial proceeding regarding a *material*, or important or substantive, matter.

perjury Making false statements under oath or affirmation.

Common law perjury had to be proven by the testimony of two witnesses. Since the two-witness rule has primarily been abandoned under modern law, most courts now require only one witness and independent corroboration, such as documents or other evidence that proves that the statement made was false. This helps prevent the problem of lying witnesses and being forced to decide solely upon one person's word against another's.

Proof of the element of intent in a perjury case requires proof that the witness believe that his or her given testimony is false. Juries are instructed to apply the objective standard to determine the witness's intent to commit perjury, then ask themselves, "Would a reasonable person believe that the witness believed that his or her testimony was false?" The prosecution carries the burden of proving this falsity beyond a reasonable doubt.

Materiality and Perjury

In the O.J. Simpson trial, Detective Mark Fuhrman was charged with perjury, following testimony in which he lied about having used racial epithets in the past. Some experts have said that even if his testimony had been a lie, it was not a "material" one. His perjury did not necessarily pertain to the defendant's guilt. The jury was not granted the opportunity to hear questions such as "Did you plant or manufacture any evidence in this case?"

SOURCE: "Perjury! The Charges and the Defenses," 36 *Duq. L. Rev.* 715, 728 (Summer 1998). *See also* Model Penal Code § 214.1 (2).

At common law, if a false statement did not take place in a judicial proceeding, it was considered a **false swearing**, which was only a misdemeanor. Modern statutes in some jurisdictions today, however, have broadened the offense of perjury so that a false swearing or statement made in *any* legal setting is perjury, even if it is not material and even though it is not presented in a judicial proceeding. Most jurisdictions, however, require that the matter be material. *Materiality* is a major aspect of perjury, and the concept of it rests on whether a witness's false testimony has a natural effect or tendency to influence, impede, or dissuade a jury from making the correct decision.

As a typical example of a modern statute, the federal perjury statute states:

Whoever:

- having taken an oath before a competent tribunal, officer, or person, in any case in which a law of the United States authorizes an oath to be administered, that he will testify, declare, depose, or certify truly, or that any written testimony, declaration, or certificate by him subscribed, is true, willfully and contrary to such oath states or subscribes any material matter which he does not believe to be true; or
- in any declaration, certificate, verification, or statement under penalty of perjury as permitted under section 1746 of title 28, USC, willfully subscribes as true any material matter which he does not believe to be true.[14]

Compare this with the Model Penal Code's definition of the felony of perjury. Under the MPC, a person commits perjury "if in any official proceeding he makes a false statement under oath or equivalent affirmation, or swears or affirms the truth of a statement previously made, when the statement is material and he does not

Myth	Fact
There are no real defenses against perjury. After all, you can't prove you haven't lied.	The literal truth of a statement stands as the ultimate defense to perjury.

believe it to be true."[15] Hence, an essential element of perjury is the belief in the accused's mind that the statement was false. Again, the statement must be material.

Subornation of Perjury

Subornation of perjury is the crime of procuring another person to make a false oath. At common law, anyone who procured the making of false statements or intentionally caused another to commit perjury could be charged with subornation of perjury. Proof of guilt required that the perjurer be convicted of perjury as well as the actor charged with subornation of perjury. It also required that the perjurer knew or should have known that his or her actions would be considered perjury.[16]

subornation of perjury
The crime of procuring another person to make a false oath.

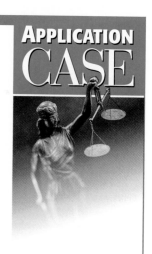

APPLICATION CASE

People v. Sharpe

In *People v. Sharpe* (1950), the defendant was convicted of perjury, conspiracy to commit perjury, and subornation of perjury. His criminal cohort Charles Barrett was convicted of subornation of perjury and conspiracy to commit perjury. The defendants were charged based upon testimony given by Sharpe and one William Gould before a grand jury. This testimony, which was false, stated that a local probation officer solicited and accepted bribes from Sharpe. The subornation of perjury charges against both defendants was based on the fact that they procured Gould to give false testimony. On appeal, the defendants argued that their convictions should have been reversed because the special prosecutor allegedly committed misconduct. They also argued that the trial court erred by sentencing them to consecutive rather than concurrent terms for the crimes of conspiracy to commit perjury and subornation of perjury.

The court of appeals found that even if the special prosecutor's actions rose to the level of misconduct, there was still substantial evidence to support the judgment against the appellants. The court also found that there was no merit to the appellants' contention that the trial court erred by sentencing them to consecutive rather than concurrent terms for their crimes. The convictions were affirmed.

Perjury

Critical Thinking Do you think the defendants deserved consecutive or concurrent sentences? Why?

SOURCE: *People v. Sharpe*, 96 Cal.App.2d 943 (Cal. Dst. Ct. App. 1950). Id. quoting *People v. Benenato*, 77 Cal.App.2d 350, 367 (Cal. Dst. Ct. App. 1946).

Proof of subornation of perjury requires three elements:

1. Perjury in fact
2. The perjured statements were procured by the accused
3. Proof that the suborner, who is the person who procures the perjury, knew or should have known that such oaths or testimony would be false

For example, federal law states:

"Whoever procures, another to commit any perjury is guilty of perjury, and shall be fined not more than $2,000 or imprisoned not more than five years, or both."[17]

Hence, not only will an accused be held liable for his or her knowingly false statement. If the accused causes another to make false statements under oath, he or she can be guilty of a distinct and separate crime of subornation of perjury. Under the Model Penal Code, it is a crime to make a false report to law enforcement with the purpose of implicating another. Under the Code, a person commits a misdemeanor when a person gives information about a crime to a law enforcement officer when they know it did not occur or pretends to provide such false information.[18]

CRIMINAL LAW *Online*

Check your answers at
cl.glencoe.com.

Self Check

1. Why do you think that the laws regarding false swearing have changed since common law?
2. What are the elements that are required for subornation of perjury?

15.4 Obstruction of Justice

Obstruction of justice, as mentioned earlier, is the act by which one or more persons attempt to prevent, or actually prevent, the execution of lawful process. As you have learned, the intent element is referred to as the *nexus* requirement. This essentially means that the act that is considered to obstruct justice must in some way have a relationship to the act of justice that the defendant is seeking to avoid.

An example of obstruction of justice occurs when an individual attempts to prevent a law enforcement official from arresting someone, whether that person is a relative, friend, or even a total stranger. Suppose that Renata pushes or physically gets in the way of a police officer who is attempting to handcuff her friend Jerome, who has committed a crime and is about to be placed under arrest. Since the officer is attempting to carry out his official duty by making an arrest, and since Renata is attempting to prevent him from doing so, Renata has committed obstruction of justice.

It should be noted, however, that if Jerome were resisting arrest, Jerome would not be charged with obstructing justice. This is because under the Model Penal Code, the obstruction of justice does not apply to those resisting arrest or flight from a crime.[19] This may seem like a contradiction: If a person is resisting arrest, isn't it logical to say that he or she is preventing an officer from carrying out official duties? The answer to that question will come later in this chapter, under the discussion of the crime of resisting arrest.

Other types of obstruction of justice include acts such as:

- Attempting to influence, intimidate, or impede any juror, witness, or officer in any court regarding the discharge of his duty
- The actual impeding or obstructing of the due administration of justice

When a statute addressing this subject encompasses more than interference with police officers and other such administrative officials, it is sometimes called *obstruction of governmental administration* or *obstructing governmental operations*.

Witness Tampering Laws

Laws that define obstruction of justice include provisions for misleading conduct with the intent to influence witness testimony, a crime that is commonly called **witness tampering**. Some of these laws were designed to address actions by organized criminals, who are known for attempting to intimidate or influence the outcome of trials and prosecutions.[20]

An example of such a law is the Victim and Witness Protection Act, which Congress enacted in 1982. This act addressed the variety of problems faced by victims and witnesses, including harassment and threats from defendants or former criminal associates. Prior to the act, victims and witnesses received minimal governmental protection. Because prosecutors realized how necessary victims and witnesses are to the successful prosecution of felons, Congress acted to provide more thorough protection. The Victim and Witness Protection Act now provides protection that lasts through the duration of the judicial proceedings.

witness tampering Illegal conduct with the intent to influence witness testimony, such as by approaching a potential witness with threats or other means to prevent the witness from testifying.

To prove witness tampering charges, the government has the burden of proving that the defendant knowingly engaged in intimidation, physical force, threats, misleading conduct, or corrupt persuasion with the intent to influence, delay, or prevent testimony or cause any person to withhold a record, object, or document from an official proceeding.[21]

Although typical witness tampering cases involve approaching a potential witness with threats or other means in an attempt to prevent the witness from testifying, a defendant who attempts to frustrate the government's plan to infiltrate his or her operation can also face witness tampering charges. See Application Case on page 525 for an example of a witness tampering case.

The reasoning in *United States v. Baldyga* indicated the court's intent to broadly apply and even extend the statute for witness tampering. The court held the statute to include circumstances that might be interpreted as actions taken by the defendant to prevent and frustrate undercover operations. Clearly, the court used this broad application as a warning to others who would consider the same tactics as used by the defendant in *Baldyga*.

United States v. Baldyga

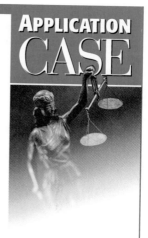
In the case of *United States v. Baldyga* (2000), the defendant was convicted of several charges: 1) multiple counts of possession of cocaine with the intent to distribute, 2) distribution of cocaine, and 3) witness tampering. During an investigation of the defendant, the DEA arranged for a cooperating witness who had purchased drugs from the defendant in the past to purchase cocaine from the defendant. During the transaction, the cooperating witness wore a wiretap device so that the DEA agents could safely monitor him.

Although the three previous sales were successful, this one was not. When the witness attempted to make the fourth sale, the defendant gave the witness a note instructing him to remain quiet and to put his hands on the wall. The witness testified that when he finished reading the note, the defendant was standing in front of him pointing a "gold-colored double gun at his face." The defendant searched the witness, discovered the listening device on his person, disabled it, and told him to leave the premises. The officers who had been monitoring the transaction approached the premises when the listening device went dead, and the defendant was arrested as he was attempting to flee the area.

The defendant appealed his conviction on the basis that his actions of confronting the witness were insufficient to support the charge of witness tampering. In affirming the defendant's conviction, the court held that while the defendant did not explicitly threaten to harm the witness, the jury could have reasonably inferred beyond a reasonable doubt that the defendant brandishing a gun and holding it to the head of the witness was an intent to deter the witness from discussing the cocaine deals with the federal authorities.

In addition, the court held that the jury could have concluded that the defendant was aware of the witness cooperating with federal agents when the defendant stated to the witness that the defendant heard that the witness would be wearing a wire and proceeded to search for it. Moreover, the jury could have further concluded that the defendant's act of ripping the wire away from the transmitter was intended to prevent or discourage the witness' cooperation with the federal agents. Hence, the defendant's actions of disconnecting the listening device satisfied the requirements under the statute because "the possibility existed that such communication would occur with the federal officials, especially in light of his prior communications with the officers."

Critical Thinking Do you agree with the defendant's conviction on witness tampering charges? Why or why not?

SOURCE: *United States v. Baldyga*, 233 F.3d 674 (1st Cir. 2000). *See also* 18 U.S.C.§ 1512(b)(3).

Suppressing Evidence

suppressing evidence A crime that occurs when a defendant, or a person working on behalf of the defendant, suppresses (hides), destroys, or refuses to produce evidence relevant to a grand jury investigation.

Suppressing evidence occurs when a defendant, or a person working on behalf of the defendant, suppresses (hides), destroys, or refuses to produce evidence relevant to a grand jury investigation. Federal law states that a defendant, in order to be convicted of obstruction of justice for the concealment of subpoenaed documents in a federal proceeding, must:

- Have knowledge of the pending grand jury investigation. Therefore, concealing or changing documentation after receiving notification of a pending grand jury investigation is a violation of this law.
- Know that particular documents are covered by a subpoena
- Willfully conceal or endeavor to conceal them from a grand jury.[22]

An example of this occurred in the case of *United States v. Brooks*, in which the Fifth Circuit Court upheld a conviction for obstruction of justice where testimony indicated that subpoenaed corporate minutes had been altered after the date of subpoena and some original minutes remained missing.[23]

CRIMINAL LAW *Online*

Check your answers at cl.glencoe.com.

Self Check

1. Should the federal witness tampering statute apply only to witnesses who are *not* involved in undercover operations? Should it apply only to classic cases of intimidating or threatening witnesses?
2. What are some ways that evidence can be suppressed? Among the participants in a trial, who seems most likely to suppress evidence?

15.5 Resisting Arrest

resisting arrest Physical efforts to oppose a lawful arrest.

An old saying holds that "Freedom is a man's natural power of doing what he pleases, so far as he is not prevented by force or law." One way that the law can restrict a person's freedom is through arrest, and resisting arrest is considered a crime. At common law, the offense of **resisting arrest** involved physical efforts to oppose a lawful arrest. It amounted to a trespass against the police officer that was similar to battery. This was because it was believed that when an officer had a legal right to arrest or restrain a private citizen, that citizen "can have no right to resist since the two rights cannot coexist." Therefore, those who resisted lawful arrests could not claim self-defense, since the officer's right to arrest them superceded their right to resist.

Since an officer at common law was not authorized to make an arrest without a warrant for a misdemeanor not committed in his presence, a defendant who killed an officer who did not have the right to arrest him or her (and was thus making an unlawful arrest) could claim the lack of a warrant as a partial defense. The result was that the offence would be reduced from murder to manslaughter.

Modern Statutes

One question that arises, and which has not been answered uniformly by the current laws throughout the United States, is how an individual should be allowed to react if he or she believes that an arrest is unlawful. Is such an individual allowed to resist an unlawful arrest?

Some laws forbid resisting arrest in any circumstances. The Model Penal Code and statutes in a number of states specify that an individual does not *ever* have the right to use force in resisting a law enforcement officer who is making an arrest. For example, California's Penal Code states:

"If a person has knowledge, or by the exercise of reasonable care should have knowledge, that he is being arrested by a peace officer, it is the duty of such person to refrain from using force or any weapon to resist such arrest."[24]

As another example, in the case of *People v. Volition*, a court affirmed the defendant's conviction of resisting arrest even though it found that the officers had engaged in an unlawful seizure. The court stated that a defendant could not use physical force to resist an arrest by a police officer, whether "authorized or unauthorized . . . when it reasonably appeared that the individual is a police officer."[25] Thus, even if the underlying charge or seizure is deemed illegal, if the defendant knowingly resists an arrest by a police officer, he will still be guilty of resisting arrest. In addition, a few statutes specify that an individual may not resist an arrest even if the arrest is unlawful.

At common law and in those states that still follow the common law rule, however, force is allowed to prevent an unlawful arrest. See Figure 15–1 on page 529 to see which states still allow individuals to resist unlawful arrest. In such a case, a suspect may use only a reasonable amount of force to ward off the arresting official. Since law enforcement personnel are rarely authorized to use deadly physical

CRIMINAL LAW Online

Resisting Arrest

Read "Resisting Arrest" on **LawInfo.com** available through the link at **cl.glencoe.com**. What is their general advice about resisting arrest, and why?

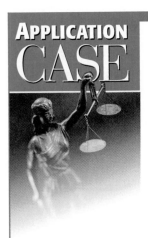
United States v. John Bad Elk

One of the earliest cases regarding the common law right to resist an unlawful arrest was *United States v. John Bad Elk* (1900). Native American law enforcement officers attempted to arrest the defendant without a warrant and without an official charge being filed against the defendant who was also Native American. It was alleged that the defendant, who was also a policeman, fired his gun in the air and refused to accompany the officers when requested. He then advised them that he would go to the police department the next morning. After more disagreement, the defendant shot and killed one of the policemen when the policeman made a move as if reaching for his gun.

The defendant was convicted of murder. The defendant argued that since the officers were not justified in arresting him, he had the right to use such force as a reasonable prudent person might use in resisting the arrest. The Supreme Court agreed with the defendant that the trial court erred instructing the jury that the deceased officer had a right to arrest the defendant and that the defendant had no right to resist the unlawful arrest. In fact, the jury should have been instructed that the defendant had the right to use such force as absolutely necessary to resist an attempted illegal arrest.

The Supreme Court held that the officer had no right to arrest the defendant without a warrant, but also stated that the defendant had no right to unnecessarily injure or kill his assailant. In the end, the Court remanded the case for the correct instructions to be given the jury and to consider whether the defendant's actions were reasonable under the circumstances.

Critical Thinking Do you think this defendant should have been acquitted? Why or why not?

SOURCE: *United States v. John Bad Elk*, 177 U.S. 529 (1900).

force to arrest a suspect, self-defense would prohibit an individual from the use of deadly physical force to resist an arrest.

There are two main reasons for this ongoing disagreement regarding resisting unlawful arrests:

1. The accused rarely knows at the time of the arrest whether it is lawful or not.
2. The unlawfully arrested individual has other recourse or remedies post arrest, including civil remedies for wrongful arrest.

FIGURE 15-1

States that Allow Individuals to Resist Unlawful Arrest

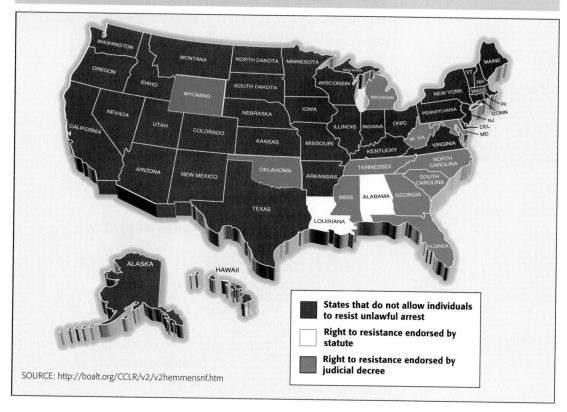

States that do not allow individuals to resist unlawful arrest

Right to resistance endorsed by statute

Right to resistance endorsed by judicial decree

SOURCE: http://boalt.org/CCLR/v2/v2hemmensnf.htm

Citizens who fear unlawful arrests should know that unlawful arrests can and do have effects upon both the civil and criminal justice system. Individuals who are wrongfully arrested can sue for damages through a civil court. In a criminal matter, an illegal seizure or unlawful arrest will result in the suppression of any evidence recovered in connection with such unlawful arrest. In other words, if

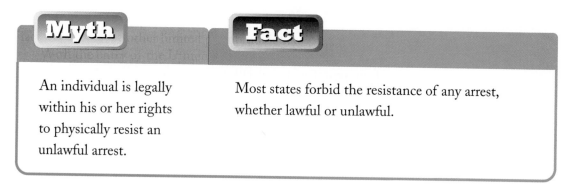

Myth

An individual is legally within his or her rights to physically resist an unlawful arrest.

Fact

Most states forbid the resistance of any arrest, whether lawful or unlawful.

officers find evidence during an unlawful arrest, that evidence cannot be admitted at trial no matter how valuable it may be to the prosecution. This concept exists to prevent police officers from benefiting in any way from illegal searches and seizures that are in violation of the individual's constitutional rights.[26]

CRIMINAL
LAW *Online*

Check your answers at
cl.glencoe.com.

Self
Check

1. Should individuals have the right to resist unlawful arrest? Why or why not?
2. What factors make it difficult for jurisdictions to decide whether resisting unlawful arrest should be legal?

15.6 Compounding and Misprision of a Felony

compounding a felony
An offense that occurs when someone refuses to report or prosecute a felony in exchange for some benefit or reward of some value.

Compounding a felony is an offense that occurs when someone refuses to report or prosecute a felony in exchange for some benefit or reward of some value. As a result, the defendant escapes conviction and punishment, which may cause greater harm to society. Public policy has always favored prosecuting all violations, and therefore a single individual should not have the sole right to overlook the harm done to society as a whole. In addition, when a felon is not held accountable for the crime, he or she is not deterred from engaging in further criminal conduct. Rather, one could argue that he or she is encouraged by the prosecution's failure to take action.

The essence of the crime of compounding a felony is the making of the unlawful agreement that causes one to decline prosecution. The Model Penal Code gives the following example of compounding a crime:

> A person commits a misdemeanor if he accepts or agrees to accept any pecuniary benefit in consideration of refraining from reporting to law enforcement authorities the commission or suspected commission of any offense or information relating to an offense. It is an affirmative defense to prosecution under this Section that the pecuniary benefit did not exceed an amount which the actor believed to be due as

ON THE JOB

Judge

Description and Duties: Apply the law to citizens and companies within one's jurisdiction. Oversee legal processes in courts of law. Sentence convicted criminals. Manage courtroom staff and budget. Interact with other judges, lawyers, defendants and victims, police officers, and court staff. Interact with the public, including people from different cultures.

Salary: Federal judges earn approximately $97,000 to $145,000. State judges earn approximately $63,000 to $122,000.

Other Information: Most judges were previously employed as lawyers. Contrary to popular belief, however, a law degree is not required to hold some lower-court judgeships in 40 states. Judges can work relatively long hours, and about one-third of all judges work 50 hours per week.

"There is a lot of humor in courts, believe it or not, despite the tragedy. You see the resilience of human beings often in horrible circumstances—people who are able to carry on and see the optimistic side of life," said Ronald Young, Judge.

Critical Thinking What qualities do you think a good judge should have?

SOURCE: Saludos.com, http://www.saludos.com/cguide/lguide.html; KiwiCareers.com, http://www.careers.co.nz/jobs/14c_law/j11510d.html.

restitution or indemnification for harm caused by the offense.[27]

For example, Patty's car is stolen. In exchange for not reporting the crime, Patty accepts a cash payment from Carol, the mother of the person who stole the car, because Carol knows that her son is a habitual criminal and she is afraid that he will go to prison again. Ordinarily, Patty's acceptance of money as part of an agreement not to report a felony would be automatically considered a crime. Under the Model Penal Code, however, she may have a defense: Since she accepted the sum equal to the value of the car, this money can be considered restitution for the stolen vehicle. If she took a much larger sum than the amount for which the car

FIGURE 15-2

Compounding Versus Misprision

South Dakota Statute SDCL Sec. 22-11-10
Compounding a felony or misdemeanor

Any person who accepts, or offers or agrees to accept any pecuniary benefit as consideration for:

- Refraining from seeking prosecution of an offender; or

- Refraining from reporting to law enforcement authorities the commission or suspected commission of any crime or information relating to a crime;

- Is guilty of compounding.

South Dakota Statute SDCL Sec. 22-11-12
Misprision of a felony

Any person who, having knowledge, which is not privileged, of the commission of a felony, conceals the same, or does not immediately disclose such felony, with the name of the perpetrator thereof, and all the facts in relation thereto, to the proper authorities, shall be guilty of misprision of a felony.

could be reasonably valued, though, restitution would not be a valid defense.

Compounding a crime differs from the offense of misprision of a felony. **Misprision of a felony** refers to the act of failing to report or prosecute a known felony, and taking positive steps to conceal the crime. The offense is defined under federal law as, "Whoever, having knowledge of the actual commission of a felony cognizable by a court of the United States, conceals and does not as soon as possible make known the same to some judge or other person or military authority under the United States, shall be fined under this title or imprisoned not more than three years, or both."[28]

The example of Carol, the mother of the felon, can be used again here. If Carol failed to report the crimes of her son with which she was familiar, and took steps to conceal that they had occurred such as by paying hush money to victims in exchange for not reporting the crime, she would be guilty of misprision of a felony.

misprision of a felony
The act of failing to report or prosecute a known felony, and taking positive steps to conceal the crime.

CRIMINAL LAW Online
Check your answers at cl.glencoe.com.

Self Check

1. Why is misprision of a felony considered a more serious crime than compounding a felony? Do you agree with this?

2. Should society be more concerned about felonies and insist that all felonies be prosecuted, as opposed to prosecuting misdemeanors?

15.7 Escape

Escape occurs when a person who is lawfully imprisoned leaves custody before he or she is entitled to freedom by due process of law. A person is guilty of this crime if, without lawful authority, he or she commits one of the following acts:

- Removes or attempts to leave official detention
- Fails to return to official detention following a temporarily granted leave

The crime of escape covers individuals who escape while in the custody of a police officer, the custody of a jail or lock-up, or the custody of any type of correctional facility. For instance, an accused who is officially under arrest and escapes from the holding cell of a local police station has committed the crime of escape.

Before a conviction for escape can be sustained, the prosecution must first prove that the person was actually under arrest. If the arrest was not completed, such as due to resistance, the accused is not guilty of the crime of escape. An accused who flees just as he or she is about to be arrested or placed in handcuff has not escaped within the meaning of the statute.

escape A crime that occurs when a person who is lawfully imprisoned leaves custody before he or she is entitled to freedom by due process of law.

People v. Trujillo

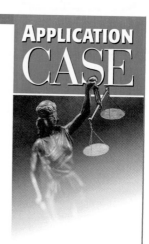

APPLICATION CASE

In *People v. Trujillo* (1978), the defendant claimed that he escaped from prison because he had been previously gang-raped by six inmates and was again being threatened by inmates who demanded sexual favors. He claimed that he reported the attack to prison officials, but nothing was done to protect his safety. At trial, the judge excluded all evidence pertaining to the gang rape and the defendant was convicted. On appeal, the conviction was reversed on the grounds that the defendant should have been allowed to introduce the evidence in support of his defense. Thus, the courts have recognized that an accused may be justified in escaping a correctional facility when he or she reasonably fears for his or her physical safety.

Critical Thinking Do you think fear for one's safety should be an affirmative defense to escape charges? Why or why not?

SOURCE: *People v. Trujillo*, 585 p. 2d 235 (Colo. Ct. App. 1978).

Defense to Escape

One important exception to the elements that form the crime of escape can be found in some recent cases, which have interpreted escape statutes to exclude inmates who escape custody as the result of reasonable fears for their safety while incarcerated. Generally, though, court decisions that have precluded convictions for escape in these types of situations have required the escapees to turn themselves in to authorities within a reasonable time after the escape.

Self Check

Under what circumstances are escape statutes interpreted to exclude certain inmates? Do you agree with this? Why or why not?

15.8 Contempt of Court

contempt of court Any affirmative act or omission that obstructs justice or attempts to negate the dignity and authority of the court.

Contempt of court is any affirmative act or omission that obstructs justice or attempts to negate the dignity and authority of the court. Courts may cite or issue summonses to individuals for contempt and civil disobedience of court orders, disruption of court proceedings, and other affronts to the courts' dignity and authority.[29] Generally contempt is divided into four categories: direct contempt, constructive or indirect contempt, criminal contempt, and civil contempt.

direct contempt A criminal form of contempt of court, which occurs in the presence of the court when a person resists the court's power.

Direct contempt occurs in the presence of the court when a person resists the court's power. Such contempt is criminal in nature. One example of direct contempt is the use of profane language toward an officer of the court. A criminal trial would be unnecessary in this case, since the judge would usually be a witness to the contemptuous behavior. In cases of direct contempt, the court has the option to impose a fine or imprisonment for a specified period of time. As with any crime, if the potential punishment for contempt is six months or more, the defendant is entitled to a jury trial.

In *Bloom v. Illinois*, the Supreme Court found:

> Serious contempts of court are so nearly like other serious crimes that they are subject to the jury trial provisions of the Constitution. We accept the judgment of our earlier cases that criminal contempt is a petty offense unless the punishment makes it a serious one; but, in our view, dispensing with the jury in the trial of contempt subjected to severe punishment represents an unacceptable construction of the Constitution.

The Court went on to find that because the defendant was given a relatively severe sentence of two years in prison, he was entitled to a jury trial.[30]

Constructive contempt, also known as *indirect contempt*, results from matters outside the court. An example of constructive contempt would be the failure to comply with a judicial order. In such a case, the judicial officer who issued the order will be called upon to enforce it against a disobedient party. This type of contempt does not present the same issues as does direct contempt because it does not attempt to openly disrupt or interfere with court proceedings as they occur.

Constructive contempt may be either civil or criminal. **Criminal contempt** is an act of disrespect toward the court or its procedures, other than direct contempt, that obstructs the administration of justice. The penalty for criminal contempt is intended as punishment, and is usually a fine or imprisonment for a specified period of time. Again, if post-conviction contempt proceedings impose sentences exceeding an aggregate of six months, a trial by jury is required. **Civil contempt** consists of the failure to do something ordered by the court for the benefit of another party to the proceedings. The penalty for civil contempt is usually payment of a fine or imprisonment for an indefinite period of time until the party in contempt agrees to perform his legal obligation.

constructive contempt Contempt of court that results from matters outside the court, such as failure to comply with court orders.

criminal contempt An act of disrespect toward the court or its procedures, other than direct contempt, that obstructs the administration of justice.

civil contempt The failure to do something ordered by the court for the benefit of another party to the proceedings.

Self Check

Can constructive contempt be as harmful as direct contempt in some circumstances? Why or why not?

CRIMINAL LAW *Online*

Check your answers at cl.glencoe.com.

Crimes Against the Administration of Justice

SUMMARY BY CHAPTER OBJECTIVES

1. Recognize the difference between the offenses of bribery and commercial bribery.

Bribery is the voluntary giving of something of value to influence performance or official duty; its essential elements are offering a gift, with the purpose to influence, and the official status of recipient. Commercial bribery is a breach of duty by an employee, in which he or she gets secret compensation from a non-employee and in return gives the briber information or rewards that he or she does not deserve.

2. Define the elements of perjury.

The three key elements of perjury are:

- Making false statements
- Under oath or affirmation
- In a legal setting

3. Define the offense of "obstruction of justice" and recognize the scope of crimes it covers.

Obstruction of justice can be generally defined as interference with law enforcement officials or the civil and criminal courts. It includes the crimes of bribery, perjury, subornation of perjury, witness tampering, suppression of evidence, and contempt.

4. Describe the crime of resisting arrest.

Resisting arrest is the offense of using physical efforts to resist a lawful arrest. Although the common law and states that still follow the common law rule permit an individual to resist an unlawful arrest, some state statutes do not allow an individual to resist an arrest even if it is unlawful.

5. Recognize the offense of compounding a felony, and explain why it is different from the offense of misprision of a felony.

Compounding a felony is an offense that occurs when someone refuses to report or prosecute a felony in exchange for some benefit or reward of some value. As a result, the defendant escapes conviction and punishment, which may cause greater harm to society. Misprision of a felony refers to the act of failing to report or prosecute a known felony. It is different because it does not involve the exchange of a benefit or reward, but does involve taking positive steps to conceal the crime.

6. Define the elements of the crime of escape.

Escape occurs when a person who is lawfully imprisoned leaves custody before he or she is entitled to freedom by due process of law. A person is guilty of this crime if, without lawful authority, he or she commits one of the following acts:

- Removes or attempts to leave official detention
- Fails to return to official detention following a temporarily granted leave

7. Recognize when constructive contempt takes place and how it differs from direct contempt.

Constructive contempt, also called indirect contempt, takes place outside of the courtroom. It results from matters concerning the court, such as a failure to comply with judi-

cial orders. This type of contempt does not present the same issues as does direct contempt because it does not attempt to openly disrupt or interfere with court proceedings as they occur.

8. Differentiate between the offenses and penalties for civil contempt and criminal contempt.

The penalty for civil contempt is usually a fine or imprisonment for an indefinite period of time, until the party in contempt agrees to perform his or her legal obligation. The penalty for criminal contempt is a fine or imprisonment for a specified period of time that is intended to punish.

KEY TERMS

obstruction of justice, page 514
bribery, page 515
quasi-bribery, page 516
commercial bribery, page 517
perjury, page 519
false swearing, page 520
subornation of perjury, page 521

witness tampering, page 523
suppressing evidence, page 526
resisting arrest, page 526
compounding a felony, page 530
misprision of a felony, page 532
escape, page 533

contempt of court, page 534
direct contempt, page 534
constructive contempt, page 535
criminal contempt, page 535
civil contempt, page 535

QUESTIONS FOR REVIEW

1. What are the elements of the offense of bribery?
2. What is quasi-bribery, and how does it differ from regular bribery? Give an example.
3. What is subornation of perjury, and how are the defendant and the perjurer punished for it?
4. In what situations does the obstruction of governmental administration occur?

5. What is witness tampering, and what are two examples of it?
6. What are the ways in which evidence can be suppressed?

Is it legal to resist an unlawful arrest?
Find it on page 528.

7. What are the laws regarding resisting lawful arrests? What about unlawful arrests?

8. In what situations may the crime of escape occur? In what situations, which are discussed in your text, is it deemed to have not occurred or is excused by the courts?

9. When and where can direct contempt take place?

10. Identify and analyze the difference between the offenses of criminal contempt and civil contempt.

PROBLEM-SOLVING EXERCISES

1. **Police Perjury** A police officer arrives at the scene of a report of an assault and observes a woman crying with a bruised eye and bloody nose. She tells the officer that her boyfriend beat her up. The officer asks the boyfriend, who is present, if he assaulted the woman. The boyfriend refuses to answer, but there is blood on his hand and nobody else in the apartment. At the trial, during the police officer's testimony, he is asked by the prosecutor, "Did you see who assaulted the woman?" The police officer replies, "Yes, it was her boyfriend," and points to the defendant. Answer the following questions:
   a) Is this perjury? Why or why not?
   b) In a situation where guilt can be proven circumstantially, such as this, does it matter if perjury is committed? Why or why not?
   c) In a situation where guilt can be proven circumstantially, such as this, are there any unnecessary risks in making the type of statement that the officer did? Why or why not?

2. **Compounding a Felony** You are a police investigator. During a routine investigation of burglaries in the neighborhood, you learn that Clyde, a 32-year

old who still lives at home, burglarized his neighbor's home. Clyde's father Darrell offers the neighbor $10,000 to replace the property stolen by Clyde, which the neighbor accepts because it is considerably more than what the property was worth. Darrell then states to the neighbor, "I hope this is the end of it and that you're not going to the police." Answer the following questions:
   a) What crime, if any, has Darrell committed?
   b) If there were no physical threats made to the neighbor, has Darrell committed a crime?
   c) Is it illegal for the neighbor to accept the money and not report the burglary to the police?
   d) What if the neighbor tells Darrell that he wants $20,000 for his "trouble and inconvenience," and that if he does not receive it, he is going to the police?

3. **Witness Tampering** You are prosecuting a defendant who stole a diamond ring worth $250,000. Your key witness overheard the defendant on the telephone, stating how and when he stole the ring. Since the defendant knows that this witness overheard his statement, he

says to his lawyer, " I am going to mess him up if he testifies that I stole the ring." The defendant then telephones the witness and says, "How are the wife and kids? I hope we all survive this mess."

a) Is this a form of witness tampering? Why or why not?

b) What factors influenced your decision?

WORKPLACE APPLICATIONS

1. **Resisting Arrest** During an abortion protest, a police officer orders Teresa and her friends to refrain from blocking the entrance of the clinic. Teresa and her friends refuse to leave and sit on the steps in front of the entrance. The officer decides to place Teresa under arrest. Answer the following questions:

   a) Is Teresa resisting arrest if she remains sitting and refuses to move at all, forcing the officer to lift and carry her away from the demonstration?

   b) Is Teresa resisting arrest if she hooks her clothing or body around a stair rail in such a way that the officer has more difficulty in pulling her away?

   c) What if the police officer is in plain-clothes and does not identify himself as a police officer?

2. **Perjury** A prosecutor charged Hosea with committing perjury when he denied giving Steve $1,000 on February 2, 2001. In fact, Hosea gave Steve $1,000 on February 3, 2001. Answer the following questions:

   a) Has Hosea committed perjury? Should Hosea's statement be considered truthful or false?

   b) Does it make a difference on what day the money was given?

   c) Should Hosea be required to voluntarily give the correct date?

3. **Resisting Arrest Versus Escape** You recently arrested a suspect who committed an assault in your presence. As you drove the suspect to the precinct, he somehow managed to open the back door of the squad car and escape. You chase and apprehend him a few blocks away.

   a) Should the defendant be charged with resisting arrest or escape? (You must first determine whether the accused escaped while under arrest.)

   b) Does it make a difference that the accused was immediately apprehended a few blocks away and that he escaped from a police vehicle and not a holding cell?

INTERNET APPLICATIONS

1. **Most Wanted** Visit the Clearwater County (ID) Sheriff's Office by clicking the link at **cl.glencoe.com** and click on "Most Wanted." Look at the information on the escapees, then answer the following questions:

   a) What information is provided on escapees? What other information would be helpful?

b) What resources do they provide for people who have information on their whereabouts?

c) Should private citizens try to apprehend these suspects themselves? Why or why not?

2. **Perjury** Read "Perjury: The Ashcroft Exemption" on About.com available through the link at **cl.glencoe.com**. Be sure to read the entire multi-page article, then answer the following questions:

a) Are charges of perjury used selectively by politicians, depending on the party of the perjurer? Why or why not?

b) Do you feel that an inconsistent application of the law should change a prosecutor's or court's decision regarding it? Why or why not?

c) Do you feel that an inconsistent application of the law has a negative effect on American society's view of the sanctity of the law? Why or why not?

ETHICS ISSUES

1. **Bribery** You work for your county's sheriff's department, and your primary duties are at the county jail. Today, you are processing new inmates who have just been brought in and are awaiting their initial appearance before the judge. Just before going off duty, the last inmate that you process offers you two free tickets to a basketball game that evening. He said that since he obviously has no use for them, you could have them instead. Answer the following questions:

a) Should you refuse or accept the tickets? Why or why not?

b) Should you accept the tickets, but offer to pay him? Why or why not?

c) What if you accept the tickets, pay for them, and explain that you can not give him any favors or preferential treatment in return?

2. **Witness Tampering** A defense attorney telephones an eyewitness, who has been subpoenaed to appear at a trial, and tells her, "If you disappear, the prosecution will not find you to testify that you saw your boyfriend steal the car. Hey, why not make everyone's life easier?"

a) Is this unethical or is the attorney acting in his client's best interests? Why?

b) Of what legal repercussions could this defense attorney be guilty?

ENDNOTES

1 "Obstruction of Justice," 36 *Am. Crim. L. Rev.* 929 (1999).

2 Extortion consists of two types: extortion by threats or fear (i.e., coercive extortion or blackmail) and extortion under the color of office. If public officials are involved or the threats of physical violence, the term *extortion* is commonly used, rather than *blackmail*. In the past, extortion under the color of office was defined as the seeking or receipt of a corrupt payment by a public official or someone pretending to be one.

3   8 Rich.2, c.3 1384, (repealed by the Statute Law Revision Act, 44 & 45 Vict., c. 59 (1881) (based on 18 Edw. 3, stat. 4[1344][oath of justices]). *See also* Royal Proclamation of Oct. 20, 1258, 3 *Eng.Hist.Doc.*369 (H. Rothwell ed., 1975).

4   *Buckley v. Valeo*, 424 U.S. 1, 28 (1976).

5   Model Penal Code § 240.5 (1 & 2).

6   Penal Law § 155.05 (2)(e)(iv).

7   *Harper*, 319.

8   A. Bequai, *White Collar Crime: A 20th Century Crisis* 42 (1978).

9   Alaska Statute (AS 11.46.660) § 11.46.660 Commercial bribe receiving, and Alaska Statute (AS 11.46.670) § 11.46.670 Commercial bribery.

10 An example of statutes that have made commercial bribery a crime is N.Y. Penal Law sections 180.00–180.08 (McKinney Supp. 1987). Federal statutes have also made commercial bribery a crime under certain instances, e.g., 18 U.S.C.A. section 215 (West Supp. 1987), bribery of bank employees; 27 U.S.C. section 205 (c) (1982), commercial bribery in the alcoholic beverage industry; and *United States v. Beckley*, 259 F.Supp. 567 (N.D. Ga. 1986), bribing an employee of telephone company to allow uncharged use of long distance service may violate the wire fraud statute.

11 15 U.S.C. sections 1–7 (1982). "Commercial bribery is an agreement or combination that has the effect of increasing prices and depriving consumers of the advantages of free competition." Section 1 of The Sherman Act was designed to prohibit this practice. *See also* "Commercial Bribery and the Sherman Act: The Case for Per Se Illegality," 42 U. *Miami L. Rev.* 365–366 (1997).

12 *Continental Ore v. Union Carbide & Carbon Corp.*, 370 U.S. 690, 702 (1962); evidence was sufficient for jury to decide whether parties violated the Sherman Act by conspiring to monopolize commerce in certain ore products. *See also United States v. Sisal Sales Corp*, 274 U.S. 268, 276 (1927), parties in a combination violated the Sherman Act by monopolizing the local and foreign sisal commerce.

13 Bribery can destroy competition in having a rippling effect. Once it affects consumer pricing in the market for service provided by the non-bribing party, this party cannot participate in free competition.

14 18 U.S.C. § 1621.

15 Model Penal Code § 241.1 (1).

16 *United States v. Standifer*, 40 M.J. 440 (1994), elements of crime of subornation of perjury under the UCMJ. Quoting the *Manual for Courts-Martial*, United States (1984).

17 18 U.S.C. § 1622.

18 Model Penal Code § 241.5 (1), (2)(a)(b).

19 Model Penal Code § 242.1.

20 "A prerequisite to a conviction [for obstruction of justice] based solely on false testimony . . . is that the government must charge in the indictment and prove at trial that the testimony had the effect of impeding justice." *United States v. Martino*, (unpublished disposition) 1988 WL 41468 (E.D. Pa., Apr. 28, 1988).

21 18 U.S.C.§ 1512(b).

22 18 U.S.C. § 1503.

23 *United States v. Brooks*, 111 F.3d 365, 373 (5th Cir. 1997).

24 California Penal Code, section 834(a).

25 *People v. Volition*, 83 N.Y.2d 192, 630 N.E.2d 641 (1994).

26 See *Wong Sun v. United States*, 371 U.S. 471 (1963), a landmark case pertaining to the Exclusionary Rule or the "fruit of the poisonous tree" doctrine. Note that an unlawful arrest predicated upon mistakes made by non-law enforcement officials will not suppress the evidence in court.

27 Model Penal Code, §242.5.

28 U.S. Code, Title 18, Section 4 (1997).

29 "Disobedience and Contempt," 75 *Wash. L. Rev.* 345 (April 2000).

30 391 U.S. 194 (1968).

Chapter Objectives

After reading this chapter, you will be able to:

1. Understand the historical development of organized crime.
2. List some typical organized crime activities.
3. List the elements of a RICO violation.
4. Understand and differentiate various laws aimed at targeting organized crime.
5. Understand the structure and activities of modern street gangs.
6. Explain the laws that target street gangs.
7. Understand the types of criminal activity that constitute terrorism.
8. Describe the various laws that target terrorism.

Chapter Outline

What laws specifically target organized crime?

Chapter 16

Organized Crime, Gangs, and Terrorism

16.1 Organized Crime

Most people base their understanding of organized crime upon movie and television images that glamorize the Mafia lifestyle and create an illusion. This illusion is that organized crime is an exciting and somehow honorable way of life, in which the only people who get hurt are the ruthless gangsters who chose to be in the Mafia. In reality, organized crime syndicates such as the Mafia have murdered countless innocent people, have brought an endless supply of drugs into the United States, and have terrorized many innocent people who are forced to live among these organizations.

Another common illusion is that only persons of Italian descent, or Mafia members, are involved in organized crime. Again, the reality is extremely different. The idea of the Mafia usually brings to mind the Italian Mafia, but almost every ethnic group in America contains organized crime syndicates. There is a Russian Mafia, a Chinese Mafia, a Jewish Mafia, and countless other ethnically distinct criminal organizations. Organized crime includes drug gangs from Latin America and the Caribbean, Chinese Tongs, and street gangs of various ethnic backgrounds. These crime syndicates pursue a multitude of criminal activities, including but not limited to drug trafficking, gambling, extortion, prostitution, pornography, and fraud.[1] In other words, organized crime is a highly dangerous crime problem that creates and contributes to numerous social problems.

CRIMINAL LAW Online

The Gotti Case

Read the entire story of John Gotti and his eventual demise on **Crime Library.com**, through the link provided at **cl.glencoe.com**. What obstacles did the FBI have to overcome in bringing him to trial? How did they succeed in having him convicted?

➤ **The Mafia Myth**
The Mafia lifestyle is presented in film as a glamorous lifestyle dominated by persons of Italian descent.
What is wrong with this portrayal?

Historical Development

Organized crime consists of individuals who associate together for the purpose of engaging in criminal activity for a sustained period of time, with an emphasis on the life of the organization. It has existed in the United States for centuries. In addition, there is a direct correlation between 1) the development of laws that criminalize a particular type of organized criminal behavior or activity, and 2) the expansion of criminal enterprises. The earliest example of this is the *lottery*. During the eighteenth and nineteenth centuries, lotteries were quite popular and, as in many states today, completely legal. States used lotteries to raise revenue for public expenditures. For example, one lottery was used to raise over a million dollars to help fund the Revolutionary War.

Over time, though, the public grew concerned that hard-working men were losing their wages because of lotteries and were left unable to provide for their families. By 1878, lotteries became illegal in most states. At this time, a syndicate of New York gamblers kept alive the Louisiana lottery by selling its lottery tickets by mail. From then until the end of the nineteenth century, many legal battles were fought over lotteries in the United States. Finally, in *Champion v. Ames* (1903), also known as the *Lottery Case*, the U.S. Supreme Court upheld Congress's power to ban lotteries under the Commerce Clause.[2] This case attempted to disable the organized criminals who were keeping lotteries alive illegally.

The early 1900s, however, saw the creation of many crime organizations throughout the country, many of which became very powerful and grew significantly in numbers. For example, this period marked the beginning of the Mafia. The reason for this growth was the criminalization of drugs and then alcohol. Rather than eradicate existing drug problems, such criminalization actually created a demand for an illegal drug trade. For example, when drugs such as morphine and opium grew in popularity during this period and many people became addicted, Congress reacted by banning the importation of opium. In 1914, Congress acted further with the Harrison Narcotics Act, which limited the lawful trade of specified narcotics such as morphine to physicians and druggists. The effect of these prohibitions was disastrous: Opium and morphine use and addiction continued as always, and criminals found an easy market in which to ply their trade.

The criminalization of drugs, however, did not help organized crime nearly as much as the prohibition of alcohol. Although it may seem hard to believe now, for decades during the late nineteenth and

organized crime
Individuals who associate together for the purpose of engaging in criminal activity on a sustained basis, with an emphasis on the life of the organization.

early twentieth century the United States had a strong *temperance*, or anti-alcohol, movement. This movement's ultimate goal was to completely outlaw the brewing, distilling, selling, and use of alcohol anywhere in the country. In 1919, this goal was achieved with the passage of the Eighteenth Amendment to the U.S. Constitution and the passage of the Volstead Act.[3] Overnight, the legitimate brewing and distilling industry became illegal. The demand for alcoholic beverages, however, continued as before, and those willing to break the law in order to provide the public with drugs and alcohol prospered. Rather than curbing the American desire for alcohol, the era of Prohibition allowed organized crime to create hugely profitable enterprises in bootlegging, which was the manufacture and sale of illegal alcohol.

Additionally, the need to drink and use drugs in secret locations known as speakeasies, where people could enjoy alcohol and entertainment, created a growing number of other illicit enterprises. Because of the secret nature of speakeasies, gambling and prostitution businesses flourished for many criminal organizations. Although the era of Prohibition ended in 1933, organized crime did not. It merely found other criminal ventures to pursue, and continued to grow and prosper throughout the country.

Elements and Participants of Organized Crime

Individuals in organized crime engage in *enterprise crime*, which usually consists of providing illegal goods and services such as drugs and prostitution. The more sophisticated groups have several different levels throughout their organization, and each is distinguished by different amounts of power and control. Most of these organizations use violence and corruption to facilitate their economic activities and usually have a dangerous reputation within their community, where others are aware of their capability of committing violence.[4]

Typical Structure   A classic example of organized crime, which illustrates the elements and participants of a typical organized crime group, would be as follows: In a neighborhood in St. Louis, Missouri, a criminal organization makes money through cocaine distribution and illegal gambling. Everyone who works for the organization must vow to protect the group at all costs, putting the group's interests before their own. When a member hears about a profit opportunity, he or she must go to his or her supervisor and report it so that the organization can decide whether it will pursue the activity.

The organization consists of three different groups:

1. Mike, the boss, and his predecessor Julio
2. About ten men and women who work directly below those two and oversee the street operations of the group. Among this group are two of Julio's brothers, one of Mike's brothers, and Mike's girlfriend Keisha. They report to Mike and, at times, Julio.
3. About 40 young men and women who work on the streets distributing the cocaine. They report directly to the ten men and women above them.

When the group is faced with the threat of competition, everyone is encouraged to do whatever it takes to protect the group's members and territory, including murdering the competitors. Everyone in the neighborhood knows about the group, and also knows never to get anyone in the organization upset because they will risk being beaten or killed.

As you can see from the basic structure shown above, a very important aspect of an organized crime syndicate is the hierarchy, or many-leveled structure, that accompanies these organizations. Each member has a role that is played within the group, each member works for a particular person, and each follows the instructions of that person in carrying out criminal activities. In this way, the organized crime structure can be compared to any type of legitimate business or organization. For example, consider a typical police department. Beat officers report to an immediate supervisor such as a sergeant for instructions or guidance, but do not usually go directly to their chief of police. In the same way, police detectives usually go to the head of detectives for their supervision. The same structure applies within organized crime groups.

The Boss and Underboss   At the very top of the crime organization is the **boss**. This person is the head of the crime "family," but usually does not involve himself in the day-to-day operations of the group. Only certain people are considered qualified to be bosses. Depending on the person's family, ethnic group, prior history with the group, and commitment to the group, a boss may be selected years before the current boss has died or stepped down. In some cases, a current boss's son may be chosen to succeed him when he dies.

boss The head or leader of an organized crime family. Usually, this person does not involve himself in the day-to-day operations of the group but is the ultimate decision-maker.

Below the boss is the **underboss**. The underboss is the second-in-command and is usually the person being groomed to be the next boss. Below the underboss is a group of middle managers and supervisors, sometimes referred to as **captains and soldiers**. These people typically work between the highest level of the organization and are usually responsible for overseeing the day-to-day operations of the organization.[5]

Crews and Other Members Most organized crime groups consist of **crews**—men and women who perform the lower, street-level work by carrying out the actual operations of the group. Crew members are not usually in a higher, decision-making position. For instance, in any drug-dealing organization, crew members usually sell and distribute the drugs. Crews usually have a crew boss who coordinates the objectives of the crew, supervises crew members, and disciplines them if necessary. A crew boss is also the person who reports the crew's activities, progress, and any problems to a higher-level person within the organization, usually a captain or soldier.

There are also people involved with the organization who maintain legitimate jobs outside of the group, but help the organization continue its goals. These people, sometimes referred to as **protectors**, consist of law enforcement officers, lawyers, bankers, and accountants who use their skills to protect the organization from government interference or criminal prosecutions. Often, a crime organization establishes legitimate businesses in order to make the organization look legal. One of the most important aspects of this is finding a way to legitimize the money that is coming in from illegal activities. This crime is called money laundering, and will be discussed later.

In such a case, an accountant may be used to change the books, set up a system that will accomplish these goals, and make it hard for the government to detect any wrongdoing. The accountant may be a willing participant in this operation because he or she is getting paid very well for his or her services. He or she also may be doing so out of fear of the organization; sometimes, a crew member or captain will approach legitimate businesspeople and let them know that if they choose not to help, there will be severe consequences. This type of threat, known as a **shakedown**, occurs when a member of the organization uses the threat of violence to get someone to do something for the group. Shakedowns can also include forcing a legitimate business owner to pay protection money to the group. For example, a crew member who offers protection services may approach the owner of a restaurant. Although the restaurant doesn't even have security problems and the owner has no need for such services, he realizes that if he refuses, his business may be destroyed and he may be physically harmed. Therefore, he feels that has no choice but to agree.

Typical Organized Crime Activities

Organized crime groups pursue all types of criminal activity, including large-scale drug operations, gambling networks, prostitution rings, and financial crimes such as money laundering and loan sharking. These crimes can be grouped under the label of **racketeering**, a system of organized crime that traditionally involves the extortion of money from businesses by intimidation, violence, or other illegal methods. It can also refer to activity in any fraudulent scheme or enterprise. The crimes that will be discussed here are drug operations, prostitution rings, loan sharking, bookmaking, and money laundering.

Drug Operations   The structure and size of a crime organization allows a family to carry out crimes that require many people to play many different roles. In a drug operation, some members may be responsible for actually bringing the drugs into the country, and others are responsible for the distribution and sales. Organizations may work with other people who are already involved with the sale of narcotics as a way to gain control of the market and distribute drugs throughout the country. Suppliers and dealers of drugs may not be members of the family, but may work for the family and help carry out the goals.

As you learned earlier, the underworld narcotics trade erupted after the passage of the Harrison Narcotics Acts of 1914, which imposed criminal sanctions for narcotics abuse. Many narcotics such as heroin cannot be grown or manufactured within the borders of the United States. Because it is necessary to import large quantities of drugs to fill the demand within the United States, investigators believe that significant organized crime financial resources are dedicated to maintaining a network of importers and suppliers of these drugs.

Prostitution Rings   One of the oldest organized crime activities is prostitution. In the past, this activity consisted primarily of importing foreign women for purposes of prostitution, which was known as the "white slave trade." The public believed that organized crime was

racketeering A system of organized crime traditionally involving the extortion of money from businesses by intimidation, violence, or other illegal methods. The practice of engaging in a fraudulent scheme or enterprise.

The Mann Act

To stop the interstate and foreign transport of women and girls for prostitution rings, Congress relied upon its powers over interstate commerce and enacted the Mann Act. In the 1913 case *Hoke v. United States*, the Supreme Court upheld this law, and the statute has existed with several changes and additions, the last one occurring in 1994. There have not, however, been many prosecutions under this statute since the *Hoke* decision.

SOURCE: 8 U.S.C. § 1328 (1994). *See also Hoke v. United States*, 227 U.S. 308, 317 (1913); and Craig M. Bradley, "Racketeering and The Federalization of Crime," 22 *Am. Crim. L. Rev.* at n.62 (1984).

FYI

Riverboat Gambling Bribes

Governor of Louisiana Edwin Edwards dominated state politics for three decades, until he was convicted of accepting more than $3 million in bribes to grant licenses for riverboat casinos. At his trial, the government argued that before and after his fourth term as governor, Edwards ran a criminal enterprise in which he, his son, and several cohorts solicited bribes to secure riverboat gambling licenses. A star witness was Edward DeBartolo Jr., former owner of the San Francisco 49ers. DeBartolo testified that Mr. Edwards slipped him a piece of paper with "Dollars 400,000" written on it, which was Edwards's demand for ensuring a Bossier City casino license for DeBartolo. DeBartolo later pleaded guilty for failure to report the felony, paid a $1 million fine, and lost control of the San Francisco 49ers.

loan sharking The practice of lending money at excessive and especially usurious rates, and threatening or using extortion to enforce repayment.

responsible for bringing the women into the country and organizing the prostitution rings. The U.S. Immigration Commission reported in 1909 that this importation was actually worse than prostitution alone, because the women coming to the United States as prostitutes were particularly disease-riddled.

In 1875, Congress invoked its power to regulate immigration and enacted a statute that made it illegal to import women into the United States for the purposes of prostitution. In 1907, Congress went further and enacted a statute that made it a crime for anyone to keep any foreign woman "for the purpose of prostitution or any other immoral purpose" for three years after she entered the United States. In addition, those found guilty of this offense were forced to provide for the woman's deportation to her home country.[6]

Today, organized crime groups control prostitution, particularly in large cities and around areas where they have other interest, such as casinos. Even in Las Vegas, Nevada, the only location in the United States where prostitution and gambling are both legal, organized criminals are heavily involved in controlling and profiting from both activities.

Loan Sharking The crime of **loan sharking,** which is also known as *criminal usury*, is the practice of lending money at excessive rates, with the use of threats or extortion to force people to repay. A loan shark normally supplies the money in cash and attaches a very high interest rate to the loan—much higher than if the person went through a bank or credit union. Unfortunately, the people who are usually the most in need of loan sharking services are people with poor or no credit, so the possibility of getting a legitimate loan is unlikely. They are forced to acquire the services of a loan shark as a way to survive.

Many people involved in the loan sharking business have no connection to organized crime. The benefit of being a loan shark associated with a crime organization is that borrowers are far more likely to take the threat of violence seriously should they fail to repay the loan. Loan sharks will often resort to violence not only because the money is not paid back, but also so that future borrowers will realize the importance of paying off the debt.

Suppose that a family living in a working-class neighborhood of Chicago has just found out that the youngest daughter in the family has cancer. The family does not have health insurance, there is no additional income to pay for expensive chemotherapy treatments, and the nearest hospital with adequate cancer treatment is unwilling to give them reasonable payment options. The father of the family has started a second job, but will not have the income from that job for a month, which will be too late.

Knowing that a neighborhood crime organization loans money at an interest rate of 23 percent, he goes to the crime organization family and requests the loan. They give him the money and a month to pay it back with interest. If the father fails to pay the money back, he will likely be seriously hurt or even killed. The loan shark is not concerned with the circumstances of why the father needs the money, even when it involves an obvious tragedy such as this. If the father does not repay the money on time, he will face serious consequences.

Bookmaking   The crime of **bookmaking** is a form of illegal gambling in which customers use bookies to place bets on horse and dog races, professional sporting competitions, and other events. A bookmaker, or bookie, charges or accepts a percentage, fee, or "vig" on the wager.

Bookmaking operations involve complicated procedures, such as using scratch sheets and other documents to keep track of the betting and determine how much the bettor owes the bookie. Crime organizations will set up bookmaking operations where residents of the community can place their bets with the organization. Like loan sharking, bookmaking is a good industry for the organized crime because people are aware of the consequences of not paying on the bet. Should a person place a bet with a bookie and lose, that person will be compelled to pay the money back or face serious consequences.

Bookmaking is a multi-million dollar industry that usually involves a complicated system for payoffs and delivery of betting information. The process usually requires establishing a physical location where the bookie can work, take, and place bets. Although a small-time criminal without a lot of resources would find it difficult to work in the industry, a crime organization could easily set up the necessary tools.[7] Bookmakers may face charges under both state and federal laws.

Money Laundering   The money received through illegal activities such as drug sales and gambling is **dirty money.** When large amounts of illegally obtained money are spent, it is usually possible for law enforcement to detect that fact—one with no legitimate source of income would not be legally able to spend large amounts of money. If such expenditures were detected, this could lead to

bookmaking The promotion of gambling by unlawfully accepting bets upon the outcomes of future contingent events from members of the public as a business, rather than in a casual or personal fashion.

dirty money The money received through illegal activities such as drug sales and gambling.

arrests and prosecutions for the illegal activities that created this money. For this reason, crime organizations avoid such detection by **money laundering**, which is filtering money through legitimate sources until it appears to be derived from these sources. Money laundering is a crime under federal law, and is a serious crime problem. Recent studies report that over $300 billion is laundered into legitimate American businesses each year.[8]

Money laundering can be accomplished in a number of ways:

- An organization can take dirty money and give it to a legitimate business, so that it looks as if the money was actually received through the business. For example, a Mafia organization that obtains large profits through drug sales may take those profits and channel them through a car wash or restaurant owned by the group. The profits from the legitimate business will be much larger than what the legitimate business actually earned, but the group may be able to wash their money for some time without detection. Law enforcement, however, may become suspicious of a small business reporting a disproportionately huge income. This may lead to an investigation and, possibly, money laundering convictions.

- Another way to cleanse the money is for an organization to pay someone else to do it. The Colombian-based Cali Cartel, one of the largest drug organizations in the world, launders their money this way. Once a large-scale drug operation is complete, the Cartel holds an auction for professional money launderers who bid on the job. The successful launderer usually has about two weeks to return the cleansed money.[9]

To avoid detection when laundering money, several steps must be taken. The first step involves changing the money derived from criminal activities into an easily manipulated and less suspicious form. Organized criminals must figure out how to move huge quantities of cash without detection. Imagine showing up at a small, family-run restaurant with suitcases full of $100 bills and asking them to launder it. Doing so would likely raise suspicions, and observers might tip off law enforcement officers that laundering is going on.

To avoid this, crime organizations may disperse the money through several different channels, so that smaller amounts are sent out and can avoid detection. Organizations can funnel some money through legitimate businesses, convert some into other instruments such as money orders, and transfer the rest to offshore or overseas accounts, where detection by U.S. law enforcement is difficult. To complicate matters, many foreign countries have strict secrecy laws that make it very difficult for American law enforcement to investigate possible money laundering.

Once money has been turned into clean money, it can be freely used, spent, and transformed into financial instruments such as letters of credit, bonds, other securities, bank notes, and guarantees that can be used and accessed anywhere in the world. Once this happens, the money, now appearing legitimate, is virtually impossible to detect as laundered money.[10]

Money laundering allows organized crime syndicates to not only prosper through illegal means, but also to hide the profits from the illegal activity. Therefore, these profits are not taxed, and the people who make the money do not have to contribute to the government like the rest of us. As a result of the growing problem of money laundering, Congress and many states have enacted statutes that directly target the crime and provide stiff penalties for committing the crime. These various laws will be discussed fully later in this chapter.

Laws That Target Organized Crime

As organized crime continued to grow throughout the twentieth century, the federal government and individual state jurisdictions enacted laws that directly targeted organized crime syndicates and the activities they pursue. In 1986, The President's Commission on Organized Crime expanded the definition of organized crime to include outside criminal organizations who protect or render services to the criminal group itself.[11] These laws offer stiff penalties for any convictions related to organized crime. Now, a defendant may be convicted of a substantive offense, such as murder or drug distribution, as well as for being part of a particular type of group criminal behavior.

Racketeer Influenced and Corrupt Organizations (RICO)

In 1970, Congress enacted the landmark **Racketeer Influenced and Corrupt Organizations (RICO)** law. RICO is a federal law that criminalizes illegal activities committed by organized crime members, and was enacted to eradicate sophisticated organized crime syndicates. (See Figure 16-2 on page 558 for the activities prohibited by RICO.) At the time of its creation, its focus was on large, east-coast Mafia families that were controlling major criminal activity throughout the country. Federal prosecutors successfully used RICO to break down the structure and sophistication of these groups by convicting and severely sentencing its leaders.[12]

Racketeer Influenced and Corrupt Organizations Act (RICO) A federal law that criminalizes illegal activities committed by organized crime members.

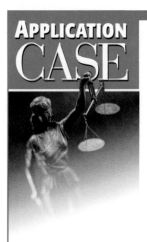

United States v. Gotti

In *United States v. Gotti* (1990), notorious boss John Gotti of New York's Gambino crime family in New York was arrested with crime family members Salvatore Gravano, Frank Locascio, and Thomas Gambino. They were charged with racketeering, murder, obstruction of justice, racketeering conspiracy, conspiracy to murder, illegal gambling, obstruction of justice, conspiracy to obstruct justice, and conspiracy to defraud the United States by obstructing its collection of income taxes. Gotti was also charged with racketeering violations, including a loansharking conspiracy.

About ten weeks before the trial began, Salvatore ("Sammy the Bull") Gravano entered into a cooperation agreement with the government and provided valuable evidence to assist its case. In 1992, the jury found John Gotti guilty on all counts. Gotti was given multiple life sentences for his violations of RICO and other crimes. He is serving his time at a maximum security federal penitentiary, and it is unlikely he will ever get out of prison. Gotti has filed countless appeals to his conviction, but higher courts have upheld the convictions on all grounds.

Critical Thinking Do you think the government would have succeeded in convicting Gotti without Gravano's help? Why or why not?

SOURCE: *United States v. Gotti*, 171 F.R.D. 19 (E.D.N.Y. 1997).

Organized Crime

Congress made RICO adaptable so that it could continuously apply to the evolving reality of organized crime in the United States. As a result, RICO's elements are fairly broad, allow for criminal prosecutions of various groups involved in a wide range of activities, and provide for both criminal and civil actions. The five elements of a criminal violation under RICO are:

1. Unlawful activity involving an enterprise
2. Two or more qualifying acts of racketeering activity
3. A showing of a pattern of such activity
4. An effect upon interstate commerce
5. The commission of the prohibited acts.[13]

For purposes of RICO, the U.S. Supreme Court has defined enterprise as any "union or group of individuals associated in fact [and] associated together for a common purpose of engaging in a course of conduct."[14] For example, if three men associate together every day by having lunch and playing pool, and all of them are

FIGURE 16-1

Racketeering Offenses

Racketeering activities include:

- Hobbs Act violations (extortion)
- Travel Act violations (interference with interstate commerce)
- Bribery
- Sports bribery
- Counterfeiting
- Embezzlement from union funds
- Loan sharking
- Mail fraud
- Wire fraud
- Obstruction of state or federal justice
- Contraband cigarettes
- Prostitution (Mann Act)
- Bankruptcy fraud
- Drug violations

SOURCE: 18 U.S.C.1961 (1) (A) (1994).

involved in criminal activity, this does not create an enterprise for purposes of the RICO statute because they must be working together on the same criminal pursuit.

When prosecuting someone for a RICO violation, the government must also show a pattern of two or more racketeering activities. A racketeering activity includes violating certain specified provisions of either federal or state criminal statutes. (See Figure 16–1.) RICO generally defines racketeering activity as:

Any act or threat involving murder, kidnapping, gambling, arson, robbery, bribery, extortion, dealing in obscene matter, or dealing in narcotic or other dangerous drugs, which is chargeable under State law and punishable by imprisonment for more than one year.

In addition, the statute lists several other violations of specific criminal statutes that constitute racketeering activity, including various acts of bribery, theft, extortion, and fraud.[15]

To prove a pattern of conduct, the prosecutor must show both relationship and continuity as separate elements. This means that the government must prove that a relationship existed between the defendants, and that they were working together to achieve a common criminal goal.[16]

To prove that the criminal act had some effect on interstate commerce, the government only needs to show that the effect of the illegal activity itself had an impact on interstate commerce. Interstate commerce does not have to involve one's physical presence in another state: Using a telephone, computer, or fax to contact someone in another state during the course of an illegal activity would constitute interstate commerce. It is very easy for the government to prove this element because almost all organized crime syndicates involve some aspect of interstate commerce. (See Figure 16–2 on page 558.)

Finally, to prove a RICO violation, the government must prove that a specific prohibited act has taken place. The statute sets forth four such prohibited acts, and at least one must be proven:

1. Investing income from a pattern of racketeering activity
2. Acquiring or maintaining an interest in an enterprise through a pattern of racketeering activity
3. Conducting the affairs of an enterprise through a pattern of racketeering activity
4. Conspiring to do any of the above[17]

In addition to stiff prison terms, a person convicted under RICO could face forfeiture of all property, heavy fines, and, under the RICO civil provisions, lawsuits brought by individuals who suffered from the RICO activity.[18]

State Versions of RICO   In addition to the Federal RICO statutes, many states have enacted their own legislation to combat organized crimes in their jurisdiction. The obvious benefit in creating such laws is that they can be used to prosecute intrastate, as opposed to interstate, commerce. In other words, organized criminal activity that is confined to a single state cannot escape prosecution simply because it lacks the element of interstate commerce. For example, Oregon's "little RICO" law defines racketeering essentially the same as the federal RICO law, and contains the same elements as the federal statute except for the requirement for interstate commerce. Under Oregon's RICO statute, a person violates this law if he or she launders money, uses threats to illegally take over a business, runs a criminal business, or operates a legitimate business though criminal means, or conspires to violate any of the above.[19]

Continuing Criminal Enterprise (CCE)   The Continuing Criminal Enterprise statute, or CCE, is similar to RICO but applies only to organized criminal activity involving drugs. This statute provides that a criminal enterprise exists when a continuing series of federal drug-related felonies are committed in concert with other crimes 1) in which the defendant occupies a managerial role and 2) from which he or she obtains a substantial income.

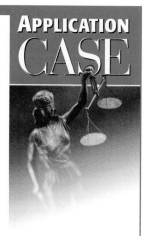
United States v. Andrews

In *United States v. Andrews*, over 80 members of the El Rukn Street gang were convicted of various RICO charges. The El Rukn gang was a highly disciplined and organized association that existed solely for the purpose of perpetrating crime. Between the late 1960s and the late 1980s, the El Rukns committed countless acts of racketeering, including 20 murders, 12 attempted murders, 11 conspiracies to murder, 1 kidnapping, wide scale drug trafficking, and numerous obstructions of justice. To protect their business, the El Rukns found it necessary to murder several rival drug dealers and rival gang members. To protect members from prosecution for some of these murders and other crimes, the El Rukns killed, intimidated, and kidnapped witnesses. These activities were carried out through a formal chain of command that was headed by Jeff Fort, an unindicted co-conspirator. Five of the defendants held positions at the second and third levels of command, and were known as either generals or officers in the organization.

In addition to the RICO charges, 37 of the defendants were convicted of conspiring to possess with intent to distribute multi-kilogram quantities of heroin and cocaine, hundreds of pounds of marijuana, thousands of amphetamine pills, and other narcotics. Several of the defendants challenged their convictions on appeal, arguing that RICO was not applicable to the conduct of a street gang and that RICO was unconstitutionally vague.

The appellate court upheld all convictions, finding that the conduct of the El Rukn gang was precisely what Congress intended to criminalize when RICO was created. The court also held that the statute was not constitutionally vague and that the government had met its burden of proving an "enterprise" for purposes of the statute. This is an important case because it was one of the first instances where federal prosecutors used the RICO statute to prosecute gangs and to recognize gangs as organized crime syndicates.

RICO & Gangs

Critical Thinking What implications does this case have for gangs and the prosecution of gang-related crime?

SOURCE: *United States v. Andrews*, 749 F.Supp 1520 (N.D. Ill. 1990).

A continuing criminal enterprise consists of five elements:

1. A felony violation of federal narcotics laws
2. as part of a continuing series of violations

FIGURE 16–2
Activities Prohibited by RICO

Sec. 1962. Prohibited activities

(a) It shall be unlawful for any person who has received any income derived, directly or indirectly, from a pattern of racketeering activity or through collection of an unlawful debt in which such person has participated as a principal within the meaning of section 2, title 18, United States Code, to use or invest, directly or indirectly, any part of such income, or the proceeds of such income, in acquisition of any interest in, or the establishment or operation of, any enterprise which is engaged in, or the activities of which affect, interstate or foreign commerce. A purchase of securities on the open market for purposes of investment, and without the intention of controlling or participating in the control of the issuer, or of assisting another to do so, shall not be unlawful under this subsection if the securities of the issuer held by the purchaser, the members of his immediate family, and his or their accomplices in any pattern or racketeering activity or the collection of an unlawful debt after such purchase do not amount in the aggregate to one percent of the outstanding securities of any one class, and do not confer, either in law or in fact, the power to elect one or more directions of the issuer.

(b) It shall be unlawful for any person through a pattern of racketeering activity or through collection of an unlawful debt to acquire or maintain, directly or indirectly, any interest in or control of any enterprise which is engaged in, or the activities of which affect, interstate or foreign commerce.

(c) It shall be unlawful for any person employed by or associated with any enterprise engaged in, or the activities of which affect, interstate or foreign commerce, to conduct or participate, directly or indirectly, in the conduct of such enterprise's affairs through a pattern of racketeering activity or collection of unlawful debt.

(d) It shall be unlawful for any person to conspire to violate any of the provisions of subsection (a), (b), or (c) of this section.

SOURCE: U.S. Code Title 18 § 1962.

3. in concert with five or more persons
4. for whom the defendant is an organizer or supervisor
5. from which the defendant obtains a substantial income.[20]

As with RICO violations, a defendant can be charged with both a substantive crime (in this case, a drug crime) and a violation of the CCE. For example, an organized crime leader would likely be charged with CCE if he or she were involved in a national drug operation with distribution centers throughout the country. He or she would likely be charged with a federal drug crime, such as possession or distribution of narcotics, in addition to the CCE charge.

Anti-Drug Abuse Act In addition to the various federal and state laws that target organized crime, there are specific statutes that target money laundering. For example, the Anti-Drug Abuse Act of 1986 holds people criminally liable for knowingly participating in money laundering schemes, and provides stiff penalties for monetary

Myth	**Fact**
A person cannot be simultaneously convicted of a substantive offense and an organized crime offense, such as RICO.	People are often convicted of substantive offenses in addition to organized crime violations, such as RICO.

manipulation that involves 1) disguising the source of proceeds of unlawful activities or 2) the failure to report income. This act also allows the government to seize and forfeit any cash or property related to such a scheme. The penalties provided are fines up to $500,000, imprisonment up to 20 years, or both. [21]

Bank Fraud Act and Bank Secrecy Act   The Bank Fraud Act and the Bank Secrecy Act require mandatory reporting provisions for financial institutions with regard to large sums of money. This legislation allows the government to monitor money laundering operations and to ensure that the money passing through these institutions is made legitimately.[22]

Money Laundering Control Act (MLCA)   The Money Laundering Control Act of 1986 (MLCA) was enacted in response to two problems that were facing significant growth:

1. Money laundering that resulted from the booming cocaine trade of the 1980s
2. Widespread non-compliance with the banking reporting statutes

Clearly, prior statutes were not working in combating the growing money laundering industry. Under the MLCA, the act of money laundering itself is criminalized, regardless of whether any reporting statutes are violated. Provisions of this act hold individuals criminally liable for knowingly spending money that is laundered even if the person was not the one involved in the laundering process. A person can be convicted under the statute for conspiring to launder money, even if he or she doesn't actually go through with it. Like RICO, the MCLA also provides for both civil and criminal forfeitures of funds or property implicated in money laundering.[23]

Criticisms   Critics of RICO and similar laws have several complaints about these laws, including:

- Although RICO is intended to target high-ranking organized crime figures, it could apply to almost anyone as long as the elements have been established.
- RICO has "federalized" virtually all criminal activities, even those normally within the jurisdiction of states' criminal statutes.
- Under RICO and similar laws, convicted persons are punished multiple times for the same offense or offenses, in violation of the prohibition against double jeopardy.
- RICO and similar offenses are too vague, and their elements are unclear.

Regarding the double jeopardy claim, a number of people convicted under these statutes have argued a violation of double jeopardy in order to challenge the validity of their convictions. Federal courts have consistently upheld their convictions on two separate grounds. First, the doctrine of dual sovereignty holds that a state prosecution does not bar a subsequent federal prosecution of the same person for the same act. This applies to people convicted under a state substantive offense and a federal organized crime offense.[24] Second, multiple offenses are valid as long as one element of the crime is different for each of the offenses.[25]

Regarding arguments about the vagueness of these laws, the federal courts have consistently rejected this argument. Federal courts have upheld these convictions and stated that an ordinary person would know that the activities of an organized crime family fell within the range of conduct, and as such could be prosecuted under RICO. In other words, Congress's original intent that these statutes cover a broad range of criminal conduct has been upheld, thus allowing for more people to be convicted under the statutes.[26]

Check your answers at
cl.glencoe.com.

Self Check

1. Why did the criminalization of drugs and, for a time, alcohol benefit criminals? Can this be undone? Why or why not?
2. Why do organized criminals need to launder money, and how is this done?

16.2 Street Gangs

Although street gangs have existed in the United States since the nineteenth century, they have grown tremendously in the last 20 years. Throughout the country, both in big cities and small rural communities, street gangs have developed into large organized crime syndicates that have influenced illegal activity in almost every state. A **criminal street gang** is any formal or informal ongoing group of three or more persons:

- whose primary activity is the commission of one or more criminal acts.
- who has an identifiable name or identifying sign or symbol.
- whose members individually or collectively engage in or have engaged in a pattern of criminal gang activity.[27]

criminal street gang Any formal or informal ongoing organization whose primary activity is the commission of one or more criminal acts, who has an identifiable name or identifying sign or symbol, and whose members individually or collectively engage in or have engaged in a pattern of criminal gang activity.

Structure of a Modern Street Gang

There are several consistent traits of a modern-day street gang. In order for a gang to maintain and prosper, there must be frequent contact between gang members. Typically, the neighborhood or area from which someone comes determines membership, which makes it easier for members to have constant interaction. A gang usually controls a specific neighborhood or territory, and members of the community are aware that the area belongs to the gang. Members may mark their territory by using graffiti to put the gangs' names on local buildings, and gang members will be quick to defend their territory should another gang try to lay a claim to it.

Another typical characteristic is that a gang faces problems or conflicts as a united group, rather than individually. For instance, if one member is being bothered or harassed by someone, the whole gang will come to his or her side and lend support. Like other organized crime groups, gangs typically have a hierarchical system. Usually, this structure is determined by the amount of time a person has been in the gang, the person's age, and the person's family ties to gang leaders or organizers. Sometimes, leadership will be determined by the dedication a member has for the group. For example, a gang member who committed a number of crimes for the group, or who is the first to physically defend the neighborhood or the gang, may quickly rise to a leadership position.

Crimes Committed by Gangs

In the past, street gang behavior was fairly innocent and was usually lawful, despite occasional instances of rival gang fistfights and small-scale criminal activity. Today, however, many modern street gangs are now involved in all kinds of criminal activity, ranging from drug dealing and distribution, gambling operations, murder, bank robberies, financial crimes, extortion, bribery, racketeering, kidnapping, and even terrorism. As the gangs become more sophisticated, so does their level of criminal activity. The crack cocaine boom of the 1980s and 1990s "is primarily responsible for transforming many fraternal, juvenile organizations into highly sophisticated organized crime entities."

The level of development of any gang's drug operation may be an accurate measurement of the overall level of sophistication of the gang. Nonetheless, the amount of drug activity engaged in by any individual gang "is, however, directly related to the size of its membership and the degree of organizational sophistication achieved by the gang. The smaller, less organized gangs are generally only involved in selling drugs at the street level. As the gang grows and becomes more structured, it develops more specialized distribution methods and expands its product."[28]

Some of the largest street gangs have made millions of dollars in drug profits through an organized system of narcotics distribution. The El Rukns, a notorious Chicago gang that has existed since the 1960s, reportedly brings in between $50,000 and $70,000 per day from narcotics sales alone.[29] In order for the El Rukns to maintain power and control over their drug monopoly, members systematically killed rival drug dealers. If they don't kill witnesses who are going to testify against them in court, their intimidation tactics usually dissuade them from testifying.

Myth	Fact
Most gang members are hardened criminals with aggressive attitudes.	Often, young men and women will join gangs as a protective measure. For example, a young person living in a gang neighborhood may experience constant harassment and abuse from local gang members until he or she joins a gang.

Identifying Gang Organizations

Although there are thousands of gangs throughout the United States, a small handful of groups have gained notoriety because of their size, power, ruthlessness, or monopoly in crime. Most people have some recognition of the notorious Los Angeles street gangs, the Bloods and the Crips. What they may not know is that there are hundreds of different Crips and Bloods gangs throughout Los Angeles, as well as Crips and Bloods scattered throughout the country.

A common misconception about street gangs relates to gender. Most people think that only males are gang members, but in fact girls have joined gangs in larger numbers this decade. The U.S. Justice Department has identified 650,000 gang members nationwide, and 10 to 15 percent of them are female. In Los Angeles County, the active gang population is now 10 to 15 percent female.[30]

Latino Gangs   Latino gangs are located primarily in the *barrios*, or Mexican-American slums, of Southern California. Most members of these gangs are either first-generation Americans or were actually born in Mexico or Central America, then immigrated to the United States as children. As with most gang organizations, Latino gangs are created based on certain neighborhoods, housing projects, or communities. By joining a gang, a young person living in a gang-infested area will have others to protect him or her. Upon membership into a Latino street gang, he or she will become a **cholo** or **chola**. In some circumstances, there will be entire cholo families where one or both parents, in addition to the children, are all members of the same gang.[31]

Latino gangs have grown in membership and power over the last few decades. The largest of these gangs, particularly the Mexican Mafia, have been responsible for large-scale drug operations throughout the country. Additionally, many of these gangs run their criminal operations inside the toughest California prisons. Although many of the Mexican Mafia's leaders are serving life sentences, they are able to designate responsibilities to members on the outside and continue to expand their operations. Additionally, members of Hispanic gangs are able to use their command of the Spanish language to facilitate the importation of drugs from Mexico and other Central American countries.[32]

cholo/chola (Especially among Mexican-Americans) A member of a Latino street gang.

Crips and Bloods   The Crips and Bloods gangs, which evolved out of Los Angeles but are now established throughout the country, have existed for over 30 years. It is believed that the Crips were first organized in 1969, and the Bloods soon after. As mentioned earlier,

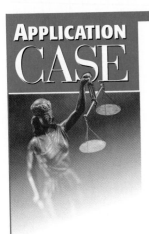
Mexican Mafia Crackdown

In 1999, over 200 law enforcement agents conducted raids throughout Los Angeles County and arrested 13 Mexican Mafia leaders on charges of murder and drug trafficking. Twenty-seven other members, including some already in prison, were charged in connection with 4 murders, 3 attempted murders, and 13 counts of conspiracy to distribute narcotics. One of the lead officers in the crackdown stated that the effort to bring down the Mexican Mafia was comparable to the 30-year effort by federal agencies to dismantle the Cosa Nostra.

During the trial, prosecutors relied heavily on the testimony of former gang members, some of whom turned to the government when they feared they would be killed by others in the gang. The jury reached its verdict after six weeks of testimony by more than 150 witnesses and five days of deliberations. During the reading of the verdicts, heavily armed federal marshals and state troopers surrounded the courthouse, and police helicopters circled over the courthouse as the defendants were taken into court. Ten Mexican Mafia members, including several high-ranking leaders, were convicted of federal racketeering and conspiracy related to multiple robberies, drug deals, and 15 murders.

> **Critical Thinking** Would you categorize the Mexican Mafia as a gang or as organized crime? Explain your answer.

SOURCE: Karen Low, "Authorities Arrest 13 Alleged Mexican Mafia Members," *Associated Press Release*, February 3, 1999, n.p.

each group is comprised of hundreds of sets, which are like gangs within the gangs. In Los Angeles County alone, officials have identified 219 different Crips gangs and 84 different Bloods gangs. Examples of the various sets comprising the Bloods and Crips in Los Angeles include the Hoover Crips, the Harlem Crips, The Grape Street Bloods, The Bounty Hunter Bloods, and the Swan Bloods. Some of these gangs are friendly and have established ties with each other, but others hold the same vindictiveness for each other as they do for rival gangs.[33]

The Crips and Bloods have many identifying characteristics that are unique to their gangs and the sets within them. For example, the Crips's color is blue, and Crips tend to wear blue clothing and other attire. Likewise, the Bloods's color is red, so Bloods tend to wear red clothing and accessories. In addition, low-wasted khaki pants with oversized t-shirts are typical gang clothing, and certain tennis shoes or jewelry may identify gang membership or association. Depending on the individual gang, members may wear a particular sports jersey or baseball cap with a team that the group adopts as a being representative of the gang.

Each gang is an independent entity that does not answer to a centralized Crips or Bloods leader. Instead, leaders known as shot-callers represent their gang when interacting with other groups. In 1993, after Los Angeles experienced the worst rioting in its history as a result of the Rodney King verdict, shot-callers throughout Los Angeles County, as well as specialized police gang units and community leaders, met to discuss the possibility of a gang truce between the Crips and the Bloods. Although gang rivalry continues in Los Angeles, and Crips and Bloods continue to war in a few communities as if nothing has changed, many believe that this gang truce was overall successful. In some areas of Los Angeles, the truce is credited with erasing two decades of violence. In others, gangs have agreed not to initiate combat, but still end up killing in the course of robberies, drug deals, dice games, and parties.[34]

While the Los Angeles gang problem may not be as serious as before, the gang problem in California is far from over. There are still countless shootings and other crimes related to gang associations. Both the Los Angeles County Sheriff's Department and the Los Angeles Police Department have specialized gang units that focus all of their attention on gang members and the crimes they commit. These officers become experts on identifying gang members, understanding which gangs are rivals, knowing the various turfs the gangs control, and are able to recognize graffiti, clothing, and other marks that may categorize an individual as a gang member.

In addition, Crips and Bloods have spread out throughout the country and are now visible in the Midwest and East Coast. Former Los Angeles gang members who have moved out of state are responsible for creating these new gang sets. As a result, crime has increased in those areas. Los Angeles gang members have been found in all regions of the United States.

Chinese Gangs Chinese gangs have experienced rapid growth since the passage of an immigration act in the 1960s that allowed many immigrants to come to the United States. These gangs, like all others, were formed as a way to make money through illegal means. Chinese gangs usually have between 25 and 50 members, with a hierarchical system based around a leader, middle supervisors, and lower ranks who commit the actual crimes. There are several characteristics that distinguish a Chinese gang from other groups, including a close

Policing and Gangs

Since even rural regions of the country now have gangs, it is likely that any police officer will work in an area with some gang activity. In order to combat the problem effectively, it will be important for him or her to have a basic understanding and knowledge of how local gangs operate and how to recognize gang members. Most law enforcement agencies have experts who provide detailed accounts of the gangs and their identifying marks, as well as those neighborhoods that have a large gang population. New officers should ask officers who specialize in gang-related issues to educate them on the problem, and should spend some time in the unit learning about what they do and how they control the problem. This information may be very important in protecting the officers' safety, as well as the safety of the community.

relationship with community organizations, investment in legitimate businesses, international connections, and control over large amounts of money. Women and girls are not usually admitted into Chinese gangs, but do associate with them and lend support.

Chinese gangs in the United States prey on people's weaknesses in their recruiting methods. They target new immigrants with limited education and skills, who need the gang's assistance to earn money. Their initiation rituals usually involve a ceremony where the new member takes an oath, then drinks a combination of blood and wine in front of the leader.

Vietnamese Gangs   Vietnamese gangs began to organize at the end of the Vietnam War, when hundreds of thousands of immigrants poured into Southern California. These groups tend to focus their criminal activities on theft, robbery, carjacking, and extortion. Vietnamese immigrants often distrust legitimate banks, and as a result are known to keep large quantities of cash in their homes. Gang members often target these homes and steal the money.[35]

Laws That Target Gangs

As gangs have evolved and become more and more violent over the last few decades, many jurisdictions have enacted legislation directly targeting gang members and their crimes. Just as RICO was established as a way to break down and destroy organized crime syndicates, gang legislation works toward the same purpose. These laws add additional penalties for gang members convicted of crimes, prohibit gang members from associating with one another, and restrict areas where gang members can associate. (See Figure 16–3 on page 569.) Some of this legislation has become quite controversial in recent years because opponents argue that many of the laws violate constitutional rights, such as freedom of association and freedom of expression. However, many of these laws have been upheld and are used throughout the country to combat gang violence.

Under federal sentencing laws, a defendant who is convicted of a narcotics offense may be given additional prison time if the prosecutor can prove that he or she is a serious gang member. This law's purpose is to enhance the sentences of defendants who participate in groups, clubs, organizations, or associations that use violence to further their ends.[36]

Over a dozen states have passed laws that make it an offense to aid or conspire to aid crimes intended to further the activities of a street gang. An Iowa statute provides that:

Federal Prosecutor

Description and Duties: Enforce federal laws, including the RICO statute. Many positions are through different federal agencies or special prosecution teams. For example, the Tobacco Litigation Team handles the lawsuit against the cigarette manufacturers to recover federal health care costs associated with tobacco use and equitable relief, including disgorgement of proceeds, under the RICO statute. Federal prosecutors for the DEA provide legal advice and support to DEA management and field offices worldwide, with an emphasis on federal criminal drug laws and related issues. Federal prosecutors for Southern District of California may work with the Border Crimes Section, where they will prosecute felony immigration and border drug smuggling cases.

Salary: Salaries are within the range of a government pay scale, but these pay levels have some flexibility. Salaries can range from GS-11 ($44,352 - $57,656) to GS-15 ($87,864 - $114,224).

Other Information: Federal prosecutors generally must possess a J.D., be an active member of the bar in any jurisdiction, and have at least two years of post- J.D. legal experience. Excellent legal research, writing and analytical skills are required. Prosecutorial experience, especially in the federal courts, is desirable.

Critical Thinking What qualities do you think a federal prosecutor should have?

SOURCE: U.S. Department of Justice, http://www.usdoj.gov/oarm/jobs/dea601criminal.html and http://www.usdoj.gov/oarm/jobs/usao301sdcarevisedinsad.html.

"A person who actively participates in or is a member of a criminal street gang and who willfully aids and abets any criminal act committed for the benefit of, at the direction of, or in association with any criminal street gang, commits a class D felony."[37]

Because California has one of the largest gang populations of any state, and because it has experienced a tremendous amount of gang-related crime in its cities and rural areas, it has also become one of the toughest states regarding the creation of legislation to combat gangs. The Street Terrorism Enforcement and Prevention Act (STEP) is an all-inclusive anti-gang law, the purpose of which is to eradicate gangs in the state.

In part, STEP provides that:

- Any adult who utilizes physical violence to coerce, induce, or solicit another person who is under 18 years of age to actively participate in any criminal street gang, as defined in subdivision (f) of Section 186.22, the members of which engage in a pattern of criminal gang activity, as defined in subdivision (e) of Section 186.22, shall be punished by imprisonment in the state prison for one, two, or three years.
- Any adult who threatens a minor with physical violence on two or more separate occasions within any 30-day period with the intent to coerce, induce, or solicit the minor to actively participate in a criminal street gang, as defined in subdivision (f) of Section 186.22, the members of which engage in a pattern of criminal gang activity, as defined in subdivision (e) of Section 186.22, shall be punished by imprisonment in the state prison for one, two, or three years or in a county jail for up to one year.
- A minor who is 16 years of age or older who commits an offense described in subdivision (a) or (b) is guilty of a misdemeanor.

STEP requires that to be convicted, the prosecutor must show that a pattern of gang activity was committed. This is defined, in the statute, as:

> the commission of, attempted commission of, or solicitation of, sustained juvenile petition for, or conviction of two or more of the following offenses, provided at least one of these offenses occurred after the effective date of this chapter and the last of those offenses occurred within three years after a prior offense, and the offenses were committed on separate occasions, or by two or more persons: [there follows 23 enumerated offenses, including homicide, robbery, and rape].[38]

Although several cases have challenged the constitutionality of the STEP statute arguing that it infringes on gang members' right to associate, the courts have consistently upheld this law.[39]

In another type of anti-gang legislation, several cities in California have enacted legislation banning gang members from associating in certain areas, such as parks. The San Fernando City Council recently passed an ordinance to this effect after a mother and her three children were killed by the crossfire of a gang shooting. This law provides that "gang members who are formally

FIGURE 16-3

State Statutory Definitions of the Term "Gang Member"

Arizona §13–105(7)

"Criminal street gang" means an ongoing formal or informal association of persons whose members or associates individually or collectively engage in the commission, attempted commission, facilitation or solicitation of any felony act and who has at least one individual who is a street gang member.

California §186.22(23)(f) (Virtually identical definitions used in Florida, Georgia, Iowa, Louisiana, Minnesota, Missouri, South Dakota, and Wisconsin)

"Criminal street gang" means any ongoing organization, association, or group of three or more persons, whether formal or informal, having as one of its primary activities the commission of one or more of the criminal acts enumerated in paragraphs (1) to (23), inclusive, of subdivision (c), having a common name or common identifying sign or symbol, and whose members individually or collectively engage in or have engaged in a pattern of criminal gang activity.

Connecticut P.A. No. 93–416 Sec. 1

"Gang" means a group of juveniles or youth who, acting in concert with each other, or with adults, engage in illegal activity.

Nevada 193.168 (6)

"Criminal gang" means any combination of persons, organized formally or informally, so constructed that the organization will continue its operation even if individual members enter or leave the organization, which

(a) has a common name or identifying symbol

(b) has particular conduct, status and customs indicative of it

(c) has as one of its common activities engaging in criminal activity punishable as a felony, other than the conduct which constitutes the primary offense

classified under STEP based on their criminal records, associates, street names, tattoos and other signs of gang involvement, and who are then served with papers notifying them of the classification are banned from using the park for sports or other non-gang activities."[40]

Arkansas, a state hard hit by Los Angeles gang transplants, enacted a statute that is modeled upon RICO but applies particularly to gang members. The Arkansas Criminal Gang, Organization, or Enterprise Act provides additional penalties for gang members convicted of crimes. This law goes beyond other state gang laws and punishes people who are acting in concert. Notably, the law specifically provides that it is not a defense to the enhanced penalty to argue that the people involved were not gang members.[41]

In addition, another part of Arkansas's gang legislation goes a step further and provides:

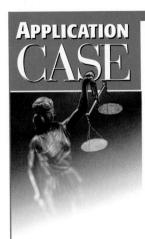
City of Chicago v. Morales

In the 1999 case of *City of Chicago v. Morales*, the U.S. Supreme Court called into question the validity of recent anti-gang laws. In 1992, the Chicago City Council enacted the Gang Congregation Ordinance, which prohibits "criminal street gang members" from "loitering" with one another or with other persons in any public place. Commission of the offense involved four predicates:

1. The police officer must reasonably believe that at least one of the two or more persons present in a "public place" is a "criminal street gang member."
2. The persons must be "loitering," which the ordinance defined as "remain[ing] in any one place with no apparent purpose."
3. The officer must then order "all" of the persons to disperse and remove themselves "from the area."
4. A person must disobey the officer's order. If any person, whether a gang member or not, disobeyed the officer's order, that person would be guilty of violating the ordinance.

The Court found the ordinance was void for vagueness on two grounds: 1) It was unconstitutionally vague in failing to provide fair notice of prohibited conduct, and 2) it was also impermissibly vague in failing to establish minimal guidelines for enforcement.

Critical Thinking Do you think the benefits of anti-gang laws like this one outweigh their constitutional vagueness?

SOURCE: *City of Chicago v. Morales*, 529 U.S. 41 (1999).

1. A person commits the offense of engaging in a continuing criminal gang, organization, or enterprise in the first degree if he:
   A. Commits or attempts to commit or solicits to commit a felony predicate criminal offense; and
   B. That offense is part of a continuing series of two (2) or more predicate criminal offenses which are undertaken by that person in concert with two (2) or more other persons with respect to whom that person occupies a position of organizer, a supervisory position, or any other position of management.

2. A person who engages in a continuing criminal gang, organization, or enterprise in the first degree is guilty of a felony two (2) classifications higher than the classification of the highest underlying predicate offense referenced in subdivision (a)(1)(A) of this section.[42]

Self Check

1. Why, in your opinion, have gang activities changed so much over the years? Are drugs solely to blame?
2. Why do you think that girls and women are more involved in gang activities?

CRIMINAL LAW *Online*

Check your answers at **cl.glencoe.com**.

16.3 Terrorism

When most people picture terrorists or terrorist activity, they imagine religious extremists blowing up buildings or airplanes. In actuality, terrorism is much more than that. People commit terrorist acts for all types of reasons, including political, religious, and social beliefs. Broadly defined, **terrorism** is any deliberate use or threat of violence by groups desiring to achieve political, social, or religious objectives. Terrorism has also been defined to include:

- The unlawful use or threatened use of force or violence by a revolutionary organization against individuals or property with the intention of coercing or intimidating governments or societies, often for political or ideological purposes
- The unlawful use of force or violence against persons or property to intimidate or coerce a government, the civilian population, or any segment thereof, in furtherance of political or social objectives
- Premeditated, politically motivated violence perpetrated against noncombatant targets by subnational groups or clandestine state agents[43]

terrorism The deliberate employment of violence or the threat of the use of violence by subnational groups and sovereign states to attain strategic and political objectives.

CRIMINAL LAW *Online*

International Crime

To learn more about the increasingly international nature of organized crime, visit the Web site of Interpol, an organization that coordinates international law enforcement, through the link provided at **cl.glencoe.com**. What information did you find on international efforts against organized crime, white-collar crime, and terrorism?

Terrorism Distinguished from Other Crimes

The main difference between terrorist crime and other types of crime is that the motive behind terrorism is political, as opposed to economic. Other criminal groups, such as gangs or organized crime syndicates, are usually only trying to achieve economic gain. For example, a gang may distribute cocaine in order to make money, but

a terrorist may bomb a building or kidnap innocent hostages in order to get the government's attention, draw a focus to their cause, or get a law changed. As another example of terrorism, a group may blow up a bus carrying innocent passengers and then tell the government that unless some of their members are released from prison, another bus will be blown up as well.

Terrorist acts could include any type of criminal behavior that uses the activity to accomplish a political or religious goal. Common examples include bombings, hijacking of airplanes or other places where large groups reside, and kidnapping innocent people or taking people hostage until a government entity gives in to the demands of the terrorists.

Regardless of the reasons or the means of carrying out the acts, terrorism is a serious threat and can take place almost anywhere. Until a few years ago, many Americans felt that terrorism only took place overseas. Unfortunately, after the Oklahoma City bombing 1995, Americans witnessed first-hand a horrible act of violence committed for political or religious reasons. As a result, laws have been enacted in order to combat terrorism and avoid the bloodshed of innocent people.

Ⱥ Oklahoma City Bombing The bombing of the federal building in Oklahoma City changed the face of terrorism in many people's minds. *How has this event changed America's ideas and U.S. policy toward terrorism?*

Laws that Target Terrorism

Congress has created several statutes that criminalize terrorist-related activity and offer stiffer penalties when a perpetrator uses violence to carry out a political agenda. Federal law defines **international terrorism** as acts of violence that "appear to be intended to intimidate or coerce" people, a government policy or conduct, and that "occur primarily outside the territorial jurisdiction of the United States, or transcend national boundaries." In 1996, Congress adopted new anti-terrorist legislation, which provided:

international terrorism
The deliberate employment of violence or the threat of the use of violence that crosses national borders.

A. Prohibited Acts

Offenses. Whoever, involving conduct transcending national boundaries and in a circumstance described in subsection (b)—

a. kills, kidnaps, maims, commits an assault resulting in serious bodily injury, or assaults with a dangerous weapon any person within the United States; or

United States v. McVeigh

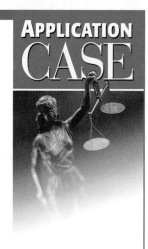

In 1995, in the worst case of domestic terrorism in United States history, Timothy McVeigh blew up the Alfred Murrah Federal Building in Oklahoma City, Oklahoma. The bombing killed 168 innocent people, including 19 children at the federal building's day care center. McVeigh was tried and convicted of 168 counts of murder, as well as other charges related to the nature of the crime.

McVeigh appealed his case to both the Federal Appellate Court and the U.S. Supreme Court, raising a total of nine separate challenges to his conviction. His attorneys argued that a new trial was warranted because of juror misconduct, an unfair exclusion of evidence, prejudicial pretrial publicity, and inflammatory testimony by victims' relatives. The 10th Circuit Court of Appeals rejected all of McVeigh's arguments that he deserved a new trial, as did the U.S. Supreme Court. McVeigh, the first federal prisoner to be executed since 1963, was executed by lethal injection on Monday, June 11, 2001.

Critical Thinking Do you agree with the courts' decisions to deny McVeigh an appeal? Why or why not?

SOURCE: *United States v. McVeigh*, 153 F.3d 1166 (10 Cir. 1998), *cert. denied*, U.S. 119 S.Ct. 1148 (1999). *See also* Andrew Cohen, "Legal Fight Won from Trenches," *Denver Post*, legal opinion, June 3, 1997, pg. A09.

Terrorism

---

b. creates a substantial risk of serious bodily injury to any other person by destroying or damaging any structure, conveyance, or other real or personal property within the United States or by attempting or conspiring to destroy or damage any structure, conveyance, or other real or personal property within the United States; in violation of the laws of any State, or the United States, shall be punished as prescribed in subsection (c).

Under the penalty provisions of this law, punishment can be as much as life imprisonment or death if the criminal conduct results in a killing. Punishment can result in various other serious terms for conduct that results in less than a killing.

Self Check

1. How have American perceptions regarding terrorism changed since the Oklahoma City bombing?
2. Which do you feel is a bigger threat to the United States: international or domestic terrorism?

CRIMINAL LAW *Online*
Check your answers at **cl.glencoe.com**.

Organized Crime, Gangs, and Terrorism

SUMMARY BY CHAPTER OBJECTIVES

1. Understand the historical development of organized crime.

Organized crime was created out of the criminalization of lotteries, prostitution rings, and the prohibition of drugs and alcohol. Since its beginning in the United States, it has evolved into a sophisticated operation that uses illegal means to accomplish a variety of economic goals.

2. List some typical organized crime activities.

Typical organized crime activities include:

- Loan sharking
- Gambling
- Prostitution rings
- Money laundering
- Drug distribution
- Bookmaking
- Extortion

3. List the elements of a RICO violation.

The five elements of a criminal violation under RICO are:

- Unlawful activity involving an enterprise
- Two or more qualifying acts of racketeering activity
- A showing of a pattern of such activity
- An effect upon interstate commerce
- The commission of the prohibited acts

4. Understand and differentiate various laws aimed at targeting organized crime.

Crimes such as the Racketeer Influenced and Corrupt Organization statute (RICO) and the Continuing Criminal Enterprise statute (CCE) were created as a way for the legislature to break down and put an end to organized crime. These statutes add stiffer penalties for people who commit crimes as part of a criminal enterprise and make the very act of participation in these groups a criminal violation.

5. Understand the structure and activities of modern street gangs.

Like many organized crime organizations, many modern street gangs have a leader, members in middle management roles, and lower-level members who commit the actual crimes. In addition, gangs also have shot-callers, who are members in leadership roles that act as liaisons with other gangs. Typical activities of modern street gangs include all kinds of criminal activity, ranging from drug dealing and distribution, gambling operations, murder, bank robberies, financial crimes, extortion, bribery, racketeering, kidnapping, and even terrorism.

6. Explain the laws that target street gangs.

Several jurisdictions have created laws that specifically address gang-related activity. One famous example is STEP, which offers stiffer penalties if a person commits a crime in association with his or her gang membership. Several cities have also enacted legislation that prohibits gang members from associating in certain areas, such as parks or sidewalks.

7. Understand the types of criminal activity that constitute terrorism.

Terrorism occurs where a group or person uses violence or other criminal means for a political or religious purpose rather than for economic motivations. Examples of common terrorist activities include:

- Hijacking
- Kidnapping
- Hostage taking
- Bombings

8. Describe the various laws that target terrorism.

Congress has created several statutes that criminalize terrorist-related activity and offer stiffer penalties when a perpetrator uses violence to carry out a political or religious agenda. In 1996, Congress adopted new anti-terrorist legislation, which provided that anyone who transcends national boundaries and kills, kidnaps, maims, commits an assault resulting in serious bodily injury, or assaults with a dangerous weapon any person within the United States can receive a punishment as severe as the death penalty.

KEY TERMS

organized crime, page 545
boss, page 547
underboss, page 548
captains and soldiers,
    page 548
crews, page 548
protectors, page 548
shakedown, page 548

racketeering, page 549
loan sharking, page 550
bookmaking, page 551
dirty money, page 551
money laundering, page 552
Racketeer Influenced and
    Corrupt Organizations
    Act (RICO), page 553

criminal street gang,
    page 561
cholo/chola, page 563
terrorism, page 571
international terrorism,
    page 572

QUESTIONS FOR REVIEW

1. How did the prohibition of drugs and alcohol help in the development of organized crime?
2. What role have lotteries played in organized crime, and how has the role of lotteries changed over the years?
3. What is loan sharking?

4. What is bookmaking, and how does a bookie make a profit?
5. Describe money laundering and the two main ways in which this crime is committed.
6. What is RICO? How do CCE and state versions of RICO differ from RICO?

7. Summarize the various laws aimed at combating money laundering.
8. How have the activities of gangs changed over the last century?
9. What is the main difference between organized crime and terrorism?
10. What are some reasons why individuals resort to terrorism?

PROBLEM-SOLVING EXERCISES

1. **Organized Crime** You have just arrested Lonnie, 25, for possession with intent to distribute cocaine. Lonnie has a large amount of drugs on him when he is caught and is charged with distribution. At the station, you ask him if he would like to call a lawyer. Lonnie replies, "Man, I can't do no more time. I could be a big help to you if we can work something out." He then goes on to say that he is working for the Williams crime family, a notorious and ruthless crime syndicate that has dominated part of your city for nearly 20 years. Authorities have been trying for years to arrest and charge one of the leaders. Lonnie offers to wear a wire when he is to meet with his supervisor, who has direct contact with Tracy Williams, the boss. Lonnie wears the wire, and the captain is taped while giving specific instructions related to pick-up points, quantities of cocaine, distribution areas, and a number of other crimes that the family has committed. Lonnie names several men who are known to be high-ranking members of the gang and describes their roles in the various operations. Lonnie, as well as several others, has two prior felony convictions for organized crimes. Answer the following questions:

a) Should criminal charges be considered against Lonnie? Why or why not?
b) What additional information do you need to know before making an arrest of the other crime family members?
c) Who can be arrested, and why?

2. **Terrorism** You are working at the reception desk of the Nebraska state capital building when you receive a call from a man with a foreign accent. He warns that in two hours a bomb will explode in your building, where hundreds of people work. The caller says that the Mission Fighters organization has planted this bomb as a way to draw attention to their cause, which is to have Montana declared a separate country where U.S. law doesn't apply and leaders of the Mission Fighters run the government. If their demands are not met, they will proceed to bomb a different state capital each week, starting with yours. Answer the following questions:

a) If a bomb is discovered, what are some possible charges the perpetrators could be convicted of?
b) If the bomb exploded and killed one or more people, what charges could be brought?
c) Considering the organization that is threatening these attacks, but also

considering the fact that the caller had a foreign accent, is it likely that international terrorists are involved as well? Why or why not?

3. **Extremism** A local extremist group has been making threats to various television stations in the area, and their actions have incited "copycat" terrorists. One of these copycat assailants, acting alone, attacked a news anchorwoman as she

walked to her car last Thursday evening. He said that he did it on behalf of the extremist group to help further their goals, but the group itself refuses to take responsibility for the attack.

a) Is the group legally liable in any way? Why or why not?

b) What actions of this lone terrorist made his act terrorism, rather than assault and battery? Why?

WORKPLACE APPLICATIONS

1. **Kids and Gangs** You have worked as a beat officer in the same neighborhood for several years. As a result, you are very familiar with most of the families, in particular a young single mother and her 11-year-old son, Jacob. The mother is working full-time and pursuing a bachelor's degree at night, and she tells you that she is concerned. She worries that her son is getting involved with the wrong crowd, will join a gang, and will pursue a life of crime. Because she works and goes to school, she is unable to monitor Jacob's activities on a regular basis. Answer the following questions:

a) Should you get involved?

b) What are some of the measures you can take to protect Jacob and make sure he doesn't join a gang?

c) Even if the mother is gone frequently, what can she do to prevent Jacob from joining a gang?

2. **Organized Crime and Extortion** You are a prosecutor who lives in the most quiet, pleasant suburb of your county. Every Thursday, you eat dinner with a

friend from work at a family-run Mexican restaurant. You know the family and like them very much. Tonight, the owner asks if he can speak with you. He explains that he has been approached by a local crime family that is demanding money for "protection." He does not have enough money to pay them, but is terrified that they will kill his only son in retaliation. He also states that he doesn't believe that the local police will do anything, since they all seem to be paid off by the crime family. Although he wants to protect his family, he assures you that he will do anything he can personally to help you end this crime ring. Answer the following questions:

a) Is there anything that he can do to help, such as wear a wiretap device? Why or why not?

b) Suppose that the charges of police corruption are true. What can you do about this? Where can you start?

c) For now, what can you do to protect his family against a criminal attack?

3. **RICO and Gangs** You are a federal prosecutor who is beginning to charge local, large-scale gangs with violating the RICO statute. You bring a case against 62 members of your city's most notorious gang, who have been distributing cocaine and crack for years. Attorneys for the defendants argue that the RICO statutes are meant to attack organized criminals such as the Mafia, not street gangs.
   a) Does this argument have any merit? Why or why not?
   b) As a federal prosecutor, do you think street gangs a worthwhile target of RICO statutes? Why or why not?

INTERNET APPLICATIONS

1. **Victims of Terrorism** Visit the National Center for Victims of Crime through the link provided at **cl.glencoe.com** and read the statistics on domestic terrorism. When you are done, answer the following questions:
   a) How do these statistics compare with your perception of terrorism in the United States?
   b) Do you think that terrorism will increase or decrease in future years? Why?
   c) Suppose that you are a terrorism specialist for your jurisdiction. Regarding these statistics, which additional information will you need to determine terrorism trends?

2. **Anti-Gang Legislation** Read "Indiana Gang-Related Legislation" available through the link provided at **cl.glencoe.com**. When you are done, answer the following questions:
   a) What crimes are covered under this legislation?
   b) What kind of enhanced penalties can a defendant face under this law?
   c) Does this legislation seem to cover everything? (Don't forget to read the section at the bottom entitled "Miscellaneous Gang Legislation.") Why or why not?
   d) Overall, are you satisfied with the scope of this legislation? Why or why not?

ETHICS ISSUES

1. **Terrorism and the Media** Your local newspaper has received a phone call from an extremist who has been responsible for at least five deaths nationwide. He asks you to publish his writings; in exchange for that, he promises not to kill any more people. State and federal government leaders have urged you to never negotiate with terrorists. On the other hand, he has been on the loose for over 12 years and police have very few leads with which to find him.
   a) What do you think your newspaper should do, and why?
   b) Is the newspaper legally liable in any way for publishing the work of this terrorist? Why or why not?

ENDNOTES

1 Craig M. Bradley, "Racketeering and The Federalization of Crime," 22 *Am. Crim. L. Rev.* 213 n.1 (1984), citing Letter from President Reagan to Senator Thurmond, January 26, 1983 reprinted in *Organized Crime in America, Hearings Before the Comm. On the Judiciary, United States Senate*, 98th Cong., 1st Sess. 3 (1983).

2 *Id.* at 215, citing J. Ezell, *Fortune's Merry Wheel: The Lottery in America* 249 (1960), and 217. See also *Stone v. Mississippi*, 101 U.S. 814 (1879) and *Champion v. Ames*, 188 U.S. 321 (1903).

3 National Prohibition Act, ch. 83, 41 Stat. 305 (1919).

4 Dorean Marguirite Koenig, "The Criminal Justice System Facting the Challenge of Organized Crime,: 44 *Wayne L. Rev.* 1351,1355, citing Darrell J. Steffensmeir, "A Public Policy Agenda for Combating Organized Crime," in *Crime and Public Policy* 269, 269–270 (Hugh D. Barlow ed., 1995).

5 Lesley Suzanne Bonnie, "The Prosecution of Sophisticated Urban Street Gangs: A Proper Application of RICO," 42 *Cath. U. L. Rev.* 579, 584 (1993).

6 Act of March 3, 1875, Ch. 141 § 3, 18 Stat. 477 (1875), superceded by the Act of March 3, 1903, ch. 1012, §2, 32 Stat. 1213 (1903); and Act of Feb. 20, 1907, ch. 1134, § 3, 34 Stat. 89 (1907).

7 Bradley, 252.

8 Scott Sultzer, "Money Laundering: The Scope of the Problem and Attempts to Combat It," 63 Tenn. L. Rev. 143, 146 n.4 (1995), citing *Federal Government's Response to Money Laundering: Hearings Before the House Committee on Banking, Finance, & Urban Affairs*, 103d Cong., 1st Sess. 546 (1993) (statement of John P. LaWare, Governor of the Board of Governors, U.S. Federal Reserve System) (citing Federal Bureau of Investigation (FBI) estimates).

9 *Id.* at 147 n.12, citing Timothy L. O'Brien, "Cash-Flow Woes: Law Firm's Downfall Exposes New Methods Of Money Laundering," *Wall Street Journal*, May 26, 1995, at A1. This article explains that the Cali cartel uses an "international network" of white collar professionals to launder its revenues.

10 *Money Laundering Legislation: Hearing of the Sen. Committee On The Judiciary*, 99th Cong., 1st Sess. 190 (1985), and *Federal Government's Response to Money Laundering: Hearings Before the House Committee on Banking, Finance, & Urban Affairs*, 103d Cong., 1st Sess. 200–01 (1993).

11 Koenig, 1351,1355, citing President's Commission on Organized Crime, *The Impact: Organized Crime Today*, Report to the President and the Attorney General 25 (Apr. 1986).

12 18 U.S.C. §§ 1961–1968 (1994). *See also* Bonnie, 579, 608, citing 18 U.S.C. § 1961 (1988) (Congressional Statement of Findings and Purpose).

13 18 U.S.C. § 1961 (1988) (Congressional Statement of Findings and Purpose). *See also* Koenig, 1351,1364, citing Glenn Beard et al., "Racketeer Influenced and Corrupt Organizations," 33 *Am. Crim. L. Rev.* 929 (1996).

14 *United States v. Turkette*, 452 U.S. 576, 580–81, 583 (1981).

15 18 U.S.C. § 1961(1)(A)-(F) (1994).

16 Koenig, 1351,1365, citing and quoting from Beard, 929, 935 (1996), relying on *H. J. Inc. v. Northwestern Bell Telephone Co.*, 429 U.S. 229, 239 (1989).

17 18 U.S.C. §§ 1962(a)-(d) (1994).

18 18 U.S.C. § 1964(c) (1994).

19 Or. Rev. Stat. §§ 166.715–166.735 (1998).

20 21 U.S.C. § 848(c) (1994). *See also* Susan W. Brenner, "RICO, CCE, and other Complex Crimes: The Transformation of American Criminal Law," 2 *Wm. & Mary Bill Rts. J.* 239 (1993).

21 18 U.S.C. § 1956 (1994).

22 18 U.S.C. § 1344 (1994), and 31 U.S.C. §§ 1829, 1951–59, 5311-26 (1994). *See also* Koenig, 1351, 1375–76, citing 18 U.S.C. § 1344 (1994).

23 18 U.S.C. § 1956 (1994). *See also* Sultzer, 143, 159, citing 18 U.S.C. § 1956 (1998).

24 *United States v. Wheeler*, 435 U.S. 313, 316–17 (1978).

25 *Blockburger v. United States*, 284 U.S. 299 (1932). See also, *United States v. Dixon*, 509 U.S. 688 (1993).

26 Bonnie, 579, 598, citing and quoting *United States v. Angiulo*, 897 F.2d 1169, 1180 (1st Cir. 1990).

27 Sanford H.Kadish and Stephen J. Schulhofer, *Criminal Law and its Processes*, 799 (6th ed. 1995), citing Iowa Code Ann. §723A.1. (1993).

28 Bonnie, 579, 599-603.

29 *United States v. Andrews*, 749 F. Supp. 1520 (N.D. Ill. 1990).

30 Rachelle Q. Ayuyang, "Hard Girlz: Filipino Girls in Gangs," *Filipinas Magazine*, August 31, 1998, v. 7 n. 76.

31 *Id.*

32 Karen Low, *Authorities Arrest 13 Alleged Mexican Mafia Members*, Associated Press Release, Wednesday, February 3, 1999 (page unavailable).

33 Louis Holland, "Can Gang Recruitment be Stopped? An Analysis of the Social and Legal Factors Affecting Anti-Gang Legislation," 21 *J. Contemp. L.* 259, 271 (1995).

34 Jesse Katz, *Violence Punctuates Truce Between Bloods and Crips Gangs: Rivalry-based killings have declined since the spring accord. But other reasons can lead to slayings*, L.A. Times, September 13, 1992, Part-A; Metro Desk.

35 Holland, 274.

36 18 U.S.C. § 521 (1994).

37 Kadish and Schulhofer, 799, citing and quoting Iowa Code Ann. § 723A.2 (1993).

38 Cal. Penal Code § 186.26, § 186.22(a) and (e) (West 1998).

39 *See* Beth Bjerrejaard, *The Constitutionality of Anti-Gang Legislation*, 21 Camb. L. Rev. 31, 40 n.51 (1998) and cases cited therein.

40 Alexander Molina, *California's Anti-Gang Street Terrorism Enforcement and Prevention Act: One Step Forward, Two Steps Back?*, 22 Sw. U. L. Rev. 457, 477 n. 139 (1993), citing Sebastian Rotella, *Gangs Question Their Exile From Park*, L.A. Times (Valley ed.) Sept. 18, 1991, at B3.

41 Ark. Code Ann. § 5-74-108 (Michie 1997).

42 Ark. Code. Ann. § 5-74-104 (Michie 1997)

43 *Id.* at 240 n.4, citing James P. Terry, *Legal Aspects of Terrorism*, in International Military and Defense Encyclopedia 2732 (1993).

What laws specifically target organized crime?
Find it on page 553.

A

Abandoned property Property over which a person voluntarily gives up permanent possession or ownership.

Abandonment (renunciation) An affirmative defense to the crime of attempt; valid only if the defendant voluntarily and completely renounces his or her criminal purpose.

Abatement When applied to a nuisance, the ending or eliminating of that nuisance.

Accessory after the fact One who intentionally aids another whom he or she knows committed a felony, in order for the person assisted to avoid criminal prosecution and punishment.

Accessory before the fact One who intentionally counsels, solicits, or commands another in the commission of a crime.

Accessory One who aids in the commission of a crime without being present when the crime is committed.

Accomplice liability The accountability of one individual for the criminal act or acts of another.

Accomplice Someone who knowingly and willingly associates with the commission of a criminal offense, and who intentionally assists another in the commission of a crime.

Actual possession When a controlled substance is on the defendant's person or within an area of his or her immediate control and reach, or when the controlled substance is within a container that the defendant may be carrying or has within his or her reach.

Actus reus A willed unlawful act, which can be an affirmative act or an omission, and which comprises the physical components of a crime; generally must be coupled with *mens rea* to establish criminal liability.

Adequate provocation When the acts or conduct of the person killed would be sufficient to cause a person of reasonable, ordinary temperament to lose self-control.

Adulteration When the ingredients of a food, drug, cosmetic, or device are poisonous, filthy, putrid, otherwise unsanitary, or have been contaminated.

Adultery Sexual relations with someone other than a spouse when the person is married.

Affirmative defense A defense in which the defendant admits to the existence of all of the necessary legal elements for criminal liability, but offers one or more legally recognized reasons why he or she should nonetheless be acquitted.

Agency theory The theory that all conspirators act as the agents of (and represent) their co-conspirators involved in a criminal scheme, and thus are liable for all criminal acts committed by other co-conspirators.

Agent provocateur Someone who intends for the principal to fail in his or her illegal venture and, because of this lack of causation, is not an accomplice.

Aggravated assault Assault with intent to kill, rob, or rape; also, assaults with specified deadly weapons. A felony in most states.

Aggravated battery A battery accompanied by an intent to kill or rape; usually a specific intent crime. A felony in many states.

Aggressor One who first employs hostile force, either by threatening or striking another, which justifies a like response.

Aid and abet To assist or facilitate a person in accomplishing a crime.

Antitrust laws Laws that ensure and preserve a competitive economy by protecting trade and commerce from restraints, monopolies, price-fixing, and price discrimination.

Armed robbery Robbery accomplished by means of a dangerous or deadly weapon, robbery in the first degree, or aggravated robbery.

Arraignment and plea The defendant's appearance to respond formally to the charges.

Assault Either attempted battery or the intentional scaring of another person.

Assault weapon Prohibited weapons named by federal legislation, such as rifles with conspicuous pistol grips, pistols with shrouds, and shotguns with a higher ammunition capacity.

Attempt to monopolize Engaging in behavior and business practices that, if successful, would create a monopoly, and that succeed in coming close enough to create a dangerous probability that a monopoly would have occurred.

Attempt When a person, with the intent to commit an offense, performs any act that constitutes a substantial step toward the commission of said offense.

B

Bail A deposit of cash, other property, or a bond, guaranteeing that the accused will appear in court.

Battered woman's syndrome A defense in many jurisdictions where a victim of ongoing abuse eventually "snaps" and kills the abuser.

Battery A misdemeanor consisting of the unlawful application of force that actually and intentionally causes the touching of another person against his or her will.

Bifurcated trial The division of the criminal trial into two parts: the first part leads to the verdict, and the second part relates to another issue, such as the sanity of the accused or whether or not the death penalty should be used.

Bill of attainder A special legislative enactment that declares a person or group of persons guilty of a crime and subject to punishment without a trial.

Bill of Rights The first ten amendments of the U.S. Constitution, which guarantees fundamental individual rights to the American citizens.

Blackmail A threat by a private citizen seeking hush money, which is payment to remain silent.

Bond A written promise to pay the bail sum that is posted by a financially responsible person, usually a professional bonds agent.

Bookmaking The promotion of gambling by unlawfully accepting bets from members of the public as a business, rather than in a casual or personal fashion.

Born-Alive rule The common law rule defining the beginning of life for purposes of criminal homicide, which states that human life begins with the birth of a live child.

Boss The head or leader of an organized crime family; usually not involved in day-to-day group operations, but the ultimate decision-maker.

Brain death syndrome The modern rule for defining death, which is characterized by absence of receptivity, absence of spontaneous movements or breathing, and absence of reflex activity.

Bribery The voluntarily giving or receiving anything of value as unlawful payment for the commission of an official act.

Burden of proof The onus of producing evidence and also of persuading the jury with the required level of proof, which in a criminal case is "beyond a reasonable doubt."

But-For test The test that asks the question of whether the result of a crime would have occurred if the defendant had not acted.

C

Capital murder A charge of murder with the maximum punishment of death; often called first-degree murder.

Captains and soldiers A group of middle managers and supervisors below the underboss of an organized crime family.

Cause-in-Fact The cause of the social harm in a criminal act that is determined by the but-for test.

Child abuse Any intentional or neglectful physical or emotional injury imposed on a child, including sexual molestation.

Child molestation Any sexual conduct by an adult with a child.

Cholo/chola (Especially among Mexican-Americans) A member of a Latino street gang.

Churning When a stockbroker excessively purchases and sells securities for a client without regard or concern for the client's investment objectives, but rather to advance his own interests, usually that of generating commissions.

Civil contempt The failure to do something ordered by the court for the benefit of another party.

Civil Law Law that deals with matters that are considered to be private concerns between individuals.

Coercion A type of duress, under which the law presumed that a woman who acted in her husband's presence was coerced; a common law defense.

Commercial bribery The giving, receiving, or soliciting of anything of value to influence an employee or professional in the performance of his or her duties.

Common law Law created by judicial opinion; also called *case law*. Historically, law from America's colonial and English past, which has set precedents that are still sometimes followed today.

Compounding a felony An offense that occurs when someone refuses to report or prosecute a felony in exchange for some benefit or reward of some value.

Conditional assault An assault where the actor threatens harm only under certain conditions, such as the failure of the victim to act a certain way demanded by the actor.

Consent A defense where, in certain circumstances, the victim agrees to the actor's conduct; this defense negates an element of the offense or precludes infliction of the harm to be prevented by the law defining the offense.

Conspiracy A partnership in crime that is an agreement between two or more people to achieve a criminal purpose or to achieve a lawful purpose using unlawful means; also called a *common criminal enterprise.*

Constructive contempt Contempt of court that results from matters outside the court, such as failure to comply with court orders.

Constructive possession A relationship between the defendant and either drugs or stolen goods, in which it is reasonable to treat the extent of the defendant's dominion and control over the property as if it were actual possession.

Constructive presence Where an individual is within the vicinity of the crime and is able to assist the primary actor if necessary.

Contempt of court Any affirmative act or omission that obstructs justice or attempts to negate the dignity and authority of the court.

Controlled substances Any substances that are strictly regulated or outlawed because of their potential for abuse or addiction.

Corpus delicti The requirement of proof for any crime; in homicide cases, this usually means the corpse of the victim.

Crews The men and women in an organized crime organization who carry out the group's actual street operations.

Crime An act or omission that the law makes punishable, generally by fine, penalty, forfeiture, or confinement.

Criminal abortion The artificially induced expulsion of a fetus by illegal means, such as spousal abuse.

Criminal contempt An act of disrespect toward the court or its procedures, other than direct contempt, that obstructs the administration of justice.

Criminal facilitation Where an individual knowingly aids another, but does not truly have a separate intent to aid in the commission of the underlying offense.

Criminal homicide Any act that causes the death of another with criminal intent and without lawful justification or excuse.

Criminal street gang Any ongoing organization whose primary activity is the commission of one or more criminal acts, who has an identifiable name or identifying sign or symbol, and whose members engage in or have engaged in a pattern of criminal gang activity.

D

Dangerous proximity test The test that determines that a person is guilty of attempt when his or her conduct, though not having advanced so far as the last act, is dangerously close to success, or when a criminal act is so near completion that the danger of its success is very great.

Deadly force Force that is likely or intended to cause death or great bodily harm.

Defense Either a failure of proof by the prosecution, or a defendant's reason why the prosecutor has no valid case against him or her.

Delivery of a controlled substance The transfer of a controlled substance from one person to another.

Diminished capacity A term used to describe two circumstances in which a mental condition short of insanity will lead to an acquittal or lessened charges: 1) where the accused raises the condition as a failure of proof defense, and 2) a true partial defense, where the crime of murder can be mitigated by the defense to manslaughter.

Direct contempt A criminal form of contempt of court that occurs when a person in the presence of the court resists the court's power.

Dirty money Money received through illegal activities, such as drug sales and illegal gambling.

Disorderly conduct A loosely defined offense addressing behavior that disturbs the safety, health, or morals of others, or that is intended only to annoy another person.

Dram shop acts Legislative acts that impose strict liability upon the seller of intoxicating beverages when the sale results in harm to a third party's person, property, or means of support.

Driving under the influence (DUI) Operating a motor vehicle while under the influence of a substance or with a blood or breath alcohol concentration above a prohibited level.

Drug conspiracies Agreements between two or more people to commit a criminal drug-related act, or to commit an otherwise lawful drug-related act by criminal or unlawful means.

Drug loitering When some public action is taken that manifests the intent to engage in illegal drug activity, such as loitering at a street corner known for drug transactions.

Drug paraphernalia Any equipment, product, or material that is primarily intended or designed for use with a controlled substance, such as bongs, pipes, rolling papers, scales, and hypodermic needles.

Drug transportation Transporting a controlled substance in a vehicle; a crime in every state.

DUI manslaughter The death of any human being caused by an individual who is driving under the influence.

Duress A defense that arises when a person commits an unlawful act because of a threat of imminent death or serious bodily injury to himself or another, unless the actor intentionally kills an innocent third person.

E

Elder abuse The abuse, mistreatment, or financial exploitation of elderly persons.

Embezzlement The unlawful taking or misuse of property by persons, typically employees, who lawfully come into possession of this property and therefore do not meet the theft or larceny requirement of wrongfully obtaining the property.

Entrapment When officers or agents of the government, for the purpose of instituting a criminal prosecution against a person, induce an otherwise innocent person to commit a crime that he or she had not contemplated.

Escape When a person who is lawfully imprisoned leaves custody before he or she is entitled to freedom by due process of law.

***Ex post facto* law** A law that: 1) makes an act committed before passage of the law, and which was innocent when committed, criminal, and provides for punishment of this act; 2) aggravates a crime, or makes it greater than it was, when committed; or 3) changes the punishment, and inflicts a greater punishment, than the law imposed upon the crime when committed.

Excuse A defense where the criminal actor has committed an unjustified crime, but there is a reason for not holding him or her personally accountable for it.

Exhibitionism Intentional acts of exposing the genitals to an unexpected stranger for the purpose of achieving sexual excitement.

Extortion The gaining of money, property, or something of value by threat of physical harm to a person or property by a public official using the status of his or her office.

F

Factual impossibility When a person intends to commit a crime, but fails to consummate the offense because of an attendant circumstance that is unknown or beyond his or her control; a defense to the crime of attempt.

Failure of proof A defense in which the defense counsel makes a motion for an acquittal or the defendant introduces evidence that shows that the prosecution's case is lacking.

Fair notice The due process requirement that people are entitled to know what behavior is forbidden, so that they may shape their conduct accordingly.

False imprisonment Knowingly and unlawfully restraining a person so as to substantially interfere with his or her liberty.

False pretenses A crime that occurs when title or ownership of the property is passed to the defendant in reliance of the defendant's misrepresentation.

False swearing The giving of a false oath during any proceeding or matter in which an oath is required by law.

Fear or intimidation The use of threat, either implied or explicit and either verbal or nonverbal, to do immediate bodily injury or harm to the victim, family member, or to someone else who is present.

Federal test The federal statutory definition of insanity, which provides that a person is excused by reason of insanity if he or she proves by clear and convincing evidence that at the time of the offense, as a result of a severe mental disease or defect, he or she was unable to appreciate the nature and quality of his or her act, or the wrongfulness of his or her conduct.

Federalism The system of American government whereby all power resides in the state governments unless specifically granted to the federal government.

Felony A serious crime that is usually punishable by imprisonment of more than one year or by death.

Felony murder rule The rule that when the accused kills one or more persons in the course of committing a felony, the *mens rea* for murder is present from the intent to commit the felony and therefore murder has been committed.

Feticide The illegal killing of a fetus.

Firearm Any weapon that can, is designed to, or may readily be converted to expel a projectile by the action of an explosive; in general, any destructive device other than standard rifles, shotguns, and handguns.

Force The actual use of physical power against the victim to aid in obtaining the money or property.

Forgery The making or altering of a writing in such a way as to convey a false impression concerning its authenticity is guilty of forgery.

Fornication Voluntary, unlawful sexual intercourse under circumstances not constituting adultery.

Fraudulent making Creating a document that is not authentic.

G

Gambling The act of staking or risking something of value on the outcome of a contest of chance, or on a future event of chance that is not under the gambler's control or influence; illegal in most forms and in most jurisdictions.

General deterrence When punishment of a specific offender causes other people in the community to refrain from committing the same crime.

General intent The intent only to commit the *actus reus* of a crime without any additional intention to do some future act or to achieve some further consequences beyond the conduct or result of the offense, or without the awareness of a statutory attendant circumstance.

Grand jury A panel of private citizens chosen to review a criminal investigation, to sometimes conduct criminal investigations, and to decide whether to charge crimes in the cases presented to them or investigated by them.

Grand theft Theft that is usually defined by statute to be the felonious taking of property valued above a set monetary amount, or the theft of motor vehicle. More serious than petty theft.

H

Homicide The killing of one human being by another human being.

Horizontal price-fixing Direct or indirect agreements made between market participants at the same level within a given market, regarding the prices they will charge for a similar product that all of them sell.

"Hybrid" legal impossibility A case of factual impossibility, as distinguished from cases of true legal impossibility.

I

Imperfect self-defense A partial self-defense, where the claim of self-defense partially fails because it is not objectively reasonable but is honestly believed by the accused; reduces a murder charge to voluntary manslaughter.

Inchoate crime A crime that generally leads to another crime. The principal modern inchoate crimes are attempt, conspiracy, and solicitation.

Inchoate offense A step towards the commission of another crime, which is itself defined as a crime because the step in itself is serious enough to merit punishment.

Incompetency The lack of capacity to rationally consult with an attorney, or the accused person's inability to understand the nature of the proceedings against him or her.

Indecent exposure An offensive display of one's body in public, especially one's genitals or the female breasts.

Indictment The paper issued by a grand jury that charges an accused with a felony; used in about half of the 50 states.

Indispensable element test A test that determines that no attempt has occurred when a suspect has not yet gained control over an indispensable instrumentality of the criminal plan.

Individual deterrence When an imposition of punishment upon the wrongdoer causes him or her to refrain from repeating the act.

Information The paper issued by a prosecutor that charges an accused of a felony; used in about half of the 50 states.

Inherently dangerous felonies Felonies that require conduct that is inherently dangerous to human life, such as rape, arson, and armed robbery.

Innocent agent or instrumentality An object, animal, or person, such as an insane person or a child, that is used by a principal to commit a crime and cannot be culpable under the law.

Insanity A defense wherein the law recognizes that the accused is suffering from mental disease when the crime occurred, and thus may be relieved of criminal responsibility.

Insider trading A type of fraud that involves the purchase and sale of securities based on material, nonpublic information.

Intangible rights theory A type of prosecution under mail fraud that is primarily used to protect citizens from dishonest public officials.

International terrorism The deliberate employment of violence or the threat of violence in a manner that crosses national borders.

Intoxication A disturbance of mental or physical capacities resulting from the introduction of certain substances into the body.

Involuntary intoxication Intoxication that occurs when the actor does not voluntarily consume drugs or alcohol, or when the actor is not to blame for becoming intoxicated, such as where he or she has an unanticipated reaction to drugs or alcohol.

Involuntary manslaughter A criminal homicide that encompasses a killing done without intent to kill, and without such indifference to human life as to constitute implied malice; occurs as a result of criminally negligent conduct on the part of the defendant.

Irresistible impulse test A test for insanity that permits a verdict of not guilty by reason of insanity if the fact-finder concludes that the accused had a mental disease that prevented him or her from controlling his or her conduct.

J

Joyriding The unlawful taking, using, or operating of a motor vehicle without the consent of the owner.

Jurisdiction The power or authority of the court to act upon the case before it.

Jury nullification (In a criminal case) The power of the jury to declare a verdict that ignores the law or the facts of the case.

Justification A defense that, because of the circumstances of the case, renders criminal conduct lawful and therefore exempts the actor from criminal sanctions.

K

Kidnapping A felony defined as the act of illegally taking another person by force or fraud; usually accompanied by a demand for ransom money.

Knowingly causes a result Committing an act in the awareness that it is practically certain that his or her conduct will cause such a result.

Knowingly with respect to conduct and attendant circumstances Committing a criminal act with the awareness that his or her conduct is of criminal nature, or that such circumstances exist as to make the conduct criminal.

L

Larceny The taking and carrying away of property of another without consent, with the purpose of stealing or permanently depriving the owner of possession.

Larceny from the person A statutory offense of taking property from the person of another; the penalty is usually greater than that of simple larceny.

Last act test The test that determines that an attempt has occurred when a person has performed all of the acts that he or she believed were necessary to commit the underlying offense.

Law enforcement defense The defense that authorizes the use of force by law enforcement officers in various circumstances.

Law The federal, state, or local enactments of legislative bodies; known decisions of the courts of the federal and state governments; rules and regulations proclaimed by government bodies; and proclamations by executives of the federal, state, or local government.

Legal impossibility A defense to attempt in which the defendant's intended acts, even if completed, would not amount to a crime.

Legality The first principle of criminal law, which holds that conduct may not be treated as criminal unless it has been legally defined as such before the conduct has taken place.

Loan sharking The practice of lending money at excessive interest rates, then making threats or using extortion to enforce repayment.

M

M'Naghten test A rule used to establish an insanity defense, under which it must be clearly proved that, at the time of the offense, the accused was so mentally ill that he or she did not know the nature and quality of what he or she was doing; or, if he or she did know it, it was without knowing what was wrong.

Mail fraud A form of fraud that uses a mail service to disseminate materials that deceive people.

Mala in se Crimes that are inherently wrong, such as rape and murder.

Mala prohibita Crimes that are wrong only because the law says they are wrong in order to protect the general public; this includes gambling, prostitution, and drug use.

Malice A state of mind involving an "abandoned and malignant heart"; not limited to the specific intent to kill, since even a wanton or reckless state of mind may constitute malice.

Malice aforethought Under modern law, any one of four mental states that reveal the intent to: 1) kill, 2) inflict grievous bodily injury, 3) show extreme reckless disregard for human life, or 4) commit a felony that results in another's death.

Mann Act A federal act that prohibits the knowing interstate or foreign transportation of any individual, male or female, with the intent that such individual engage in prostitution or any sexual activity.

Manslaughter The killing of another without the mental element of malice aforethought.

Mayhem A felony defined as the violent disablement or removal or a person's limb or of an essential body part, such as an eye; today, a felony in jurisdictions that have not replaced it with aggravated battery.

Megan's Law A statute, enacted in many states, which requires community notification by authorities when convicted sex offenders are released from prison.

Mens rea A guilty state of mind that the prosecution, to secure a conviction, must prove that a defendant had when committing a crime.

Misappropriation The wrongful misuse or stealing of another's property that has been entrusted to an embezzler.

Misdemeanor A crime that is less serious then a felony and is usually punishable by fine, penalty, forfeiture, or confinement in a jail for less than one year.

Misprision of a felony The act of failing to report or prosecute a known felony, and of taking positive steps to conceal the crime.

Mitigation The reduction of a penalty or punishment imposed by law.

Model Penal Code (MPC) A comprehensive recodification of the principles of American criminal responsiblity.

Money laundering The transfer of illegally obtained money through legitimate persons or accounts, so that its original source can not be traced; a crime under federal law.

Monopolize To obtain the power to control and dominate interstate trade and commerce in a particular industry, such as oil or computer software.

Motive The emotion that prompts a person to act; not an element that is required to prove criminal liability, but may be shown in order to identify the perpetrator of a crime or explain his or her reason for acting.

MPC (ALI) test A test for insanity that provides that an actor is not responsible for his or her criminal conduct if found lacking in substantial capacity to 1) appreciate the criminality of his or her conduct, or 2) conform his or her conduct to the requirements of the law.

Murder The killing of another with the mental element of malice aforethought.

N

Narcotics addiction The repeated or uncontrolled use of controlled substances; also called *drug dependency*.

Natural and probable consequences doctrine A doctrine that holds an accomplice liable not only for the offense he or she intended to facilitate or encourage, but also of any natural and foreseeable additional offenses committed by the principal to whom he or she is an accomplice.

Necessity A defense where a person, under the pressure of circumstances, commits a justifiable action; valid only when the harm produced is less than the harm that would have occurred without the action.

Negligent homicide A criminal homicide committed by a person who has neglected to exercise the degree of care that an ordinary person would have exercised under the same circumstances.

Negligently Committing an act when one should have been aware of a substantial and unjustifiable risk that a crime exists or will result from such conduct.

Nonproxyable offense A crime committed by an action that can only be done through the actor's own conduct, not through an agent's.

Nuisance Anything that endangers life or health, gives offense to the senses, violates laws of decency, or obstructs the reasonable and comfortable use of property.

O

Obscenity Sexually explicit material that falls outside the protection of the First Amendment and therefore may be punished under a criminal statute.

Obstruction of justice When one or more persons attempt to or actually prevent the execution of a lawful process.

Omissions Circumstances in which a failure to act is viewed as a criminal act.

Organized crime Individuals who associate together for the purpose of engaging in criminal activity on a sustained basis, with an emphasis on the life of the organization.

P

Pandering Either procuring a prostitute for a place of prostitution or procuring a place for a prostitute in which he or she can engage in prostitution.

Perjury Making false statements under oath or affirmation.

Petty theft Theft that is usually statutorily defined as the misdemeanor taking of property under a set monetary amount; less serious than **grand theft**.

Pimping Promoting prostitution, living off of the earnings of prostitutes, and in some cases coercing individuals to work as prostitutes.

Pinkerton **doctrine** The doctrine that holds a person associated with a conspiracy is responsible for any criminal act committed by a co-conspirator if the act is within the scope of the conspiracy and is a foreseeable result of the criminal scheme.

Possession with intent to deliver A drug offense that may be proven circumstantially by proof of a sizable quantity of drugs, possession of manufacturing or packaging implements, and the activities or statements of the person(s) in possession of the substance.

Preliminary hearing A post-arrest, pre-trial judicial proceeding, during which the judge decides whether there is probable cause to prosecute the accused. In some jurisdictions, the preliminary hearing is minimal; in others, it is a mini-trial.

Premeditation and deliberation A mental state that implies a cold-blooded killing in which the intent can be achieved in numerous ways; raises second-degree murder to first-degree murder in jurisdictions that classify murder into two or more levels.

Principal One who is present at and participates in the crime charged, or who procures an innocent agent to commit the crime.

Principal in the first degree Usually the primary actor or perpetrator of the crime.

Principal in the second degree One who intentionally assists in the commission of a crime in his or her presence; such presence is either actual or constructive.

Probable cause Evidence that indicates a fair probability that the suspect committed a crime; required for an arrest of a suspect by a law enforcement officer.

Procedural criminal law The rules governing how the criminal law is administered.

Proportionality The constitutional principle that the punishment should fit the crime, as expressed in the Eighth Amendment's cruel and unusual punishment clause.

Prostitution A crime that is committed when one person agrees to engage in sexual intercourse in return for something of value, usually money.

Protectors Law enforcement officers, lawyers, bank officials, and accountants who illegally use their skills to protect a crime organization from government interference or criminal prosecutions.

Proximate cause That cause, from among all of the causes-in-fact that may exist, that is the legal cause of the social harm.

Public order and safety offenses Offenses that deal with behavior that is not necessarily immoral, but nonetheless affects the peace and safety of the community.

Punishment When an agent of the government, using authority granted by virtue of a legal criminal conviction, intentionally inflicts pain, loss of liberty, or some other unpleasant consequence on the person who has been convicted of a crime.

Pure legal impossibility Where the law does not define as criminal the goal the defendant sought to achieve; a valid defense to the crime of attempt.

Purposely with respect to attendant circumstances When the actor is aware of the existence of such circumstances, or he or she believes or hopes that they exist.

Purposely with respect to result or conduct The actor's conscious object to engage in conduct of that nature or to cause such a result.

Q

Quasi-bribery An extension of the crime of bribery that covers people other than public officials whose functions are also important to the public welfare.

R

Racketeer Influenced and Corrupt Organizations Act (RICO) A federal law that criminalizes illegal activities committed by organized crime members.

Racketeering A system of organized crime that traditionally involves the extortion of money from businesses by intimidation, violence, or other illegal methods; also, the practice of engaging in a fraudulent scheme or enterprise.

Rape A felony that consists of forcible sexual intercourse with a person against his or her will.

Rape trauma syndrome A condition observed in some rape victims, in which the victim develops phobias and physical problems as a result of having been raped.

Receiving Illegally acquiring possession, control, or title of stolen goods.

Reckless driving Driving that involves the willful and wanton disregard for the safety of persons or property.

Recklessly Committing an act that consciously disregards a substantial and unjustified risk that a crime exists or will result from the actor's conduct.

Recognizance A promise to appear in court.

Reform A by-product of punishment that is characterized by therapy and education, which causes a convicted criminal to lose the desire to commit further criminal acts; also called *rehabilitation*.

Resisting arrest Physical efforts to oppose a lawful arrest.

Retributive justification A justification for punishment based on the theory that a wrongdoer deserves punishment for punishment's sake.

Riot A tumultuous disturbance of the peace by three or more persons, who are assembling in the execution of a lawful or unlawful act and committing it in a violent and turbulent manner.

Robbery A common law crime that consists of larceny committed by the use of force or fear, where the property taken is either taken from the person of the victim or within his or her immediate presence.

Rout An unlawful assembly that is escalating, but does not reach, the level of a riot; an attempted riot.

S

Securities fraud A criminal, civil, or administrative offense with the following elements: substantive fraud that is found in the offer, purchase, or sale of a security or in connection therewith; the use of interstate commerce or the mails; and willfulness.

Self-defense The justified use of reasonable force by one who is not an aggressor, when the actor reasonably believed it was necessary to defend against what he or she reasonably perceived to be an unlawful and imminent physical attack.

Shakedown When a member of a crime organization uses the threat of violence to get a person to do something for the organization.

Shopkeeper's rule An exception to false imprisonment laws that provides a shopkeeper with the right to restrain a person if the shopkeeper possesses a reasonable belief that the customer has not paid a bill or has shoplifted an item.

Shoplifting A crime defined by a specific theft statute to address thefts of merchandise, concealment of merchandise, altering price tags, and retail theft.

Simulated controlled substance A substance resembling a controlled substance in its nature, packaging, or appearance, which would lead a reasonable person to believe it to be a controlled substance.

Sodomy The sexual penetration of the anus or mouth of one person by the penis of another; illegal in some jurisdictions.

Solicitation The act of seeking to persuade someone else to commit a crime with the intent that the crime be committed; also, the act of offering to pay another, or receive payment from another, for sex.

Specific intent The intent to commit an act for the purpose of committing an additional future act, to achieve some further consequences, or with the awareness of a statutory attendant circumstance.

Spousal abuse Long-term physical abuse by the victim's spouse or partner.

Spousal rape Nonconsensual sex between a woman and her husband, ex-husband, or partner.

Statutory law Law that is created through the American State and Federal legislatures.

Statutory rape A form of rape involving sexual intercourse between an adult and a child that is usually between the ages of 13 and 17.

Subornation of perjury The crime of procuring another person to make a false oath.

Substantial step test The MPC test to determine whether the *actus reus* of attempt has occurred, which requires that the suspect must have committed an act or omission that constitutes "a substantial step" in the commission of the substantive offense.

Substantive criminal law The section of criminal law that defines criminal acts.

Suppressing evidence When a defendant, or a person working on behalf of the defendant, illegally suppresses (hides), destroys, or refuses to produce evidence relevant to a grand jury investigation.

T

Tax deficiency When the proper amount of tax to be paid is greater than the amount shown on a taxpayer's tax return.

Tax evasion The willful attempt to avoid paying legally due taxes; a specific intent crime that is also called *tax fraud*.

Terrorism The deliberate employment of violence or the threat of violence by subnational groups and sovereign states, in order to attain strategic and political objectives.

Theft A broad category of misconduct against property that include the crimes of larceny, embezzlement, theft by false pretenses, shoplifting, robbery, and receiving stolen goods.

Thief A person who commits an act of larceny or theft, who is principal in the original taking of property, and who is not merely a subsequent receiver of the property.

Three-Strike laws Laws that impose sentences of 25 years to life for those who have been convicted of certain serious offenses three times.

Tort A civil wrong for which a remedy may be obtained, usually in the form of fines or punitive damages.

Transferred intent A doctrine that holds a person criminally liable even when the consequence of his or her action is not what the actor actually intended.

Treason The felony crime of waging war against the United States or allying with, aiding, or otherwise comforting its enemies.

True defense A defense that, if proved, results in the acquittal of a defendant, even though the prosecutor has proved the defendant's guilt beyond a reasonable doubt.

Tying arrangement An agreement that a purchaser must buy additional (or tied) products along with the one product that he or she desires; at the very least, the purchaser must agree to not buy this tied product from any other supplier.

U

Under color of authority or office A requirement for the crime of extortion, which holds that the action must be taken by the perpetrator in his or her capacity as a public official.

Underboss The second-in-command of an organized crime family; usually the person being groomed to take the boss's position in the event of death or incarceration.

Unequivocality test A test that determines that an attempt has occurred when a person's conduct, standing alone, unambiguously manifests his or her criminal intent.

Unlawful assembly A gathering together of three or more persons with the common intent to achieve a lawful or unlawful purpose in a tumultuous manner.

Utilitarian justification A justification for punishment based on the notion that a social practice is desirable if it promotes the greatest good for the largest number of people.

Uttering When a person presents a forged writing and attempts to use it to deceive others.

V

Vagrancy A crime that is vaguely defined as being idle and without visible means of support; no longer a crime in most jurisdictions due to the unconstitutionality of past vagrancy laws.

Vehicular manslaughter A criminal homicide, in which the perpetrator caused a death while operating a motor vehicle either grossly negligently or while under the influence of alcohol or other drugs.

Vehicular manslaughter The killing of a human being by the operation of a motor vehicle in a reckless manner that is likely to cause death or great bodily harm to another.

Vengeance The imposition of a punishment that is perceived as equal to the crime, such as in the phrase, "An eye for an eye, a tooth for a tooth."

Vertical price-fixing Direct or indirect agreements made between market participants at different levels within a given market, regarding the price at which their product will be resold.

Viability The point at which a fetus can reasonably live outside its mother's womb, with or without artificial support.

Voluntary intoxication The voluntary act of introducing substances into one's body that one knows or should know are likely to have intoxicating effects.

Voluntary manslaughter An intentional, unlawful killing of a human being without malice aforethought.

W

White-Collar crime A broad category of nonviolent misconduct involving commercial and financial fraud.

Willfulness For tax evasion purposes, the voluntary and intentional violation of a known legal duty regarding a taxpayer's knowledge that he or she should have reported more income than he or she actually did.

Witness tampering The intent to illegally influence witness testimony, such as by approaching a potential witness with threats or other means to prevent the witness from testifying.

Y

Year-And-A-Day Rule The causation rule that requires that, in order to classify a killing as a homicide, the victim must die within a year and a day after the act causing death occurred.

* English case

PHOTO CREDITS